Encounter Groups

ENCOUNTER

GROUPS: FIRST FACTS

Morton A. Lieberman
Irvin D. Yalom
Matthew B. Miles

BASIC BOOKS, INC., PUBLISHERS

NEW YORK

To our favorite groups . . .
Grace, Leslie, Daniel, David
Marilyn, Eve, Reid, Victor, Benjamin
Betty, Sara, David, Ellen

PREFACE

Anyone aware of the burgeoning accumulation of literature on encounter groups may well ask, "Is this book necessary?" Our answer has been affirmative because the explosive expansion of the use of groups for personal change has not been matched by corresponding concern for information about what such groups do and how well they do it. Innovation has exceeded evaluation. Much so-called encounter group theory has been contributed by expert, often prestigious, practitioners in an effort to abstract the essence of their own skill. Often the very artfulness and perspicacity of the originators has too sharply shaped their perspective, rendering their theories into self-fulfilling prophecies. The time seemed at hand for a comparative investigation of the broad range of theories and methods currently brought together under the rubric of encounter.

Our efforts have centered on discovering what actually happens to people in encounter groups: Who benefits, who is harmed, and what aspects of the group experience, the behavior of the leader, and of the person himself, explain these effects? The first chapter describes how we approached these problems and Chapter 2 depicts the groups we studied. Chapters 3 through 6 document changes in the participants as evidenced in several measures of change and in case analyses.

The next three chapters focus on effects of group process on the participants: Effects of leaders, of group normative structure, of group cohesiveness, and of interpersonal climate. The focus is shifted in Chapters 10 and 11 from the group to the individual, raising the question of the effects on outcome of the attitudes, expectations, and personality characteristics of the individual member, as well as of the influence of his relationship to the group—how attracted he is to the group, how deviant, how active, how influential, and so on. Chapter 12 looks at a number of experiences emphasized in both therapy and encounter circles as the core mechanisms which induce learning, such as expressivity, self-disclosure, insight, and feedback.

Chapters 13 through 15 present the findings of substudies on the effects of encounter group experience on racial attitudes, on the contribution of structured exercises to encounter group learning, and on how participants maintain what they learn in the groups.

The final two chapters are intended to render some general meanings from the findings. Chapter 16 suggests practical applications for leaders and participants. Chapter 17 evaluates the overall effectiveness of encounter groups as a medium of personal change.

This book represents a collaborative effort. The authors worked closely together during all phases of the project. Chapters 7, 10, 11, 12, 13, 14, 15, and 17 were primarily the responsibility of Morton A. Lieberman; Chapters 2, 4, and 5 of Irvin D. Yalom; and Chapters 6, 8, and 9 of Matthew B. Miles. Morton A. Lieberman and Matthew B. Miles shared responsibility for Chapter 3 and Matthew B. Miles and Irvin D. Yalom for Chapter 16.

An inestimable debt must be acknowledged to a large number of individuals and institutions whose active support made the study possible. The time of the principal investigator to devote exclusively to research away from home base was freed through the aid of a Research Career Development Award, National Institute of Child Health and Human Development, and the good will of his colleagues at The University of Chicago. Matthew B. Miles' participation in the first year of the study was made possible through a senior post-doctoral research fellowship from the U. S. Office of Education. Grants awarded by Stanford University from the Ford Foundation Special Innovations in Education Fund and from the Mary Reynolds Babcock Foundation supported the study in its early days. Subsequent support was generously made available by the National Institute of Mental Health, MH19212, the W. Clement and Jesse B. Stone Foundation, the Carnegie Corporation of New York, the Foundations Fund for Research in Psychiatry, the Grant Foundation, Stanford University Medical School General Research Funds, General Research Funds of The University of Chicago Division of Biological Sciences, and General Research Funds of The University of Chicago Social Science Research Committee. We are particularly indebted to Stanford University for permission to use its facilities for actualizing the design of this study and to both Stanford University and The University of Chicago for the provision of encouragement and a facilitative environment, as well as funds, space, and untold amounts of computer time. We also wish to express our appreciation to the Program in Humanistic Education, State University of New York at Albany, and to the Center for Policy Research, New York City, for secretarial assistance.

Many people have contributed actively and directly to the final product. We are indebted to Dr. Peggy Golde of Stanford University for her contributions in the early stages of the research, particularly her work on the issues of measuring racial attitudes and group norms, and in providing information on the leaders from an anthropological perspective. Without the energy, skill, and total devotion to the project of Herbert Wong, who served as project coordinator during the crucial first year of the study, we are certain we would never have completed our task. During that first active year when data were being collected at Stanford University, Lea Freedman contributed indefatigably both her research and administrative skills. We are grateful to Bonnie Weil, whose secretarial and artistic skills helped create a viable climate for organizing the groups and resolving countless administrative concerns. In particular, we would like to acknowledge the skills of the observers who, despite brief training, demonstrated reliability and sensitivity plus the willingness to serve at odd hours and distant places: Dr. Thomas Bittker, Roger Enfield, Michael Evans, Marvin Gerst, Carol Green, Laura Grinneks, Jon Kangas, Barry Kinney, Alan Levy, Frederic Levy, Jill McCleave, Joan Meisel, Dr. Dick Metzner, Barbara Phillips, John Rhead, Charles Richardson, Adam Rochmes, Peter Rogers, Cynthia Schwartz, Jeffery Schwartz, Ronald Schwartz, Dr. Saul Wasserman, Ronald Weisberg, Sylvia Weiner.

When the study entered its second and third year, several others added substantial contributions to the substantive findings. We would particularly like to acknowledge the contribution of Dr. Ruth Kraines of The University of Chicago and several University of Chicago students: Dr. Betty Goldiamond contributed substantially to the chapter on race, Dr. Susanne Drury is to be thanked for conceiving and executing the study of structured exercises, and Dr. Jan Allen for conceiving and executing the study of maintenance of change. Dr. Arthur Roberts made the initial explorations on self-disclosure, and Dr. Kitch Childs those on aspects of the person which influence learning. Steven Miller and Clifford Straley, at Stanford University, provided the basic data with regard respectively to "dropouts" and the utilization of critical incidents. Jackson Kytle at Teachers College, Columbia University, did the basic scaling on student militancy and political preference.

We have been aided by a number of people in our statistical analyses and would particularly like to thank (but not hold responsible) Dr. Helena Kraemer of Stanford University and Drs. Darrel Bock, David Wiley, and Donald Fiske of The University of Chicago, as well as Mrs. Louise Rehling, whose unusual skill as a programmer forestalled or resolved countless battles with the computer. Paul Amer, of the State University at Albany, provided competent computing assistance in final analyses of data on group norms, group conditions, and college effects. Other group conditions computations were carried out by Joel Millman at Teachers College. We are grateful to Barbara Hill for her perseverance in the face of innumerable changes in the manuscript and for her uncanny ability to commute the most illegible pages hastily into clean copy. This book would not have been possible in its present form without the yeoman services of Grace Lieberman, who served as content editor. To the extent that our style is tolerable and our meaning is clear we owe a debt to her. Finally, we would like to thank the participants who permitted the interruptions of their meaningful personal experience for the intervention of research and, most particularly, the group leaders who made the study possible. It is unusual for seasoned professionals to allow themselves to be examined as minutely as we have studied these leaders. We are grateful.

Morton A. Lieberman
Irvin D. Yalom
Matthew B. Miles

CONTENTS

Encounter Groups

CHAPTER 1

Intentions and Approaches

Today's American is fairly likely to come face to face with the question of membership in an encounter group. If he is not personally considering enrollment in a "growth center" or joining a "living room group," he may be evaluating encounter groups connected with his work or with his church, or he may be puzzling over a request from his offspring to sign a permission slip for participation in a school group. If any one of these is the case, he is likely to raise the questions that have been the target of the present study: What are encounter groups? What do they do for participants? How do they do it? Do they do it well? What are the risks? If he begins to make further exploration, he should soon add, "Should it be a T-group, a Transactional Analysis, Gestalt, or Sensory Awareness group? Should the leader be a psychiatrist, an artist, a tape recorder, one of us?"

The answers that have here or there been offered are as exhaustive as the questions. Encounter groups have varyingly been looked at as an antidote to alienation, a modern-day revival without the deity, fun and games for adults who cannot play without a token offering to the Protestant ethic, an inexpensive form of psychotherapy for the masses, a Communist plot to undermine American morals, a way out of the havoc of the industrial revolution. Those who have made themselves available to lead encounter groups may have been prepared by long years of training in a prestigious professional institution, by participation in a two-week institute, or purely by personal commitment.

In the varying forms it takes, the encounter movement is an enigma. It employs the newest, the oldest; its strategies sometimes stress safety, sometimes danger; it reveres anger and love, words and deeds, old Western drama, old Eastern meditation. Encounter groups are the interpersonal equivalent of skydiving. They are high-risk, high-adrenalin endeavors, partially controlled, semiregulated surprises. All participants share some idea

3

of what will unfold, but there is sufficient ignorance of the details to lend qualities of mystery and uneasy adventure into the unknowns of self and others.

The encounter movement exists largely outside the traditional help-giving institutions of society. Its strong egalitarian and anti-intellectual overtones may represent a reaction against many of the traditional institutional forms of help-giving and the dependence on the professional help-giver. Yet there is nothing new in the idea of using groups to make life better. Since time began small groups have flourished as healing agents whenever old values and behavior patterns were no longer working, and people were forced to question life and look at it anew. Religious healers have always relied heavily on the use of group forces to inspire hope, increase morale, offer emotional support, renew confidence in the benevolence of the universe, and, thus, counteract many psychic and bodily ills. Only as the healing function has passed from the priesthood to the secular professions has the conscious use of group forces declined concomitantly with increasing reverence of the doctor-patient relationship.

Despite their varied form and function, encounter groups do share common features. They attempt to provide an intensive, high contact, group experience; they are generally small enough (six to twenty members) to permit considerable face-to-face interaction; they focus on the here-and-now (the behavior of the members as it unfolds in the group); they encourage openness, honesty, interpersonal confrontation, self-disclosure, and strong emotional expression. The participant is usually not labeled a "patient" and the experience is not ordinarily labeled "therapy," though the groups strive to increase self and social awareness and to change behavior. The specific goals of the groups may vary from reducing juvenile delinquency to reducing weight. Occasionally they seek only to entertain, to "turn-on," to give experience in joy, but generally the overall goals involve some type of personal change—change of behavior, of attitudes, of values, of life-style.

The Emergent Scene

The first well-known forerunner of the present-day encounter group took place in 1946. After passing a Fair Employment Practice Act, the state of Connecticut asked a team of social psychologists and educators led by Kurt Lewin to conduct a workshop to train leaders to deal effectively with community interracial tensions. The participants were assigned to small discussion groups to analyze problems group members had experienced in their home communities. In each group recorders kept process records that were fed back to the workshop staff in evening planning sessions. At the request of some of the participants the evening meetings were open to permit the participants to share in the recorders' observations. Before long, all parties were involved in the analysis and interpretation of the dynamics operating in the workshop groups. The participants agreed that these evening meetings aided their understanding of their own behavior and its impact on the problems they were addressing in the workshop. The staff realized they had, perhaps inadvertently, discovered a powerful technique of human relations training. Group members might profit enormously from observations on how groups worked and about their own behavior and its effects on others.

The small group which was the center of the Connecticut workshop became the bellwether of subsequent annual summer laboratories sponsored by the National Training Laboratories, an organization founded by the staff of that first 1946 session. This basic human relations training group or, later, "T-group" ("T" for training) or sensitivity-training group, evolved through the years into an increasingly refined educational instrument. Group leaders employed concepts such as "feedback," the giving and receiving of interpersonal perceptions, and "participant-observation," the conscious study of the process of a group of which one is a member. They also designed numerous new techniques or exercises to explicate the dynamics of the small group at work.

The modern, swinging, "let it all hang out" encounter group appeared only as a speck on the horizon before the early 1960s. It derived from many sources. An important impetus toward the development of the new encounter group occurred when several West Coast group development leaders questioned the limitation of the use of human relations training to the acquisition of interpersonal and leadership skills. They proposed a more humanistically based redefinition of goals emphasizing personal growth, the development of full potential of the individual, the discovery and enjoyment of hidden, untapped resources. The emphasis shifted from learning about people in groups to learning about oneself.

No single source of the current encounter movement can be identified. California in the sixties was fertile soil for an experience which offered a promise of intimacy and a sense of community. Nowhere more than in California had there been such an inexorable breakdown of the institutions which traditionally have provided stability and intimacy. The nuclear family as well as the extended family, the stable neighborhood or work group, the local merchants and the family doctor, the neighborhood church in place after place had fallen prey to the demands of progress and a runaway technocracy. The encounter group became a social oasis where people could drop the facade of competence demanded by a fast moving, competitive society, and let loose their doubts and fears and disappointments. Harmonious forces in the newer psychologies of such men as Rogers and Maslow, which offered a positive, humanistic view of man, provided impetus for the personal growth group. From yet another direction, more traditional psychotherapists increasingly employed the group method, sometimes in simple response to the growing number wishing to be served, sometimes out of the conviction that the group, itself, posed a powerful curative force.

Other derivative streams arose simultaneously but independently: Synanon, Gestalt therapy, the Marathon, alternate life-style systems. All suggested that all people were patients. The disease was the runaway dehumanizing technocratic culture; the remedy was the return to grappling with the human condition; the vehicle of treatment was ideally the small group, "group therapy for normals." The differentiation between mental illness and health grew as vague as the distinction between treatment and change. Personal growth group leaders claimed simultaneously that patienthood is ubiquitous and that one need not be sick to get better.

The Issues

The T-group or experiential group, rechristened by Carl Rogers as the basic encounter group, snowballed in the mid-1960s until it reached the near epidemic proportions it had begun to assume in 1967 when the present study was conceived. The events of the fifteen years since the first Connecticut workshop have been the backdrop against which the basic questions and the methodology of the study have been shaped. It seemed time to gather the broad-gauged, comparative data required to examine whether the many conventional labels for personal growth groups reflected real differences, to develop beginning ideas of the specific processes through which such groups affect participants, and to understand the several aspects of the experience claimed to be the essential ingredients of personal change—the leader, the group culture, the personal characteristics of the participants, the activities or learning mechanisms employed to effect change.

The social relevance of the issue of casualties in encounter groups and the dearth of systematic information led to a concerted effort to identify all individuals who might have been psychologically harmed by the experience. The evidence is distressingly limited, but there is no dearth of emotional reaction to the issue of psychological risk. On the one hand, there is a tendency to see only the hazards of encounter group techniques. Some mental health specialists who have seen psychiatric casualties from encounter groups have responded by labeling the entire human relations field as dangerous and irresponsible. At the other extreme, there is a tendency to ignore, or to disregard, rather compelling evidence of adverse consequences of the encounter group experience. Many group leaders and growth centers are hardly aware of their casualties. Their contact with their clients is intense but brief; generally the format of the group does not include follow-up, and knowledge of untoward responses to the experience is, therefore, unavailable. Furthermore, some group leaders reject the medical or psychiatric definition of adverse effects. They assert that stressing members to the point of such discomfort that they require professional help is an accomplishment, not a danger of the encounter group. These leaders believe that such members, although temporarily worse, have in fact undergone a growth experience that will in the long run help them to be more fully integrated individuals. The evidence supporting either of these positions is meager.[1]

The questions which underlie the study design are schematically represented in Figure 1-1. The figure charts the sequence of events that might lead to or influence individual learning or change. The diagram is not meant to imply that all changes are equivalent, or that the same relationships are invariant for all changes; these are matters for empirical examination. What is implied is a causal sequence of events associated with outcome.

Starting at the bottom, outcomes (F) are most closely associated with the experiences (E) of the participant in the group. Experience is meant to include both how the participant related to the group—how active he is, how attracted, how influential, and so on—and his activities in the group, such as self-disclosure, receiving feedback, gaining insight, and so on.

What conditions bring about such experiences? Why do participants have them in some groups and not others? Why are some individuals in some groups more active than others? The focus in (D) is on characteristics of the group. Relationship between differences in group characteristics (D) and the participants' experience (E) is illustrated by such questions as: What is the association between the amount an individual self-discloses and the level of group cohesiveness? What is the relationship between receiving useful feedback and the existence of certain group norms?

The critical "experimental variable" that was assumed to make a difference among groups was, of course, the behavior of the leader. The hypothesized sequence relates leader variables (C) to group characteristics (D). Leaders were studied from the following perspectives—their actual behavior in the group and the perception of the participant of the leader's charisma, warmth, and so on. We also examined the relationship between the leader's theoretical or technological orientation (B) and his actual behavior. Finally, the personal characteristics of individual members (A) were tested for their influence on outcome (F). The line from (A) to (F) represents these relationships. The association may be more complex; personal characteristics, such as anticipations and expectations, may interact with group type. Or the relationship may be mediated through the participants' experience [expressed in terms of (A)–(E)] in which the degree of revelation, for example, may depend more on personal characteristics than on particular group conditions.

7

FIGURE 1–1

Schematic Overview of the Study

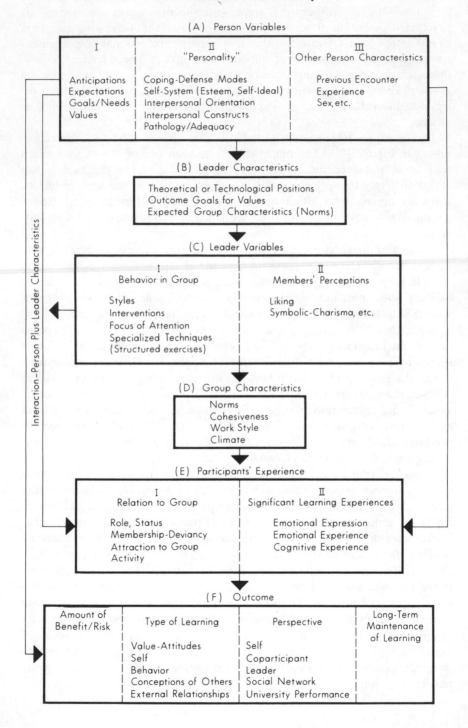

(A) Person Variables

I	II "Personality"	III Other Person Characteristics
Anticipations Expectations Goals/Needs Values	Coping-Defense Modes Self-System (Esteem, Self-Ideal) Interpersonal Orientation Interpersonal Constructs Pathology/Adequacy	Previous Encounter Experience Sex, etc.

(B) Leader Characteristics

Theoretical or Technological Positions
Outcome Goals for Values
Expected Group Characteristics (Norms)

(C) Leader Variables

I Behavior in Group	II Members' Perceptions
Styles Interventions Focus of Attention Specialized Techniques (Structured exercises)	Liking Symbolic-Charisma, etc.

(D) Group Characteristics

Norms
Cohesiveness
Work Style
Climate

(E) Participants' Experience

I Relation to Group	II Significant Learning Experiences
Role, Status Membership-Deviancy Attraction to Group Activity	Emotional Expression Emotional Experience Cognitive Experience

(F) Outcome

Amount of Benefit/Risk	Type of Learning	Perspective	Long-Term Maintenance of Learning
	Value-Attitudes Self Behavior Conceptions of Others External Relationships	Self Coparticipant Leader Social Network University Performance	

Interaction–Person Plus Leader Characteristics

The Methods

The style of the inquiry was shaped by general methodological and practical considerations. The initial intention was to undertake a field study, traveling to various centers of group activity to participate in, observe, and interview ongoing groups in their natural settings. Preliminary probes suggested serious limitations to such a strategy. The encounter group movement has a strong anti-intellectual flavor, a bias that might make leaders and participants less than ideal research subjects. A more important consideration was likely to be the selective influence of population differences across different types of encounter groups. A sample randomization to the various group types was critical to usable outcome research. The need to control population created the dilemma of how to accomplish this goal while minimizing the effects of "being researched" so that both participants and leaders could have a genuine experience.

This dilemma was resolved by a fortunate happenstance. The instructors of an experimental course at Stanford University on "Race and Prejudice" approached the investigators with questions of how to make the course more relevant from the students' point of view.[2] In the then current quarter, weekly "laboratory" sessions had turned into racial confrontations with explosive results. This situation suggested that the research interests could be combined with the University's interest in evaluating experienced-based educational activities. Highly experienced encounter group leaders, both black and white, were recruited to offer personal-growth programs to interested students from the course, as well as to other undergraduates interested in personal-growth experiences. The contract with the students was open: They were offered the opportunity to participate in groups composed of all-white or all-black students as well as mixed groups composed of black and white students; thus, they could use the group experience to explore both racial issues and other areas of interest. The encounter leaders were informed of the general research interests, as well as the intention to evaluate the effects of encounter groups on racial attitudes.

THE PARTICIPANTS AND CONTROLS

Students were recruited to participate in the experimental encounter groups through letters and presentations to those currently registered for the Race and Prejudice course, articles in student publications, and posters placed around the campus. These notices also briefly described the functions of the groups, and made clear that interested students could register for the encounter groups for three units of academic credit. (This arrangement had been made with the University both to legitimize the educational functions of the endeavor for the students, and to establish grounds for a realistic research contract with them.)

9

Students who expressed interest in the course were invited to a series of meetings in which the research staff discussed in depth the purposes of the inquiry and the nature of the experience to be offered. A microlab technique was employed at these meetings to illustrate the "feel" of encounter groups. In small groups of four or five, students engaged in various exercises chosen to demonstrate here-and-now communication, feedback techniques, and fantasy and personal revelation techniques. The students were told that the encounter groups would offer the opportunity to explore racial issues, but that they would be free to pursue any personal learning goals. The staff emphasized in these orientation meetings that the experience might be emotionally taxing and occasionally upsetting, and described the arrangements that had been made to make University mental health facilities available to participants if the groups became emotionally stressful.

Of the 251 students who registered for the encounter group course, fifty had been enrolled in the Race and Prejudice course. The original study design anticipated some all-black groups, some all-white groups, and several mixed black-white groups to test the influence of racial composition on racial attitude as well as on other dimensions of personal change. The timing of the study was unfortunate in this regard since racial tensions, which had been increasing on the campus for weeks, reached a critical point just at the time of registration. Only ten black students registered for the course; each was assigned to one of four groups, two of which were led by black leaders. The limited participation of black students meant of course that research expectations relative to questions concerning race had to be restricted to those appropriate to study under mixed racial conditions.

In all, 210 students were assigned to the eighteen encounter groups. The assignments were based on a stratified random sampling of sex, class year, and previous encounter group experience.[3] A control group was composed of thirty-eight students who had registered for the Race and Prejudice course but could not be accommodated in the encounter groups because of size limitations or schedule conflicts, and thirty-one demographically matched students who were randomly selected from names generated through a questionnaire which had asked participants to name six friends who "may have interest in the group experience but who cannot participate next quarter and will be here at Stanford next Fall." These sixty-nine students were offered payment to take the same psychological test batteries as the students in the groups and to commit themselves to follow-up testing sessions at the end of the Spring Quarter, and again six months later.[4]

THE GROUPS AND THEIR LEADERS

In the interest of representing major theoretical differences in approaches to the encounter experience, sixteen leaders were retained to represent nine widely used group technologies. The tenth type, the Tape Group, required no leaders.

Because all too often inquiry into growth-oriented group experiences has been based on the work of inexperienced leaders, considerable care was given to the selection of group leaders. From a list of sixty experienced leaders representing the nine approaches, professionals most familiar with each approach were asked "Who are the two best leaders in the Bay area?" The sixteen leaders selected were mostly psychiatrists or psychologists. All were highly experienced group leaders, and were uniformly esteemed by their colleagues as representing the best of their approach.

A time limit of thirty hours was set for the duration of all the groups. The other restriction on format was that only those leaders selected to conduct marathons could utilize their total time in a continuous manner if they so chose. To encourage the leaders to feel unrestricted in fully utilizing their skills, flexibility was permitted wherever possible. Some leaders preferred to meet twice a week for ten weeks, others began with a six-hour session followed by shorter weekly sessions and a six-hour terminal session.

The leaders were informed that the research was an outgrowth of the Race and Prejudice course. It was emphasized, however, that they were expected to "do their thing," to conduct the groups in the same manner they normally did to enhance the possibility of their group members' personal growth. What was unusual about the experience for most of the leaders was the heavy load of research tasks involved. Each leader was asked to fill out a number of questionnaires before, during, and after the research experience, as well as to permit tape recording and ongoing observation of his group. Yet, at the same time, the research dimension was part of the attraction of the assignment for most of the leaders.

The ten approaches represented in the study groups were:

National Training Laboratory (Basic Human Relations Group, T-group, Sensivitivy Group). The traditional NTL-modeled group in which the leader's role is seen as helping members understand themselves and others within and through the group process. The leader characteristically focuses on the group as a whole and on the members' transactions with each other. He attempts to explicate what is happening to the group as a whole, focusing on such issues as group maintenance, cohesiveness, power and work distribution, subgrouping, scapegoating, and so on.

Gestalt Therapy. Gestalt therapy has been a militant, proselytizing movement with major centers in New York, California, and Cleveland. Gestalt stresses the wholeness of the individual. Change is viewed as a subintellectual process which is mediated by helping the individual get in touch with the primitive wisdom of the body. When the late Fritz Perls, founder of the Gestalt school, operated Gestalt groups, there was little use of the group, or, for that matter, the other group members. There was an empty chair, "the hot seat," next to the leader to which the members came one by one to "work" with the leader. In Gestalt-oriented encounter, much emphasis is placed on heightened emotionality, on understanding what the body is telling one by its posture, by its numerous autonomic and muscular-skeletal messages. The leader often helps members to resolve inner conflict by holding dialogues between the disparate parts of the psyche. The participation of the other members is minimal; often their primary function is simply to verify by their presence, like the all-seeing Greek chorus.

Transactional Analytic. Eric Berne (1961) first introduced the term "transactional analysis" and a distinct style of small group leadership based on this method. Not unlike the Gestalt groups, the "work" is done by the leader with each of the group members in turn. Berne often spoke of therapy *in* a group rather than *with* a group. The term transactional analysis refers to the transactions between ego states (parent, child, and adult) *within* one individual rather than transactions among individuals.

Esalen Eclectic. William Schultz in his book *Joy* (1967) describes a basic approach to the encounter group and a number of techniques for accelerating the developmental pace of the group. These include an emphasis both on the experiencing and deepening of interpersonal relationships and on the liberating of somatic restrictions. By breaking free from social and muscular inhibitions, people learn to experience their own bodies and other people in a different and fuller sense. The group leader's focus is on both the individual and the interpersonal relationships within the group. Often structural interventions may be suggested by the leader to help members shuck constricting inhibitions. The emphasis is on doing and experiencing; the cause, the meaning of the persisting restrictions is of minor consequence.

Personal Growth (*National Training Laboratory Groups, Western Style*). Personal growth leaders are grounded in the NTL sensitivity group approach, but have shifted their emphasis from the group to a Rogerian conception of the individual. Most of the leader's attention is centered on interpersonal or intrapersonal dynamics; rarely does he focus on "the group." He has a liberating model of personal development and does not object to the concept of group therapy for normals. Most leaders of this school see little distinction between personal growth and psychotherapy.

Synanon. The Synanon group (referred to as the Synanon game) is grossly different from any of the other types. It emphasizes the expression of anger; the game is "put" on each member in turn, and the other members systematically explore and attack him, presumably in the belief that if one is attacked in his weakest areas long enough he will grow stronger in them. It is termed a game perhaps because once the group is over the atmosphere changes quickly to one of warm support.

Psychodrama. To consider psychodrama as a type of encounter group is to introduce slippage in logic, since psychodrama or role-playing is used as an aid, or an auxiliary technique, in many encounter formats. Some encounter group leaders, however, structure their groups predominantly as psychodrama or role-playing experiences. (The Moreno purist may shudder at this vulgarization, since these groups are obviously not employing psychodrama in its classic sense.)

Marathon. The marathon or time-extended group meeting, first introduced by George Bach, has become a household concept in the crazy quilt world of the encounter group. A marathon group meets for long stretches of time: twelve, twenty-four, or, occasionally, an heroic forty-eight hours without pause. Members may take short sleep periods but generally the group is continuous. Intensive psychological contact together with sheer physical exhaustion serve to accelerate the movement and the pace of interaction. "Marathon-oriented" encounter leaders claim that the power generated by this hyperbolical togetherness can in a single weekend induce more personal change than months, even years, of spaced, "diluted" meetings. The marathon format implies more than sheer form. Affixed to the form are certain core substantive principles: high intensity, involvement, interpersonal honesty, and confrontation. Defense mechanisms are not tolerated; the members must quickly jettison them or the group strips or vigorously sands them away.

Psychoanalytically Oriented. The term "psychoanalytic encounter group" would have persuaded Fenichel that the American Philistines had overrun the last bastion of the classical psychoanalytic edifice. This category is intended to represent encounter groups led by conservative, analytically oriented clinicians. These groups are generally, but not always, led for students in the helping professions; they focus on the dynamics and the individual in the group, especially from the perspective of his personal historical development. They tend to be less emotionally charged, more rationally based with heavier focus on intellectual mastery of group dynamics as well as inter- and intrapersonal forces operating in the group.

Encounter Tapes (Leaderless Groups). Many encounter groups are self-directed; they have no officially designated leader, though often an unofficial leader emerges from the ranks of the members. Elizabeth Berzon investigated several methods of increasing the efficacy of leaderless groups, attempting to understand the precise contributions of the leader and to build these functions into the group through some artificial means. She has developed a highly sophisticated set of tape recordings which members play during each meeting of an encounter group. These tapes are marketed under the trade name of "Encountertapes" by Bell and Howell, and have gained widespread use. The tape program uses a variety of structured exercises (prescribed sets of interaction among members as a total group, among pairs, and occasionally as individuals in meditation) to construct a cohesive, "warm," and unthreatening group climate. Members are taught through doing as well as through explanations to emphasize relationships, feedback, and reflection.

THE MEASURES

Studies of educational and therapeutic outcomes are chronically plagued by problems of when to measure, how to measure, and what to measure. These problems were magnified in the present case because of the range of leader orientations and participant goals. Three basic intentions guided the process of assessment. First, any imbalance in data collection should be on the side of too many to handle rather than too few to be meaningful; the consequent "data bank" could be drawn upon as issues and questions which might have been unanticipated in the planning stage but arose out of the analysis. The second principle was to insure that the encounter experience could be evaluated not only through the eyes of the participants, but also from the vantage point of the leaders, the coparticipants, and friends of the participants who might be sensitive to some of its effects upon participants. Finally, it was deemed essential to assess not only immediate outcome differences, but also the maintenance of learning over a relatively long term. Thus a number of outcome measures were administered to participants and controls before the groups began, immediately after they were terminated, and six months after termination.

Needless to say such intentions necessitated many more measurement instruments than merit detailed description here. Most are reproduced in the Appendices for the interested reader. Wherever possible, instruments were used that have been developed by other investigators, but the special qualities of the encounter experience made it necessary to develop many new measures.

Assessment of Outcomes. Outcome was measured in terms of the role of encounter experience in the life of each participant. In order to acknowledge that people may enter encounter groups with varied expectations and goals, the strategy was to test a multiplicity of conceivable learnings. Some effects of the experience could be expected to be described as diffuse and general changes in the person as a whole, others as discrete behavioral changes. Some were likely to show up only in information gained directly from the participants; others might be detected or checked through other sources, such as leaders, other participants, or friends.

For some participants the central importance of what is taken from the encounter group may be reflected in "oceanic, enthusiastic, conversion-like" feelings—a "peak experience" that only the participant senses, but which he views as a landmark having long-term implications, an anchor point, a goad to further experience, or a determinant in life-planning. Such responses were identified by providing participants with a paragraph-long description of "peak experience." They were asked whether they had ever had such an experience and under what conditions it occurred.

As a consequence of the encounter experience a person may become more or less critical of others, more or less tolerant; he may come to view people as more complex, less detailed. He may increase or decrease his belief that interpersonal difficulties can be worked out. The device used to measure this dimension ("Personal Description Questionnaire") was an adaptation of Harrison's adaptation of the Kelly REP test (Harrison, 1962).

Three procedures were employed to assess issues related to self. Self-ideal discrepancy was measured on the same scales used to measure interpersonal constructs; the Rosenberg scales (Rosenberg, 1965) and the self-description ratings on the Personal Description Questionnaire provided two measures of self-esteem; the congruence between self-perception in the group situation and others' views of self was assessed during the early and late meetings of the group by means of a twenty-one-item sociometric covering various roles and statuses of members of the group ("The Members of This Group").

The meaningfulness of encounter experience may also be reflected in a reordering or reorientation of perceptions of what is personally important. Two realms of values were sampled: Participants were asked the importance to them of seven types of personal behavior, stressed in encounter, such as spontaneity and expression of feelings ("Personal Anticipations"). They were asked to indicate on a "Life-Space Questionnaire" their most important life goals now and as they imagined they would be seven years hence. People often join encounter groups when they are facing life crises, such as a change of career or the break-up of a marriage, that require them to make major decisions. For such people the most salient aspect of the group experience may be the work done in resolving such dilemmas. To trace these changes, participants were asked to indicate on the "Life-Space Questionnaire" whether they were contemplating any change in life space related to salient goals, such as altering a direction, making a new choice, entering into new activities, or giving up old activities or relationships.

The encounter group experience may also open up new ways of dealing with personal dilemmas. For example, a person may learn that paying attention to his inner life aids coping; he may utilize the world of feelings more frequently; or he may find that establishing symmetric feedback relationships aids problem-solving. Learning new modalities or broadening one's problem-solving approach to personal issues may be the prime learning carried away from the experience. The "Personal Dilemma Questionnaire" was developed to assess this area.

Three approaches were employed to assess changes in interpersonal relationships. Prior to participation, participants rated "where they were now" and "where they hoped to be at the end of the group" with respect to expression of affection and anger, spontaneity, and thirteen other similar issues. At the end of the experience, these forms were returned to each participant, and he was asked to indicate where he was now. A similar format describing situational opportunities for such behavior as expression of feeling, spontaneity, was also administered before and after the experience ("Personal Anticipations"). The FIRO-B (Schutz, 1966) was used to measure preferred interpersonal style. Finally, a "Friendship Question-naire" was administered to assess both the extensiveness and intensity of friendships outside of the group.

The degree to which the individual perceived the encounter group experience as dangerous / safe, genuine / phony, socially relevant / irrelevant, and so on was measured by a twenty-four-item "Index of Encounter Group Attitudes." Participants were asked to evaluate the personal relevance of the experience by means of open-ended questions as well as scales.

We also measured the impact of the encounter groups on participants through the eyes of leaders, coparticipants, and friends. Many psychotherapy and T-group research reports suggest that, despite the potential biases of the therapist or trainer, professional judgments of change have proved to be a useful, valid source of information. In this study, group leaders were asked to rate changes they felt in each member in nine areas, such as spontaneity, happiness, and interpersonal sensitivity ("Leader Evaluation"). Coparticipants in the group provided another perspective for assessing member change. Several times during the course of the group experience, participants filled out a sociometric questionnaire rank-ordering each group member relative to the amount of learning achieved as well as for specific group behaviors. At the onset of the study, both participants and controls were asked for the names of five to seven individuals who knew them quite well ("Social Network"). At the six-month follow-up, letters were sent to each participant's and control's "social network" asking whether the person had changed over the past six months. If the respondent indicated "yes," he was asked to describe the nature of the changes. This procedure offered an external checkpoint on whether changes reported by leaders, coparticipants, or self were of sufficient magnitude to be perceived by people in close contact with the participant (see Miles, 1965; Bunker, 1965).

Approximately half the participants were interviewed a few months after the end of their group experience. Those who had dropped out of their groups, or were suspected to have had an exceptionally rewarding experience, or to have suffered psychological damage were interviewed intensively. (A few facts were gleaned from the Stanford University records—pre- and postgroup grade point averages, incidence of dropout from school, and date of graduation.)

Assessments of Leader and Group Characteristics. An essential assumption of the study was that what happened to participants would be heavily influenced by crucial aspects of the leader's behavior, as well as salient characteristics of the group as an entity. A "Leadership Questionnaire" asked the participant to answer ten questions about his leader, choosing for each question from four words he thought best described the leader: Charisma-oriented, love-oriented, peer-oriented, and skill-oriented. And, certain group characteristics could be assessed only through participant reports. At the end of an early, middle, and late session, group norms were assessed by asking the participant to indicate whether particular behaviors involving intimacy, aggression, confidentiality, and so on, would be appropriate in his group at the present time ("Checklist of Do's and Don'ts"). Group cohesiveness was measured by asking participants to rate such items as, "Since the last session I have thought about the group all the time . . . not at all," (Yalom *et al.*, 1967).

Each participant's "personal" response to his experience in the group was assessed through a "Critical Incident Questionnaire," administered at the end of every meeting, which asked: "Of the events that occurred in the meeting today, which one do you feel was the most significant to you personally and why was this experience significant to you?" At the last group meeting participants ranked fourteen aspects of the group experience they felt were personally helpful in growth or learning ("Curative Factors Questionnaire"). Items included such dimensions as expressing feelings, using others as models, understanding one's own impact on others, and so on.

A number of other crucial dimensions of leadership and group conditions were assessed through ratings of trained clinicians who attended each meeting in pairs. These observers [5] provided data for each meeting on discussion content, predominant work patterns, nonverbal procedures, extent of personal revelation, group climate (twelve Osgood scales), dominant issues confronting the group ("Themes Ratings"), group norms (similar to participant checklist of Do's and Don'ts), leader interventions ("Checklist of Leader Behavior"), focus of leader's attention (group, individual, or interpersonal) and leader style, in terms of nine overall categories such as releaser of emotions, personal leader, teacher, challenger ("Leader Style Ratings"). Observers were also asked to rate their own personal reactions to the leader after each meeting on eight Osgood scales.

THE CHALLENGE

Whatever controversy may obtain regarding the utility, the effectiveness, the risk of encounter ·groups, most observers attest that they contain a quality which induces involvement, excitement, often enthusiasm. There is evidence throughout the succeeding pages that encounter groups can work mood magic on those who partake of them. One of the most challenging tasks of the study has been to try to understand why and how encounter groups have such power to move people emotionally and to examine this effect judiciously, neither dismissing it prematurely as meaningless nor accepting it as evidence of meaning sufficient unto itself.

As for all events endowed with magical qualities, sifting the real from the unreal, the substantial from the gossamer is the first problem, the first responsibility of inquiry. In the encounter movement, widespread enthusiasm of both purveyors and consumers has all too often combined to discourage, at times even actively oppose such an effort. Yet only through

17

systematic information on how well the innovations which characterize the movement actually serve the goal of positive personal change may what magic inheres in the process be harnessed most effectively.

NOTES

1. The data relating to encounter group casualties are in a chaotic state and extraordinarily difficult to evaluate (News and Reports, 1969; Sata, 1967; Gottschalk and Pattison, 1969; Jaffe and Sherl, 1969). Systematic follow-up studies are scarce. Much of the material is anecdotal; a large number of participants in a group or a laboratory increases the likelihood of multiple reporting. If fifty laboratory participants report the same single negative (or positive) event, it soon takes on massive proportions.

2. Stanford is a private university with an undergraduate body of approximately 8,000 students. The student body is preponderantly middle- and upper-class. The academic standards are high and the average standard achievement test score is over 650. Although Stanford had been relatively tranquil and nonmilitant in the past, there was considerable student unrest stirring on the Stanford campus during the year the experiment was conducted. Interest in encounter groups on campus was exceedingly high at the time of the project. Some lecturers who took informal polls of their classrooms found that approximately 50 percent of Stanford students had attended at least one encounter group. There was abundant evidence of encounter group activity on the campus: encounter groups were advertised in the *Stanford Daily* newspaper, on bulletin boards, and on posters widely distributed around the campus.

3. Slightly over two-thirds of the participants were males (a bit under the 3:1 male-female ratio of undergraduates at Stanford). Over 90 percent of their parents had had some college education. Their own Standard Achievement Test Scores averaged in the mid-600s. All the participants were undergraduates and came about equally from the four class years (the Junior year was slightly underrepresented). Except for ten black and five Oriental participants, all were white; most were Protestant, 13 percent were Jewish, and 12 percent were Catholic. Most of the participants were majoring in the social sciences, or humanities, about half had been in an encounter group before, and 80 percent had at least one close friend who had been in an encounter group.

Overall, the participants viewed encounter groups with a cautious positiveness before the groups began. Two-thirds of the participants viewed the encounter group as more safe than dangerous, as more socially beneficial than irrelevant to social issues, and as more genuine than phony.

On a series of ten-point scales (0–9, with the midpoint at 4.5) on which they rated their behavior on expressivity, awareness of others, adequacy of relationships, intimacy, inner understanding, sensitivity, and spontaneity, participants emphasized their relative satisfaction with their ability to express emotions, to understand themselves, to be sensitive and spontaneous. (The means on these four scales were slightly above the midpoint, though the variations were large. Two-thirds of the participants scored between a rating of 7.5 and a low of 2.5.) They expressed more difficulties in their ability to be aware of others' feelings, to get close to others, and, particularly, to relate to people (mean of 3.3).

On a series of ten-point measures of opportunities in their interpersonal environment (0–9, with a midpoint of 4.5), participants indicated that they had numerous opportunities for novel experiences and for situations where they could trust others (the only two scales above the midpoint), a reasonable number of opportunities for being open, sharing with their peers, and expressing feelings directly (at midpoint), and fewer opportunities for the availability of feedback from others about their behavior, for expressing anger, and, to some extent, for getting to know others deeply. These ratings suggest that the desire for feedback and for expression of anger were uppermost in the majority of the participants' minds, when considering the encounter groups; these were closely followed by needs for a situation to express closeness. Being able to trust and having novel experiences were two areas that participants would be unlikely to emphasize in the encounter groups.

Furthermore, as a group, the participants emphasized changing the way they related to people, feedback (learning how others view them), flexibility (letting things happen), and sharing with their peers as the most important goals in the encounter group. Being able to express their feelings and having new experiences were moderately important to them. Expressing anger directly to people was distinctly unimportant.

Prior to the beginning of the encounter group the average participant listed approximately seven value items on a life-space questionnaire (What are the most important things in your life?). A little over two-thirds of the value items concerned content focusing on self—issues of identity, self-acceptance, need achievement, skills, academic concerns, career, life-styles, and the like. A little over a quarter of the value items focused on interpersonal issues and relationships. The remaining value items were concerned with social or political issues.

Within the self area, of the seven items the average person found important, 1.7 were concerned with issues of identity, self-understanding, philosophy, self-acceptance, life-style, self-expression, and new experiences; 1.9 were concerned with the external world, specifically achievement, motivation, material objects, physical health, academic and career issues; and .9 were concerned with issues of hedonism such as new experiences, novelty, adventure, leisure, pleasure, nature, and esthetics. The average person cited approximately two values focusing on interpersonal relationships. Obviously, individual differences were predominate in this area and it is difficult to characterize the entire population except to note that issues of development and change were central. Over one-quarter of the issues presented in the participants' listing of values concerned important life decisions. Approximately half of the students said that at least one decision confronted them. Clearly the students were involved in changing, growing, developing.

4. The sixty-nine control subjects closely paralleled the participants in sex and class level distribution. They had had slightly more contact with encounter groups through their own participation or that of friends. There were fewer Jewish and more Catholic students in the control population. A larger number majored in engineering, and fewer were in the social sciences. They had a lower mean SAT math score (639) than the experimentals (664); the mean SAT verbal score was virtually identical (controls 638, experimentals 635). Although the control group was made up of students recruited in two different ways, analysis of pretests demonstrated that they did not differ significantly on any of the pretest variables, so that they have been treated as a single group in subsequent analyses.

5. A team of twenty-nine observers including the research staff observed each meeting. The observers were pre- or postdoctoral clinical psychology interns at a local hospital, graduate students in clinical psychology, psychiatric residents, or, in a few instances, practicing clinicians. All had led or participated in encounter groups. The observers were trained for a total of approximately fifteen hours, twelve hours prior to first observation and three hours after the third observation. Training consisted of orientation to the study, microlab techniques for team building, practice use of instruments on the data produced in the microlabs, and systematic definition of scales and practice of observation skills using encounter group films.

The large number of group hours required a methodology for making the data gathered by the observers directly transformable for computer processing. The observation tasks were therefore cast at a macroscopic level. Observers made no ratings during the meetings. A log sheet was used to make notes. Immediately after the end of the standard three-hour observation period each observer reviewed his notes and filled out a set of rating forms. The departure of the observation techniques from more conventional ones may be illustrated by the process employed to assess group themes of covert emotional issues in the group, modeled after focal conflict theory (Whitaker and Lieberman, 1965). The usual procedures for this analysis require judgments based on a transcript, a detailed and obviously time-consuming procedure. For the present study, a form was constructed that presented the observer with an ordered sequence of possible conflicts. The observer indicated his relatively complex judgments in codeable form. Thus, the observer data represent midlevel abstractions, rather than microscopic ratings, of the interaction of the group. The use of such procedures was based on the assumption that relatively sophisticated clinicians can process complex group events, and make reasonable and reliable judgments upon reflection.

The complexity of the tasks to be performed by the observers placed a high demand on their energies and skills (174 judgments had to be made after each session). A further risk was that the compelling quality of encountering might draw the observers into the emotional drama causing them to lose their objectivity. To circumvent such influences and increase the reliability of observer judgments, two observers were assigned to each three-hour session. Furthermore, observers and observer pairs were systematically rotated among the groups and from one session to another. In most cases, the same observer pairs never met more than one observation period, and most observers saw the same group only once or twice in its lifetime. These systematic rotations, although losing some of the quality of information gained as an observer "gets to know a group," did correct for personal biases and provide relative uniformity of information across groups. After making their independent ratings of each observer period, the observer pairs met, discussed their ratings, and attempted to resolve any differences in their judgments. Thus for each meeting there were two independent observations plus a third rating based on observer discussions. Observers made ratings related only to the behavior of the leader and the characteristics of the groups; they made no judgments used to assess outcomes to participants.

Observers were strongly urged to remain *nonparticipants,* and to resist any efforts by the group members or leaders to pull them into the flux of the group. They were not to be totally mute, however, if muteness acted as an irritant to the leader or member who was confronting them; they attempted merely to remind all parties that the contract they had made with the research staff required that they be nonparticipant observers. Each leader had access, if he wished, to the informal notes (the "log sheet") made by the two observers during the meetings, but he was unaware of the ratings the observers made after the end of each meeting. The leaders received no feedback from the observers.

CHAPTER 2

The Groups in Profile

The group participants shared many experiences: they were recruited and oriented en masse; they were confronted with the same research questionnaires; they all met in groups which were tape recorded and scrutinized by two silent note-taking observers; they were all studied immediately at the end of the group and again six months later for follow-up purposes. Beyond these common features the experience of the participants differed sharply. Each of the seventeen groups had its own unique life cycle. The life of each group and the experience of each participant within that life was so complex that we can only hope to approximate it, to schematize it, in the following pages.

This overview of each group was derived from many sources: questionnaire data, observers' notations, interviews with members and leaders, attendance records, and transcribed excerpts from tape recordings of the meetings.

Group #1—T-Group

Solid, hard-working, garden variety, training-type encounter group: Low profile, supportive leader. . . .

Group #1 met eight times in a sparsely furnished dormitory lounge, where members sat on the floor. Although two of the six men and three women who made up the group were black, the group was not primarily focused on racial issues. All but one member attended every session, and no one dropped out of the group. The leader had had fifteen years of experience with sensitivity-training groups, staff development programs, racial encounter groups, and therapy groups.

Leader #1 said he thought of a group as a collection of individuals who are moving toward forming relationships with one another, and who become a group with its own standards, values, and norms after a period of evolution. He reported that initially he offers minimal guidelines, becomes increasingly active as the group progresses, but still tends to limit his interventions to interpretations about the here-and-now. He said that he used the group to get feedback about himself by checking with the members about their view of things he said or did. He described his goals as wanting to help the members become closer to one another, and to develop skill in communicating more adequately.

According to the observers, Leader #1 generally oriented his remarks toward interpersonal relations in the group, and rarely focused on one member's fantasies, history, or current personal problems. Among all leaders, observers rated him about midway in calling attention to the group as a whole. In the observers' view, Leader #1 tended to protect, support, and befriend the group members. He often revealed his own here-and-now feelings; much less frequently, his personal values. He rarely challenged, confronted, or exhorted members of the group; he questioned them, invited them to participate, or made explanatory comments. Occasionally he offered concepts to help understand behavior.

The observers rated his overall style as that of a "resource leader," there to be used as the group would like to use him, while he himself had nothing overt that he wanted the group to do; a noninterventionist. Whenever he did manage the group, it was to focus its attention on what was happening. Occasionally he suggested some sort of procedure. Although he participated, he did not characteristically draw attention to himself as the leader. Observers ranked only five leaders as having less charisma; only two as more caring and supportive.

Some verbatim comments by the leader culled from the last meeting may add to the picture of Leader #1:

My impression is that she is very close to you, Jim. Does anyone else share that impression? How do you all account for her willingness to take a risk for Jim? It seemed to me she cared a great deal to be willing to risk losing something. . . . Was your heart pounding when you did it? . . . When you take a risk like that it takes a hell of a lot of caring for someone and there is not apathy in that relationship. . . . Why don't you ask her how she felt about it? . . . Is he right? Is that valid? Does that confirm the way you're thinking? . . . Now you're being protective. . . . I was really tickled by your willingness to encounter. That was a genuine encounter last week, no mistake about it.

. . . What's important for me in the group? It is that somehow we build a kind of climate that will permit us to share whatever feelings exist in here.

. . . Jerry, you seem to have backed off quite a bit. . . . I want to hear more about the loneliness and longing, the longing that shows in your face. To me, I see you as a very attractive male and that's something intriguing. Well, maybe not intriguing, let's say warm and feeling. I like you, that's what I'm saying. I feel a lot of sensitivity that doesn't get released and I felt a lot of yearning that gets avoided somehow; and yet somehow it doesn't connect.

(The leader later in this group suggested an exercise in which one of the members was cradled by the others.) . . . Do you have any feelings that we might drop you? . . . What I was trying to convey with this was that the group was willing and able to cradle one of its members and to let them hold you, and that person can give herself to the group.

I get a great sense of your affection, John. . . . When I embrace a guy I feel his manliness. The question is whether I am afraid of it or not or whether there is some sort of erotic implication to this.

Leader #1 was rated about midway among the leaders in his use of structured exercises. Some examples:

Let's do an experiment in knowing. Get in a very small circle, see and be seen for a few minutes. No talking. Communicate with each other nonverbally.

Be a kid and say what a kid feels. Be a frightened little girl. What does she say?

Set up a pile of hands. Recognize what your hands are saying. Let yourselves be seen and try to see. Move your hands around slowly.

I'd like to have you try visualizing who you feel close to and distant from. Try to place each of us in the group according to how you feel to us. In other words, those that you feel closest to put close to you; those that you feel furthest from put far away from you. Just put us where we go; anywhere you choose. Move us around and change us as you see fit, like an interior decorator. Now let the rest of us look around as she places us and think in terms of how close we feel to her. Where would we put ourselves, one at a time.

GROUP PROCESSES

In the first meetings there was some focus on the members' outside lives. As the group proceeded, the amount of here-and-now material gradually increased. Overall, the group was eighth of the seventeen groups in percentage of time spent on here-and-now topics. This was one of the very few groups (along with Groups #2 and #8) in which there was a clearcut developmental progression from outside material to inside material.

When the group talked about outside material, it usually pertained to racial or personal issues that were then current in the lives of the members, rather than to more abstract social topics or personal historical material. When the group discussed inside issues, they frequently discussed "the group." In fact, the members of only one other group discussed "the group" more often. The rest of the inside material related to interpersonal issues. This group spent more time discussing inside material on interpersonal issues than any other group. They seldom discussed themselves as individuals or the leader.

The group was relatively unstructured; the most typical mode of communication was a rather general unfocused discussion. It was very rare that the group used some type of formal go-around. Very rarely did one member monopolize the group. Lengthy dialogue between two group members was not unusual, however. In the later meetings, members tended to reveal their here-and-now feelings more than the members in the majority of other groups, although there was still little talk about past history or current outside issues. Members described their group as not very cohesive (it ranked as one of the least cohesive groups), and said, furthermore, that the cohesion at meeting eight was lower than in meeting four.

When asked about the events in the group most important to them, members of Group #1 usually selected some type of expression of feeling, citing occasions when they openly expressed some strong emotion like anger, warmth, closeness. Group events (group expressing a feeling, mastering a certain issue, or getting over a certain roadblock) were selected more commonly in this group than in other groups. They also cited expressing feelings as their most important learning; helping others, second (although the average rank was seventh).

LOOKING BACK

When the group was terminated, the members did not rate their group experience as a very positive one. Compared with the other groups, the members of Group #1 found their group less pleasant, less turned-on, less constructive, and one in which they regarded themselves as learning relatively little. Nor did they think too highly of their leader. They rated him below the mean of other members' ratings of other leaders on their opinions of his competence, on whether they would like to be in another group with him, on their admiration of him as a person, on their approval of his techniques, on their feeling that he understood the group, and on the ratings of his effectiveness. Only three of the other fifteen leaders were rated less favorably by their group members. The observers felt much more positive about the leader and rated only three leaders more highly on the same dimensions on which the group members had been asked to rate their leaders.

Some of the members stated that the leader was just too vague and should have supplied more direction, more push, more dynamic energy to the group. They felt that he was too passive and should have done more teaching. One group member, however, seen several months after the end of the group, had a much more positive feeling about the group than earlier.

Overall, Leader #1 had positive feelings about the group. He felt that the pace was good and that they achieved a level of sharing and strong support. Although there was some testing of anger, by and large it was a low conflict group compared with other groups that he had led. Were he to lead the group again, he did not feel that he would change his techniques in any important way.

Group #2—T-Group

Classic, old school, sensitivity group, members frustrated, straining at bit; leader patient, firmly holding reins. . . .

Group #2 met seven times. The first and the fourth meetings were six hours long, the other five were three hours long. The first two meetings were in a dormitory lounge, and the last five in the living room of a member's on-campus apartment. The setting was informal; all sat on the floor. The three women and seven men in the group attended regularly.

Leader #2 was a clinical psychologist who had been deeply involved in sensitivity training for eleven years, and was nationally recognized as an expert in the area of group function and group dynamics. He stressed the importance of molding the group and of the members' participation and understanding of the process of group formation so that they could begin to understand other social environments in which they had to function. He said it was important for him that individuals in the group work toward greater humaneness toward others and more openness and honesty with themselves; he wanted them to enjoy the others in the group. He described himself as deliberately less active than many leaders because he felt that a group should struggle with its internal problems and have the satisfaction of resolving them, rather than being constantly removed from the cocoon of group forces by a well-meaning, but too active and tantalizing, leader. He saw himself as both a leader and member: "I am somewhere between a teacher in the broadest sense, and a member of the community which develops."

Observers rated Leader #2 third among the leaders in the attention he focused on the entire group, second in attention to interpersonal material. Observers reported that he often invited members to participate, questioned them, or reflected something back to them, but he rarely directly challenged or confronted them. He provided cognitive structure by comparing members one to another or inviting them to seek feedback from the other members, although he did not often explain, or summarize, or offer members a specific suggestion about how to understand themselves. He did support members of the group occasionally, but rarely explicitly protected or befriended a member. He did not participate as a member of the group, and he rarely revealed his own personal values or his own here-and-now feelings, but he did tend to draw attention to himself as a leader.

The observers found him a "social engineer and releaser of emotions by

25

suggestion." He attempted to focus attention on how the group as a whole should move ahead, rather than on the private problems of individual members. He often was seen to manage the group by stopping it, or blocking something, or focusing on a particularly important thing, or pacing the group, or by calling attention to a decision that the group had to make.

These statements come from the beginning of the first meeting:

Does anybody have any ideas on how we might start? Shall we have introductions? . . . How do you feel about what's going on so far? . . . How did you feel as this was going on? . . . Gee, I didn't have that feeling at all. I was touched by what you said. How do you feel about that?

I think we should bring this thing into the present, into the now, instead of thinking about it as just a discussion we are having. It sounded like you had a lot of feelings about me. . . . I don't know yet if I want to be a member of the group. . . . I guess the leader is always the assumed central part of a group somehow. . . .

From Session 5:

Is a discussion about getting involved here a kind of red hot topic? . . . Do you feel any ties here at all, I'm asking each of you? Is it hard to talk about them, about how you feel toward people in the room?

Do you think that you can react physically with this group? I'll ask you if there's any physical technique that you'd want to use if you don't want to react verbally with the group. . . . I'm sure that each person will find his own way to express himself, I don't care how. We're not limited to verbal expression. There's your face, your body, anyway. I wouldn't make a game or a gimmick out of it, but if you actually want to express yourself, by all means it's open to you.

Jim, can I share a feeling I have about you? I have the impression that you're just bursting to be the leader of this group. In one way or another that would make you happy. . . . I'd like to check this out with you. How do you feel about being the leader of this group, because it's a hunch on my part? . . . I don't know of a simple lecture to give you.

. . . I want to describe my role as I do it, and I think I reserve the option to do this. From time to time I'll offer what I think are suggestions, about the way in which I think you can work usefully. It may not work, but I will do what I can along that line. The other important thing is I think it's useful to you individually and collectively to find out where I am because I really can't tell you. . . . I know I don't want to lead you. I think the responsibility is with each of you. . . . I want to feel free to make suggestions and do things to increase the way in which you can learn here. . . . I still don't know where I am in my relationship to you. . . . I think you're fighting the position that reflects your attitudes toward me. I looked around and I saw you and Ted lying down and everybody else except Ted was up on his elbows conscious.

Leader #2 used approximately twenty-three exercises during the life span of the group, about midway among the seventeen leaders. Examples of his exercises:

26

Close your eyes. Visualize the people in the group. Who would be easy to communicate with? Who difficult? Now, go up to the person and tell them why you could or couldn't communicate with them.

Everyone shout somebody's name . . . whose name was shouted the most? Okay, Jan, if you're talking about being straight, can you go around and identify the straight people in this group.

Can you say it with more bite? Can you tell them how you really feel?

Don't move. Everyone look at Bill. Tell him what it says to you. Describe him.

Would you all take some partner and step outside and share one thing with that partner that you've censored here in the group.

Everybody space out, close your eyes, feel the space around you and push it aside. Now curl up in the tiniest space you can, slowly come out, shake your shell off.

GROUP PROCESSES

Only three other groups spent more time focusing on inside material. When Group #2 did focus on outside material, it was almost entirely personal and current in the lives of members. The group did not discuss personal historical material, nor was there much discussion of racial or other social issues. The inside material mostly concerned the leader or the total group.

In contrast to many of the groups, Group #2 rarely focused on one person, although dialogues and general unfocused discussion were frequent. Both the observers and the members rated this group as about midway in terms of intimate disclosure of material and expression of feelings. The observers rated Group #2 as relatively low profile in terms of emotional climate. They saw it as a relatively harmonious, informal group; dull, quiet, slow, and somewhat uninvolved. The general picture of the normative quality is that warm, nonconfrontational, feelingful behavior was clearly approved in the group. Members saw Group #2 as a moderately cohesive group which increased somewhat over time.

LOOKING BACK

Immediately after the group ended, the members rated it in the top third of the seventeen groups on these dimensions: they found it a pleasant experience, were turned on by it, thought it constructive, and felt they learned a great deal. They did not rate their leader highly. He ranked slightly below the average on—thought him competent, would like to be in a group with him again, admired him as a person, approved of his techniques and effectiveness. He rated slightly above average on understanding his group. The members felt that he was too remote and passive. As with Leader #1, the observers rated him as much more competent than did the group members. Only three leaders were rated higher.

Group #2 members, much more frequently than any other group, cited feedback as the most significant event in a given meeting. They also chose obtaining of insight and self-disclosure. They mentioned more frequently than any other groups that helping someone else in the group was important. The members of Group #2 felt, as did the members of the majority of the other groups, that the most important learning was that the group "helped me understand my impact on others." The second most important learning to Group #2 members was that they felt that they were involved members of a group, and felt close to the other members (rated eighth on the average of all seventeen groups). They deviated from all other groups in that they were able to use *other* members as models.

The group members had many differing opinions about their group experience. Some were angry at the leader for not being more active and directive. Others felt the group, which at first had seemed artificial and phony, had in the long run been extremely constructive.

The observers noted that Leader #2, in contrast to many, exercised considerable patience. He had no particular investment in helping members achieve a personal breakthrough and was perfectly prepared to be inactive for long periods of time until he felt there was an opportunity to do some teaching, or when intervention seemed to be needed. Unlike many other leaders, he helped the group focus on certain basic issues such as competition among the members for leadership, dissatisfaction with the leader, formulating the goals of the group, group discouragement, and frustration.

Group#3—Gestalt

Love fest, letting it all hang out, pretend the pillow is her and let her have it, everything goes, fun, funny. . . .

Group #3 met for three time-extended meetings. The first six-hour meeting was followed a week later by another. The last meeting, two weeks later, was for eighteen hours. The first meetings were held in a dormitory lounge; the last in a reading room. The eleven members sat on the floor on pillows or mattresses; they attended regularly.

Leader #3 was a clinical psychologist who had been running therapy groups for about eight years. One innovation of his has been the open sharing of his own fantasies and dreams. He reported that he pays careful attention to posture shifts, and helps members get in touch with themselves through these observations. He prefers to do group work because he finds it more exciting. He considers himself innovative and radical. He wants each member to have increased awareness about his own behavior and greater understanding of the "why" of such behaviors. He hopes that each member of the group will be able to choose to make of his life what he wishes. He feels that it's important to frustrate members of the group in order to help them assume responsibility for their own acts. He tends to focus as much as possible on the here-and-now.

Leader #3 was a very high support, high challenge, anti-intellectual leader who revealed himself freely, as observers saw him. The focus of his attention was fairly evenly distributed among interpersonal, intrapersonal, and group behaviors and midway among the leaders. He often invited questions and confronted members in an effort to "open them up." However, he gave a great deal of support (he and Leader #8 were the highest). He offered friendship, as well as protection, to group members. With Leader #4 he was the highest of the leaders in his use of self. He revealed his here-and-now feelings and his own personal values, often drew attention to himself as a person and as a leader, and in many ways participated as a member of the group.

He gave less attention than any other leader to any type of coherence-aiding statement, whether explanation, clarification, or interpretation. He managed the group by focusing on members or issues, or by suggesting some type of structural procedure.

The observers rated his global style as "challenger," as "releaser of emotions by demonstration," and as a "personal leader," one who expressed considerable warmth, acceptance, genuineness, and caring for other human beings.

These remarks were selected from the beginning of the first meeting:

Let's begin. I'm. . . . Can you tell me your expectations for our group? I'll tell you what my ground rules are: (1) there's no subgrouping, and subgrouping is bad. If you have something to say, say it. I hear some of you whispering. (2) No drugs. No dope, tranquilizers. (3) The last rule is no physical violence that will be injurious. . . .

I haven't the foggiest idea what the research is about. I am as much in doubt as you are. . . . I filled out the same forms, by the way. . . . I'm in favor of getting all the hidden agendas out in the open. If you have something to say, say it. I'll lay it right out and I hope you do the same. . . .

This is what I do. I lead groups. I lead groups on a regular basis. . . . One of the things I don't do is give lectures on what groups are like and stuff like that.

Let's go around the room and each of you find somebody that you think is interesting. Go sit by the person. . . . When you get together with your partner, get a little space between you, don't cram together. Just sit together for a few minutes and get to know the person you're sitting with without using any words.

This is a little experiment in awareness. Don't go somewhere else. Get in touch with what you're thinking. Let your attention go there. Keep in touch with your awareness. Don't try and change anything. Just stay in touch. We're going to take a little trip together. Innerspace travel, like you are shrunk down and traveling in your blood stream. Imagine a little tiny you entering your body. . . .

We've got about seven more minutes. I'd like you to experiment by telling the other three people in your group something you've been holding back, something like a secret.

Excerpts from the final session:

What are you experiencing right now? . . . There is heavy stuff going on here and there's a lot not being said. I can feel it. A cloud is hanging over it. . . . You're gossiping. . . . You're still gossiping. . . . You're pussyfooting. It's obvious you have very different points of view but you're saying it so carefully like maybe she's going to fall apart.

Make believe your girlfriend is sitting right here, and talk to her. . . . Stay with it. . . . You're holding back. . . . Keep telling her. . . . Okay, now switch seats, and you play your girlfriend and see what she says. . . . Yell back if you want to. . . . Pound your fists. . . . Louder. . . . louder . . . Why don't you tell her, "I give you the power to make me feel guilty"? . . . Do you resent that? . . . Say, "I'm just putty in your hands."

What do you mean, being crazy? . . . How would you be like if you went crazy? What's your fantasy? . . . And then? . . . Bullshit . . . you're being so calm and collected. . . . I'm entitled not to believe you. . . . I think you're a prick. . . . Because when I tell you that I don't believe you you're so calm . . . and so nice. . . . Now, what's going on inside? I think you want to drive me crazy. . . . Well, I don't feel like explaining myself. . . . Tough. I don't want to do it. I'd rather drive you crazy than have you drive me crazy. . . . I am being obnoxious. . . . I'm a rat. You're a rat. He's a rat. . . . He's not a rat. Is that what I said? I never heard me say that. . . . You're an elephant. . . . I'd like to see you two guys drive each other crazy. You're both the same way. I'm getting out of here.

Leader #3 used a high number of structured exercises, approximately sixty. Only two leaders used as many or more:

Form small groups of four people. Take turns introducing yourselves nonverbally. Take five minutes to decide how you want to do it. Try to come up with a name for your group.

Be a little metal box. Imagine you're empty; you're a shell. How do you feel?

I'd like some feedback. Tell me what you feel. Go around on me, on the leader.

Let's all try to bring you to a boil. I'd like to hear what the mind-fuck sounds like out loud.

Get in touch with your headache. Be your headache and talk to him. Say that's your headache.

GROUP PROCESSES

The members of Group #3 spent much of their time discussing inside, here-and-now material; only four groups spent more time. When the group did discuss outside material, it was generally a discussion of personal current events. Past historical material, or abstract issues, or current social issues were rarely discussed. The inside here-and-now material was fairly evenly distributed between interpersonal and intrapersonal issues. Only three groups spent more time discussing intrapersonal material. The group spent a relatively high proportion of time discussing its feelings toward the *leader, both as a leader and as a person.

The members spent much of their time in leader-organized subgroup discussions. Not infrequently, they discussed one particular member. Rarely were there prolonged monologues or dialogues. The leader himself was quite active. The members disclosed a great deal about their here-and-now feelings; in only two groups was there more self-disclosure. Self-disclosure was very high in the very first meeting and then tapered off. The observers noted that Group #3 was unusually harmonious, unusually informal, and highly open. Group #3 ranked highest of the seventeen groups at the two administrations of the cohesion questionnaire. The cohesion was higher at the eighth meeting than at the fourth.

Intense emotional expression (kissing, touching, expressing caring, commenting on likeability, crying, pleading for help) was much approved. Sexual, dream/fantasy material, problems with outsiders, were seen as appropriate content. Group #3 was also high on approval of advice-giving, trying to convince others, judging another's behavior as wrong, telling another he was unlikeable, and shouting with anger.

Much more frequently than in most groups, members of Group #3 frequently cited situations which involved expressing a positive ("warm," "close") feeling as the most important events in group meetings. Insight or some type of cognitive gain were very infrequently mentioned. Group #3 emphasized understanding their impact on others and expressing their feelings as primary learnings. (These two factors ranked one and three, respectively, for the entire study population.) They reported that they also gained from understanding why they felt and thought the way they did, and from discovering previously unknown parts of themselves.

LOOKING BACK

At the end of the group, the members were exceedingly enthusiastic. They found their group a pleasant experience (first among the seventeen); they were "turned on" by the group (first among the seventeen); they considered it to be a constructive experience (tied for first among the seventeen); they felt that they learned a great deal (second among the seventeen groups). They ranked Leader #3 as competent (fifth among the fifteen); they would like to be in a group with him again (second); they admired

31

him as a person (tied for fourth); they approved of his techniques (tied for second); they felt that he understood the group (third); they felt he was effective (fourth). Overall, he was rated second. The observers on the average rated him almost as high. When the leader was interviewed some months after, his view was that it had been about an average group for him, although he did not get into the "heavy" intrapersonal material on which he usually focuses in groups. He felt that ordinarily he works with more facets of himself.

Group #4—Gestalt

Leader star. Nothing in moderation. Role-playing, encounter, feeling. Startle. Ridicule. Dangerous, high-risk. . . .

Group #4 started with ten men and three women. Two men dropped out of the group after the first meeting. The group met for a first, ten-hour session, followed by a sixteen-hour session, and the final four-hour session. Meetings were held at the home of a group member, a few minutes from the Stanford campus.

The leader was a clinical psychologist who had had considerable experience leading encounter groups and Gestalt therapy groups. He said he didn't play games. He was convinced that people really don't want to change and refused to get himself placed in a position of trying to change them. Instead, he said that he tried to help them take responsibility for themselves and reach a point where they can make some free choices about the way to live. He pointed out that he is not a traditional therapist. He does not make interpretations but, instead, offers observations on others' behavior, and in so doing he hoped to lead his patients to greater awareness of themselves. He felt he often frustrates people's expectations and said that it is inevitable, and that he has no hope or desire necessarily to give individuals a satisfying or pleasant experience.

The leader brought a cotherapist with him. He insisted that this was the only way he could work. The coleader was subordinate to the leader and very similar in his comments and approaches. He often mirrored the leader's statements or praised the leader for his courageous contributions. Observers saw Leader #4 as being extremely unpredictable. They reported that he seemed to have no clear plan, and used almost every technique of group leadership one could imagine; that he gave a kind of lumbering sense of searching around to get something started; that he was constantly the center of the group interaction, and should something go on in the group for any period of time in which he was not centrally involved, he would intervene to bring himself back into the center of the group light. At times, observers said, he was very melodramatic and would fall asleep or feign sleeping for ten to fifteen minutes, leaving the group quite confused and not knowing how to proceed. His participation rate was extremely high half of the total time. The observers felt that he enjoyed the adoration he got from some members.

The observers felt that he maintained considerable control in the group by his unpredictability. He would suddenly ridicule or jump up and hug or kiss members. He tended to use a great number of four-letter words. He was extremely uninhibited. On one occasion he jumped up to one of the male members saying, "You turn me on," lunged on top of him, hugged him on the ground for a few minutes, and kissed him on the cheek. He then said he had been turned on to homosexuality when he was interacting with his own sons. He also interacted sexually with the women. For example, at the end of one meeting, one of the female members came up to him and kissed him for a long period of time on the lips. He encouraged this and appeared to enjoy stroking her buttocks during the kiss. He tended to use a great deal of humor and occasionally would burst into song. He rejected the role of expert and, when asked questions, he would say, "Beats me," or "I give up, what is it?" He revealed his own feelings frequently. He discussed his own sexual behavior, and his pleasure about being appointed to the Stanford faculty for the purposes of the study, saying that he would be sure to use it on his curriculum vita for future applications.

More than any of the other leaders, he attempted to taunt the observers, and to undermine the research. At times he would scream into the microphone to the tape recorder. He counselled the students not to take the research forms too seriously and, unlike other leaders, refused to fill his out at the end of the meeting.

According to observer ratings, Leader #4 very rarely used coherence-making statements. He often taunted people for attempts to understand anything intellectually. He challenged individuals more often than most of the leaders. In every meeting he invited questions and confronted members. On a couple of instances he gave the group some frame of reference in which to consider things, such as "No one can make you happy or unhappy. Only you can do that to yourself." He gave a fairly high level of support in the group, either protecting or supporting an individual, or more often offering his love or friendship. He revealed his here-and-now feelings more openly than almost any group member, and participated as a member much more frequently than most of the other leaders. He revealed his own personal values and drew attention to himself very frequently.

Here are some verbatim comments made in the second meeting (the third to the sixth hour):

Are you crying? . . . I feel you're holding back. Something or somebody . . . I'll come closer. . . . Crying is a woman's second best weapon. . . . All right, close your eyes and imagine you are holding something back. What are you holding back in your past? . . . Okay, stay in that position, exaggerate it.

Now imagine you are taking a peek in your hands. What do you see? . . . A little metal box? So you're hiding all that emptiness. Imagine you are empty, a shell, nothing inside. . . . Make believe you are your hands right now. What are they saying to you? . . . Go ahead, but be your hands.

I'll tell you where I got started in this field. . . . I had a friend who was a psychologist. I visited him once, and they had a party at a psychiatric clinic, and I saw this big party full of psychiatrists, psychologists, social workers, and I thought to myself, "By God, without even going to school, I'm better at this than they are," and I figured I'd better go back to school, and finish up, and make my mark in the world. I thought they were nuts, they were so peculiar. That's when I decided. I really started therapy when I was fifteen. I had my friends lie down and tell me their problems.

Well, we're going to encourage squealing. By squealing, I mean that when a group is not together like this we try to find little tidbits about one another. A good example of a squealer is Sam here, who has been sitting around the room like a deadhead; you know like he hasn't got an emotion in his body. He was so turned on by that feeding, and by getting fed by Jill. You were alive, Sam, you were really alive. . . . Have fun here man, you are fun when you have fun. You're dead when you don't. Has anybody got a squeal? . . . Who is that prick who is eating with his fork? . . . What do you do when you put somebody's cock in your mouth, like when you are married, of course? . . .

You are laying something on us, baby. Get yourself off the hook. . . . Fuck you, tell him to stay off the hook but don't tell me to let him off.

(To the observer.) Okay, when I say something that's really important I'll tell you to write that, because sometimes I'll say something really important and it won't appear important. Just a little phrase like "of course", or "is that so?" can be very important. Everything I say is important. Sometimes I'm just bullshitting.

(To the observer.) You're a very competent looking guy. What is your name? . . . You look like a Jewish guy. Are you Jewish? Good, I like Jewish people. . . . Where do you work? Are you a psychologist there or teaching assistant? What, speak louder, we're not picking up your voice very well on the tape. . . . You look uncomfortable. . . . What's going on with you?

Excerpts from Session 8:

I think this set a record—about ten or twelve hours without a single incident. Maybe we should run the group until seven o'clock tomorrow night. See if we can keep it going. Keep it going for twenty-four hours without a single thing happening. . . . I think we're at a stalemate. . . . In the past I've gotten angry at groups like this, but I'm not even bored. I'm tired. It's one of the most amazing groups I've ever seen. Constantly, sometimes like a conspiracy of silence. I like it a lot. I can really say there is no person in the group whom I dislike. . . . I couldn't criticize any of you. I keep asking myself, "What has led us into disharmony?" Fine, we'll have a group grope. Okay, get the light out. . . . I think I'm on the bottom of this pile. . . . Where is the observer? . . . He's on the bottom, he was taking notes on the bottom of the pile. . . .

Everybody be quiet, and get on your hands and knees, and close your eyes. Start moving slowly to the center of the group. Same old scintillating group. . . . I just thought of a great thing for us to do. Turn the tape recorder back and listen to the last three hours.

Leader #4 used approximately sixty structured exercises. He tied for second in frequency with Leader #3. Some examples:

Why don't you stand up? Close your eyes. Pay attention to how you're standing, sitting, and breathing.

I want you to fantasize out loud a situation in which a guy has to make a decision, stick with yourself and talk about it.

Prick with fork, cock in mouth, go ahead and have a fantasy about that and tell us about it.

Close your eyes and feel, identify with me. Start the next three sentences with "here, now, I am . . ."

We're going to divide into groups, choose a team. We want each of you to work with your group, get in touch with your group mind.

Okay, why don't you go ahead and tell her why you are better than she is. Go ahead, spell it out.

GROUP PROCESSES

The member focus on both inside (here-and-now) and outside material was about average. When inside material was discussed it was primarily interpersonal and personal material and the group as a whole. This group spent more time talking about individual material than most of the others. When they discussed outside material, they talked about current personal events in their lives and also personal historical material. In every meeting, some time was spent discussing the leader.

As there was a great use of structured exercises by the leader, there was considerable highly stylized communication. For example, the group would spend a fourth to a third of the meeting in some type of go-around where each person gave systematic feedback to someone else. A large portion of the meeting would be spent exploring, and helping one member explore himself.

The observers rated Group #4 above average on the amount of self-disclosure of past or current events in one's life.

The observer's ratings of climate fluctuated widely. Some meetings were extremely involved and others extremely uninvolved. The members rated their group as one of the least cohesive groups.

When group members cited the most significant event of each meeting, it was almost always an incident involving the describer himself. Usually, it related to some type of feeling (usually positive) that was experienced or expressed. The second most common incident was a negative feeling of being rejected or angry or frustrated. Also common was the disclosure by someone else of some important past historical material. The reason given for this incident's importance was usually one of feeling closeness, empathy, or having gained some insight. They felt they gained through understanding their impact on others and understanding their own thinking and feelings. Furthermore, they indicated more often than members of any other group that they realized their ultimate responsibility for their own lives. They also valued the experimentation with new behavior.

LOOKING BACK

The members of only one other group rated the experience as less pleasant than Group #4 members. They felt average in being "turned on," and for having had some personal learning in the group and below average in considering the constructive experience. The members felt ambivalent about their group leader. They thought that he was relatively competent; they admired him as a person; they approved of some of his techniques; but they also declared that they would not like to be in a group with him again, and that he was too obtrusive. The observers felt more critical of Leader #4 than the members. They did not admire him as a person; they saw him as ineffective and as not understanding his group.

The group members had very mixed feelings about their experience in the group. Some of the comments were extremely critical. One felt that the leader had been quite destructive. He "called me a dumb shit because I didn't know how to participate." Another member felt that the leader demanded a deep instant type of intimacy which made her feel empty because she was not able to respond to his demands.

Other members liked the leader, but stated that they greatly feared his disapproval and tried to say things in a way that would gain approval. Several commented that the group moved too quickly, that it was too intense, that there was too much strain and deep feeling, and that this was an unsettling experience.

When an investigator attempted to describe to Leader #4 the psychological injuries suffered by members of the group, he constantly interrupted with sarcastic comments like, "Great. That's wonderful."

When asked about his retrospective view of the group, he said that he still talks about it because it was the most stubborn group he had ever had. The group refused to form a contract with him, either to change, or to work, or even to see it through to its end. "All I remember was that there were two or three people who were quite delightful and wanted to work, and the rest of them didn't want to do anything. So, what I did was just go ahead and have a good time for myself." The leader was quite discouraged by the group and was perplexed about why so many were so unwilling to work. He did not feel that he should have changed any of his techniques or general approach, but tended to place the blame for the failure upon the members' resistance and reluctance to participate in work in the group.

Group #5—Psychodrama

*Sanitary, distant, low-key, low-conflict group. Serious
psychiatrist leader. Frustration, resistance, silence.*

Group #5 started off with ten members, but one member dropped out
after the fourth meeting; another attended most of the meetings, but withdrew from the group near the end. Attendance was generally poor; two to
three people were absent at each meeting. The group met in a dormitory
lounge for ten three-hour sessions; this was one of the very few groups
that did not have at least one time-extended session.

Leader #5, a psychiatrist with about six years experience leading psychotherapy groups, was selected to represent the psychodrama approach.
He placed considerable emphasis on the interactional aspects of the group
and considered that he used psychodramatic techniques to facilitate the
group's interaction, rather than as a primary emphasis. He described himself as a relatively inactive leader who liked to wait and see what happened between himself and the group members. He did not believe that he
could change others, but rather that change is most likely to occur when
one is not actively forcing it. He felt it important to create a safe group in
which people experience and try a wide range of behavior. He also believed that much of the help that groups offer comes from its members. He
thought groups usually perceived him as nonjudgmental, protective, warm,
but somewhat difficult to get close to.

The observers saw Leader #5 as a bit withdrawn, somewhat authoritarian, as someone who expressed practically no warmth or personal affect, but repeatedly asked people to express what he himself was not saying. He focused on the entire group to a much greater extent than any
other leaders. He was among the two lowest in frequency of interpersonal
comment; observers' ratings corroborated the recollections of group members about the leader's reluctance to focus on what was happening between
two or more members in the group. Many of his interventions were involved with managing the group in one way or another.

Observers saw him as a low-support leader who rarely challenged or confronted the members, but quite frequently called on them, questioned
them, or invited them to participate. He was more prone to summarize
than any of the other leaders, but did not often invite feedback, and never
gave the members a conceptual framework or taught them how to understand certain phenomena that were occurring. Occasionally he offered
affection, or support, or encouragement. He never actively protected.
More than other group leaders he focused the attention of the group onto
something that happened, or something that someone said. He very fre-

quently managed the time or pacing of the group, pointing out that there was only so much time left or they were getting away from the topic.

Although members perceived him as aloof, observers felt he tended to reveal his here-and-now feelings (usually about tension or feeling uncomfortable in the group or feeling distant or close to an individual member), and occasionally his personal values. The observers characterized his overall group style as that of a social engineer.

At the very beginning of the group he said:

I wouldn't mind knowing a little bit about each one of you as we get going. Just how you see these meetings, how you got into them. . . . Can you give any examples today, John, about your feelings on campus and the feelings you have inside of you that could help us understand what you're getting at? . . . Where are you from, John? Can you tell us a little bit about your background?

Well, okay, the task we have then, having heard a little bit about the background, and there is some spread among us, although we are all white. That's one general characteristic among us in the group. The task we have to look at is the racist attitudes we have. I think many observers of the scene say that we are all racists, and we have to try and identify within ourselves our own racist attitudes. . . . Who is aware of their own racist attitudes? What are your racist attitudes? . . . Would you tell us about them? . . . Can you show us that by any chance? . . . Yeah, let's see how he'd act out that experience with that guy you're telling us about.

How does that sound, folks? I think he's saying that the black man seems to have aggressiveness, I imagine sexual potency, a lot of spontaneity that he doesn't have. These are dangerous qualities. Was I paraphrasing too much?

Has anything that John showed us rung any bells with people here about their own experience? Mary, you shook your head. Who else is aware of some particular qualities that seem to be racist like John told us about his?

. . . This time okay for you people? I'd say the task again is getting at your racist feelings that we probably have. And seeing if you can change them in this group. It's a pretty clear task perhaps.

. . . I see part of my task in trying to keep this from being too much of a discussion. For example tonight we, I think you, we, I think you came out, and told us a great deal about yourself and where you're at in trying to deal with it. It's hard to do.

. . . Okay, well what do you say that we knock it off?

From Session 3:

Can you use your own life as an illustration? . . . What have you seen so far in this group? . . . What do you see in regard to Bob's behavior?

. . . I am groping. How do others see it? . . . (Summarizes previous statements.) . . . How does the group feel toward Jim? . . . How come you didn't tell him that last week? . . . Are you protecting Jim? How come you're protecting him? . . . Can you see any connections to this to the problems of prejudice around here?

. . . John, Jim, and Ann seem to keep the ball rolling around here.

. . . The meeting is different tonight, it's got a lot more silences. . . . We want to encounter each other and yet we seem to resist this. I don't understand it.

The leader of Group #5 used approximately fifteen structured exercises during his group, almost all of them psychodrama scenes. In the first couple of meetings he tended to focus on clarifying racial attitudes; since there were no blacks in the group, he asked members to role-play blacks. Later he suggested role-playing involving the life of one of the group members. These were relatively minor aspects of the group and several meetings occurred in which there were no structured exercises at all. He asked one of the members to arm-wrestle with him on one occasion and once asked all members to express their feelings toward one group member.

GROUP PROCESSES

Group #5 began by spending much of its time on outside issues; gradually and consistently as the group progressed it dealt more and more with inside material. When the group talked about outside material it generally pertained to personal, current, or historical material in the lives of each of the members. Occasionally, there was a good deal of abstract discussion in the group and, rarely, a discussion of social issues. Although all members were white, there was some discussion of race; the leader attempted to work on racial attitudes in the first four meetings. When the group talked about inside material, they did not focus heavily on interpersonal or intrapersonal material. Instead, they spent more time than did most of the others talking about the group as a whole and about their feelings toward the leader. There was a heavy focus on the leader, especially during the last four meetings, primarily critical in nature. The group attacked him for frustrating them by refusing to become one of the members.

Much of the group was run in a general, unfocused manner, or in dialogue between the leader and a member or between two members. There was relatively little focusing on one person, on monologues, or on subgroup structured exercises.

According to the observers, the members revealed less about their here-and-now feelings than members of the great majority of groups. Only one other group was rated as having less self-disclosure. There was more disclosure of past material, according to the observers and members. Members and observers agreed few feelings were expressed in the group.

The observers saw Group #5 as being closed, cold, uninvolved, dull, slow, and weak. The members scored the group as low on cohesiveness. More often than almost any other group, the group members selected as critical, incidents in which they themselves were not active participants, such as *other* people's discussing something, and most frequently revealing something about themselves. A typical critical incident for a member of this group was that some other member revealed an important event of feeling in his life (not a feeling toward a member of the group) which resulted in that individual's gaining an important aspect of his own problem. It was also more common in Group #5 than in other groups for members to select as significant an abstract discussion which resulted in their obtaining information.

Like the majority in other groups, the members of Group #5 felt that the group had helped them understand their impact on others, that they had learned that everyone was in the same boat, and that they had expressed their feelings. Unlike other groups, however, these members did not feel that they had learned by being involved as a member of a group.

LOOKING BACK

Immediately after the experience, the members gave Group #5 relatively low ratings. In comparison to the other groups, they saw it as an unpleasant, turned-off, nonconstructive experience in which they had learned little. There were only two groups which received lower overall ratings.

The members' rating of the leader was similarly low. In comparison to other groups' members, they saw their leader as being incompetent and ineffective. They reported that they would not like to be in a group with him again, they did not admire him as a person, they disapproved of his techniques, and they felt he did not understand the group. Furthermore, they said he was too remote and too passive. He was similarly unpopular among the observers, who rated only three leaders less effective.

The most consistent report of the members was that their leader was too aloof, and that the group spent a great deal of time in sparring and intellectualizing before finally getting down to important feeling issues. This was by no means unanimous; some members felt that the leader had done an excellent job, and that they had had a very positive experience. All members sensed that the leader was trying hard to get around the feeling of coldness without much success until the end of each meeting.

Although they felt that they had not talked about personal things, when the members described the issues that were discussed they mentioned some very intensely personal issues. For example, a girl talked about her virginity, another about some incest that had occurred in the family, others about frustrated romances or their identity confusion, one about having just learned that he was half Jewish. The members did not perceive the leader as really trying to help the group go to where the intense feeling was. They felt he tended to be quite formal and often started the meeting with a short summary of what had happened in the preceding meeting.

When the leader was interviewed sometime after the end of the group, he stated that he felt some pressure from the research design to use more psychodrama, and to focus more on black-white issues than he might have done ordinarily. He mentioned that he found it a real problem when students tried to engage him as a peer and he felt that, were he to accept their invitations, he would be allying himself with their resistance to the real work of the group. He knew that the negative feelings toward him increased as a result of this particular stance, but in retrospect he felt there was little else he could have done. Were he to do it over again, he felt he would not change his presentation of himself, but that he might help the students get more into their fantasy life or use more structured exercises.

Group #6—Psychodrama

Leader who made things happen, who could not easily be forgotten. "The group marathon is like an ocean voyage; we will leave together and we will return to port together."

In addition to twelve members, Group #6 usually included at least two assistants who helped the leader run the group. Two initial three-hour meetings were followed a week later by a twenty-four-hour marathon; two three-hour sessions followed. Two members dropped out.

The leader was the most unconventional of all the leaders. The director of a growing center, he had less formal training than other leaders, holding a Master's degree in psychology. He had also studied with J. Moreno and was selected for the study to represent the psychodrama technique. He was a controversial figure, not only because of the large number of people in the area who had attended his marathons, but because of his aggressive confrontation techniques. He particularly valued the expression of rage and his groups became known as "psychological karate groups."

A striking figure, flamboyantly dressed, Leader #6 characterized himself as a "tourist guide" or an "antenna" for the group. He expressed the opinion that people attended groups because of their great need to be close and to be loved by others . . . because groups fill a gap which is not met elsewhere in the community. The groups create a new sense of community, and provide help by allowing people to touch, to be touched, to experience catharsis, and to experience the reality of emotional needs. He commented that for him the group was an art medium which he used in much the same way that others would create paintings or sculpture.

Leader #6 rated highest of all leaders in the amount of challenge and confrontation he used. In one meeting he "challenged" a relatively silent member of the group:

> How come you don't say anything? Why do I always have to come to you? What's going on in your gut? . . . Why don't you be direct? Why do you use sarcasm like that? . . . We've got to find out who you are and what you feel. . . . I get so fuckin' tired of having to push you and find out what you're like.

Do you want us to be all like you? How long do you want us to go? Twenty-four hours without saying anything?

The leader then threw his cup of coffee across the room, slapped the student hard in the face, and pushed him around a bit.

Observers saw him as highly mobile; he wandered around the group looking for points to intervene. He could be silent for long periods of time, but generally he was exceedingly active. It seemed important for him to bring members to the point of breakthrough or breakdown. The breakthrough was a type of episode where the member gave a verbal or nonverbal signal that he had reached some new level of awareness. Or the student might break down by dissolving into tears. If these events failed to happen, the leader might then launch into a short lecture, or he might suggest they break for coffee. The leader used recorded music which reflected the mood of a particular member, or elicited the feeling he was hoping to evoke.

In addition to his high challenging, he was a highly supportive leader, and offered members his own personal love or friendship. Only Leaders #7 and #8 spent more time exploring interpersonal issues, but very little time focusing on the group as a whole. He rarely attempted to clarify, or explain, or make some type of coherence-aiding interpretation, although he could occasionally deliver a short lecture on how to change or understand feelings.

Leader #6 ran the group; observers felt no doubt about his forcefulness as a leader. He directed the group's focus on an issue, or on a person, or he told the group to stop at such and such a point, or suggested some type of procedure.

He was highly self-revealing; he not only revealed his own here-and-now feelings, but material from his own current and past life as well as his own personal values. He seldom discussed himself as the leader of the group, however, or helped members to explore their feelings toward him. In addition to being the most charismatic leader, the observers characterized his style as that of a challenger and a releaser of emotions by demonstration.

From Session 1:

I'd like to ask you some questions right now. Do most of you know what this is all about? I do a lot of marathon, sensitivity-training, and psychodrama groups. Mainly during the twenty-four-hour marathon we all have to be together. All you need is a sleeping bag and we'll let you know where it's going to be. The intention of this is to try and get very close to each other, intimate. We'll probably arrange some free sandwiches and you won't sleep very much. The sleeping bag is so you can crawl in and hide.

Any of you ever heard of psychodrama? It's a very simple thing we use and as we go along I'll explain it. But basically we don't explain too much, we just jump into it. We want to get as intense as possible and as close as possible. Any of you choose to stand behind somebody else, and say some of the things you think that person would say. Then you're called a double. The double is like another voice inside of you. Your conscience, your id, whatever you want to call it, and sometimes you have a kind of dialogue with yourself. You'll find out as we go along that we want all of you to participate as much as possible. I may come in and out of it. Sometimes we won't do anything. Sometimes we'll create a kind of a tension which we call psychological karate. Put you in a super double-bind position where you're forced to respond in some way. And in the marathon or in the three-hour sessions as we get into it, you can take your glasses off, or your shoes, or anything that might restrain you or hurt you. Any physical pain going on, say the two of you decide to wrestle, and the rest of the group use your body as a cushion to protect the action in the center so the bodies don't bump against the wall or bump against a chair. During the marathon and also during the shorter periods, no marijuana, no aspirin, no psychedelics, no drugs of any kind. What we're trying is to get people to turn on to people. What happens during the marathon is that somebody might get high for three hours, and then it wears off, then you're yourself and you're all alone. . . . No drugs, even tranquilizers.

Do any of you know each other? . . . Okay, so in effect we're all total strangers. Okay. Let's pull the chairs back and all of you sit in a big circle. If you want to take off your shoes, go ahead. Form a tight small circle and put the shoes in the center. Okay, we're going to tell the names now. Make sure that you can see each other. Introduce each other, and say whatever you want to say. I think we ought to organize. I don't know how, I'd just like to organize.

(After several minutes.) Ho hum. What a drag. It's all so safe. What a safe issue, what a safe issue. What a goddamn safe issue. Isn't that nice. Did you really know each other? Really, really? (Sarcastically.) . . . Do you really know each other now that you're talking about the sit-in?

What are you avoiding about each other? . . . This is a Race and Prejudice course and there's a Chinaman and there's a Nigger in it, and nobody says anything about it. You've answered all the questions and now you sit and talk about sit-ins.

. . . How do you feel about being the only Korean here? How do you folks feel about her? How do you feel about the obvious majority? . . . Who the hell is she? Some Stanford bitch? That's exactly what I meant. What do you want to get caught with this one? I bet she cuts my balls off. Are you a bitch? I bet she's not a virgin. . . . Stanford kids always analyze the here-and-now before the here-and-now begins. You're doing a whole analysis. You people are head trippers and questioners. That's Stanford chicks. The Stanford chicks have a very quick mind, and will analyze anything else and that's a whole defensive bullshit.

From later sessions:

It really is irrelevant whether you squirmed or not just then. It really doesn't matter. The point is that she doesn't like the position of watching a person squirm. The question we're asking her is how did she avoid all the nasty filthy shit that's going on in the earth. We know the earth is not a goddamn pretty fucking sight. Now maybe you were raised in a nunnery.

. . . (Sets up a psychodrama.) Okay, I'm a heavy. I drive down the street and try to pick you up, and try and score with you. You know what I mean? Do you ever meet con men, you ever meet freaks, you ever meet insane people? You never meet geniuses, you never meet super crazies, and superlove crazy? . . . I'm a super freak. . . . (During the psychodrama, one of the members begins to cry. One of the members tells him to stop it.) Now wait a minute, you tell me, what did I do? . . . I hurt her feelings. How did I do that? . . . By being me? . . . I feel kind of helpless myself too, shit. . . . I guess I never went through college trying to analyze everything. . . . I never could figure out college students. They're always asking why. . . . I don't know what's going on here. What the fuck is going on? . . . You think I'm a selfish sonofabitch? . . . Well, thank you for your analysis. How're you going to help me get off my selfish sonofabitchiness? Well, you know selfish sonofabitches don't listen to anyone. (Continues role-playing.)

Okay, let's have some feedback. What's happened? (Signaling an official end to the role-playing.) That's right, you just rejected me. You tried to persuade and manipulate me to go to her. You didn't ask how I felt. You insisted that you wanted me to go to her, and comfort her. But I wasn't going to go where I had no idea, no intention of going. The role I played wasn't just exactly a role. It was a great part of me. For a long time I had to restrain myself from being my real me. Very few people can stand pure raw experience.

Joan, how come you're out of it? You're concerned for Joan, aren't you? You're supposed to be the one who cares. You want everyone to love one another, but when something comes up that has love in it you stay out. Maybe all you guys in the group are right. Maybe Joan is hiding behind politics. If it's beautiful, Joan stays out of it. If it's ugly, Joan's right in it. . . . You give the appearance that you give and care, but you don't. . . . Bullshit, you just can't wait till the group is over so you can pour your energy into the love movement at Stanford. . . . Do you want to change your world? Bullshit, you want to burn it. Why don't you change yourself before you change the world. You sound like a Nazi. Only words are different, but they burned it . . . (At this point the leader put on a record of Nazi marching music which was blaring loudly in the room and he was walking around the group saying, "Heil Hitler, Heil Hitler.")

GROUP PROCESSES

Observer ratings indicated that the group focused almost entirely on inside material, intrapersonal revelation and interpersonal issues. There was very little discussion of the group as a whole, or of the leader.

More than 60 percent of the time was spent focusing on one person. Occasionally, there was a dialogue but very rarely was there the generally unfocused discussion characteristic of so many of the other groups. Group #6 members had a higher rate of self-disclosure of here-and-now feelings and personal historical material than any of the other groups. These observer conclusions are roughly corroborated by the group members themselves. The observers saw Group #6 as strong, intense, alive, informal, involved, close, and warm. To a somewhat lesser degree the group was also seen as sad, open, aggressive, and tense.

Like Group #3, Group #6 had norms characterized as "intense, disclosing confrontation." Its members approved positively toned emotional behaviors like kissing, touching, caring, crying. Unlike any other group, they approved hitting another member and making threatening remarks. They considered discussing sex life, dreams/fantasies, and problems with outsiders as appropriate content; they also approved advice-giving, probing, interruption, shouting with anger, and commenting on another's unlikability.

Group #6 ranked among the lower third in cohesiveness despite high attendance and the high degree of enthusiasm and excitement generated in the group.

The members of Group #6, far more than the members of any of the other groups, cited some type of strong, negative or positive expression of feeling as the most important incident of the meeting. They responded to this incident by feeling positive towards the other members or by gaining some kind of insight into their behavior. Significant by their absence were critical incidents which reflected group mastery: gaining information, obtaining feedback, or helping of other members.

The members of this group differed from most of the other groups by de-emphasizing the importance of understanding their own impact on others. More than members of most groups, they stressed that they were helped to understand their thoughts and feelings, and to discover and accept previously hidden parts of themselves. More often than those in most groups, they felt that they had received some type of advice from the group. Curiously, the members did not mention the expression of feeling as important.

Some of the other groups had a small number of dramatic incidents; Group #6 seemed to have nothing *but* dramatic incidents. The leader supplied an extraordinary amount of energy for the task of making things happen in the group. Any intellectualized or abstract discussion was quickly halted, usually through ridicule or direct command. The group was highly dramatic and the leader possessed considerable dramatic skill.

LOOKING BACK

The testimony questionnaires the students filled out reflected that they felt very positive about the group. They were turned on (fourth among groups), considered it constructive (tied for first), and they felt they had learned a great deal (first among all the group). Yet, nine other groups rated their groups as more pleasant.

The members regarded their leader highly. (He tied for second among leaders.) He was considered to be competent (tied for first) and effective (tied for fourth) and the members approved of his techniques (fourth among the leaders). They admired him as a person (tied for second) and they would like to be in a group with him again (fifth among the leaders) but they tended also to rank him as too active and too intrusive (first among the fifteen leaders).

Members described him in near superhuman terms. "He's pretty forceful. I thought he was amazingly insightful. We'd do whatever we were doing, and he'd step in and say . . . here's where I think you're at . . . and he'd tell you exactly what you were thinking. He's incredible." "He just kind of got vibrations from people, really sensitive feelings . . . he's got some sort of psychic powers or something." "When I think about the group I think mainly about how strong he was, and how resourceful, and how he kind of encouraged people to be that vigorous and just live it."

Group #6 was a high-risk group which generated two serious casualties, and also evoked such negative comments from members as: "This group approach is verbal obliteration. . . ." "The leader lacked the sensitivity to see that some people are more precarious and couldn't take it . . . ." "The leader didn't bring out people's feelings, he was telling them what their feelings were. . . ." "I wasn't hurt so much as mad. . . ." "One guy was questioned by the leader about his potency, and he challenged him to say whether or not he could turn on the girls in the group. . . ." "This specific group opened us up too deeply. It hurt us. It opened up problems within one another but did not draw us very close together as other groups did. I don't know, maybe it did accomplish something different in its own violent way."

The ratings of the observers were quite similar to the testimony of the group members. Their competence ratings placed him second among fifteen leaders.

Group #7—Psychoanalytic

Gentle, soft-spoken, traditional psychiatrist leader. Limited group goals. Slow-moving, uninvolved group.

Group #7 started with eleven members, all white. Three women dropped out after one session, and a man left at the sixth session. The group met for ten three-hour meetings, in a fairly comfortable dormitory lounge.

The leader was a psychoanalyst who had been practicing and teaching group therapy for over twenty years. He felt it was important to use past historical material to clarify the present. He stated that he is generally fairly inactive in the group, and rarely will speak more than ten percent of the time. He felt that it was important for people in the group to feel free to work on and to talk about what they wanted to talk about, and saw himself as exerting extremely little pressure on individuals.

Leader #7 expressed some concern about the short duration of the group and felt that ten sessions seemed to be an extraordinarily short time in which to accomplish anything but said he hoped to use the time to "make a beginning of something important."

Observers rated Leader #7 the most conservative of all the leaders. He had a very low key, formal, intellectual style. Only one other leader did less challenging, or less confrontation of members. Leader #7 did not take charge and did very little limiting of discussion. He did not actively try to open up members nor did he offer support. He was one of the leaders rated higher in terms of conceptual input; he was one of the two leaders who occasionally summarized events.

Leader #7 generally focused on the intrapersonal level, rarely commenting on what was happening between two members of the group. He invited, questioned, or reflected something the members said. He offered relatively little support or positive feeling and almost no challenge or negative feeling. He used his own person to a relatively low degree. Occasionally toward the end he revealed some aspects of his own life.

Here are some verbatim excerpts from Session 1:

I guess we can officially start now. I suppose it really started when you first got here—all sorts of thoughts and feelings running through your minds. I'm not sure what has been told to you and what expectations you have. We can discover where our mutual expectations are. Maybe we can get started by going around the room and telling everybody who we are. You all know that I'm Dr. X. There is no particular agenda and I thought we would say whatever we like here. . . . What were you hoping would happen here? Did you have any expectations?

I think there are things going on in the room which you are not quite ready to share yet. Your eyes met for a second and then you turned away. Well, silences are difficult. I think maybe in a silence I wish someone would say something. . . . Somebody other than me—and each one of us I guess is hoping the other will express something very startling so we can react to it. You left out the girls as you were talking, were you referring to everyone, girls as well as boys? . . . I think you're copping out on that one. . . . Are you responding to dress or to manner? . . . A few minutes ago I thought you were irritated with those two on the side of you.

Something real did happen and it's hard to say. It's hard to look when you're instructed to look for something. Because it was just a fraction of a second when your eyes met here. It has a certain connotation. You're using the word embarrassment; why should it be embarrassing? Can you imagine if you had kept your eyes there, what would have happened; what would you have experienced? . . . You gave me the feeling you thought if you kept looking at him, he could shun you. You used the word shun—is that what you meant—that he could shun you? . . .

Do you have some second thoughts about coming back? . . . There is one more objective here, and I hope you'll all have this objective. And that's to get to know yourself better too. You're discovering already how hard it is to let yourself go. Does anyone have a kind of impression from this first session? I know I don't have a great experience in encounter groups, but I feel there's a lot I know about me. We can think and talk about how we feel and what we think. I would give the highest priority to spontaneous expression of all the important feelings that we have. It isn't easy and I hope we can help each other do that. . . .

People have their own likes and dislikes about the way groups are run. For example, if we were to ask you to pair off and look into each other's eyes, or to Indian wrestle, or to fall backward in each other's arms and so on, some might like it. I am more familiar with easing into it, and we'll see if we can get that to work for us. If we should need devices, we can talk about it. Let's arrange to meet here next time.

From Session 5:

This is a very different session from last week . . . I think somebody has to be willing to get a little closer or maybe hurting enough to break up the first deadlock.

Yes, there are many descriptions made about the creative experience, but in studying psychological studies of great artists or creative people, it seems that they have the capacity to fuse with the whole universe on a large cosmic scale of some kind, to fuse with nature.

. . . We were talking about the choice of careers; we were talking about boyfriends and girlfriends and I think there may be something you are seeking, or something that's bothering you in connection with these choices. . . . You may not realize it but you're searching; you're trying to solve something. It's an escape from reality that's very pleasant but reality always comes back. There was a little more talk today about boyfriends and girlfriends; does anyone feel tied up with this? . . . Well, maybe what I have to say is irrelevant. I thought that there was a kind of searching for more meaning in relationships.

From Session 7:

I was kind of thinking that you are having a hard time getting started because no one wants to be exposed. . . . There's always competition in the world. I was thinking back to a mother with half a dozen children. Isn't there a competition for the mother's attention? . . . There's the situation of a newborn baby in the family where there are children already, and there's a very strong reaction on the part of the older children. . . . If we were to transfer this scene into the family scene and try to get under the psychological thing like the fact that some kids can compete better than others. And I'm not talking about skills now but their concerns about competition. . . . What was the competition like in your family? . . . Mark said his parents didn't stress grades. How did the rest of your parents handle that? . . . I think Neal was talking about his sister and his parents stressing grades. I was wondering if it made a difference in the relationship with them. I was thinking about Neal's sister; she might represent mother's values so much that she doesn't want to do well in school.

The problem is that you still have to be relevant to the community. You should be maybe one step ahead instead of ten where you'd like to be. Maybe then you could lead in a certain direction instead of inflaming everyone. Try not to use such extremes because the people are not ready for that yet. . . . Okay, wear a coat and tie as you need for an interview. Don't debate them on that issue.

I've been thinking that what bothers me is that this conversation hasn't been as personal as last week. I want to find out what happened to his girlfriend and we've just gone around in the broad circles. I keep debating whether or not to ask him. What do you say about the situation?

Leader #7 introduced no structural interventions aside from asking in the first meeting that members go around the group to introduce themselves and to describe their expectations of the group.

GROUP BEHAVIOR AND PROCESSES

This group focused on outside material eighty percent of the time—more than any of the others. It was lowest in the amount of time spent discussing intrapersonal issues; the members did not attempt to discuss or to work out personal feelings among themselves.

The group often discussed personal material dealing with "current life," such as a problem someone was having with other people or with school or a career choice. Less frequently the members discussed some social issue, or dealt with personal historical material of one of the members. There was no emphasis on any kind of nonverbal interaction. The general communication style was unfocused discussion with somewhat more of a tendency than most groups for one member to hold monologue, or for the group to focus entirely on one member. There was no formal "going around" the group, nor was there any discussion in formal subgroups. There was virtually no physical contact among members.

According to the observers, this group had the least disclosure of here-and-now feelings about one another, of fantasies, and feelings about themselves at the moment. The members themselves felt they disclosed somewhat more. They did not feel they had expressed their feelings in the group.

Observers saw Group #7 in almost the exact reverse of Group #6, as being weak, slow, dull, distant, closed, quiet, uninvolved, and cold. Though items such as sex, dreams, and problems with outsiders were all appropriate to talk about, acting in an explicitly *feelingful* way, except for telling others of one's caring, was not approved (or disapproved). Behaviors such as touching warmly and telling others of their likability did not receive endorsement. "Talking without showing feelings," a behavior almost universally disapproved in other groups, was neither good nor bad. The members approved advice-giving and convincing; they saw shouting with anger, pushing, probing, or judging others negatively as neither good nor bad. The level of cohesiveness grew steadily, ranking eighth initially, fifth toward the end of the meetings.

The events picked as most important by the members reflected the non-confrontative, intellectualized approach of the group. Typical incidents cited were:

Getting out problems I have been thinking about for a long time; using the group as a sounding board and hearing a little bit more about the validity of my own personal convictions about life.

Talking about dorm life, reasons for being in school and marriage.

There was no group in which the expression of affect was less frequently chosen as a significant incident. By far the most common critical incident described by the members of Group #7 involved some type of general discussion on an outside issue in which the whole group was involved, and from which the members said they invariably profited by obtaining information. The members of Group #7 did not see interpersonal understanding, the most widely chosen factor in other groups, as important. They felt that they learned most from advice and suggestions, a factor only moderately important in most of the other groups.

LOOKING BACK

Group #7 thought negatively of their group experience. They did not find it pleasant (eleventh out of seventeen groups), they did not feel it was a particularly constructive experience (ninth out of seventeen groups). They also gave relatively negative ratings to their group leader. In competence he ranked twelfth; in effectiveness, thirteenth; in understanding of the group, twelfth; in approval of his techniques, fourteenth; admiration of him as a person, thirteenth; in desire to be in a group with him again, fifteenth. They considered him passive and very remote. He was equally unpopular with the observers and on all these dimensions was rated fourteenth of the fifteen leaders. The group members felt that he was too formal, too intellectualized, that he didn't participate as a real person and didn't seem to be "with it." They saw him, though, as kind and sincere, and as someone who couldn't possibly harm anyone. Despite the apparent dissatisfaction members felt with the group, they reported a long-term positive effect as greater than one might anticipate from these evaluations.

The leader's view of the group after it was over was that it was a worthwhile experience, but extremely hard work. He felt that at times it took the group a long time to get warmed up. He stated that he functioned differently in this group than in ordinary therapy groups because he was more active, worked harder, felt a time pressure; he talked more and perhaps a bit differently in that he was more prone to use illustrations from his own life and be more self-disclosing than in prior groups. He perceived the group as functioning optimally when they were trying to deal with certain acute types of problems, more closely approximating the type he would face in a therapy setting.

Group # 8—Transactional Analysis

Wide range but firmly balanced, nothing in excess. Gestalt, sensitivity, leader an insightful, expert bundle of happiness.

Group #8 started off with thirteen members, two of whom dropped out. There were three weekly, three-hour meetings followed by a twenty-two-hour marathon over a weekend. The first three meetings were held in the carpeted lounge of a dormitory; the marathon meeting was held at a nearby institute.

Leader #8 was a psychiatrist, well-known as an expert in Transactional Analysis, who had had extensive experience leading groups for ten years. He stated his aim in a group as personal growth of the members and their assumption of personal responsibility for that growth. He described himself as little concerned about group dynamics; or the growth of the group.

Observers considered the most characteristic aspects of Leader #8's behavior to be that he summarized, supported, and provided high conceptual input to the group. He generally focused on intrapsychic material; according to the observer ratings, more of his statements attended to the intrapersonal lives of each of his members than those of the other leaders. He ranked last of the leaders in focus on group process material, approximately midway in terms of how frequently he commented on interpersonal processes. Leader #8 did not frequently challenge or confront members; he usually questioned them, invited them, reflected on something they had said, or called on someone in the group. He was one of the highest support leaders. He occasionally offered friendship and, less rarely, protected members. He provided the members with concepts through which they could understand their behavior. He invited feedback, made comparisons, and explained what was happening.

He did not call attention to himself as leader. Although he often revealed his personal values, he did not often reveal his own here-and-now feelings, or participate as a member. He maintained boundaries between himself and the members. The observers rated his overall style as charismatic. The sheer weight of his personal attractiveness seemed to make people in the group move.

Excerpts toward the end of the marathon:

Something's on your mind, B. . . . Can I bring into the group questions you were asking me last night? I had the feeling that some of the things you were asking had to do with your own discomfort. Do you want to talk about that at all? When you were talking about peer pressures, I thought you were talking about yourself and some of your own ideas. Is that accurate? Is there much pressure on you in your fraternity? . . . Let me push my fantasy a little further. If it doesn't fit again, we'll drop it. My feeling was that you were in a very conservative college, and that you would not be one of the campus radicals. . . . I have a strong hunch you are afraid of disapproval. How do you feel about being talked about? . . . Is that why you're afraid of arguing? . . . Who hollers at you at home when you give your own opinion? . . . What sort of things do you argue about? . . . Are your parents narrow-minded? How are you going to try and change you? . . . Hold it. D., what do you feel about this? (Leader asked everyone in the group about how they felt about what was happening.)

Would you do an experiment? . . . Would you get up and say to each person in the room something positive about him or her? . . . Are you aware of how adept you were at picking out the strong points of everyone here? I think the important issue is that you don't have to look for funny things to say in order for people to listen to you. You are really in tune with what's going on. . . . Who do you feel he's closest to? . . . You and J., want to sit in a room and talk about it for a few minutes? . . . What are you feeling now? . . . Any more things you want to say? . . . Anything else you want to do, B.? (This is extremely typical of the leader's behavior, asking each student whether or not he has gone far enough, or whether he wants to do anything else.)

 . . . You've got two choices about how to handle that. One is not to tell them about it and the other is to tell them about it. If you play along you feel badly and if you don't play along you feel bad too. . . . See you're playing "kick me". If you tell them and they respond, you feel bad. . . . If you make decisions based on what is best for you, not upon child desires but upon what's important, then it's up to them to handle it. . . . Well, that's the point. Do you want to go the rest of your life behaving in a way that will not hurt other people? It's actually their choice to feel hurt. They also have the choice of respecting you for making your own decisions. . . . It sounds to me as if what's happened to you has put you in the position where no matter what you do, they're going to feel badly. If you don't tell them what you're doing, they'll feel badly because you don't tell them. If you tell them, they feel badly because you're doing what they don't want you to do. . . . You've got to give that some thought, about their being hurt and your being hurt. . . . Will you keep in mind that you are not in charge of their feelings? . . . They are in charge of their own feelings and you're in charge of yours.

Leader #8 ranked with the lowest in the frequency with which he used structured exercises in his group (approximately eleven exercises during the thirty hours of group meetings). Some of these were:

You have a dialogue in your head now. Act out the dialogue where you have a conversation with your family.

J., sit in the center, and one by one let everyone in the group come by, and try to be close to you.

Who are you least close to? Sit in the middle of the room and talk about it.

Encounter groups have value in what one takes away from them. To crystallize it, go around the room. Every person will try to say what he is going to do differently.

GROUP PROCESSES

The members of Group #8 spent a great deal of time focusing on outside material; only two groups were higher. The outside material was usually related to the current personal life of members. Some personal, historical material was discussed; and much less often social or abstract issues were discussed. When the group discussed inside material, it was both intrapersonal and interpersonal. Almost never was "the group" discussed. Monologues were not uncommon, but general unfocused discussion was relatively uncommon. There was no formalized subgroup discussion, and very little structured interaction, such as the group "going around" on a certain issue.

According to the observers, Group #8 was a moderately high group for self-disclosure of here-and-now feelings and moderately high for discussing past material in the group. The members did not feel that they expressed emotions as freely and as thoroughly as did members of most other groups. The observers rated the emotional climate much like Group #7, though not to such an extreme degree. It was seen as moderately weak, slow, quiet, dull, harmonious, relaxed. The members generally approved expression of positive feelings, disclosure, and moderate confrontation. They saw the group as cohesive.

More commonly than any other, the group selected as critical an event which represented some cognitive insight or some form of self-disclosure which resulted in insight or learning for the individual. They did not choose events in which they expressed feelings, or received feedback from others. Members of Group #8 were quite clear that gaining insight into hangups, understanding their thinking and feelings, and receiving advice were most important for their learning. Some factors which were chosen very heavily by other groups were not chosen at all by the members of Group #8; for example, "The group helped me to understand my impact on others," or, "I was able to express my feelings very fully; I was able to say what I felt rather than holding it in," or, "The important issue was that I was an involved member of a group; I felt close to the other members."

LOOKING BACK

The members of Group #8 were highly enthusiastic about their group at the end of the thirty hours. They rated their group as—a constructive experience (tied for first rank among the groups), personally learned a great deal (ranked first), turned-on (ranked third), a pleasant experience (ranked second). Their ratings of their leader were equally high, (ranked highest over all leader dimensions). He was ranked as competent (tied for first), effective (third), high in understanding his group (first), an admirable person (first); they would like to be in his group again (first), and they approved of his techniques (much higher than any of the other leaders). The observers thought less highly of the leader; their overall ratings on the same dimensions placed him seventh among the leaders.

Before the marathon, many of the students were much less positive in their feelings about the group. The leader himself, several months after the group ended, stated that in retrospect he felt it was a successful group, and that he was well-satisfied with the outcome. In his opinion, this group represented the typical kind of outcome that he had had in a group; he had had no particular problem with the group, nor would he have changed his techniques in any way were he to do the group over again.

Group #9—Transactional Analysis

Leader interpreter of "games people play." Low-energy group: members spaced throughout the room, no boundaries, no helmsman.

Four members of the fourteen members of Group #9 dropped out during the first four meetings. Two dropped out later. The attendance was extremely poor. The group met eight times in a dormitory lounge. People sat on the floor, often not in a circle, but spread about sometimes in a far corner of the room.

Leader #9, a psychiatrist, had been involved in groups for eight years, but had never previously led a nonpatient group. He voiced goals that differed from other leaders' in that he felt that the expression of feelings was far less important. He also de-emphasized getting close to other members, sharing with peers, expressing anger, experiencing joy, or being shaken in the groups. What he said he did consider important was to become flexible, to become sensitive to others, to have new experiences, to have a greater sense of self-worth, and to form a more effective means of relating to others.

Observers rated his repertoire of interventions as narrow. He entered quickly into an interaction to point out the kind of game that the members were playing, and then retreated. Observers considered him quite inactive in the group compared to other leaders. Many of his comments attempted to provide some type of cognitive input for the members. He often explained, summarized, or gave them a concept to understand their behavior, but rarely confronted or challenged a member. At times, he questioned, exhorted, or preached. He was approximately midway among the leaders in the amount of support he gave, and this support was fairly well-distributed among three different modes: protection of the members, support of the members, and the offer of personal affection. He did not often reveal his own personal values, or draw attention to himself as a leader, or participate as a member of the group. He was perceived by the observers as less charismatic than any of the other leaders. A central notion of his was that each group member should arrive at a contract with the therapist about what he wished to accomplish. He felt that the work was primarily to be accomplished between the group leader and the individual, with each person receiving his turn. He did not focus on the dynamics of the entire group, or on the group process. Other members of the group might help one another and learn from one another but he felt the leader had the major responsibility for the group effort. He used a straightforward transactional analytic approach to analyze the transactions which occur among the three ego states of the individual, parent, child, and adult, as well as to analyze the games that are played between individuals.

Here are some verbatim excerpts from the first meeting:

Let me say something about the group. Now you can do anything you want as far as I'm concerned. I just don't want anyone to get violent with me and I think we should extend that to everybody unless someone doesn't mind. . . . One person said I belong to a fraternity and everybody hammered him. No one was waiting for the clues he gave to show his individuality. . . . That's a game to me. And the game is that you can let a guy talk for ten minutes and you can find out what you want. You can find what you want to criticize.

. . . In my therapy groups I'm a very strong leader; I'm very, very active in that group. . . . I don't think this group would last very long without a leader. . . . Does everyone want me to be a leader or is there anyone who doesn't want me to? . . . The leader sets the rules. He has the prerogative of calling time and showing his own prejudice . . . I'll be the group leader then. Does anyone disagree? . . . You can fight with each other, or you can disagree with me. My picture of a group is that we are all sitting in a circle, and we have an external boundary like the room. All groups have to have an external boundary. There are all sorts of different kinds of leaders like the army has— generals, sergeants, and corporals. Now if you just have an external boundary, then all you have is a party, and there is no leadership. Then you get people in masses who are just wandering around. Okay. We've got the leader and the external boundary. Okay, the next thing is that you have six things you can do in a group and when you're with another person, and you can only do one of these six things. The six things you can do when you're in a social setting— you can withdraw; that's one thing . . .

And then there are games. And games are this. You play something on one level but it means something on another level; then you get a payoff for it. A payoff is "Well, I don't care about this or that" and what it does is psychologically reinforce you. . . . The sixth thing—I don't know if it will happen here —is intimacy. Intimacy has been happening for 3,000 years. You get very close to someone. . . . (Student asks, "Could we fire you if we wanted to?") Maybe. I think the easiest thing would be not to come. You don't have to come. The only thing I'm going to do is come to the room next Tuesday and if nobody's there, I can't do anything about it . . .

Excerpts from Session 4:

We have eight out of thirteen. What's that percentage? . . . The normal attendance of an ordinary group function is 86.7 percent throughout the world. That was arrived at by a group therapy project. . . . George is kind of a half-assed conformist. Aren't you going to put your feet in the middle, George, like everybody else, wouldn't you feel better?

I'm really intrigued by what those observers are doing. . . . The only thing I know about the project is how many groups there are: seventeen . . . The only thing I know is they asked different psychiatrists to come down and lead groups. . . . I'm a transactionist. You're supposed to really like this. It's the greatest thing that ever happened. . . . The two guys who talk the most were Jim and Joe and the group got them. Joe was playing "kick me" and he was saying "here's my real problem" and would go on and on. I could only say shut up, which is kick me . . .

Now what's happening? You and he are going through just like a panel discussion. Okay, that ought to keep us from doing much. . . . Do you want a confrontation? . . . Are your parents feeding you? . . . Okay, then you're not entitled to bitch about it. . . .

Excerpts from Session 6:

George started out saying something, and then you went into this great big thing. People asked you questions. You finally got one and a half compliments, and as soon as you got that you changed the subject. Like, can you take only one and a half compliments? Is that all you can take in an hour? . . . You blocked it off. You mean if I don't say something complimentary to George, like he doesn't really count; it doesn't make any difference? Did you get a compliment today? Or did somebody say something nice to you? . . . What did she say? . . . What makes you smile, George? . . . Look, George, what would you say to us if you weren't telling us how fucked up you were? I mean, what else could you say? . . . Let me tell you what happens. You set yourself up as a target and your payoff is that you're entitled to say, "I don't feel that" . . . Can anybody in the group say something new or meaningful to Gary? . . .

What I think we're having now is called an interesting evening. The main topics for an interesting evening are (1) sex, (2) drugs, and (3) everything else, like politics. . . . I'm sort of wondering whether you are intelligent or not. Why don't you just make good grades? Why don't you just do that and forget whether or not you are intelligent? . . . Anybody have a new twist on this? . . . Maybe you can say something about this to us next week. I wanted to see if anybody else had anything they wanted to say. Do you want to say something tonight? . . . Do you figure you could ever figure out the way you want the group to go? Does anybody else have anything to say?

Leader #9 introduced only about five structured exercises during the entire group. These were:

Tell me the first thing that comes to your mind.

Whoever hasn't said anything, say something now.

Say something nice to each other or I'm going to take over.

Everyone say something straight to her—wait until after they all say something to you to respond to them.

Change something right now, or change the course of things that are occurring in this room.

GROUP PROCESSES

The group divided its time equally between discussing inside and outside material. The outside subjects generally involved personal current material in the lives of the members. There was relatively little discussion of abstract or social issues, and no discussion of racial issues. When members talked about inside material they talked about their personal feelings. They did not discuss feelings that existed among the members of the group. The group spent much more time than most other groups in discussing the group itself.

The leader preferred to work with one person, with the rest of the group observing. This pattern held true in the beginning. As the group proceeded, however, it spent an increasing amount of time in unfocused general discussion about trouble the group was in. Very little time was spent in formal go-arounds or subgroups.

Although Group #9 was not a high self-disclosing group, it was higher than several of the other groups. The members felt that they had disclosed far fewer intimate details of their lives than had the members of most of the other groups. Furthermore, they did not feel that they had expressed feelings in the group.

The observers described Group #9 (like Groups #7 and #5) as slow, dull, distant, closed, informal, uninvolved, quiet, sad, cold, and aggressive. Apparently, all groups led by psychiatrists had similar emotional climates in this project. On the other hand the climate of this group, unlike several of the other more uninvolved groups, was considered aggressive rather than harmonious. It was seen by many of the members as a somewhat uncomfortable, slightly dangerous place.

Members gave clear approval to positive behavior such as kissing, touching, expressing, caring, commenting on likability, as well as of crying and pleading for help—but not to threatening remarks. They thought sexual material could be discussed, although repeated bringing in of "outside topics" was discouraged. Advice-giving, probing silent members, shouting with anger, and commenting on another's unlikability were all approved, but putting down another who had just opened up was seen as inappropriate. Group #9 was the least cohesive of all groups.

The members of Group #9 generally chose some type of expression of feeling—either positive or negative—as the critical incidents. They usually commented that their response to a critical event was a negative feeling—hostility or frustration, or a feeling of exclusion. The members rarely stated that they obtained information or insight from the event, and they rarely chose a critical event involving self-disclosure. Only Group #9 stated as most important that the group was helpful to them because they were able to help others. They also cited receiving advice and realizing their impact as important, two categories frequently chosen by all the other groups.

LOOKING BACK

The testimony of the members at the end of the group was exceptionally negative. They considered Group #9 unpleasant (tied for seventeenth place), turned-off (seventeenth place), nonconstructive (tied for seventeenth place), an experience in which they learned very little (sixteenth place), and unsuccessful (seventeenth place). They evaluated their leader in roughly the same fashion. On the global ratings of leaders, he was ranked fourteenth of fifteen leaders in competence, in effectiveness (fifteenth), not understanding of group (fifteenth), they did not admire him as a person (fourteenth), want to be in a group with him again (fifteenth), or approve of his techniques (fourteenth tied). The observers rated only two leaders as more inept. Interviews with members corroborated their questionnaire responses. The students said they would characterize the group as "boring" or "plodding." There was rarely any attention, any energy, any pitch of excitement. The leader just sat around for long periods of time, making comments about the games the group was playing.

An event that greatly influenced the course of group #9 was the occurrence of a manic psychosis in one of the members. Two meetings were devoted to discussing him and the members' emotional responses to the event (see Chapter 5).

When the leader was interviewed several months after the group ended, he stated that the group was not all that it could have been, primarily due to "poor structure." He saw the major problem of the group to be that there were too many things going on around the University. If he were to do it over again, he would have tried to screen out unstable members, be more active, structure the group more by, for example, setting up psychodrama episodes in each meeting. He also felt that he would have worked out a contract with each member more thoroughly. He realized that the students in the group were not, in general, satisfied with the whole group experience, but did not really feel that it was important for the group to have been successful. He did feel that there were some satisfied members in the group and he recalled at least two or three members who, in his opinion, learned a great deal.

Group #10—Esalen Eclectic

*Psychological calisthenics. Programmed, obedient group.
Rules. Unsynchronized. Forced, rapid intimacy.*

Group #10 started off with eleven members, but one woman dropped
out after the first meeting. Attendance was good. The group met in a dormitory lounge for an initial three-hour session, then a twelve-hour marathon session, and then five weekly three-hour sessions.

Leader #10 had a professional background quite different from that of
any of the other group leaders. A musician, he became interested in encounter groups through his interest in creativity. Ten years earlier he spent
a year in a special program on creative behavior at the Esalen Institute.
He began coleading groups; and had led one marathon group (an entire
weekend) almost every month. He stated that he did a great deal of Gestalt
work and was especially interested in the relationship between body sensa-
tions, body movements, body awareness, and personality and creativity. He
did not focus on the group as a system, but described himself as a one-to-
one trainer with whomever he is working on in the group. He said he felt
it was important to help individuals "get into themselves" by becoming
aware of how they breathe. He felt that breathing is a characteristic way
of blocking and if people are anxious they will have a particular type of
shortness of breath. Only through working with the body posture, position,
and attitude can one get to "where the subject is." He felt the important
thing is to get into the "blocks"—the impasse.

The observers described Leader #10 as being particularly stiff, ill-at-
ease, and trying extremely hard. He seemed to have a preplanned script of
exercises he had decided to use in a particular meeting. He placed tremendous emphasis on the "breakthrough," and worked hard on various members to pass a certain point which would be reflected by a burst of self-ex-
posure, tears, or some other sign. Leader #10's rate of activity seemed to
be extreme: in some meetings he accounted for as much as a third of all
the words spoken. He did not involve himself in the group in the same
way as other leaders. Very few leaders focused more on intrapersonal material than Leader #10. The observers rated him a very low support
leader; only two leaders were less supportive. He did relatively little challenging or confrontation, but he frequently questioned individuals or invited them to participate in the group. In the observers' view, he was a
highly managerial, highly structuring leader who made little use of his own
person. He almost never drew any attention to himself or participated as a
member. In most meetings he revealed to a minor extent some of his own
here-and-now feelings. He often attempted to give the members of the

group a type of framework on how to change. He also frequently invited feedback from the other members for one member of the group.

Leader #10 led the group in a characteristic way that was extremely different from any of the other leaders. He used a great number of structured exercises, and in every meeting put the group through certain paces.

From Session 1:

Anyone here, can you give us some feedback why you came and your expectations? . . . So that was the issue that brought you here. . . . Does anybody else have any similar or especially different idea?

You know we are being very general right now, and later on we're going to have to have some specific rules against being general. . . .

Well, you think I'm philosophizing, do you? Okay, so now we will set up our model for our group. We'll call this a basic encounter group, sensitivity group, and it won't be based on any special technique. Rather, it's a mixture. We will try a series of techniques and a series of processes, the ones that I know. The ones that I can think of immediately are sensitivity training, body awareness, and a few other encounter group techniques. I see this as an Esalen-type encounter group. We would call it more generally a plain encounter group. Does that meet most of your expectations?

. . . Okay, I would like to lay out some rules. Once we get started there will be specific ways of acting which, I think, are productive and growth-inducing. First of all, the assumption is that we're here to change. Each one of us, me included, as a leader, because I learn in the process as well as you learn. Now the assumption goes like this: that most of us get stuck at certain points in our lives; at almost any point in our lives we have attitudes and we have ways of behaving that become stereotyped. We kind of get into the group, and respond to certain situations in certain ways, because of the fact that it's safe for us to do that . . .

We're conditioned. We have to try to find and discover that there are many avenues for behavior which have been shut off to us for one reason or another. Every single human being has a desire not to take a chance or a risk and try new behavior. An example would be if there's someone in the group that I don't like and I just say straight away, "I don't like you," and I don't say why, or if I'm angry and I don't want to express my anger because that shows I'm an angry person, so I hold it back. Now to learn to express joy, love, anger, fear, anxiety, to say to other people our embarrassments, is a way of releasing a lot of the things that have been holding us back, that really prevent us from living, and so basically the whole idea of the encounter group is to take a chance. So that's what we're here for; we're a learning group working toward changes. That's really all there is to it. Any questions on that? . . .

In the encounter group, the idea is to stay in the here-and-now, so when you say things, don't say "one wonders" or "one wishes" or "you would like to know,"—"you" meaning "me," see. If you use the word "you," don't use it in the third person general, "you" meaning the whole world. Practice talking to people in the third person singular. Practice your pronouns. Direct your pronouns somewhere, then own your own feelings. Let's start off with a short exercise. Now for a few minutes we are going to walk around, and the idea is to really look at everybody with your eyes, but no talking. It's called meandering. Meander around the room and look at people. Don't focus. Allow them to come into your awareness and walk past them and see if you can find ways of discovering the other people with your eyes. After we do this for a few minutes, I'll go on with further instruction about what follows.

From Session 7:

I've been having the idea right along that I've been in complete control over the group, leading it, so I feel tonight I would rather not do that. I'd rather have you people start without my intervening so much—and controlling. Not that I think that you're all waiting for me, but we've done a lot of that . . . To be a little more specific, I feel like I'm playing a cat-and-mouse game. It's been exclusively stated that each time we're here to get into contact with our feelings, and now we've had thoughts about feelings . . .

Come on, you guys, what's happening? Let's have a process check right now. What's happening right now? What do you think happened? . . . Does anyone here remember the rules we set up in the first two or three meetings? . . . What were some of the primary rules we were going to operate this group on? . . . What else? . . .

Let's try a here-and-now thing. There's an even number of people here, so if we get five in the middle and five on the outside—you middle people face out. This will be a here-and-now practice. Now you people on the inside tell your partner how you feel about each other. . . . How are your own feelings? . . . What do you feel? . . . What did we learn, what did we learn before?

Leader #10 was in a completely different class from any of the other leaders in use of structured exercises. During the thirty hours of the group he used over eighty.

Take your shoes off, wander around, find the person you know least, and have a back-to-back conversation.

Close your eyes, touch each other's faces, know through your fingertips.

Now break up in groups of three and get to know each other by looking at each other.

Imagine children meeting, fighting and making up.

Make each person an animal. What kind of animal are you?

Suggests nonverbal exercises including breathing, rocking on one's pelvis, focusing on areas of the body that are tight.

Raise and lower your partner's feet. Touch them as a lover, a parent, etc.

Split into groups of four to invent a new way of introduction to one another.

Each person think of the most joyous moment of your life and then think of a way to describe it. . . . First verbally and then by action.

Be your hands, you're hard to work. Resist it. What are your hands doing? . . . Be your hands and talk to the confusion . . . Tell everybody how dumb you are.

Get into contact with your inner self of violence . . . Have a fantasy fight between your weak self and your strong self. See yourself in the fight. Describe it . . . Get up and be the weak person.

Tell us how you can feel more as a woman. Look in the mirror often. Try and see yourself as a woman. Try to be more female within.

GROUP PROCESSES

The group members spent more time than fifteen of the other sixteen groups on inside material. The very small amount of outside material that was brought in generally pertained to personal material in the lives of the students. The inside material was both intrapersonal and interpersonal, very rarely on an abstract or social issue. Very rarely was "the group" as a whole discussed. The leader managed the exercises, waited until they were finished, and then asked for some reactions. He often spent large proportions of the meeting focused on one member. There was rarely unfocused general discussion among all the members.

According to the observers, there was relatively little self-disclosure in Group #10. The group members, however, felt that they had disclosed intimate details of their lives (seventh among the groups). They felt that they had expressed feelings to a much greater degree. By the eighth meeting, they felt they had expressed more feelings than the members of any of the other groups.

The observers' ratings gave Group #10 this profile: weak, quiet, dull, distant, informal, relaxed, harmonious, and closed. Half of the meetings were rated as extremely involved, half as extremely uninvolved.

Touching, caring expression, comments on liability, pleading for help, and crying were all seen as good. Making threatening remarks was disapproved. Though dreams and fantasy reports were approved, there was clear disapproval of bringing in outside topics, or for bringing friends to sessions. Group #10 was the only group which disapproved the behavior of "showing one has no intention of changing." Advice-giving, probing silent members, and commenting on unlikability were approved, but putting down someone who had just opened up was seen as wrong. At the end of the fourth meeting, Group #10 was the third most cohesive. This decreased considerably. Unlike a strong, naturally developing group which increases in cohesiveness as it proceeds, Group #10 proceeded in the opposite way, from strong feelings about the group in the very first meetings to disenchantment at later sessions.

As might be expected, the members often cited as significant events involving some type of group game entailing expression of feeling or self-disclosure (more frequently cited as significant than by members of any other group). The members' response to these events was usually a sense of universality—that they were like other people, or that they had made a breakthrough and were able to do something they previously were not able to do. At the end of the entire group experience, the members of Group #10 felt, as did the members of most of the other groups, that "the group helped me to understand my impact on others." Group #10 felt more often than any other group that the group had encouraged them to experiment with new kinds of behavior.

LOOKING BACK

As compared with other groups, Group #10 found their group to be moderately pleasant (seventh out of seventeen); somewhat turned off (tied for eleventh place); somewhat constructive (ninth out of seventeen); and moderately educative (tied for eighth place). They rated their leader similarly at about the mean of the fifteen leaders. Compared to other leaders, he was rated low on competence (tied for seventh place), effectiveness (tied for eighth place), understanding of his group (tied for sixth place), approval of his techniques (tied for eighth place), admiration of him as a person (tied for sixth place), desire to be in a group with him again (tenth place). More than the members of any other group, the members thought their leader was far too active and far too intrusive.

The observers felt far more negatively toward Leader #10. On the global ratings of leadership effectiveness he ranked sixteenth of the seventeen groups. In their ratings of his style, observers reflected an opinion of Leader #10 as lacking appreciation of "timing," of the "needs of the group."

In interviews with the group members, some members felt strongly that the leader was playing some "pseudo-sensitivity games" with them. They felt that they had to come up with the correct answers for him and that he was pressuring them unduly to express the kinds of feelings he wanted to hear. One member stated that he saw the group as a very constructive one at first; however, at the end, great boredom set in. He attributed this, however, more to the failure of the other members to involve themselves in the group than to the leader's failure. One member who dropped out stated, "How dumb—and so what?" She felt that this leader expected some instant closeness and this was very unrealistic for her since she had to make friends on a more gradual basis.

When the leader was interviewed several months after the end of the group, he expressed dissatisfaction with his leadership. In his view, it was a flat group; he was too structured and too self-conscious about the observers in the room. He felt there was also a great deal of flatness in the group members; they had a strong resistance and reticence about them which he was unable to break through. Ordinarily, he structured a group very heavily at first, and then allowed the group to go where it felt the need to go. He never let this particular group go because he felt that he was needed at all times. He had a tendency, he said, to hold himself totally responsible for the group and immediately to feel pressure to take over if the group was not moving. He stated that he was not concerned about any lack of short-term enthusiasm because he was really working for longer-lasting and deeper levels of integration. It was his prediction that the six-month follow-up would demonstrate that many members would have a definite residue of change.

Group #11—Rogerian Marathon

Resistive, fearful, silent, play-safe group members. Leader hard-working, frustrated, eventually impatient.

Group #11 began with twelve members, had only two twelve-hour meetings with the leader scheduled four weeks apart. Between the two meetings, the group had been asked to meet for a six-hour leaderless session, but they met for only three hours. Each meeting was held in a comfortable, informal lounge.

The leader, a clinical psychologist, represented the marathon method of encounter. His basic orientation was Rogerian, and he had been leading groups for about twelve years—at least four therapy groups during the week and from three to five encounter groups a month. The observers described Leader #11 as extremely active in the group; he modelled continuously for the other members by disclosing his own feelings, especially about the predicament in which he found himself in the group. He struck the observers as being hard-working, honest, accepting at first, very careful not to offend others, and demonstrating considerable respect for members' opinions and feelings. He did not strike observers as having to work through some of his own problems. He focused on interpersonal behavior and on the group as a whole and only infrequently on intrapersonal issues. He was not challenging or confronting, but he rarely made warm or supportive comments. He invited members to participate and he often questioned them. He did not spend a great deal of his time providing cognitive structure. He rarely summarized meetings or gave the group a conceptual framework about how to understand themselves. It is clear from the verbatim transcripts that the leader gradually became quite disappointed and frustrated and expressed his disappointment openly.

From Session 1:

I have been imported by the establishment from _____ at considerable expense and maybe you are wondering why. One thing I want you to know about me right off the bat is that I have been sick lately. I almost didn't come. I have been running a high fever the early part of the week, and I'm on antibiotics, and I've been dragging the last couple of days. I feel better this morning but I might fade away during the day and need to take a nap at some point.

What do you think will happen today? . . . What's your fantasy about what might happen? . . . Are you a participant or an observer? . . . You look as if, well, you're sitting as though you're an observer.

Those people in the back are observers. That's part of a weird feeling I have —observers and tape. Outside there is a lot of distraction. I'd like to get rid of the tape recorder. . . .

I think what I'd like to do now is to direct you for a short period of body awareness. You'll have a chance to be more in touch with your own emotions and you'll have a lot better chance of getting in touch with each other. So I'd like to have you take off your shoes, glasses, and socks if you want to, and anything else that feels restraining. I don't know if this is actually physically possible, but let's give it a try. . . . I want each of you to lie on your back. Put your arms at your sides; cross your legs. Feel you yourself as a body lying on the floor. Let your thoughts pass by and leave you in the here-and-now. Feel the parts of your body that are pressing against the floor. Feel the floor pressing up against your body. Make a careful survey of your body. Feel where the tension centers are. Find a part that's tense. Go right into it. Focus your attention on the center of the tension. Just feel how it feels inside there. Focus on your breathing . . . (He continued with sensory awareness exercises for a few minutes more.)

. . . I want to shift my own role now from directing to letting you go ahead. I'll respond rather than initiate it. Do anything you want . . .

You actually didn't ask a question, you made a statement. . . . While something happened to you, you were talking about moving slowly. What does that mean? . . . Are you the kind of a guy who usually doesn't move slowly? The thing that strikes me is that you were the first one here today . . . You tend to be impatient; you wish we could get on with something. Do you have any sense of impatience in regard to this group? . . . Would you be willing to say what kind of vibes you are getting from any particular person? . . . It seems like it's difficult for Neal to express his point of view because as soon as he starts he gets hammered at . . .

I'm interested about other people thinking about distance. How distant does each of you think about the other people in the group? What if you were to rate on a seven-point scale? Seven is very close, and one is very distant. How do you rate everyone? Well, Sharon, do you feel close to anyone? . . . Who do you feel most distant from? . . . There is something I notice about you, you seem to talk to me a lot . . .

Chris, do you have any reaction to those girls, or feelings toward girls? . . . What kind of vibes do you get from them? . . . I'm suddenly having the feeling that everyone is somewhat shy . . .

Excerpts from the twelfth hour: (this is the beginning of the second marathon session, four weeks after the first one):

You all look familiar, but I don't remember any of your names . . . Do you know each others' names? . . .

I think I'd like to wait for a while before setting up any structure . . . I'd like to know what you've done since last time. . . . Do you feel guilty in telling me that you only met for three hours rather than six? . . . Yeah, you're doing it with an apologetic smile . . .

I didn't want to come back today. Last time the group was a drag. I was sick but the group made me worse. What are we going to do with the group today? . . . There are no blacks in the group. Had I known this originally in advance a little bit more I probably wouldn't have come to the group. . . . We are stuck here until nine p.m.; food will be brought in. . . . It's not clear what we're going to do with all this time . . . I feel like I'm talking to a bunch of mummies who are all dead . . .

Anything you want to happen today? . . . I'd like to see what the rest of you want to do today . . . (The group has a go-around on this question.)

. . . I feel like a nigger today. I feel prejudiced against by all of you. Everybody is talking and sort of shunning me, pushing me out . . .

I feel annoyed at the three of you coming in late. I feel annoyed at you and you and you . . .

Could you start that again by saying, "I feel"? I'd like some reaction from you. You sit around like dummies . . .

Excerpts from the twenty-first hour:

I'd like people to describe how they see themselves and how they think they've changed since the last session . . .

Is there anything you can do in this group to make people happier, if that's really what you want to do in life? . . .

How do you feel about her being disappointed in you? . . . Well, we have run out of bullshit. . . . It's been a long time since I've felt as helpless as I do here in this group. . . . Are you saying it's that way for you too, Jay? . . .

It's as if I were on another planet and I had a group of androids, a kind of mechanical person without emotions. . . .

I find myself vacillating between not giving a damn and feeling hopeless and irritated and feeling hopeful. . . . There's a deadness here in this group. Yes, we could get together and dance and have a party and tell jokes, but that's not relevant to the feeling I have here like we're slogging through heavy mud . . .

Are you saying that you don't feel it, Ted? Yes, the part outside of the room when we were walking felt good. I found a lot of my tension dissipated. As soon as we came back in here and tried to talk with each other it all came back again. It just doesn't seem to happen . . .

Who in this group is readiest to be touched? Who shuts it off the most? Who needs to be unshut-off?

Well, I tell you that I feel helpless as a leader in this group. You say that you're sorry for letting me down. Like I don't want you to feel guilty. You just didn't know that I felt helpless, but I'm not laying it on you. Well, I'm not. That isn't the main thing. I'm just saying that I feel helpless.

Leader #11 used twenty-one exercises, mostly during the first six hours. He used several nonverbal exercises where he asked members to try to become more aware of their body, to feel where their tension centers were, or to focus on their breathing. Occasionally he had the group "go around" on some person, expressing their feelings about the behavior of the individual. The most significant structured exercise from the standpoint of the members was a "trust walk." The group was broken into dyads, and asked to take a walk with one another. One member of a dyad was blind-folded and was led by the other and then the roles were reversed.

GROUP PROCESSES

The group spent approximately 75 percent of its time dealing with outside issues such as the draft, the war, and, to a lesser extent, racial issues, despite the leader's focus on interpersonal issues. When the group did discuss inside issues there was a moderate amount of focus on the leader, a result of his own efforts to focus the group on himself. They spent relatively little time discussing interpersonal issues among the members of the group, or focusing on one person. In the beginning the group spent most of its time in a general, unfocused discussion. Later, considerable time was spent in structured subgroups. Occasionally, a good deal of time would be spent in a formal go-around.

There was exceedingly little self-disclosure in Group #11, either of the here-and-now feelings or of there-and-then feelings. The observers rated it one of the two or three least self-revealing groups, although during the first half of the group the members felt to some degree they had revealed intimate details of their lives. Nor did members feel that they expressed their feelings. The observers considered Group #11 to be slow, quiet, harmonious, distant, weak, and uninvolved. In striking contrast to most other groups, there was *no* norm favoring *intense feeling expression*—touching, expressing caring, crying were disapproved, along with hitting or threatening other members. The members of Group #11 also disapproved of bringing friends to the sessions. Advice-giving, convincing, probing silent members were slightly approved, but pushing one who'd "had enough," and putting down others who had opened up were seen as wrong. At the end of the first half of the group, the group had scored about midway on cohesiveness. By the end of the group there was a precipitous drop.

The members of Group #11 seldom selected a negative incident as significant. They frequently reported that they gained information from discussion of some abstract issue. Very rarely did the group members say that they had obtained insight or that they had revealed themselves. Group #11 members were quite similar to the members of the other groups in feeling that the group helped them to appreciate their impact on other people, to learn that they were similar to others, to feel that they were in the same boat as other people. Like members of other groups, they reported they had benefited by being an involved member of a group. They differed from the other groups in devaluing understanding themselves, or revealing anything embarrassing about themselves and still being accepted.

LOOKING BACK

The members of this group were dissatisfied customers. They did not find it a pleasant experience (tied for eleventh place among the seventeen groups), they were not turned on by the group (sixteenth place), they did not find it a particularly constructive experience (tied for twelfth place), they did not feel that they had learned very much (tied for thirteenth place). The overall testimony ranked this group thirteenth. They felt less negative about the leader, rating him midway among the leaders. They felt he was too passive and slightly remote. The observers rated Leader #11 more highly. Only five leaders were more favorably rated by the observers in terms of liking him as a person, or their feelings about his general effectiveness, competence, and understanding of the group. They felt the group was an intellectualized one which never got into a feeling, or confrontation mode.

What went wrong? Many offered the suggestion that there was something wrong in the composition of the group; there were too many "naive, unaware people" who were unmotivated to take risks, to explore themselves, to work for some kind of change.

When the leader was interviewed many months after the group ended, he stated that it was one of the worst groups he had ever run, that the whole group was a drag. He said the people in the group were not motivated for an encounter group, and what they wanted was some kind of directed experience. "There was a sort of deadness and passiveness about the group." If he gave them some exercises or structural interventions, they responded well but otherwise all they did was to sit there and "play it cool." In retrospect he felt there was nothing he could have done differently except not take the group. He stated that he would avoid ever again running a group of nonmotivated people.

Group #12—Eclectic Marathon

Revealing, trusting, well-jelled, tightly knit.

The group met three times: a two-hour meeting, followed two weeks later by a twenty-hour marathon meeting and a final two-hour meeting ten days later. The marathon meeting was held in the leader's home; the short meetings in the dormitory lounge. The group started with fifteen members; one woman dropped out.

The leader was a psychiatrist who had been leading groups for seventeen years. He had experimented with innovative approaches. For the last three years, for example, he had held marathons with large groups—all his individual patients, and their spouses. Most of his work had been done with patients, but occasionally he had run groups of nonpatients. He described his heavy commitment to his patients. He is not only willing to see a patient who is in psychological difficulty at any hour of the day or night, but he would also wake up members of the group so that they might hold a group meeting to help the individual work through his dilemma. He stated that he works on the individual person rather than on the group, turning an imaginary spotlight on a member to make him the center of attention for as little as thirty minutes, or as much as three hours. He claimed little patience with any conventions which slow up the level of intimacy and honesty which can be produced. He felt that he showed a great deal of himself, not only his own here-and-now feelings and his values, but also his personal life. His ground rules are simple; honesty in the group and informality. He encourages members to meet outside the group without him.

Observers indicated that Leader #12 focused very heavily on personal issues (second among the leaders); structured fantasy was quite characteristic of his approach. Correspondingly, he was quite low among the leaders in comments about the entire group or interpersonal issues. Although he didn't challenge members he generally invited them to speak, or questioned them. He very openly supported or protected members. Observers felt he revealed his personal life and his own personal values more frequently than most of the other leaders, but his here-and-now feelings less. He rarely drew attention to his role as a leader. He was not a charismatic leader, and was considered as a kind of a teacher by some of the observers. On many occasions he attempted to give the members of the group an individual cognitive framework by which to understand their behavior. Only Leaders #6 and #8 provided more cognitive input than he did.

From Session 1:

What I'd like to do is give an introductory thing. Introduce ourselves and find out where we're going. I'm Ed _____ and I'd rather be called Ed than Dr., or anything like that. I'm a psychiatrist and I do not work for Stanford, and have no connection whatsoever with the official administration. What I'm primarily involved in is working with people and talking freely and openly without fear that someone will censure you. Say what you please. . . . I'm here to find out what you want.

Let's go around the room, then, and tell a little about yourselves and about what you want out of this class. One thought that I had concerning the black-white parts of this study is that someone could pretend that he was black . . . It might be good for you to see what it's like to be a black militant . . .

As far as an encounter group goes, I don't mind using any techniques.

I can understand your feeling of wanting to drop out, not because I'm a psychiatrist but because it's part of my own life. Some part of me wants to drop out. . . . Does that mean you don't have any feelings about what he said? . . . That's not what I asked. Do you have any feelings? . . . Yes, that's what I'm trying to get. I think that's bullshit, and I think you have a lot of feelings, and I think you're hiding your anger behind yourself. It's your responsibility to tell us your feelings. I'd like to go with that as being something we can establish as the basis of this group. Just to illustrate—if you've been to see a movie, and I ask you how you feel about it, and you say it was great camera work, well-conceived, etc., you haven't told me how you felt. Would you say you were bored by it, excited by it, turned on by it, depressed by it—you are telling me how you feel. I'd like to leave this open. We can tell each other our thoughts and feelings. Thoughts are what you do all day long but feelings are different . . .

I'm sticking to the issue of what you are feeling at any particular moment. Apparently you were feeling bad that we were pounding him. . . . Why should I resolve it? Why don't you resolve it? . . . I think what you're doing is interrupting a conflict . . .

Excerpts from Session 7:

There's something I'd like to know. Is anybody hurt? Emotionally or soulfully sore? Anybody feeling uptight? How do you feel about the last hour? . . . I wish you would have said something if you were feeling resentful toward me. I didn't know that. You seem to have gone from a deep thing to a superficial thing. I wasn't sure if you felt good about what was happening. . . . Do you have anything to say about the last two hours? It's been too intellectual in a sense. . . . Were you feeling hostile anywhere within the session that you didn't express it? . . .

(Following his suggestion for a black-white fantasy trip.) . . . Okay, I've got one quick reaction to what we've just heard. Nobody made love. . . . There weren't any sexual scenes I can remember, except yours. Is it really threatening to think of a black-white love thing?

P., you're so full of shit. It's coming out of your ears. You know you can't even imagine your girl screwing a black guy without some kind of magic happening, without her getting used. You can't imagine your girl really liking a black guy, it offends you. You're a racist. It comes out of your every pore. You're just pretending you're not. Even your attitude shows in your fantasy. . . . How come you chose to play a black that could only say fuck you? . . . Well, why didn't you play a black who wasn't foolish? . . . Because that's all you think of blacks, that they're stupid. . . . Oh, you couldn't play a smart black, could you? That would be giving it too much. You didn't try it on your own.

Leader #12 used approximately twenty to twenty-five structured exercises during the course of his group; only four leaders used structured exercises more frequently. Here are some examples:

Let's go around the room and tell something about ourselves.

Could you play a scene and ask for something?

Think of your three worst secrets. Imagine the reaction, and tell your neighbor in gibberish.

Fantasy yourself being shrunk to the size of a pin and enter a trip inside your body. Try to imagine what you smell, feel like. Try to imagine what you find. Travel to any part of your body that you're having a problem with. Try to examine the problem. Now imagine yourself exiting from your body at any point. Okay, open your eyes. Who wants to share a trip?

GROUP PROCESSES

Group #12 spent an unusual amount of time on discussion of outside personal material, their past and current lives. More than any other group, they invested considerable time discussing fantasies. According to the observers, Group #12 was a high revealing group, both as to here-and-now material, and to personal material from outside the group. It increased progressively. The observers considered the group an exceedingly informal, harmonious, and relaxed one. It was not considered to be fast-moving, alive, and intense.

Kissing, touching, telling others of their likability, expressing caring, pleading for help, and crying were all positively valued. Sex, dreams, and problems with outsiders were seen as legitimate content. Probing silent members, mentioning unlikability, shouting with anger were seen as good, but continuing to push members or putting down someone who had opened up were seen as wrong. Group #12 ranked second among the groups in cohesiveness.

Group #12 members very frequently selected some type of self-disclosure as the significant incident of each meeting. Members responded to these self-disclosures with feelings of warmth, love, or empathy, or by obtaining increased insight. They felt the most positive effects had been that the group helped them to appreciate their impact on others and to realize that everyone was in the same boat. What was unusual was that they felt they had achieved insight into themselves and into the sources of their conflicts. They felt that they had learned to recognize and accept hidden parts of themselves, and to make some type of link between the past and the present. They were also one of the very few groups whose members said the group had helped them to understand some things that had happened in their nuclear family, and that they had relived many old conflicts with their families.

LOOKING BACK

The members of Group #12 found it to be a pleasant experience; turned-on, constructive, educative. The average ratings placed it third among the seventeen groups. The members also rated their leader highly.

They felt he was highly competent, effective, and understood his group, and they approved of his techniques, although they did not admire him as a person as much as several of the other groups admired their leaders. Overall, the ratings they gave their leader placed him fifth among the leaders. The observers saw Leader #12 more positively. They admired his competence, his skill, and his degree of understanding of the group, and rated him first among the leaders.

The great majority of members felt extremely positive about the group and about the leader. One of them stated: "He's a fantastic man; if I have any problems at all, he's the person I would turn to. He was not attacking at any time, was willing to help, was not intrusive. . . . If you wanted to be silent, he let you be silent." Another member pointed out that the group was especially helpful to him because he had worked out his problems with his parents by a psychodrama episode in which the leader played him, and he played his parents. One member stated an opposite view; his own experience was one of exclusion. He felt that there was an inner circle in the group which "mouthed radical jargon, and was very much into the drug culture." He himself couldn't get into this, and felt that he was never really accepted by the leader. Furthermore, he was troubled by the discussions of homosexuality in the group and by the challenging of his traditional hierarchy of life values.

Group #13—Synanon

Different group every week. Relentless attack, verbal dogfight, ridicule, scorn. No leaders, many leaders.

The setting of the Synanon groups was entirely different from that of any of the other groups in the project; participants were bussed to the Synanon branch at Oakland. The group met in weekly three-hour sessions for eight weeks. Twenty-three students started Synanon. Ten dropped out before attending half of the meetings. The attendance rate among the others was generally poor.

The students were in a different group every week at Synanon. They were assigned to a group composed the evening of their meeting. Each group consisted of four or five Stanford students, and nine or ten experienced Synanon group members. Although the Synanon group members were not members of a continuous group, they were members of the Synanon community and knew each other well. Two senior Synanon members were designated as the executive leaders of the Stanford "tribe," and filled out the leader questionnaires for the two groups they led. After each meeting some of the students chose to participate in a social hour for the entire Synanon community.

The shadow of Synanon, the institution, loomed large in each of these groups. In recent years, Synanon has shifted its basic goals from offering an effective treatment for drug addiction to that of offering an alternative way of life. People with any type of severe problem in living, or in fact, any people who want to participate in the Synanon way of life are accepted. Small groups are omnipresent and are always referred to as the "Synanon game." The Synanon leaders describe the game as a verbal dogfight in which people are attacked bitterly for all the phoniness and softness that they have. Members attempt to attack each person's weak spots time and time again, in the belief that through the attack he will become strong. There are no official leaders; leadership emerges from among the most experienced game players. There did indeed appear to be one figure who assumed a leadership role in each of the Synanon groups to which the Stanford students were assigned. These individuals seemed to be the cleverest, most perceptive, and most indestructible members. Their statements carried more weight than others, and they made the decision to "put the game" on someone else when someone seemed to have had enough.

Observers saw the leaders as high-challenge, low-support, and highly active. They taunted, ridiculed, used a great deal of humor. They would suddenly move off the person they were attacking, and move on to another person. There was virtually no support, no attempt to draw similarities between members, no gentle invitation to members to engage in the group. Leaders provided a framework to the members on how to change, or occasionally gave explanatory statements on how to play the game. The leaders generally did not manage the group aside from shifting the game from one person to another two or three times during the meeting. They were extremely free in revealing their own here-and-now feelings and their personal values, and more than the leaders of any of the other groups, participated fully as members of the groups. The leaders' statements were generally focused on interpersonal and intrapersonal issues. They almost never made statements about "the group," although not infrequently they would make statements about Synanon.

One of the acknowledged leaders of the Stanford groups was a woman in her early thirties who had been in Synanon for over five years. A dedicated member of the community, she had worked her way up to a position of considerable responsibility, and said that she would be dead if not for Synanon. She said she would like very much to convert at least some of the Stanford students into Synanon citizens, and planned to give them literature.

Here are some verbatim excerpts of this leader's statements at the second session:

You know, you kids do not understand this one thing; it is too much for any one little asshole to crawl into Synanon, and do anything to it. They can't slow it up; they can't damage it; they can't fuck it up; they can't do anything

73

except sit around and hope they learn something. . . . Sit down and calm down about ten decibels in your tone. . . . Now, can we reason with you a little bit? It won't tax your brain too much? . . . Okay, when did you find out there were going to be conflicts in your schedule? I mean, what time today was there supposed to be a class and you wouldn't be in it? . . . Lower your tone when you talk to me. . . . Well, listen, you sit back and listen to her, she's got a lot more time in Synanon than you have. She has information. Listen to it. No, I'm serious. It's not a game, this is not a cute little thing here. . . . You were playing the Synanon game and you were fucking it up. Now listen, listen, listen . . .

Like you've got this bird nest on your head, you know, and you're sort of fat and you're kind of spastic and you jerk and then you've got these cowboy boots you've been wearing for a long time, and that dirty shirt. Do you have any socks on when you get up at night? Don't you just sort of stand your clothes up? Then I ask you about public figures and you name a couple of white authors. . . . I ask you about yourself, you as a man, and you want to take me on a goddamn trip. And this trip, you are so fucked up, you are trying so hard to be white. . . . I don't want to know about your background, I can tell you about your life. . . . You put on this funny style of shirt that all you want is to get into white society, you want to be white. That's where you are. You got very uptight last week, and when we quit this thing you got all involved about your uninvolvedness. What did you think about when you got back to campus? What were your feelings about it? . . .

We have a lot of funny things that happen in the game. We don't try to set ourselves up as parents. In a game there is no leader. The leader emerges, and it's this leader for a moment, and it keeps switching around. The game attempts to do only one thing, to talk about the obvious things to talk about a person. Now your appearance offends me. You go on and talk about it . . .

Well, let's talk to this kid over there. What's your name? . . . Billy, you look like you're very uptight. What's wrong? . . . Is this your first game here? . . . Well, it takes experience to play games. What you can do is this. If I sit in a game, and see someone attacking Carol, and I didn't like what they were doing I wouldn't come to her defense. It's up to her to defend herself as best she can. Later when that game is over I'll turn to that individual, and I'll tell him exactly what I thought of the attack on Carol. Now that's the way you play the game . . .

Let's go around the room. Start with the girls on your right. Give everyone your feeling about them . . . I think what I'm hearing is the rise of the bullshit . . . Lie down, animals, lie down. Since I have been at Synanon I've always noted that when a newcomer comes into the game you do not attack, you try to inject a little information into the newcomer . . .

Now you want to get some feelings. If none of you other motherfuckers will be honest I'll tell you something. It disgusts me when some little dingbat hole like this one comes up to me, and she comes on by trying to do her cute feminine little thing, and I'm supposed to be charmed with it all. . . . I don't want her getting into my private life. I don't want to be bothered with it. . . . To sum it up, you've got a lot of growing up to do. In the meantime you're a pain in the ass. . . . It's time somebody spanked your ass and put you in your fucking place . . .

Excerpts from Session 5:

I'm talking to you. Do you think that's right, does that sit right with you? . . . Have you read the Synanon book yet? . . . Are you going to be tested on it? . . . Wait a minute; how could you read the Synanon book and only read parts of it? It really isn't like episodes. . . . Why don't you just read the first couple of pages? How can you skip around the book? I don't understand that . . .

Why don't you tell us about Synanon? . . . Talk slower, that's number one. We'll understand you better. . . . Why are you so goddamn serious? I mean, really, we're having a ball. We're rolling around on the floor. . . . Actually, all that studying, all that work has put you in a room with twelve ordinary people, and you can't even look at someone in this room and say "hey, you must be having some fears because you just broke up with your boyfriend". . . . That's all we talked about tonight. . . . Well, let's fill in the rest of the picture. You're a virgin. And it's morally imperative to you that you remain so until you're married. You break up your big-time love life at the age of ten. You've been deadly serious since then. You sit in games and intellectualize. You go out with lots of girls. You don't have sex with them. It's beginning to boggle my mind. We keep hearing about sexual freedom and make love not war, and I run into virgins here at Stanford by the dozen. . . . You know the reason that they're bombing the campus and burning down the buildings is because all the students should be home fucking instead. . . . Well, we can't change your morals, but there's a bit of information that bothers me. You keep saying you don't think it's necessary to know how, and yet I think it takes a couple of years for a guy and a girl making it to develop a halfway serious sex relationship. . . . (And so the game continued. This student was taunted by the other members about being a virgin and then taunted twice as hard for never having masturbated.)

The Synanon leaders used no structured exercises aside from an occasional and informal go-around where some members were asked to give their feelings toward everybody in the group.

GROUP PROCESSES

Since Synanon groups had a life span of only a single meeting, there was little sense of past history. The ongoing relationship was to Synanon; the new group which met every week resembled a group that met a number of times, except that most of the people were different. The groups generally spent much time focusing on outside material. Occasionally abstract, or racial, or social issues were discussed. Very few groups in the study spent more time on current personal material outside of the group. When the group did focus on inside material it was generally on how a member was feeling toward himself at that moment. There was an intense focus on one individual lasting from a few minutes to forty-five minutes, then a shift to another person. There were no dialogues, monologues, subgroups, or general unfocused discussion.

Synanon was a high self-disclosure group, both in the amount of inside and of outside material. The observers felt that in only one other group was there a higher intensity of self-disclosure, although the students' ratings of self-disclosure placed Synanon sixth among the groups. The average student rating of Synanon on expression of feeling placed it only about midway among the seventeen groups. The observers described the emotional climate of Synanon groups as: strong, fast, alive, aggressive, involved, informal, and alternately tense and relaxed, remarkably similar to Group #6, the psychodrama marathon group.

The members felt that crying or mentioning another's likability were both appropriate. But (unlike the majority of other groups) there was no positive consensus about such behavior as touching, kissing, or showing caring. Talking about one's sex life, and bringing in problems with outsiders were both favored. Approval for confrontation (criticizing another's behavior, convincing, probing, commenting on unlikability, and shouting with anger) tied with two other groups for first place.

The members of Synanon exclusively selected as critical events some type of expression of negative feeling (often someone else's) through which they felt they gained some information or feeling that they were like other people, or got over some hurdle that had been blocking them. The gaining of insight was rarely mentioned. The members of the Synanon groups selected different factors from those chosen by members of the other groups as crucial in their learning. They reported that they had received advice and that they had revealed embarrassing things about themselves, and still had been accepted by the others. They did not feel that they learned about their impact on others, nor obtained any insight into their behavior. They did feel that expressing feelings very fully rather than holding them in had been useful to them.

LOOKING BACK

Subjects attending the Synanon group considered their experience to have been positive, about midway among the seventeen groups. They also ranked the Synanon leaders midway among the fifteen leaders. Synanon, more than any other group, evoked a bimodal response from the group members. Some felt extremely negative toward their experience in the group whereas others felt quite positive and, in fact, continued their contact with Synanon long after the end of the project.

The students who looked back at their group experience as positive emphasized the diversity of experience they had at Synanon. One said, "I was really overwhelmed by the great diversity of characters in the group, their strength, their weakness. It made me feel that all strengths and weaknesses are beautiful." Another: "First of all, the people around the campus are not like those at Synanon. I really appreciate the honesty of those people. They think in terms of black and white, whereas Stanford people usually think in terms of gray." One student who had disliked the group very much when he was in it stated that, looking back on it, he felt that perhaps it was a useful experience. He appreciated now how humorous and clever Synanon people were, and admired their great skill in cutting through the Stanford intellectualization in a matter of minutes. Another subject pointed out the support that occurred after the group meetings.

Others felt less positively. One pointed out that she had never gotten involved in the group because the game was never put on her. "If you are always honest whenever any questions come up and you answer without covering yourself up, then the game doesn't get turned on you." Another commented that she was bored with the group, and it was unreal to go to a group week after week and immediately be exposed to yelling and shouting and fighting. Another student felt much more negatively, commenting that "the group was really heavy. They attacked very viciously. In fact, all the girls were attacked on sexual issues; if they were virgins, they were attacked about that; if they weren't virgins, they were attacked for that."

Another stated, "the whole group was a fake. The more experienced players picked on the least experienced players. They tried to pretend it was good for you, but I thought it was just sadism. I didn't like the attacks on me, and I didn't want to attack others, so I just withdrew."

Group # 14—Personal Growth

Black-white encounter fizzle; crisis of disappointment, apathy. Leader sorry he came.

The group began with nine members, four white men, two white women, one black man, and two black women. A black man and a white woman dropped out of the group. General attendance was quite poor. Group # 14 met for only twenty-four hours. The first two meetings were two hours each, one week apart. These were followed by three five-hour meetings at two-week intervals. The sixth meeting, one week later, lasted for five hours. The group planned to meet for an additional five-hour session, but the leader decided to cancel, partly because of scheduling difficulties, but primarily because he felt the group wasn't getting anywhere.

The leader was a clinical psychologist selected both because he was black, and because he represented a West Coast personal growth group style. He had had extensive experience in directing sensitivity and encounter groups, many of which were black-white confrontation groups. He was deeply committed to working on racial issues in community settings. He stated that one of his primary goals was to help people attain "tolerance

77

for or humane interest in people dissimilar to oneself." Observers considered Leader #14 to be primarily concerned with members' attitudes toward racial issues. He directed most of his energies toward evoking emotions from the group members through questions or challenges. In contrast to some of the other high-challenge leaders, he ranked as one of the least supportive of the leaders. He frequently expressed his own feelings, drew attention to himself as a leader, and also revealed his own values or some personal material from his own background. Observers rated his focus as predominantly on the individual.

From the very beginning of the first meeting:

> One person will not be able to be here today. The original composition of the group was to be four black and six white. At this point I don't really consider that we have a black-white group and if this isn't changed the group will either have to be dismantled or we'll have to bring in some new people. The best I can suggest for today is, since we're here, we have a session.

> This should be a very different experience from any other class or almost any other group, unless you have been in anything that approaches an encounter group before. What happens here is that I push everyone to be very open and honest, and come out and say and do the things we generally don't do. Stop playing the games that we always play in the classroom, or in a social situation, or at home or whatever. Just really strip down and let it all hang out, and relate to each other in terms of what's on your mind, what you're thinking, and what you're feeling about.

> Okay, so honesty and openness are the key words and this makes for sometimes very intense and very upsetting, sometimes very hurtful experience, but usually very worthwhile, so it's not going to be an all pleasant experience. It should be very meaningful, however. And sort of a lot of bucking down and getting with it, if that's necessary. Some of the things that might come out might be very personal. Usually the more personal you are, the more meaningful . . .

> Things that go on here are very important. They should not be taken lightly outside. I think you should not discuss what goes on, especially with people's names attached to them . . .

> The major focus is to be what's going on here. The here-and-now, instead of getting on a soapbox and talking intellectually or politically or whatnot. We will try to zero in on what's going on between us . . .

> Maybe one way of getting started is to sort of try to come out honestly with your reactions, feelings, about people in the room right now. Don't play the games but come on out with what you think and what you feel . . . You're talking a lot out there now. How about in here? Relationships out there are one thing but in here is something else. Right? . . .

> Those are a lot of words. I don't know what you're saying, though. What do you mean? . . . What's the difference between the way you feel about her and me? . . .

There's a lot going on and you're not saying a damn thing. Come out with it. . . . You lose the conversation at just the point where it gets intense. Now you're telling me when you walk in the room and see the difference between people that you don't want to see any difference. . . . What do you mean, just a person? . . . What color is just a person? . . . That's a bunch of bullshit. . . . Do you agree with this? . . .

Do you want comfort? I don't. I wouldn't take this class if I wanted comfort. I'd sit in a lecture, write down notes, take the final, turn it in . . .

From Session 6:

You hide behind what you say. Why don't you try relaxing? You're getting so you can't think too well. Lilia is stepping on you. There's a nervousness about the way in which you look. You can't really look at me straight.

. . . There's a lot of the teacher relationship here, and I guess it goes back to some of the earlier things you were saying. How much you really look to me to do things so that you can get out of it. Well, that's another part of why I've been acting the way I've been acting that doesn't have anything to do with leadership. That's my own personal reaction; the aloofness, the part that is mine, not really grooving, either with this type of group or you as individuals. So I've kept myself back on both of those. . . . I feel much more removed from the white people than the black, although the black people in the group I think are turned off to me . . .

But teachers are a challenge even when they pick on you . . . What about people bigger than you? . . . That could be a copout. . . . Sounds like you're saying that you're using pride to avoid the whole issue. . . . You're also saying that it's not good to win. . . . He must be pretty nasty underneath. . . .

Are you convinced that you're going to lose all the time? . . . What did you get out of that arm wrestle? . . . How about the whole competitiveness? You were feeling very comfortable for a number of reasons. What you really did was to suggest a situation where you were competing with me. Very directly, since someone had to win and someone had to lose unless you were setting it up so that you would lose . . .

You would never fight blacks? So you say that intellectually you would never fight blacks? Emotionally? Do you want to offer us anything? . . .

I'm sure it looked like there was some anger involved. It was used in sort of getting her to change. That frequently doesn't work very well. Anger usually doesn't work in changing a person. I was wondering if you had ever tried any other emotions. . . . You don't think it's right to change people? . . . You are saying it's not good to be angry and it's not good to change people? . . .

Leader #14 used a few nonverbal techniques in the first four meetings, but practically none after that. He suggested an arm wrestle, and that students explore their feelings while embracing another member. A couple of sensory awareness exercises were also suggested.

GROUP PROCESSES

In some meetings, the group focused almost entirely on inside, here-and-now material, or on the leader. Other meetings focused almost entirely on outside material. When the focus was primarily on the here-and-now, it was generally in terms of race and the racial bias that existed among the black and white members of the group. In the first few meetings there was considerable focus on the leader, much more than in most other groups.

When the group focused on outside material, there was once again a large concern with racial issues either in the personal history of the lives of the members or as an abstract issue. The observers noted that early in the group there was considerable self-disclosure about both here-and-now feelings and personal details of members' lives outside the group, but little later on in the group life. The members' ratings placed the group at twelfth of the seventeen groups in self-revelation, although they felt that they did express emotions in the group. The emotional climate of Group #14 was, according to the observers, dull, quiet, slow, weak, informal, distant from one another, and closed with their feelings. At times, ratings of involvement fluctuated widely from meeting to meeting.

The members moderately approved kissing, touching, commenting on another's likability and crying, but the normative focus was sternly and sharply on the here-and-now. Group #14 was the only group to consider that frequent joking was inappropriate behavior. The members considered advice-giving, saying another's behavior was wrong, convincing, probing silent members, commenting on unlikability, and shouting with anger extremely appropriate. The average cohesiveness score rated by members of the group at the end of the fourth meeting placed Group #14 at a twelfth place tie. The dropout rate and absenteeism corroborate the judgment that this group was low in cohesiveness.

By and large, the group felt that they were helped by being able to express their feelings rather than holding them in; secondly, they thought that they benefited by gaining some insight into their thinking and feeling. Although both these items were chosen by all groups, they were more often selected by members of Group #14.

LOOKING BACK

The members of Group #14 felt that their group was an unpleasant, turned off, destructive experience in which they learned very little (last among the seventeen groups). The members' overall ratings of the leader and the observers' evaluations place him tied for ninth among the fifteen leaders. The members of Group #14 who were interviewed said the group never got going. They felt that the leader didn't want to be a leader but a peer, a member of the group. Some complained that he demanded instantaneous feelings from the group, as though they were to "switch feeling on and off like a light switch." One black member stated that the white members of the group had certain unrealized expectations—they had gone into the group wanting to be close, and wanting to understand everything about the blacks quickly. "Their compassion towards us was a pseudo-compassion in that we became a type of lab specimen for them." Other subjects suggested that at the beginning of the group the leader was an extremely strong and active leader who "exhorted us to give our whole life story in five minutes"; however, later he withdrew, fell back, and "should have been more dominating, giving the group ideas where it was going; he stayed on the sidelines too much."

In an interview several months after the group ended, Leader #14 stated, "That was the most unsuccessful group I've ever had . . . there weren't enough blacks for a true black-white encounter group and that's where I was in my interest . . . if I couldn't do what I wanted to do, I didn't feel like doing much of anything. . . . I just wasn't interested in a plain encounter group." He stated that he let the group know about his disappointment, but that others didn't reciprocate by expressing their true feelings. In fact, no one in the group really exposed himself. Nor did the group develop the kind of atmosphere which allowed the members to get close, or to feel supported by one another. He felt he had been hostile in the group, but stated that he was usually like that, and that he deliberately models honesty so that others can follow his lead.

Group #15—Personal Growth

Cold, distant, sharp; a black and a white group within a group. Cold anger, penetrating insight.

Ten members started in Group #15, three black men, one black woman, four white men and two white women. One member committed suicide after the second meeting. The black woman and three white men dropped out of the group before it was half over. The group met for a total of six sessions, four weekly three-hour sessions, followed by a twelve-hour all-day meeting a few days later and a final six-hour meeting three weeks later.

Leader #15 was a black clinical psychologist, who had been heavily involved leading therapy groups, T-groups, and black-white encounter groups. He ran his therapy groups very much like his encounter groups, and found it increasingly difficult to differentiate the two. He felt it was important for him to play an active part in the group, and although he involved himself in the group, he felt it was important to make it clear that he was the leader. It was not important, in his view, that the members experience closeness, trust, or "joy." Consequently, it was rare for him to say, "I'm feeling good about you"; one would much more frequently hear him say, "Did everyone hear that the same way?" He felt that his groups saw him as an irritating, arrogant, perhaps even overtly hostile leader, rather than as a conciliator who was tender or caring. He preferred that the members of the group walk out thinking and preoccupied about what happened in the meeting, and what would happen in the next one. He did not like to use touch, or physical embraces in the group. Instead of making friends, he would prefer that members find ways to understand what they're doing with one another.

Observers rated Leader #15 as making few supportive comments or gestures. He challenged and confronted more than most other leaders, and also interviewed or questioned the group members. He often entered into the group as a member, aligning himself with a black member as "us" or "we." His own personal values, especially those involving racial issues, were freely shared with the group. He rarely attempted to help members understand their behavior, or to provide them with a cognitive framework by which to understand their personal dilemmas. He tended to summarize at the end of a meeting, more than almost any of the other leaders. The observers saw him as a leader with a somewhat charismatic personal style, carrying the group members along by the force of his own personality.

Some verbatim excerpts from the beginning of the first session:

My understanding of this group is that it will focus on black-white issues. Is that everybody else's understanding?

One thing I'm getting for this is money. Does anybody else have any understanding?

I think we ought to set a rule to stay throughout the whole three-hour session and throughout the whole thing. . . . If somebody must leave he must return the following week and tell why. Okay? There are just two other points or three. The first two are pretty basic. No fighting. . . . Yes, and no sexual behavior . . . I guess the only other thing I haven't said is that honesty is a very broad term, but that's what people would try to get to in terms of an encounter group, being as honest as you can be. . . . Levels of honesty can be reached, and the best is when you can lay yourself out and look at it, and let other people look at it. I think it's time to meet one another . . .

Do you have any impressions other than what we have indicated about what we can do to sit down and rap with blacks? Is it worth it? . . .

All the white people get in a circle on the floor and talk amongst yourself about how you feel about black people. . . . Why do you feel uncomfortable down there? . . . Okay, let's get the blacks in the middle . . .

Excerpts from the twenty-first hour (last three hours of the twelve-hour marathon):

Let's look back on today. What do people think happened the previous nine hours? . . . Do people notice how everyone gets very verbal during lunch and dinner and then comes back here and everything stops? . . . Paul, you haven't said much lately . . . How do you feel when you have to say "nigger"? . . . How have the white people felt lately? . . . How about the good things about black people? . . .

I can't think of any good points about white people. I guess it's probably the ability to impress people effectively. . . . The four black people here can't come up with nothing much nice to say about white people. . . . Let's all us black people get in the center. . . . (Here the leader gave a long personal account of his childhood, lasting about ten minutes, and talking about the way he worshipped white heroes like Tarzan and Johnny Appleseed, and how he never thought for a moment that he could have chosen some black heroes who might have done the same things.) The thing that blew my mind was when my family was first refused service at a restaurant. My father, who was a tough customer, just acquiesced. Driving the car afterward I asked why neither my mother nor father would say anything and my mother cried. . . . This kind of shit lasted so long, all my life, it was just incessant. . . . My adviser at college advised me against grad school. . . . It's hard to shake that kind of shit. I always look for that adviser at psychology conventions to get his ass . . .

(The leader at this point went around the group asking for statements about what each member had learned. One of the white girls commented she hadn't learned very much because she thought the group never finished any issue. He responded to this by angrily challenging her to state what it was that she wanted to finish.) . . . Anyone else feel the way Jean feels? Well . . . why don't you say what you mean? . . . Maybe next week we'll try and read your mind again for you . . .

Leader #15 used relatively few structured exercises. His most common technique was a fishbowling format in which the black members held a group meeting in the center with the white members around the outside watching and listening; he then reversed the positions. Afterward each group discussed what they felt when they heard the other. Occasionally the leader used structured go-arounds in order to give people some consensual validation about their own observations.

GROUP PROCESSES

Group #15 talked about race more than any other group (more than half the time). There was relatively little interpersonal confrontation within the group, however, and much of the discussion was abstract personal history. The focus was rarely on the here-and-now. They discussed outside material more than almost any other group. Frequently, the leader broke the group into a black group and a white group; each subgroup was instructed to discuss a certain issue—their feelings about blacks or what it was like when they grew up. Sometimes one member offered a long monologue describing his own personal history.

According to the observers, very little self-disclosure occurred in the course of the group. There was only a slightly higher level of disclosure of there-and-then past historical material, or material about members' current lives outside the group. The members felt, however, that they had disclosed many intimate details of their lives. They also felt that they had expressed feelings in the group to a moderate degree. According to the observers, Group #15 was weak, slow, dull, sad, cold, very distant, and closed. The members seemed to be extremely involved.

Group #15 was one of the few groups where "talking without showing feelings" was not seen as inappropriate. Though they approved discussing dreams and fantasies, they indicated few norms relating to feeling expression. Bringing friends to sessions was disapproved, as was refusing to be bound by a group decision. Probing a silent member and shouting with anger were seen as appropriate, though putting down one who had just opened up was seen as inappropriate. Members ratings placed that group fourth among the seventeen in cohesiveness, in sharp contrast to the observers rating of the group as uninvolved and uncommitted.

Group #15 members often cited an incident which reflected a racial issue as being the most significant event of a meeting. They commonly chose some type of abstract discussion as the critical event, and their response to it was either a report of some negative feeling or some information gained from the discussion. It was exceedingly rare that the members selected some type of incident reflecting positive affect. The members of Group #15 felt that expressing feelings, and feeling involved as group members were important to their learning. Less frequently than other groups, they cited learning something about their interpersonal impact as important.

LOOKING BACK

Group #15 must be understood around two important issues: (1) the extremely heavy racial emphasis, and (2) the suicide of one of the members. (The facts surrounding this tragedy are described in detail in Chapter 5.) It came as a great shock to the leader and to most of the members of the group when they learned that he had killed himself a few days after the second meeting. The group felt extremely upset and changed from an encounter group to a therapy group for several sessions before it went back to its typical course.

Those members who were still in the group at the end of the thirty hours felt rather positively about their experience. They rated the group as being pleasant, turned-on, constructive, and an experience in which they had learned a great deal; this placed Group #15 fifth among the seventeen groups. The members were even more positive about the leader and their ratings placed him fourth among the leaders. The observers placed Leader #15 eighth among the leaders.

Members' comments on the experience varied widely, depending to a great extent upon whether the person was white or black. A black girl said, "The first two sessions were dull but by the fourth session we really got into things. It was exciting and not intellectual—so unusual for Stanford. But we never got through the guardedness. The blacks would attack

84

the whites, who withdrew, and refused to defend themselves." Another black member said, "We spent half of each session breaking through our defenses." Another said, "I was sorry the group spent so much time on the black-white thing; you had to take sides." A black member spoke for many in describing the leader: "I loved him, he was great. I was impressed because he was a very learned black man; I felt a personal pride because he was so educated and yet so black. He was at the same time not trying to be black by wearing a dashiki, or trying to talk black." White members of the group did not convey this sense of enthusiasm. One said he dropped out because he "wasn't getting anything from it but uptightness. . . . I felt hostile to everyone there but there was no way I could let it out. If I had stayed in I'd have blown or exploded."

At the end of the group, the leader felt that his primary problems were the suicide, which disrupted the group, and the failure of the white students to commit themselves to the plan. He was also annoyed with the research interventions since he thought that the postgroup questionnaires served to erase the events of the group from the members' minds at the end of each meeting. He saw lack of resolution of the racial issue as part of the general education of individuals to find out that they are more racist than they think and that black-white prejudices run very deep.

Groups # 16 and # 17—Tape Program

The members of these leaderless groups followed tape-recorded instructions in each of ten sessions. During the first meeting, a member of the research staff met with the groups to introduce the members to the Encountertape Personal Growth Program. The tape "leader" began the first meeting with some further orientation and beginning exercises:

. . . In this session, you're going to have a series of short meetings in which you'll be doing things that have worked in the past to get groups such as yours off to a fast start. I'll keep time for you.

Incidentally, it's important for the success of this session that you stop what you are doing when I call time, even though it might interrupt you—perhaps even in the midst of a sentence. I'm sorry when this becomes annoying but the timing itself helps to make the session work.

You're probably sitting in a circle. Will you make that circle smaller, until you are sitting close to each other? I'll wait a few seconds for you to do this. (Five-second pause.)

Now, to try yourselves out, will you please have a five-minute meeting. You might do two things during this time. If you don't already know each other, go around and tell your first names. Then ask yourselves, "How do I feel right now?" and tell the rest of the group about it. I'll let you know when five minutes are up. Go ahead. (Five-minute pause.)

Please stop. If you were like most groups doing this for the first time, you might have found it hard to do. Maybe it was easier to talk about something else, rather than how you felt. Maybe you really aren't sure what it means to talk about how you feel.

Well, first of all, it means that you tune in to what's happening inside you right now, and then you talk about it. Are you scared, resentful, excited or curious about being here . . . and what's going to happen next? Like, right now, I feel a little self-conscious—wondering about how my voice is coming over to you.

Whatever it is that is happening inside you, tune in to it. Then, tell the rest of the group about it as best you can.

Now, try it again. I'll tell you when the five minutes are up. Go ahead . . .

In the fourth session, the tape asked for a review of progress and problems. Some of the suggestions were:

Do people in this group seem to know what they are feeling? . . . Do they tune in to what's going on inside of them when they are in the group? . . . Do they talk up about it? . . . Are they with it? . . . Do you speak for yourselves here? Do you say "I" when you mean I? . . . Are you looking at each other when you talk? . . . Are you talking directly to each other, calling each other by name? . . . So now I would like you to report to yourselves about your own progress about these things. Go ahead. I'll come back on the tape in about ten minutes and make some further suggestions.

I wonder if you're as tuned in a group as you'd like to be? If not, perhaps you can help each other and find out what the roadblocks are. . . . For instance, the group sometimes tiptoes around certain things. . . . Like individuals who are not as tuned in as others, or those who knock everything, or those who are quiet. . . . In my experience in groups, I have found it is much better to deal with such things head-on so the air can be cleared and more progress can be made. Maybe that will mean expressing angry feelings. . . . Angry feelings certainly have a place in relationships. When someone is angry at someone else and says so, it means that he has a real stake in what's happening. . . . He cares about what's going on between himself and the other person. Now I suggest you spend the rest of the session trying to deal head-on with anything that appears to be standing in your way of progress as a group. You might want to repeat things you've done here before, or you might just want to talk about where you are and how you're doing . . .

Other sessions offered instructional exercises and comments on such issues as feedback, intellectualization vs. here-and-now content, self-disclosure, and so forth. In Session 6, for example, a breaking-out exercise was used. Members of the group were asked to stand in a tight circle while one member in the center tried to break out of the group. After each member broke out he became part of the circle again. After this exercise, members were asked to spend the rest of the session talking about how they felt about the exercises, following a guide like this:

86

Watch for and talk about these things especially: What did you feel when you were trying to break out? What different ways did people use in trying to break out? Did this experience remind you of anything else that you might have done recently, for example, the way you've tried to break out of another problem? Remember, when you talk about this, tune into your feelings and talk up about them.

In Session 9, the emphasis was on giving and receiving, on letting people experience saying good things about one another. The group was asked to choose three people whom they saw as having the most trouble letting the group into them, letting people get close to them. Each of these people was asked to go to the center of the circle and stand there while the other group members in turn were asked to express some good feelings they had toward him, without using words.

I should like to repeat, *without using words*. You might want to touch him, put your arms around him, or really embrace and hug him. The person who is receiving the good feelings doesn't return them, he just stands there silently receiving, but not giving. . . . Don't rush through this, take your time. It's a little embarrassing, but if you're willing to try it you might learn some interesting things about yourself.

In the tenth and last session, the group was run as a microlab. Each group member was asked to stand in front of each other person, to touch him in some way, make contact with him or call him by his name, and then to tell how he felt about doing this. Then the group was given a period of time to discuss feelings about this exercise. Following this a structured cradling exercise was proposed: a member was placed in the middle of the group with everyone closely bunched around him; he was directed to fall while the group caught him, and then passed him around from person to person. Following this there was work on termination. The tape asked people to say goodbye to one another and talk about the ways in which they had seen people in the group change in order to help people retain some of the things they had learned about themselves.

Group #16—Tape-led Group

Obedient, responsible, low-conflict, cautious here-and-now,
programmed warmth and support.

Eleven members attended Group #16. One member dropped out of the group after the sixth session. Attendance was good. The group met for eight sessions in a dormitory lounge.

GROUP PROCESSES

Group #16 was an obedient group. Only toward the end of a couple of meetings did members ignore the tape, or turn off the machine. The group dealt almost entirely with interpersonal inside here-and-now material. Little time was spent on individual issues and total group issues. The group spent considerable time following the exercises prescribed by the taped instructions. Communication was divided between general unfocused discussion and focus on one person. According to the observers, Group #16 ranked about midway among the groups in the amount of self-disclosure. According to the members, however, there was little disclosure of intimate details of their lives. The members also felt that they had not expressed their feelings and the group ranked in the lower third of the groups in this dimension.

Observers said the group was extremely quiet, slow-moving, weak, distant, and closed. Kissing, touching, expressing caring, telling another of his likability, and pleading for help were all seen as appropriate. Though dreams and private fantasies could appropriately be discussed, bringing in outside topics and bringing a friend to the sessions were thought inappropriate. Probing a silent member and shouting with anger were approved, but interrupting a dialogue or putting down a member who had opened up were not.

Group #16 was a highly cohesive group. The members' ratings of cohesiveness placed it in the upper quarter of all the groups. The members of Group #16 very frequently saw feedback situations as the critical incidents of the meeting. It was rare for them to suggest incidents involving self-disclosure or insight. They felt that the most important experiences were those that helped them understand their impact on others and to experiment with new behavior. They rated this exceptionally high as compared with the other groups. Many members of the group felt it had been useful to them in helping them to understand their thoughts and feelings. Very few stated that they had been helped by expressing feelings ordinarily held in.

LOOKING BACK

At the end of the group experience, the members' ratings indicated that their group was a pleasant, turned-on, constructive experience in which they learned something about themselves. The average rating placed Group #16 midway among the seventeen groups. Group #16 members, like those in the other tape-led group, felt resentful about the tape recorder. They felt that they had been cheated; they resented that they did not have a "live" leader, who, they were convinced, might have taken them much deeper. They resented having not only the one tape recorder giving directions, but another recorder recording *it* (this second recorder being a research recording of the group meeting itself). In the fourth meeting one member was attacked, and became quite tearful and ran out of the meeting. She returned to the group, and the incident was not mentioned again. When members were interviewed at the end of the group, they stated that this type of thing would not have happened had they had a leader. They felt a leader would have helped the group and the member investigate her feelings and utilize the opportunity for learning. The group talked about having a reunion after the group sessions were over, but never did. The members did make a point of stating that they had made some friends in the group, however, and reported even many months after the group that they could still stop and talk to one another for long periods of time. At the six-month follow-up, the members of the two Tape Groups remembered the names of all members of the group to a much greater extent than those in the majority of other groups.

Group #17—Tape-led Group

Outspoken, "disobedient" group. We used "George," our tape recorder leader when we felt like it.

Group #17 started with thirteen members, three of whom dropped out. Two time-extended meetings were held in the apartment of one of the members, the rest in a dormitory lounge. Attendance was good.

GROUP PROCESSES

Group #17 was considerably different from the other tape group. It was far less placid; the members more often expressed their dissatisfaction with the tape recorder. They would refer to the tape program as "George" in jocular, ridiculing fashion. When the tape suggested, for instance, that they do a certain exercise, someone would interrupt to say, "Oh, that's a great idea, George." In the last three meetings, the group played the tape all the way through at the beginning of the meeting, and then decided whether or not there was any part of the taped instructions they wished to follow for the day. This was counter to basic instructions, which were to play the tape and follow its own instructions about when it should be turned off and on during the meeting.

The members spent about a third of their time discussing outside issues (quite unlike Group #16, which spent practically its total time on the here-and-now). The outside material was primarily personal current material in the lives of the members or some abstract issue. Discussion of personal historical material was less common. Two-thirds of the time was spent focusing on inside material, either on the group as a whole or on the interactions among members. There was considerable discussion about the leader or the lack of a leader. The group's work style was heavily structured, although in the final meetings more time was spent in a general discussion format. The observers rated the self-disclosure of here-and-now material in Group #17 as considerable (sixth among the groups). The members felt that they disclosed many intimate details of their lives; their ratings placed Group #17 fifth among the groups.

The observers rated the climate as harmonious and informal, as well as stronger, faster, more alive, more involved, and warm than the majority of groups. They also noted that for some of the taped instructions the members were highly committed. More than in many other groups, members were permitted to withdraw, and not forced to participate actively. Touching, expressing caring, and telling another of his likability were considered appropriate. Hitting and threatening were disapproved of; other emotionally toned behavior was left unregulated. The members felt it was wrong to keep probing others, to judge another's behavior as wrong, to interrupt, to tell another he was unlikable, or to put down someone who had opened up. Group #17 was one of the few groups whose members felt it was wrong for a member to refuse to be bound by a group decision. The cohesiveness ratings of the members placed Group #17 in the upper half of the seventeen groups. There was, however, a bimodal distribution of attraction to the group; some members felt it was silly, and refused to participate or to follow the instructions of the tape recorder. Others were deeply committed to the group.

A striking aspect of the events selected as critical by the members of Group #17 was that they so frequently mentioned "the group," such as that the group had mastered a stage or gotten over an obstacle. They tended to stress insight more and feedback less than the members of the other tape group. They felt that the group had helped them to understand their interpersonal impact on others, to express their feelings, and to learn that everyone else was in the same boat. Group #17 differed from the other tape group in placing a greater emphasis on catharsis and on revealing embarrassing things to the others, and still being accepted.

LOOKING BACK

The members of Group #17 rated their experience as better than average. They considered the group to be pleasant (fifth of seventeen groups), turned-on (eighth of seventeen), constructive (eighth of seventeen), and a group in which they learned a great deal (tenth of seventeen). The disappointments expressed by the members of this group centered around the slow pace and shallow, artificial flow of the group. Some of the members wanted the group to move faster, and to be able to deal more penetratingly with issues. One of the members pointed out that they had a good deal of ambivalence about assuming more autonomy: "We wanted intimacy and intensity, but I guess we also wanted safety and structure. We were afraid to really go off on our own." The early meetings were especially unsatisfactory to the members in that they provided a sense of incompleteness.

For example, two people got into an argument early in the group, and the rest of the group felt constrained to continue with the tape, following instructions which were inappropriate at that particular time. The members felt most antagonistic toward the tape when unexpected incidents like this arose, and were angry that they had no leader or any guideline about which to resolve them. They resembled Group #16 in their pervasive resentment of the tape recorder as leader. As one member put it, "I'll be damned if I'm going to let a machine tell me how to be more human." Many expressed a feeling of having been gypped by the research staff; that if they had only had a leader they could have done a great deal better.

In summary, Group #17 came face to face with basic authority issues. At one level, they made a bid to become more involved and intense with one another, and to rebel against the structure which had been placed upon them; on the other level, they felt relieved at the safety and comfort provided by the programmed tape recording. When a task seemed appropriate they entered into it with considerable energy. There was little pressure placed on uninvolved members. Hostility was rare, and never pursued to some level of resolution. Consequently, Group #17, like the other tape group, appeared to be a rather safe place in which no one was pushed further than he desired to travel.

CHAPTER 3

Outcomes: The Impact of the Experience

Encounter groups are people-changing groups. Though they can be said to have a "task," it is rather unlike the task of the missile-launch team, or the sales conference. And though encounter groups do have a restorative function, it is not as central as it is at cocktail parties and church services, or in dramatic productions. Encounter groups, like classrooms and like therapy groups, exist for the purpose of transforming their members in some hoped-for ways.

The question of how to assess the changes effected through encounter groups is not a simple one. While such groups are both educational and therapeutic, they are claimed in theory to be both more affectively oriented than traditionally cognitive classrooms and less curatively oriented than therapy groups. Researchers on human relations training have thus tended to employ a wider range of outcome measures than has been customary in educational or therapeutic research. Gibb (1971), for example, has organized research on the effects of human relations training under six major rubrics: sensitivity (greater awareness of the feelings and perceptions of others); managing feelings (awareness and acceptance of the feeling component of one's own actions); managing motivations (e.g., clear communications of one's own motives to others); functional attitudes toward self (self-acceptance, self-esteem); functional attitudes toward others (e.g., decreased authoritarianism; prejudice, collaborative orientation); and interdependent behavior (e.g., interpersonal competence, teamwork).[1]

Criteria such as these overlap somewhat with, but are not identical to, criteria used in the assessment of psychotherapy. Kelman and Parloff (1957), for example, discuss three major classes of therapeutic outcome: comfort (relief of distress or symptoms); effectiveness (social role performance, management of transactions with others); and self-awareness (acquisition of insight, correction of perceptual distortions, and the release of repressions). The last outcome domain, and more especially the first, ordinarily receive little attention in studies of nontherapeutic groups. The criteria suggested by Gibb, it should be noted, also overlap with, but are not identical to, outcome variables of concern in education. The Gibb variables stress attitudes, the expression and sensing of feelings, and behavioral competence. Little or no attention is paid to strictly intellectual outcomes, like those that might ensue from a course in interpersonal relations or group behavior (for example, clearer concepts, knowledge of generalizations, or retention of facts and specific information).

The variety of outcome variables in the relevant literature, and the diverse orientations of the leaders in the groups under study, suggested tapping as many potential outcomes as feasible. The assessment of change involved two major steps. The first was to develop a series of measures that reflected the possibility that individuals might change in many different ways. The second step was to determine whether the patterns of change were assignable to group effects or individual differences. At times the answer to such questions was a matter of comparing differences among the seventeen groups on the diverse dimensions: Did different encounter groups have different effects on participants? At times the answer lay in a comparison of differences between the participants and their matched controls.

The specification of which participants changed, how much they changed, and in what ways, required a method that could classify individuals without obscuring the diverse ways that encounter groups might affect individuals. For this purpose, a composite Index of Change was devised. The Index, which is described more fully later on, was based on each prospective participant's test scores on a plethora of measures, as well as on assessments of change made by four sets of people immediately after the groups terminated and again six months later. As is witnessed everyday in informal evaluation processes, the answers to such questions always reflect in some part who it is that answers them—the subject of the evaluation, the person responsible for effecting change, or others in a position to respond to the change. In an effort to take into account such differences in vantage point, the Index of Change employed four perspectives: benefits as seen by the participants immediately after the group and six months later, benefits as seen by the group leaders, by friends or relatives of the participant, and by coparticipants.

SELF-VIEW OF CHANGE

Reports of the participants, themselves, about the consequences of their experience in encounter groups constitute the most immediate, often the most poignant, data about group effects. Participants' reactions may seem overly enthusiastic, incomplete, or unduly pessimistic against the judgment of others, but the fact is that people do have feelings and reactions about the impact of encounter groups on them. At termination, participants rated such reactions on four seven-point scales (one high, seven low); personally found it a pleasant/unpleasant experience; was turned-on/turned-off; overall, a constructive, destructive experience; for the amount of time involved, personally learned a great deal/very little.

Of those who completed the groups, 65 percent found them pleasant (above midpoint four), 50 percent testified to having been turned-on to the group, 78 percent thought the experience constructive, and 61 percent thought they had learned a great deal. Since the intercorrelations of the four scales were high (gammas ranged from a low of .59 to a high of .87), the scores from the four scales were summed so that a score of twelve or less (an average of 3.0 or less on each scale) was considered positive, thirteen to nineteen, neutral; and twenty or higher, negative. On these overall evaluations 57 percent of the participants who completed the groups gave positive testimony, 29 percent were neutral, and 14 percent were negative.[2]

At the six-month follow-up, the number of positive evaluations dropped. Of 125 participants for whom there were data, 56 percent saw the experience as pleasant, 48 percent were turned-on, 64 percent perceived it as constructive, and 51 percent indicated that they had learned something. Summing the four scales, 46 percent were positive, 32 percent were neutral, and 21 percent were negative.

Another perspective on self-reported change is afforded from the responses to several open-ended questions: "For you personally, what was the value of the group? Has it resulted in any changes in yourself? (Describe.) Do you expect these changes to be lasting? Why?" The proportion of those describing positive changes in answering these questions were 61 percent at termination and 55 percent six months later.

At termination, 106 of the participants of the 163 who responded to these questions identified one or more positive changes; seven participants indicated negative and positive changes, four negative changes, and forty-six indicated no change. Comparable figures six months later for 114 participants were sixty-six positive, five mixed, six negative, and thirty-seven no change.

Was the reduction in self-reported positive changes noted from short post to long post a real one or does it reflect a selective failure to return the long-post instruments? When responses of a true panel of persons (N = 120) who had completed both sets of measurements were examined, the drop in self-reported changes was maintained; 18 percent moved toward more negative evaluations (no change, mixed, or negative change) while only 8 percent moved toward a more positive estimation.

So much for the numbers of self-reported changes. What, in fact, was their content? At both Time 2 (termination) and at Time 3 (six- to eight-month follow-up), the most frequently reported positive changes were increased openness and honesty in communication (25 percent of those reporting positive change). Almost as often, participants cited increased intimacy and acceptance of others, as well as increased awareness of self and others, and proactiveness in interpersonal settings (spontaneousness, confidence, talkativeness). The number of responses in each category was small, so that generalizing about changes from Time 2 to Time 3 reports is risky, but a slight increase was evidenced in talkativeness, self-acceptance, and ease, and perhaps a decrease in reports of intimacy and tolerance.

Of those persons who did report some change at termination, 72 percent expected the change to be lasting, 7 percent thought it might possibly last, 16 percent didn't know, and 5 percent said it wouldn't last. It is of interest that so few participants anticipated difficulties in maintaining change. The overriding reason given for expecting the changes to endure was that they provided continuing reward and reinforcement: "because they are good;" "I have found they bring me personally closer, sooner, to others;" "because I liked the change;" "because I find them rewarding;" "I have already been confronted with the situation of being more honest and open, expressing my feelings, and both parties found it beneficial and enjoyable." No central theme appeared in the comments of the thirteen people who did not expect to maintain their changes.

Summarizing the participants' own views of change: of those who completed the encounter groups, approximately 50 to 70 percent (depending somewhat on the mode of gathering self-evaluations) indicated at the end of the group experience that some positive change had taken place. The self-ratings reflect a reasonably satisfied clientele who felt that they had changed and believed at the termination of the encounter group that such change would endure. These findings are not surprising; they mirror our everyday experience that encounter group participants are generally positively inclined toward the experience, and believe that it has been useful to them. While participants expected the change to be lasting, positive evaluations of change dropped six months later, so that for every participant who evaluated the experience negatively, 2.3 participants perceived it as productive, whereas the comparable ratio at termination had been 4.7 to 1. The decrease in positive evaluations may indicate an "overvaluation" immediately following the group which was "corrected" by the passage of time, or it may suggest that participants felt some of the changes they had made disappeared with time, an issue considered in more detail later in the chapter.

LEADER ESTIMATIONS OF MEMBER LEARNING

Leader estimations of individual change were obtained at termination by asking each leader to rate each member of his group on nine eleven-point scales. The leader was asked to compare each member with three people from groups he had led in the past: an average changed participant (position five on the scales), one who was changed much less than most (position two), and one much more changed than most (position eight). The leaders were asked first to rate the participant's behavior as it appeared to them when the groups had been completed, and then as he recalled the participant during the first couple of meetings ("poorer, the same, or better than the person's current behavior"). The distance between these "now" and "then" judgments was the measure of interest.[3]

Intercorrelations of each leader's ratings on the nine scales made clear that a simple summation of the scores for each participant would be an unreliable index of outcome; for one leader changes in ability to express anger were highly related to increased collaboration, while for another leader anger and collaboration appeared to be negatively related. In short, the factor structure of the rating instrument was a function of the interpersonal and personal schemata of the leaders. As might be expected, leaders also varied considerably in the range of the scale they used, and in which particular dimensions they saw members changing most. Accordingly, for each leader, subscales were developed; one represented the four scales most sensitive to positive change for that leader (Impact Scale); the other (Tri Cluster Scale) consisted of the three items most highly correlated with one another. This scale was more sensitive to change in a negative direction. Table 3–1 presents the items used in the two subscales (and provides, incidentally, an empirical index of what changes leaders felt had occurred most intensively in members of their groups, as contrasted with prototypical participants from past groups).[4] It is of some interest to note that all but two leaders (#8 and #12) used the *openness* dimension, and all but three leaders (#2, #7, and #14) used the self-understanding dimension. *Closeness* came next, with nine of the fifteen group leaders using it as the dimension of maximum impact. (Although leaders were not asked to assess on which dimensions most change had occurred, this finding emerged from a study of the empirical ratings given members.)

On the Impact Scale, leaders rated 3 percent of their participants as having shown a negative change, 8 percent as having shown no change, and 89 percent as having shown some positive change. The 89 percent figure is gross in that it ranges across participants in whom leaders saw anywhere from a modest to a considerable amount of movement. To obtain a more exact index of leaders' estimates of high positive gain, this level of change was arbitrarily defined as requiring a movement of at least two points per scale used (that is, two-thirds of the distance between the average and ineffective member or two-thirds of the distance between the average and the more effective member). Viewed in these terms, a shade less than one-third (30 percent) of the participants were judged by the leaders as having shown considerable benefit at the end of the encounter group experience. Thus, although 89 percent of the participants were judged by the leaders as having shown some positive change, high change was noted only in a third of the total participants.

The number of persons changed decreased on the Tri Cluster scales so that 9 percent of the participants were judged by the leaders as having

TABLE 3-1

Rating Dimensions Used by Leaders to Evaluate Outcome

	Group Numbers														
	1	2	3	4	5	6	7	8	9	10	11	12	13	14	15
1. *Openness*, directness, revelation of own feelings and thoughts, self-disclosure	X O	X	X	X O	X	X	X	O	X O	X	X	O	X	X O	X O
2. *Sensitivity* to others' feelings and reactions, understanding of others	X			X	X		O	O		X O	X	O	X	O	X
3. *Spontaneity*, flexibility, ability to act freely and creatively	X	X O	O	O	O		X		X		X		O	O	O
4. *Self-Understanding*, being in touch with own inner feelings, seeing self clearly	X		X	X	X O	X O		X	X	X	X O	X	X O	X	
5. *Closeness*, ability to be warm, affectionate, intimate with others	O	X	X	X		X	X	X O		X		X		X	
6. *Anger*, ability to fight, attack others without feeling conflicted or upset about it	O		X O		X O		O		O					X	
7. *Collaboration*, ability to work easily and cooperatively with others, help the group move along in its work		X			X		X O	X	O			X O		X	
8. *Positive Self-Image*, self-esteem, liking, and acceptance of self as one is		O	O		O				X	O	O	X	O		X
9. *Happiness*, feeling good about one's life and what is happening in it, joy, pleasure in existence	O		O		O			X		O	O		X		O

KEY: X = Four scales most sensitive to change in a positive direction.

O = Three clustered scales.

shown negative change, 14 percent as having shown no change, and 73 percent as showing some change. Clearly, the leaders emphasized positive change and saw the vast majority of participants as showing some positive change. They perceived one-third as having experienced considerable benefit.

SOCIAL NETWORK ESTIMATION OF CHANGE

At six-month follow-up, every participant and control, and from three to five people nominated by them as able to describe their behavior, received a letter (Social Network Questionnaire) asking them to describe changes they had noticed since June 1969, in the participant's (or their own) behavior, ways of relating to others, and so on.

Looking first at the self-reports of participants and controls to the Social Network Questionnaire, 56 percent of the 133 participants and 52 percent of the fifty-two controls for whom there were data said that at least one change had occurred in their behavior. Thus, roughly half of this total population could point to some change in behavior in the preceding six months, whether or not they had been in an encounter group. Two or more such changes were reported by 41 percent of the participants, 35 percent of the controls. Three or more changes were reported by 23 percent of participants and 19 percent of controls. Overall, the number of participants who felt they had changed, as well as the number of changes mentioned, did not differ from the controls. These findings stand in some contrast to the findings of earlier studies using this measure. Miles (1965), for example, found that 82 percent of the adult members of a two-week training laboratory reported one or more changes, while control group percentages were only 33 percent. In the present case, the insignificant differences between experimentals and controls may indicate that students are more likely to see themselves as changing, regardless of special experiences.

"Social network respondents" who were sent the Social Network Questionnaire were, characteristically, close friends, associates, parents, or other relatives who took the request to reply to the Social Network Questionnaire quite seriously, often supplying lengthy, thoughtful, even poignant replies. For 111 members of the experimental group, 1.6 respondents per person returned the Social Network Questionnaire and for forty-one controls, two respondents per person. Most participants *and* controls were perceived by those in their social network as having made some positive change (participants, 80 percent; controls, 83 percent). The average number of positive changes mentioned for the control group members was 1.1 and for experimentals 1.5, a negligible difference. Social network respondents mentioned negative changes for 27 percent of the experimentals and 14 percent of the controls.

A "net" change score was compiled by subtracting average negative mentions from average positive mentions. Net positive change was defined as a score of 1.5 or higher (to allow for the control group base rate). Differences between experimentals and controls in net positive change, as perceived by their social network, were negligible (not statistically significant); 43 percent of the experimentals exceeded this figure and 36 percent of controls exceeded the 1.5 score. A minority of both groups were perceived as undergoing a *net negative* change (7 percent for experimentals, 5 percent for controls). An item-by-item analysis to determine the existence of "verified" changes (when the self-described change was also described by at least one member of the social network) revealed that about half of both the participants and their controls reported a specific change which was independently verified by the report of someone in their social network.[5]

In sum, the belief in change in the college population as a whole appears to be endemic. At any rate, the encounter experience as it manifested itself in perceptions of participants' behavior by significant others did not demonstrate unique effects. Participants and controls alike were perceived as changing by those in their social network.

COPARTICIPANTS' RATINGS OF LEARNING

At the end of an early meeting (usually the third or fourth) and again at the end of the eighth meeting, members of each group rated one another on a series of sociometric questions. These questions included one specifically indexed for peer judgments of learning: "rank everyone in the group including yourself from most to least on the amount of learning they have made in this group." Evidence (presented in Chapter 11) that coparticipant ratings of learning were relatively independent of other sociometric judgments, along with some evidence (presented in Chapter 5) which reflects the accuracy of coparticipant perceptions of who in their group had undergone negative psychological changes, implies that coparticipants may have been especially able to identify those who benefited from the groups. Participants whom coparticipants viewed as having learned were defined as those whose average rank order position was in the sixtieth percentile or better. Based on this criterion, 37 percent of the participants were judged by their peers to have learned.

At this point the reader may be having an experience akin to watching a "shell game." The number of people considered to change as a result of their participation in encounter groups is at one point substantial, at another minor, and then, once again, major. In part, these variations can be attributed to arbitrary necessities involved in deciding how high a rating needs to be to represent change. A more serious problem, however, is that the number of people who change depends on from which perspective change is viewed: the participants', the leaders', the coparticipants', or the person's social network. These sources not only yield different percentages of how many changed; they do not even overlap. People whom the leaders perceived as having changed are more often than not different from those whom coparticipants judged to have changed. Correlations among leader ratings of change, participants' judgments of their own change, and coparticipants' judgments of change hovered around zero, reaching a maximum of .20.

A method was needed that would overcome the disabilities of perspective in classifying participants according to the amount of benefit or loss. Interviews with the participants suggest that individuals use encounter groups in a variety of ways, and no single measure of change can do. Some participants sharply altered their view of themselves, either in a positive or negative direction; others appeared to undergo radical value transformations. Still others learned new strategies for dealing with interpersonal issues. Some decreased in personal comfort. Because of the variety of response, any final assessment of who benefited, and who changed for the worse required an index based on a variety of perspectives as well as a range of types of change. Thus, change was defined in terms of the extensiveness of alterations that took place in people in several areas and from several perspectives: objective measures on a wide range of variables, as well as others' views, and one's own view of change.

Measures of Types of Change

As described in Chapter 1, data were available on a series of areas of change thought to be relevant to the encounter group experience: the person's values; his attitudes toward such experiences; his behavior as reflected in coping strategies and interpersonal style; aspects of self-view, such as level of self-esteem, the content of his self-image, and the congruence between his ideal image and self-image; view of others as reflected in how the person looked at significant others, and whether he viewed his interpersonal world as simple or complex; how many dimensions he used to view others and certain characteristics of the person's interpersonal relationships outside the encounter group, such as changes in his view of the environmental opportunities for important interpersonal relationships as well as friendship patterns.

Tests and questionnaires administered to both participants and controls before the group, after the group ended, and six months later yielded scores on seventy-eight measures. These seventy-eight scores were reduced to a basic set of thirty-three measures through a series of procedures outlined in Table 3–2. (The instruments and questionnaires as well as a Table of Correlations appear in Appendix I.) These thirty-three measures were used to identify who changed, and to establish a basic index of change. They are also used in most of the subsequent chapters when variables such as leader style and norms are examined against the criterion of change.

Index of Change

Several measures representing the four perspectives—self, coparticipants, leader, and social network, as well as a number of others derived from tests and questionnaires were used to define a cummulative index of

TABLE 3-2

The Measures of Change

Variable	Values and Attitudes	
	Test Description	Operation
1. Safe/Dangerous Direct expression of feelings are criticisms; encouraged to be open and frank too fast; individuality is pushed aside; people get hurt; detract from individual responsibility; forced to reveal things; too intense for some; cruel and irresponsible behavior	Attitudes toward encounter groups; twenty-four Likert scales	Homogeneity analysis
2. Socially Beneficial Breaks down barriers between people; not relevant to the real world; preparation for life in a democratic society; help improve world; open up communication among the races; an educational innovation; too personal and emotional for solving social problems; humanize bureaucratic institutions.		
3. Genuine/Phony Playing the sensitivity game; directness in feelings is artificial; illusion of contact; genuine feelings can be expressed; an adult plaything; modern equivalent of lonely hearts; one can become truly himself; people express their genuine selves		
4. Experiencing Directness (.58)[a], novelty (.65); flexibility (.76); expressing anger (.60); sharing with peers (.72)	Encounter group values: eleven seven-point scales; degree of importance; examples: directness, novelty	Principle component factor analysis, first factor, 60% variance, second, 22%
5. Changing Feedback (.45); changing ways I relate (.44)		

TABLE 3-2 (continued)

Variable	Values and Attitudes	
	Test Description	Operation
6. *Self-Orientation* Self-acceptance; identity; self-understanding; philosophical and religious concerns; life-styles; positive maturation processes	Life-Space Questionnaire; list (up to ten items) the aspects of your life currently important to you	Content analysis
6a. *Hedonism* New experiences; novelty; adventure; leisure; travel; nature; esthetics		Hedonism is a subclass of Self-Orientation
7. *Instrumental-External* Academic skills; career; other need-achievement themes; material objects possession; income; physical		
7a. *Specific Academic Issues*		Specific Academic Issues and Social-Political Values are a subclass of Instrumental-External values
7b. *Social-Political* War; race; prejudice; environment		
8. *Interpersonal Relationships* Friendships, empathy, sensitivity, understanding, giving and helping, being respected by others		
9. *Intimacy*		
10. *Growth Orientation* Proportion of all life-space items which were indicative of growth, change, development, learning		

TABLE 3-2 (continued)

Variable	Behavior Test Description	Operation
11. *Interpersonal Adequacy* Able to express inner feelings (.70); knows how others feel about me (.70); satisfied with the way I relate (.78); easy to get close (.75); spontaneous	Self-rated behavior; seven ten-point scales; examples: expression of feeling, sensitivity	Principal component factor analysis first factor, 60% variance, second, 21%
12. *Feeling Sensitivity* Understand my inner feelings (.62); sensitive to others (.61)		
13. *Adequate-Active Coping* Scales reflecting use of interpersonal perspective (.65); interpersonal problem solving (.63); understanding and empathy (.77); gaining perspective from authoritative sources (.48); spontaneous action (.42); taking some positive concerted action (.72); making planned alternatives (.67)	Personal Dilemma Questionnaire; describe three actual problem situations, indicate how they were "solved"; on a series of nineteen seven-point scales (very likely to unlikely) indicate how solved if the same problem were to occur tomorrow	Factor analyses for each of the nineteen items independently on the three problems, rotated to simple structure, correspondence of factors on all three problem situations, twelve final scales, scales subjected to another factor analysis yielding two principal component scores, first factor, 49% variance, second, 20%
14. *Defensive Coping* Scales reflecting the use of humor-minimization (.48); tension reduction through flight (.46); escape (.48); expecting the worst (.42); denial (.54)		
15. *Expressing Controlling Behavior toward Others*	FIRO (Schutz, 1958)	
16. *Acceptance and Desire of Control from Others*	Four Gutmann scales assessing interpersonal relationship orientation (thirty-six items)	
17. *Expressing Affection toward Others*		
18. *Acceptance and Desire of Affection from Others*		

TABLE 3-2 (continued)

	Self	
Variable	Test Description	Operation
19. *Self-Esteem*	Eleven-item Gutmann scale, Rosenberg (1965)	
20. *Positive Self-Concept* Mental health (.73); honesty (.64); responsibility (.52); ability (.59); status (.60); active-enthusiasm (.74)	Personal Description Questionnaire, based on the REP Test modification by Harrison (1964). Thirty-five seven-point scales: e.g., lenient-strict, responsible-irresponsible, described self and ideal self	Factor analyses of self scores, rotation to simple structure yielded seven scales: *Mental Health,* comfortable with others, relaxed, well-adjusted, unworried, optimistic, happy; *Consideration,* accepts suggestion, sympathetic, accepts help, accommodating; *Honesty,* genuine, shows feeling, frank, sincere; *Permissiveness,* lenient, undemanding, nondirective; *Responsible,* reliable, constructive, thorough, dependable; *Ability,* able, competent, informed; *Status,* influential, prestige. Self scores on the seven scales factor analyzed and two principal component scores developed, first 46% of the variance, the second, 22%
21. *Self as Lenient* Considerate (.60); permissive (.80)		
22. *Self-Ideal Congruence (Interpersonal)*		Sum of differences on mental health, consideration, honesty, permissiveness
23. *Self-Ideal Congruence (Instrumental)*		Sum of differences on responsibility, status, and ability
24. *Positive Conception of Others* Mental health (.67); honesty (.73); responsibility (.68); ability (.72); status (.50); activity-enthusiasm (.79)	Personal Description Questionnaire; same thirty-five scales described previously. Subject asked to describe four people whom he knows well	Factor analysis yielded seven basic scales previously described for self. Scales subjected to second factor analysis to produce principal component scores, first 61% variance, second 23%
25. *Others as Lenient*		

TABLE 3-2 (continued)

Self

Variable	Test Description	Operation
26. *Interpersonal Complexity* Degree of differentiation in viewing others in interpersonal areas. Sum of differences in scores on mental health, consideration, honesty, and permissiveness		Total number of concepts person used to describe significant others, score based on number of differences on the thirty-five scales, if all four seem as equal on a scale, score = 0, maximum differentiation = 7
27. *Instrumental Complexity* Degree of differentiation in viewing others in work related areas. Sum of difference score on responsibility, status, and ability		
28. *Conception of Best Friend*	Semantic Differential Scales; good, pleasurable, successful, important, free, calm, warm	Face validity

External Relationships

Variable	Test Description	Operation
29. *Opportunity, Open Peer Communication* Feedback (.61); know others deeply (.79); open and honest encounter (.76); share with peers (.75); novelty (.66); directness (.70)	Eight ten-point scales, describe current environment. Opportunities for you to have such experiences, e.g., to know others deeply, novelty	Factor analysis, two principal components, first factor 81% variance, second 19%
30. *Opportunity, Expression of Anger* Trust (.56); anger (.60)		
31. *Number of Close Friends*	Friendship Questionnaire	Face validity
32. *Hours Spent with Close Friends*		
33. *Explicit Decisions*	Life-Space Questionnaire (described previously); indicate whether explicit decisions made during past six months regarding items subject roted in life space	Content analysis

[a] In this and subsequent variables based on principal component analysis, numbers in parentheses are factor loading. Only ones shown are items used to name variable.

TABLE 3-3

Outcome Index

	Indices	
Changes	Time 2	Time 3
Values and Attitudes	1. Attitude Encounter Group 2. Change Orientation 3. Amount of Value Change	1. Attitude Encounter Group 2. Change Orientation 3. Amount of Value Change
Behavior	4. Interpersonal Adequacy 5. Coping	4. Interpersonal Adequacy 5. Coping
Self	6. Self-Regard 7. Sociometric Congruence	6. Self-Regard —
Others	8. Conceptions of Others	8. Conceptions of Others
Various Perspectives on Amount of Change	9. Testimony (Self-Rating) 10. Peer Rating of Learning 11. Leader Ratings —	9. Testimony (Self-Rating) — — 12. Social Network
View of Environment	—	13. View of Interpersonal Environment

SCORE KEY:

1. Attitude Encounter Group (Safe/Dangerous, Socially Beneficial, Genuine/Phony). Cutoff points determined by critical ratio (CR). Scored 0 if no two identical signs, if two or three signs 0, or if two signs 0, one + or −; scored + if three signs + or two +, one 0; scored − if three signs − or two −, one 0.

2. Change Orientation Changing (#5), Growth Orientation (#10). Scored same as CR if two signs identical; if signs differed, +2 or greater scored +, −2 or greater scored −, otherwise 0.

3. Amount of Value Change Self-Orientation (#6), Instrumental External (#7), Interpersonal Relationships (#8), and Experiencing (#4). At least three positive signs scored +; less than three, 0. Negative signs were not considered. Thus this is essentially index of changing without regard to directionality.

4. Interpersonal Adequacy Interpersonal Adequacy (#11), CR sign.

5. Coping Adequate-Active Coping (#13), CR sign.

6. Self-Regard Self-Esteem (#19) and Self-ideal Congruence—Interpersonal (#22). CR sign, if both signs identical. Scored + if one sign +, one 0, scored − if one sign +, one −.

7. Sociometric Congruence Score based on the VCIA role (see Chapter 11) as judged by peers compared to the same set of sociometric items in which the self is described. CR used to define +, 0, and − cutoff points.

8. Conceptions of Others Positive Conceptions of Others (#24); +, 0, − based on the CR.

9. Testimony (Self-Rating) Score of twelve or less, positive; thirteen-nineteen, 0; and twenty or greater, negative.

10. Peer Rating of Learning Scored + if sixty percent agreement among peers of having learned; otherwise 0.

11. Leader Ratings Impact scale. Scored − if negative sign, scored 0 if 0-7, + if eight or more.

12. Social Network Scored if ≥ 2 respondents viewed participant as having changed.

13. View of Interpersonal Environment Opportunity for Open Peer Communication (#29) and Conception of Best Friend (#28). Scored CR sign if two identical; scored 0 if one sign =, one −. If one + or −, the other 0, scored the sign for Open Peer Communication.

change. The criteria used to select "signs of change" were based on several considerations: (a) Inclusion of indicators from the various perspectives; (b) Relative independence among measures (based on intercorrelations);

(c) Theoretical unambiguousness; (d) Inclusion of measures summarizing a large body of data, such as the sociometric questionnaire.

Table 3–3 shows the measures used at Time 2 and Time 3. (It should be noted that some measures such as social network were available only for Time 3.) On each sign of change listed in Table 3–3, each participant could receive one of three possible scores: a positive change (+), unchanged (0), negative change (−). (The actual score for each of these indices was converted to a sign based on the critical ratio procedure for describing when a change had occurred.) [6] Interviews which were available were added to the aforementioned indices for approximately half the participants. These were people who had been interviewed for special substudies: Dropouts, casualty suspects, or visible learners, for the issue of maintenance of change.

A case-by-case adjudication process was instituted to render a final change assessment for each participant. Each principal investigator looked first at the Time 2 data for each participant, and made a careful critical judgment of the impact of the group experience upon him. Most weight was given to change which occurred in the behavioral and self areas. Discussion among the three investigators rendered a final decision. A similar judgment process was applied to Time 3 data. Through this process, participants were classified into five basic outcome categories. [7]

The category *Negative Changer* was assigned where the judgment was that the person had experienced downward shifts on three or more signs on the change indicators. The category *Unchanged* was employed when it appeared that, by and large, the person had experienced no positive or negative gain from the experience, or when the change signs showed inconsistent patterns (some up and some down, a few unchanged). The category *Moderate Changer* was applied where it was clear that the person had experienced predominately positive shifts (on the change signs), with a few or no negative changes. The category *High Learner* was applied when it was clear that a substantial amount of positive change had occurred, usually on five to six of the change indicators, and only rarely were negative signs in evidence. Dropouts and Casualties were maintained as separate outcome categories. The criteria for these categories are discussed in Chapter 5.

Table 3–4 shows the results of assignment to these categories. Of those who entered the groups, approximately a third showed positive gain, and a little over a third showed no change; the remainder underwent some form of negative experience. They were Negative Changers or Casualties, or had dropped out for psychological reasons. Thus, of those who began the encounter groups, 66 percent did not benefit while 34 percent benefited. It should be emphasized that the criteria used to assess change were stringent. If the 34 percent figure were compared with rates of positive outcome reported in the psychotherapy literature, it might seem quite small. This could, of course, be accounted for by differences in effectiveness, but

TABLE 3-4

Index of Change—Outcome Classification
Total Sample[a]

	Casualties	Negative Changer	Dropouts	Unchanged	Moderate Changer	High Learner	Total
Short Post							
Participants	16 (08%)	17 (08%)	27 (13%)	78 (38%)	40 (20%)	28 (14%)	206
Controls		16 (23%)		41 (60%)	9 (13%)	3 (04%)	69
Long Post							
Participants	16 (10%)	13 (08%)	27 (17%)	52 (33%)	37 (23%)	15 (09%)	160
Controls		7 (15%)		32 (68%)	5 (11%)	3 (06%)	47

Index of Change for Those Who Completed Group
(N = 179 Short Post, 133 Long Post)

	Casualties	Negative Changer	Unchanged	Moderate Changer	High Learner
Short Post	09%	10%	44%	22%	16%
Long Post	12%	10%	39%	28%	11%

[a]Four participants were judged from interview data to have left for "physical" reasons (e.g., schedule conflicts). Five persons designated as Casualties in fact dropped out before group completion.

may also be explained by differences in the outcome criteria applied; much of the psychotherapeutic outcome research is based only on therapist judgments or self-judgments (similar criteria in this study produce rates of positive change over twice that of the 34 percent figure), as well as on one-dimensional rather than multidimensional indices.

Table 3–4 also shows the status of the control group. It should be mentioned that several indices were not available for the control groups (such as, of course, leader judgments or coparticipant judgments), nor were there extensive interviews of any of the control group members to help adjudicate outcome classification. Thus, less significance can be attached to differences among controls and participants. Suffice it to say that fewer controls showed positive gain, and more showed unchanged status as well as negative change when compared to the participants.

The picture at Time 3 is similar: 32 percent of experimentals and 15 percent of controls were judged to have experienced positive impact (39 percent of those who meaningfully completed the groups). Once again, as with the self-report and social network data reviewed earlier, it can be seen that control group base rates of change are clearly not zero. The percentage of unchanged controls rose to 68 at Time 3, while 33 percent of experimentals fell into that category. The proportion of participants sustaining undesired outcomes (negative or casualty) was stable.

The question naturally arises whether the Time 3 data were affected by nonreturn of the research instruments. The experimental population did shrink from 204 to 179, or 12 percent. Controls dropped from sixty-nine to forty-seven, or 32 percent. A comparison of the outcome status at Time 2 of participants and controls who returned at Time 3 revealed that seventeen out of twenty-eight High Learners returned (60 percent), thirty-one of the forty Moderate Changers (77 percent), fifty-seven of the seventy-eight Unchanged (73 percent), and twelve of the seventeen Negative Changers (70 percent). For the controls, three of the three High Learners (100 percent), six of the nine Moderate Changers (66 percent), twenty-eight of the forty-one Unchanged (68 percent), and ten of the sixteen Negative Changers (62 percent). The distribution suggests that, for both experimentals and controls, the distribution of outcome groups returning data at Time 3 did not differ in any substantial way from the distribution of outcome groups at Time 2. In general, we may trust the finding that encounter group experience appeared to induce short-run positive changes in about a third of those beginning the groups, left slightly over a third unchanged, and produced undesired changes (negative or casualty) in about 15 percent. Somewhat over 10 percent of those who entered the groups dropped out along the way. Meanwhile, it is important to remember that 15 percent or so of controls were reported to have made positive changes during the same time period.

The picture at the six month follow-up was approximately the same. All in all, this assessment, carried out using a range of data from the self, group peers, the group leader, and associates from outside the group, gives a somewhat more conservative picture of changes than the self-reports alone, which were positive for 60 percent of those who stayed with the groups.

Change Maintenance

How durable were the Time 2 changes six to eight months later? Table 3–5 shows the status of both the participants and controls for whom there were both Time 2 and Time 3 data. The rate of maintained positive change among experimentals (28 percent of the total that began the group), while double that of controls, is considerably less than the self-report data on estimate change maintenance noted earlier. Adding to this those who first showed positive change at Time 3 gives a total of 39 percent, still double the control group rate, but much less than the figures drawn from self-estimates. For those who changed positively, three out of four were able to maintain these positive benefits—a high and perhaps enviable record of maintenance. Although the rates of change were modest, the stability of such change when it did occur is impressive.

Encounter group practitioners often cite cases of "late blooming," probably in the belief that a period of "sorting out" has to take place before

TABLE 3-5

Panel Final Outcome Classifications

	Participants N = 133	Controls N = 47
Casualty	16 (12.0%)	—
Negative, Maintained	8 (5.9%)	6 (12.8%)
Unchanged	46 (34.4%)	30 (63.8%)
Backsliders[a]	11 (8.3%)	3 (6.4%)
Late Bloomers[b]	15 (11.3%)	2 (4.3%)
Positive Change, Maintained[c]	37 (27.8%)	6 (12.8%)

[a]Moved from positive change to no change or negative.

[b]Moved from negative to positive, or moved from no change to positive.

[c]Received change or high change, and retained change or high change.

learnings are stabilized. The findings certainly do not suggest that this phenomenon is widespread. Only *one* person in the sample succeeded in moving from a negative change at Time 2 to positive at Time 3; of all those classified as unchanged at termination, only 25 percent were "late bloomers." Thus, "late blooming," offered as a possible expectation to a participant who has experienced poor outcomes, appears more a hope than a probability. There is about 75 percent chance, whether immediate outcomes are nil, positive, or negative that they will be essentially the same six months later (reasons for different degrees of maintenance of change are discussed in Chapter 14 where samples of "maintainers" and "non-maintainers" are looked at in depth).

The classification of participants based upon the indices of change represents one of the two basic approaches used for examining outcome in relationship to other group conditions, such as leadership and group norms. Inasmuch as this measure is crucial, some basic data on the particular indices used to make this component score are presented in the next few pages. Figures 3–1 and 3–2 show the interrelationships among these indices as well as the "contribution" of each index to the classifications of High Learner, Moderate Changer, Unchanged, Negative Changer, Casualty.

Table 3–6 shows the percentage of participants and controls significantly increasing or decreasing on each index at both Time 2 and 3. Thus, for example, Index 5, Adequate Coping, may be read as follows: 21 percent of the participants increased significantly over their Time 1 score in Adequate Coping, while 24 percent decreased. In contrast, the controls showed an increase of only 12 percent and a decrease of 35 percent. Similarly for changes measured six to eight months later, 20 percent of the participants increased in Adequate Coping, while 22 percent decreased in comparison to their Time 1 scores; 21 percent of the controls increased on this scale, 28 percent decreased.

Outcomes: The Impact of the Experience

The most stable change sign from Time 2 to Time 3 was Testimony (the sign most closely related to the final outcome classification). Considering all participants, 65 percent maintained the same position at Time 3 (negative, no change, or positive) as they had had at Time 2. Other relatively stable signs were Adequate Coping (63 percent) and Attitudes to Encounter Groups (55 percent). The Attitude drop-off was asymmetrical: of those with initial negative changes, 77 percent maintained them; of those with positive changes, only 50 percent maintained them. Thus, the glow wears off, but attitudes changed for the worse are more durable.

Self-regard and self-view of behavior showed somewhat less stability, with 56 percent and 52 percent of maintenance, respectively. Self-regard appeared to be one of substantial recoveries on the part of those who had originally experienced losses; of this group 37 percent maintained a negative change, 40 percent recovered from their initial drop, and 23 percent showed positive change. Of those who experienced an initial *increase* in

FIGURE 3–1

Clusters of Components of Outcome[a]: Time 2 (Short Post)

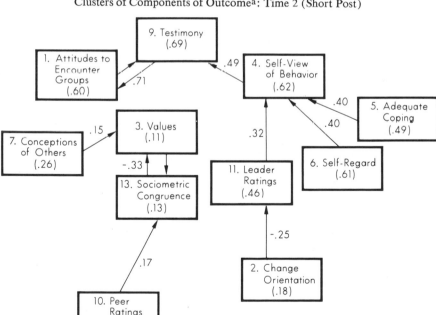

[a] McQuitty's elementary linkage analysis was used to form clusters, using the gamma statistic. Variables more closely related are plotted closer together; the gamma figure is shown on the arrow connecting two variables. The boldface figure after each variable label shows the gamma between it and the final classification (Casualty, Negative Changer, Unchanged, Moderate Changer, High Learner). Arrows indicate which variables are most closely related. For examples, Self-View of Behavior is more closely related to Testimony (gamma = .49) than it is to any other variable.

FIGURE 3–2

Clusters of Components of Outcome[a]: Time 3 (Long Post)

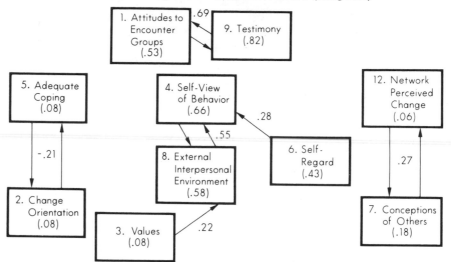

[a] McQuitty's elementary linkage analysis was used to form clusters, using the gamma statistic. Variables more closely related are plotted closer together; the gamma figure is shown on the arrow connecting two variables. The boldface figure after each variable label shows the gamma between it and the final classification (Casualty, Negative Changer, Unchanged, Moderate Changer, High Learner). Arrows indicate which variables are most closely related. For example, Self-Regard is more highly related to Self-View of Behavior (gamma = .28) than to any other variable.

self-regard, 67 percent retained it, with 24 percent dropping back to no change, and 9 percent moving to a negative change.

A roughly similar pattern obtains in self-ratings of Interpersonal Adequacy, a moderately changing outcome component. Of those who initially experienced a decrease, 30 percent retained it, 57 percent recovered, and 5 percent moved to an increase. Of those initially experiencing an increase, 66 percent maintained it, 31 percent moved back to no change, and 3 percent dropped. The healing, and to a lesser extent, sobering effects of time are clearly evident in these data.

Experimental-Control Differences in Outcome[8]

The indicators of change as discussed thus far suggest that, with respect to the gross impact of encounter groups, participants experienced changes beyond those noted in the control group. The encounter group experience is thus not a neutral one, though it certainly appears to fall short of the extensive claims ordinarily made by advocates. Readers with a broadly clinical bent might be satisfied at this point with the evidence on outcome. Oth-

TABLE 3-6

"Change Signs" Making Up Final Outcome Classification
(Percentages)[a]

	Time 1-2			Time 1-3		
	−	0	+	−	0	+
1. *Attitudes to Encounter Groups*						
Participants	19	52	29	31	43	26
Controls	14	70	16	21	70	9
2. *Change Orientation*						
Participants	26	52	22	33	37	30
Controls	36	42	22	41	36	23
3. *Values*						
Participants	—	55	45	—	48	52
Controls	—	52	48	—	47	53
4. *Self-Rating of Behavior:*						
Interpersonal Adequacy						
Participants	18	58	24	18	51	30
Controls	29	57	14	30	49	21
5. *Adequate Coping*						
Participants	24	55	21	22	58	20
Controls	35	54	12	28	51	21
6. *Self-Regard*						
Participants	25	32	43	20	35	45
Controls	36	39	25	41	30	30
7. *Conceptions of Others*						
Participants	26	49	25	29	52	19
Controls	22	58	20	23	64	13
8. *View of Interpersonal*						
Environment						
Participants	—	—	—	23	50	26
Controls	—	—	—	17	66	17
9. *Testimony (Self-rated Gain)*						
Participants	14	29	57	21	32	46
Controls	—	—	—	—	—	—
10. *Peer-rated Learning*						
Participants	—	63	37	—	—	—
Controls	—	—	—	—	—	—
11. *Trainer-rated Learning*						
Participants	3	66	30	—	—	—
Controls	—	—	—	—	—	—
12. *Social Network*[b]						
Participants	—	—	—	5	51	43
Controls	—	—	—	5	59	36
13. *Sociometric: Self-*						
Other Congruence						
Participants	24	59	17	—	—	—
Controls	—	—	—	—	—	—

[a]Ns for this table are: Time 1-2, Participants = 174, Controls = 69; Time 1-3, Participants = 125, Controls = 47.

[b]Ns for this table are: 111 for Participants, 41 for Controls.

ers may desire a somewhat more precise view of statistical differences among experimentals and controls.[9]

Differences among the participants and their controls were examined relative to the thirty-three indices described earlier, which were organized into five areas: Values and Attitudes, Behavior, Self, Conceptions of Others, and External Relationships. A multivariate analysis of covariance [10] indicated that at Time 2, three of the five areas showed significant differences among the participants and the controls: in order of the strength of differences, Values and Attitudes ($p = .002$),[11] Behavior ($p = .04$), and Self ($p = .07$). No statistically significant differences were found in the areas of Conceptions of Others ($p = .36$) or External Relationships ($p = .37$). Table 3–7 shows those specific indicators in which the changes among the participants were significantly different from the changes found in the control group. In all, seven of the thirty-three variables showed statistically significant experimental-control differences, five beyond the .01 level. These findings can be considered as maximally conservative since the analysis held pretest differences constant.

To summarize the Time 2 changes of experimentals: (1) in Values and Attitudes they increased slightly in the importance of such "change-oriented" values as "learning how others view me" and "changing some of the ways I relate to people," while the control group decreased; (2) they maintained their level of "growth-orientation" (aspects of their life space involving growing, learning, and becoming), while controls, who were less growth-oriented to begin with, dropped even more; (3) they came to see encounter groups as more safe, while controls saw them as more dangerous; (4) in the Self Area experimentals saw themselves as somewhat more "lenient" (considerate, permissive), while controls saw themselves as less so; (5) the discrepancy between their self-picture and ideal self in the interpersonal domain (mentally healthy, considerate, honest, permissive) decreased, while that of controls increased; (6) they saw their own behavior as more interpersonally adequate, while controls decreased; and (7) they became more likely to use an active coping style (behavior such as taking action, interpersonal discussion, and problem-solving), while controls became less likely. It is noteworthy that on six of seven change indicators, experimentals improved (by the *a priori* definition of improvement as positive change) while controls worsened on all seven.

What were these differences like six to eight months later? A multivariate analysis of covariance was again used to compare participants and controls on differences between Time 1 and Time 3 scores. A number of the differences noted previously were attenuated or totally disappeared. The overall levels of change in the five areas at Time 3 were as follows: Values and Attitudes ($p = .14$); Behavior ($p = .47$); Self ($p = .08$); Conceptions of Others ($p = .21$); and External Relationships ($p = .87$). Overall, there was a much lower probability of finding experimental-control differences at the long-post follow-up. Table 3–7 shows the levels of signifi-

TABLE 3-7
Significant Experimental/Control Differences

	Signifi- cance Level Time 1-2	Signifi- cance Level Time 1-3	Unadjusted Time 1	Time 2	Adjusted	Unadjusted Time 1	Time 3	Adjusted
VALUES AND ATTITUDES								
Values: Change Orientation[a]								
Participants	.04		0.00	-0.06	0.00	0.04	-0.05	0.00
Controls		.14	-0.01	0.18	0.29	-0.03	0.14	0.26
Life Space: Growth Orientation								
Participants	.001		28.62	27.10	0.00	29.9	26.3	0.00
Controls		.42	16.67	11.85	-12.44	21.8	18.9	-5.02
Attitudes to Encounter: Safety								
Participants	.001		26.61	27.94	0.00	26.34	26.38	0.00
Controls		.09	26.13	25.77	-1.91	25.96	24.74	-1.26
BEHAVIOR								
Self-Rating: Interpersonal Adequacy								
Participants	.01		0.00	0.21	0.0C	-0.10	0.06	0.00
Controls		.03	0.00	-0.18	-0.29	0.00	-0.16	-0.30
Coping Strategy: Adequate								
Participants	.01		0.01	0.10	0.0C	0.01	0.02	0.00
Controls		.31	-0.03	-0.24	-0.31	0.04	-0.07	-0.07
SELF								
Self-Concept: Leniency								
Participants	.01		0.02	0.10	0.00	0.06	0.11	0.00
Controls		.10	-0.06	-0.25	-0.30	-0.22	-0.29	-0.25
Self-ideal Discrepancy: Interpersonal								
Participants	.10		15.92	12.67	0.00	16.2	13.0	0.00
Controls		.12	9.45	18.49	7.50	8.4	20.5	5.10

[a]Low score equals greater change orientation.

cance for the seven variables that had previously discriminated the participants from the controls at Time 2. No other "new variables" statistically insignificant at Time 2 became significant at Time 3. There is attenuation (drop in significance levels) on all of these seven indices; life-space, growth orientation, and adequacy of coping style show the largest drops, from previously high levels of significance to totally insignificant differences between participants and controls.[12] Differences thus were still noted in the Self area and to some extent in the Values and Attitudes area.[13]

It is of interest to briefly look at the areas that did not show overall experimental-control group differences. It has long been assumed, particularly in T-group theory and lore, that major effects should be expected in how the individual views others. The findings presented here, however, indicate that overall the encounter groups did not substantially alter participants' conceptions of their interpersonal world, either in terms of its content (the kinds of concepts the person had about significant others), or in terms of its complexity (the schemata he brought to bear in viewing others). Nor were overall differences found in how the individual perceived his interpersonal environment (whether he saw it as a place where increased opportunities for certain kinds of interpersonal behavior were to be found). The findings yield no direct evidence that participants changed their relationships with close friends, or perceived their close friends in different terms prior to the encounter group.

These findings suggest that the overall effects of encounter groups are primarily in the Value-Attitude area, and in the way a person thinks about and perceives the self. In some sense, these are "internal changes," changes that may or may not be apparent to outsiders. Behavioral manifestations, the index to others that an individual had changed, are not pronounced as overall effects of encounter groups.

Examination of experimental-control differences in respect to life decisions reported (variable thirty-three), revealed no significant differences between the number of life decisions made by participants, and the number made by controls. At the long post (as additional information not reflected in the thirty-three variables), both participants and controls were asked whether they had experienced a major event, or made some major decision in the preceding year and, if so, to describe them. The number of such decisions was similar for both participants and controls—54 percent of the participants, 52 percent of the controls. A content analysis of the decisions made indicated some interesting differences, 34 percent of the participants had made decisions concerning the formation of new relationships (falling in love, marriage) compared to only 18 percent of the controls. On the other hand, controls appeared to have made more decisions about their instrumental world, military-related decisions, career decisions. Of all the decisions reported, 41 percent of the participants made decisions about relationships compared to 29 percent of the controls; conversely, 49 percent of the controls, compared to 36 percent of the participants, made decisions having to do with instrumental areas, military, career, school and such things as the Peace Corps. Thus, although the number of life decisions did not differ between the participants and their controls, one effect of the encounter group was to emphasize decisions having to do with relationships, a finding that closely parallels the major value orientation of such groups.

Before considering comparisons among groups, one additional measure —Peak Experience—is worthy of consideration in terms of the impact of the encounter experiences. Immediately after the group experience, participants were given a description of a peak experience, and were asked whether or not they had had such an experience in the preceding six months. If they said yes, they were asked to report whether it had occurred in the encounter group, or in a number of other situations, such as with friends, alone, or facilitated by drugs. Although 60 percent of the participants reported having such experiences, only seventeen (16 percent) indicated that the experience had occurred in an encounter group. (The figure for "with a group of friends," was 15 percent; for "with one other person," 51 percent; for "alone," 45 percent; and for "facilitated by drugs," 27 percent.) It thus seems that encounter group experiences were not a major influence in the production of peak experiences in contrast to other settings. It is of some interest that a majority of the participants claimed to have had peak experiences, even when defined in the questionnaire in relatively extreme and mystical terms. Perhaps these college students were going through important and intense experiences regardless of the input which project groups represented in their lives.

All in all, experimental-control differences were modest, even though possibly meaningful. Seen as a large "black box" which our participants metaphorically entered and left, the encounter group experience in gross terms did not transform persons strikingly on a large number of variables. There is little basis, however, for assuming that there is *an* experience labeled "encounter group" which is a standard "black box," or that people interact with particular group experiences in a standard way, or that all types of group experience are equally effective in inducing change. The seventeen groups differed rather substantially among themselves, and, as later chapters demonstrate, these differences accounted for more variance in outcome than the sheer fact of participation, alone, in an encounter group.

Contrasts among Groups, Effects on Outcome

Up to this point, outcome has been discussed as if encounter groups were a unitary event. This is only a fictional convenience. More striking than experimental and control differences were contrasts among the seventeen groups studied. Some left the participants unchanged. One group (#10) did not yield even one positively changed person; from that particular group, many left happy and contented, but unchanged. Another group (#8) yielded ten who changed in a positive direction out of twelve who began. Still a third group (#4) produced negative reactions of some kind in seven of the thirteen who began.

In reality, the study examined seventeen learning environments which differed considerably in the behavior of the leader, the working procedures of the group, the levels of cohesiveness, the group norms, climate, and use of time. An overview of the outcome differences among the groups can best be gained by examining the proportion of participants who showed various outcome statuses: High Learners, Moderate Changers, Unchanged, Dropouts, Negative Changers, and Casualties. Table 3–8 shows the array of group-by-group differences for the short and long post-test.

A "yield" score summarizing the data presented in Table 3–8 was computed by weighting six outcome categories. Each person who dropped out of a group for psychological reasons was weighted (− 1) on the assumption that dropping out represented a mild negative outcome. This assumption

TABLE 3-8

Number of People Showing Benefit and Risk by Group

Group	Starting N	Dropouts[a]	Casual- ties	Negative Changers	Unchanged	Moderate Changers	High Learners
1	9 (7)	0	0	3 (1)	3 (4)	1 (1)	2 (1)
2	10 (7)	0	1	2 (1)	4 (2)	0 (1)	3 (2)
3	11 (8)	0	0	0 (0)	7 (4)	2 (3)	2 (1)
4	13[a] (11)	1[a]	3	3 (3)	3 (2)	2 (2)	1 (0)
5	11 (6)	1	1	2 (1)	3 (1)	1 (2)	3 (0)
6	14 (10)	2	2	0 (0)	3 (0)	3 (5)	4 (1)
7	11 (10)	4	0	0 (0)	5 (3)	1 (1)	1 (2)
8	12[b] (9)	1	0	0 (0)	1 (3)	5 (3)	5 (2)
9	14[a] (10)	3[a]	2	0 (1)	8 (2)	0 (2)	1 (0)
10	11 (9)	2	1	1 (1)	7 (4)	0 (1)	0 (0)
11	12 (9)	0	1	1 (1)	8 (6)	1 (1)	1 (0)
12	15 (11)	2	1	0 (1)	4 (1)	7 (4)	1 (2)
13	21[b] (18)	6[a]	2	1 (0)	6 (5)	5 (4)	1 (1)
14	9 (8)	2	1	1 (1)	3 (2)	2 (1)	0 (1)
15	9[b] (5)	2[a]	1	1 (1)	0 (0)	5 (1)	0 (0)
16	11 (10)	0	0	2 (1)	6 (6)	3 (3)	0 (0)
17	13 (12)	1	0	0 (0)	7 (7)	2 (2)	3 (2)
Totals	206[b] (160)	27	16	17 (13)	78 (52)	40 (37)	28 (15)

[a]Subtracted from this list are four Dropouts who were in fact Casualties.

[b]This list includes all those who "meaningfully" began the groups. In Groups #8 and #15 one additional person each was initially signed up but left for "physical," nonpsychological reasons. Two such persons began in Group #13. The overall beginning total was thus 210.

NOTE: Numbers in parentheses = Time 3, corrected N represents those persons for whom information was available at Long Post.

FIGURE 3–3

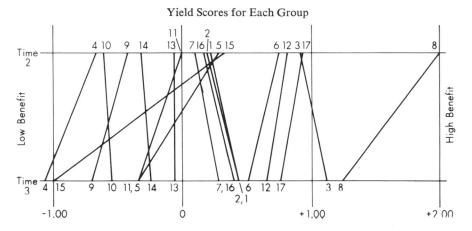

Yield Scores for Each Group

was supported by interviews with Dropouts (see Chapter 5). Negative Changers were weighted (− 2). Each Casualty was weighted (− 3). People classified as Unchanged were weighted (0), as were Moderate Changers (+ 2), and High Learners (+ 3). Thus the extreme positive and negative categories, as well as the two intermediate categories were assigned equivalent weight.

Figure 3–3 illustrates how few groups changed their relative position significantly from Time 2 to Time 3. (The rank-order correlation was .79. This stability, of course, in part occurred because the Dropout and Casualty figures served as a base common to both yield computations.) The substantial drop of Group #8 is accounted for by three High Changers in that group who did not return for Time 3 data. The Group #5 score was influenced not only by nonreturners, but by two backsliders as well. The substantial "drop" in Group #15 is an artifact; five Moderate Changers in that group did not return post data.

The Time 2 yield scores displayed in Figure 3–3 indicate that Group #8 (Transactional Analysis) was clearly the most productive group. Other relatively high-yield groups were Group #17 (Tape), Group #3 (Gestalt), Group #12 (Eclectic Marathon), and Group #6 (Psychodrama). Another cluster of groups in which more participants showed positive than negative outcomes is made up of Group #15 (Personal Growth T-group), Group #5 (Psychodrama), Group #1 (NTL T-group), Group #2 (NTL T-group), Group #16 (Tape), and Group #7 (Psychoanalytic). All the other groups did not, on balance, show a surplus of benefit compared to negative outcomes. Group #11 (Rogerian Marathon), Group #13 (Synanon), showed an almost equal balance between negative outcomes and positive change. Groups #14 (Personal Growth), #9 (Transactional Analysis), #10 (Esalen Eclectic), and #4 (Gestalt) all yielded a higher number of negative outcomes than positive outcomes. Clearly, the

119

"school" or ideological labels attached to the groups meant very little in connection with their productivity. One of the highest-yield groups, for example, turned out to be a Gestalt group (#3) as did the lowest yield group (#4). Similarly, one Transactional Analysis group (#8) was the most productive group; the other ranked next to the last in Yield (#9). Through many of the remaining chapters, evidence is brought to bear that yield is a function of particular conditions, processes, and phenomena which are uncorrelated with the ideological bent of the leader.

SPECIAL EFFECTS OF THE SEVENTEEN GROUPS

Comparisons among groups using proportions of benefit and risk are, of course, only crude indicators of the effects of each encounter group on its participants. The basic thirty-three change measures in the five realms of Values and Attitudes, Behavior, Self, Conceptions of Others, and External Relationships were examined to determine discrete effects of each of the groups, as well as to examine those psychological areas most affected by differences in the various encounter groups. The statistical method used compared each group, one at a time, against the average of all the other groups in the experimental sample.[14] It was thus a relatively strict, conservative method of discovering those groups which showed positive or negative changes distinctly different from those of the remaining groups. Table 3–9 shows the variables that discriminated among the groups at both Time 2 and Time 3. As an aid to surveying this information, Figure 3–4 shows the corrected means and the relative position of each group to the control population.

As is shown in Table 3–9, the changes in Values and Attitudes discriminated most sharply among the seventeen groups, a finding similar to that which reported differences for participants versus controls. Also, as in the comparisons between participants and controls, measures of Self show overall significance among the seventeen groups. However, in contrast, to the experimental-control comparisons, the Behavior realm does not show overall differences among the groups, while External Relationships do show differences not found between participants and controls. Nine specific dimensions showed significant overall differences among the groups: the three Attitude scales, the valuation of change, self-oriented values, self-ratings of interpersonal adequacy, a lenient self-image, self-ideal discrepancy, and environmental opportunity for peer communication.

The discrete effects of each group are illustrated in Figure 3–4 which displays each group contrasted with the average of all other groups. Under the contrast method, certain variables that did not discriminate overall among the groups can locate several groups that differed significantly from the rest. Such cases are indicated by an asterisk (p. $\leq$ .10) next to the group number. As an aid to examining Figure 3–4, the significant effects of each group are briefly portrayed:

Group #1 (T-group) participants saw encounter groups as more dan-

TABLE 3-9

Overall Effects: Covariance Analysis among Groups

Variable	Time 1-2 (N = 174)	Time 1-3 (N = 125)
1. Safety/Danger	.0001	.03
2. Social Benefit	.0002	
3. Genuine/Phony	.0001	
4. Value Experiencing		.07
5. Value Change		
6. Value Growth		
7. Self-Orientation	.02	
8. Value Instrumental-External	.08	.05
9. Value Interpersonal		
10. Value Intimacy		.05
Overall p	.0001	.03
11. Interpersonal Adequacy	.06	
12. Feeling Sensitivity		
13. Adequate Coping	.13	
14. Defensive Coping		
15. Acceptance of Control	.12	
16. Expression of Control	.18	
17. Acceptance of Affection		
18. Expression of Affection		
Overall p	.22	.52
19. Self-Esteem	.13	
20. Self-Concept		
21. Lenient Self-Image	.03	.09
22. Self-ideal Discrepancy (Interpersonal)	.05	
23. Self-ideal Discrepancy (Instrumental)		
Overall p	.02	.41
24. Concepts of Others		.15
25. Perception of Others As Lenient		
26. Complexity (Interpersonal)		
27. Complexity (Instrumental)		
28. Concept of Best Friend		.07
Overall p	.52	.03
29. Opportunity for Open Peer Communication	.0001	.11
30. Opportunity for Expression of Anger		.14
31. Number of Close Friends	.19	
32. Hours Spent with Close Friends		.18
33. Number of Life Decisions		
Overall p	.03	.14

gerous, decreased in their Self-Orientation, and increased in external-instrumental values—in other words, the effect of Group #1 may be seen in a movement away from the inner value concern to values having more to do with the world out there. There was a concomitant increase in values having to do with interpersonal relationships and, in particular, intimacy.

FIGURE 3-4

Mean Changes for the Seventeen Groups

Values and Attitudes

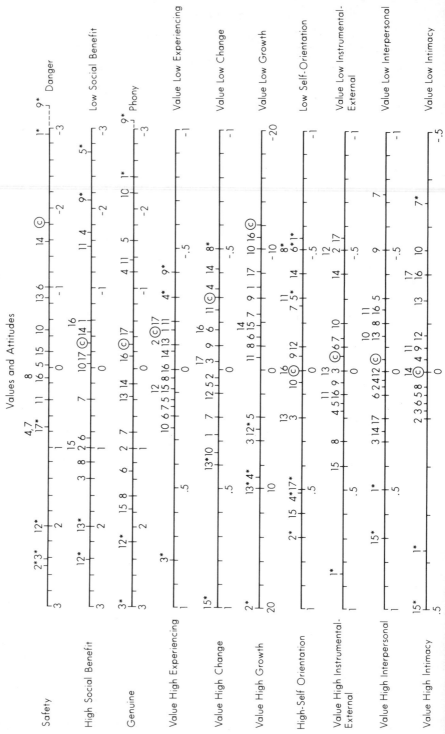

FIGURE 3–4 (*Cont'd*)

Mean Changes for the Seventeen Groups

Interpersonal Behavior

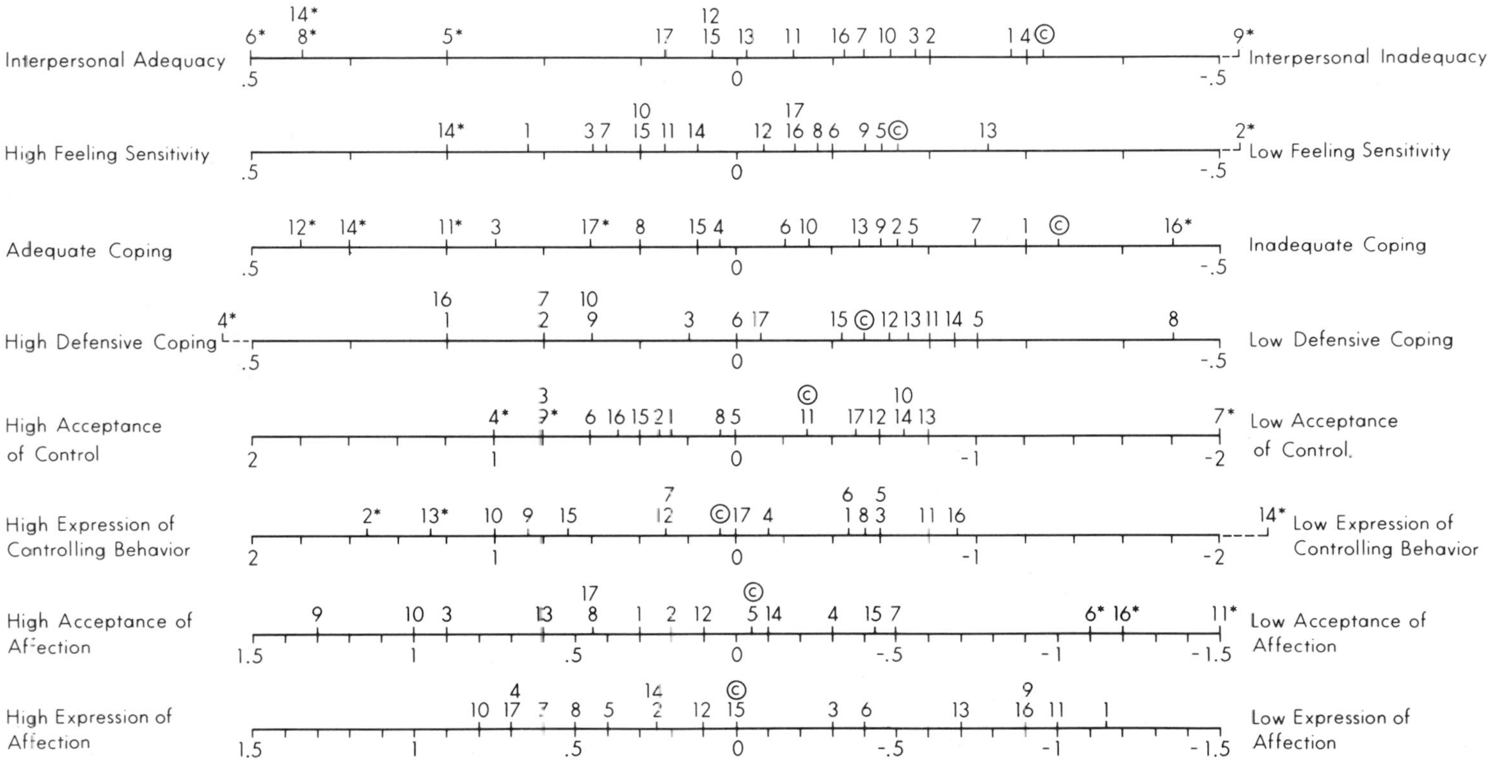

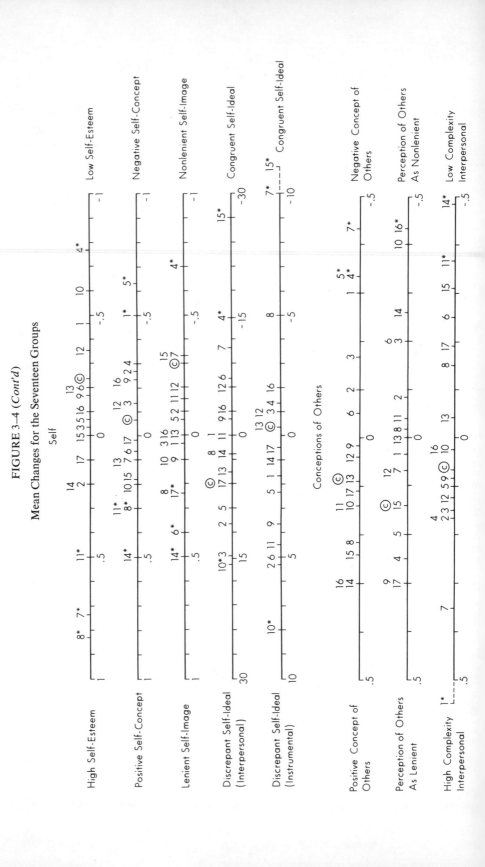

FIGURE 3–4 (Cont'd)

Mean Changes for the Seventeen Groups

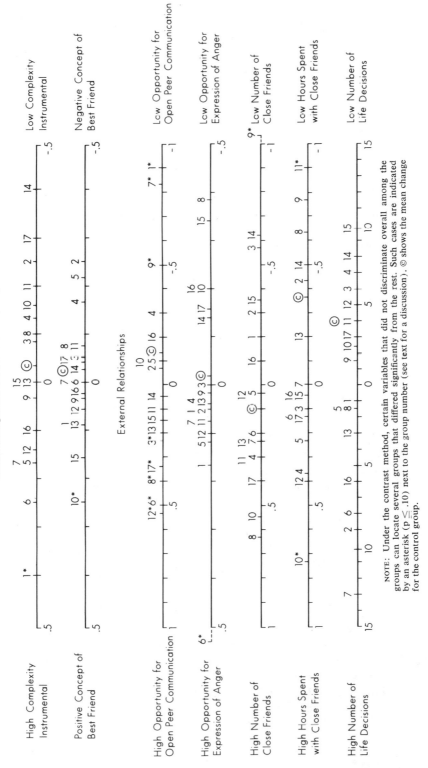

FIGURE 3-4 (Cont'd)

Mean Changes for the Seventeen Groups

External Relationships

NOTE: Under the contrast method, certain variables that did not discriminate overall among the groups can locate several groups that differed significantly from the rest. Such cases are indicated by an asterisk (p ≤ .10) next to the group number (see text for a discussion). ⓒ shows the mean change for the control group.

Members of Group #1 were significantly affected in their Conceptions of Others, being more likely to see the significant interpersonal world as complex; they had a more differentiated view of others. Finally, these participants felt their environment contained fewer opportunities for open peer communication.

Group #2 (T-group) participants viewed encounter groups as safer and more genuine. In the Value area, they increased in their emphasis on growth and self-oriented values. In the Behavioral area, they judged their level of feeling sensitivity to be decreased, and were more willing to express directive or controlling behavior. Thus the major changes for the participants in Group #2 were expressed in the Values and Attitudes area and in Behavior, the latter in the direction of becoming "harder."

Group #3 (Gestalt) members perceived the encounter group as safer and more genuine. Their Value change was in emphasizing experiencing as a dominant value, a value that reflects a motif of many encounter ideologies, but which showed a significant increment only in this group. Aside from these changes in the Values and Attitudes area, the only other change noted for the members of Group #3 was in their view that the environment offered more opportunities for open peer communication.

Group #4 (Gestalt) participants increased in their valuation of growth and values focusing on self-orientation. The members of this group underwent a few changes in the Self area: they decreased in their self-esteem, their self-concept became less lenient, and their self and ideal images became more congruent. The final change in this group was in their perceptions of others in their environment as less lenient. Of interest is that despite the high stimulation and here-and-now orientation of Group #4 (see Chapter 2), participants declined in their valuing of experiencing and became much more self-oriented and growth-oriented.

Group #5 (Psychodrama) participants perceived encounter groups as less socially beneficial after the experience than before they started the group. They were not as interested in self-oriented values. Despite their increased sense of interpersonal adequacy, they viewed themselves with less self-regard.

Group #6 (Psychodrama) members showed a wide variety of changes. In the Value area, they were less interested in self-development. Behaviorally, they increased in their sense of interpersonal adequacy and decreased in the amount of affection they required from others. Their only change in the Self area was their view of self as more lenient. Their conceptions of others became less complex. Finally, they perceived their environments as having increased in the opportunities for open peer communication and for the expression of anger. Thus, Group #6 evidenced significant modifications in at least one dimension of each of the five areas assessed.

Group #7 (Psychoanalytic) members decreased their emphasis on interpersonal values in the Value area. Behaviorally, they were less willing to accept controlling behavior from others. They showed greatest change in the Self area, increasing in their self-esteem and in self-ideal congruence, particularly in instrumental or task aspects. They viewed their environments as containing fewer opportunities for open peer communication.

Group #8 (Transactional Analysis) underwent interesting and somewhat confusing changes in the Value area. Although this group was the most successful in overall amount of change, the degree in which members valued change decreased. The degree in which they valued focus on self also decreased. In the Behavior area, they increased in their sense of interpersonal adequacy, and decreased in maladaptive or defensive coping strategies. In the Self area, they showed an increase in self-esteem, as well as a more positive self-concept. They saw others more positively, and also perceived more opportunities in their environment for open peer communication, but fewer opportunities for the expression of anger. Overall, members of Group #8 changed in a large number of dimensions.

Group #9 (Transactional Analysis) individuals perceived encounter groups as more dangerous, less socially beneficial, and less genuine. They placed less emphasis on values having to do with experience. Behaviorally, they felt decreased in interpersonal adequacy, and they perceived fewer opportunities in their environment for open peer communication. Clearly, the discrete changes noted among the members of Group #9 mirror their overall rating as an unsuccessful group.

Group #10 (Esalen Eclectic) members show only one significant change, a more positive view of their closest friend. The lack of any significant departures again mirrors the overall rating of this group as unsuccessful in yielding change.

Group #11 (Rogerian Marathon) members decreased in the amount of affection they required from others. In the Self area, their self-concept became more positive. Their view of others moved toward seeing them as less complex, and they indicated that they spent less time with friends outside of the group.

Group #12 (Eclectic Marathon) participants saw encounter groups as safer, more beneficial, and more genuine. Behaviorally, they increased in their utilization of adequate-active coping strategies, and viewed their environments as containing more opportunities for open peer communication. These specific changes mirror the relative overall success of this group.

Group #13 (Synanon) members, perhaps befitting their instrumental orientation, increased their view of the encounter group as socially beneficial, and valued change more. Interpersonally, they were more willing to express controlling behavior. They also valued growth more.

Group #14 (Personal Growth) members increased in their positive conceptions of self. Behaviorally, they were less willing to express controlling behavior, and they saw others in their environment as being complex interpersonally.

Group #15 (Personal Growth) members showed changes in two areas.

In Values, they increased their evaluation of change and their emphasis on interpersonal relationships, particularly intimate ones. In the Self area, their self-ideal became more congruent both in the interpersonal and task aspects.

Group #16 (Tape) members showed decreased sense of adequacy in coping, decreased need for affection from others, and a decreased tendency to view others as lenient.

Group #17 (Tape) stands in sharp contrast to the previous Tape group. Members of this group increased values focusing on the self, increased in their sense of adequate or active coping strategies, viewed themselves as more lenient, and perceived the environment as offering increased opportunities for open peer communication.

It is perhaps superfluous to say that this overview of changes characteristic of each group does not meet a prime requirement of science—to abstract and generalize. Clearly, the themes of individual change are complex, so that if the group is treated as a unit few generalizations are apparent. The data presented in Figure 3–4 bring home the message that the seventeen groups were in fact distinct learning environments which provided distinctive experiences and outcomes for the participants. The variations in outcome among the seventeen groups are the point of departure for subsequent chapters, where the attempt is made to understand the diversity of outcomes in relationship to style of leadership, norms and other group conditions, the experiences presented in the group which were thought to lead to growth or learning, and the personal characteristics of the participants.[15]

The high variation in effects that is so convincingly demonstrated by the measures of personal change is in some way disappointing both to the scientist and to the practitioner, each of whom could enjoy a firmer footing for prediction regarding the conditions of inducing personal change. In another way, the recognition of the persistent problems attendant on the search for broad relationships between experience and outcome may in reality be the most useful knowledge, pointing not only to the cumulative complexity of individuals in groups, but also to the futility of searching for the "best manual," the "correct method," or the "foolproof formula" to "guarantee" the goals of personal change through groups.

Summary Findings

Viewed from the perspective of the participants, at the termination of the encounter groups somewhat over 60 percent of those who completed the groups saw themselves as having benefited. Six months later, 10 to 20 percent of this group were less enthusiastic about the positive change they previously perceived. Leaders were the most optimistic about the number of individuals who changed, perceiving some change in almost 90 percent of those who participated. When assessed in terms of "high" benefit, however, the figure of 90 percent was considerably reduced and only one-third of those who participated were seen by leaders as having made substantial gain. Benefit, viewed from the different perspectives, self, leader, coparticipants, social networks, was found to be unrelated to one another. The unique effects of the encounter experience in the view of the participants' social network is questionable, for friends and relatives saw change in as many controls as participants. Those in the social network perceived over three-quarters of both participants and controls as having changed during the six months after the groups ended.

The lack of correspondence among the various perspectives on amount of change led to the development of a cumulative index as a means of identifying benefit as well as negative outcomes. The index, based on the variety of perspectives on change as well as a series of indices developed from test measures covering a number of types of changes, revealed that one-third of those who participated in the groups benefited from them, a little over one-third remained unchanged, and the remainder experienced some form of negative outcome; dropping out of the group for psychological reasons, making negative changes, or experiencing psychological decompensation.

The status of the participant at the end of the experience reflects the participants' status six to eight months later. Of those who experienced positive benefit as a consequence of their participation in the group, three-quarters maintained such learning. A similar percentage was found for those who changed in a negative direction. Only 10 percent of the participants who showed no positive change at the end of the encounter group showed signs of benefit six months later, indicating that the notion of "late blooming" is not a viable concept for explaining much of the utility of encounter groups. Those who did show gain six to eight months later were drawn from those who had originally been classified as unchanged; individuals who had a negative experience did not turn out six to eight months later as showing positive gain.

Type of change or area of change was examined by comparing participants and controls on a series of thirty-three measures. Differences between participants and controls were greater at the end of the group than they were six to eight months later. The most important and stable areas of change were in Values and Attitudes and in Self. Participants were more likely to shift their Value structure in the direction of being more change-oriented and more growth-oriented. Their self-images moved toward perceiving themselves as more lenient, and toward increased congruency between their ideal image and their self. Behavioral changes appeared to be less stable, so that, although at termination participants increased in their coping adequacy and perceived their behavior as more interpersonally adequate, only the latter maintained the significant difference at long post.

Based both on the number of individuals who experienced benefit from the groups and on the comparison of the different areas in participants and their controls, it was concluded that overall, encounter groups show a modest positive impact, an impact much less than has been portrayed by their supporters and an impact significantly lower than participants' view of their own change would lead one to assume.

To a considerable extent, the modesty of the gain can be attributed to the wide differences among the various groups studied. Some groups were highly productive learning environments, others were innocuous, providing a certain degree of pleasurable stimulation but little learning as measured here. Still others were on balance destructive, leaving more of their participants psychologically harmed than psychologically benefited. Differences among groups were more substantial both in the number of people affected and in the type or area of change than were differences between those who participated in them and those who did not.

NOTES

1. Other useful reviews of the literature on the assessment of outcome in the intensive group experience (which have appeared with most frequency in the area of human relations laboratory training) have been made by Stock-Whitaker (1964), Campbell and Dunnette (1968), Buchanan (1964), and House (1967).

2. Men were more likely than women to give positive testimony at the short post (p < .02); 64 percent of men were positive and 41 percent of women. However, this difference receded to the p < .10 level at the long post-test (51 percent vs. 36 percent).

3. This measure was adapted from one originally developed by Miles (1965) where a correlation of .55 was obtained between leader ratings before and after a two-week training laboratory and behavior change as seen by associates on the job six months after the laboratory. It is unknown whether the retrospective technique used in the present cases is more or less valid than the earlier mode.

4. Table 3–1 is also interesting, in passing, for those dimensions which, by and large, do not show across-the-board impact, as rated by leaders: emotional modes, such as happiness and anger; spontaneity; and positive self-image. This is especially striking, not only in view of the claims of the encounter group movement, but in light of the leaders' initial goals for participants, which included "increasing self-worth" as third in a hierarchy of seventeen possible goals, and "getting close to others" as fifteenth. The initial goals for participants as seen by leaders do not necessarily correspond with those areas most frequently noted as showing up in changed behavior of participants.

5. Moscow (1971), using the same measure, found that 50 percent of a sample of persons in a two-week training laboratory in the Netherlands had at least one "verified" change, along with 33 percent and 37 percent of two control groups. He also quotes verified-change rates of 59 percent and 58 percent for laboratories held in the U.K. and the U.S.A.

6. Following McNemar's (1949) formula, the critical ratio was defined as $D/\frac{\delta d}{N}$,

where D = mean difference (change score, δ d = standard deviation of the difference, and N = number of cases). Positive changes larger than the critical ratio were called "plus," negative ones "minus," and all other changes were defined as "no change."

7. Persons who had been found to be casualties through interviews were not included in this judgment process.

8. The experimental population was composed of sixty-five women and 144 men. An analysis of variance at Time 1, which showed that the percentage of variance variables, suggested that a multivariate analysis of covariance on the thirty-three added by sex ranged from 4 to 15 percent on a total of seventeen different outcome variables might be revealing of more discrete sex differences in types of changes. Only one of the thirty-three change measures, when Time 1 scores were adjusted, proved to discriminate among men and women. The change signs and the outcome classifications were also reviewed for male-female differences. By and large, they did not prove to be substantial.

9. Experimental-control differences at Time 1 were evaluated by tests of differences in outcome indicators collected at Time 1. Of seventy-eight indicators, only three showed significant differences ($p \leq .05$), a number which establishes confidence that the two populations did not differ at outset. Even so, for the analyses in this and later sections, multivariate analysis of covariance was employed to hold constant the pretest level of all variables. Similar tests were performed to determine whether the 125 persons in the Time 1–3 panel were any different from the forty-nine persons who provided only Time 1–2 data.

10. Multivariate Analysis of Covariance, Time 1 scores entered as covariates (MESA 98).

11. These are overall p values for a linear combination of indices within each change area.

12. Looking at the changes in the Time 1–2 panel and nonreturner populations, only four of seventy-three variables showed significant differences ($p \leq .05$), yielding confidence that the changes noted in the Time 1–3 panel were representative of the changes which would have been found had the total experimental population returned instruments at the long post. In comparison with those who did not return data, panel members: (1) showed more of an increase in self-rated awareness of other's feelings toward them; (2) showed more of an increase in self-rated opportunities to share with others; (3) showed a smaller increase in number of categories used to view others' work-oriented characteristics; and (4) decreased slightly in hours spent with close friends (while nonreturners increased). The general picture on these four significant differences is not consistent; the first three suggest more peer orientation on the part of panel members, and the last, less.

13. Here, too, there were few statistically significant sex differences. At Time 2, (pre- to short post): (1) women tended to use withdrawal/denial less than did men, but shifted slightly in the male direction, (2) women wished for more controlling behavior from others than men, and increased this wish from Time 1 to 2, while men decreased, (3) women's expression of control toward others was at a lower level than men's, but both men and women increased their expression of control, (4) women used fewer cognitive categories than did men to describe others in work-oriented respects, but increased more on this than did men, and (5) women, starting at about the same level as men, increased more than men on the "decisiveness" variable—the proportion of one's life space about which decisions had been made. No sex differences in Time 1–2 changes occurred in the domain of attitudes and values, or in self-picture. At Time 1–3 (pre- to long post): (1) women were less likely to use withdrawal/denial than were men, but shifted slightly in the male direction, (2) women began with slightly higher levels of wishing to receive affection from others, but dropped substantially below the male level by Time 3, (3) women began with higher levels of expressed affection (as seen by the self) than men, and dropped, while men rose (at Time 3 men were higher than women), (4) women began with higher levels of expressed affection (as seen by the self) than men, and dropped, while men rose (at Time 3 men were higher than women), (4) women began with higher self-esteem than men, and maintained their level; men rose and exceeded women on this measure at Time 3, (5) women felt their relationship with their

closest friend had improved, while men felt it had worsened, and (6) both men and women improved their perceived opportunities for communicating with peers in their interpersonal environment, but women started from a much higher position (had more opportunities available, as they saw it), and improved a bit more than did men. No sex differences were found in changes in the attitudes and values area.

The picture is mixed: women moved away from the stereotyped "female" position on three variables (denial, received affection, expressed affection), and toward the stereotyped "female" position on two (improved relationship with friend and peer communication opportunities). Women were initially higher than men in self-esteem, though gained more in self-esteem. Though the short post evidence suggests that encounter group experience, when it does affect men and women differently, may have a freeing, "de-stereotyping" effect, the long post evidence is mixed on this count.

14. Multivariate Analysis of Covariance, Contrast Analysis; Time 1 scores entered as covariates (MESA 98).

15. Can we generalize to other groups run by these same leaders? Were the groups studied typical, more effective, or less so than usual? Leaders were requested to rate the degree to which a series of seventeen learning goals had been achieved, in comparison with the achievement in their usual groups. The mean rated goal achievement corresponded to "Somewhat below average when compared to my usual groups." Goals such as "becoming sensitive to others' feelings," "seeing others in more human terms," "sharing with peers," "learning how others view them," and "discovering more means of relating to others" were best achieved—though all fell below the point "About average when compared to my usual groups." Least well achieved were goals such as "becoming more spontaneous," "understanding inner feelings," "getting to know others deeply," and "expressing anger directly to people." In the leaders' view, the Stanford groups enabled interpersonal transactions and contact at a slightly below average level, but fell a good bit short of the more intense interpersonal contact and inner understanding to which the leaders claimed they had been accustomed.

When the leaders were asked, after the groups, to assess the norms which had been characteristic of their groups, again on a comparative basis, they felt the Stanford groups had been less open, less feelingful, less self-disclosing, and less involved than their usual groups, and more withdrawing, resistant, and dependent.

Can these judgments be trusted? Possibly not. The leaders were being closely scrutinized and may have wished not to be judged on the basis of the present groups. It should be recalled that they tended to miss or minimize casualties in their groups, which supports this possibility. Leaders' self-images as competent would be maintained by the claim that their usual groups were better. But the judgments may also be trustworthy; these were respected professionals with much comparative group experience. Although the analysis showed low correlations between individual member judgments of change and leaders' evaluations, the leaders' judgments of average individual member gain correlated .30 (not significant) with group yield at the short post, suggesting some relationship. And the leaders' judgment of the degree to which their groups had achieved learning goals they felt were important correlated .44 with group yield.

Perhaps perceived factors in the Stanford population might account for the leaders' ratings. In the leaders' view, the Stanford students were rated as brighter, but less sensitive than their usual group members; the leaders also felt that they were slightly less able to spot pathology (though they felt there was less of it than usual). There were no differences in average ability to understand the students, or in how much the leader himself had learned.

Perhaps features of the research situation, such as the questionnaires, the fact that the groups carried credit, observers' presence, tape recordings, or poor meeting rooms might have led to lower ratings. However, only the research questionnaires and the meeting rooms were rated, on the average, as having "some" influence. An analysis of high-yield and low-yield groups showed no relationship between the rated influence of questionnaires, or rooms, and group yield. There was, on the other hand, some relationship between a leader's view of the questionnaires and his rating of goal achievement. Of the seven lower-rating leaders, five said the questionnaires had had quite a bit or a great deal of influence. Only one of the five higher-rating leaders said so. This lends weight to the look-good hypothesis, as well as to the idea that leaders who felt frustrated with their groups blamed the research questionnaires as the contributing factor. Finally, perhaps the fact that the group meetings were more spaced out in time than these leaders' usual groups (which for most leaders were more typically run on weekends on a residential basis) accounted for lower ratings. On balance, similar (or possibly better) positive outcomes might be expected from these leaders in their ordinary circumstances.

Would there be more or fewer casualties in their usual groups? We do not know: Leaders undernoticed and underplayed casualties in the study situation. They were probably less likely to use high-risk techniques (heavy confrontation, challenge) under such close scrutiny, so that more casualties might be likely in their usual groups. On the other hand, random-assignment in the study may have exposed some persons to high-risk environments who, in usual groups, would be eliminated by self-selection. All in all, the evidence remains ambiguous with regard to the adequacy of the sample of leader behavior.

CHAPTER 4

High Learners

In this chapter we shall look at the "High Learners," individuals who had a highly constructive experience in the group, the effects of which were still apparent six months later. How did we identify them? The procedure described in Chapter 3 rated the outcome of the 174 individuals who completed the group sessions. Each participant's change in a number of major areas (eleven immediately postgroup, ten at the six-month follow-up, thirteen in all) was examined and a final judgment made as to whether he was a Negative Changer, Unchanged, a Moderate Changer or a High Learner. Two separate and independent ratings were made, one the individual's status at the end of the group, and another for his status six months later.

The participants whose outcome tallies were convincingly positive underwent positive change in five or more areas with little, if any, offsetting negative change. Fifteen individuals could be identified by this definition as High Learners at the six-month follow-up; nineteen others who were High Learners at the end of the group either backslid or did not return for the six-month follow-up.

Consider some illustrative examples at the long post (see Table 4–1): F. D. improved significantly in his view of self, in the use of mature adaptive styles of coping with dilemmas, in his perception of the availability of social opportunities in his environment, and in his ability to perceive others in more complex ways; he viewed encounter groups as safer, more genuine, and of more social benefit; he explicitly stated that the group had been a constructive experience in which he learned a great deal. He commented, "I am more aware now, because of the group experience, of my feelings at a given moment toward someone, and am aware when I am not expressing them, and when I'm playing social games. Because of this awareness I think I more often express my true feelings." One of his closest friends described him as having become more "involved with life," more sensitive, and more interested in developing and utilizing his personal resources, more "interested in nature, people, and experience."

TABLE 4-1
Change Signs for High Learners—Six Months Post Group

Group Number	Subject Number	Attitudes	Change Orientation	Value Change System	Self-View of Behavior	Coping	Self-Esteem	Conceptions of Others	External Interpersonal Environment	Testimony	Social Network
1	9 N. V.	+	0	+	+	0	+	0	0	+	0
2	11 F. D.	+	0	0	0	+	+	+	+	+	+
2	18 C. V.	0	0	0	+	0	+	+	M	+	0
3	22 N. C.	+	+	0	0	0	+	0	+	+	0
6	62 F. Y.	+	+	+	+	0	0	0	+	+	M
7	68 N. K.	0	0	+	+	0	+	+	0	0	M
7	70 D. T.	+	+	0	0	−	+	0	0	+	+
8	76 C. N.	+	0	+	+	0	−	0	+	+	M
8	79 E. T.	+	+	+	+	−	0	0	M	+	0
12	119 L. L.	−	−	+	+	+	+	0	0	+	+
13	129 L. C.	+	0	0	+	0	+	−	M	+	M
14	142 M. Q.	+	0	0	+	+	+	+	M	0	M
14	144 R. C.	0	0	+	0	+	+	0	+	+	0
17	166 D. G.	+	+	0	+	+	0	0	M	+	+
17	173 S. V.	+	−	+	+	+	−	0	+	+	0

KEY:

+ = significant positive change; 0 = unchanged; − = significant decrement; M = missing. Signs of change (+, 0, −, M) are, as previously discussed in Chapter 3, based on a statistic developed from a critical ratio procedure.

F. Y. improved significantly in her self-perceived interpersonal behavior and in her perception of the availability of opportunities in her environment for more productive and satisfying relationships. She underwent a significant value shift as she increasingly turned her attention to personal growth and fulfillment. She, too, viewed encounter groups as safer, more genuine, and of more social benefit. On the testimony questionnaires, she rated her experience as having been extremely rewarding and constructive. In her own words:

I found that the experiences in the group started me thinking and facing myself in a new way, a way I never risked before for fear of the weaknesses or incompleteness that I'd find. However, since facing them, recognizing more my needs and more which direction I needed to start or try to start in, I started acting on my thoughts, not just thinking them. Also the experience has helped me face and interact with people in a new and more honest forthright way. I'm not as sweet and acquiescent as before and I no longer docilely tolerate or overlook the games that people attempt to play with me. It's so beautiful, so exciting to not only think but to know that people can experience deeper levels with each other, and not just with their closest, most trusted friends. But one can't just think about this ideal or hope, one has to try to live its reality.

The identification of High Learners was not a mechanical process of summing the number of instruments that showed a significant positive change. The entire profile of the outcome instrument results for each individual was considered along with all available ancillary data. (This included, for example, interview data on over 50 percent of the participants stemming from separate investigations of casualty suspects, dropouts, and highly visible learners.) Furthermore, as Chapter 3 describes, not all instruments or areas of change were equally weighted.

These methods of identifying High Learners were conservative. The individuals considered to be High Learners have convincing change profiles. Is it possible that our methodology was too stringent and failed to identify all individuals with highly positive outcomes? Might not a participant have made extraordinary gains in only a single outcome sector, such as self-esteem? And would he then have failed to meet the criteria? This is not probable. Personal change is rarely sector-tight. It is doubtful that an individual can undergo *marked* shifts in one area, for example self-esteem, without changing also in such areas as interpersonal presentation of self, ability to establish closer relationships, coping styles, etc.

Our definition of high change is not synonymous with high enthusiasm, a conversion experience, or massive positive transference to the leader. Although most of the High Learners spoke very positively of their group and their leader, high testimony was not a requirement of the High Learner status. One High Learner, F. D., rated his leader as passive and ineffectual, and cryptically describes him as "A nice guy but not cut out to be a leader." Another, D. T., rated his leader as incompetent, ineffective, remote, and passive: "He had little understanding of the group, many times tried to push interpretations and direct our searchings to inappropriate areas." The High Learners who were in the leaderless encounter tape groups felt highly dissatisfied with their automatized leader.

Conversely, many who were enthusiastic about the group, extolled their leaders, and encouraged large numbers of acquaintances to enter encounter groups had little evidence of positive change.

Table 3–4 in Chapter 3 shows the postgroup and six-month follow-up outcome results. Fifteen individuals had enough significant positive change to warrant being called High Learners. Nine of these had been High Learners immediately after the end of the group and had maintained their learning; five had been Moderate Changers and one had been considered Unchanged at the end of the group, but six months later had a High Learner profile of change.

Consider the subjects rated High Learners on the basis of outcome data immediately at the end of their group: Of the total of twenty-eight, eleven did not return for the six-month follow-up,[1] nine maintained their High Learner status, four slipped back slightly to Moderate Learner status, three slipped even farther to Unchanged status, and one subject radically altered his change profile to the position of Negative Changer. Thus, of those High Learners who returned for follow-up, slightly over half retained their High Learner status, and 75 percent retained some positive change position.

Note that there are no High Learners at the six-month follow-up who at the end of the group were Negative Learners, and only one who was unchanged at the end of the group. This finding is contrary to the often expressed sentiment that an individual who appears not to have profited, or who may even seem shaken up immediately after the group may in the ensuing months "put it all together" and eventually profit greatly from the experience. Our data indicate that, to a great extent, individuals who at the end of the group are either negatively changed or untouched tend to remain that way. We do not imply that the High Learners invariably had a tranquil course following their group experience. Changes in their environment, either fortuitous or occasioned by changes in behavior, often precipitated short-lived personal storms. Had they been examined during the eye of the storm, the changes might not have appeared to be tending in a positive direction. For example, one High Learner, C. N., was interviewed as a casualty suspect because he started psychotherapy after the group. Following the group he returned home for the summer, was separated from his girlfriend, and re-entered a highly conflictual living arrangement with his parents. A depression ensued, he consulted a psychiatrist, and felt that he made excellent use of the four therapy sessions he had. He pointed out that one of the benefits of the group was that he learned it was possible to obtain help through talking about his problems with friends as well as with experts in the area. He soon learned to cope more adaptively with his highly restrictive, negating mother, and on return to school in the fall he continued to make good personal progress. (C. N. will be discussed in greater detail later in this chapter.)

Types of Learning

Table 4–1 depicts the results of the questionnaire data for each High Learner. There are in-depth interviews with half of the High Learners on the nature of the group experience, the types of changes they underwent, and the maintenance of these changes. Most of the quotations in this chapter are from transcriptions of these interviews.

In addition, for each there are several "open-ended" impressionistic questionnaires. For example, they were asked whether the group had induced any changes in them, and if so, to describe the changes. The same question was asked in two different forms at the six-month follow-up. They were asked for their opinions about the group and leader; they were asked to describe the most significant event of each meeting and of the whole experience, and in a number of ways they were encouraged to expand their answers to the structured questionnaires.

INTERPERSONAL OPENNESS

The single most prevalent description of change was in the general area of interpersonal openness. Participant after participant described his greater openness, honesty, confrontation, directness, or simply his ability to "let it all hang out." As one stated, "The most important thing I learned in the group was that complete honesty is of the utmost importance in sustaining a relationship with another person." Others learned that telling another what you thought of him, "cleared the air" and enabled them to relate more closely. "I told another girl in the dorm who had intimidated me for months that I found her intimidating and that it made me feel I wasn't worth as much as she. We get along a lot better now." And another said, "All year there's this chick upstairs who keeps asking me to do her favors. I finally told her I wished she'd stop asking me to do things for her and instead come down and just talk to me sometimes. One of the intense pleasures I have in life now is talking straight to people. That pleasure simply wasn't open to me before." Another said, "I know that others don't get my feelings through osmosis without my having to tell them. Now I know I have to tell people what I want them to know; they can't mind-read."

An extreme example of expressing feelings was offered by L. C., a participant in Synanon. More than anything else he learned to "follow a gut reaction," and described a fracas in a traffic jam where he finally got out of his car and vigorously told off another driver. "It was nice to get something out that was all penned up inside, and besides it's a lot better than putting it all on my wife."

Others coupled openness with the process of "feedback." They were now open enough to ask others directly about how they feel about them, or, as one High Learner, N. C., put it: "I can tell people when I dislike them or disagree with something they're doing. I like to get this kind of feedback and I know that others appreciate hearing it from me."

A few qualified the desirability of openness or placed limits on it; they caution against blind allegiance to the idol of total honesty. One said, "What I've really learned is that I must be honest with others to achieve a complete relationship. But I know that there is also a place for tact and I don't think you should be honest to the point of needlessly hurting others." Others learned too late; one subject (not a High Learner) stated: "I have a bitter attitude towards encounter groups and the ideal of frankness, since under the influence of the frankness concept I said things that really hurt my girlfriend and then I broke up with her." A friend of one of the participants commented even more starkly on this risk: "John has been changed by the group but in a bad direction. Under the guise of honesty and openness he has become cruel and thoughtless of others. He's fine at getting things off his chest, but rather thoughtless about others." A parent of another participant (not a High Learner) echoed this comment:

> Frankly I was upset at his one visit home a year ago when he was in your course. He seemed to be very callous about tactfulness, kindness, and consideration to others. He had never been this way until he was exposed to your group therapy that seemed to think "frankness" was *everything!* It is *NOT.* Good manners must still exist. Many immature adolescents are not prepared to be criticized and *told* which of their faults need "improvement" before a group. Jim survived it. He did not complain. But, I do not approve such an approach for everyone and anyone!

In summary then, many High Learners changed in their methods of relating to others: They behaved in a more trusting, open, honest manner; they hid less of themselves; they expressed their opinions more forthrightly; they gave feedback to others, and requested it for themselves. They also perceived that adaptive openness is curvilinear; too much as well as too little can jeopardize human relationships.

CONCEPTION OF SELF

Table 4–1 indicates that ten of the fifteen High Learners showed a significant positive shift in their self-system. Their self-esteem and sense of personal worth increased. They became more self-directed and less other-directed; the center of their self-regard was now positioned within their ego boundaries, rather than in the perceived appraisals of others. The words used to describe this shift were very different, but this basic theme was the same:

I have a lot more self-confidence. I used to feel like I was hiding a lot of stuff from everyone. I don't have to hold back now. I'm not scared anymore; I'm more spontaneous. It used to be really important to me whether someone liked me, and now that's not so because I realize everyone can't like you.

Another High Learner said that the group was the first time in his life where he has been in a situation where people told him honestly what they felt about him. He was well-received by them and generalized that to other situations with people. "I never thought others regarded me well, and now I see that this was projection and that the acts I thought were hostile to me weren't true. I used to play a role, keep up a front, and put across an image of myself based on my accomplishments. I just don't feel that's necessary any longer."

Another said, "I have to be what I am and not what other people want me to be. Everyone is different. Some people can do things better than me —I can do some things better than them."

And, "I'm no longer concerned that much about my image. I'm more comfortable with me. I don't have to play roles anymore. I am myself in all roles and, man, that's a big difference."

A greater centering of the self usually results in greater stability of esteem. Self-concept is for some High Learners no longer a fickle, bobbing balloon prey to the winds of others' judgments. "I don't really need others to validate me. In the past if others shunned me I'd be wiped out for a week."

One participant phrased it eloquently:

As a result of the encounter group I am more inner-directed. It's not that I'm impervious to what others are thinking, but I don't receive my ultimate sense of value from others. *Before the group the fear of rejection was the organizing principle for my behavior.* I just couldn't take any rejection of myself. Now I know that others can't give me a self and can't give me a life.

Most High Learners developed a sense of their own worth which was outside of petty day-by-day failures or successes. This stability permitted more self-extension and more risk-taking. "I could take chances with others. I don't have to hide in corners anymore to avoid getting hurt. This has really been great with girls and I have a good love relationship now with a girl." Another participant had always been terrified of groups, but after a very positive experience in a group which let him know of their acceptance of him, he now moves in and out of groups with relative ease. Another stated:

I can be myself more and not try to hide things I think other people wouldn't approve of. I used to do this all the time. People didn't accept me the way I was, so obviously there was no reason why I should even want to have anything to do with them. There's not any sense in having them accept me wearing a mask, so I don't say anymore, "What would they think of me if I did this, or maybe I'd better not do it." I've gone out of my way to meet new people that I wouldn't have thought about meeting before. If people just can't accept me where I am that's just too bad. You don't have to be anything except just what you are.

ASSUMPTION OF RESPONSIBILITY FOR SELF

A few High Learners reported that they felt more in charge of themselves; they realized that others can't really manipulate one's own feelings unless they are allowed to "bug" them, put them down, frighten them, belittle them, make them lonely, etc. One subject reported that he learned to separate his emotional responses into those that were intrinsic, over which he had little or no power like hunger and sex, and into those that he could change in some way, like his need always to be best or to be right.

ACCEPTANCE OF OTHERS

Several High Learners reported a greater respect and tolerance for the ways, opinions, and foibles of others. "I used to tell people what they should think and how they should feel. Now I can say 'Here's what I feel and what you feel is up to you.' What others feel may be okay for them." Others talked about a destereotyping process. They had often put people into boxes and kept them there by not attending to other evidence, or by reacting to them in such a way that a narrow and corroborating band of behavior was evoked from them. The group allowed them an opportunity to humanize others. One phrased it, "I can put up with others a lot easier now without trying to force them to change or without having to try and burn down their house or something like that." Another spoke of how he was initially turned off to an "uptight" 4.0 (straight A) student bound for Law School. "He disgusted me—that type always does. But I got to know him in the group. He smokes grass, has his own hang-ups, and I learned that in his way he's a neat guy." Another had come from a conservative, somewhat bigoted home. He worked through a strong initial dislike of a radical boy in the group, and found himself more accepting and understanding of those who are different.

One High Learner began the group with the cruel tendency to mock others and, by the end of the experience, had left much adolescent baggage behind him: "One of my first impressions in the group was about this twenty-two-year-old freaky kid who looked like a sixteen-year-old bright-eyed dropin from Mars. I wondered 'How can anyone who looks like this really be real?' But gradually I began to see that this was a really nice, alive, wonderful person." Several in the same manner altered and humanized their attitudes toward their parents. Some began to view their parents as struggling, uncertain, but nonetheless caring individuals. Others went further and began a new and open dialogue with their parents which awakened long dormant parent-child tenderness.

COPING

Table 4–1 displays the results of the coping questionnaire described in Chapter 3. When confronted with personal dilemmas, six High Learners made highly significant changes in their coping strategies. Rather than avoid the problem by denial, flight into substitute activity, or some other evasive tactic, they more often confronted the issue in an adaptive fashion.

In interviews, several High Learners gratuitously offered this shift as an important aspect of their learning. In general they described the development of diagnostic skills which they could use for their own as well as others' problems. They learned to remove themselves from the swirling vortex of a personal storm, to figure out what was going on and how to take sensible steps to change the situation. They rarely learned a specific method of diagnostic framework; rather, they learned how to assume the diagnostic pose.

One High Learner, E. T., who had been in a transactional-analysis group remarked that although his leader used the Berne parent-child-adult schema, he did not himself use those concepts. "I do try to analyze and understand why I'm unhappy or tense, and then try to change it. I didn't get a particular solution from my group, but a framework in which to work out a solution." He gave as an example a recent situation in which his parents had come for a prolonged visit. He grew increasingly "uptight," the whole family soon began growling at one another, and the resumption of overt internecine hostilities seemed imminent. He then backed away psychologically from the situation, tried to look dispassionately at his spiraling irritation, and decided that he resented spending every afternoon, evening, and weekend with his parents; he had other important relationships, he had school demands, and, too, he missed his occasional grass. However, he felt guilty about not wanting to see his parents since they had come so far to see him. Bolstered by his encounter experience he confronted his anxiety and his parents by telling them about his internal state, and about the strain between his need for more time of his own and his desire to see them. The result was a gratifying one: not only was a reasonable scheduling compromise worked out, but he felt closer to his parents.

Another High Learner, C. N., also in a transactional-analysis group, stated:

The technique of my leader was transactional analysis—the Parent-Child type thing—and sometimes when I'm really confused about things I stop and ask myself, "What the hell is making me do that? . . . My God, is it in response to all the shitty things my mother did to me as a kid, you know how I feel about that, or was it a response that I'm making on my own accord?" That's a fairly complicated theory and I didn't learn it totally by him explaining it for an hour or two during the group, but it kind of gave me some guidelines to go on. It does help a bit and makes you think back. Part of that technique was in saying, "Well, what would so and so think about you if you did this?" and I'd kind of ask myself that and say, "Well, he thinks this, but what would I think?" and I'd get straightened out in my head as to who was thinking what. It was like the decision was going to affect me, not whoever was thinking that about me, or whatever.

In a similar vein, another High Learner was faced with the loss of a girlfriend who went to Europe for six months. He stated, "My first move was to just get stoned, and race around frantically contacting other people to avoid being alone. I knew this was the same old bag I always put myself in. I stopped everything and started really asking, 'Why are you doing this to yourself?' I've gotten to a lot stronger position since."

One High Learner talked about being faced with an important life decision (whether to go to Europe for a year with his girlfriend) which previously would have driven him to distraction. He tried an approach he had seen his group leader use: he objectively tabulated all the advantages and disadvantages of the possible decisions and then made a choice which felt good to him. He disclosed that he actively resisted a typical response method: hitching down to Big Sur and getting away from everything until chance made the decision for him.

Another subject gave this example: His roommates accused him of some deceit about a financial matter (concerning the rent money). Rather than rushing off hot-faced to hide in the library and gnaw at his entrails, he went to his roommates, engaged in a lengthy discourse with them, and got to the bottom of the issue and the surrounding feelings. He stated that he was much more able to live with himself after that.

The change that occurred was, in general, the instillation of an observing, diagnosing ego and, usually, the employment of a confrontation mode of problem solution rather than some form of problem denial or evasion.

VALUE SHIFT

Table 4–1 suggests that eight of the fifteen High Learners underwent a significant shift in their value system, as measured by value instruments (see Chapter 3 for details). In interviews, many reported some value shift toward the direction of "consciousness III." They described a greater devotion to humanistic aims and a greater resistance to confinement by the technocratic establishment. As one put it:

The group helped me to understand what things in this life really mean anything to me; and what was limiting me that shouldn't be. It's made me determined to resist the impositions of other people that interfere with the kind of life I think I should lead. For example, I've decided to resist the draft and absolutely refuse military duty.

Or another: "I believe I'm doing more what I want to do rather than make others feel that I have picked the mold they have made for me. I feel much less urgency today." Or yet another: "The best part of the group was the weekend we spent together. We were so open and free. I inwardly revolted against having to return to Stanford's artificial walled-in world." The most cryptic commentary on this subject was an answer given by one girl to the question (at the six-month follow-up), "Have you made any major life decisions in the past six months?" She penned in, "No decision seems major anymore!" A friend of one of the Time 1 High Learners wrote in the social network questionnaire, "John is less studious, more degenerate, does less, but enjoys it more." (This participant was one who did not return for the six-month follow-up.)

Many (nine) High Learners tended to make important life decisions that reflected a shift in values:

Decided to go to medical school, rather than enter the Peace Corps. Teach —get competent experience in mainstream of American life before leaving and complaining. . . . Dropped out of Stanford. . . . Decided to stay in school for a while. . . . Shacked up with a chick for a while. . . . Decided to spend this summer and fall in Vietnam as Volunteer in Asia. . . . Got married. . . . Moved from California. . . . Draft, school, and marriage. . . . Decided to spend the summer on my own, staying alone, visiting parents. . . . I accepted my grandfather's death. . . . I decided the mystic spiritual path was the way to true freedom for me, and that I should spend my life following it. I made the decision to drop out of school because I felt it to be contrary to this goal. . . . I was almost drowned. I started a cool thing with this girl that we intensify each time we see each other.

The task, however, of judging whether the change is a constructive or destructive one is a nightmarish chore for the researcher. We can illustrate this by considering one High Learner, C. N., in detail:

C. N. was rated a High Learner because of improvement at the six-month follow-up in a number of areas including his self-perceived impersonal behavior, his extremely high testimony as to the constructive value of the group, his appraisal of an increased number of social opportunities in his environment, his greater "humanization" of others ("more interested in people as individuals and respect for them for what they are—not for what I think they should be").

His values and life-styles also underwent some drastic change which was easily observable in his relationship to athletics. He was an outstanding athlete and had come to the University on a full tuition swimming scholarship. His work in the group radically altered his perspective. In an interview he stated:

"My swimming went beyond the swimming itself, like it was kind of an ego type thing because I didn't have a lot of friends and I was somehow kind of justifying my existence by winning a race or something, plus trying to cut down on my sex drives and that sort of thing by swimming all the time. But I kind of came to grips with myself and saw that swimming was taking me away from people and that's where I wanted to be. Like I was out swimming eight hours a day, swimming in the morning, swimming in the afternoon, exhausted in the evening, and what kind of relationships can you have with people when you're exhausted all the time and gone all the time? I just couldn't stand that anymore. I was getting into myself and realizing why I was trying to win races and be competitive and all that sort of thing. I'm kind of out of sports right now consequently, and I am confident about this decision."

It's hard to quarrel with the fact that C. N. underwent some profound and, from an eight-month vantage point, enduring change. He altered his interpersonal coping style from an evasive, distancing mode to a direct, confrontative personal mode which resulted in a number of new, close friends and the establishment of an important love relationship. His self-image, too, has altered:

"I suppose I'm not as concerned about the image I present to people. When you're wound up in a thing like swimming, they're almost selling you a way of life in terms of appearance and attitudes, and, you know, the competitive spirit and things like that. You're worried about your self-image if you're always competing because you're trying to show people, 'Look at me; I'm better than you' or something like that. Although there is, I admit, a satisfaction to competition. In fact, I really can't see myself competing anymore. It's really strange; I haven't been in a race since last spring, haven't swum competitively."

His new set of values soon brought him into conflict with his traditional environment. His relationship with his rather inflexible parents grew even more strained during a stormy visit home. To maintain his $2,000 scholarship he had only to make a token appearance at swim practice, but declined to assume that form of hypocritical liaison with the establishment. He answered the six-month follow-up question, "Have you made any major life decisions?" by noting, "Yes, have decided it's useless to play follow-the-leader."

Although he has had periods of discomfort he feels he has grown considerably. Viewed from others' perspective, however, the changes in C. N. were less sanguine. His college athletic coach lost a star performer who, in his eyes, had "defected to the crazies." One can imagine the reaction of his high school swim coach who devoted endless hours and, no doubt, was much invested in C. N.'s future success. Imagine, too, the reactions of his conservative parents who now must pay the $2,000 tuition, have witnessed a partial radicalization of their son, and have had to adjust to C. N.'s experimentation with such total honesty that he revealed to them his experiences with drugs and sex.

Another striking example of a High Learner undergoing a controversial shift in values and life-style is C. V. His case is discussed in greater detail later in this chapter; but note here that, though the group was an exceedingly constructive experience for him, he answered the question about whether he had made any major life decisions thusly: "I decided that the mystic spiritual path was the way to true freedom for me, and that I should spend my life following it. I made the decision to drop out of school because it was contrary to this goal." The shift in values appeared to be at variance with C. V.'s gains. Further investigation, however, revealed that he embarked upon a period of serious questioning—a "psychosocial moratorium," to use Erikson's term, which eventually proved to be of considerable value in his personal search for identity.

It was quite difficult to evaluate the value change in one participant (a High Learner who did not return for his six-month follow-up). He became so involved in antiwar activity that he dropped out of college and

145

alienated many of his old friends with the ferocity of his dedication. He accepted these losses, however, in the service of the peace cause:

> When I approach a person it's not in an "I want to meet you" way, but "How do I get my ideas across to you?" There are only twenty-four hours in a day and it's just a matter of time. Right now I'm just not interested in what people think of me personally; I'm more interested in getting my ideas across to them.

When we compare the value shifts of the High Learners to the shifts in some of the Unchanged or Negative Learners, the contrast is striking. For example, one participant responded to the major life decision query, "Decided to settle for less, decided to lower my goals in life, decided to act as responsible as I could, join the navy, all occurred the same day." This subject had a number of negative ratings and appraised his group experience as a destructive one. Given his overall change profile, it becomes easier to evaluate his shift in life-style as impulsive and maladaptive.

Another subject reported a value shift in an entirely different direction. He converted to a fundamentalist Christian religion and was leading an unusually orderly, even obsessive, life in which he spent considerable time praying for relief of his distress. He was interviewed at length since there were several indices which suggested he might have been a Casualty. We did not have quite enough evidence to consider him such, although it is certain he experienced considerable discomfort immediately following the group and eventually obtained solace from depression and anxiety through a religious conversion. Most observers would consider his change in life-style as a defensive maneuver, rather than an indication of or an accompaniment to growth.

An Unchanged subject struggled with a value conflict with no constructive resolution. A friend remarked on the "social network" questionnaire:

> He seems to be more concerned about the incongruity of living in a way which is unconcerned with material goods and directed toward helping other people (i.e. simple clothes, interest in Teacher Corps) and at the same time being very attracted to goals such as owning a Porsche and skiing frequently. . . . In his behavior, for example, last fall quarter he was on a "Spartan" kick of just wearing one pair of jeans and spending as little money as possible. Yet, at the same time, he would avidly talk about such goals as returning to Europe for a summer and owning a good sports car.

Some High Learners' major shifts in life-style, for example, increased militancy or dropping out of school, would not be evaluated by every observer as positive change. Shall we say of these participants that they learned a great deal and happened also to be struggling with the normal youthful search for an alternative life-style? Or shall we say that for some the encounter group was the incubator for dormant antiestablishment feelings? Or, is positive change in the young necessarily accompanied by signs of searching and defiance? Although our data does not contain an answer to this riddle, it does tell us that a nomothetic approach is inadequate. Each individual must be studied separately. Not all the High Learners experienced this value shift.

For some subjects, a period of intense value shuffling may well be a sign of growth; indeed initially some were fixed too low in the hierarchy of needs, too concerned about their acceptability, lovability, or ability to love or accept, even to consider the possibility that they might have the right to ask larger questions of themselves and others. Others may have moved too far and too quickly in their competence-achievement sphere without having resolved or even considered some important issues of identity. For these individuals, a "psychosocial moratorium" may be an extremely salubrious event.

We do not know how enduring or, for that matter, how "real" were the value shifts. We do note that, despite the avowed allegiance of some High Learners to experiencing and being, their achievement levels did not decline; they maintained their grade-point averages after the group. (This is discussed fully in Chapter 6.)

These personal changes, interpersonal openness, conception of self, responsibility for self, acceptance of others, coping styles, and value shifts have been selected for discussion because the High Learners stressed these areas. The list is not exhaustive and does not do justice to the rich complexity of patterns of change for some participants.

High Learners—Who Gets the Credit?

Our method of selecting High Learners differs in one particularly interesting manner from our identification of Casualties. By definition a Casualty had a negative psychological reaction that was both enduring and, to the best of our judgment, *a direct result of their encounter group experience.* Not so with the High Learners! We required only that they demonstrate significant positive learning at a point in time, approximately six months after the end of the group. If improvement occurred, we made an *a priori* assumption that the group was *the* or *a* responsible agent of change; we did not demand or expect any proof. Naturally our *a priori* mode is a treacherous one; how can we really ever know that the group was instrumental in the positive change present six months later?

One important indication that this may in fact be legitimate is that the data presented in Chapter 3 demonstrate that three times as many experimental subjects as control subjects had high positive change. To be sure there was less information available on the control population (for example, there were no interviews of control subjects), but, this factor would work to *reduce,* not to magnify, differences between the control and experimental populations. For the control population, high change on questionnaires automatically labeled a subject as High Learner, whereas for the experimental subjects, questionnaire evidence was necessary but not always sufficient. Negative ancillary information, such as evidence from an interview could, even in the face of high changes on the questionnaire, remove an experimental participant from the rolls of the High Learners. The reverse could not occur. Evidence of high learning from interview data alone was not sufficient to define an individual as a high changer; corroboration from highly positive change on the outcome instruments was necessary.

Did the subjects themselves award credit to the groups for their change? By no means! Several subjects were labelled High Learners despite their explicit denial that the group had been an important factor. Although, on written questionnaires, fourteen of the sixteen High Learners rated their group experience as having been positive and constructive, on interview many gratuitously offered that the group had been just a minor cog in the gears of change. We may illustrate these points by examining the alternative causes credited by the subjects.

GOOD TIMING

Some claimed that the group experience came at a "good" time, i.e. at a time when change would have occurred anyway; one High Learner vigorously denied that the group was a factor in his growth. He claimed instead that his change was due to "the process of growing up." He came to Stanford directly from an English public school, and he stressed the difficulty of obtaining skills in human relationships in the English authoritarian school system. In his first year at Stanford, he was having a difficult time finding his way socially and just at this point entered the encounter group. In the ensuing months he gradually acclimated himself to the Stanford social scene, made friends, and grew comfortable with his interpersonal relationships.

One subject was a transfer student from another campus and made the identical point: His awkwardness and discomfort at being in a new situation would have improved with or without the encounter group.

Another High Learner said he had been in "the tail end of the sophomore slump" when he entered the group. He's feeling a lot better now, but thinks it may be because he's simply "in another place" in his education.

Two High Learners emphasized that the group was perfectly timed; both had been through the throes of a severe identity crisis, and at the time of the group were emerging with a new sense of self. One stated, "The group came at a kind of good time for me so I think the progress I've made since then has not been directly as a result of the group. It's hard to weed out what is a result of the group and what isn't." The other, E. T., had left school prior to the group for a six-month solitary sojourn in the mountains. During this time he thought about himself, his relations to others, and the purpose of his life. In his solitary communion with nature he felt he achieved a state of peace with himself: he could be content, he realized, by being alone in a beautiful place; nothing else was essential; others weren't necessary for his well-being; he alone had the capacity to make himself happy or miserable. After he had assimilated these understandings he decided he could go back and relate to people differently, not because he needed their validation but because it would be "cool to be happy like that with others".

He returned to school immediately before the beginning of the encounter group, and found that the group offered an ideal opportunity to test out new ways of being and behaving with others, and to obtain feedback from these others which permitted him to make adaptive corrections.

There is little question but that six months later he had undergone highly significant positive change. Was it, we asked him, a result of the encounter group?

I don't know. It's really difficult to actually pinpoint it to the group. I understand that you learn by the situations you are placed in, and that it doesn't happen in any one place. I expect that the encounter group helped me in some particular ways, but I would be very hard-put to give you an exact accounting. I don't see a causal relationship between the encounter group and being happy, and relaxed and at peace with oneself. This year I've started a candle store, and I've done a lot more things that last year I wouldn't have considered doing. I don't know how much of that you can credit the encounter group. As a matter of fact, I would attribute it much more to my experience while being here.

Despite his disclaimers, we noted in an interview with him six months after termination, that the group and the leader were very much alive psychologically for him. He made good use of his experience in the group in his maintenance of learning. To give one brief illustration: Often when he finds himself caught in a dilemma he will remember the way someone in the group or the leader would have approached the same problem, or he might remember the leader's voice saying, "If you do something and you feel good about it, then it's what you should be doing and it's a good thing."

LIFE EVENTS FOLLOWING THE GROUP

Several High Learners pointed out that, although they had greatly changed during the time of the study, it was not due to the group (or not primarily to the group) but to other important events which occurred after the group. One High Learner (and several other subjects who were Moderate Changers) attributed his personal growth to a six-month stay at one of the Stanford-in-Europe campuses. (The size, less than 100, and close living arrangement of these campuses encourages considerable intimacy with other students and faculty, and often results in the individual becoming an involved member of a closely bonded cohesive group.)

Two High Learners claimed to have profited from a social psychology course they took the quarter following the group. Their new knowledge of motivational influences enabled them to maintain objectivity by observing and analyzing others. To illustrate, one described how he was able to apply behavioral analysis to interpersonal dilemmas. Recently in an argument with his grandfather in which his grandfather had been attacking radicals, he managed to keep his cool by objectively considering the fact that his grandfather had been reinforced for such behavior in the past.

Another pointed out that in the year following the group he had an entirely different type of school experience. For three years prior to that he had been taking a heavy load of science courses. In the next year he had nothing but humanities and a very light load. He felt this had been very important in the new and more positive way he felt about himself.

Another subject went through a severe crisis in his life where he experimented with extreme radicalism. During this time he established an important and ongoing relationship with a professor who was exceedingly helpful to him.

Were any High Learners helped by another encounter group following their experience in the project? Whereas 20 percent of the other experimental subjects had been in at least one other group, of the thirteen High Learners on whom we have this information, *not one* was in an encounter group in the six months following the project. Some of our interview data permit us to speculate on this finding. The High Learners may not have needed further encounter groups. They successfully mastered the task of transfer of learning, developed opportunties, and methods of applying their learning in their natural life space. Others who may have been stirred but not deeply changed by the group sought out additional encounter groups because they were not yet able to create social relationships conducive for continued learning.

Were any helped by psychotherapy? Of the thirteen High Learners on whom this information is available, two sought psychotherapy during the six months following the group. One of these saw a therapist only once and received some medication for a mild anxiety-depressive state. The other, however, had a positive experience with a therapist which probably contributed to his learning. We have already discussed this High Learner, C. N., who, due to a three-way collision between his altered life values, his tactlessness, and his conservative, alarmed parents, had a depressive episode for which he saw a therapist for several visits.

How then to evaluate the role of the group in the change process? We find it hardly surprising that the High Learners emphasize other factors that occurred in their lives. Our investigation of the maintenance of learning (see Chapter 14) revealed that change is more enduring if it is practiced and reinforced outside of the group. This is by no means a novel concept; the very first T-group leaders recognized the importance of transfer of learning and considerable emphasis was placed on helping individuals find ways to apply their in-group learning to their back-home situation. Nor is it unexpected that postgroup events should be deemed more salient. The postgroup period was, first of all, "real"; no matter how intense the encounter group seems, the participants know that the group is but a dress rehearsal for life. Many deny or attempt to deny that the encounter group is temporary; our interviews and group protocols indicate that a large number of subjects joined the groups with the explicit purpose of establishing permanent friendships, and with the unstated or unconscious one of finding a permanent group. If they do not evolve past this point and do not appreciate that the function of the encounter group is not sheer relating but learning *how to* relate, not living but learning *how to* live, then we would expect their gains to be evanescent. Although many participants reported in their interviews that they felt good in meeting, even months later, someone from their group, or that they felt a special kind of bond with fellow members, not one reported a single, meaningful, enduring friendship which had issued from the encounter groups.

Immediately following the group, one High Learner, N. C., formed an encounterlike group with three of his close friends (and roommates) and credited this second group with much of his change. He described the process in these terms:

> The one thing that really surprised me was that two weeks after the encounter group was over I didn't care about the people in that group so much; it was like in that context we could be very close, but in the outside world, in a social context, we couldn't be because we didn't have the same interests and we weren't very similar people. In a forced situation we could be close. The people that are my friends are people whom I've lived with closely, and people I've seen since. It was good to know you could talk to strangers and have them really get close to you in a short time. Knowing that with your friends with whom you've developed much more deep and longer lasting things is even more important; you could re-evaluate those ties in terms of things you've learned through the group. It was sort of disappointing; you look at those people and say, "yeah, we had something once that was really strange and close," but it doesn't seem real. . . .

How often do we note the same phenomenon in the investigation of psychotherapy (and especially brief therapy) outcome (Yalom, 1970)? Patients may report that they are better, but cite a number of external or environmental ameliorating factors: new friends, new social groups, a love relationship, greater satisfaction and greater achievement at work, etc. We cannot suggest that these factors were unimportant in the positive change that occurred, but we must not ignore the fact that the potential friends, the new social groups, the work satisfaction were always "out there" waiting for the individual. Not until the group experience mobilized him to take advantage of these resources was he able to exploit them for his satisfaction and personal growth.

We gain some clarity on this issue when we realize that the group cannot and need not accomplish the entire task of change. Many individuals receive a slight boost from the group which may come, for example, as a result of risk taking, of disclosing to others a hidden and presumably unacceptable part of themselves; the result is often that he is so accepted by the group members that he is willing to take a similar risk with others outside the group. This process (the very reverse of the vicious circle in which many psychiatric patients are enmeshed) may be referred to as an adaptive spiral which, once set into motion gains inertia, but whose origins in the encounter group experience may be either forgotten or deemed feeble in comparison with powerful real life events.

What of the opposite argument? Is it not possible that undergraduate students are in such terment, are passing through a period of life when marked changes are the rule rather than the exception, that introducing an encounter group into an undergraduate's life (and crediting it with change) is not totally unlike starting an electric fan in a monsoon and measuring the ensuing breeze? The undergraduate years are a time of great turbulence. The social network data presented in Chapter 3 indicate that three-fourths of the subjects, both controls and group participants, were viewed by acquaintances as having changed over a six-month period. This is a considerably higher percentage than reported for adults on the same measuring instrument (Miles, 1965). The "major decision" questionnaire is witness also to the flux of this life stage: over half of all subjects, both controls and group participants, considered that they had made some significant, major decision over a six-month period.

Though the arguments cannot be dismissed, we can bring some further data to bear on the issue. Chapter 3 indicates that, despite the movement in the entire undergraduate population, the experimental participants change much more than the controls. Only 4 percent of the control subjects (High Learners) made extensive positive shifts on change measures, as compared with 16 percent of the participants who completed the group experience.

If the groups had little causal relationship to outcome, if the High Learners achieved their gains because of good "timing" or because of fortuitous subsequent life events, then one would expect to find the fifteen High Learners (or the original twenty-eight at the group's ending) evenly distributed among the seventeen groups. But the distribution is not random. Several groups produced multiple High Learners, while seven produced none at all.

HIGH LEARNERS' PERCEPTIONS OF IMPORTANT CHANGE
EXPERIENCES

In the eyes of the High Learners what were the valuable or productive occurrences in the group? Data bearing on this question come from several sources: the "How Do Encounter Groups Work" instrument, the "Critical Event" instrument, Self-Disclosure instruments, and retrospective interviews.

"How Do Encounter Groups Work?" is a questionnaire described in detail in Chapter 12. Basically it consists of a list of fourteen descriptions of mechanisms by which groups effect change. Each participant was asked whether each mechanism: (1) did not apply to his learning in the group; (2) applied somewhat; and (3) was an important part of his learning experience. He was then asked to select the two most important learning factors.

There are few striking differences between the High Learners' explanation of how their group worked and the explanations of those who were unchanged. We note that Item 7 ("The group helped me understand the type of impact I have on others; they told me honestly what they thought of me and how I came across") is considered most important by both High Learners and Unchanged participants. All subjects valued such items as "universality" ("I learned that we're all in the same boat. My problems, feelings, fears are not unique and I share much with others in the group.") and "catharsis" ("I was able to express feelings very fully; I was able to say what I felt rather than holding it in; I was able to express negative and/or positive feelings toward others").

The one major difference between the High Learners and the Unchanged group was that the Learners placed much more value on insight ("getting insight into the cause or sources of my hang-ups; learning that some of the things I am are related to earlier periods of my life"). Many instruments demonstrated the unexpectedly important role that cognitive factors played in personal learning in the encounter group. We discuss this in depth in Chapter 12. Conversely, some High Learners attributed no importance whatsoever to insight. Obviously there are different pathways through the learning experience offered by the encounter group.

THE MOST SIGNIFICANT EVENT OF THE GROUP

The diversity of learning pathways is illustrated by considering another question: What did each subject consider the most significant event that occurred in the entire thirty hours of the group and why? The twelve High Learners who answered this question described these events:

Group #7: When Jan was discussing her dilemma of whether or not to stay in school and why, she explained a number of conflicts between her own desires (as they appeared to me) and the desires of her parents (and even grandparents!). Naturally, this allowed me to further understand or emotionally grasp the dynamics of some of my own hang-ups of this variety.

This subject stresses cognitive gains. Through vicarious, or spectator therapy, he acquired some cognitive structure which he can apply to some of his personal dilemmas.

Group #1: Someone told me I was just "not aware," that everything out in the world is not peaches and cream like I felt it was. First, it shook me and I felt bitter. But after more explanation, I appreciated it since it has made me more aware that things, objects and events are *not* always the way I picture them to be.

This subject expresses the importance to her of feedback. She is a relatively sheltered upper-class black girl who was "awakened" by the group to face many of the social and psychological unpleasantries that she had previously refused to notice.

Group #8: When we said goodbye to each other I felt able to express what I felt for the people in my group more fully than in almost any other situation I've been in.

Group #8: During the marathon session when everyone would get involved with problems and four hours would go by like four minutes, it made me happy in the confident way I could relate to the people in the group. Or when I realized I could and should change situations by positive rational action.

Both underscore the sheer intrinsic pleasure that results from being close to others and being an involved member of a group. The second also expresses a sense of mastery, a sense that he is not a passive spectator to his human predicament but can change it through rational means.

Group #17: It was when I first looked at the people in the group and knew we could be perfectly open with each other from the first word. It was really good, in many ways, to really be able to *talk* right away, although it is also necessary to go through the trivia to give a basis of understanding.

This is a view commonly held by many of the participants: an opportunity is offered for them to be open.

Group #3: "That girl" breaking down and crying. I think crying in front of a group of people for the reason of distrust or shame in herself was a very strong emotion to show.

The expression of a strong emotion, not by the subject but by another member, is considered the most significant event of the thirty-hour life of the group. The statement is too cryptic for us to extract its full meaning, but it conveys some sense of admiration, or even wish to emulate the member.

Group #14, M. Q.: When our group split up into black/white sections and talked. . . . the other group just sitting quietly while one member of a race talked to another of the same. I see that even though encounter groups do help there is still a barrier. Because when blacks or whites talk among themselves, things get said that don't when there is a mixed group. I know that I was able to say things I wouldn't have if I had felt like the whites were really in the discussion.

Group #7: When one of the girls said she had wished to come to a group meeting with a problem, but felt she didn't have the necessary rapport to the group: the relation to us by her of this. Shows that despite being in a situation where people knew they could actively relate personally to near strangers, to relate in a satisfying way, the people remained passive and uninterested. Not the girl above, but most of the group toward her and each other. Significant to me by showing what couldn't be accomplished under a favorable situation.

High Learners

These two, both High Learners, report critical incidents that curiously seem negatively valenced. Both comment soberly on the limitations of encounter groups or on the impossibility of consummately free black/white communication. The second subject, interestingly, on the previous questionnaire cited Item 11 ("The experience that despite the availability of others, I must still face life alone and take ultimate responsibility for the way I live; I learned to face the basic issues of life and death, thus living a life less cluttered with trivialities") as the most salient mechanism of change for him. It is as though he realized what could not be done for him by the group or by any kind of environmental "arrangement" and thereby appreciated what he had to do for himself and by himself.

Group #2: The particular moment when I found that the people in the group liked me. It showed me that I do have some personal traits, that I am not disliked, but mostly it removed the doubt and tension about how I was being received.

Group #12: People said they liked me! Groups always have frightened me because I thought few people would like me.

Group #17: The time they picked the most reticent people (one of whom was me) and had everyone react to them. This was significant because of the personal attention.

These subjects have had an experience of caring, and being cared for, of basic acceptance and validation by others; they apparently had significant doubts about their worth and acceptability and it was with considerable relief they had these doubts disconfirmed.

Group #6, F. Y.: During our twenty-four-hour marathon, following an incident when a very reticent and seemingly deep boy broke out into tears . . . eventually the whole group (with the exception of Ellie) gathered close together, all touching, no speaking but just *together*—swaying a little and all feeling ourselves surrounded by others.

This was most significant to me as it pointed up so poignantly, both so beautifully and so sadly, people's loneliness, their need for touching, need for nearness. So much was communicated, in those minutes of silent togetherness, so much more than barrier-building words could ever have expressed. It pointed up to me, also, though that one of our greatest problems has been a super overemphasis on the individual and his uniqueness, his apartness—as so vividly demonstrated by L's hanging onto her separateness, her individuality, by not joining the group. One sees the almost starving need to be reached out to, to be accepted just as a human being and no more definition than that. But this experience, at the same time, pointed out to me that basically each man *is* alone—and he must try different ways of bridging that aloneness, though he must never try to hide from his aloneness by surrounding himself with people.

And finally, what the whole group experience, as most aptly demonstrated in this specific event, showed me was that man's problem, man's walls go much, incredibly much deeper than color barriers, race barriers—his problem which is one of insecurity, lack or inability of self-acceptance, must be dealt with and resolved first—before color, race prejudice can be considered, since really the latter are truly outgrowths of the former. Certainly, race, color, was dealt with some in the group experience, but the group didn't really resolve anything along those lines—it just pointed up more on just the human-to-human level, where all the growth needs to be nourished.

The twelve descriptions portray a universe of learning experiences: cognition, feedback, a sense of community, being accepted, expressing strong emotion, taking responsibility for oneself, a sense of mastery, and the sheer pleasure of being close to others and being cared for by them. These accounts remind us once again of the limitations of even a comprehensive research design. Each individual experiences the group in a rich and uniquely human way which the scoring templates, the computerized data processing, and sophisticated statistical techniques cannot fully reflect.

THE INTENSIVE GROUP EXPERIENCE

Many of these "significant incidents" describe the "intensive group experience," that core emotional matrix which almost all small interactional groups share. What are its characteristics? Some examples given by High Learners:

We tried an experiment of first staring at each other without saying anything and also by placing our hands on top of the others. During the hand experiment most everyone was concentrating on that alone and therefore pulled their guards down and were open. As a result, I felt closer to everyone in the group, as if they could possibly understand me.

I think we were feeling more together as a group than ever before. Trust and warmth are definitely growing. Very warm and happy feelings to this.

Getting to love all of the beautifulness that can be in the lives of all of us. Getting close when you want to get close. I hope to change my life; so that I will be close and unafraid to be close. To recognize the things that keep people apart and say, "fuck them" without reserve.

Ruth became aware of how even though she's been outwardly pushing for the group to get going, actually she's stopped things when they have gotten too close to something she didn't want to talk about. It will be good to Ruth now that it's in the open.

The feeling of the community created between the nine of us was very warm and human. People were beginning to communicate honestly. It's great to be alive and be able to know people in such a context. So many problems could be solved if we could all do it all the time.

Touching; a guy opposite me and I shook hands, tested our strength. It was interesting since I had never met him nor had I talked to him before. It evoked new thoughts.

The final group hug—I felt real honest togetherness and closeness; love, warmth, friendship.

I can't separate any one thing out as most important. Everything we did, telling our reactions to the marathon, receiving feedback from everyone in the group on how we perceived each other, and saying farewell, meant a lot to me. During the whole session, especially at the end, I felt excitement, pleasure, and love for everyone in the group. I especially felt that I was better than usual at choosing the right words for communicating my feelings, and that the people around me were more perceptive of and responsive to my feelings.

For people who feel isolated and out of touch with others, the group offers a warm haven with an emotional atmosphere reminiscent of the primary family. Many come to the group looking for validation. Am I okay? Am I acceptable? Am I lovable? Many people have not found an opportunity or the audience to whom to address these questions since leaving their primary family. The encounter group not only permits such questions but encourages them; it works toward establishing an atmosphere where everyone feels free to request and to give feedback. On the "How Do Encounter Groups Work?" questionnaire, the great majority of subjects considered feedback ("the group helped me understand the type of impact I have on others; they told me honestly what they thought of me and how I came across;") as the most important mechanism of change in the group.

Most groups provide these experiences: openness, closeness, a feeling of being a part of the group, a chance to find out others' usually hidden perceptions and feelings about oneself, an arena in which considerable catharsis can occur, a trusting atmosphere in which one may disclose usually hidden parts of himself. This intensive group experience occurs as an integral part of the small group process; even members of the unsuccessful groups reported this type of experience. It takes a particularly potent and misguided leader, or highly unpropitious norm-setting event to obstruct the development of the intensive group experience.

Thus it is not unexpected that so many of the High Learners describe having had an intensive group experience. It is necessary but not sufficient for substantial and enduring change (see Chapter 12). The participant must reinforce his experience actively after the group, and/or augment the intensive group experience with other types of learning in the group.

OTHER SIGNIFICANT EVENTS

The experience of being found acceptable is cited as an important experience by many of the High Learners. Acceptance by the encounter group is often a different type of experience than is the acceptance in the outside world caused by role, accomplishments, or presentation of self. Acceptance on this basis still leaves one murmuring, "But what if they really knew"? An encounter group requires that the multi-layered socio-cultural facade be deposited at the door; acceptance in the group is, if the subject feels he has not dissimulated, tantamount to acceptance of his core self. As one High Learner, N. C., phrased it:

The here-and-now focus was really important. I went into the group and started applying my usual role, and put across an image of myself based on my past accomplishments. I talked about experiences that I'd been having and things that I thought were me, and the leader pointed out that he thought this was kind of an imaginary thing, that I had picked to lay out in front of people as an image of myself, what I thought were the best elements of me. He didn't think I needed to do this with others.

This participant ended the group with a much clearer sense of his basic worth and with much less need to conceal from others that fictitious despicable gnome he had considered as his "real" self.

Self-Disclosure. Many cited the experience of having self-disclosed parts of themselves that they usually keep hidden. We investigated self-disclosure by questionnaire at the six-month follow-up.[2] The High Learners on the average revealed more of themselves in more areas than did the others. (For example, 30 percent of the High Learners' disclosures had been revealed to only one or two people before, as compared to 18 percent of all other participants' disclosures.) Half of the High Learners disclosed material that they had previously revealed to only one or two close friends about their fears, weaknesses, and feelings of inadequacy as compared to 28 percent of the others; in the area of sexual feelings, the figures are 33 percent of High Learners versus 16 percent of the others; "details of past life," 50 percent of High Learners versus 18 percent of others.

Of the thirteen High Learners on whom we have data on amount of self-disclosure, ten revealed more than the average number of their group. There is evidence to suggest that High Learners were high disclosers. But not all high disclosers were High Learners; neither were all High Learners high disclosers. Three disclosed very little of themselves.

Modeling. In interviews three of the High Learners gratuitously offered examples of modeling, of having taken for one's own some behavioral trait or some general problem-solving strategy. Either the leader or another group member was used as a model:

Sometimes when I'm in a conversation, or someone's asking me for advice or I'm confused about something, the way B_____(the leader) handled things —how he'd put his finger on some of the really important things when struggling with a decision. I remember how important it is to get a lot of information out on the table; sometimes I even say things out loud—that helps me to clarify what's important and what's unimportant in the same way B_____did.

There was one guy in the group whom I still use as a model. He felt he didn't have to worry about what other people thought or felt about him since he couldn't be anything other than what he was. I tried and still try to make that change for myself and whenever I'm working on it I still think of that guy; he serves as a sort of example for me.

One High Learner described a curious instance of negative identification often referred to as a "mirror reaction."

I could see myself in Sue, one of the girls in the group. She wanted to change everyone else, and make them live the kind of life she lived and feel the way she felt. I didn't like what I saw and even now if I sense myself slipping back, I put her back in my mind as a sort of reference point.

These participants seem to have acquired and maintained personal learning by tethering it to some particular person and event in the group.

Experimentation. Some High Learners stressed the opportunity for experimentation. They were encouraged to take risks, to say and do things which, in their wildest dreams, they never envisioned doing. One member who had difficulty expressing himself with any spontaneity was helped, he claimed, by being given certain tasks in the group such as going around the group and giving each member a compliment.

One High Learner reminded us not to overlook the effectiveness of the "Dale Carnegie" aspects of the encounter group. The leader pointed out his tendency to start any sentence with "I don't know" and to drop his voice at the end of his sentences. It helped him appreciate that his style of delivery persuaded his listeners that he had little of value to say.

Profile of a High Learner

Much of this chapter may be summarized by presenting a detailed description of one of the High Learners. Our information on C.V., a 19-year-old sophomore in Group #2, comes from the entire battery of questionnaires that he filled out, questionnaires filled out by his leader and some of his acquaintances, an in-depth clinical interview six months after the group, and a shorter interview two years later.

Table 4–1 indicates that six months after the group, C. V. had made positive shifts in his conception of his self-system; he perceived others in more complex ways; his testimony of the value of the group was highly positive; and his perception of his interpersonal behavior was considerably more positive.

Group #2 was a moderately successful group led by a "high support, social engineer" leader (see Chapter 7).

C. V. was an active, involved member who obviously profited from the group in a variety of ways. Some of the "most significant incident" questionnaires that he filled out at the end of each meeting reflect both his involvement and the richness of his experience:

I was describing my own experiences with drugs and how I had stopped using them, when I realized that this was a story I gave to everyone, that it was about all I had to talk about.

It explained why people get rid of me, and it gave me an important insight into my own personality. (Third meeting)

159

Three of the members were discussing depression when the leader started to break in. He said he was going to criticize the group. A girl said she resented this because he did nothing to help the group. He continued to say that he didn't like us to bring in outside material.

I thought this refocused the group to deal with relationships and activities that were present and available experience to all the group members. It made the group become more meaningful. (Fourth meeting)

The leader finally came out and made a definite stand on what the group should do to accomplish what it wanted. He said that the group should be together for work, which might be difficult, and that working together was important. Unfortunately, I can't remember more details.

I felt glad that the leader finally made a positive statement, and I felt that it gave the group much more direction. (Sixth meeting)

The group had just started. I was the center of attention. I said I wanted feedback about what others thought of me, but I became confused since I thought there was a big difference between my self-image and the image I was projecting.

I found out that there was not as much of a discrepancy as I had thought. (Seventh meeting)

We became aware that it is hard to deal with positive feelings—this gave us something to work on.

I thought this was a very valuable point to pursue—it has a lot to do with my own experiences. (Eighth meeting)

We were concentrating on helping Bill. I felt that I was making an effort to help him by directing questions at him, hoping to help him out of an inferior position with his friends that he reconciled himself to.

I felt very strong reservations about spontaneously questioning him like this, since I had not thought about what I was saying, and also for this reason I felt very exposed to criticism. At the same time, I felt that perhaps I was helping him, and that I had suffered similar problems and that he would profit by my experiences. (Ninth meeting)

These comments suggest that C. V. took the group very seriously. He was relieved and grateful when the leader blocked group flight, and refocused the group on its primary task. He learned a great deal about his interpersonal presentation of self, e. g. the ways he bored people and how others viewed him. He was validated by others, and learned to have greater confidence in his own perception of self. He struggled with problems concerning the experiencing and perception of positive feeling. He had the experience of being thoughtful and helpful to others in the group.

At the end of the group C. V. was moderately enthusiastic about his experience. On the testimony questionnaire he rated the group as a pleasant, turned-on, constructive, high learning experience; however, he did not use the highest ratings of the scale on any of these dimensions. (Six months later his testimony ratings had slipped slightly, though he still evaluated the group positively.) His feelings about his leader were mixed, though he considered him to be competent, admirable, and he approved of his leadership techniques; nevertheless, he considered him to be very ineffective, remote and passive. On the "How Encounter Groups Work" questionnaire (see Chapter 12) administered at the end of the group, he felt that the most important factors in his learning were:

1. Being an involved member of a group.
2. Appreciating his interpersonal impact on others (mediated through feedback).
3. Universality (learning that others share his problems, feelings, and fears).
4. Revealing embarrassing things about himself and still being accepted.

Six months later he considered the first two of these mechanisms of learning as having paramount importance. When C. V. viewed the group from a very long-term perspective (two years later), the facet of the experience that stands out most sharply in his memory is "feedback":

In the past and still now I am obsessed, no, that's too strong a word, I would say "concerned" about my impression on others. I keep having to put it out of my mind; but the best way to put it out of my mind is to mentally go back to the group and remember the good kinds of feedback I got from the people there who really knew me. This is the first and maybe the only time I got this kind of accurate feedback from others; it helps me to feel good about myself and to know that I don't really need it anymore.

C. V. was an active participant and a high self-discloser in the group. In fact, he felt that he revealed more of himself (past life details, here-and-now feelings, aspects in which he takes pride, sexual feelings, fears, and personal goals) than anyone else in his group. In most of these areas he confided material to the group which he had only shared with one or two friends in the past.

When C. V. was asked about the types of learning he experienced, he volunteered several types of changes. He recalled that before he entered the group he felt that he had to put up a front or play a role in most social situations:

I had to put across an image of myself based on my past accomplishments, and the group helped me change this. When I first went into the group, I talked a lot about what I had been doing, experiences I had been having, and things that I thought were me, and the leader pointed out that he thought this was kind of an imaginary thing, not really significant, that I had picked out to lay in front of people, as my image of myself, what I thought were the best elements. He didn't necessarily think this was really me. That kind of made me think a lot. Later on I tried to put this aside. . . . The whole thing with our group was just reacting to the group as it was in a particular situation and not bringing in outside things. All of this little partial self was based on outside things, so I had to drop it. When I found myself just reacting in the situation as it was, I found out that people had a more positive reaction to that than to the stuff I brought in and presented as "me." So that really helped a lot. I still do it, sometimes, but it's more a protective mechanism. It has pertinence when you're first getting to meet people. Then you can put it aside later on when you have had a chance to sound them out. There always has to be some kind of holding back a little bit before you're really ready to expose yourself at a deep level.

He also emphasized that he got a much clearer view of how others perceive him:

More or less it's a sort of gaining insight into other people's reactions and unless you can really get in an unusual situation where people are actually telling you how they perceive you, what they think about you, and really doing it so you know they're being honest and there are no projections of your own onto them and things like that, they are more or less filtered out. Just seeing that, and then generalizing from that one situation to other situations you run into from then on, I think that's really helped.

His own sense of self stabilized, he was less prone to define himself as he perceived others to be defining him (often inaccurately, as he came to learn). Furthermore his relations to others were less burdened by parataxic distortions. In his own words:

I used to have the feeling that I wasn't being well-received by people I thought were my friends. Thinking about this, I can think that before the group I would have projected a lot onto them, but now I don't think it was really there—like feelings and fear that they don't like you. But as a result of the group I kind of have a more intuitive grasp of the fact that this is projection, that all these little acts that you interpret as hostile are not; they are just your perception of them. When I was in the group I started out with a lot of projections on people and felt a lot of feelings of hostility toward me and lack of acceptance and things like this, and when we got to where we could actually open up to each other, I found out that this was a projection, a kind of imaginary thing on my part, and the people weren't really this way.

I can get more specific than that. About three weeks ago there were two or three friends of mine that were living in a house, and I had been living at home and always used to go over there. We had a lot of common interests and things; they were all together in a living unit and I was coming in; I would come over every day and after a while I got to thinking maybe they really don't want me to come over here, like maybe I'm not really part of this thing they have, and I started really wondering. One of these guys I had gone to Alaska with before, and apparently on that trip I had really brought him down without realizing it and we were talking about Alaska one day and he said, "Wow, you really bummed us out on that Alaskan thing"; and he was really emphatic about it. That just really shattered me, and for about a week I didn't know what was going on, because I thought this guy was my best friend. But after a while I talked to another friend, and he didn't have this impression of our Alaskan trip at all. So I realized maybe it's that guy's imagination, and it's not really the truth about me.

C. V. learned to deal with some life problems from a cognitive perspective. For example, he stated that he has learned to categorize his emotional drives into two clusters: those basic drives like sex over which he has no control, and those drives or attitudes which he can change or alter in some beneficial fashion.

He described an important shift toward greater tolerance of others' right to be different:

I've really changed my attitudes toward other people. It's made me have a lot more respect for them than before. I don't feel like ousting people just because they have an opinion that varies with mine or something like that. . . . I'd say the main thing was that I haven't been trying to force my views on people and things like that, and I've just let it stand, and tried to avoid getting into arguments and things like that. Then people can see how you are different without having it forced down their throats.

Was it the group that really was responsible for C. V.'s positive change? Six months later he said:

I feel I've made a lot of progress since the group. The group came at kind of a good time, so I think a lot of the progress I've made since then has not been directly as a result of the group. It's really hard to weed out what is a direct result of the group and what isn't, especially since it was so long ago.

Since the group, say six months or so after it, I really started developing my own philosophy of life, and attitude toward life. This has been really big for me, it's had a lot more effect on me than the group, I would say, but the two are kind of intermingled.

There were several individuals who were High Learners at the end of the group, only to have the gains slip away during the months following the group. C. V. maintained his learning, and six months later his overall outcome picture was as strongly positive as it had been at the end of the group. He rated himself "four or five" on a five-point scale for maintenance of learning (five was defined as total maintenance). When we interviewed C. V. to explore his methods of maintenance, we were struck by his extremely active posture towards transfer of learning. He had a pronounced tendency not only to generalize his feelings toward himself and the other members to situations outside the group, but also was willing to take risks to try out new behaviors based on his learning.

You can draw an analogy between the situation in the group and situations outside the group. My experience in the group gave me a kind of boost for this. . . . I think more than anything else, I had a really positive experience with that particular group because I found out they all really liked me and when you find that out in one situation, you think maybe it's true in another, so you start looking for positive-type reactions to you in other situations too, and you realize that although you may not perceive it that way, this may be the way it is. And it's usually turned out that way, so it's kind of a self-fulfilling thing. It cuts down a lot of the fear; a little of it is still there, but you realize that most of the time you've had a good experience as a result of asking what's happening. It's given me more self-confidence.

. . . I remember one time when I was seeing some friends I really expressed "What are you talking about?", and I don't think I would have been able to talk like that before I got into the group where I had a kind of positive reaction to my saying, "What do you think of me?" I feel like I can focus what's happening between me and a friend, say, to a point where I can ask things like this and it will seem perfectly natural.

Although he has made no permanent ongoing friends from the group, nevertheless he continues to use his comembers to maintain his change. He sees them occasionally and still thinks of them. Their memory provides an inner source of warmth upon which he can draw.

I've thought often of this one girl who was really the first one to say that she reacted positively to me as a person. When I think of her I feel good, like I shouldn't doubt myself. . . . I don't really know the people in the group as well as some on the outside, just from the standpoint of how long I've known them. But there is a real closeness there—you just walk up to them and right away, just like that. I don't know why that is; I guess from just having been in a close situation like that, for six weeks, once a week. I think there really is something special there. It somehow is more spontaneous; like when you see a person from your group you go up to him right away and hug him or her and that kind of thing.

Perhaps C. V.'s most striking trait was his ability to apply his encounter group learning in an appropriate tactful manner:

The main thing in any kind of encounter experience in applying it to the outside, is that you have to use a little bit of detachment in your personal relationships, like you can't just react very suddenly to things that they say to you or impressions they have of you, or impressions you have of them. It's okay to react, but at the same time you have to kind of put aside that reaction a little bit and look at it and say what's really happening here is. . . . That, I think, is really the key to successfully applying the encounter experience to everyday life. If you just react you are going to fall into the pattern you were in before. Of course, after a while what you learn becomes very natural to you and you don't need to do this. I think at first you do. It's a very quick thing when it actually occurs; it takes effort to do it like it takes effort to break out of any pattern. It doesn't take much time to do it, it's just a matter of attitude really.

C. V. describes here some crucial aspects of change maintenance. If one is to change, one must, he says, take a slightly detached posture in personal relationships. React, but also delay for a moment to reflect upon and understand the reaction. Effort and practice is needed at first, but eventually the maneuver becomes automatic. To C. V. the maintenance of change is not an emotional process as much as it is a deliberate, cognitive one: "Look at it and say, 'What's really happening here is' . . ."

There was evidence of another important change in C. V. which gave us some measure of concern: unlike his other changes, this one might not have been a change for the better. Six months after the group he was asked to describe any major decisions he had made in the previous six months. He wrote:

I decided the mystical spiritual path was the way to true freedom for me, and that I should spend my life following it. I made the decision to drop out of school because I felt it to be contrary to this goal.

We checked his school record and found that C. V. did indeed drop out of school. Although one might read ominous overtones into his mystical conversion and his school dropout, we had so much reason to believe that C. V. had changed in a positive way that we chose to view these facts under the umbrella of the young adult search for identity, one aspect of which is the declaration of a psychosocial moratorium.

A friend (one of the members of C. V.'s social network whom we polled) contributed some information which suggested that, on balance, the upheaval in values and life-style shift were indeed positive moves:

In the previous school year C. V. was known as a "bummer," even among his friends. He could bring anyone down, just by walking into the room. He had the unfortunate habit of kicking people unintentionally and not excusing himself. "That's what you get" was his favorite phrase. Since June, C. V. has dropped out of school, bought a motorcycle and got a job. Whereas before I felt like I saw too much of him, I never see enough of him now. He is now a far gentler and more responsive person.

Our supposition proved to be a correct one. We interviewed C. V. two years after the end of the group and learned that the apparent upheaval was indeed a sign of a vigorous and growth-inducing inner search. For six months he "lived at home, worked at two jobs, and thought." He realized that he had been expecting too much from school; he had previously planned on a religious study major in the hope of obtaining a greater degree of self-knowledge and inner peace. He returned to school with a more realistic approach to his curriculum, worked more effectively, improved his grade point average, and graduated at the appropriate time.

C. V. blushed a bit as he recalled his past romance with the mystical pathway in life. He has, he says, sobered and assumed a more realistic appraisal of the role of the mystical in his life:

That part of my life is still important to me, but I know now that the mundane world continues to exist and I must continue to deal with it. . . . I was very disappointed in my mystical searching because I never experienced a dramatic change of consciousness. I know now that I was expecting too much, too quickly. I continued working with a Zen Master for about a year, but I've decided to stop now; I realize I'm not in the right place psychologically for that anymore, although I recognize its value and also continue to feel respect for others involved in it. What I've taken away from it is a different kind of attitude toward life. I can stand back and take a long view of things to see the whole span of my life and my place in the universe.

The story of C. V. shows how one High Learner was able to use the positive aspects of the encounter group experience to change his life and to maintain that change. The experience of the individuals described in the next chapter will provide a striking contrast, for these are the Casualties, those who suffered negative effects from the group experience.

NOTES

1. While it is unfortunate that eleven High Learners did not return for the six-month follow-up, this follow-up percentage is approximately the same for each outcome category. (See the discussion of panel constitution in Chapter 3.)

2. We inquired about the amount of self-disclosure in six different areas: 1) details of my past life; 2) how I felt at the moment; 3) things about which I felt happy or proud; 4) my sex life or sexual feelings; 5) my fears, weaknesses, and feelings of inadequacy; and 6) my personal goals, wishes and plans. Each rated his disclosures in each area on a six-point defined scale, (e.g. 1 = disclosed things that I had never told anyone before and 6 = did not talk about this at all to the group). In general there was less self-disclosure than is popularly assumed. For example, only two of thirteen High Learners made any "first time" disclosures (revealed material they had never told anyone before) in the group.

CHAPTER 5

Hazards of Encounter Groups

How dangerous are encounter groups? Are the gains worth the hazards? What types of negative outcomes occur? How do injuries occur? What kind of groups appear to have the greatest risk for participants?

For several years, mental health professionals have been in the uncomfortable position of having to answer these questions without information. Despite the lack of knowledge, there has been no dearth of polemics.

The battle lines are starkly drawn. On the one side are those individuals, often mental health professionals, who, having seen or heard about encounter group members who have suffered damage as a result of their group experience, have generalized and branded the whole field as dangerous (Gottschalk and Pattison, 1969; Jaffe and Sherl, 1969). Many local medical societies have issued strongly worded statements describing potential hazards. The Committee on Mental Health of the Michigan State Medical Society issued a statement that the hazards of encounter groups are so considerable that all group leaders should be professional experts, trained in the fields of mental illness and mental health (Jeffries, 1969). Several state legislatures have passed or introduced legislation to restrict encounter group practice.

Right-wing groups have labeled sensitivity-training as a communistic technique to undermine national loyalty and to encourage sexual promiscuity (*Congressional Record,* June 10, 1969, pp. H4666–4679). Sensitivity-training became an important election year issue for California school supervisory boards; sensitivity, sin, and sex were combined in a campaign motto urging the elimination of the three S's from California school systems. In 1969 a 30,000 word entry in the United States *Congressional Record* likened all forms of small group practices to Bolshevistic brainwashing techniques (*Congressional Record,* June 10, 1969).

A contrasting view has been espoused by many growth centers and encounter group leaders who deny the existence of any risk to participants. Some, for example, have packaged their product into games which may be purchased at department stores by the general public, and played with one's friends in the absence of any trained individuals.

The factors responsible for both positions are clear. Clinicians' views, on the one hand, are based on heavily skewed information. They see casualties of encounter groups but rarely see members who have had a productive experience. They often learn of the existence of a group only through its casualty spinoff; groups which are safe, either because they are low impact or because they are highly effective, never come to their attention. Some professional clinical associations have attempted to garner relevant evidence by polling members for a list of all the casualties they have seen (Henry Work, M.D., written communication, 1971). Such an approach can demonstrate the existence but not the degree of risk. Knowing the number of casualties without knowing the total number of participants from which the casualties issue offers useful but severely limited information. Anecdotal case reporting has another intrinsic flaw: multiple reporting may spuriously inflate casualty rates. An untoward outcome in a group member is generally a striking event not easily forgotten by the other members. If the other fifteen members all describe this event to colleagues or friends, the single casualty soon assumes alarming proportions.

On the other hand, a number of factors may cause proponents of encounter groups to err in the opposite way and vastly minimize the dangers. Most encounter group leaders and growth center administrators are limited in their source of information. Their groups are generally intensive but brief; once ended, members scatter, and there is little opportunity or inclination to collect follow-up data. Any psychological decompensation manifesting itself after the end of the group would be unlikely to come to their attention.

There are ideological sources of bias. Many encounter group leaders reject medical model definitions of psychological injury or "adverse effect;" they feel that extreme psychological discomfort, even to the degree where professional aid is required, may not be a failure but an accomplishment of the group. They view psychological decompensation, like the legendary "night journey," as a stage of personal growth, a method of assimilating previously split-off parts of themselves. The most extreme view holds with Laing (1967) that a psychotic experience may permit the individual to realize his true potential more fully. In some quarters this approaches the advocacy of psychotic experience as a desideratum of personal growth.

Other leaders express a lack of interest in adverse effects, since their ideological base stresses the necessity and ability of each individual to assume responsibility for himself. They believe that the leader who takes responsibility for the welfare of a group member infantilizes him and impedes his growth.

These concerns motivated the American Psychiatric Association to establish a task force in 1969 to survey the present state of knowledge in the field. The task force report ("Encounter Groups and Psychiatry," 1970) emphasized that, despite strongly held opinions, there was virtually no controlled research in the field. The literature consisted primarily of anecdotal reports or nonsystematic evaluations lacking even meager follow-up study. The little available outcome research, and that often without adequate controls, involved National Training Laboratory groups generally led by trained, professional behavioral scientists; there had been no attempt to assess the effects of the new encounter group formats.

With these considerations in mind, the research design of the present study was constituted to give careful attention to the hazards of encounter groups. A number of contingencies were built into the project to maximize the likelihood that all students who suffered psychological injury could be identified, studied, and, if necessary, referred to agencies which would provide psychotherapy.

The study of encounter group risks presented basic ethical problems. The desire to do an *in vivo* study of encounter group hazards conflicted with a sense of ethical responsibility to the participants. It was clear, however, that to study the potential risks of a reputedly high-risk procedure required the study of groups that used techniques (fighting, verbal onslaught, considerable physical contact, extreme self-disclosure) considered distasteful, unsound or even dangerous within the mental health profession and by the general public.

A rather sizable proportion (approximately 50 percent) of Stanford students had at the time of this project already had some type of previous encounter group experience. This state of affairs assuaged but did not eliminate concern about sponsoring a University course that might have psychological risk to the participants. The dilemma was solved through a compromise.

1. To protect the participants:
    A. In the orientation session considerable information was conveyed about the nature of the encounter experience. including a simulation of its emotional impact (a microlab exercise).
    B. Before they committed themselves to the course, the students were cautioned that the groups could be stressful and could provoke emotional upset. This message was given in writing to all subjects, and in addition, orally, to those (approximately 80 percent) who attended the pregroup briefing.
    C. The students were informed of sources of help should they become emotionally distressed. These included the student health service, the Department of Psychiatry, and the name of one of the principal investigators.
    D. The same information was given to the group leaders. After the suicide of one of the group members, the leaders were informed and urged again to refer troubled students to appropriate sources of help. Most leaders read this letter aloud to their groups.
    E. Discretion was exercised in the choice of leaders. A leader known to be

irresponsible and dangerous would have been rejected. Our only serious question was in regard to Leader #6 (see Chapter 2) who was, in the eyes of the professional medical community, a high-risk leader, highly impactful but not irresponsible.

F. Research conditions imposed on the group leaders tended to increase restraint. All meetings were observed by two members of the research team; all meetings were tape recorded. The leaders were aware that they were being closely scrutinized. With the exception of Synanon, all leaders met their groups on or near the Stanford Campus.

2. To insure realism:

A. In line with the standard practice of the encounter groups studied, no screening of members was performed, and all students who applied for the course were accepted. Seniors were discouraged only because they would be less available for long-term follow-up.

B. There was absolutely no intervention by the observers or the principal investigators during the course of the group. The observers were nonparticipants; though they may have had strong reactions to such group activities as physical fighting, scapegoating, or, in one group meeting, the use of marijuana, they kept their feelings to themselves. Although some leaders asked for feedback or validation at the end of a meeting, observers strictly avoided comment.

C. Although some students might have preferred to be in certain groups, all assignment was randomized aside from even distribution of sex, race, and previous encounter group experience.

What was the overall effect of the research design on the casualty rate? It is possible that some aspects increased the risk. For example, the random assignment of subjects to groups may have resulted in some subjects joining a "poor fit" group that they intuitively would have avoided in the free marketplace. Secondly, it is possible that the participants, in order to receive their three academic units, may have been under more pressure to continue in an incompatible group than might be present in a natural setting. We learned from interviews, however, that the three credits appeared to be only a minor theme for the vast majority of subjects. Furthermore all subjects, aside from a few that attended only a meeting or two, received credit for the course and the dropout rate, 17 percent, was appreciable.

In the judgment of the researchers the overall effect of the research design acted to reduce the potential casualty rate. The leaders, by agreeing to participate in this project, placed themselves on professional display. They were well aware of many factors: their behavior was under the closest scrutiny; the outcome of their efforts was being assessed; their work was being compared with other leaders; professional publications would stem from the study. The cumulative effect of these factors was to put the leaders on their best behavior. They seemed to be more cautious, more conservative, and less inclined to avoid extreme techniques (for example, nudity, excessive physical contact, and so on) that might be used in other encounter group settings.

Identification of Casualties

A casualty was defined as an individual who, as a direct result of his experience in the encounter group, became more psychologically distressed and/or employed more maladaptive mechanisms of defense. Furthermore, to be so defined this negative change must not be transient, but enduring, as judged eight months after the group experience.

Since it was not possible to interview in depth all 210 subjects who began the groups, eight criteria were used to identify a potentially high-risk subsample, who could then be studied more intensively:

1. *Request for Psychiatric Aid*. The most obvious mode of identifying a casualty, and the one used in most previous research, is the request for emergency aid during the course of the group.
2. *Dropouts from Groups*. We assumed that some of those who dropped out of groups early might have done so because of a noxious group experience.
3. *Peer Evaluation*. At the end of the group, all members were asked: "Can you think of people in your group who were hurt (made worse, became overly upset) by the experience? Please describe what happened and to whom it happened. (Include yourself. if this question is appropriate to you.)" All subjects mentioned were considered casualty suspects.
4. *Self-esteem Drop*. The Rosenberg self-esteem measure was used as one measure of outcome. We calculated the pre-post change in self-esteem and interviewed the lowest 10 percent (the seventeen subjects who decreased the most in self-esteem).
5. *Low Testimony*. The lowest 10 percent of the participants rated their group experience as being low on learning, more destructive than constructive, unpleasant, and as being turned off.
6. *Psychotherapy*. At the six-month follow-up, all subjects were asked whether they had started psychotherapy since the beginning of the group, or whether anything had happened in their group to make them think they needed psychotherapy. All subjects answering affirmatively were studied.
7. *Leaders' Ratings*. The leaders were asked at the end of the group to rate each student on the amount of progress he had made on a number of dimensions (e.g. self-understanding, positive self-image, happiness, openness, sensitivity. ability to collaborate with others. ability to be close with others. etc.). The 10 percent of the subjects who had the lowest leader ratings were included in the high-risk population. Positive self-image and happiness were more heavily weighted than the other items.
8. *Miscellaneous*. For example, the observers occasionally reported concern about some member of a group whom they observed. or subjects during an interview expressed concern about another member. One casualty was discovered when he was interviewed as one of the thirty subjects with the most positive self- and leader-defined outcome. He had scored himself highly on questionnaires in a self-deceptive attempt to turn a destructive experience into a constructive one. It was clear that he had *not* benefited from the group but in fact had had a very negative experience.

Interviews of Casualty Suspects

Once a list (n = 104) of casualty suspects was compiled, the next phase of the project began. Approximately eight months after the end of the group sessions, each suspect who could be reached was interviewed for fifteen or twenty minutes by phone. If there was any suspicion that the subject had a psychologically destructive experience, he was given in-depth interview in person or by telephone.

The interviewer informed the subject that the investigators, in their study of the effects of the encounter groups, were interviewing a large number of students to obtain their retrospective view of the group. Did they now view the group as an overall constructive, neutral, or destructive experience? Was the group stressful to them? Had they been made uncomfortable by the group? For how long a period? In which ways? Specific inquiries were made about interpersonal functioning, academic effectiveness, and self-concept. If the group had a negative effect, had they by now (eight months later) recovered to the level of comfort or adaptation that was present before the group? Were there concurrent life circumstances that may have also been responsible for the subject's deterioration during the period of the study? Had they sought help from professional or informal sources?

To enhance the flow of information, we often mentioned our mode of identification (e. g. decreased self-esteem on their self-administered questionnaires, or comembers citing the subject as having been harmed by the group) and proceeded to investigate these areas. To refresh the memories of dropouts who had been in the group for only a couple of sessions, a tape recording of their last meeting was played. In general, however, no prodding was necessary; we were struck by the vivid recall eight months later, even by those who described the group as dull and plodding.

Our definition of casualty was fairly stringent; not only must the group member have undergone some psychological decompensation but this must have been persistent and there must have been evidence that the group experience was the responsible agent. We did not consider as casualties several subjects who were shaken up and severely distressed by the group but who, a few days later, had recovered their equilibrium. Nor did we include several subjects who during the group or in the six months following had some significant psychological decompensation that appeared to be due not to the encounter group but to other circumstances in the life of the individual.

The case of D. A. is illustrative. D. A. was the major tragedy of the study. A few days after his second meeting he committed suicide through an overdose of sleeping pills. It would have been easy to impugn the group as the responsible agent. However, upon study, we learned that he had a long history of psychiatric disturbance and had, during the course of the group and over the preceding three years, sought help from a number of sources for his chronic depression, loneliness, and dissatisfaction with his interpersonal relationships. (In fact, the main reason he had recently transferred to Stanford was because he heard that the student health psychiatric service was excellent.) In the months preceding the project he had been in a number of local encounter groups. In his therapy group he generally assumed the role of the neediest, sickest member. At times he was bizarre in the group and arrived under the influence of marijuana which he used, he stated, to control his anxiety. Not only was he in two forms of psychotherapy while he was in the project, but we learned from a friend that he was, concurrently, in another encounter group in a nearby growth institute.

He attended two meetings of Group #15, a group which focused heavily on black-white issues. We reviewed the notes and tapes of these meetings and concluded that they were low affect, cautious meetings. The group leader reported that D. A. had, if anything, been optimistic and was involved in a constructive manner. In his questionnaire which he filled out at the end of the first meeting D. A. commented: "I am inhibited emotionally when I talk, especially because of the reactions I think this makes in others: they don't believe what I'm saying, I'm faking, I'm covering up, I'm on a head trip, I'm talking to myself, etc., etc. I used to see my discussion behavior in groups as extremely intelligent and worthwhile but this year an encounter group convinced me I could speak only shit. I'm now very anxious about sounding out of it, being an intellectual asshole. In this new group I was trying to start by being really feeling, and emotional, and honest, instead of analytic and evaluative. J., who seemed a cool guy and one who would be impatient with bullshit really made me feel good with the simple indication that I was worth listening to."

A few days following the second meeting he visited the room of two women who were in the project but in other encounter groups, and invited them to accompany him to a film. Both declined explaining that they had set this time aside for studying. Later that same evening he ingested several bottles of sedatives and hypnotics, and was dead the following morning. (Both of these women were, of course, strongly affected by the incident and both dropped out of their encounter groups.)

After we reviewed this information, we decided that we could not label D. A. a "casualty" of the encounter group. It is obvious that he was a seriously disturbed young man who had been reaching out for help from a number of different sources. We considered that his presence in the group was more a manifestation than a cause of his distress. The encounter group seemed no more responsible for his suicide than his therapy group or his individual psychotherapy. To complicate matters even more, there was an important but unstable relationship between S. C. (a casualty in Group #9; see below) and D. A. His group therapist reported that D. A. was disturbed by his friend's increasingly severe illness. S. C.'s manic episode preceded D. A.'s suicide by approximately one week. Nevertheless, it is impossible to conclude with certainty that the experience in the group did not in some way contribute to the ultimate outcome. The suicide note which D. A. left is an angry indictment of past and present therapists, encounter group leaders, and comembers, all of whom, he felt, had failed to listen, to understand and to help:

I felt great pain that I could not stop any other way. It would have been helpful if there had been anyone to understand and care about my pain, but there wasn't. People did not believe me when I told them about my problems or pain or else that it was just self-pity; or if there had been someone to share my feelings with, but all they said was that I was hiding myself, not showing my true feelings, talking to myself. They kept saying this no matter how hard I tried to reach them. This is what I mean when I say they do not understand or care about my pain; they just discredited it or ignored it and I was left alone with it. I ask that anyone who asks about me see this; it is my last request.

There were several other individuals who six months after the group seemed to be more troubled than before they started the group. Some like D. A. joined the group looking for help. None of these was considered a casualty unless we had some evidence that the group was in some way responsible for his decompensation.

To summarize, then, we defined a casualty as a member whose group experience was destructive. During and/or following the group he was more uncomfortable and/or utilized more maladaptive defenses and this negative change was relatively enduring. Finally, in our opinion the encounter group could be impugned as the responsible agent.

A total of 104 casualty suspects were identified. Of these, twenty-five were unavailable by telephone or through the mails. Seventy-nine participants were interviewed by phone by a clinically experienced member of the research team. As a result of the first contact, those participants who seemed particularly high risk were invited for a personal interview. Forty-nine were interviewed in depth by the same interviewer.[1]

By these methods, sixteen participants were identified who, by the above definition, suffered psychological harm from their group experience. *Thus, of the 206 participants starting the groups,[2] sixteen (7.8 percent of the total, and 9.1 percent of those who completed 50 percent of the group meetings [3]) suffered significant psychological injury.*

Table 5–1 indicates that the casualties are not randomly distributed among the seventeen groups: Six groups (#1, #3, #7, #8, #16, #17) had no casualties; seven groups (#2, #5, #10, #11, #12, #14, #15) had one casualty while four groups (#4, #6, #9, #13) had more than one casualty. Note that three of the four high-risk groups (#4, #6, and #13) were led by a leader whose style is characterized by high aggressive stimulation, high charisma, high individual focus, high support, and high confrontation (see Chapter 7).

TABLE 5-1
Mode of Casualty Identification

Group Identification	Request Emergency Psychiatric Aid	Dropout from Group	Peer Evaluation "Who Got hurt?"	Self-esteem Drop	Low Testimony	Therapy Began During or Within Six Months Group	Low Leader Ratings	Miscellaneous
#2 T. G.								X
#4 V. C.		X	X					
#4 N. I.			X					
#4 B. V.					X			
#5 O. O.			X	X	X			
#6 L. L.			X		X	X		
#6 E. L.			X				X	
#9 E. D.			X	X	X	X		
#9 S. C.	X	X	X			X		
#10 H. P.			X		X		X	
#11 M. A.					X			
#12 H. I.						X[a]		
#13 C. L.	X	X	X			X		
#13 D. R.			X	X	X	X		
#14 M. M.		X	X			X		
#15 D. H.		X	X			X		
Total positive signs for Casualties	2	5	12	3	7	8	2	1
Total positive signs for Noncasualties	0	29	18	15	11	11	17	0

[a]Did not begin therapy but stated that as a result of the group was seriously considering it.

MODES OF IDENTIFICATION

How successful were each of the modes of identifying casualties? Table 5-1 presents the methods through which each casualty was traced. The traditional methods of casualty-finding (request for emergency aid and leaders' ratings) were particularly ineffective. Only two subjects came to our attention because emergency psychiatric aid was needed: one appeared at the emergency room in an anxiety depressive state, and the other was involuntarily hospitalized with a manic psychosis. The leaders were particularly insensitive in casualty identification: of the twenty-four subjects who were rated by the leaders as having decreased the most in mental health areas, only two were casualties. Or, to put it in another way, of the sixteen casualties only two were seen by the leaders as having significantly worsened.[4] During a postgroup interview when the leaders were informed that some subjects in the group had had a negative effect, they were still unable to identify them.

Eighteen participants began psychotherapy during or within six months after the end of the group; seven (39 percent) of these were casualties. Thus of the sixteen casualties, seven (44 percent) were correctly identified by this method.

By far the single most effective method was to ask the group members at the end of the group: "Who was hurt by the group?" This method successfully identified twelve of the sixteen casualties. The group members named a total of thirty different individuals who, they thought, had been hurt. Of these thirty, eleven were named by more than one person in their group. Of these eleven, eight were casualties. Four casualties identified by this method had only a single nomination; of these four, three named themselves. Only one casualty (E. L.) was chosen by only one person. Thus *if a subject is perceived as having been hurt by more than one member of his group (or so perceived himself), it is highly probable that he represents a casualty of the group experience.* Furthermore, all the severe casualties were identified by this method.

There were only three false positives, three multiple-chosen subjects who were not casualties. The wording of the statements pertaining to these three was clearly attenuated compared to the statements describing the casualties: (1) "C. W. cried and left the group when she was criticized;" "Started crying at mild criticism . . . it didn't seem permanent or to affect strongly her later behavior in the group." (2) "M. M. probably became a little upset because we attacked him so much." "I was a bit disturbed by being told I wasn't very friendly." (3) "T. F. realized he had been deceiving himself about his feelings toward blacks." "I think I was more upset than anyone in the group because a very elaborate ego-structure I had concocted was shattered, but I am glad it happened for I learned how much I'd been kidding myself."

This last participant, T. F., a twenty-year-old junior, is worthy of a brief digression since he illustrates many of the problems in determining whether psychological injury had occurred as a result of the group.

In an interview several months after the group, it was readily apparent that he was under considerable tension; his speech was pressured, he was clearly anxious and plaintively searching for support and approval. He used the dynamisms of denial, reaction formation, and obsessive doing and undoing liberally and especially in the area of his not inconsiderable hostility. Much of this is evident in his account of his group experience: "I was more open than I'd ever been, the leader (Group #12) really saw what was eating at me, only two people attacked me at the time. I wanted to avoid and deny what they said but I couldn't. I felt very alone. I was shattered." He was deeply depressed for four days following the group but stated that he pulled himself together by "internal dialogue" and by talking to friends. He now considered the whole ordeal as "an important learning experience." Nevertheless, it was the interviewer's judgment that in the long run he had in fact learned little and remained exceedingly uncomfortable. Following the group he had joined a Christian fundamentalist sect and volunteered that he spent considerable time praying for relief from tension and depression, hardly a coping mode advocated by the encounter group. The interviewer was sufficiently concerned about him that he recommended to him that he seek psychotherapy.

Nevertheless we did *not* consider T. F. and many similar subjects as casualties. We knew that he had been tense and depressed before joining the group (he had sought psychotherapy four months before the group experience). Secondly he had had a traumatic life event just preceding the group—the breakup of an important relationship with a girl—which may have been responsible or contributed to his dysphoria. Thirdly, he stated explicitly that the group was a positive experience and, although it is a defensible investigatory position to disregard the conscious and attend to the denial and reaction formation of which there was abundant evidence, we chose instead to operate at a *low* inferential level which may have resulted in our underestimating the number of casualties.

Table 5–1 indicates that the testimony of the subject himself identified only seven of sixteen casualties. (Recall that the testimony instrument asked the subjects to rate their group on four seven-point scales as to whether it was a pleasant-unpleasant, turned on-turned off, constructive-destructive, high learning-nonlearning experience.) Two other indices, entering psychotherapy after the group and dropping out of the group, were only moderately effective in identifying casualties.

Casualties were likely to have been identified by more than one of our modes of identification. Sixty-two percent (nine of the sixteen) of the casualties were identified by multiple indicators (three or four different modes); compared to only 3 percent of casualty suspects who subsequently, upon interview, were not considered to be casualties. Two suspects (out of 88) with three indices of suspicion could not be located for interview. This raised the possibility (again) that our reported casualty rate is a low estimate.

Description of the Casualties

In the discussion section and in Chapter 7 we shall discuss the relationship between leadership style and psychological risk. We shall now describe each of the sixteen casualties. (See Chapter 2 for description of the character of each of the groups.)

Group #2.

T. G. is the curious instance of a casualty who would never have been identified had a research assistant not been interviewing the subjects whose postgroup, self-report questionnaires suggested that they were the highest learners. T. G., a sophomore, had been distressed before joining the group and saw the student health psychiatrist twice, approximately three weeks before the beginning of the encounter group, because of unsatisfactory interpersonal relationships, loneliness, free-floating anxiety, feelings of worthlessness, and inability to study. He felt that his brief contact with the psychiatrist was helpful and he explicitly stated that he joined the group looking for further personal help, as well as for a friend. He began optimistically, hoping to change his methods of presenting himself and his modes of relating to others, but dismally failed in these aims. "I was not really there in the group. I just played around in the past. It only reinforced what I had always been. I wanted to say things in the group, I wanted to get close to people, but I ended up saying irrelevant things. I wanted to make contact especially with G., who was like me. But I was out of touch with him and out of touch with myself. I was alienated from the group." He was convinced that the group made him worse. His fantasies of changing, of doing things in the group were not realized. He stated that afterwards he felt empty, that he was unable to make an impression on others, less accepting of himself, and more cynical that things would ever be different. He stated that *if he couldn't reach himself and others in the group, then he despaired of doing it elsewhere.* The summer immediately following the group was an extremely bad one for him: he withdrew, lapsed into apathy and pointedly avoided interpersonal contacts. He was unable to perform when he returned to school, and eventually dropped out of college altogether.

He was unclear why he rated himself and the group so positively immediately following the group, except to say that he wanted so much to have a good experience that he deceived himself. Furthermore, it was only some weeks later that he realized the full impact of the failure. At the eight-month follow-up interview, T. G. was referred for psychotherapy. He made good progress in individual therapy.

T. G. represents a specific type of casualty. He faults the leader on grounds of omission rather than commission. He entered the group with moderately severe schizoid characterological problems and with extremely unrealistic expectations of the group. He hoped for therapy, and unattainably rapid therapy at that, and he hoped to form some enduring friendships. His expectations were doomed to fail; he left the group more troubled and more discouraged than before. The unfavorable outcome is more a function of the subject's unrealistic expectations fostered by the current encounter group mystique than of specific events in the group.

Group #4.

V. C. was identified by three indices: he dropped out of the group, he needed therapy after the group, and he was selected by six members (including himself) as having been harmed by the group. Some comments were: "V. C. was scapegoated by the leader." "V. C. was so shaken by the rejection he received he never came back. He simply didn't know how to respond comfortably to the new situation. It was very annoying though sad." His own answer was, "Myself. Without knowing why, I became very depressed and afraid."

V. C. dropped out of the group after the first session (a time-extended, nine-hour meeting). He had an extraordinarily negative reaction to the group experience. and may be considered as one of the severest casualties. He stated. "I was very scared during the meeting; I withdrew. The leader told me I was a dumb shit because I didn't know how to participate. I felt really outside and really hurt, alienated from other people in the group." He stated that he was attacked by the leader and by one of the female members of the group. Somehow he still felt some warmth emanating from the leader but not at all from the other members. He felt different from the other members because he hadn't experimented with drugs, nor had he been in encounter groups before. He felt the leader put him down because of his lack of experience in these areas. There was an absolute lack of support from other members of the group, and furthermore he felt that the leader was dangerously unpredictable: at times he might be sensitive and supportive, but the very next minute he was frightening and punitive. In short, he summarized his experience as, "I was an outsider; I was treated as the lowest thing on earth; my opinions were not valid; I was just a toy being played with." The effects of this group experience were cataclysmic for him, he stated. He lost his "sureness about self," and the kind of identity that he had been building for some time. Following the group he stated that he went into an extreme depression characterized by depressed affect, by severe insomnia. by weight loss (40 pounds. from 180 to 140—the subject was over six feet tall), and by occasional suicidal ideation. This depression lasted approximately six months until finally with the help of psychotherapy he was able to return to his pregroup level.

It is difficult for V. C. to think of a single positive aspect of the group. Looking back at the group after several months he feels that one important thing that the leader said to him was, "there is no one who can make you happy or unhappy; it's all within yourself." He stated that this comment comes back to him from time to time and carries with it some meaning for him, but that it had no meaning within the context of the group experience.

V. C. is a severe casualty. He entered the group with unrealistic expectations, and his unfavorable outcome was related to aggressive, intrusive, and rejecting behavior by other members following the model of the group leader.

Group #4.

N. I. was identified by the "who was hurt" index. She cited herself: "I personally became rather destructively upset out of a combination of boredom and nerves." She stated that the group had a paradoxical effect on her, and she finished the group feeling less comfortable, less sure of herself, and more concerned about her "inner core of emptiness." When there was silence or relative inactivity in the group, she sensed the leader's expectations of the group for depth and profound intimacy. Her reaction at this juncture was self-critical, she felt empty, and convinced that she lacked depth and the ability to care for others. The carry-over to her relationships outside the group was marked: she felt such an internal void when she attempted to get close to others that she maintained an interpersonal wariness and distance. N. I. reports a decreased level of self-esteem and self-regard. She is convinced that the group leader neither liked nor accepted her. Often she sent him "distress signals" which he ignored. "He was much more important to me than the other members of the group, and when someone important doesn't care for me obviously I'm going to care less for myself." Although she has tried to put this out of her mind, it is yet a vital issue; for example, six months after the group when taking an examination, she mistakenly put the name of the group leader on her paper instead of her professor's name. Her explicit judgment of the group was extremely negative: She was disappointed with the experience and ended up less open, less "in touch" with herself and others. She was not so distressed that she sought therapy, but often after the meetings she had to seek out friends to "pull myself together and to convince myself that there is something likable and acceptable about me."

We consider N. I. a minor casualty, whose negative experience was related to the style of the leader whom she experienced as rejecting, and who attempted to accelerate the group into a state of advanced intimacy.

Group #4.
B. V. was interviewed because of his low scores on the postgroup testimony instrument. He explicitly evaluated the group as a negative, destructive experience for himself, and warned others about encounter groups in general and about the leader of his group in particular. His pregroup expectations were high and therapeutic in nature: he stated he had reached the nadir of his existence, was involved with drugs and political activism, had abandoned his academic interests, and was in despair about his passive stance towards life. "I wanted some reassurance about my existence. I wanted to be found acceptable, to be told I was okay, to go ahead and dig myself the way I was." He did not, he stated, get that acceptance from the group. Instead he left the group feeling more unsettled, more depressed, more self-negating, and more unacceptable than when he entered. Much of this he attributed to the leader's scorn and reductionistic dismissal of his whole way of life as a "rejection of authority." He could not relate to anyone else in the group, and experienced it as a static, meaningless endeavor. The depression and loss of self-esteem was not profound; six months later he denied that many negative effects of the experience still persisted.

We regard B. V. as a minor casualty. His negative experience was related both to his unrealistic expectations of the group and to the leader's aggressive judgmentalism.

Group #5.
O. O. was a freshman, Mexican-American student who was identified as a casualty suspect by three indices: self-esteem, testimony, and "who was hurt." On the "who was hurt" questionnaire he answered, with no further elaboration, "myself." He states unequivocally that the group was a negative and harmful experience for him with no positive offsetting features. To his mind the group was a subdued, fragmented one that seemed to coalesce only through banding

together to attack someone in the group. He was the group scapegoat, and experienced massive rejection. Although everyone else in the group was given considerable encouragement to speak, he felt that midway through the group he received a strong message to be quiet. He heard the group tell him that he was only "rapping" pointlessly and irrelevantly, that what he had to say was not worthwhile. "I felt defeated, deflated, and alienated, like a zero. I never really understood why the group silenced me but I knew that I could be accepted by the group only by being quiet." He felt too threatened either to oppose the group interdiction, or to get further information from the group. He states that he would have dropped out of the group long before the end had it not been for the fact that he wanted and needed the academic credits.

The experience was particularly detrimental for O. O. because it reverberated with similar experiences that he was having at college. In his high school he associated only with noncaucasians, e. g. Chicanos, blacks, orientals. At college he felt alienated from the occidental students, drifted through the first two quarters, and signed up for the group because he wanted to improve his methods of relating to white students. The group, however, only reinforced his feelings of alienation and inadequacy. He grew increasingly tense during the course of the group; his ability to concentrate, his academic performance and his social relationships deteriorated.

He felt the detrimental effects of the group continued for several months; he became irritable, defensive and, to use his term, "paranoid." Prior to the group he could generally shrug off others not liking him as "their bag." No longer! He accepts their unfavorable appraisal now, and ruminates about his personality defects. He attributes these pernicious developments to his bad experience in the group. Although he has considered psychotherapy on a couple of occasions he has never followed through with this. Several months after the encounter group he joined a Chicano, social, quasi-encounter group which has, to a small degree, given him a sense of identity.

We consider O. O. a moderately severe casualty. His negative experience in the group was a function partly of his unrealistic goals, and partly of the failure of the leader to help the group and the subject to transform caustic criticism into constructive feedback. The subject could not, without assistance, objectify the experience; he could not make use of the comments about his interpersonal style because he experienced his behavior and his self-concept as inextricably interwoven. Any attack on his behavior was an attack on his core. Moreover he failed to communicate his distress; neither the leader nor the other members appreciated the extent of his discomfort.

Group #6.

L. L. was identified by three indices: low testimony, seeking psychotherapy during the group, and "who was hurt." Five group members, including herself, cited her as having been hurt. Some of the comments were: "She thought that deep down inside she wasn't worth anything, and decided it was better not to know." "L withdrew and became very afraid." "L was hurt because the group attacked her on her 'passiveness.' " "Everybody in the group was attacked but

181

it only really hurt L and S." "Yes. I was hurt. Absolutely down. left with desperate feelings. Shook up."

L. L. is unequivocal in her evaluation of the group as a destructive experience. She had been in encounter groups previously, and found them helpful. She signed up for the project because of "vague feelings of needing something," without being able to specify more clearly the source or nature of her uneasiness. The group, following the model of the leader, was an intensely aggressive one which undertook to help L. L., a passive, gentle individual. to "get in touch with" her anger. The group attacked her in many ways, including a physical assault by one of the female members. Most of all, however, she remembers the leader's attack on her. At one point he cryptically remarked that she "was on the verge of schizophrenia." He would not elaborate further, and the pronouncement echoed ominously within her for many months. On two occasions she sought help from the student health clinic, but was assigned to a medical student, and did not find her sessions helpful. For several months she remained extremely depressed, and withdrew markedly from her family and friends. She was insomniac; she obsessed so much about her leader's schizophrenia remark that she dreaded going to bed because she knew her mind would focus on this point of terror. Often she lapsed into daydreams in which she relived, with a more satisfying ending. some event in the group. She stated that the only benefit of the experience was to help her appreciate how lonely she was: however. her discomfort had been so great that she had been unable to make use of this knowledge.

We consider L. L. a severe casualty. At the interview eight months after the end of the group, she felt that she was gradually reintegrating herself, but was not yet back to the point she was before the group began. Her negative experience was a result of an aggressive, intrusive leadership style. The leader attempted to change her value system by battering down her characterologic defenses.

Group #6.

E. L. was identified by two indices: the group leader's ratings and the "who was hurt" questionnaire. One member stated, "E. L. seemed to become and remain very sad and insecure in the group." Other indices were unavailable since he did not complete postgroup questionnaires except for one portentous cryptic note: "Total renunciation of the validity of self. Total loss of the meaning of defense and control. No reference points."

The evaluation of this subject was difficult since at the time of the interview (eight months postgroup) he was confused and disorganized. The interviewer suspected that he was either in an acute schizophrenic state or under the influence of drugs (a possibility which the subject categorically denied.) He was vague, abstract, spoke in a low mumble, and it was very difficult to obtain clarity about any of the issues in the group. Furthermore, the examiner found it difficult to disentangle the effects of the group from external events that occurred in the subject's life during the time of the group. During the course of the group, E. L. moved to a rather "freak-out" dorm, and took LSD for the first time. He stated that at the end of the group he had had a "three-week schizophrenic break." This was the worst three weeks that he had ever spent in his life, but he somehow managed to get through it and through his final examinations without professional help. He had difficulty describing this episode except to state that "my vowels seemed very long; I felt alienated from my body like Hamlet's mortal coil, and wanted to shuck my skin. My lungs felt polluted from smoking, and I couldn't study." He was smoking marijuana frequently during this period of time. His sleep was fitful and disrupted by early morning awakenings.

He found it difficult to pin down why the group experience was unsettling for him. The most untoward thing that happened was once when he had stated that he was just observing the group, the leader stated, "Well, each to his own thing." E. L. understood the leader to be saying that he was going to be an observer all the rest of his life. "The leader just wrote me off at this point." It was a mistake for him to go into the group, he said. "Things were too unsettled for me already, and I didn't need to spend time in a chaotic group standing on shaky ground." There were, he insisted, many other negative things about the group which he could not clearly describe. Not many people were helped by it, and he felt he above all was certainly not helped. The interviewer felt so concerned about this student that he strongly urged him to seek professional help, a referral which E. L. did not accept.

We consider E. L. a severe casualty, but found it difficult to establish the degree of the group's responsibility. Undoubtedly E. L. was a troubled individual before the group, and some significant coincidental life changes occurred during the course of the group. Nevertheless we cannot discount the fact that immediately following the group he entered a state of extreme disorganization from which he had not yet, eight months later, recovered. It is to be noted that E. L., very much like L. L., responded similarly to the leader. Each overvalued his statements. Each of them was upset by a comment of the leader which they assumed to be one of very serious and unfavorable prognostic intent.

Group #9.

E. D. was identified by four indices: "who was hurt," decreased self-esteem, unfavorable testimony, and seeking psychotherapy after the group. One subject, and E. D. himself, cited him as having been hurt: "E. D. very nervous and upset when grilled with questions. Everyone else was equipped with socially acceptable, ego-building defense mechanisms." "Me. The last meeting I didn't want to come to, and came out of 'responsibility.' I was not in the mood for 'encountering,' and was almost forced to. I don't trust anyone in the group, and felt threatened by it. I came away feeling insecure and having many self-doubts, without being able to resolve them within the group. I overheard another member of the group describing my actions with his roommate, and he was reinforcing my own self-doubts about myself. I didn't want to participate, was forced to participate unnaturally, and then was emotionally upset by the experience for several days afterwards. Our group had no cohesion, no group feeling, no real understanding, and I felt pressured to 'produce' and show myself at the last meeting. I shouldn't have gone to it. In fact, I should have dropped out several times before."

E. D. had recently transferred to Stanford from another campus. For a long time before the group he had felt inadequate and isolated, and had seen a psychotherapist several times. These feelings were responsible for his transfer to Stanford, since his only friend had recently moved to Stanford. At Stanford he felt socially isolated and had joined the group looking for friends, since he feels best when he can relate deeply with people.

He depicts his group experience as a catastrophe. He was unable to trust the other members, whom he perceived as aggressive and dominant. The group lacked cohesiveness and a feeling of warmth and support. The leader, he felt, was simply "crummy" and lacked any idea of how to deal with people. The last meeting was particularly bitter for him since he was vigorously attacked for his passivity and uninvolvement. He recalls nervously picking at the carpet during the onslaught; he was criticized for this, and when he stopped picking at the carpet, was criticized for passivity and suggestability. He was so shaken that he soon misinterpreted most comments directed toward him, and perceived everything as criticism. The group had a postgroup beach party, but he did not attend because he felt so antagonistic to the members. E. D. stated that were it not for the last meeting he might have escaped relatively unscathed since he had previously rationalized his failure in the group by his refusing either to take the group seriously or to involve himself emotionally.

At the end of the group he was asked, "What was the most significant event for you personally?" He replied bitterly:

> The last meeting when I was attacked for my silence in the group. This guy, whose name I can't remember, was trying to play amateur psychiatrist and "break me down" to the point where I supposedly would "open up." However, my feelings were then, and are now, that it is very hard for me to react when I can't trust people, and in a group which is set up for a certain time, and is scheduled to break up, it is very hard for me to react. I need a sense of commitment. It destroyed me for several days. I wanted to resolve what had been left hanging and couldn't, and what I had thought all along had been true—if I had opened up and expressed all my frustrations they would have been lost on people who merely are taking the class for credit. Unless people are going to have a permanent place in your present life, opening up in an encounter group is useless and even harmful, at least for me. However, I think this is a personal hang-up with myself because of many feelings of inferiority.

Following the group he felt deeply depressed for about a week. Following this he was left with a residue of deflation, helplessness, self-disgust, and discouragement. Even months later he continued to feel anxious, depressed, and less trustful of others. His isolation increased and he made plans for transferring to yet another college. He has avoided participation in encounter groups, but several months after the end of the group he sought psychiatric help. After some brief individual therapy he made excellent progress in ten months of group therapy.

We consider E. D. a moderately severe casualty. His negative outcome was a function of several factors. Prior to the group he had relatively severe psychiatric problems, and he began the group with unrealistic psychotherapy goals and hopes of forming enduring friendships with the other group members. He experienced the group as so dangerous and untrustworthy that he chose not to disclose his homosexual feelings or, for that matter, any feelings at all. This deviant, nonparticipant role generated even more anxiety, and reinforced his alienation and negative self-concept. The group, a fragmented, low-support group led by a laissez-faire leader, had no appreciation of his discomfort and first coaxed, then ignored, and finally scapegoated and frontally assaulted him.

Group #9.

S. C., a twenty-year old sophomore, was the most visible of all the casualties. During the course of the group he developed a severe manic psychosis. At the time of the eight-month follow-up, he was still moderately disturbed and refused an interview. Our material thus comes from his psychiatrist, his medical records, and the group leader.

S. C. was not an identified patient before entering the group. He had distinguished himself athletically and performed well academically. In the first meeting his behavior was entirely rational, and the leader stated that he would have been unable to screen him in a pregroup interview. In retrospect, the pregroup test battery might have provided some clues. For example, on one questionnaire he wrote an inappropriate lengthy comment: "I have wanted to try to liberate myself from some of the old value systems that have been imposed upon me by society. I have wanted to raise myself above winning and losing, thus elevating my mind above the petty discrepancies that can drag life down to a low level of subsistence. I have needed to rearrange my present pattern of living to actually find life itself. I have asked questions. I have smoked weed. I have done what my emotions told me to do. I took chances in trusting people. I tried to strip away the facade that the outside saw as 'me' and I am still trying. . . ."

The more structured pregroup questionnaires were of little value, probably because of S. C.'s high denial. For example, he rated himself as high as possible on the self-image questionnaire.

Although he was entirely rational during the first meeting, he took a controversial conservative stance which evoked considerable reaction from the liberal-radical students in the group. During the second meeting S. C. again was rational, but slightly hyperactive, and again was the center of the group focus. After the end of the meeting, he approached the leader and, somewhat inappropriately, told him to be firm and strong. At the third meeting he was clearly hypomanic, and discoursed at length on political, social, and sexual issues. He revealed more of himself than seemed appropriate for that stage of the group. The leader, a psychiatrist, saw him privately after the meeting, and advised him to seek aid at the student health service, and not to return to the group. Between the third and fourth meeting, S. C. became very manic and bizarre: he stole a bicycle, climbed the scaffolding at the women's dorm, bought an expensive motorcycle with a bad check, etc. At the fourth meeting he arrived thirty minutes late with two companions in an obviously psychotic state. The group spent the remainder of the session getting him out of the room and into prompt medical treatment. He was hospitalized and later returned to the University maintaining a very precarious adjustment.

Should S. C. be considered a casualty of the group? It is entirely possible that the onset of his manic psychosis was inevitable, and that the three encounter group meetings he attended were irrelevant and coincidental. Or is it possible that he joined the group because he heard, and heeded, the first inner rumblings of disquiet? We shall with certainty never know. The leader of Group #9, an experienced clinician, expressed the view that the group bore considerable responsibility for the onset and severity of S. C.'s psychosis. He stated: "I feel the psychosis would have occurred nonetheless, but S. C.'s experience in the group. . . . the intense stimulation, the negative feedback, the pressure to open up, the nonviable social role he created for himself in the group, all undoubtedly hastened the course of his psychosis."

Group #10.

H. P. was identified by three indices: the group leader's ratings, low testimony, and the "who was hurt" question. Two students cited H. P. as having been hurt: "H. P. hates me because I honestly told him he meant nothing to me and if he didn't exist I wouldn't care a bit." "I don't think H. P. is any better for it. In fact he may be uptight because of the group. I think there was a definite lack of mutual cooperation and understanding between H. P. and the group."

H. P. entered the group with explicit personal change goals: "I'm too much in control of my emotions and unwilling to make close relationships for fear of being hurt; I wanted to get rid of some of my defenses." Like many members of Group #10, H. P. was intrigued at first by the leader's structured interventions, but gradually he withdrew. "I had strong positive feelings toward others at first, but after the marathon, the best that I could feel was simply apathetic. First I liked the leader but after the midpoint I didn't—he was too structured. I felt I had to overcome my defenses as best I could, but couldn't do it. The leader kept pressuring me to express my feelings, but I didn't know what I felt. When I said this, I was attacked as a phony. This reinforced my defenses, so later in the sessions I just withdrew and watched. My feeling at the end was disgust and frustration. It just didn't do me any good, and I should have defended myself more." He stated that he did have positive feelings toward the others, and wanted to be friends with them, but felt very discouraged about his failure to do so. "I felt I made a fool of myself, a phony. I tried to express emotions, and the others believed it, but I felt helpless and phony. Perhaps groups may have some potential for good, but usually they are superficial and phony. This group was a destructive experience for me."

During and following the group, H. P. felt himself progressively alienated from others and more discouraged about making changes in himself. Obviously, the group had a noxious influence on him and reinforced many of his negative feelings about himself. Although following the group he reintegrated himself to some degree, some three months later he again lapsed into a depression for reasons unclear to him but "connected with distrust for other people." Despite his dysphoria he had procrastinated about seeking professional help.

In summary, H. P. (and T. G., Case 1) had an experience very similar to that described for schizoid patients who drop out of group therapy (Yalom, 1970). These individuals gradually become aware of their inability to experience and express emotions; they feel distant from others, and enter therapy with a resolution to change their modes of expression and relating. In the group they encounter themselves, and slowly grow to appreciate the chimerical nature of their resolution; they often leave deeply frustrated, more discouraged, and nihilistic than ever about the possibility of obtaining help in the future. Enthusiastic group members and impatient, demanding leaders merely hasten this process by placing undue pressure on the subject to "breakthrough" rapidly. H. P. acquiesced to the pressure by a sham display of emotion which he realized was artificial and resulted only in reinforcing his own feelings of duplicity and his distrust of others.

Group #11.

M. A. was identified by only one index: his low testimony. He stated that the group was a poor experience for him with virtually no redeeming features. His reasons for joining the group were, in his own words, "I was at a lost point in life. I was down, had been rejected by my girlfriend, lost my self-confidence, and I thought the encounter group experience would give me a chance to find myself." He was not sure why the group was a negative experience. He blamed the "group" and the other members rather than the leader. He had regarded himself as flexible and radical, whereas the other members seemed so young, boring, trite, rigid, and set in their own ways. One of the things the group did for him was to make him realize that he was "merely" a Stanford student, that he was like the others, and yet somehow not a member of either the radical or the square group. Following the meetings he felt "useless and lost—like I didn't belong anywhere."

He pointed out that another adverse experience for him in the group was that the leader did not like him and was "down" on him. The leader disliked him for "making a mockery of the group." In a sense, M. A. and the leader seemed to be in competition, but the leader "had all the troops." He felt that the leader considered him to be a divisive force in the group and was angry at him for derailing the group and for subtly discouraging members from talking personally. M. A. stated that he engaged in a lot of self-disclosure in the group, but that he had done this before and it was nothing new or helpful for him. He had a talk with the leader after the end of the group, and felt the leader had been very disappointed with him. He realized that he hadn't handled himself in the group nor was he handling himself very well in life. (An interview with the leader corroborated some of M. A.'s impressions. The leader did view him as a divisive force. He was surprised though, that M. A. had been adversely affected, since he thought he was a "con man" who let all comments roll off his back.)

The end of the group found him, M. A. stated, with less self-esteem than when he started. The lowered self-esteem has endured, persisting to the time of the interview six months later. The summer following the group was a bad one for him; he was living with a girl whom he did not like, wanted to get away but was somehow afraid of hurting her. He suffered considerable anxiety, attempted to go to summer school, but was unable to concentrate. He has been in no further groups because he had been so turned off by the group experience in the project. He has never been in psychotherapy, but has been considering it and asked the interviewer's opinion.

We consider M. A. a minor casualty. His poor experience occurred as a result of a deviant, nonviable role he created for himself in the group. It appears that he entered the group feeling anxious and nonconfident of himself, and handled this maladaptively by responding to the other students with derision, disinterest, and scorn; a vicious circle resulted as the other members displayed similar behavior towards him. These events all occurred in the context of a group which in the eyes of both leader and members was an unsuccessful one. The leader did not conceal his dissatisfaction and on several occasions berated the group. He seemed to feel especially threatened and angry at this member who appeared bent on disrupting the integrity of the group.

Group #12.

H. I. was identified by only one index: he responded positively to the question, "Did anything occur in the group that made you consider entering psychotherapy?" He stated:

> To some degree, yes. I realized that I was fairly unusual. It disturbed me to see people reject me when I started opening up. Even more the leader's lack of genuine warmth unsettled me. The group became much more hostile to me the more I participated, and it was hard for me to feel a part of the group. I was mostly irritated with the way the leader sponsored a clique within the group. I felt like I was at a fraternity rush party, and had to b.s. in order to make it. I would not have felt sincere if I had tried to be accepted thusly.

H. I. stated that the group interested him and taught him something about human relationships but was not a positive personal experience. "It was disappointing and possibly harmful. I had more self-confidence before the group than after. Until the group I had been satisfied with my relationships with others." In the group, however, he felt he was rejected by both members and leader. According to H. I., the leader formed a rather in-group clique of students who "mouthed radical jargon and were very much in the drug culture." He and some other peripheral members of the group couldn't quite get into this inner circle, a state of affairs which he found quite anxiety-provoking. He said that perhaps it should have been enlightening to learn that he couldn't relate to everyone, but nevertheless it was not constructive.

For a long period of time after the group he felt less confident of himself in social situations, especially when male-female relationships, the drug culture, or homosexuality were being discussed. This lack of confidence lasted at least a couple of months and even eight months later there were still some traces left. Because of his negative experiences, he never joined another group. The group stirred up many important issues, for example sexual codes and life values, without offering coping stategies. Two homosexuals in the group discussed their sexual lives quite openly. Although he states he is not troubled about homosexuality, he remains vaguely troubled by the discussion pertaining to homosexuality. Similarly, he remains puzzled about the value of the success-oriented life.

We consider H. I. a minor casualty. The negative experience appears to be a result of a lack of acceptance by the leader and other members, and by a challenge to his value system.

Group #13.

C. L. was one of our most obvious casualties. She requested psychiatric aid at the emergency room at the hospital following the third group meeting. In addition to dropping out and requesting therapy, she was identified by eight group members as having been hurt by the experience, e. g. "C. L. got blasted for being fat." "A girl was fat and everybody told her so. It hurt her, but it was true. It was pretty sad." "One girl was constantly called a fat Italian mama, was extremely hurt, and quit the group."

She stated that the group was an extremely destructive one for her. The group operated by everybody "ganging up on one another, thirteen to one, and bulldozing them until they were left on the ground panting." She was bitterly attacked by the group and finally dropped out after an attack on her in which she was labeled "a fat Italian mama with a big shiny nose." She was also told that she probably had "a hell of a time getting any man to look at her". She was very distressed by the fact that she was unable to respond coherently to these attacks, was even further distressed by the failure of the other group members to come to her defense. Returning home from the meeting that evening she cried for almost an hour and realized that the Synanon members had been all too accurate in their perceptions of her. The effect of the experience was to reinforce her already considerable self-contempt. During the next four days she grew progressively more depressed, had many solitary crying spells, slept very fitfully, awakened around 4:00 a.m., and found herself unable to control her appetite and at this point requested psychiatric aid.

She was seen for six emergency psychotherapy sessions in the Stanford Psychiatry Clinic. Following the summer she was seen for five months in therapy, during which she made some moderate strides by losing weight, and gradually increasing her self-confidence.

C. L.'s problems obviously did not begin with the encounter group. On two occasions the previous year she sought psychotherapeutic aid because of her low self-concept and her obesity. She entered the group for similar reasons. Nevertheless, there is little doubt that her experience in the group was destructive. She sought psychotherapy not electively but as an emergency measure to undo the injury to her already deficient self-image.

189

Group #13.

D. R. was identified as a casualty suspect by four indices: decrease in self-esteem. low testimony. seeking psychotherapy. and "who was hurt." He said. "Myself. I was cut down, totally unable to defend. I desperately needed a chance to rebuild, but was ignored, felt totally, completely inadequate."

D. R. stated that he was severely attacked by the Synanon group as part of the routine procedure, and then was attacked again because he refused to play the Synanon game and attack others. He underscored the fact that he especially abhors violence. During the last meeting the members lashed out at him, and he withdrew, felt hopeless and "just sank into a kind of withdrawal." This withdrawal and depression lasted for several days until he saw a psychiatrist for a single interview which was helpful for him. Some months later he saw a psychiatrist again for two interviews for another depression which resulted from a minor slight from a female. He pointed out that over the long term the group experience had not been helpful. Before the group he was more on top of relationships; now he seems to have less intimate and less rewarding friendships. He thinks more about his method of relating to others and in so doing strips himself of spontaneity. Furthermore he is more sensitive to the slightest rebuff to which he responds with depression and withdrawal. At one point in the interview he expressed the belief that things must get better soon since they can't get worse. He pointed out that perhaps Synanon was useful in that it took him off his pedestal, shook him out of his complacency, and exposed him to a broader world perspective than the white, middle-class ethos.

The interviewer noted that D. R. was a tense, depressed and tightly constricted young man. He was markedly conflicted in the area of aggressiveness, and could not easily express anger or even disapproval. His critical comments about his group were thus cloaked in vague platitudes. Synanon highly values the free expression of anger, and places considerable pressure on people to defend themselves and to attack others. He responded by psychological resignation from the group which evoked even further attack.

D. R. was sufficiently depressed during the follow-up interview to be referred for psychotherapy. We consider D. R. to be a moderate casualty.

Recall that Synanon differed from the other groups in that there was no stable group composition, and therefore less of an opportunity for small group cohesiveness to develop. The cohesiveness that Synanon generates is not small-group-centered, but involves the entire organization. The subjects in the project did not have enough contact with Synanon to develop these feelings. Although there was a social hour scheduled after each meeting to engender positive feelings, and to serve as an implicit reminder to the participants that the group attack was indeed a "game," the subjects were not reassured and the casualty and dropout rate in Synanon were high. It is interesting to note that the mechanism of injury for the two subjects in Synanon differed considerably. C. L. was heavily attacked in the very areas in which she felt most uncertain. It was as though her fantasy of the most dreaded calamity came to pass in the group. D. R., however, suffered not so much from an attack on his person but from the group's encouraging him to attack others. His well-entrenched characterologic structure was such that he handled his aggressive urges by denial and reaction formation. Group pressure which demanded that he suddenly change resulted only in dysphoria and a reinforcement of defenses.

Group #14.

M. M. was identified as a casualty suspect by three indices: She began therapy after the group, she dropped out of the group, she was cited by three other members as having been hurt. They commented: "She backed herself into a hole by not admitting that our criticism was valid." "M. M. seemed to be hurt when she was focused upon hard, but she denied it." "M. M. was pushed, she shut up completely."

At the time of the eight-month follow-up, M. M. was highly disturbed psychologically and most uncooperative with the investigators. She failed to keep several appointments, but was eventually interviewed in her dormitory. At that time she was frankly paranoid, extremely hostile, resistive to any type of inquiry, and inconsistent in her answers. She stated that she felt quite isolated in the group, especially when "different attentions were being brought to others." She stated that she herself wasn't attacked, but at other times she alluded to attacks upon herself. Perhaps the thing that was worst for her was "being looked into." She mentioned that she was upset after the group, that she has continued to be upset months later, but that it is very difficult to know whether or not this is directly related to her group experience. On further questioning, she stomped out of the room shouting: "See my parents if you want any further information about me. See my parents."

Fortunately we have some ancillary information about her from other group members and from her psychiatrist. One of the other casualty suspects in her group who was interviewed stated that M. M. was "belted" so badly in the first meeting that she did not return for several meetings. She was placed in the "hot seat" for at least the final thirty minutes of that session, and was vigorously attacked for wearing a mask, and putting up a false front. He felt she was deeply injured by the group; when she finally returned she never fully reentered the group but remained an observer.

We learned that, in the month following the group, M. M.'s parents grew very concerned about her bizarre driving, and consulted a psychiatrist. We interviewed the psychiatrist, and learned that he diagnosed her as an acute paranoid schizophrenic and hospitalized her. Her psychiatrist discussed the encounter group with her, and concluded that the group experience contributed to her psychotic episode, by overstimulating her, and imposing values of freedom upon her which she could ill manage at the time. On the contrary, he stated, she needed reinforcement of repressive and suppressive mechanisms, not liberation.

Unfortunately, we could not obtain information about her psychological condition before entering the group or about her reasons for joining the group. Most likely she was disturbed before beginning the group. However, the fact that she was heavily traumatized in the group, that she was so disturbed afterwards that hospitalization was required, and that her psychiatrist gratuitously stated that the group had been harmful to her, all lead us to consider M. M. a severe casualty of long duration.

Group #15.

D. H., the sixteenth and final casualty, was identified by four indices: the group leader's ratings, seeking psychotherapy, dropping out of the group, and "who was hurt." Two members cited her as having been harmed: 'Yes. D. H. opened up her personal life and a negative experience with a boy as well as other issues which would seem to keep her from returning to the group." "D. H. revealed some things about her relationship with a boy—demeaning for her."

D. H. stated that the group was a negative experience for her with few redeeming features. She was aware of the fact that she had racist feelings, and disclosed these to the group, only to be placed on trial and punished without being helped to change, work through, or understand her feelings. Furthermore she revaled some intimate sexual problems, and again received nothing in return except callous disinterest on the part of the group. She feels she learned some things from the group but of a nihilistic nature, i. e. "that blacks and whites will never be able to trust one another." She also learned a bit about the feelings of blacks, what it's like to be a member of the black race as well as something about the magnitude of white guilt. But her learning was limited to nonpersonal things, and she learned nothing useful about herself. She attributes this to the leader whom she feels was extremely ineffectual and highly biased against the white members of the group. He too merely listened to what she had to say without offering anything positive in return. Because of her disappointment and fear of the group she missed the final two sessions.

For months following the group D. H. was burdened with many negative feelings about herself. She experienced considerable shame; it was difficult for her to take pride in herself after an experience she perceived as public humiliation. She took a risk, uncloseted her skeletons, discussed for example her feelings about her sexual relations with black males, and was neither rewarded nor reassured by the group. (The group in fact, did not respond dispassionately to her. Another member of Group #15 was interviewed and referred to D. H. as "that sex maniac.") She states that her lack of pride was a problem for her before the group, and it has been greatly aggravated since then. She has had difficulty in trusting groups of people again, and asserts that she will never again join a group. "I don't think there will ever be enough trust amongst a group of people for me to ever try this again." She finds her relationship with blacks is far less adaptive, satisfactory, and intact, and she has tended to avoid black people since the group. Some of the negative aspects of the group were neutralized by the fact that she had a very positive relationship with a male student existing before and after the group, and in many ways this has carried her through quite well.

Three months after the group she sought psychotherapy because of a sexual problem and for general feelings of inadequacy—problems of long-standing duration which, however, were probably aggravated by the group. She visited the therapist only once and did not return because she felt intuitively that the therapist would not be useful to her.

We consider D. H. a casualty of moderate severity. Many of the ingredients of a therapeutic brew were present in her group experience: she took a risk; she plunged into the group; she disclosed copious intimate material. What D. H. felt was absent, however, was mutual trust and acceptance to support such revelations.

DISCUSSION

What have we learned from our study of these unfortunate individuals? Their existence and their number alarm us. A casualty rate approaching 10 percent is alarming and unacceptable in an endeavor calculated to foster positive growth. Some perspective may be cast on the finding by asking, "What is the comparable casualty rate in the control sample?"

In the most rigorous sense our controls for the study of casualties are insufficient: we could not employ comparably exhaustive methods of scanning the control subjects for psychological decompensation. Most of our techniques of casualty identification were not applicable for the controls; for example, group leader ratings, "Who was hurt by the group," global evaluations of the group, dropouts. We do know, however, that very few controls requested psychotherapy in the eight-month follow-up period.

Had a large number of control subjects been interviewed for evidence of subtle psychological changes in the same eight-month period, several might have been identified. However, there would still remain an insoluble methodological problem since our definition of casualty states that the encounter group must be an important contributing factor to the subject's psychological distress. Sheer psychological decompensation is not enough to warrant the title "casualty"; earlier we gave some illustrative examples of seriously troubled subjects who were not labeled casualties.

Overall our impression is that the risk factor in several of the groups was considerable. Furthermore, we wish to underscore the point that our rates may err on the conservative side; the true rates may yet be higher. Our definition was stringent. The net we threw out may have missed some subjects. The fact that one of our casualties, T. G., was thought at first to be a High Learner and was identified fortuitously, raises our index of suspicion. There were several high-risk subjects who could not be located for follow-up. Finally, several conditions were imposed on the groups to reduce risk to the participants.

METHOD OF INJURY

The case summaries vividly illustrate that the phenomenon of psychological injury is a complex and varied one. Further, some individuals who had similar experiences to those of the casualties were left untouched or benefited. Some casualties are group-specific: the individual most likely would have had a different outcome in another group; others are individual-specific: the individual carried the seeds of the outcome within himself and would have planted them in any group.

We shall attempt to clarify these points by first summarizing the mechanisms of injury, and then shall discuss the strategies by which other group members avoided injury. Our discussion stems from our interviews with the casualties, with other group members, and from ancillary data about each group.

The various mechanisms of injury include: (1) Attack by leader or by group, (2) rejection by leader or by group, (3) failure to attain unrealistic goals, (4) coercive expectations, and (5) input overload or value shuffle. These are, of course, arbitrary *post hoc* categories. At times the boundaries between them are unclear. Attack usually implies lack of acceptance, whereas the reverse is not necessarily the case. Some subjects experienced such a massive attack that the lack of acceptance was, oddly enough, not a crucial issue: the subject either dropped out of the group or was, in a figurative sense, too concerned about survival to afford himself the luxury of asking for love.

Attack. Ten of the sixteen casualties were adversely affected by an attack by the leader or by the group. For six subjects the leader was experienced as personally attacking. These six subjects were in Groups #4, #6, and #13, each of which had leaders with a similar style ("energizers"— see Chapter 7). The subjects' descriptions of their experience in these three groups are virtually interchangeable: "The leader told me I was a dumb shit." "I was treated as the lowest thing on earth." "The leader dismissed me and my whole way of life." "The leader said I was on the verge of schizophrenia." "The leader just wrote me off. The message was I was going to be an observer the rest of my life." Group #13 (Synanon) differed from the other groups in that there were several leaders or veteran game players (see Chapter 2). The content of the comments was the same, however, "They gang up on you, tear you down, and leave you on the ground, raw and bleeding." One subject was, "cut down, totally unable to defend myself."

Our data suggest that with few exceptions these six students entered the group with goals appropriate for a personal growth group. B. V. came closest to expressing overt therapeutic goals and entered the group in a troubled state, "the nadir of my existence." Our limited information about E. L. also suggests that at the time he entered the group he may have been approaching a crisis in his life. The three group leaders for these six subjects were all charismatic, highly personal, self-revealing, intrusive, and challenging; they focused on the individual in the group. Their demands were severe. Leaders #4 and #6 could be quite supportive if the members proceeded at the leader-prescribed rate, but even then they retained their aura, power, and charisma through their unpredictability.

All three exerted considerable influence and pressure on their members. Each used a format in which each member was "worked on" one at a time. In Groups #4 and #6 there was no place to hide, and each member received his turn. Regardless of initial expectations, the leaders' rules of procedure were imposed. Leader #6 made this very clear at the beginning of the group as he compared the group to a ship voyage. They would, he stated, all depart together and return to port together. Members of the group were literally not permitted to leave during the twenty-four-hour marathon. Group #13 (Synanon) had no single leader, but the aggregate leadership operated in a similar manner. However, since a new group formed every week, it was possible to elude the spotlight, by behaving as if one had already had the "game put on him."

Other casualties also suffered from attack. These subjects, however, reported being attacked only by the other members and not by the leader. The groups (#5, #9, #14) from which these casualties came were cold and uninvolved, with low cohesiveness and low trust. Their leaders were relatively distant, nonsupportive, and according to both observers and to the leaders themselves, were unaware of the impact of the attack or attempted, unsuccessfully, to halt it.

Two of these subjects were obviously troubled and immediately assumed the deviant role. S. C. in the very first meetings monopolized the group time, and espoused unpopular, ultraconservative positions on the issues the group discussed. M. M.'s interpersonal style was similarly bizarre; she displayed so much irritation, distrust, and contempt that in the initial meeting she drew a massive group attack upon herself.

The other two casualties who were attacked by the group members suffered injury in different ways. O. O. entered the group in a vulnerable state and was inordinately uneasy about his relationship to white students. The group gave him some criticism which the laissez-faire leader failed to help convert into constructive feedback. O. O. suffered in silence. At follow-up, Leader #5, an experienced clinical psychiatrist, was considerably surprised at hearing of O. O.'s negative response. E. D. in Group #9 had an unrewarding experience throughout, but states he might have escaped unscathed had it not been for the attack on him in the last meeting.

Group #9 was from every perspective one of the least successful groups. Its dropout rate was high; only eight of the original fourteen members finished. Cohesiveness was poor. The group had been hampered in its development by cancelled meetings, by the manic psychosis of S. C. (see Chapter 2). The group floundered for much of its life and then appeared to make a belated rescue attempt. E. D. had been, throughout, one of the most uninvolved, least committed members of the group. In its terminal thrashing about, the group appeared to scapegoat E. D. as the prototype, symbol, or indeed cause, of its failure.

Rejection. Rejection played a role in the negative outcome of six of the sixteen casualties. For several, the experience of rejection and attack are so similar that the difference is but a semantic subtlety. B. V. and O. O., however, explicitly reported both attack and rejection. B. V., for example, stated, "I wanted some reassurance about my existence . . . to be found acceptable . . . to be told I was okay . . . to dig myself. . . ." He did not get that acceptance from the group and left feeling even more negatively about himself. O. O. similarly entered the group searching for acceptance, especially from Caucasian students. He was so sensitized and so expectant of rejection that he perceived criticism of his circumlocution and his failure to discuss his here-and-now feelings as a total, blanket rejection of his core self.

Three others (M. A., H. I., and D. H.) experienced rejection without the occurrence of overt attack. M. A. and H. I. both felt that true membership had been denied them. H. I. described the group as consisting of a center clique and another purgatorial ring of members. He felt that the leader admitted only members with values similar to his own. Anticipating the rejection from the group, M. A. struck first, and so derided and scorned the other members that his prophecy was fulfilled as the other members reciprocated with rejecting behavior.

D. H., in Group #15, courted acceptance too vigorously. She had planned her agenda in advance, for she was weighted down with guilt about her sexual behavior and her negative feelings to blacks. She promiscuously revealed herself to a group that was not yet prepared for such intimate material, and she was insensitive to the receptivity of the individuals to whom she disclosed herself. In its first meetings, Group #15, a mixed black-white group with a black leader, was occupied with defining boundaries, with establishing trust, with easing black-white tensions; it was not yet ready for the degree of intimacy D. H. demanded. Interviews with the leader and other members indicated that they withdrew from her, and experienced her as a problem, "a sex maniac," rather than as a person whom they knew and liked who had some serious life problems. This sequence of events was particularly noxious for D. H., who had longstanding problems in the areas of guilt and shame. Her sense of shame particularly was reinforced, and she found it far more difficult to trust and to confide in others after the group experience.

Failure to Achieve Unrealistic Goals. Four individuals (T. G., O. O., E. D., and H. P.) entered the group with unrealistically high expectations. Their needs and goals were extensive, and would have been an appropriate ticket of admission to any psychotherapy group. For example, E. D. had transferred to Stanford simply because his only friend had recently done so. He felt alienated both from others and from himself. He had strong schizoid trends and experienced a sense of restriction on his emotions and an inability to reach out to relate and empathize with others. He had previously sought psychotherapy for these very problems.

T. G., H. P. and O. O. can be described in almost identical terms. They all entered the group with great expectations. They all hoped to learn to relate, to break through their restrictive schizoid straitjackets, and to get in touch with their emotions. Each explicitly stated that they hoped to find friends in the encounter group. T. G. and E. D. had had previous individual therapy; H. P. and O. O. were seeking help for the first time. None of

196

the four had ever been in a group before. Despite their vigorous personal resolutions to do things differently, resolutions which were probably abetted by the then current optimistic mystique surrounding the encounter group, they found, to their great dismay, that their behavior was more locked, rigid, and repetitive than they had known. They soon re-created and re-experienced in their groups the same interpersonal environment from which they had fled in the outside world. They were flooded with discouragement, and abandoned their abortive attempts to communicate and relate differently. All of them left the group more discouraged and more pessimistic about ever changing.

Often the leader and the group collude in the expectational set. They amplify the subject's unbounded initial optimism and grasp strenuously for the ever-elusive, will-of-the-wisp of the encounter group—the "breakthrough." H. P. stated it explicitly: "I tried to overcome my defenses as best I could, but I couldn't do it. The leader kept pressuring me to express my feelings but I didn't know what I felt. When I said this, I was attacked as a phony. This reinforced my defenses so later in the sessions I just withdrew and watched." Other factors in addition to the interplay of unrealistic expectations and a schizoid character structure contributed to the negative outcome. E. D., for example, was plagued by homosexual drives which he was unable to discuss in the group. Not infrequently when there is something important that one *cannot* talk about in a group, the result is a total inhibition. The individual is stripped of his spontaneity and unconsciously monitors all his responses lest he let the secret slip through.

Coercive Expectations. Two subjects (N. I. and H. P.) reported unusual reactions to the group. As a result of being unable to meet the leader's or the group's demands for emotional display, they both ended the group with a personal sense of hollowness. N. I. stated that her group leader had powerful expectations that the group would move quickly to a level of profound sensitivity and intimacy. She could not match his apparent depth of feeling, and responded in a self-critical fashion by a growing conviction that she lacked both depth of feeling and the ability to care for others. The other subject, H. P., a schizoid individual, had a very similar experience. He responded to the group pressure for expressive display by sham emotion which resulted in his considering himself not only emotionally void but artificial and phony as well.

The phenomenon is well known. Groups often set up norms which demand a vigorously sensitive display of feeling. If there are some experienced encounter groupers among the members who, like a Pavlovian canine salivating to a bell, begin to "feel" in the early minutes of the first meeting, then some problems are posed for group beginners. They may respond to the group pressure by actually experiencing deep feelings, or simulating the same. A hardy soul may resist the group current by honestly expressing his skepticism. Occasionally, participants, like N. I. and H. P., deeply concerned about their emotional shallowness and lacking the skills to obtain consensual validation, are convinced of their difference from the other members and use this information to berate themselves.

Input Overload. Several subjects seemed to have been traumatized by "overstimulation" by their encounter group. This is a mode of injury as vague as it is inferential. The subjects involved (E. L., S. C., and M. M.) were still too highly disturbed at the time of the follow-up interview to cooperate in the research. The evidence for overstimulation derives from their psychiatrists and group leaders. These three subjects all experienced psychotic episodes. Group Leader #9 expressed the opinion that, although he felt S. C. would have had a manic psychosis even had he not been in a group, the "intense stimulation, the negative feedback, the pressure to open up" all helped stir an already too turbulent cauldron and accelerated the onset of his illness. M. M.'s psychiatrist similarly impugned the group for overstimulating her and imposing values of freedom, when what she needed was "not liberation but reinforcement of repressive and suppressive mechanisms." E. L. was already shaky when he entered Group #6 which, along with Synanon, was the most highly confrontational, explosive group. He seemed to have been stirred into a whirlpool of confusion. He stated that it was a mistake to enter the group. "Things were too unsettled for me already, and I didn't need to spend time in a chaotic group standing on shaky ground."

H. I. was affected in a different manner, yet he too was "stirred up" in a manner that did not prove constructive to him. He was disturbed by the open discussion of homosexuality in the group. Although he denies personal homosexual concern, the investigators felt that some unresolved sexual conflicts were awakened with which he could not deal. Secondly, his hierarchy of values was shaken as the leader challenged his success-orientation. In neither instance was the subject able to do more than feel shaken. He lacked the opportunity or ability to work through this issue either inside or outside of the group.

PROTECTIVE MECHANISMS OF NONCASUALTIES

Obviously there is yet another dimension to these mechanisms of injury. Many participants found the groups to be productive learning environments. Not everyone who was attacked, rejected, or overstimulated suffered harm. Many individuals sailed through high-risk groups or high-risk experiences either unscathed or with evident profit. This is in part accounted for by personality variables and will be discussed in detail in Chapter 10.

There are a number of other factors which served as protective mechanisms. In the many interviews with casualty suspects who did not suffer injury, we addressed the question of how each dealt with a potentially noxious experience. It seemed clear that many of these individuals viewed the group far more casually than the sixteen casualties. They had no pressing need for, nor great expectations of, the group. The three easy academic credits often entered into the discussion of their reasons for joining the group; loneliness, depression, or other psychological "hang-ups" rarely were mentioned. Many described an intellectual curiosity about groups or a desire for training as a leader.

Several participants mentioned "uninvolvement." They stayed out of the vortex of the group, they "did not take it seriously," the group was "artificial," "not meaningful," "boring," "plodding." One subject in Synanon stated, "It's unreal, you know, for a group of strangers to meet once a week and scream at one another. How can you really take it seriously?" These participants maintained a pose of objectivity and distance. They detoxified the risk quotient of the group by forming an alliance with an observing ego which kept before them the fact that the group was an artificial time-limited aggregation in which deliberate magnification of emotions occurred. Others disengaged themselves physically and dropped out of the group. Obviously, extreme lack of involvement which reflects a safety or a survival orientation also diminished the possibility of positive, constructive gain.

These participants were not devastated by an attack. Many could rely upon their highly positive self-concept to evaluate critical feedback by the other members. Their center of gravity remained within themselves, unlike many of the casualties who had low stores of self-esteem, and whose sense of worth rocketed up and plummeted down with the appraisal of others.

Other members used an outside reference group for validation. For example, a subject in Group #4 (a high-risk, highly aggressive, confrontational group) was an experienced grouper; when she felt pressured in the group she would either work it through by referring to internalized phantoms of past groups, or would actively work it out with members of the commune where she lived. Her commune functioned as a slightly attenuated but perpetual encounter group and dwarfed the emotional impact of the leader or members of Group #4 on her. Another well-integrated girl responded adaptively to the same Synanon attacks which devastated others. She stated that the group pointed out the "dark sides" of herself and she also realized the universality of these aspects. She maintained her ability to objectify: "Yes, they attacked me for being a virgin, but I know that they have different cultural backgrounds and different attitudes to sex. I didn't let it fluster me." The group turned out to be an "eye-opener" for her. She had led a sheltered life and found the group to be an educational venture which, though smacking of a slumming experience, was a personally meaningful, integrative one.

Others discovered ways to get through high-risk groups with a minimum of discomfort. One participant in Group #4 said she could write a treatise on "how to get through an encounter group unscathed." She was open, disarming, nondefensive in the early meetings and remained fairly, but not inappropriately, inactive and inconspicuous the rest of the time. Some Synanon members were successful in avoiding the "hot seat" because the composition of the groups changed every week (see Chapter 2). There-fore it was possible to attend the ten meetings with no one realizing that the "game had never been put on" a certain individual. One member max-imized the possibility of hiding by playing the game to the degree of mild assaults on the current target of the group. Only the most skillful could hide indefinitely in Synanon, and a large number of subjects (as we shall discuss shortly) dropped out of Synanon after the game had been played on them or when their number was coming up.

Some participants were fortunate in their group assignment. They seemed fragile, frightened individuals who benefited from the group expe-rience even though to the observers they appeared to be only peripheral members. They participated to a degree that was optimal for them, bene-fited from vicarious experience, and profited from a sense of belonging-ness. One subject, in Group #12, expressed great gratitude to her leader for permitting her to participate at her own pace. He invited her in, but was not intrusive, demanding, or punitive when she did not participate at his pace. This young woman might have had an outcome similar to L. L. in Group #6, or C. L. in Synanon, were she in a group with a confronta-tional, intrusive leader.

Another subject may have had a negative outcome had not his group leader (#2) responded very sensitively to him. He would have been a thorn in the side of any leader. He was an encounter group buff, who con-stantly competed with the leader and inappropriately urged the group into deeper levels of forced intimacy and catharsis by suggesting a series of group exercises. Furthermore he was extremely vulnerable, and joined the group for therapeutic purposes when in the midst of a severe identity crisis. We suspect that without firm leader intervention, he would soon have created a nonviable role for himself and evoked a withering degree of group hostility. The leader very deliberately "kept the lid on." Leader #2 felt that it was his task to suppress him and guide him into a different, al-beit less colorful, role in the group. The subject's reaction to the experi-ence was one of annoyance at the leader's suppression, and guilt that he hadn't asserted himself more and moved the group faster and in a more helpful direction for the other participants. He ended the group with a sense of disappointment, uninvolvement, and some displeasure at the ex-tent of his own need to control, but with no psychological decompensation.

Other participants displayed remarkably tenacious protective defenses. A severely schizoid member in Group #1 was interviewed because other members labeled him as having been hurt. The research team had had considerable concern about him since the first meeting when his bizarre behavior was noted by the observers. He not only did not verbally partici-pate in the group, aside from a few cryptic and enigmatic comments, but took copious written notes, a highly sophisticated way of committing sui-cide in a California encounter group. We predicted that no group would long tolerate this behavior, and that strenuous efforts would be made to change him which, if unsuccessful, would be followed by efforts to exclude him. In the early meetings the group did focus heavily upon him, but soon, as is usually the case with extreme and unyielding deviants, withdrew from him. The leader, mild, accepting, and nonconfrontational, helped to establish tolerant, gentle, nondemanding norms. Though the member continued much of this behavior throughout the meetings, the others were able to accept him as he was without experiencing a sense of failure because they hadn't broken through his defenses. In the six-month follow-up, he remained elusive and noncommittal, but overall expressed a positive attitude toward the group experience.

ENCOUNTER GROUPS AND PSYCHOTHERAPY

There was relatively little difference between the controls and the experimentals when one examined the incidence of psychotherapy begun prior to the encounter group experience—16 percent experimentals versus 21 percent controls (data were available for 143 participants and 51 controls). There was, however, a decided difference between the experimental and control group in the nine months after the beginning of the groups. Eighteen experimental subjects (13 percent), of whom seven were casualties, began psychotherapy during this time as compared with only two (4 percent) control subjects. Over *three times* as many experimental subjects as controls entered therapy after the onset of the encounter group.[5]

We attempted to understand the meaning of this difference by interviewing the eighteen experimental subjects who began psychotherapy during or following their encounter group experience. (Perhaps one might, more accurately, say *sought* psychotherapy since the therapy experience of some of the subjects was limited to only a few sessions.) Fourteen of the eighteen subjects were interviewed.

The information flowing from the interviews of these fourteen participants suggests four types of relationships between the encounter group experience and psychotherapy.

Psychotherapy to Repair the Damage of the Encounter Group. Five of the fourteen subjects interviewed fit into this category. They (L. L., S. C., C. L., D. R., and M. M.) were all casualties of the groups and have been described in detail earlier. Two of the five (L. L. and D. R.) saw a psychiatrist only for a couple of emergency sessions in the midst of an acute anxiety attack or depressive episode, and did not continue therapy. C. L. continued outpatient therapy for several months with considerable benefit. S. C. and M. M. continued under psychiatric care only so long as they were hospitalized for psychotic episodes. There is, in addition, one other subject (V. C.) who should be mentioned here. He does not appear among the eighteen since he began therapy *before* the group and continued it during and subsequent to the group. However, as we noted earlier, he was severely disturbed by the group and the nature of his therapy changed from an optional self-exploratory venture to a necessary treatment of a profound depression.

Some Participants Sought Psychotherapy for the Same Reasons They Started the Encounter Group. Application for the encounter group and the request for psychotherapy were both manifestations of the individual's psychological distress. The participant considered encounter as a mode of therapy or at least as an opportunity to combat loneliness and to make friends. Six participants fall into this category. Two of them have already been described as casualties (E. D., and D. H.). Both sought therapy some months following the group experience; both had had a history of psychological disturbance existing long before the encounter group.

Another example of this category is L. C., a participant in Group #11 whom we did not consider a casualty. He was a passive, shy individual who complained of no sense of direction in life, and described himself as friendless, lonely, and unable to seize the chances that life provided. He joined the group because of his loneliness and his inability to talk to people, and had hoped that in the group he would be able to change these aspects of himself. He states that the group was a disappointment to him in this way, and that he had even passed up an opportunity to meet one person in the group after the end. In many ways the group was a failure experience for him in that he merely repeated his patterns of passivity and uninvolvement in the group. "What was destructive in the group was my failure to get into the group. It was my failure, not the group's. . . . I was a coward." However, he stated that he also received a good deal of positive feedback in the group, and he ended the group on a very positive note. The positive feeling evaporated, however, after a few weeks and he returned to his habitual frame of mind. Four months later when the summer quarter began, he saw a psychologist several times for the same reasons that he had sought help in the group: his feelings of loneliness, inadequacy, and inability to form intimate relationships.

Two Participants Had a Constructive Experience in the Group and Sought Therapy to Continue Work Which Had Been Initiated in the Group. C. N., a participant in Group #8, had sought psychotherapy several months prior to the group for anxiety, conflict with parents over issues of his independence, and for global feelings of inferiority. He did not feel the therapist could help him, and saw him only one time. He joined the encounter group for the same reasons that he had previously sought help and emphatically declared that the encounter group experience was a constructive one for him. He felt very well for the month following the group. However, he returned home during the summer and states that he went through a very severe depression which was "the worst period of my life." During this time he had severe anorexia and suicidal thoughts, but managed to continue functioning throughout the summer on a job. He saw a psychiatrist approximately four times, was benefited by his work with the therapist, and also by his relationship with a girlfriend whom he saw for the next six months. However, when she left to go overseas he once again sought therapy, which again has been useful to him. One is tempted to classify this student as a casualty when considering only the bare facts, i. e. an extremely severe depression beginning approximately four weeks after the end of the group experience. However, this was examined in depth with the subject who feels strongly that the two were not causally related. He states that, had he not returned home to live with his parents, he is certain the depression would not have occurred. His previous relationship with his parents had been an extraordinarily conflicted one for which he had sought therapy before going into the group. To his mind the group was totally constructive: it made him aware of problem areas that he had not previously considered. At the same time, however, it made him realize and fully understand that talking to someone about his psychological problems could be of value. Since his group experience, he has been able to use psychological aid far better than on his previous attempt. His relationships with others have improved; he is more honest, more personal, more self-assured with his peers and with females. He considers these changes in himself to be dramatic ones.

E. C., a participant in Group #4, sought psychotherapy following the encounter group experience, and stated that the encounter group aroused a need for psychotherapy. He stated, however, that overall this was an extremely positive, constructive experience. He had entered searching for help for his depression, high level of anxiety, apathy, inability to relate to others, and lack of motivation in his work. The group was an intense, somewhat uncomfortable experience for him. He stated that the leader quickly created considerable emotional strain in the group. E. C. did not totally integrate himself into the group, and felt alienated during the meetings and unsettled for months after. Nevertheless he considers the encounter group a good experience because he realized a great deal more about the kinds of problems he had and, furthermore, felt very optimistic about working on these problems. He felt it was too much to ask of an encounter group that met for a relatively brief period of time to work through or to solve problems. His group was successful both in making him aware of his major problems and of the possibility of getting help for them. Consequently, following the group experience, he applied for group therapy. Again one is tempted to consider him a casualty because the bare facts are that he experienced discomfort in the group, and had more discomfort following the group than he had before he entered. Nevertheless, our summary view is that the group was a constructive experience for him. It propelled him into further exploratory therapy which he appears to be utilizing well.

One Student Sought Psychotherapy Subsequent to the Group for Reasons Entirely Unrelated to the Group. B. T., a participant in Group #7, joined the group because his career goal was to become a psychiatrist. Curiosity, too, was an instigating factor since he alone of all his friends had never attended one. Before joining, he had had a short course of therapy for a mild depressive episode. He had a positive experience in the encounter group; the leader, he said, had a remarkably "soft touch" and no one could have been harmed. Several months later he experienced another depressive episode which was treated successfully with antidepression medication. He stated unequivocally that the group was a positive experience for him and was unrelated to his depression several months later.

To summarize, encounter group subjects may seek psychotherapy following their group experience for a number of reasons: (1) to repair the damage of a destructive group experience; (2) for the same reasons that brought them to the group; (3) because the group was a constructive experience which helped them understand the need for therapy; (4) for reasons unrelated to the group; and (5) most important of all, the possibility of getting help through psychological means. Perhaps the point to be underscored is that when an individual begins psychotherapy following an encounter group experience, one should not conclude that the group was a destructive experience. In fact, this was true for only five of the fourteen participants who began therapy.

DROPOUTS

An intensive study was made of the subjects who dropped out of the seventeen groups. It was assumed that a large number of casualties would be found among the dropout sample, and the study of group dropouts was considered of intrinsic importance. Often, a large number of dropouts betokens a dual failure, that of the group and that of the individual. Those who terminate a group prematurely are generally not helped by the experience; furthermore, the occurrence of a dropout is often demoralizing for the group, which must spend time considering the reasons for the dropouts or dealing with guilt for having driven the member out of the group.

Dropouts were defined as members who missed the last two meetings of their group.[6] After we identified the dropouts by screening attendance records, we attempted to interview them to understand their reasons.

The interview schedule ran as follows: First, to revivify the group for them, a thirty-minute excerpt of a tape recording of the last meeting they had attended was played. After listening to the tape the subject was asked to sort sixty-five cards, each stating some reason drawn from our clinical experience and from the small-group literature for dropping out of a group, into three piles labeled "very important, somewhat important, and unimportant" for dropping out. They were then asked to choose and rank order the five most important items in the "very important" pile. The subject was then interviewed by a research assistant who used the rankings as a guide for the interview. The dropouts were not well-motivated to participate in any follow-up aspects of the study; consequently, we paid them an appropriate fee for their time.

Of the thirty-five dropouts, eighteen attended only three or fewer meetings, while seventeen attended more than three meetings. Our expectation that the dropouts would be a high-risk sample was not entirely borne out: of the thirty-five dropouts, only five were casualties. However, some individuals dropped out to protect themselves, and may have suffered some harm had they continued in the group.

Many of our conclusions about the dropout population are hampered by our relatively poor follow-up rate. Only twenty-three of the thirty-five dropouts could be interviewed; the remaining twelve could not be located, or, in a few instances, refused to come for an interview.

The reasons offered by those interviewed fell into four major categories:

Concern About the Group's Attack, Anger, or Rejection. This is the major reason for dropouts. Eleven subjects cited this as a primary reason for leaving the group. Nine had either anticipated or had experienced an attack or rejection by the group as a whole or by one or more members. Two subjects dropped out because they specifically feared the anger of the leader; both of these subjects were in Group #4, a high confrontation, high-risk group. The experience of its casualties has already been described earlier in the chapter.

These are the words of one case in this category:

> The group had special people they always brought into the conversation—I was not one of them. I was ill at ease with all the people in the group; I didn't feel they were like me or could understand. They left me and several other people who didn't talk much in the group out. Hardly anyone could say anything without being attacked, and I got into a vicious circle of not saying anything, becoming more uncomfortable, and feeling even more inhibited about saying anything.

Two subjects who were roommates, though they were in different groups, both decided to drop out after the suicide of D. A. He had come to their room the night he killed himself to ask them to go to the movies. They were both studying and declined. D. A.'s death not only evoked considerable personal guilt, but it also augmented many fears they had of their groups. The one in Group #2 said that she knew he had probably opened himself up to his group; they had not come to his help; and they were responsible for his death. She described fantasies she had of being "mobbed" by her group. Nine months earlier she had participated in a sixty-hour marathon group which had profoundly shaken her up and whose effects she was still feeling. The next meeting of her group was to be a twenty-hour marathon, and she decided to heed her fears and drop out of the group. The roommate had a similar response. She mentioned that she knew that D. A. was, in addition to being in Group #15, in another group outside of the study. "This group was extremely brutal and contributed to his suicide. He looked so many places for satisfaction, and was rejected so many times. He was rejected by his encounter groups too, and I didn't want to be part of something that could hurt another person like that." She had in her first meeting told two people she liked them; and had been ignored in return. "I felt more rejected than I ever remember." D. A.'s suicide helped her to decide that she wanted nothing more to do with groups.

Fear of One's Own Anger. Seven subjects expressed concern about losing control and expressing anger. Some expressed this explicitly, others more implicitly. There is heavy overlap between this category and the previous one. All these subjects also feared being attacked by the group. The interviewer described these subjects as tight, controlled, and restricted. They were often obsequiously polite and appeared to have little access to their rage. In the group they were made uncomfortable when urged to express their feelings; they often dropped out of the group after they experienced their own anger. It was difficult for them to return to the group because of a free-floating sense of danger. The subjects seemed to fear two possible consequences: either they would explode with rage and commit acts they would always regret, or they would encounter massive and withering retaliation from the rest of the group. An excerpt from the interviewer's summary on a subject who dropped out of Synanon after six lessons is illustrative:

On this sorting task he indicated that the reason that he dropped out of the group was primarily because there was too much anger and hostility in the group, too much "gutsy expression" in the group; somewhat less important were the facts that there was no leader and no control in the group. However, when we investigated a bit more about there being too much anger in the group, it became clear that he feared the attack and anger of the group less than he feared the group's insistence that he participate in expressing his own anger. Our clinical judgement suggests that this is an individual who is distant from his anger and quite threatened by it. He has a mincing, effeminate quality to his speech and his gestures. He is very obsequious in his relationship to us. He was surprised and overly thankful to us for paying him for his time. He has been in psychotherapy two summers ago and one of the things that he worked out was his inability to be aggressive. During the interview, as he spoke about Synanon, he was very condescending about the other people in the group. He states that these were not the kind of people he would ordinarily associate with in life, in fact they were the very kind of people he would avoid. As he spoke about them there was a sneer about his lips, which again denoted a good deal of unconscious anger and hostility. He says he usually expresses anger passively, by total withdrawal or by a cold steely stare rather than any kind of overt expression.

Fear of Intimacy and/or Self-Disclosure. The two subjects in this category were made uncomfortable by the intimacy or revelation in the group and the demands for the same from them. Though at one level they desired closeness, they also feared it. They were schizoid, self-abnegating individuals with low self-esteem who dreaded the thought of self-disclosure because of their conviction that inwardly they were evil and shameful.

Desire for More Intimacy. These four subjects were impatient; they wanted to move faster than the rest of the group; they wanted closeness and intimacy, and wanted it quickly. They criticized the leaders for being too uninvolved and too passive. This criticism was particularly levied at Leaders #7 and #9 who, as Chapter 2 describes, were intellectualized, non-confrontational, and laissez-faire. They criticized the physical arrangements: the cavernous, sterile rooms; the tightly scheduled meetings; the research accoutrements, tape recorder, observers, and questionnaires. These subjects were experienced "groupers." One had just completed an intimate fast-moving group to which she compared her new group most unfavorably.

DROPPING OUT: IMPLICATIONS FOR THE GROUPS

Let us now consider the dropouts from the group perspective. There are marked differences among the seventeen groups (see Table 3–8, Chapter 3). Five had no dropouts. (Three of these groups may have been artificially low in dropouts since Groups #3, #6 and #11 were marathon groups. Group #11 had only two long meetings, while Groups #3 and #6 had fifteen- and twenty-four-hour marathons respectively right at the end, thus reducing the likelihood that dropouts, as we have defined them, could occur since it is extremely unlikely that a member will leave the group in the midst of a meeting. Group #6 had strong prohibitions about dropping out, and a member would have been physically prevented from leaving the marathon.)

That Groups #1 and #2 had no dropouts was not surprising to the research team. Both leaders were nonintrusive, supportive leaders; both tended more than others to think in terms of group cohesiveness, group integrity, and of building a maximally effective social organization. Leader #1 was highly group-oriented.

The high-dropout groups were #7, #9, #13 (Synanon), and #15. Synanon lost eight members (recall that Synanon was a double group with twenty-one original members). Many reasons can be advanced to explain Synanon's high dropout rate. It was an uncomfortable, high attack group. There was no support during the meeting; although a postmeeting socializing period was offered, many subjects made only marginal use of it. There was little opportunity for group cohesiveness to develop since the subjects were in a different group weekly. There was no sense that they "owed" it to the group to attend, that the other members would be disappointed, or that the group would disintegrate without them. Note also that Synanon demanded more time since they had to travel approximately sixty minutes on a chartered bus to the Synanon in Oakland.

Groups #9 and #15 encountered problems early in their course (see

Chapter 2). A participant developed a manic psychosis in Group #9, while a participant committed suicide in Group #15. Both leaders in post-group interviews stressed the demoralizing effects of these events on the subsequent course of the group and on the dropout rate. Group #15 was a mixed black-white group with a black leader. The tension level was high and the white subjects in particular were consistently guarded and uncomfortable. Groups #7 and #9 were the least "hip" groups; they were led by psychiatrists each with a strongly held conceptual framework (Psychoanalytic Group Leader #7 and Transaction Analytic Leader #9). The distant, aloof posture of these leaders turned off many students who found the groups dull and uneventful.

PREGROUP DIFFERENCES BETWEEN DROPOUTS AND GROUP CONTINUERS

The intergroup differences in dropout rate are so great that, as with casualties, the best predictor for dropout potential is "What group were they in?" Nevertheless, we investigated whether the dropouts differed from group completors on some pregroup measurements.

We used a paired-control method. For each dropout a paired control was selected—a subject who was in the same group, of the same sex, and had had the same amount of prior encounter group experience. Then the subjects who dropped out for similar reasons were compared with their matched-pairs on *pregroup variables* hypothesized to be relevant.

The eleven who dropped out because they feared the group's anger or rejection were compared with their paired controls on ten psychological characteristics thought to be relevant to issues of anger measured before the group experience. These variables were: (1) perceived danger of encounter groups; (2) self-rating of spontaneity; (3) perceived opportunities in their environment for "putting others straight"; (4) opportunities for expressing anger; (5) the value they place on expressing feelings; (6) the value of expressing angry feelings; (7) the FIRO scales of acceptance of control from others; and (8) expressing controlling behavior. The sign test (Siegel, 1956) was used for these comparisons.

Of the eight variables examined, five of them were significant at or above the .10 level in a direction consistent with our hypothesis. The subjects who dropped out of their groups because they feared the group's anger or rejection differed from their matched pairs in: perceived themselves as having few opportunities to put others straight; perceived themselves as having few opportunities to express anger; felt it was less important to express their feelings; felt it was less important to express their anger directly to people; and were less controlling of others.

A comparison of those who dropped out because they feared their own anger on the same eight variables revealed that three were significant in the expected direction: They less often perceive opportunity to put others straight; it is less important for them to express all their feelings; and they attempt to control others less. There is heavy overlap between the participants in the previous category and in this one, and the similarities in the psychological dimension reflects not only this fact but also the fact that both reasons for dropping out revolved around feelings of anger and fear of it.

Four students dropped out of the groups because they desired more intimacy. They were compared with their matched controls on the following measures thought to be relevant to the issue of intimacy: (1) genuineness of encounter groups; (2) ease of intimacy; (3) opportunities to be intimate; (4) opportunities to share with peers; (5) opportunities to be in trusting situations; (6) value of expressing feeling; (7) value of being close; (8) value of sharing with peers; and (9–10) the FIRO wanted and expressed affection scales. Because the N is small, no significance tests could be computed. The subjects who dropped out because the groups did not provide them with enough immediate intimacy differed from their control pairs in the following ways: they perceived encounter groups as less genuine; they found it more difficult to get close to others; they usually did not see themselves as having enough opportunities to know others deeply; it was less important for them to express their feelings but more important for them to become close to others and share with their peers. On the FIRO they expressed and accepted less affection from others.

These findings are consistent with the impressions of the clinical interview in that it was felt that the students who desired more intimacy at a quicker pace were in fact heavily conflicted in this area. Although they felt it was important to be in situations where they could express intimacy, they nevertheless perceived the encounter group situation with considerable mistrust. They also rated themselves as wanting less affection and expressing less affection. Although they behave as though they wish to plunge into intimate relationships with others, their behavior at the same time precludes such eventuality.

These findings suggest that the students who were destined to drop out, compared with others in the same group, had certain distinguishing features which contributed to their decision. The ultimate decision to drop out is, of course, a subtle interplay of the existing personality characteristics, the interpersonal needs, and the norms which their group will establish. The students who most deplore their lack of opportunities to be close to others will be most disenchanted if they are placed in a group with an aloof, detached, nonpersonal leader. The students who are highly conflicted about aggression, who are fearful of the expression of anger, who do not feel it is important to express anger or to confront others directly, will be highly stressed if they are placed in a highly confrontive, assaultive group.

NOTES

1. There were two subjects not interviewed personally, about whom we had considerable ancillary information from psychotherapists. They included the young man who committed suicide during the course of the group and S. C., who developed a manic psychosis during the group.

2. Two hundred ten subjects started the group but four dropped out for unavoidable physical reasons.

3. This figure includes five casualties who did not actually finish the group.

4. However two other casualties were grossly disturbed and were probably recognized as such by their leaders. The leaders neglected to include them (because of early dropout) in their postgroup evaluations.

5. What percentage of the entire student body seeks psychotherapy during a ten-month (academic year) period? The student health center can supply no accurate figures but offers an estimate in the range of 8 percent. Our experiment group is much higher than that figure but the control group is lower. Note however that a slightly larger number of control (21 percent) had had prior therapy than the experimental population.

6. Throughout the rest of this work we have used another definition of dropouts, i.e. members who attended less than 50 percent of the group meetings. The reason for the difference is that in this particular aspect of the study we are more interested in identifying and studying those individuals who, because of dissatisfaction, left their groups. Elsewhere, where we examine outcome we are more interested in the total amount of time an individual is exposed to the learning situation. Hence in this section but not elsewhere, an individual is defined as a dropout if he missed his final two meetings, even though he attended the first eight meetings of his group.

What difference does this make in the numbers of individuals categorized as dropouts? By the definition used in this section, thirty-nine individuals are defined as dropouts. Throughout the rest of this work we have identified thirty-five dropouts. The two definitions have, however, a heavy overlap: twenty-eight individuals are considered dropouts by both definitions.

CHAPTER 6

Encounter Groups in the College Setting

It is the rare college or university today in which encounter group experiences, T-groups, or courses centering around interpersonal and group interaction, are not available. Most institutions of higher education include faculty members who lead encounter groups as a legitimate part of the instructional or cocurricular program. Typically, such faculty members come from departments of psychology, sociology, or speech; from professional schools such as education, nursing, business, or public health; or from the staff of student counselling services.

Faculty, administration, and students making decisions about whether to offer, sponsor, or participate in encounter groups are faced with a number of questions about probable benefits and costs. There are several reasons for uncertainty on the part of anyone in higher education who must make such decisions.[1] First, there is a good deal of factual uncertainty about what such groups really "are." For faculty members committed to a "knowledge transmission" model of education, such groups certainly do not seem like education. To the psychologist, psychiatrist, or counselor, encounter groups are not the same as "psychotherapy" or "counseling." Most encounter group practitioners claim to be doing something more intensive than education, and less reparative and distress-relieving than therapy. Yet such distinctions remain fuzzy in the mind of many inhabitants of college campuses.

There is also a good deal of uncertainty about what encounter groups actually accomplish for their members. Do they contribute to or inhibit the traditional intellectual outcomes expected of college? Do they help students to be more mentally healthy, or actually cause damage? The emotional intensity surrounding encounter groups tends to encourage participants to report dramatic experiences, including negative ones, which move into the informal social network of campuses and produce a range of un-

211

verified images and stereotypes among students, faculty and administrators who have not been involved in the groups. Few objective data are available to check such impressions.[2]

Underneath such uncertainties may lie a deeper one: What are the aims of collegiate education? The college and university have traditionally been transmitters of the methods and concepts of the intellectual disciplines and professions. Humanistic or psychological outcomes have often been actively resisted by faculties as inappropriate to higher education, or used by colleges to correct deficiencies which prevent students from giving full attention to the acquisition of knowledge. Yet even for the latter group, there remains a good deal of ambiguity about how institutions of higher education should try to induce affective changes.

The affective education of the young supposedly took place, once upon a time, in the supportive bosom of an extended family, in a reasonably stable neighborhood or community undergirded by the church and surrounded by a less pluralistic and more coherent set of values than those now in force. Whether such a straightforward and complementary set of socializing influences on the affective life of the young ever did exist is not known. In any case, higher education institutions today can hardly be said to deal with young people who have grown up in such a context. Alienation, anomie, incoherence seem more the rule; the nuclear family is variously damned as being pathogenic and ineffectual; church membership declines rapidly, drugs abound, and mass media document, extend, and accelerate whatever processes, beneficent or otherwise, happen to be occurring.

Thus, the uncertainties centering around the use of encounter groups in higher education are part and parcel of the uncertainties surrounding the present-day task of higher education. Should colleges and universities devote themselves to such affective outcomes as heightened self-esteem, increased self-awareness, value clarification, greater expressiveness, increased relatedness? College faculties have frequently split on these matters on campuses where encounter groups have been used vigorously and extensively. The underlying issues are not minor, even when allowances are made for the natural vested interests of discipline-oriented academics and enthusiastic encounter group advocates. Meanwhile, the groups go on, whether or not they are blessed by curriculum committees, deans, or student health services. And students' needs for growth, relief from disabling concerns, and a sense of connectedness to others continue, whether or not encounter groups can in fact meet these needs. It is useful, therefore, to search out what can be said about the relationship of encounter groups to educational objectives.

Encounter Groups and Grade Point Average

At the most gross level, the question can be asked: Do encounter groups help or hurt grades, the most commonly used measure of learning in colleges? No experimental-control differences in grade point averages were significant the year before the groups were offered, the year of 1968–1969, or the following year. From 1967–1968 (the year prior to the encounter groups) experimentals averaged 2.93 Fall, 3.03 Winter, 3.07 Spring; controls 2.90, 3.08, 3.16, for the same time periods. During the 1968–1969 year (the encounter groups took place in the Spring) experimentals averaged 2.99 Fall, 3.08 Winter, 3.10 Spring; controls 2.99, 2.04, 3.07 for the same time period. In the academic year, subsequent to the encounter groups, the experimentals averaged 3.01 Fall, 3.09 Winter, 2.94 Spring; controls 2.87, 3.19, and 2.95.

If encounter groups did not influence academic achievement across the board, advocates might still claim that a high-impact experience could release more goal-directed energy for productive pursuits, whereas critics might assert that strong positive impact could damage achievement motivation and the will to study, or that strong negative impact could disable the student. When grade point averages were plotted for each outcome classification and compared with those of controls, there were only two cases (both negative outcomes) in which grade point averages were significantly different from control averages. In the Spring of 1967–1968 (one year prior to the encounter groups), those who became casualties had a GPA of 2.66 compared to controls 3.16 ($p \leq .10$). One year after the groups, those who experienced negative change in connection with their group experience showed a low grade point average during the Spring semester (2.20 compared to controls 2.95).

An examination of changes over time of each outcome group is shown in Figure 6–1. While High Learners or Moderate Changers experienced a gain in Fall and Spring of the year following the encounter groups, as contrasted with the two years before, this trend began in the Fall before the onset of the encounter groups. A similar pattern occurred for those who underwent no change from the groups, with the exception that Spring scores did not show a parallel gain.

Negative Changers, interestingly enough, showed a gain during the Fall-Winter of 1969–1970 over their parallel scores in the previous year. In the Spring of 1969–1970, however, they showed a precipitous drop in comparison with the preceding Spring; this difference held true even when Spring and Winter scores were averaged together. It does not seem reasonable to conclude that the Spring, 1969–1970 drop was caused by the negative change received in the encounter group, however, since the negative grade-point changes would be likely to have been manifested immediately,

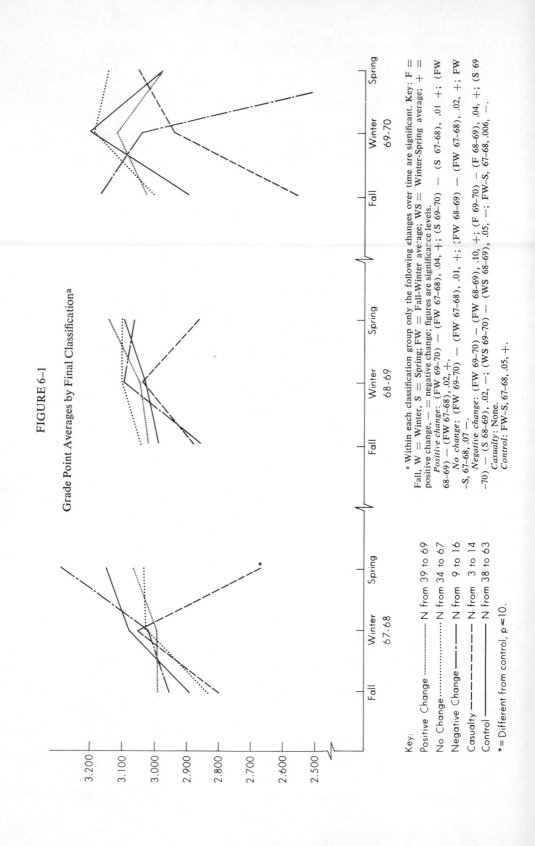

FIGURE 6–1

Grade Point Averages by Final Classification[a]

[a] Within each classification group only the following changes over time are significant. **Key:** F = Fall, W = Winter, S = Spring; FW = Fall-Winter average; WS = Winter-Spring average; + = positive change, — = negative change; figures are significance levels.
 Positive change: (FW 69–70) — (FW 67–68), .04, +; (S 69–70) — (S 67–68), .01 +; (FW 68–69) — (FW 67–68), .02, +.
 No change: (FW 69–70) — (FW 67–68), .01, +; (FW 68–69) — (FW 67–68), .02, +; FW –S, 67–68, .07 —.
 Negative change: (FW 69–70) — (FW 68–69), .10, +; (F 69–70) — (F 68–69), .04, +; (S 69 –70) — (S 68–69), .02, —; (WS 69–70) — (WS 68–69), .05, —; FW–S, 67–68, .006, —.
 Casualty: None.
 Control: FW–S, 67–68, .05, +.

Key:
Positive Change ——————— N from 39 to 69
No Change ⋯⋯⋯⋯⋯⋯⋯ N from 34 to 67
Negative Change —·—·—·— N from 9 to 16
Casualty — — — — — N from 3 to 14
Control —————— N from 38 to 63

* = Different from control, p<10.

during the Fall and Winter of 1969–1970. Negative Changers showed an increase in grade-point average during this period over the preceding Fall. It could be argued that there is a general Spring "slump," as the control data suggest, and that the Negative Changers were in some way influenced by the encounter group experience, so that they "slumped" more when Spring rolled around. Such reasoning seems unwarranted, however, since the Casualties did not receive poorer grades in the same period. The changes over time noted for Casualties were not significant; the same is true for controls, with the exception of the Spring of 1967–1968, a year prior to the group experience.

It appears, then, that for those who experienced no change, or positive change, the group experience did not interfere with grade point average gains which had been made over the prior year. These GPA changes occurred during a time when control group grade point averages were unchanging. Interestingly enough, Casualties did not experience significant changes in grade point averages. Negative Changers had rising grade point averages in the Fall immediately after the encounter group experience, followed by a very substantial drop in the Spring one year after the group experience, which would be difficult to assign to the encounter group experience.

Dropping Out of College

Did participation in encounter groups in some way encourage students to leave Stanford? The status of both the participants and the controls as of the summer of 1971 (about two years after the encounter groups) showed that of the 208 who had begun the encounter groups, 164 (78.8 percent) had either graduated Stanford or were still attending, compared to 59 of the 69 controls (85.6 percent). Twelve participants (7.8 percent) dropped out of college temporarily subsequent to the encounter group, compared to 2 (2.9 percent) of the controls. This difference is not statistically significant. We did find, however, that 28 (13.4 percent) participants dropped out of Stanford, and did not return subsequent to the encounter groups, compared with 5 (7.2 percent) of the control group. This difference approaches significance ($p = .18$).[3]

The practical significance of the difference of dropout rates between the participants and controls was not minor, and over half the participant dropouts occurred in the year immediately after the groups, suggesting the possibility of group-related effects. The dropout rates from college were tabulated for the entire Stanford classes comparable to the participants in our study. The figures reveal that dropout rate for Stanford freshmen who entered in 1968–1969 was 13.8 percent, compared to a rate of 20 percent for the comparable two-year period for those freshmen who participated in

the encounter groups. To put that another way, of the twenty-eight participants in the encounter group project who dropped out of school and did
not return, thirteen (46 percent) were freshmen; they represent a disproportionate share in the population of study participants of whom only 30
percent were freshmen. Comparison between other class years reveals
only small differences between overall Stanford drop rates for the two-year
period in question and our participants. That is, the differences for sopho-
mores and juniors are negligible. Although again the differences between
the freshman participant dropout rate and overall Stanford dropout rates
are not significant, the figures are suggestive that dropping out may be one
consequence of participation in encounter groups. Our figures also suggest
that it is not the peculiarities of sample selection—i.e., that those who
come to encounter groups represent a dropout-prone population; if this
were so, the control group rates, a comparable group of students, would be
higher. In fact, the control group rate for freshmen was a low 8 percent,
contrasted to the 20 percent for the participants.

Finally the dropout rates were compared to the various outcome categories, to determine whether differential rates existed for those who had negative outcomes in the encounter group compared to those who had positive. The results of such an analysis indicated that students who dropped
out were not differentially represented in different outcome classifications.
(Of the sixteen Casualties, one dropped out of college; two of the Negative
Changers dropped out, eleven of the Unchanged, and ten of the High
Learners or Moderate Changers.)

Use of Psychotherapy Services

Eight months after the groups began, participants and controls were asked
whether they had ever been in "psychotherapy or psychological counseling," and (if yes) when they had started. Of the 143 experimentals who returned questionnaires, 16 percent, as compared to 21 percent of 51 controls who returned questionnaires, reported that they had been in
psychotherapy or counseling prior to April, 1969, when the groups began.
Those starting therapy in the eight-month period from when the encounter
groups began included 13 percent for participants and 4 percent for controls, a difference significant at p = .12. Thus the encounter group experience appears associated slightly with increased rates of seeking psychological help. Some of this increase is a direct function of having
received negative impact: seven (54 percent) of the thirteen Casualties who
filled out the questionnaire said they had sought psychotherapy or counseling. When Casualties were not included, however, the rate for participants
was still 8 percent, slightly more than the control rate.

Some experimental group members reported that they sought help because the group experience launched a desire to work constructively on one's own problems; others went for reasons essentially unrelated to the group. All in all, however, it can be expected that providing encounter group experience on a college campus may increase the rate of seeking psychotherapy or counselling.

Impact on Intellectual Dimensions

Colleges and universities aim at outcomes primarily associated with the mastery of the various disciplines, and the development of skills necessary for the use or acquisition of knowledge. It would be idle to claim that encounter group experiences make any contribution to such outcomes.

Liberal arts colleges, however, have traditionally aimed also at broader intellectual outcomes, such as helping students to clarify personal philosophy and values, make wiser life and career decisions, be more able to learn from experience, acquire a more sophisticated view of man in the social environment, and so on.

Outcomes like these might conceivably be affected by encounter group experience. Whether they are or not, college faculty, administration (and students, even) have fears that encounter group experience may have negative effects on such outcomes. Those opposing the use of encounter groups on college campuses suggest that they tend to encourage anti-intellectualism since they espouse a kind of "gut" orientation which is opposed to thought. What worries this group is that in encounter groups the adjective "heady" has a pejorative connotation, all efforts to be rational are treated as "intellectualizing," and proponents make the ahistorical assertion that "all we need to know is right here in this room."

The fear has also been expressed by educators that encounter group experiences, perhaps because they emphasize pleasure, joy, and interpersonal closeness, may decrease achievement motivation, or cause students to become impatient with disciplined inquiry and move away from intellectual concerns and the pursuit of excellence.

A third fear is that encounter groups, designed as they are along generally egalitarian lines, with interaction modes being both intense and informal, may somehow encourage students to resist traditional role-taking by teachers and themselves. The legitimate authority of the teacher may be eroded. In the encounter group, every man is an authority on his own feelings and feels free to comment not only on them, but also on the visible behavior (and often the inferred feelings) of other group members and the leader. The distance between leader and group member is generally considerably smaller than the distance between faculty member and student.

The worry, then, is that students, full of the glow of the egalitarian, emotion-laden group experience, may rebel against or withdraw from traditional student and teacher roles.

A number of the discrete outcome findings reported in Chapter 3 bear, at least partially, on the evaluation of the impact of encounter groups on these hopes and fears of those responsible for collegiate education. It will be recalled that, across the board, the most distinctive difference between experimentals and controls appeared in the greater emphasis of participants on the values of change and growth as a way of life. No significant changes were noted for either participants or controls in achievement need, academic skills, career issues, or in the number of life decisions reported before or during the life of the groups. Although at termination participants felt more adequate than controls to cope with life problems, this difference was not maintained at follow-up. The measure of conception of others, which has some redundance to the aim of acquiring new views of man in the social environment, was unaffected by encounter experience.

The fear concerning the anti-intellectual effects of encounter groups is that work orientation will decrease because interpersonal orientation has increased. Data from the Personal Description Questionnaire indicate that the work orientation dropped slightly ($-.47$) for experimentals, while controls rose (.22), but the difference is not significant. Both experimentals and controls rose in interpersonal orientation (2.78 and 2.77). Thus there is no support for the myth that encounter group experience decreases work orientation, or increases interpersonal orientation. Though a few less participants mentioned achievement themes after the group experience, neither participants nor controls shifted significantly in self-ideal discrepancies in instrumental orientation ($-.71$ experimentals, -1.16 controls), suggesting that educators need not worry about encounter experiences decreasing achievement motivation.

Scores combining responses on two items from the coping questionnaire "seek some professional help or advice" and "seek additional information by reading up on the situation" showed a mean change for participants of 1.48, while the average control score dropped $-.69$. These differences are not significant, but they certainly do not suggest a turning away from established authority or books as information sources as a result of encounter group experience.

Affective Components of Educational Goals

Most colleges and universities today consider that generalized mental health goals are legitimate, and do take some responsibility for the affective life and the mental health of their students. Most offer counselling services to "protect" the intellectual achievements of students. Sometimes outcomes in the affective area are directly sought as valued objectives of the college experience. Social adjustment is valued in most colleges both intrinsically and as instrumental to facilitating the student's ability to work effectively with peers and teachers. Gains in self-esteem are also seen as important subgoals of higher education. The negative effects of technical achievement on human dimensions of the person has increasingly been voiced as a relevant issue for the liberal arts college. Educators have expressed fear that the development of technical competence has devalued introspection and acknowledgment of human feeling; they have expressed interest in efforts to integrate technical and human aspects of the person.

Because encounter group experience involves introspective attention to body and to emotional states, as well as the questioning of many characteristics of daily life, educators sometimes fear that it may result in a turning inward of attention and cathexis, increasing the incidence of personal moratoria, reducing interest in studies, and the like. The linkage of encounter group experience to religious and philosophical concerns may also, it is felt, encourage diffuse exploration of traditional or esoteric religious systems, with resulting diversion of energy from the concerns of academics. A kindred fear is that students will "go overboard" toward the affective side of their lives, rejecting thought, and spending all their energy in more and more encounter groups, and in courses which have an affective flavor, perhaps deserting more traditional academic subjects en masse. "Love is not enough," say encounter group critics, "Students need skills, competence, mastery . . ."

What do the findings imply regarding the effects of encounter groups on such affective aspects of collegiate life? Since only a third of the students who completed the study groups made unambiguous positive gains, encounter groups on the campus cannot be expected to lift the general level of mental health. Their potential for inducing negative effects has been extensively discussed in the preceding chapter. Relative to more specific descriptions of mental health measured in the Personal Description Questionnaire (relaxed/tense, well adjusted/maladjusted, unworried/anxious, happy/sad) no significant differences were registered between experimentals and controls when the groups terminated. Nor were there significant experimental-control differences in self-esteem upon completion of the experience. Participants, however, saw themselves as more considerate and accepting, less demanding, then did controls at both termination and follow-up.

If encounter groups could be claimed to facilitate integration of interpersonal and instrumental orientations, gains should be expected in measures of each, or at least one should not change at the expense of the other. In fact, participants reduced self-ideal discrepancy in the interpersonal, but not in the instrumental, area. Thus while interpersonal orientation did not change at the expense of instrumental, neither can it be said that the encounter experience linked the two aspects in the sense of inducing gains in both. Nor did participants undergo change in either the instrumental or interpersonal area in their views of significant others. These findings hardly constitute evidence that encounter groups remedy the polarization of instrumental and interpersonal aspects of the person.

Changes in life-space dimensions dealing with emphasis on self were examined to test the extent to which encounter group experience increased valuation of feelings and inner life. In the eight months from when groups were begun until follow-up, both participants and controls declined in overall percentage of emphasis on items dealing with the self (22 to 20 percent and 28 to 21 percent, respectively). Although participants declined slightly less in their valuation of self-aspects, there is no evidence to support a view that encounter groups increase such valuation. Nor do the findings warrant the fear that encounter groups will turn students "away from the world," inasmuch as no experimental-control differences were obtained either on a measure of sensitivity to one's own and others' feelings, or in focus on environmental aspects of the life-space.

Relative to social adjustment, a self-report measure of interpersonal adequacy showed clear differences between participants and controls, both at termination and follow-up, in contrast with reports of friends and associates which, as noted in Chapter 3, yielded no experimental-control differences. At termination, 24 percent of the participants saw themselves as more interpersonally competent, compared to 14 percent of the controls; at follow-up, 30 percent of the participants and 21 percent of the controls saw themselves as more interpersonally adequate. At both administrations, 18 percent of the participants and 30 percent of the controls indicated they felt less interpersonally inadequate.

There was no evidence that encounter experience might make participants go overboard toward the affective, immersing themselves in such experiences out of proportion to other things. When the groups ended, only seven participants mentioned the group experience as part of their total life space, at follow-up only one. No controls mentioned an encounter group experience. At follow-up, 7 percent of participants and 8 percent of controls indicated that they had attended another encounter group since the study groups had begun; this is not sufficient evidence that encounter group addicts were created by participation in the study.

Encounter groups have often been cited as an antidote to alienation, a problem of concern on college campuses, judging from the increased attention to existential writings. While participants were not known to be especially alienated to begin with, the findings on changes in their relationships to others do not constitute a case for saying that the group experience made them feel less isolated or more able to relate closely to others. No differences obtained, for example, in the degree to which participants and controls viewed their interpersonal environments as providing opportunities to be honest, sharing, trusting, and in deep contact with others. Neither were there experimental-control differences in emphasis on intimacy as a feature of interpersonal relationships, or on FIRO measures of expressed and wanted affection. When students were asked how much time they spent with close friends, 20 percent of the participants and 13 percent of the controls indicated an increase in time when the groups ended, but this difference disappeared at follow-up (20 and 21 percent, respectively). Prior to beginning the groups, 29 percent of controls and 51 percent of participants said they had made three or more new close friends during the preceding six months, but at termination, neither group evidenced change in the number of friends. When participants were asked at follow-up if they had formed durable friendships with other group members, 22 percent of the 125 responding said they had. Participants also said they had formed new love relationships more often than did nonparticipants. Taken together, these findings do not substantiate the supposition that the effects of encounter experience for decreasing alienation and loneliness are as powerful as has been claimed.

Looking generally at the impact of encounter on the affective aspects of college life, it can be said that although participants became more lenient in their self-concept and some perceived themselves as improving in social adjustment, across the board gains in mental health did not occur, and some psychological damage did. Changes in the interpersonal area neither blocked nor facilitated changes in the instrumental area. The valuation of inner feelings increased only slightly, and there was no evidence of excessive introspection or disproportionate emphasis on affective experience. Significant shifts in relatedness to others occurred neither in participants or controls. It thus may be said that neither the hopes or fears concerning encounter effects on college students were realized.

Encounter and Student Activism

Active participation of students in political life is a central issue among many concerned with higher education. Analyses of the meaning of student dissent range very widely. Those, who are, so to speak, on the educational and psychological right (for example, Feuer, 1969) suggest that familiar psychological forces, such as rebellion against father figures, are involved. Persons nearer the center (for example, Keniston, 1968) suggest that dissenting students have simply incorporated and pushed further the permissive, democratic, equalitarian values of their parents. Voices of the "left," like Reich (1970), suggest that major value transformations are occurring in American society, and that students are the harbingers of better things to come. Most college faculties would divide almost immediately on the question of whether politicization of students is a desirable or undesirable outcome of the college experience. It will be recalled that student activism was at a new height at the time of the present study, so that the climate provided incentive to examine the relationship between political activism and encounter experience.

Over the two and one half months of the group experience, both experimentals and controls tended to increase in militancy scores.[4] Congruent with the events occurring on the Stanford campus at the time, both participants and controls increased in willingness to engage in militant activities (40 and 35 percent, respectively, increased, 16 and 25 percent, respectively, decreased). Neither was militancy or political preference a significant predictor of who entered the groups, who completed them, who was benefited or harmed from the experience, or who found the group attractive, or what kinds of learnings were realized.[5] Thus, encounter group experience cannot be said to radicalize students, to attract a biased sample of students as far as political preference and militancy goes; nor is student activism or political orientation related to outcome.

Should Encounter Groups Be on Campus?

Encounter group experience did not help or hurt grade point averages, even for those students who received strong positive or negative outcomes. There seemed to be a marginal positive relationship at best between encounter group experience and dropping out of college; in particular, freshmen dropped out of college more frequently. Those in groups were somewhat more likely to seek psychotherapy in the six months after the group than were controls.

In the intellectual domain, participants as a whole experienced change in values favoring change and growth, but little else. Fears of negative effects of encounter groups on valuation of achievement or intellectuality were not realized, however. On the affective side, little evidence was established either for massive positive or negative effects. Whether an administrator is for or against activism in student life, he need not take this issue into account in considering the place of encounter groups. On balance, the contribution of encounter groups to the intellectual and affective aims of collegiate experience seem insufficient to encourage colleges to develop encounter groups as an active part of their programs.

There is a real sense, however, in which the question of whether encounter groups should be on campus is academic. The groups will undoubtedly continue with or without official sanction. Whatever the implications of the present investigation regarding their impact on the intellectual or affective growth of the Stanford participants, the students themselves were overwhelmingly of the view that encounter groups ought to be part of college life. When participants were asked at termination whether such experiences should be available to students, 94 percent said they should be offered as a regular elective; only 9 percent, however, believed they should be part of the required curriculum. The proportions six months later were strikingly similar; 90 and 9 percent, respectively.

Students offered a number of comments about the function of encounter groups in the University curriculum:

A lot of people can really benefit from direct, honest confrontation with others—especially college-age people. Part of the University's purpose, besides training us, should be to make such opportunities available.

The University should be a place where people can learn about themselves and grow as individuals. Encounter groups are a unique way in which people can find out about themselves and others.

It enables you to see yourself in an important light—makes you more realistic, and if the experience occurred early enough, you could work on it during these important college years.

Although a major value of the college experience is personal growth, it has no place in the curriculum, but should.

The experience of learning about the people with whom you go to classes is equally as important as the class. Group experience does expand interpersonal relationships somewhat, and could possibly help individuals see better how they affect other people around them and what other courses are relevant to their lives.

About 10 percent of the comments explicitly compared encounter groups and other learning experiences in the college environment, usually to the detriment of the latter.

It gives you a different way of evaluating yourself apart from academic success.

People are too uptight now from studying and forget how to be human.

It gives the student a personal learning experience which is unmatched by anything in a classroom. The most important thing in life is to understand yourself, and the group gives everyone a chance to do this.

It is more like reality than what is usually taught.

It is a human addition to the devastatingly *inhuman* formal educational process.

With faculty, student, administrator, black, mixed groups, untold amounts of understanding would be revealed in time (if encounter groups were elective). Misunderstanding screws up everybody's life. *Real* communication is more important than a foreign language or Western Civ.

I think the group experience is extremely relevant to education, in that it offers an alternative to the highly structured teacher-class learning situation.

What I most wanted out of college was an understanding of myself, a place to experiment with my personality, a place to grow personally. What I've got instead is a place where I can learn to be a scholar of trivia or a dropout. Encounter groups could be a beginning in providing other possibilities for college.

223

The reasons for not requiring the experience most frequently centered around the label "required." Over and over again, students said: "Nothing should be required;" "All courses should be voluntary." Beyond this generalized rejection of involuntary entrance to learning environments, however, a number of rather specific qualifiers were proposed. About 10 percent of the students suggested that there was probably a large fraction of persons who would not learn, who would be uninterested, would be bored, would think the group was a joke, wouldn't like it, would be too cynical or closed, wouldn't be geared to it, wouldn't dig it, and the like. Another 10 percent pointed out that it would be difficult for an encounter group to work effectively under circumstances of forced participation, because investment and willingness to learn would be low, and dealing with low-investment participants would use up energy, spoil the group, and waste time. About 6 percent mentioned the possibility of damage or negative outcomes to participants who were required to participate.

Given this sort of student interest in the encounter experience, and remembering that in the present investigation some students did benefit, and some groups were much richer learning environments than others, administrators may be best advised to legitimate encounter groups on campus, but to maintain at least as much control over them as they do over other courses. Offering encounter groups as an elective course means that the usual, legitimate channels (for example, departmental structures or student health services) used to select faculty and maintain quality control would serve to clarify the precise nature of the offering and to provide for informed consent of the participants, as well as to insure the availability of needed supportive services. If such a stance can help to maximize those benefits reaped in the more successful groups described in this volume, and to reduce casualty rates, it may be more sensible than officially ignoring or censoring encounter group experiences so that students seek them "underground."

NOTES

1. The interested reader is referred to the thoughtful discussion by Harrison and Hopkins (1967) of differences between the didactic knowledge-transmission view of educative experience and the inductive, discovery-oriented, self-analytic approach inherent in encounter groups.

2. One case study of encounter groups in a Catholic college (Shaevitz and Barr, 1970) primarily examined generalized effects on the college environment and did not assess the impact on particular students. Another more comprehensive study, the Talent in Interpersonal Exploration Project (Bebout, 1971), is examining the processes and outcomes of encounter groups led by students and others who had received a modest level of supportive training.

3. The participant group of 208 included 34 who dropped out of the encounter groups and four individuals for whom we did not have information or who were suspended or transferred; the controls included three individuals for whom we had no information. A comparison of those who dropped out of the encounter groups and those who completed encounter groups revealed that similar rates of dropping out of school obtained in both types of participants (14.7 percent for the Dropouts and 13.2 percent for the participants who completed the encounter groups).

4. The instrument asked for attitudes toward the following "alternative means for accomplishing one's desired ends": peaceful demonstrations. strikes. occupying offices. destructive acts, confrontations with demands and threats, and guerilla warfare. For each of these tactics the respondent was asked whether he would participate; whether it was "O.K. for others but not for me"; whether he had no clear opinion. or was "somewhat against them for others." or "strongly against them for everyone." The data from this instrument were subjected to Guttman scaling by Jackson Kytle.

The best product obtainable was a four-item scale with these items: peaceful demonstrations (I have no clear opinion. O.K. for others, or I would participate coded as accept); strikes (O.K. for others, or I would participate); destructive acts (O.K. for others, or I would participate); and confrontation with demands and threats (O.K. for others, or I would participate). The coefficient of reproducability of the scale was .84. which falls just short of the usual .90 standard.

This measure proved to be meaningfully related to political preferences: militancy was highest for students who described themselves as revolutionary radicals and New Left. lower for liberals. Democrats. and independents. and least of all for Republicans and conservatives.

5. Did our activism measures relate to any personality variables? We found faint relationships with self-esteem: radicals and militants had slightly higher self-esteem. partially supporting Etzioni's (1968) ideas about alienation. We also found a moderate relation to clinically-rated pathology. as judged from a sentence completion test: 24 percent of radicals were rated as disturbed. as contrasted with 13.7 percent of conservative and liberal students.

Looked at from the point of view of the right, this finding confirms the notion that militant student radicals are simply acting out or attempting to work through inner conflicts by political activity without regard to the merits of the situation. From the left. the data can be seen as confirming the notion that classical clinical diagnoses reflect "adjustment" to the status quo and that the only truly sane person is one actively engaged in attempting to reconstruct a sick society. We do not have additional data with which these alternative interpretations could be fruitfully pursued.

CHAPTER 7

The Leaders: Their Behavior and Impact

How do encounter leaders change people? The styles of sixteen encounter leaders were studied widely. Some were primarily analytic and interpretative; others saw the management of group forces as their distinctive function; still others offered instructional, often nonverbal, exercises almost exclusively. Some of the leaders believed passionately in love; others just as passionately in hate. For one leader, the basic stuff of change stemmed from the experience of primary rage; for another, the idea that humans were dependent was anathema. Some leaders depended solely on talk-therapy; others used music, lights, the clench of human bodies.

The leaders were deliberately chosen, of course, to emphasize such differences in style, methodology, and philosophy. Part of the reason for ensuring this divergence was to discover whether the conventional labels they represented, labels such as Gestalt, sensory awareness, T-group, and so on, had any real meaning in describing what they actually did as encounter leaders. The more challenging goal behind the design, however, was that of generating the sort of data about leadership differences that would allow the development of an empirical taxonomy of encounter leadership methodologies. The resulting typology might ultimately be related to differing types or degrees of personal learning or change.

The intention to elaborate a typology of encounter group leadership placed rigorous demands on the experimental design. As the major experimental variable, it was necessary that the leaders' behaviors be classified in a way that would make them truly capable of being associated with varying outcomes. Because of the diversity of orientations represented among the leaders, the methods of observation had both to be sensitive to the discrete characteristics of each orientation, and yet sufficiently abstract to work for several cases and allow comparison. The relatively large number of leaders and their methodological differences suggested that the study of the apparent function of their behavior held more promise for understanding its effect on outcome than would the analysis of their personality characteristics—a variable less likely to be associated with school of thought or ideological orientation.[1]

Several observational schedules were developed which employed differing magnitudes in the units of observation. At the more microscopic end, observers rated how frequently leaders displayed each of twenty-eight discrete behaviors. At the other extreme, observers at the end of each meeting recorded their overall impressions of "how the leader came across" to them in terms of rather broad categories of leadership style. Three other assessments, made by observers or participants or both, struck at the midpoint of the continuum, measuring the focus of the leader's attention (whether group, interpersonal, or intrapsychic), his interpersonal attractiveness, and his symbolic meaning to the participants.[2]

A Look at What Encounter Leaders Do

LEADER BEHAVIOR

The behavior of the leaders was first assessed for how often they did such things as "challenge," "interpret," or "stop an interaction among members" (see Appendix II for complete list of twenty-eight items making up the Observer Checklist of Leader Behavior and Observer Reliability). These discrete behaviors were grouped into five areas, in terms of the function they seemed intended to perform: (1) *Evocative Behavior,* behavior seemingly designed to get members to respond; (2) *Coherence-Making,* behavior apparently aimed at altering cognitive perspectives; (3) *Support,* as evidenced in positive affective gestures;[3] (4) *Management,* interventions concerning how people worked with one another or how the group was functioning as a whole; and (5) *Use of Self,* behavior involving demonstration or modeling by the leader. Evocative behaviors were most frequently used (29 percent), and next most frequent were those involving Use of Self (22 percent). Supportive behaviors were used the least (12 percent). Coherence-making (19 percent) and Management (17 percent) were midway in percent of use.

While differences occurred among the leaders in their use of one or another of the five types of behavior, much that is similar can also be noted, particularly in their use of evocative behavior. This is not surprising; despite their differences in philosophy and personal style, the functions the leader serves through these behaviors are generally necessary in order for any group of people to develop conditions useful for growth. All leaders must pay some attention to how their groups are working; all leaders perceive the necessity of generating responsiveness in the members, and so on.

227

TABLE 7-1

Items from Factor Analyses of Leader Behavior

Item Number and Item	Factor Loading Weights
Factor 1 *Intrusive Modeling*	
25. Reveals Feelings	.80
5. Challenging	.65
6. Confrontation	.66
26. Reveals His Personal Values, Attitudes, Beliefs	.62
28. Participates As a Member in the Group	.58
77. Exhortation	.54
27. Draws Attention to Himself	.51
Factor 2 *Cognitizing*	
13. Providing Concepts for How to Understand	.75
8. Explaining, Clarifying, Interpreting	.59
12. Providing Framework for How to Change	.54
Factor 3 *Command Stimulation*	
1. Inviting, Eliciting	−.66
2. Questioning	−.64
18. Suggesting Procedure for the Group or a Person	−.61
23. Decision Task	−.52
Factor 4 *Managing* or *Limit-Setting*	
21. Suggesting or Setting Rules, Limits, Norms	−.76
22. Setting Goals or Directions of Movement	−.67
19. Managing Time, Sequence, Pacing, Starting, and Stopping	−.46
17. Stopping, Blocking, Interceding	−.41
Factor 5 *Attention Focusing*	
9. Comparing, Contrasting, Finding Similarities	−.66
20. Focusing	−.57
4. Calling On	−.54
Factor 6 *Mirroring*	
10. Summarization	.69
24. Decision-Making	.47
3. Reflecting	.44
Factor 7 *Affective Support*	
14. Protecting	−.69
16. Offering Friendship, Love, Affection	−.61
11. Inviting Members to Seek Feedback	−.50
15. Support, Praise, Encouragement	−.43

The differences in behavior among the leaders become more evident when the specific behaviors within one of the five functional areas are examined for the kind of evocative behavior the leader used, the forms of coherence-making or managing behavior, and so on. The best sense of the variation among leaders in their preference for one type of behavior over another may be gained from counting the sessions at which each leader called on a particular sort of behavior.[4] Here, for most of the five types of behavior, leaders range from expressing no, or only occasional, examples of the behavior during a meeting to consistent use at every meeting.

Though this type of analysis goes slightly beyond what can be known through unaided observation, the five types of leadership behavior which it assigns are not intended to have any necessary theoretical meaning, nor are they considered equivalent or in the same metric. They represent a common sense ordering, based solely on what has seemed to be the function of what leaders commonly do in groups to effect personal change. To provide a more systematic ordering, the leaders' scores on the twenty-eight observable behaviors were factor analyzed.[5] The seven clusters produced were assigned brief descriptive labels. Table 7–1 presents the seven factored dimensions of leadership behavior and the items, in order of factor loadings, on each dimension.[6]

Three of the seven factored dimensions of leadership behavior appear designed to elicit participants' response. *Intrusive Modeling* represents behavior that gets response through direct, energetic demands via challenges, confrontation, and exhortation; this is also behavior that involves the intense participation of the leader as a self-revealing member of the group.[7] *Command Stimulation* groups behavior that directly requests members to respond immediately and, often, in a particular form. It is probably associated with leaders who are termed "directive" in a psychotherapeutic parlance. *Attention Focusing* clusters behavior which solicits response more indirectly than the first two types; it permits greater latitude to respond or not, or to choose from several types of responses.[8]

Of the four other dimensions, *Cognitizing* consists of teaching or instructional behaviors, and includes the more traditional interpretative behavior. Several behaviors pragmatically considered coherence-making, such as comparing, summarizing, and inviting feedback, did not appear under Cognitizing, suggesting that they may play a smaller role in the realm of cognitive behavior than had been assumed. *Managing* or *Limit-Setting* represents behavior relating to the conditions of the group as a social system. Again, some of the behaviors initially thought to be managing are not included in this dimension, suggesting that procedures and attention-focusing were more associated with stimulation than with the management of group process. *Affective Support,* the seventh factor, clusters positive affect behaviors: protection, friendship, love, affection, support, praise, encouragement. Inviting members to seek feedback, originally classified as coherence-making, appears on this dimension as a supportive behavior. *Mirroring,* the most puzzling dimension, combines summarizing, decision-making, and reflective behavior, all originally grouped under different functions. Conceivably, this dimension represents a cluster of leader behaviors that were reactive rather than proactive.

The differences among the leaders in their tendency to use one or another of the seven dimensions are depicted in Table 7–2, Variables 1–7. The groups are shown in order of their similarity to one another. On the three response-oriented factors, leaders who stemmed from the older, more traditional forms of sensitivity training and group therapy were distinguished by their scores from leaders associated with schools that have

TABLE 7-2

Measures on Leaders

Variables	#10 Esalen Eclectic	#9 Transactional Analysis	#7 Psychoanalytic	#15 Personal Growth	#14 Verbal Encounter	#11 Rogerian Marathon	#5 Psychodrama	#2 T-Group	#12 Eclectic Marathon	#8 Transactional Analysis	#1 T-Group	#13 Synanon	#6 Psychodrama	#4 Gestalt	#3 Gestalt
Behavior Factors															
1. Intrusive Modeling	59	77	52	92	101	56	72	37	81	50	68	182	160	125	134
2. Cognitizing	153	94	109	54	76	49	44	53	119	170	118	107	125	98	92
3. Command Stimulation	178	75	55	64	87	122	70	136	122	77	111	65	91	121	150
4. Limit-Setting	151	91	74	84	85	78	91	137	72	78	101	133	95	106	109
5. Attention Focusing	74	64	98	97	128	40	110	114	57	127	99	140	153	85	59
6. Support	83	94	50	57	80	90	72	102	59	135	147	79	128	142	174
7. Mirroring	104	94	138	135	107	113	120	108	62	142	105	66	86	63	68
Style															
8. Interpreter of Reality	2.6	4.0	4.0	3.2	3.0	2.3	3.4	2.9	4.5	4.4	4.2	3.8	3.7	1.8	2.0
9. Release of Emotion by Suggestion	5.2	0.0	1.3	2.6	2.4	2.0	3.0	3.6	2.3	2.2	4.0	2.8	4.3	3.6	3.4
10. Release of Emotion by Demonstration	1.0	0.0	0.0	1.8	1.2	1.8	1.6	0.4	2.0	1.0	1.2	4.0	5.0	4.0	3.0
11. Personal	1.4	1.3	1.3	0.4	1.0	1.0	2.0	1.6	2.3	4.6	2.2	0.0	2.5	3.1	2.6
12. Social Engineer	1.8	1.0	0.2	2.0	1.2	1.0	2.8	3.1	0.8	0.6	1.4	0.5	0.0	1.1	0.8
13. Charismatic Leader	1.4	0.0	0.4	2.6	0.4	0.0	0.4	0.4	0.5	2.6	0.0	1.5	5.0	3.8	2.2
14. Teacher	5.2	2.5	2.9	1.0	1.0	0.5	2.0	3.1	3.8	3.6	3.0	1.3	1.2	2.2	2.6
15. Resource	0.0	2.5	2.2	0.4	1.0	2.5	1.4	2.4	1.3	1.8	1.8	0.0	0.2	0.2	1.2
16. Challenger	0.6	0.5	0.4	2.4	1.8	0.5	0.8	0.9	2.3	1.2	1.6	4.3	5.2	3.3	2.6
17. Model	2.5	2.1	2.3	2.4	1.7	2.9	3.3	2.0	2.9	2.8	2.8	3.7	3.3	3.6	2.7
Focus															
18. Group	20.0	22.5	16.0	36.3	11.0	17.5	51.7	30.0	11.4	1.2	16.0	3.8	11.7	17.3	10.0
19. Interpersonal	27.7	32.5	6.0	17.5	27.7	47.5	17.5	52.5	18.6	23.8	48.0	36.3	23.3	42.2	42.5
20. Intrapersonal	50.0	35.0	77.6	23.7	48.0	35.0	25.8	17.5	61.3	71.3	30.0	55.0	61.7	35.6	40.0
21. Evaluation, Observer	5.3	3.5	4.0	6.2	5.1	5.2	3.1	4.9	6.0	6.6	4.8	5.3	6.3	5.3	6.3
22. Evaluation, Participant	3.1	3.2	3.1	4.2	4.1	4.3	3.4	4.8	5.9	4.3	4.8	4.3	5.7	4.2	5.5
23. Nonverbal Exercises	2.70	0.28	0.00	0.11	0.71	1.25	0.00	1.37	0.37	0.00	1.30	00.0	1.90	2.00	1.55
Symbol															
24. Charisma	4.0	0.7	0.4	4.0	4.0	1.6	4.5	1.0	2.1	2.4	1.5	6.0	8.1	3.2	2.0
25. Love	3.8	0.8	2.2	0.8	1.3	3.7	3.6	4.0	3.8	3.8	3.6	2.7	2.4	3.2	3.9
26. Peer	1.6	5.6	2.2	3.2	1.3	7.0	6.4	4.0	2.6	2.6	3.2	1.6	0.5	1.6	5.7
27. Technical	4.2	3.4	3.8	4.8	3.8	2.2	2.4	3.0	3.5	2.6	2.4	4.2	2.6	3.5	1.6

come into prominence in the last decade. Intense stimulation through intrusive modeling or command stimulation was more characteristic of the latter group, whereas those in the older traditions are better described by attention-focusing; they seldom exhibited intrusive modeling and make only moderate use of command stimulation. This conclusion was tested by summing each of the leaders' scores on these three stimulation dimensions, an operation which yielded the following rank order from high to low: #6 Psychodrama, #13 Synanon, #3 and #4 Gestalt, #14 Personal Growth, #10 Esalen Eclectic, #2 T-group, #1 T-group, #7 Psychoanalytic, #9 Transactional Analysis, #11 Rogerian Marathon, #5 Psychodrama, #8 Transactional Analysis, #12 Eclectic Marathon, #15 Personal Growth.

Again, these findings are not surprising. Traditional T-groups conceived of change as requiring group self-analysis and nondirective leadership. They considered it crucial that participants establish their own goals and learning rates (see Argyris, 1967, for a detailed theoretical discussion of this point of view). The more traditional forms of group therapy generally have maintained an historically ingrained perspective of the group as a stimulating, "regression-inducing" environment, in which the primary role of the therapist is to help individuals understand and cope with these affective states as they arise in the interpersonal interplay of the group, rather than to induce or stimulate them.

On the cognitive factor the distinction collapses between representatives of older and newer forms. Some cognitive structuring is characteristic of most of the leaders, although the particular behaviors differ. The two leaders who cognitized most did so in different ways; Leader #8 representing Transactional Analysis stressed the teaching of concepts, whereas the other high scorer, the Esalen Leader, #10, emphasized instructional exercises. The Rogerian Leader, #11, one of the Psychodrama Leaders, #5, a T-group Leader, #2, and a Personal Growth Leader, #15, made the least use of the cognitive dimension.

On the whole, the more traditionally oriented group psychotherapists were less likely to display managing behavior than were the T-group leaders and those representing the newer forms.[9] The levels of supportive behavior for each leader were unrelated in any way to differences in theoretical orientation. Differences in frequency of supportive expression are probably more reflective of personality than of differences in the leaders' theoretical positions.

LEADER STYLE

A broader and more personal perspective on the leaders was afforded by the observer's impressions of their overall style for each meeting. (See Appendix II for the nine categories of leadership style used for this evaluation.) As was to be expected, leaders showed greater uniformity in their characteristic overall style than in their employment of the more discrete categories of behavior; yet, the observers' ratings of leadership style in great part paralleled and complemented the findings on the behavioral items. (Table 7–2, Variables 8–17, presents leader scores on the nine style categories averaged over all meetings.)

FOCUS

There were considerable differences in the amount of time they focused their attention on total group, interpersonal, or intrapersonal issues.[10] One leader almost never focused on the group as a whole; another did so more than half the time (Table 7–2, Variables 18–20), overall averaging just under one-third. Intrapersonal yielded a smaller range. On the average, leaders gave such issues close to half their time; but one leader focused on an individual well under a fourth of his time while another did so more than three-fourths of the time.

LIKING OF LEADER

The overall interpersonal attractiveness of the leaders was assessed through the reactions of both observers and participants—observers for each meeting, participants for the total series. For this assessment both groups were asked to rate the leader on seven-point scales in respect to his competence, whether they would like to be in a group with him, whether they admired him or were repelled by him as a person, whether they approved of his techniques, how much they felt he understood the group, and whether they considered him effective or ineffective. Table 7–2 (Variables 21–22), shows the mean rating of each leader on interpersonal attractiveness; as can be seen, participants leaned toward the positive view more than observers.[11]

LEADERS' SYMBOLIC VALUE

In change-oriented groups, leaders have the capacity to create surplus meaning or possess symbolic value for those within their purview.[12] To assess symbolic value, a forty-item Leadership Questionnaire was devised; participants selected the word best describing the leader from ten sets of four words. Each set contained a word associated with charisma, with a love orientation, a peer orientation, and a technical orientation (see Appendix II).[13]

Interest in charisma has waxed and waned in modern-day psychology; it has generally been introduced into the psychological literature as conceived by Weber regarding political ideology, and it has been used from time to time by political scientists interested in the psychological relationships of charismatic political leaders to the governed.[14] The central properties of charisma in this view are a belief in the magical properties of the leader: a sense that he is uniquely endowed; the sense of having a special or a unique relationship to him; and the willingness to be influenced by him. Phrases that have often been used to describe the charismatic leader refer to his inspirational sense of a personal mission, his vision, buoyant confidence, sanctity, devotion, exemplary character, exceptional or divine power, or supernatural or superhuman ability. He presents an appearance of an unconflicted belief in himself and what he is doing. As portrayed in the literature of political science, charismatic leaders evidence a capacity to sustain a shift from traditional norms or to maintain adherents from a position somewhat outside the normative system of the society. The charismatic leader gives meaning to others' behavior; he validates the disciple's action and sanctions otherwise unsanctionable acts. The charismatic leader's person and ideology are intertwined and inseparable.

Following such themes in the social science literature, a charismatic encounter leader, on this assessment, was presented as one who was inspiring, imposing, stimulating, believed in himself, and had a vision or sense of mission. A love-oriented leader was defined as one who symbolized giving, understanding, genuineness, caring, sympathy, warmth, openness, kindness; members wanted to be with him. The peer-oriented leader was defined as one who created little social distance: a "nice guy," related, relaxed, easy-going, "one of us," a friend, easy to get close to. The technically oriented leader was defined as one who expressed expertise, intelligence, solidity, decisiveness, competence, knowledge, skill. Table 7–2 (Variables 24–27) presents each leader's score on these four qualities.

Four Basic Leadership Functions

It has been implicitly suggested by these differing levels and kinds of assessments of leadership behavior that there is some redundance in what they tapped, although till now they have been discussed as separate approaches to describing leader behavior. In order to establish higher-order abstractions from the plethora of information yielded by these assessments, the twenty-seven variables describing leader behavior were intercorrelated.

In presenting the twenty-seven variables and their intercorrelations, Table 7–3 makes clear that a number of strong associations obtain, for example, between participants' views of leaders as charismatic and the observers' ratings of charismatic style, or between observers' ratings of social-engineering style and the group as the focus of leader attention. The number of high positive and negative correlations among the twenty-seven variables suggested that the number of variables needed to describe leader behavior could be considerably reduced. When the twenty-seven variables were factor analyzed,[15] four clusters emerged which accounted for 74 percent of the variance. Table 7–4 shows the four rotated factors and the loadings on each of the twenty-seven variables.

Much of what the leaders do, as both participants and observers see them, can be subsumed under four basic functions: *Emotional Stimulation, Caring, Meaning-Attribution,* and *Executive Function.* These four dimen-

TABLE 7-3
Correlations Among Leader Variables[a]

Variable	#	1	2	3	4	5	6	7	8	9	10	11	12	13	14	15	16	17	18	19	20	21	22	23	24	25	26	27
Leader Behavior Factors																												
Intrusive Modeling	1																											
Cognitizing	2	07																										
Command Stimulation	3	-15	15																									
Limit-Setting	4	18	11	54																								
Attention Focusing	5	36	17	-49	14																							
Mirroring	6	-66	-09	-40	-32	18																						
Support	7	25	28	40	20	02	-32																					
Leader Style																												
Interpreter of Reality	8	-14	40	-55	-37	33	24	-30																				
Release of Emotion by Suggestion	9	21	22	61	63	24	-23	37	-36																			
Release of Emotion by Demonstration	10	87	08	06	14	29	-63	37	-27	44																		
Personal	11	-15	51	19	-21	-06	-00	-17	09	17	11																	
Social Engineer	12	-46	-56	23	36	39	26	42	-27	25	-38	-18																
Charismatic Leader	13	58	33	01	08	-35	-23	08	-21	42	75	40	-35															
Teacher	14	-45	62	50	34	48	-00	-03	20	26	-40	41	13	-14														
Resource	15	-69	-26	-11	-39	14	40	29	23	-60	-70	10	14	-66	05													
Challenger	16	91	17	-10	13	04	-60	24	-03	36	92	04	-43	74	-38	-71												
Model	17	56	16	-06	09	10	-45	-13	-04	31	76	23	-26	47	-16	-47	59											
Leader Focus																												
Group	18	-35	-67	-10	03	-11	34	-36	-17	03	-28	-26	80	-23	-10	12	-36	-11										
Interpersonal	19	05	-22	52	46	-20	-38	60	-47	26	14	02	24	-11	-10	19	04	06	-14									
Intrapersonal	20	14	72	-23	-28	23	03	-13	46	-16	10	26	-79	22	24	-13	18	12	-68	-57								
Observer Reactions/Member Ratings																												
Observer Liking	21	37	08	28	-10	04	-50	42	05	31	54	31	-24	35	-10	-13	59	25	-37	27	06							
Participant Liking	22	32	40	28	00	10	-19	36	-09	36	48	33	-36	62	01	-42	54	16	-57	08	28	68						
Games																												
Games	23	42	19	88	75	-42	-51	28	-77	75	53	-05	15	51	45	-86	38	22	-09	32	-18	06	38					
Leadership Questionnaire																												
Charisma	24	66	24	-09	18	61	-22	11	-01	51	74	06	-20	76	-26	-80	76	46	-10	-22	07	26	42	60				
Love	25	-33	22	57	18	-15	-12	51	-10	45	-01	61	16	-07	48	26	-16	24	-14	45	-03	37	14	20	-27			
Peer	26	-35	-48	04	-16	-57	12	11	-15	-47	-41	-04	33	-54	-10	66	-56	-20	35	33	-50	-17	-39	-33	-60	-78		
Technical	27	-04	-02	-46	-22	01	21	-63	26	-54	-35	-54	-19	-17	-09	-02	-13	-49	01	-50	22	-46	-23	-26	-13	07	-22	

[a]N = 128.

TABLE 7-4
Rotated Factors of Leader Variables

Variable	1(30%)[a]	2(20%)	3(14%)	4(10%)
Leader Behavior Factors				
1. Intrusive Modeling	0.91	0.16	−0.11	−0.00
2. Cognitizing	0.03	−0.23	−0.87	−0.27
3. Command Stimulation	−0.12	−0.35	0.02	−0.71
4. Limit-Setting	0.10	0.00	0.13	−0.86
5. Attention Focusing	0.31	0.03	−0.05	0.02
6. Mirroring	−0.58	0.09	0.17	0.21
7. Support	0.20	−0.69	−0.04	−0.10
Leader Style				
8. Interpreter of Reality	−0.20	0.04	−0.50	0.38
9. Release of Emotion by Suggestion	0.32	−0.37	0.13	−0.76
10. Release of Emotion by Demonstration	0.96	−0.18	−0.02	−0.05
11. Personal	−0.02	−0.82	−0.32	0.08
12. Social Engineer	−0.36	−0.08	0.77	−0.37
13. Charismatic Leader	0.71	−0.19	−0.13	−0.12
14. Teacher	−0.44	−0.29	−0.47	−0.59
15. Resource	−0.77	−0.20	0.09	0.51
16. Challenger	0.90	−0.01	−0.15	−0.03
17. Model	0.76	−0.41	−0.07	0.04
Leader Focus				
18. Group	−0.15	0.08	0.79	−0.03
19. Interpersonal	−0.04	−0.36	0.33	−0.24
20. Intrapersonal	0.10	0.06	−0.89	0.15
Interpersonal Attraction				
21. Observer Liking	0.34	−0.43	−0.13	0.10
22. Member Liking	0.32	−0.21	−0.31	−0.12
23. Games	0.44	−0.03	0.04	−0.89
Member Perception				
24. Charisma	0.78	0.04	−0.03	−0.25
25. Love	−0.22	−0.86	−0.08	−0.26
26. Peer	−0.40	−0.18	0.44	0.37
27. Technical	−0.18	0.88	−0.22	0.15

[a]Percentage of variance extracted by factor.

sions may constitute an empirically derived taxonomy for examining leadership in all forms of groups aimed at personal change, be they therapy or personal growth groups. Figure 7–1 shows the scores of each of the leaders on the four basic dimensions. They suggest that these dimensions are capable of discriminating among leaders of highly varied orientation.

Emotional Stimulation represents leader behavior which emphasizes revealing feelings, challenging, confrontation, revelation of personal values, attitudes, beliefs, frequent participation as a member in the group, exhortation, and drawing attention to self. Stylistically, stimulation represents the emphasis on the release of emotions by demonstration—the leader becomes a risk-taker, expressing the anger, warmth, or the love by showing how it is to be done. Stimulation also represents a very personal style of leadership where the leader is at the center of the group's universe. It is through the leader's personal powers and force of personality that the group moves ahead and that people in it have specific experiences. People are made to move by the sheer weight of the leader's "personal attractiveness" and personal powers. Another aspect of the stimulative leader style is the emphasis on challenging—such leaders may be characterized by frequent dialogues with individual members. A value is placed on personal confrontation; shaking-up or unsettling may be considered a primary learning condition. Challenging assumptions participants hold about them-

FIGURE 7–1

Leader Scores on the Four Basic Dimensions

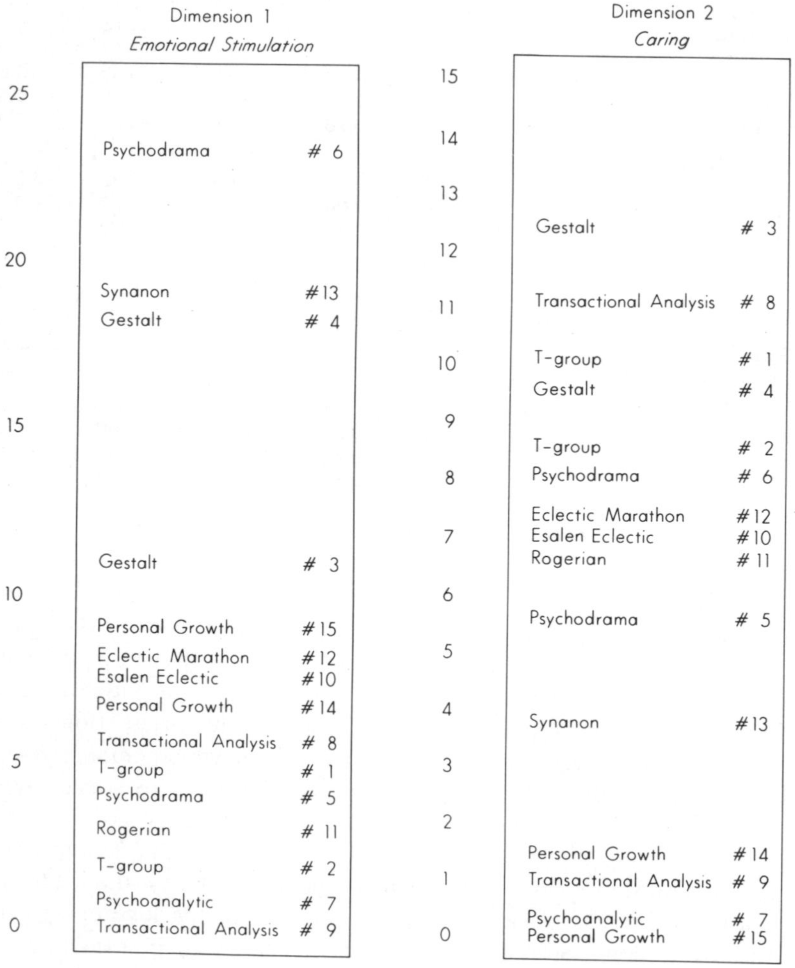

Dimension 1 Emotional Stimulation			Dimension 2 Caring		
25			15		
	Psychodrama	# 6	14		
			13		
				Gestalt	# 3
20			12		
	Synanon	#13	11	Transactional Analysis	# 8
	Gestalt	# 4			
			10	T-group	# 1
				Gestalt	# 4
15			9		
				T-group	# 2
			8	Psychodrama	# 6
				Eclectic Marathon	#12
			7	Esalen Eclectic	#10
	Gestalt	# 3		Rogerian	#11
10			6		
	Personal Growth	#15		Psychodrama	# 5
	Eclectic Marathon	#12	5		
	Esalen Eclectic	#10			
	Personal Growth	#14	4	Synanon	#13
	Transactional Analysis	# 8			
5	T-group	# 1	3		
	Psychodrama	# 5			
	Rogerian	#11	2		
	T-group	# 2		Personal Growth	#14
	Psychoanalytic	# 7	1	Transactional Analysis	# 9
0	Transactional Analysis	# 9	0	Psychoanalytic	# 7
				Personal Growth	#15

FIGURE 7–1 (*Cont'd*)

Leader Scores on the Four Basic Dimensions

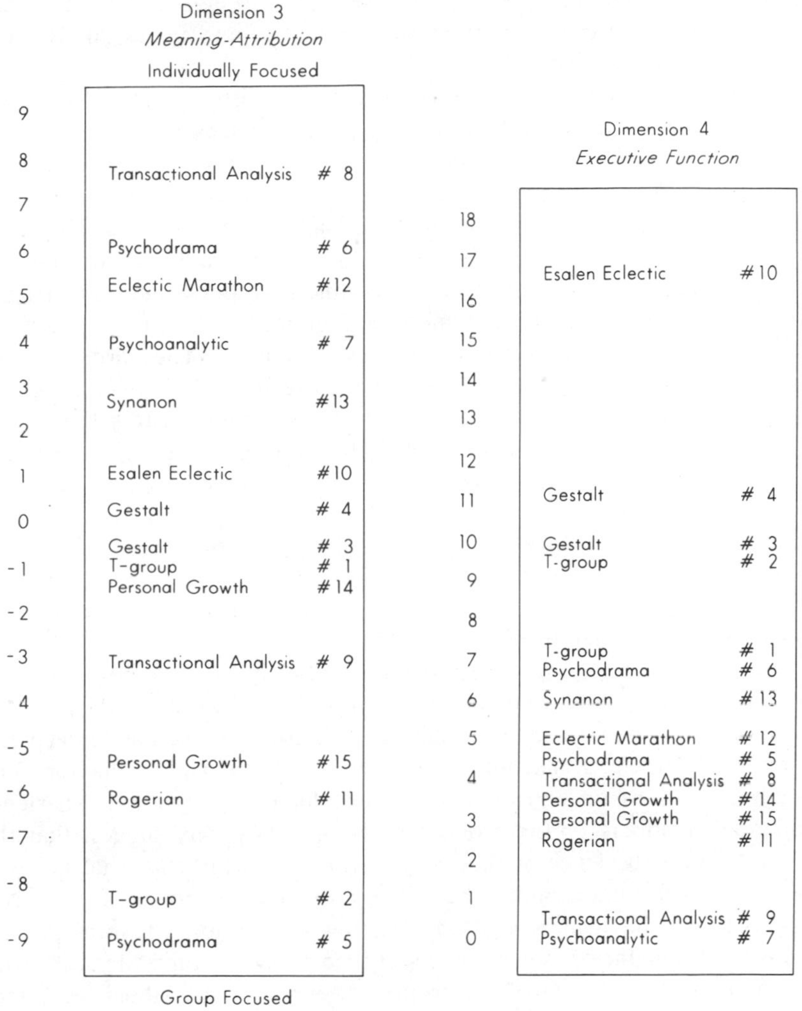

Dimension 3
Meaning-Attribution
Individually Focused

Scale	Dimension 3	
9		
8	Transactional Analysis	# 8
7		
6	Psychodrama	# 6
5	Eclectic Marathon	#12
4	Psychoanalytic	# 7
3	Synanon	#13
2		
1	Esalen Eclectic	#10
0	Gestalt	# 4
-1	Gestalt	# 3
	T-group	# 1
	Personal Growth	#14
-2		
-3	Transactional Analysis	# 9
-4		
-5	Personal Growth	#15
-6	Rogerian	# 11
-7		
-8		
	T-group	# 2
-9	Psychodrama	# 5

Group Focused

Dimension 4
Executive Function

Scale	Dimension 4	
18		
17	Esalen Eclectic	#10
16		
15		
14		
13		
12		
11	Gestalt	# 4
10	Gestalt	# 3
	T-group	# 2
9		
8		
7	T-group	# 1
	Psychodrama	# 6
6	Synanon	# 13
5	Eclectic Marathon	# 12
	Psychodrama	# 5
4	Transactional Analysis	# 8
	Personal Growth	#14
3	Personal Growth	#15
	Rogerian	# 11
2		
1		
0	Transactional Analysis	# 9
	Psychoanalytic	# 7

selves, and at times refusing to accept members' views of themselves, are also characteristic. A last aspect of Stimulation as a leader style is the emphasis on intrusive modeling, and use of self. The stimulative leader signals participants to be like him in style, values, behavior, and beliefs. Leaders who are high on Stimulation are perceived as charismatic, inspiring, imposing, stimulating, believing in themselves, and possessing a vision or a sense of mission. Mirroring, teaching and resource function, and participant perceptions of peer-orientation are negatively associated with this style. Emotional Stimulation appears to be a style centered in the person of the leader; the very presence of the leader is a salient feature of the group experience. This dimension organizes behavior which sends psychological signals that add up to "be like me," "see me," "I am here—omnipresent." Emotional Stimulation is a high input dimension characterized by manifold uses of self.

Caring as a leader style involves protecting, offering friendship, love, affection, and frequent invitations for members to seek feedback as well as support, praise, and encouragement. Stylistically, such leaders express considerable warmth, acceptance, genuineness, and a real concern for other human beings in the group. The style is characterized by the establishment of specific, definable, personal relationships to particular group members who the leader works with in a caring manner. Leaders high on Caring are perceived by the members as symbolizing giving, understanding, genuineness, caring, sympathy, warmth, openness, kindness. They are at the opposite pole from what members perceive as technically proficient, expert, decisive, solid, competent or knowledgeable. Caring clusters the support items of the Behavior Checklist, the stylistic rating of the Personal Leader as seen by observers, and Love-oriented as perceived by participants; a technical orientation is negatively associated. Caring is clearly a warm/cold, love/not-love dimension. This dimension should not be confused with interpersonal attractiveness, for the members' feelings about the leader are not associated with it. Liking the leader is more related to Emotional Stimulation than to Caring.

Meaning-Attribution involves cognitizing behavior—providing concepts for how to understand, explaining, clarifying, interpreting, and providing frameworks for how to change. Such leaders are perceived as "interpreters of reality," attaching meaning to a person or a group's behavior. They offer explanations for consideration. These leaders may name experiences individual members or the group are having, they may suggest that they look into the experience or they may tell a person directly what he's feeling. In general, understanding how it is and what people are feeling is an important goal for leaders high on Meaning-Attribution. Meaning-Attribution is a bipolar factor; some leaders characterized by high Meaning-Attribution emphasize aspects of the group as a whole while others focus more on the individual. Leaders whose interpretations generally focus on the group as a whole emphasize cognitive recognition of group climate, how the group is working, and so forth. Such leaders often raise issues or ask the group to reflect on its behavior—to take a cognitive or reflective stance toward group experiences. Leaders who are high on Meaning-Attribution directed at individual behavior request a similar stance relative to intrapersonal issues. Meaning-Attribution represents the naming function of leader behavior, wherein the leader gives meaning to experiences that members undergo. It refers to the translation of feelings and behavior into ideas. The perception of members that leaders who do not assume this function are more like peers suggests that qualities of parent, priest, or pedagogue may be associated with this dimension. Meaning-Attribution, however, does not have the emotional valence of charisma, as seen from the leader scores in Table 7–4 where charisma is clearly on a separate dimension.

The fourth dimension of leadership, *Executive Function,* is defined in terms of behaviors such as limit-setting, suggesting or setting rules, limits, norms setting goals or directions of movement, managing time, sequencing, pacing, stopping, blocking, interceding, as well as such behaviors as inviting, eliciting, questioning, suggesting procedures for the group or a person, and dealing with decision-making. Leaders high on Executive Function emphasize the expression or release of emotions through suggestions rather than, for example, through demonstration. They are perceived as taking a "movie-director" approach, stopping the action and focusing on a particular behavior either of the group or of an individual. The intent of stopping the action is to have the participants learn about particular behavior cues, emotions, personal learning, and so forth. Essentially these leaders ask the group to reflect upon some action, but unlike the "interpreter of reality" they are more likely to ask the group to provide the answers than to provide the answers themselves. The emphasis is on prescriptive behavior in which the form and type of actions are constructed by the leader. Executive Function clusters two categories of the Leader Behavior Checklist: Limit-Setting and Command Response. It is associated with observer-style ratings of Releasing Emotion by Suggestion and member perceptions of a Teacher orientation, as well as with the use of structured exercises or games. The observer-style rating of Resource Leader is negatively associated. Executive Function represents behavior primarily directed toward management of the group as a social system, and makes heavy use of structured material as a mechanism for goal achievement.

These four dimensions are basic in the sense that all leaders exhibited some of the behavior encompassed in each dimension. One further dimension emerged which accounted for a smaller percent of the variance: the leader's interpersonal attractiveness.[16] It does not have the same properties as these basic dimensions, as it is a derivative dimension, representing the evaluation of the leader's behavior rather than the behavior itself.

The Relationship of the Four Basic Dimensions of Leader Behavior to Outcome

Figure 7–1 shows the characteristics of each of the leaders in relation to Emotional Stimulation, Caring, Meaning-Attribution, and Executive Function. The weighted outcome scores described in Chapter 3 were used to characterize groups that were low, medium, and high on each of these four dimensions.[17] Leaders low on Stimulation had a mean outcome score of

− 04, moderate Stimulation + 33, and high Stimulation + 20. Leaders low on Caring scored − 12, moderate Caring + 23, and high Caring + 55. Low Executive Function leaders showed a mean yield level of − 09, moderate + 61, and high Executive Function + 05. Leaders who exhibited very little Meaning-Attribution had a mean yield of − 16, those who showed high Meaning-Attribution directed toward the group + 17, and those who showed high Meaning-Attribution directed toward individuals + 65.

On this basis, the most effective leadership style would be displayed by leaders who are moderate in amount of Stimulation, high in Caring, utilize Meaning-Attribution, and are moderate in expression of Executive Functions. Conversely, the less effective leaders would be those who are very low or very high in Stimulation, low in Caring, do very little Meaning-Attribution, and display too little or too much Executive behavior.

Another way of demonstrating these findings is to examine the relationship between four basic leader dimensions and outcome, using correlations. Rank order correlations indicate that outcome relates to Stimulation rho = .16, Caring rho = .46, Meaning-Attribution of either kind rho = .61, and Executive Function rho = .05. As a scatter plot of leader behavior and outcome suggested that the levels of correlation are greatly affected by one deviant group, a new rank-order correlation was computed for each of the four dimensions omitting in each case the most deviant group. These new correlations are Stimulation .24, Caring .60, Meaning-Attribution .70, and Executive Function .20. It is thus apparent from the analysis that Stimulation is associated with outcome in a curvilinear fashion; leaders who have too much or too little of it are unsuccessful. Similarly for the Executive Function—leaders who have too much or too little tend to be unsuccessful. The Caring dimensions showed a linear relationship; overall success is associated with high Caring. Meaning-Attribution is a linear relationship in the sense that Meaning-Attribution of either kind is associated with success, but a low level of Meaning-Attribution is associated with failure.

In the next section, when these four dimensions will be used to create leader typologies, some patterns of effective and ineffective leader style become more apparent. High Stimulation combined with high Caring behavior takes on a different meaning when the leader also carries out extremely high levels of Executive Function rather than moderate ones. The absence of Meaning-Attribution appears to spell the difference between the relatively low levels of success of the leader with high Caring behavior and greater success of another who carries on high Caring behavior, and provides a cognitive framework as well. Thus, Leader #1 and Leader #8 are both moderate (see Figure 7–1) on Stimulation; they are both high in Caring; and both engage in a moderate amount of Executive Function; they differ in that Leader #8 provides a high level of Meaning-Attribution while this is absent in the behavior of Leader #1. It seems that, although

Caring is a critical function of leaders, alone it is not sufficient to insure high success.

Another illustration is provided by examining (Figure 7–1) the scores of Leader #12 and Leader #8. Both leaders mirror one another on level of Stimulation, Meaning-Attribution, and Executive Function. They differ in that Leader #12 has a moderate degree of Caring, compared to the high level of Leader #8. Their outcome scores are both positive; however, Leader #8 is far and beyond the most successful leader in our study, while Leader #12 is fourth in positive outcome.

It appears that the two central functions, without which leaders rarely were successful, are sufficient Caring and Meaning-Attribution. A combination of high levels of affectional behavior and high levels of cognitive input are critical.

LEADERS' THEORETICAL ORIENTATIONS

It has been mentioned earlier that in examining the behavior of encounter leaders of divergent orientation, one question of interest was to assess whether conventional labels like Gestalt, T-group, sensory awareness, and so on, were meaningful descriptions of methodological differences. The findings generated by the factor analysis which has just been described give the answer. Using scores on the basic behavioral dimensions, a statistical clustering procedure yielded these groupings: [18] a Personal Growth leader and one T-group leader; the Eclectic Marathon leader, a Transactional Analysis leader, and one T-group leader; the Rogerian Marathon leader, one Psychodrama leader, and one T-group leader; the Psychoanalytic leader and one Transactional Analysis leader; one Psychodrama leader and the two Synanon leaders; and the two Gestalt leaders. The Esalen Eclectic leader did not resemble any of the other leaders.

Clearly, clusters do not support the view that leaders labeled similarly behave similarly in encounter groups. A less stringent method used to evaluate actual similarity was to look at the degree of the similarity among leaders who might be expected to be similar. The three T-group leaders, for example, were compared to determine their similarity to each other compared with their similarity to other leaders. This procedure produced two ranks per pair; [19] for example, T-group Leader #1 and T-group Leader #2 had a rank of nine; eight other leaders were closer to Leader #1 than Leader #2; Leader #2, however, was ranked third with Leader #15, so that only two other leaders were closer to Leader #2 than Leader #15. The mean rank for these three T-group leaders was 5.3. The second pairing expected would be the two Gestalt leaders who were paired by the clustering method. The rank for them was 1.0. The two Psychodrama leaders, #5 and #6, had a mean rank of 12.0. The two Transactional Analysis leaders had a mean rank of 8.0. The two Marathon leaders, #11 and #12, had a mean rank of 7.0. Overall, except for the

241

two Gestalt leaders, the similarities based upon orientation were indeed weak, if existent at all. Whatever the labels of the diverse encounter leaders, the findings are indisputable that conventional categories of leader orientation are poor predictors of leader behavior.

While the finding that encounter leaders' behavior is highly varied diverges from that generally reported in the literature on individual psychotherapy (to the effect that experienced psychotherapists tend to behave much the same, as opposed to novitiates), it is no surprise that in a new field characterized by heavy borrowing, on the one hand, and the affirmation of "doing one's own thing," on the other, orthodoxy has little influence. Marked similarities existed in how leaders approached the task of running an encounter group, but these similarities were not associated with school of thought.

Leader Types

To develop an empirical typology of leaders derived from the twenty-seven behavioral variables, leaders who shared similar profiles were grouped. Scores for each leader on Emotional Stimulation, Caring, Meaning-Attribution, and Executive Function were plotted on a series of graphs to provide a visual image of the ways in which leaders were similar to one another. Leaders #3, #4, #6, and #13, for example, could be grouped as high in Emotional Stimulation and Meaning-Attribution (Figure 7–1, Dimensions 1 and 3). A more exact statistical procedure [20] for developing a typology produced the same groups of leader types as the inspection method. Six clusters or leader types were identified from the two clustering methods: Type A—Leaders #3 and #4 (Gestalt), #6 (Psychodrama), and #13 (Synanon); Type B—Leader #12 (Eclectic Marathon), #8 (Transactional Analysis), and #1 (T-group); Type C—Leader #2 (T-group), #5 (Psychodrama), and #11 (Rogerian Marathon); Type D— Leader #14 and #15 (Personal Growth); Type E—Leader #7 (Psychoanalytic) and #9 (Transactional Analysis); and Type F—Leader #10 (Esalen Eclectic) did not resemble any other leader, but represented a single type.

TYPE A—ENERGIZERS

The definitive characteristic of these leaders is intense Emotional Stimulation. They all gave moderate to high attention to Executive Function and, with the exception of the two Synanon leaders, they were similarly high on Caring. They were perceived as the most charismatic. It is of interest to note that, among those studied, only these leaders were strongly attached to an articulated belief-system, as well as emotionally tied to the founder of their school of thought. For example, subsequent to leading this encounter group, Leader #6 was reportedly persuaded by the head of a Far Eastern religious sect to give up leading encounter groups because they elicited behaviors which the head of the sect felt to be "narcissistic" and not in keeping with the belief-system.

Synanon clearly shares characteristics of a revitalization movement and is more nearly influenced by the charismatic qualities of its founder than any of the other types of encounter groups studied. Despite examples of other influences in the Synanon format, Synanon leaders perceive the founder of the movement as the originator of all innovations for changing individuals. Synanon rituals include a formal prayer, suggestive of the heavy religious overtones of the movement. The Gestalt school, founded by Fritz Perls, also has a sectlike flavor. Witness the published posters of Perls' sayings which have taken on the character of a Gestalt prayer.

The parallels among these five men as encounter leaders and as followers of "religiostic" movements are striking. All five of these leaders communicate a faith beyond that which characterizes members of the healing professions as a whole. This is not to imply that other leaders possessed no similar qualities, nor that the zealousness of the charismatic type was not mixed with some of the more characteristic qualities of the traditional mental health professional. However, the religious quality of the behavior was dominant in the charismatic type, allowing them to feel assured enough to take over for participants and assert firm control. They felt ready, willing, and able to guide participants forward, to "turn them on" the road to salvation. They may even have seen this form of help as their most signal contribution.

As might be expected, the level of proselytizing behavior was highest for members of groups led by charismatic leaders. This again supports the grouping of these leaders under the banner of charisma (see this chapter, page 259).

TYPE B—PROVIDERS

Leaders of this type specialize in Caring and Meaning-Attribution (two of these leaders were high on individually oriented Meaning-Attribution, one moderate). They evidence moderate use of Emotional Stimulation and Executive Function.

These were individually focused leaders who gave love, as well as information and ideas about how to change. They exuded a quality of enlightened paternalism. They subscribed to a systematic theory about how individuals learn which they used in the group but did not press.

TYPE C—SOCIAL ENGINEERS

The definitive characteristic of these leaders was their use of group oriented Meaning-Attribution. These leaders were group-focused, and observers saw them as concerned with how people related to the social system. These leaders were not "personal in style" in the sense that the Providers were, but they did exhibit a moderate amount of Caring indicating relatively high levels of support and affection. Type C leaders were uniformly low on Emotional Stimulation. They ranged from little to frequent exercise of Executive Function. They operated in some ways as "social engineers." It appears that these leaders mainly offered the communication of support and the steering of the work of the group as a whole, rather than aid on individual or interpersonal issues. Their group members saw these leaders as low in charisma and high in peer-orientation.

TYPE D—IMPERSONALS

These leaders were distant, aggressive stimulators. They were moderately high on Emotional Stimulation, low on Caring and Executive Function. In a word, they were "impersonal." Neither of the Type D leaders were particularly high on Meaning-Attribution, although the differences in their scores on this dimension indicate that one was more group-oriented and one more individually oriented.

TYPE E—LAISSEZ-FAIRES

These leaders obtained the lowest scores on three of the four basic dimensions: Emotional Stimulation, Caring (their behavior was characteristically impersonal), and Executive Function. They got moderate to high scores only on Meaning-Attribution. These leaders ape the classical descriptions of laissez-faire leaders because of the absence of a cluster of any of the behaviors assessed in the study: they were generally low on input; they neither stimulated emotions nor controlled group conditions, nor did they offer support. They were "generalists" insofar as their behavior revealed no consistent pattern of the dimensions employed in the study. The symbolic meaning of the Type E leaders to their group members was as technicians. They had some views about how people learn in the encounter situation and communicated some ideas to group members, as shown by their relatively high scores on Meaning-Attribution. This communication, however, was not reinforced through behavior tapped by the other three dimensions.

TYPE F—MANAGERS

This leader was uniquely characterized by his extreme score on the Executive dimension. Unusual degrees of control were exercised on how, about what, and for how long members interacted with one another. The use of frequent structured exercises (an average of eight per group session) was the major, but not the only, form of control the leader used. The observers informally labeled him "Top Sergeant," which perhaps, better than any other data, characterizes the stance of this leader.

The Consequences of Differences in Leader Types

The initial section of this chapter discussed the development of a method for looking at leader behavior and ended with the characterization of the groups studied into six basic types. By the use of outcome data, as well as the reactions of participants during the group, this section will consider the following questions: (1) Overall amount of effect: How successful was each type in producing change? How many learners, how many unchanged people, and what proportion of negative outcomes occurred in groups led by the various types. (2) What are the specific or unique effects on outcome of particular leader types? For example, were some more likely to change values and others more likely to change the self-image? (3) To what extent do particular leader types generate enthusiasm, and to what extent is such enthusiasm converted into postgroup proselytizing behavior? Finally, (4) What are the perceptions of the participants during the time they were participating in the group? What did they emphasize as unique to the experience?

COMPARATIVE EFFECTIVENESS OF LEADER STYLES:
AMOUNT OF CHANGE

At the end of the experience, each participant was classified as having been a High Learner, a Moderate Changer, or relatively Unchanged; as showing patterns of predominately negative changes, as dropping out prior to termination for psychological reasons, or as becoming a psychiatric casualty. Table 7–5 shows these outcomes for the six leader types and the tape groups (G).

Clearly, Providers (B) were the most effective in producing positive

TABLE 7-5

Leader Type and Outcome

Leader Type	N	High Learner	Moderate Changer	Un- changed	Negative Changer	Drop- out	Casualty	Weighted Impact Average
A Energizers	59	8 - 14%	12 - 20%	19 - 32%	4 - 07%	9 - 15%	7 - 12%	+.17
B Providers	37	8 - 22%	13 - 35%	8 - 22%	3 - 08%	3 - 08%	1 - 03%	+1.03
C Social Engineers	32	6 - 19%	3 - 09%	14 - 44%	6 - 19%	1 - 03%	2 - 06%	+.16
D Impersonals	18	0 - 00%	7 - 39%	3 - 17%	2 - 11%	4 - 22%	2 - 11%	00
E Laissez-Faires	25	2 - 08%	1 - 04%	13 - 52%	0 - 00%	7 - 28%	2 - 08%	−.20
F Managers	11	0 - 00%	0 - 00%	8 - 70%	0 - 00%	2 - 10%	1 - 10%	−.45
G Tape Groups	24	3 - 13%	5 - 21%	13 - 54%	2 - 08%	1 - 04%	0 - 00%	+.58
Total	206							

changes while minimizing the number of participants who had Negative Outcomes. The Tape Groups showed the next highest *relative* gain score. Their score reflects their extremely low number of Negative Outcomes, combined with only a moderate number of High Learners and Moderate Changers. Social Engineers (C) displayed a relatively balanced picture of few Dropouts and some Casualties, balanced off by a large number of High Learners. Energizers (A) produced some High Learners and many Moderate Changers, but also a high number of Casualties and Dropouts. On balance, then, Providers (B), Social Engineers (C), and Energizers (A) as well as the Tape Groups (G) produced a relative gain. Impersonals (D), Laissez-Faires (E), and Managers (F) all produced a relative loss; that is, a higher percentage of negative than positive or neutral outcomes. Impersonals (D) and Managers (F) produced no High Learners at all; Laissez-Faires (E) had a few High Learners who were balanced by an equal number of Casualties and a large number of Dropouts. The poorest leader style is clearly the Manager (F); not one participant showed positive change, there were no High Learners nor Moderate Changers, most participants were untouched, and there were a few Negative Outcomes.

A not infrequent statement in the encounter group field is that the most successful encounter leaders use high-risk procedures; high-risk procedures are seen as being the most productive for major learning or change. There has been an association between high risk and high yield. When one looks at the percentage of High Learners or Casualties produced by each of the six leader types, however, it becomes clear that the Providers (B) and Social Engineers (C) who were not especially associated with risk, were the most productive of high learning; one-fifth of all the participants in their groups were High Learners at the end of the experience. The highest risk leaders, the Energizers (A) and the Impersonals (D) produced fewer High Learners. A rank-order correlation between percentages of High Learners and percentages of Casualties indicates that they were correlated $-.33$, clearly indicating that the data lend little credence to the notion that high risk is necessary in order to achieve a high level of growth.

Both Energizers (A) and Impersonals (D) conducted groups with high casualty rates; both types were characterized by aggressive stimulation and relatively high charisma. The relatively high number of Casualties in groups led by the Laissez-Faires (E) was most likely the consequence of omission rather than a direct result of leader behavior itself. It may be recalled (see Chapter 5 on input overload) that a case examination of individual Casualties suggested overstimulation by the group leader as a primary pathway toward Casualty status. Situations in which the leader inadequately protected someone under attack by other members of the group were also cited as signal in contributing to Casualty status.

Aside from the Tape Groups (G), Providers (B) produced the smallest number of Casualties; it is useful to recall that the Providers' behavior combined high support and moderate structuring with lower levels of stimulation. The Tape Groups (G) which produced no Casualties, may provide a key to understanding the relationship of leader behavior to casualty status. An analysis of leader "behavior" in the Tape Groups indicates that prototypical interventions are Meaning-Attribution and Executive Function. Thus, on one hand, the Tape Groups (G) differ markedly from Energizers (A) in that they provide low levels of stimulation; on the other hand, they do not resemble the Laissez-Faires (E) in that the Tape Groups provide a highly structured environment with clear guidelines for behavior. The observer reports for the Tape Groups indicated that they tended to avoid intense conflict, an observation lending credence to the notion that it was the absence of high leader induced stimulation, and perhaps the high degree of structure, that made the Tape Groups safe.

LONG-RANGE EFFECTS: THE LONG POST

The discussion thus far has been limited to describing relationships between leader style and outcome as assessed at the termination of the encounter groups. What about the status of participants six to eight months later? Are these relationships between leader style and outcome still detectable nearly a year after participants began the encounter groups? Is maintenance of learning a product of events in the group and, in particular, leadership style? The data brought to bear on such questions offer little substance on which to posit such connections; overall maintenance appears to be a property of the strategies a person utilizes subsequent to the encounter group (see Chapter 14). The data are relatively mute with regard to specific conditions created by the group that would lead to maintenance or nonmaintenance of learning, perhaps in part because of the lack of theoretical guidelines regarding what types of learning experiences may be more expected to remain secure far after the learning experience is terminated. It seems clear that participants who maintain learning develop strategies that are somewhat different from those who did not maintain the learning. The data do not lend themselves to discovering how these strategies are developed and how or whether they relate to events in the group or to what leaders do.

Table 7–6 shows rates of maintenance for each of the six leader types and the tape groups. The data are imperfect, for approximately one-fourth of the participants did not return for the long post. Whether a participant did return or not appears not to be a result of what he took away from the encounter experience. High Learners were no more likely to return than those who had a negative experience.[21] The rate of nonreturners ranged from a high of 41 percent for the Impersonals to a low of 9 percent for the Tape Groups. These are extremes, however, and, for most groups, approximately 25 percent did not return. Column 2, Table 7–6 shows the number of Moderate and High Learners who had maintained change. Unfortunately, the distributions were not equal, so that, for example, the apparent lack of maintenance for Social Engineers (C) could be an artifact of

TABLE 7-6
Leader Type and Long-Range Effects

Leader Type	Percent Not Returning	Change Maintenance	Late Bloomers[a]	Recovers[b]	Negative Decliners
A Energizers	28	10/14 71%	2/23 09%	2/4	N = 1
B Providers	28	11/15 73%	6/17 35%	1/2	N = 1
C Social Engineers	37	2/5 40%	3/12 25%	0/1	N = 0
D Impersonals	41	3/3 100%	1/5 20%	0/2	N = 1
E Laissez-Faires	31	2/3 67%	2/9 22%	0/0	N = 0
F Managers	25	No Change in Subjects	1/5 20%	0/1	N = 0
G Tape Groups	9	5/7 71%	2/17 12%	1/2	N = 0

[a]N based on number of Time 3 returners who were at Time 2, Unchanged, or Negatively Changed or who have moved from a change classification to a High Learner classification.

[b]N based on number of Time 3 returners who were classified at Time 2 as Negative Changers.

the small number of participants available for examination. One case could make all the difference. From the data displayed in Table 7–6 it would seem that the vast majority of participants who did learn were able to maintain their learning, regardless of the leader style to which they had been exposed.

What about others whose status showed change at long-term assessment? Although overall (see Chapter 3) the number of late bloomers (participants who mainfested learning only at follow-up) is not impressive, where such effects did occur, the data presented in Column 3 suggest that they were associated with all types of leadership style, although more frequently with the Providers. The effectiveness of the Providers is again emphasized; more individuals learned in the Providers' groups, and there was a tendency for more to show manifestations of learning at Time 3 than any other group members.

What about recovery from negative effects of the groups? Column 4 of Table 7–6, which shows the number of individuals originally classified as Negative Changers whose status at follow-up was judged as not negative (almost invariably they were judged as unchanged), makes clear that there were far too few such cases to allow any reasonable conclusions to be drawn about the relationship between leader style and subsequent recovery from negative status. A similar situation exists for individuals who manifested negative status at follow-up, but who had not shown such a pattern at termination; there were very few such cases altogether and never more than one for any particular leader type. Thus, the conclusions reached about the effects of leader style on outcomes as measured after the termination of the encounter groups are the same conclusions that can be reached about the relative effectiveness of leader style from the long post data. Although this is in part due to data imperfections (sample attrition), it is primarily an effect of change stability. Most individuals did not alter their outcome status six to eight months after the groups terminated.

Specific Effects of Leader Style

It seems clear that leader types differ in the overall effects they produce. Some leader styles arc more successful than others; some entail higher risk than others. But what of more microscopic dimensions of change? To what extent are discrete outcomes systematically related to leader behavior? It may be recalled that in Chapter 3 a basic set of thirty-three dimensions was developed to describe personal change in attitudes, values, behavior, aspects of self, conceptions of others, and external relationships. In the present section these dimensions are examined for their relationship to leader style. Are some styles of leadership more likely to effect changes in values and attitudes? Are others' styles more likely to change the conceptions participants have of other human beings?

The methodological problems entailed in such a question are fairly obvious, considering that leadership is only one of several relevant dimensions characterizing the groups studied, whereas the unit of analysis relative to the effects (outcomes) of the group experience is the group itself. Outcomes could as easily be investigated in relationship to other characteristic dimensions of the groups, such as their norms or whether they used massed or spaced meeting time. In order to "isolate" the specific contribution of leader style to particular areas of behavioral change, a rather complicated and in some senses arbitrary set of statistical procedures were employed which, in effect, made it possible to look analytically at the impact of leader style while holding "constant" two other group characteristics, norms and massed vs. spaced meeting time.[22]

With this limitation in mind, let us turn to an examination of the specific outcome effects of leader style. As is evident from Table 7–7, of the five areas of change examined, change in values and attitudes were the most systematically related to differences in leader style. Issues of self showed several important systematic relationships to leader style and there were some strong associations between external relationships and differences in leader style. Conceptions of others were not related to differences in leader style, and few systematic relationships were evidenced between leader style and behavior change.

Figure 7–2 shows the means score (amount of change from the covari-

TABLE 7-7

Leader Type and Specific Outcomes
Multivariate Analysis of Covariance—Levels of Significance

	Time 1-2	Time 1-3
Values and Attitudes		
Value Experiencing		.17
Value Change	.002	
Value Growth	.10	.14
Self-Orientation	.13	
Value Social-Political		
Value Interpersonal		.14
Value Intimacy		
Safety-Danger		.11
Social Benefit	.15	
Genuine-Phony		
Overall p	.06	.21
Interpersonal Behavior		
Interpersonal Adequacy		
Feeling Sensitivity		
Adequate Coping		.03
Defensive Coping		
Acceptance of Control		
Expression of Controlling Behavior	.12	
Acceptance of Affection		
Expression of Affection		
Overall p	.53	.37
Self		
Self-Concept	.19	
Self-Image		
Self-Esteem		
Self-Ideal (Interpersonal)	.08	.19
Self-Ideal (Instrumental)	.05	
Overall p	.27	.86
Conceptions of Others		
Positive Concept of Others		.09
Perception of Others As Lenient		
Complexity (Interpersonal)		.16
Complexity (Instrumental)		
Positive Concept of Best Friend	.18	
Overall p	.78	.19
External Relations		
Opportunity for Open Peer Communication	.05	
Opportunity for Expression of Anger		.10
Number of Life Decisions		
Number of Close Friends	.07	
Hours Spent with Close Friends		
Overall p	.17	.27

ance analysis) of each leader type. In using them it is helpful to recall that the Type A, B, and C leaders represent those who showed overall gain in outcome; in contrast, Types D, E, and F showed relative loss. Types A, B, and C are the most frequent, representing eleven of the sixteen leaders. In examining the data, it should be borne in mind that more weight can probably be given to the effects of these three leader styles than to other styles. In addition, in some senses, the Type D, E, and F leaders are imperfect variants of the three basic types. For example, the Type D (Impersonal), showed considerable similarities to Type A (Energizers), excepting that the Type D did not express the warmth contained in Type A behavior. Both Type D and A leaders are high stimulation, charismatic leaders.

VALUE AND ATTITUDE CHANGE

At the end of the encounter group experience participants in A (Energizers) groups changed their attitudes toward encounter groups in the direction of seeing them as more Socially Beneficial and Genuine than they had at the outset. They also placed increased value on Experiencing, and showed an increased interest in Growth. Participants in B (Providers) groups showed a similar change in their attitude system, seeing encounter groups as more Socially Beneficial and Genuine. Changes in their value system focus around a lowered valuation of Self-oriented values and a heightened valuation of values centering around things External to Self. They increased in the value they placed on Intimacy as a part of their lives. Participants in C (Social Engineers) groups perceived encounter groups as safer, but showed no other attitude changes. Only one major change in their value system was noted, an increase in valuing Growth. Participants in groups led by D (Impersonals) changed in their attitudes toward encounter groups, seeing them as more Dangerous on one hand and more Genuine on the other. In the value area they were more interested in Changing and saw Intimacy and Interpersonal Relationships as more important. Participants in E (Laissez-Faires) groups perceived encounter groups as more Dangerous. Small changes were apparent in their movement away from Self-oriented values and from the importance they placed upon Interpersonal Relationships. For F (Managers) groups, no major effects were noted on participants' attitudes toward encounter groups; major value changes occurred in their increased belief in the importance of Experiencing and Changing.

Overall, participants in groups led by A, B, and D leaders showed the most extensive changes in their values and attitudes. With A and B leaders, participants' attitudes toward encounter groups became more positive; those in the D and E groups became increasingly ambivalent or plainly more negative. How the leader behaves appears to affect how intensely the participants perceive growth as an important or unimportant dimension in their lives. The styles of leadership of the A and C leaders were particularly effective in increasing the value placed upon growth. Members of the

FIGURE 7-2

Leader Types and Specific Outcomes

Attitudes and Values

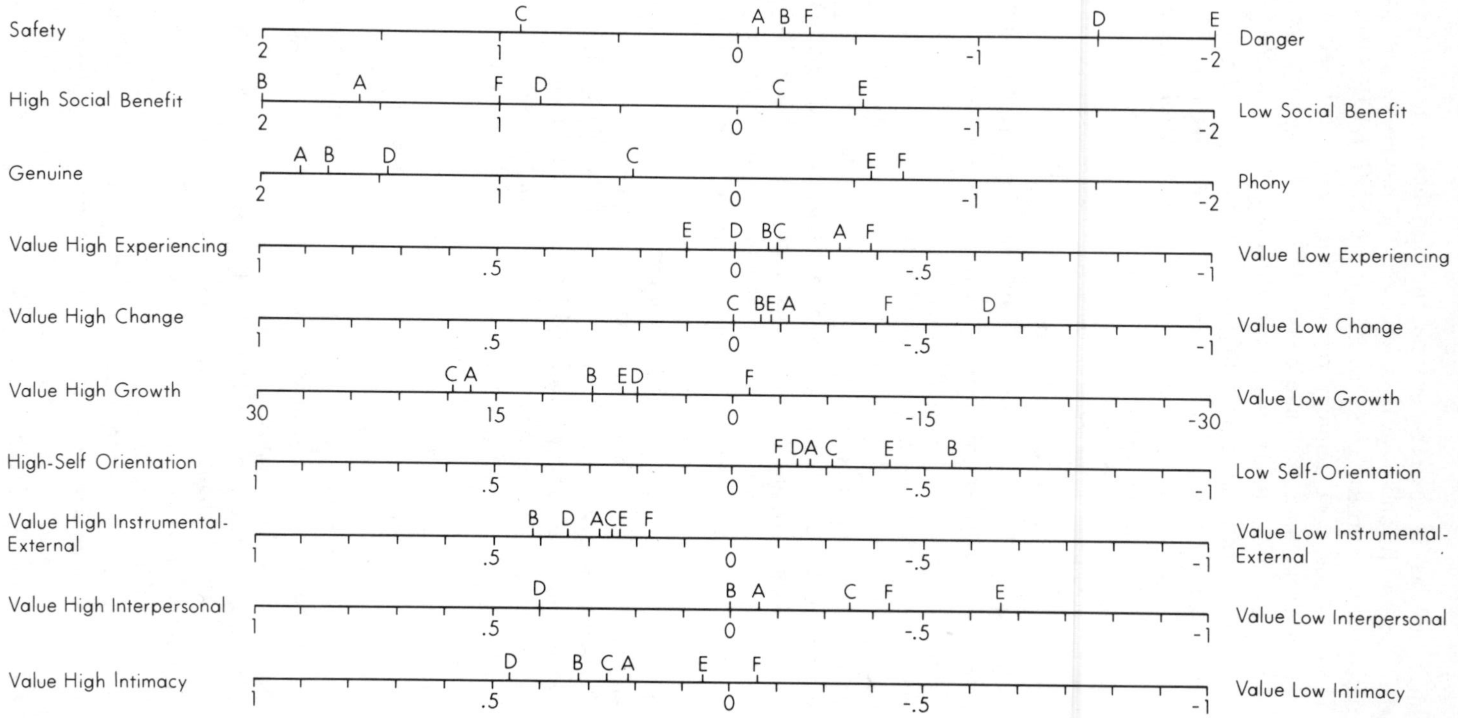

Safety

High Social Benefit

Genuine

Value High Experiencing

Value High Change

Value High Growth

High-Self Orientation

Value High Instrumental-External

Value High Interpersonal

Value High Intimacy

Danger

Low Social Benefit

Phony

Value Low Experiencing

Value Low Change

Value Low Growth

Low Self-Orientation

Value Low Instrumental-External

Value Low Interpersonal

Value Low Intimacy

FIGURE 7-2 (Cont'd)

Leader Types and Specific Outcomes

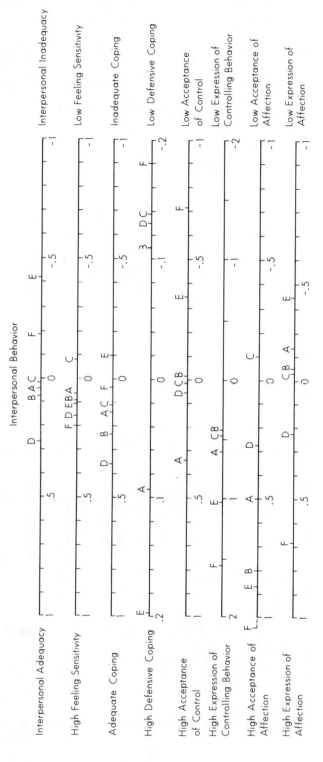

FIGURE 7-2 (Cont'd)

Leader Types and Specific Outcomes

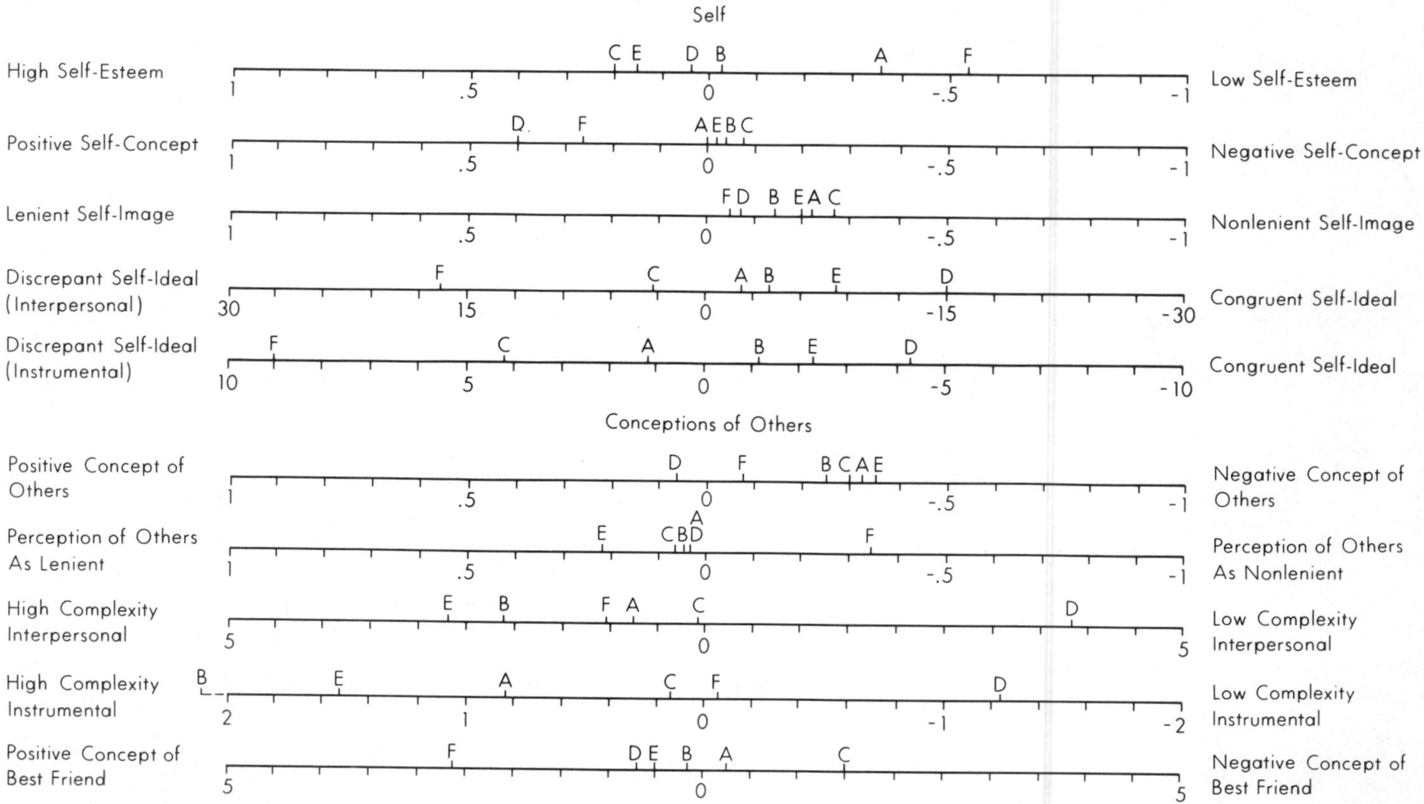

Self

High Self-Esteem	Low Self-Esteem
Positive Self-Concept	Negative Self-Concept
Lenient Self-Image	Nonlenient Self-Image
Discrepant Self-Ideal (Interpersonal)	Congruent Self-Ideal
Discrepant Self-Ideal (Instrumental)	Congruent Self-Ideal

Conceptions of Others

Positive Concept of Others	Negative Concept of Others
Perception of Others As Lenient	Perception of Others As Nonlenient
High Complexity Interpersonal	Low Complexity Interpersonal
High Complexity Instrumental	Low Complexity Instrumental
Positive Concept of Best Friend	Negative Concept of Best Friend

FIGURE 7-2 (*Cont'd*)

Leader Types and Specific Outcomes

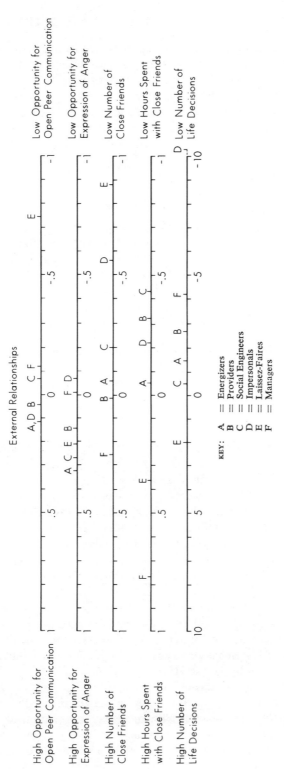

KEY: A = Energizers
      B = Providers
      C = Social Engineers
      D = Impersonals
      E = Laissez-Faires
      F = Managers

group led by the F, "authoritarian," leader decreased interest in growth.

Values centering on change were also influenced by leader style. D and F leaders, the two styles that had the least positive effect on Growth scores, also had a dampening effect on interest in Change. In an overall way the pattern of leader influence on values and attitudes mirrors the findings on amount of change presented in the preceding section; A (Energizers), B (Providers), and C (Social Engineers) were the three leader styles that showed overall relative gain. In analyzing specific indices of change, we note that it is these three leader styles that tended to influence the values and attitudes in similar directions.

It is perhaps not surprising that leader influence showed its most marked effects in the value/attitude area. Although we do not have the data to specify particular aspects of leader behavior and changes in values and attitudes, it seems reasonable to speculate that encounter leaders have highly articulate value structures which are directly and consciously communicated to the participants. Leaders perceive their task as one of creating a new consciousness leading to a new life-style. In this sense, they are emotional revolutionaries, and for them value change is not the Gordian knot it presents to classical therapists. It is a desired and sought-after goal. Our own data presented here and in other sections of the book would support this view of the encounter group. An interesting side note is that, despite the effectiveness of the tape-led groups, they are not effective as value changers.

BEHAVIORAL CHANGE

In general, systematic associations between leader style and change in behavior did not occur (see Table 7–7 and Figure 7–2, Interpersonal Behavior). The lack of significant findings is dramatic in its contrast to the systematic relationship between norm type and behavioral change that is discussed in the following chapter. An examination of Figure 7–2 (Interpersonal Behavior), suggests that, unlike the value area in which the successful leader styles (A, B, and C) appeared to have more influence than the unsuccessful leader styles, behavior seems to be more influenced by Types D, E, and F. Of course the influence was often, although not always, in a negative direction.

Laissez-Faires (E) and Managers (F) share some striking similarities and differences; participants in both their groups decreased in Interpersonal Adequacy and in Acceptance of Influence from others, while increasing in Expression of Controlling Behavior. They are markedly dissimilar in that participants in groups led by Laissez-Faire (E) leaders increased markedly in Defensive Coping, while those in Managers' (F) groups show a marked decrease in defensive behavior. They are again markedly dissimilar in that F leadership is associated with increased Expression of Affection, E with decreased Expression of Affection.

Although sharing a similar overall decrement in amount of learning,

256

participants in groups led by E leaders are often the mirror opposites of the D and F: they are high on Interpersonal Adequacy, low on Expression of Controlling Behavior, relatively low on Acceptance of Affection, etc. Although the patterns are complex, the results pictured in Figure 7–2 suggest that the three failure styles of leadership are quite distinctive from one another, and have very different specific effects.

The three successful leader styles, A, B, and C, show primarily similar patterns of change or no change on the various indices of interpersonal behavior, excepting that the A leader appears to increase Defensive Coping. Could this be a result of the high stimulation so characteristic of this style of leadership?

EFFECTS OF LEADER BEHAVIOR ON THE SELF-SYSTEM

Changes in the degree of discrepancy between the participants' views of self and ideal self-image showed the greatest influence of leader style. Some leader styles significantly decreased the discrepancy between the person's ideal self and his described self, while other leader styles had the opposite effect of making the discrepancy between self and ideal greater. Participants in groups led by B, D, and E leaders showed less discrepancy between their self-concept and ideal image; members of groups led by F leaders showed markedly more discrepancy between self and ideal; participants in C groups (Social Engineers) showed slightly more discrepancy.

Social Engineers (C) had the most impact on increases in Self-Esteem; the level of Self-Esteem decreased under Energizers (A), and even more under Managers (F). Leader style was relatively unrelated to the content of the self-image, except that members of groups led by Impersonals (D) were more likely to change toward an improved self-concept.

Similar to our analysis of Interpersonal Behavior, there is no simple relationship between successful and unsuccessful groups and their impact on self. The most striking finding in this area is that the Impersonal (D) and Laissez-Faire (E) leaders appear to have the most beneficial effects on the self, particularly in regard to Self-ideal discrepancies and the positive-negativeness of the self-concept. The Managers (F) present a sharp contrast to the changes of participants led by Laissez-Faires (E) and Impersonals (D). Managers (F) show a decrement in Self-Esteem and a large Self-ideal discrepancy. Again, aside from the discrepant score for the Energizers (A) in that they lower self-esteem (perhaps again in terms of the high stimulation), the three successful leader styles, A, B, and C, are relatively similar while the unsuccessful styles of leader show wide differences among themselves.

CONCEPTIONS OF OTHERS

The overall direct effects of leader style on Interpersonal Conceptions is small. Although such changes occurred (see Chapter 3) the processes involved were not directly associated to style of leadership or to the normative structure of the group. The most noteworthy relationship between leader style and conceptions of others occurred in relation to Interpersonal Complexity; participants in Provider (B) and Laissez-Faire (E) groups saw others as more complex than at the outset, while participants in Impersonal (D) groups saw others as less complex than at the outset. Some effects were also noted in regard to perceptions of one's closest friend. Participants in Social Engineer (C) groups changed toward less positive conceptions of their closest friends, while those in Manager (F) groups increased their positive conceptions of their closest friends.

EXTERNAL RELATIONSHIPS

The relationship between leader style and effects on External Relationships, again suggests relative homogeneity of the three successful leader styles and the heterogeneity of the unsuccessful leader styles. In general, successful leaders (A, B, and C) increased participants' perception of opportunities in their interpersonal environment; unsuccessful leaders decreased perception of such opportunities. Relationships with friends outside of the encounter group show some interesting patterns: participants in the group led by the Managers (F) showed marked increases in their relationships outside of the group, even though the opportunities presented by this social network are lowered. The predominant style of this leader incorporated highly organized structured exercises with little time or opportunity in the group for relating outside of the group structure. Could it be that their increased emphasis on external relationships reflects one of the probable needs many participants brought to the encounter groups? The need to relate to others in close intimate ways perhaps could not be serviced in such a highly structured setting as the Manager (F) leader style.

Overall attempts to relate particular areas of change with leader style are disappointing. The systematic relationship between the style of the leader and outcome effects are few and far between, except in the value area.

These observations do not necessarily detract from the thesis that leadership style is central in its effect on participants and on outcome: Overall success or failure in learning is clearly associated with leader style. Rather, it suggests that, aside from the value area, the specific relationship between types of effects or outcome and leader style is mediated by other factors. Clearly, the normative characteristics of the group play a role (see Chapter 8); just as clearly, the leader style plays a role in shaping a group's norms. The normative characteristics of a group, however, are not identical with leader inputs, as is discussed more fully in Chapter 8.

Perhaps the most useful way of thinking about leader style is in terms of the overall impact it has on learning rather than in terms of specific areas in which people may change. Leader style creates a condition or a setting under which individuals can learn. The particular kinds of change that take place are probably mediated by many other conditions, such as the individual's initial level and interests or the particular kinds of learning experiences (mechanisms) that occur to the person in the group.[23]

LEADER TYPE AND ENTHUSIASM

Enthusiasm, "being turned on," is a psychological state which for many is synonymous with being a participant in encounter groups. Back (1972), in a recent treatise on encounter groups, has described such an affect state in terms of religiosity. Reflections on encounter groups that have appeared in the mass media clearly mirror high enthusiasm (as, for example, the movie *Bob and Carol and Ted and Alice*). The information presented in Chapter 3, which indicated that the majority of participants in the Stanford study were found to be enthusiastic at the end of the group, reflects the same theme.[24]

Chapter 3 showed, however, that there was no correlation between enthusiasm and judgments of change by peers or by the leader. Enthusiasm was asymmetrically related to change as measured by other tests, so that, while positive changes in many of the test indices were associated with enthusiasm about the experience, many enthusiastic participants did not show change despite their enthusiasm.

What of the relationship between "being turned on" and leader style? When the groups ended, all participants were asked to indicate the degree to which they saw the experience as pleasant, turned on, constructive, beneficial to their learning. Mean scores (on a 7-point scale with $7 =$ high) were: Type $A = 4.9$, Type $B = 5.0$, Type $C = 4.2$, Type $D = 4.2$, Type $E = 3.2$, and Type $F = 3.1$. Overall, participants expressed relative enthusiasm, with A and B leaders producing the highest degree of enthusiasm among their participants. Upon readministration of the same questionnaire six months later, there was some decline in the degree of enthusiasm, with large drops in the level of enthusiasm expressed by those with A leaders and in the Tape Groups and moderate drops for those with C and D leaders. Evaluations of those with B and F leaders remained stable.

These positive evaluations, or course, are not necessarily equivalent to the behavior and psychological meaning intended by Back (1972) in attributing a characteristic of religiosity, nor are they necessarily reflective of the feelings mirrored in popular descriptions of encounter groups. Six to eight months after the encounter groups terminated, a questionnaire to assess "proselytizing behavior" was administered to all participants. The hope was to understand the type of psychological response to encounter groups that is expressed in becoming a convert, "wanting to spread the word." The participants were asked, "since your group experience, have you encouraged others to participate in encounter groups?" The responses could range from "No, I've actively discouraged people" to "I frequently find myself encouraging people to get an experience in an encounter group." Proselytizing behavior was defined as frequently encouraging people. Of the 15 percent of all participants who indicated that they had proselytized, 24 percent represented Type A leaders; 20 percent Type B; 7 percent Type C; 10 percent Type D; 0 percent Type E; 17 percent Type F; and 10 percent Tape Groups. Clearly, these responses were not randomly distributed among leader types.

These observations on proselytizing behavior are not surprising. The description of Type A leaders as charismatic would lead one to expect their participants to behave as disciples. The enthusiasm generated in the Type B leader groups and the high number of learners in those groups make understandable the positive aura and tendency to proselytize of participants. Of less obvious character is the reaction of 17 percent of the members in Type F leader groups who engaged in proselytizing behavior, despite the absence of any learners.

Clearly there are several alternative pathways to proselytizing behavior and "conversion," not all necessarily dependent on positive outcomes for the participant. The high amount of proselytizing demonstrated particularly by members of A, B, and F leader groups suggests that charismatic leaders, the experience of significant positive change, and highly structured activities ("games") all have some role in leading to what has been described frequently as conversion behavior. No wonder, then, that the encounter group movement has created a rapidly expanding "cultlike" group. It is more than likely that the prototype of the Type A leader is characteristic of a large number of encounter leaders; this was the most common style of leadership employed by the study leaders. When, prior to launching the study groups, each leader was asked to indicate on the leader questionnaire how he felt he was usually seen by the groups he led, more of the encounter leaders saw themselves as charismatic than as characterized by any other emotional symbol. Often leaders saw themselves as more charismatic than they were seen to be by participants or observers.

A bit of reflection on the development of the encounter group movement and on the observations of its dominant leaders suggests that with few exceptions encounter groups involve activities and expectations heavily influenced by charismatic founders. The movement appears to attract a number of leaders who share or desire to emulate such qualities as are found in the founders. The total amount of enthusiasm observed cannot be associated specifically with the leaders, for some derives from activities (see Chapter 15). But leaders, particularly if they are "charismatic," play an important role in creating a self-perpetuating movement by producing converts who wish to induce others to undergo the experience. As noted in Chapter 5, even some of those participants who suffered intense psychological harm from being in an encounter group were still quite willing to endorse encounter groups and saw them as useful for others.

PARTICIPANTS' PERCEPTIONS OF THE GROUP AND LEADER STYLE

Another perspective on the effects of the diverse leader styles is offered by the members' perceptions of the group during the life of the group.

What kinds of psychological opportunities did the various leader styles offer to the members of their groups? Group provision for feedback, for knowing others deeply, for open and honest encounters with their peers, for being able to share with their peers, for novel experiences, for opportunities to express trust or anger or being direct,[25] revealed significant differences among leader types.

Participants in Energizers' (A) groups emphasized the increased opportunities for novel experiences and for the expression of anger. Providers' (B) groups emphasized the increased opportunities to share with their peers. Social Engineers (C) stressed the increased opportunity for obtaining feedback about their behavior. Members of Impersonals' (D) groups evidenced no distinct reaction; they reflect the average scores for the total participant population. Those in the Laissez-Faires' (E) groups were the most highly distinguished; they rated the experience as decreasing the opportunity for feedback, knowing others deeply, sharing with peers, having novel experiences, and getting out their anger. Participants in the Managers' (F) group stressed the lowered opportunity to share with peers and express anger. Those who were in the Tape Groups reported on increased opportunity to know others deeply and share with peers.

These differing perceptions of the groups by the participants are consonant with the underlying behavior patterns of the leaders. It is not surprising that the intense stimulation and charisma of Type A leaders would lead participants to view their groups as providing the increased opportunity for novel experiences and for the expression of angry feelings frequently associated with intense stimulating behavior. The stress on increased sharing with peers by participants in B groups mirrors their characterization as displaying high caring behavior, high meaning attribution with moderate levels of stimulation, and an emphasis on moderated conflict and on closeness or warmth. Similarly the emphasis of the C leaders on group conditions corresponds to the members' perception of the groups as ones that increase the availability of feedback. The participants in groups with Laissez-Faire (E) leadership, reflect their disappointment in the experience in their uniformly low ratings of opportunities, perhaps because the character of the experience in no large way met their expectations of the special qualities they associated with encounter groups. The Type F leader, characterized by high controlling behavior, reflected actual problems in getting at other issues, such as relationships with peers and the expression of anger. Members of the Tape Groups, those without an actual leader, mirrored an obvious peer emphasis in their opportunity ratings, knowing one another deeply, and sharing with their peers.

Another perspective of participants' perceptions may be gained by ex-

TABLE 7-8

*The Effects of Leader Style
on Participants' Perception of Their Group Experience*

		Leader Type							
		A	B	C	D	E	F	G (Tapes)	Overall Mean
	Event								
1.	Expression of Feeling, Unspecified	12%	16%	13%	20%	19%	24%	21%	16%
2.	Expression of Positive Feeling	09%	08%	04%	05%	03%	01%	04%	06%
3.	Expression of Negative Feeling[a]	21%	13%	10%	18%	17%	05%	12%	15%
4.	Experience of Positive Feeling[a]	08%	04%	10%	03%	05%	03%	09%	07%
5.	Experience of Negative Feeling[a]	05%	02%	04%	00%	01%	04%	10%	04%
6.	Feedback[a]	10%	08%	18%	14%	11%	18%	19%	13%
7.	Insight	06%	08%	04%	05%	02%	06%	05%	05%
8.	Self-Disclosure[a]	16%	23%	22%	11%	18%	33%	11%	19%
9.	Abstract Discussion[a]	13%	18%	15%	23%	24%	05%	10%	15%
	Target								
10.	Active Self	28%	27%	28%	24%	35%	38%	33%	29%
11.	Passive Self	14%	08%	13%	13%	10%	14%	11%	12%
12.	Not Self[a]	36%	39%	33%	50%	26%	31%	19%	34%
13.	Group[a]	21%	26%	26%	13%	30%	19%	36%	25%
	Personal Meaning								
14.	Love[a]	20%	20%	18%	04%	14%	12%	19%	17%
15.	I'm Like Others	04%	04%	02%	00%	06%	07%	05%	04%
16.	Altruism	02%	04%	04%	00%	01%	03%	00%	02%
17.	Personal Mastery[a]	10%	05%	08%	04%	07%	15%	09%	08%
18.	Group Mastery[a]	06%	06%	12%	14%	16%	08%	14%	10%
19.	Empathy	06%	04%	04%	07%	02%	05%	01%	04%
20.	All Negative Feeling	18%	19%	17%	25%	26%	20%	25%	20%
21.	Insight	18%	20%	14%	21%	10%	15%	13%	16%
22.	Information	14%	18%	22%	26%	19%	15%	13%	18%

[a]Significant at p = .05, one way analysis of variance.

NOTE: Percents add to 100% for each classification; Event, Target, Personal Meaning.

amining the critical incident reports. At the end of each meeting participants were asked to indicate what event in the group they felt most important for them personally and in what ways it was important. These critical incidents were categorized in terms of the event referred to, the target of the event, and the meaning attributed to it. The nine event categories, the four target categories, and the nine categories used to classify the personal meaning the event had for participants are presented in Table 7–8. This shows the percentage of total responses for each of the leader types and the Tape Groups. The last column shows the overall mean for the total group of participants (approximately 1500 critical events were scored).[26]

Participants in groups conducted by Energizers (A) emphasized the expression of negative feelings and experiencing of emotions as a prototypical event when compared to groups led by other types of leaders. The feeling of love and personal mastery were the most common meaning of the events cited as critical.

Participants in groups led by Providers (B) did not emphasize the experiencing aspects of events and were not likely to see feedback as crucial. The events they most emphasized related to self-disclosure. Similar to the A groups, participants in B groups emphasized love as a meaningful response and did not see personal mastery as crucial in their experience. Participants in Social Engineers' (C) groups selected out events of feedback and self-disclosure as crucial, and did not see the expression of feelings, particularly positive ones, as central. Similar to participants in A and B groups, they emphasized love. They stressed, however, group mastery in contrast to Type A's emphasis on personal mastery.

Participants in D groups, Impersonals, selected out discussions as the prototypical event and emphasized the expression of negative feelings. Frequently participants in such groups chose events that happened to other individuals as the most critical for themselves. Unlike many of the participants in other types of groups, they did not emphasize group-level events. For participants of groups with Type D leaders, the meaning attached to the critical events differed in several important respects from all other participants. The response of love was almost totally absent; the emphasis was on group mastery as a meaningful aspect of their experience. Then too, participants in groups led by Type D leaders did not emphasize self-disclosure or experiencing as salient events.

Participants in groups led by Laissez-Faire (E) leaders emphasized events characterized by discussions and the expression of negative feelings, but not the experience of affects. They were more likely than most to emphasize as critical those events which involved the whole group; their most salient distinguishing response was group mastery.

Participants in groups led by Managers (F) emphasized self-disclosure and feedback, and gave little importance to the expression of feelings (particularly negative ones), the experience of positive feelings, and the discussion. For these participants, the distinguishing prototypical response, that is the meaning events had to them, was an emphasis on personal mastery. They were less likely to emphasize the feeling of love as a salient meaning of the event, and they were less likely to emphasize group mastery. The members of the two Tape Groups emphasized the experiencing aspects of events and feedback, and tended not to see self-disclosure as central in their experience. More often than any of the participants under other leadership conditions, they emphasized group events. The meaning tended to be love, personal mastery, and group mastery.

Table 7–8 shows that considerable communality existed among all the participants regarding the meaning of events, as well as the target, and, to some extent, the events themselves. There also were important differences in the participants' feelings of groups under different leader types. There were uniform experiences associated with being a participant in a group led by a particular style of leader. The type of leader one had did have some impact on the experience as seen through the eyes of the participants. The implications for learning of these critical events are discussed in detail in Chapter 11.

Summary

The analysis of the behavior of leaders in encounter groups indicates that how leaders conduct themselves does make a substantive difference in the relative benefit or harm group members experience. Differences in what leaders do in their groups, however, were shown to be unrelated to differences in their theoretical orientations or to the labels conventionally used to describe diverse schools of thought regarding encounter group technique. Four basic dimensions were found to underly a variety of leader behaviors—Stimulation, Caring, Meaning-Attribution, and Executive Function. Caring and, particularly, Meaning-Attribution were found to be associated with beneficial effects, whereas excessive Stimulation or inordinate attention to Executive Function were associated with negative outcomes.

Using the four basic dimensions of leader behavior, a typology was developed describing six leadership styles. Three of these styles—those of the Provider, the Social Engineer, and the Energizer—were found to be successful. The Laissez-Faire, Manager, and Impersonal styles were found to be unsuccessful.

NOTES

1. For all the analyses presented in this chapter, the two Synanon leaders are treated as a single unit. The Synanon format involved changing the composition of the group at each session. Thus, the participants met varyingly with one or another of the two leaders.

2. It should be apparent that the observation schedules also differed in the degree of personal judgment expected or permitted. The Leader-Behavior Checklist required only a rating on a five-point scale, whereas other schedules expressly solicited the personal reactions of the observer or participants. Stylistic judgments were midway; schedules provided external reference points, but required the observer to filter out a single evaluation from a number of choices.

3. Differentiations in this area are crude and do not reflect subtler aspects possible in the affective relationship between leader and members. The decision to limit this area of assessment to the more obvious expressions of positive affect grew out of

the assumption that observers were insufficiently trained to make fine discriminations, within a positive valence, among supportive behaviors.

4. Number of meetings in which this behavior appeared: *evocation area,* (1) inviting, 42 percent–100 percent; (2) questioning, 67 percent–100 percent; (3) reflecting, 0 percent–90 percent; (4) calling on, 37 percent–91 percent; (5) challenge, 12 percent–100 percent; (6) confrontation, 0 percent–100 percent; (7) exhortation, 0 percent–78 percent; *coherence-making area,* (8) explaining, interpreting, 30 percent–90 percent; (9) comparing, 0 percent–78 percent; (10) summarizing, 0 percent–70 percent; (12) framework, how to change, 12 percent–90 percent; (13) concepts, 0 percent–80 percent; *support area,* (14) protection, 0 percent–42 percent; (15) support, 0 percent–90 percent; (16) friendship, 0 percent–63 percent; managerial area, (17) stop, block, 10 percent–85 percent; (18) suggesting procedures, 22 percent–80 percent; (19) timing, pacing, 9 percent–100 percent; (20) focusing, 0 percent–80 percent; (21) rules, 0 percent–50 percent; (22) goals, 0 percent–50 percent; (23) decision task, 0 percent–50 percent; (24) decision-making, 0 percent–30 percent; in the *uses of self,* revealing, here and now, 22 percent–92 percent; (26) personal values, 25 percent–80 percent; (27) calling attention to the self, 0 percent–67 percent; (28) participating as a member, 0 percent–80 percent.

5. The principle component was factor analysis with varimax rotation to simple structure. Scores on the twenty-eight behavioral categories for every meeting were entered into the matrix, yielding a 15×128 matrix (fifteen leaders, 128 meetings overall). Scores were derived from the following transformation of observer ratings: observers rated 0 if the behavior was absent during the meeting, 1 if it occurred at least once, 2 for an occurrence of several times and 3 if the behavior was typical. On the assumption that most weight should be given to occurrence or lack of occurrence, the scores were transformed as follows: 0, 1 for 1, 1.5 for the observer ratings of several times, and 1.75 for frequently or typical.

6. In all but one case the variables selected to represent a factor were those items that had the highest loading, and in no instance was an item used on more than one factor. The one exception was Item 15 (support and encouragement) which showed approximately equal loadings on two dimensions. Item assignment in this case was made for conceptual clarity.

7. The clustering of behaviors grouped under Use of Self and Evocative behavior, which had appeared distinct, suggests that high self-disclosure by leaders may have an effect similar to that of confrontation by the leader, insofar as it places an intense demand on members to reciprocate.

8. All three of these patterns of behavior appear intended to stimulate response from the participants, differing mainly in their style and in the degree of freedom participants probably experience in whether and how to respond. The observation that so much of encounter leader behavior is focused on getting members to respond is of more than passing interest. Although common to all forms of encounter groups, stimulation as a prime function of leaders is perhaps the most unexamined characteristic of this movement; yet, historically, emotional contagion was the first phenomenon of groups to interest investigators. Le Bon, MacDougall, and Freud were all intrigued with the powerful primitive affects that could be released in groups. Until the recent advent of encounter groups, however, most work with individuals in a group context emphasized the examination and management of such affects rather than the stimulus potential of the leader. It is this emphasis on stimulation that perhaps most truly differentiates the activity of the encounter leader from other forms of help-giving through groups. This radical departure in conception of the leader's role undoubtedly explains some of the controversy and concern which the encounter movement has aroused in many professional and lay circles.

9. Of interest is the probable complementarity of the managing and cognitive dimensions; both emphasize structured behaviors of a highly specific and often unemotional character. Some of the leaders who were low in cognitizing appeared relatively high in managing behavior. One of the T-group leaders provided structure through managing rather than cognitive functions, whereas one of the Transactional leaders provided structure in his group through cognitive but not managing functions. High scores on both cognitive and managing dimensions, as with the sensory-

awareness (Esalen) leader, indicate a leader who "runs a tight ship," employing highly structured sequences of behavior. Leaders who were low on both of these dimensions, such as the Rogerian leader, exemplified a leader style of low control.

10. This method of categorizing the leader's focus of attention does not in any precise way join the issue of group interpretations versus individual interpretations rampant in the group psychotherapy literature. These ratings represent an effort to obtain a much cruder measure of what sorts of things the leader paid attention to when he intervened.

11. A Pearson intercorrelation across groups between the participant and observer evaluations yielded an r of .68.

12. Entire systems of psychotherapy (e.g. psychoanalysis) are based upon the symbolic meaning a therapist has for the patient relative to transference phenomena. The present research has largely ignored this view of leadership because a strict transference perspective would quickly require a consideration of those led (participants). Phenomena would be explained, not in terms of properties of the leader, but of the members. In this research the symbolic value of the leader is looked at for its relevance to his charismatic attributes.

It may be worth considering some distinctions between positive transference in psythotherapy and the influence of charisma. Perhaps the most meaningful is that positive transference implies properties or characteristics primarily of the patient and not of the therapist. In contrast, in the relationship of encounter group members to charismatic leaders, the locus of analysis is the characteristics of the leader and not of the member. The second critical difference is that an operational definition of charisma rests upon the assumption of unanimity of perception in the led. To define the qualities of a charismatic leader, one needs to define a set of perceptions that members share. A positive transference model permits variations in perception which do not fit the concept of charisma.

13. Correlations between the Leadership Questionnaire and observer ratings of leader style partially established the validity of this scale. The leadership style of Charisma was correlated .76 with high scores on Charisma as perceived by members; observer ratings of a Personal Leader were correlated .61 with participant perception of a Love-oriented Leader. Peer-orientation as perceived by participants correlated .66 with the Resource Leader style, as rated by observers. (Such leaders may overtly try to diminish the status differences implied by the role of the leader.) Participants' perceptions of a Technically oriented Leader were not confirmed by the style ratings of the observers.

14. See e.g. "Philosophers and Kings: Studies in Leadership," and Ann Ruth Wilner, "The Theory and Strategy of Charismatic Leadership," *Daedalus,* Summer, 1968.

15. Principal component BMD × 72 (varimax rotation).

16. It is of some interest that leader attractiveness to members was less related to other leader behavior variables than attractiveness to observers, who seemed more specific in both their positive and negative evaluations. Participants liked leaders who produced high amounts of Cognitive behavior and who were perceived as charismatic. They did not like the Resource or Social Engineering style of leaders or those who were Peer-oriented or group-focused. Observers liked Intrusive Modeling behavior, charismatic style, and leaders whom members perceived as Love-oriented. They did not like Mirroring behavior, group focus, or leaders who were perceived by members as technicians. Observers and participants both liked leaders who showed supportive behavior, who encouraged release of emotion by demonstration and who had a challenging style of behavior. Caution, however, should be exercised regarding these relationships. Only charismatic style and challenging style, group focus, mirroring behavior, and release of emotions by demonstration reach .05 level of significance (.50 correlations). Perhaps this means that there is some association between liking and particular behaviors, but it is not as high as one might expect.

17. Note that Meaning-Attribution is a bipolar factor. High scores on the positive end indicate high Meaning-Attribution of leaders directed toward individuals; high scores on the negative end indicate Meaning-Attribution behavior directed toward the group; low scores indicate leaders who did not engage in either of these two forms of Meaning-Attribution.

18. Computer program PGM Hi Clus.

19. Rank-order arrays, based on similarity as assessed by the D-statistic (on the scores of factored behavioral dimensions) were computed for every leader with every other leader.

20. PGM Hi Clus computer program (connectedness method). Leader scores on the 27 variables were interrelated by using a D-statistic.

21. As reported in Chapter 3, a comparison of change scores between those who returned at the long post and nonreturners indicated that the two groups were similar.

22. Mesa 98 Multivariate Analysis of Covariance in which the variance is associated with multiple classification; leader type, norm type, and massed-spaced were systematically examined.

23. This discussion has focused on the unique effects of leader style on particular outcome categories, measured immediately after the encounter group experience. Although the relevant table, Table 7–7, for this area shows the data regarding long-term changes, by and large the effects do not seem to warrant discussion. Loss of approximately 25 percent of the data at Time 3 in part influences this opinion, but primarily it rests on the observation that systematic relationships between leader style and specific outcomes were rare. It is hard to conceive of the meaningfulness of long-term outcome data in this respect given the obvious extragroup influences on the person which were magnified in the long post measurement period.

24. Our own information reflecting participant enthusiasm immediately after the encounter groups terminated indicates that of those who completed the groups, 65 percent checked the positive end (places 1, 2, 3 on the 7-point scale) as having found the group pleasant, 57 percent as having been "turned on" to the group, 78 percent as it having been a constructive experience, and 61 percent stating that they learned a great deal.

25. One-way analysis of variance.

26. The critical events for each person were converted into scores and a one-way analysis of variance was computed to assess the effects of leader types. Those critical events marked with an asterisk were significant at or above the .05 level.

CHAPTER 8

Group Norms

The concept of "norm" is an old one in social psychology and serves to organize a wide variety of behaviors. A norm is a shared idea of appropriate behavior in a particular social system. Such ideas are not only privately held by individuals, but are perceived by each person as being held by most others in the system. Behavior which violates such ideas of the good is ordinarily defined as deviant and receives sanctions—adjustive behaviors—which serve to reduce deviant behavior and return the system to its prior equilibrium. Ordinarily sanctions do not need to be exerted frequently or vigorously; rather, the *anticipation* of sanctions is often as effective in controlling deviant behavior as are actual sanctions.

Norms and the associated sanctioning system provide a certain amount of stability and predictability to social life; members of the social system know what to expect of each other. Norms also serve as a simple substitute for interpersonal pressures and *ad hoc* influence tactics, and represent a kind of social contract which can be invoked when troublesome behavior arises. In any social system, and particularly in the small group where face-to-face interaction occurs and sanctioning can be visible and prompt, norms are intimately related to goal achievement. The content of a group's norms can, in many respects, be seen as an equilibrium or balance between the hopes and goals of its members and the fears or costs that may arise or be incurred as efforts are made to move toward group goals. Since norms are, in effect, a standard set of "should's" or "should not's" for all the members of a group, they may aid (or block) movement toward group goals very decisively. Matters such as how much effort is put forward, the style in which members relate to each other (for example, how trusting or competitive they are), and even the specific procedures used (hearing from all members or only the leader, for example) are all usually regulated by norms.

Powerful or highly esteemed members of small groups not only shape group norms in the first place, but tend to be more constrained by norms.

They are seen as embodying the norms in their own behavior, thus serving to establish the norms for others. When the norms governing a situation are not completely clear, members often wait to see whether members with higher status will sanction a particular behavior. High status also carries with it some "idiosyncracy credits"—the ability to deviate temporarily without sanctions (since the high-status member or leader has done many good things for the group in the past). High-status members can thus possibly bring about change in norms more easily than can other members.

Norms can be seen to be a crucial aspect of the culture of the encounter group. The success of encounter groups depends, in large respect, on the creation of a tiny society, which is separated from and marked off from the surrounding culture. For example, in most ordinary interpersonal interaction, it is treated as a norm violation if one comments directly on the appearance or behavior of other persons, or shares one's own inner feelings. Such behavior is usually defined as "rude" and occurs rarely, even among intimates. People typically pay attention to the *content* of an interaction and allude to what has been said, but very rarely allude to the actual interpersonal processes occurring in the immediate situation. Encounter groups not only violate these norms, but create counternorms; talking about interpersonal processes or feelings is a decisively good idea, and avoidance of such self-analytic behavior is defined as bad. Similarly, encounter groups tend to be supported by norms which encourage more interpersonal closeness than is typically the case in ordinary transactions, invite the reduction of "task orientation," and favor the direct expression of anger.[1]

Little has been written on the functioning of norms in encounter groups. Gibb (1964) has outlined a theory of four modal concerns in group development, including acceptance, the flow of interpersonal data, goal orientation, and modes of control in the group. Each of these is decisively regulated by norms, dealing with specific areas such as trust, feedback, decision-making, risk-taking, and work style. The T-group or encounter group task is not only to analyze and become aware of the implicit norms in the group, but to alter them to facilitate more individual learning in the group setting.

Gibb's ideas were extended by Psathas and Hardert (1966), who classified trainer interventions according to the presumed norms they generated, along eleven basic dimensions: feedback, feeling expression, acceptance, process analysis, goal and task concern, behavior experimentation, leadership behavior, participation, trainer authority, decision-making, and concern with structure. Psathas and Hardert suggested that the trainer, as a high-status member of the social system, signaled through the content or style of his interventions "implicit norm-messages indicating to members what norms should be established in the group." Psathas and Hardert, however, did not assess the degree to which such "messages" did in fact bring about the existence of the norms presumed to exist tacitly in the leader's comments and made no analysis of the actual norms in force in the groups studied.

Recently, Luke (1972) analyzed norms in twelve T-groups; members did feel that group trainers were more influential in forming such norms than were other members. The most centrally endorsed norms were those regulating awareness, acceptance, feedback, and the expression of feelings; such norms appeared to be in place earlier in groups where members attributed high influence to their trainer.

One additional line of work in this domain should be mentioned here. Whitaker and Lieberman (1964) suggested that deviant behavior in therapy groups appears when a member interferes with a solution to a "group focal conflict" which is acceptable to most of the members. Focal conflicts include a disturbing motive (such as "the wish to be unique and to be singled out for special attention from the therapist") in conflict with a reactive motive (such as the realization that other group members won't permit this). Such a conflict will characteristically have a more or less durable solution (such as tacit agreement that "going around the group" is a useful procedure), which is actually a group norm. Whitaker and Lieberman point out that deviant behavior, when it occurs, arouses anxieties "previously held in check by the solution"; thus, to deal with these anxieties the group must either bring about conformity in the deviant, reinterpret the deviant behavior as not threatening the solution, or modify the solution (norm) so that it incorporates the deviant behavior. Norms in this sense are very decisively an equilibrating device, holding members' goals and fears in a more or less stable balance.

The present project offered an excellent opportunity to test the importance of group norms in shaping outcomes of the encounter group. No empirical work has indicated that different normative patterns do, in fact, induce different amounts or types of outcome. In this chapter the normative situation as it developed in the seventeen groups is reviewed and analyzed against outcomes for individuals. Since (to anticipate) it is apparent from these analyses that norms *do* make a difference in the prediction of outcome—a contribution at least as powerful as that of specific leader behavior—the sources and development of norms in these seventeen groups are explored.

Measuring Norms

In spite of the pervasiveness of the norm concept, there have been relatively few empirical investigations of norms, as such. The measurement mode has classically (Bates and Cloyd, 1958; COPED, 1970) been to ask group members to estimate the proportion of other group members who would endorse a particular normative statement (few, some, most), or to estimate the percentage of those likely to make such an endorsement. As Miles (1969) has shown, such estimates are frequently subject to "pluralistic ignorance." If the norm deals with innovativeness, for example, group members tend to see their system as anti-innovative, but the system turns out to be filled with innovative people, each of whom thinks he is in a minority. The tendency is for respondents to judge their systems to be more "conservative" than the privately held attitudes of members would lead one to conclude. This distortion occurs in part, of course, because private attitudes and public behavior are discrepant. Thus the perceived-endorsement approach to the measurement of norms has weaknesses.

Accordingly, a more common sense direction was taken to the problem of measuring norms—that of asking the group member to imagine that he was speaking to a new member who wanted to have an idea of what, in general, went on in the group. The respondent was asked to explain to the fantasied new member whether a particular behavior, such as "being repeatedly late," would be seen as appropriate or inappropriate by most of the group.

A large number of possible behaviors which could be seen as norm violations, such as "talked about the details of his sex life," "challenged the leader's remark," and "kissed another member," drawn from personal observation of encounter groups and the literature were employed to develop a forty-eight-item checklist of "Do's and Don'ts" (see Appendix II). These items dealt with such things as group procedures, the nature of legitimate content, the style of interaction in the group, the behavior of the leader, the relationship among group members, and boundaries on the expression of affect. Participants and leaders were asked after the third session of the group and then again in a later meeting (seventh or eighth) to judge whether a particular behavior would be seen by most members of the group as "definitely appropriate," "somewhat appropriate," would produce a "mixed reaction," be seen as "somewhat inappropriate," or as "definitely inappropriate."

This instrument was also administered to members of the control group prior to the group experience to get a generalized measure of expectations for encounter groups held by Stanford students similar to those who actually participated. The group leaders were also asked to fill out the instrument in anticipation, indicating how their usual groups typically fared on each of the forty-eight items.

Normative Dimensions

Data from the late administration of the norms instrument were factor-analyzed, using the group mean scores. The first five factors are shown in Table 8–1.

TABLE 8-1
Factor Analysis of Norm Instrument

Item	Factor Loading
Factor 1 Intense Emotional Expression (27% of Variance)	
Warmly touched another member	.96
Kissed another member	.94
With strong feelings, told another member how likable he is	.91
Told another member how much he cared for her	.89
Cried	.81
Pleaded for help	.77
Hit another member	.76
Asked for reactions or feedback ("How do you see me in this group?")	.65
Made threatening remarks to other group members	.61
Focused his comments on what was going on in the group	.58
Talked a lot without showing his real feelings	−.56
Frankly showed sexual attraction to another person in the group	.61
Factor 2 Open Boundaries: Expression of Outside and Personal Material (17% of Variance)	
Frequently joked	.88
Talked about the details of his sex life	.81
Kept bringing in topics from outside the group	.70
Brought up problems he had with others who weren't in the group	.66
Disclosed information about the group on the outside	.64
Refused to be bound by a group decision	.60
Described his dreams and private fantasies	.57
Brought a friend to the group session	.46
Factor 3 Hostile, Judgmental Confrontation (11% of Variance)	
Said another member's behavior was wrong and should be changed	.81
Challenged the leader's remarks	.82
Kept on probing or pushing another member who had said, "I've had enough"	.78
Talked about killing himself	.76
Put down another member who had just "opened up" with some personal feelings	.70
Shouted with anger at another member	.73
Told another member he was unlikable	.72
Interrupted a dialogue going on between two people	.67
Gave advice to other members about what to do	.62
Tried to convince people of the rightness of a certain point of view	.61
Told another member exactly what he thought of him	.55
Factor 4 Counterdependence/Dependence (9% of Variance)	
Said he thought the leader should have the biggest responsibility for planning and guiding group activities	−.82
Said he thought the group should take more responsibility for deciding what activities should go on	−.77
Appealed to the leader to back him up	−.66
Said little or nothing in most sessions	−.47
Factor 5 Peer Control (7% of Variance)	
Tried to take over the leadership of the group	−.92
Tried to manipulate the group to get his own way	−.84
Dominated the group's discussion for more than one session	−.74
Said little or nothing in more sessions	−.54
Wrote another member off saying he didn't matter	−.52
Acted indifferently to other members	−.51
Was often absent	−.50

Factor 1 emphasizes items dealing with warmth, closeness, and intimacy, as well as emotionally loaded behaviors including crying, pleading for help, and those associated with violence or threat; a high-intensity, emotional-expression factor.

Examination of item intercorrelations for Factor 2 indicates that groups loading high on it tended to feel that less "binding power" should be exerted on members, for example, that it was all right to joke, and that outside topics, dreams and sexual material were appropriate to discuss in the group. Groups loading low on this factor tended to forbid the introduction of outside material, to stick to the "here and now."

Factor 3 is interpreted as support for a hostile, judgmental, confrontational style. Factor 4 deals essentially with behaviors toward the group authority figure, and Factor 5 specifies that both domination and withdrawal are inappropriate behaviors, implying a sort of "one man, one vote" ideology. Groups high on Factor 5 saw peer control of extreme behavior (for example, exertion of strong personal influence, withdrawal and indifference) as appropriate.

The factor analysis proved useful in locating five basic normative dimensions, but included only thirty-eight of the forty-eight items. The full correlational matrix suggested separating the counterdependence/dependence dimension. The ten items which were not included in the first five factors were allocated, based on their correlations, to establish six dimensions or six clusters of items. For example, the item "Resisted the leader's suggestions on procedures," though not loaded heavily on the dependence/counterdependence factor, did correlate with some items in the counterdependence cluster, and was thus assigned there.[2]

To stay as close as possible to the real normative situation in the groups, a method was needed which would show whether a particular norm, such as approval of the behavior "warmly touched another member," was in force in a particular group. For each group, each norm was examined for the percentage of group members who said that most other group members would judge the behavior in question as "appropriate" or "very appropriate," "somewhat or inappropriate" or "very inappropriate." If this percentage (in either direction) exceeded 67 percent of the group members, a norm was considered to be "in force."

Table 8–2, which shows all the norm items for each group "in force," makes clear that this method provided a usefully wide range of scores, particularly on Dimensions 1, 2, 3, and 6. This method yielded a much more precise indication of the actual normative state of affairs in a particular group. Note, for example, the unusually high intensity of feeling (Dimension 1) for Group #6, along with the fact that Group #6's members believe (in striking contrast to the situation in other groups) that hitting other members and making threatening remarks to them are behaviors seen as appropriate. Similarly, in looking at Group #7, one can note a relatively low intensity of feeling (Dimension 1), but also that (Dimension 2) both

TABLE 8-2
Norms in Force in Each Group (Late Session)

Items and Norm Clusters	Low Yield												High Yield					Item Totals	
	4	10	9	14	13	11	7	16	2	1	5	15	6	12	3	17	8	A	I
1. Intense Emotional Expression																			
4. Kissed	A	A	A	A				A	A	A			A	A	A	A	A	8	0
15. Warmly touched	A	A	A	A				A	A	A			A	A	A	A	A	12	0
24. Showed sexual attraction										A			A					2	0
28. Told other he was likable	A	A	A	A				A	A	A	A		A	A	A	A	A	15	0
32. Told other how he cared for her	A	A	A	A			A	A	A	A	A		A	A	A	A	A	12	0
9. Pleaded for help	A	A	A	A				A	A	A	A		A	A	A		A	10	0
42. Cried	A	A	A	A	–			A	A	A			A	A	A	A	A	10	1
31. Hit another member		–	–	–	–	–		–			–	–	A	A			–	1	7
47. Made threatening remarks		–	–	–	–	–		–		–	–	–	A	A	A	A	–	1	8
6. Asked for feedback[a]	A	A	A	A	A	A	A	A	A	A	A	A	A	A	A	A	–	16	0
7. Focused on what was going on[a]	A	–	–	–	A	A	A	A	A	A	–	A	A	A	–	–	–	17	0
38. Talked without showing feelings	–															–	–	0	14
Total Score	7	5	6	5	1	–3	1	6	6	4	2	–1	10	7	7	2	5	4.1	
2. Open Boundaries																			
3. Brought up problems he had with outsiders					A		A			A	A		A	A	A	A		8	0
14. Disclosed information to the outside	–	–		–				–		–								0	3
23. Kept bringing in outside topic	–	–							–									0	6
2. Talked about his sex life	A	A	A		A		A			A	A		A	A	A		A	9	0
13. Described his dreams and fantasies	A	A					A	A		A	A		A	A	A		A	11	0
8. Frequently joked			–			–									A	–		1	1
25. Refused to be bound by a group decision	–	–			–						–				A			1	3
19. Brought a friend to the group session				–									–					0	10
48. Showed he had no intention of changing[a]																	–	0	1
Total Score	–1	–1	0	–3	2	–2	3	–1	–2	1	–1		2	3	5	0	2	0.5	

TABLE 8-2 (continued)

Items and Norm Clusters	Low Yield														High Yield			Item Totals	
	4	10	9	14	13	11	7	16	2	1	5	15	6	12	3	17	8	A	I
3. Hostile, Judging Confrontation																			
16. Gave advice		A		A	A	A	A			A	A		A		A		A	10	0
20. Said another's behavior was wrong		A		A	A										A	—		4	1
37. Kept on probing or pushing another	—					—								—		—	—	0	5
43. Tried to convince others of his viewpoint				A	A	A	A				A		A		A			6	0
45. Probed a silent member	A	A		A	A	A		A	A	A	A	A	A	A	A		A	15	0
18. Interrupted a dialogue	—						A	—								—		1	3
21. Told another he was unlikable		A		A	A	A					A		A		A	—		7	1
27. Shouted with anger at another		A	A	A	A			A	A	A	A				A			9	0
35. Told another exactly what he thought of him[a]	A	A	A	A	A	A	A	A	A	A	A	A	A	A	A	A	A	17	0
40. Put down another who had just "opened up"	—	—	—	—	—	—	—	—	—	—	—		—	—	—	—		0	15
22. Talked about killing himself	A						A	A					A	A				5	0
Total Score	−2	2	3	6	6	1	2	1	0	1	3	1	6	2	5	−5	0	1.9	
4. Counterdependence																			
11. Challenged the leader's remarks		A	A	A	A	A	A	A	A	A	A	A		A	A	A	A	15	0
46. Resisted the leader's procedural suggestions								A							A			2	0
12. Said he was not getting anything from being in the group	A	A		A			A	A	A		A				A	A		9	0
34. Told group off, said experience was silly, worthless											A							1	0
Total Score	0	2	1	2	1	2	2	3	2	1	3	1	1	1	3	0	2	1.6	
5. Dependence																			
10. Offered the leader a ride home		A		A			A		A	A			A		A		A	8	0
17. Appealed to the leader to back him up							A				—							1	1
41. Said group should take more responsibility[a]						A		A							A			3	0
44. Said leader should have biggest responsibility[a]																		0	0
Total Score	0	1	0	1	0	0	1	0	1	1	0	−1	2	0	1	0	1	0.5	

TABLE 8-2 (continued)

Items and Norm Clusters	Low Yield										High Yield							Item Totals	
	4	10	9	14	13	11	7	16	2	1	5	15	6	12	3	17	8	A	I
6. Peer Control																			
5. Tried to take over group leadership																I	I	0	2
30. Tried to manipulate the group		I	I						I	I		I		I		I		0	7
39. Dominated for more than one session		I														I		0	2
1. Said little or nothing in most sessions	I	I		I	I	I	I	I				I		I		I	I	0	11
29. Wrote another member off		I	I		A	I	I	I	I			I		I		I	I	1	10
36. Acted indifferently to others	I	I			I			I						I		I		0	6
26. Was often absent		I	I	I	I	I	I	I	I		I	I	I	I	I	I	I	0	15
33. Talked about social or political questions				A	A	A	A		I	I			A	A				6	2
Total Score	2	6	3	1	1	2	2	4	4	2	1	4	0	4	1	7	4	2.8	
Norms Total	18	27	22	26	19	20	18	25	20	23	22	18	28	26	27	23	27		

KEY: A = 2/3 or more of the group members considered this behavior appropriate.

I = 2/3 or more of the group members considered this behavior inappropriate.

aNot used in score totals since common to nearly all groups.

sexual and dream-fantasy material are seen as appropriate for discussion.

Encounter Group "Universals." As Table 8–2 shows, certain norms appeared in nearly all groups. In all but one group, it was seen as appropriate to ask for reactions or feedback ("How do you see me in this group?"). In all groups "focusing one's comments on what is going on in the group" was seen as appropriate. In fifteen groups, "telling another member how likable he is," "challenging the leader's remarks," and "probing a member who has been silent" were judged as appropriate; all seventeen groups judged "telling another member exactly what one thinks of him" as being appropriate. Certain other behaviors were almost universally seen as inappropriate: "putting down another member who has 'just opened up' with personal feelings (for fifteen groups), "talking a lot without showing one's real feelings" (fourteen groups), and "being absent from the group frequently" (fifteen groups).

In general, regardless of other differences among the groups, participants expected a "feelingful" analysis of here-and-now behavior, giving and receiving feedback in the process. This process was seen as active (for example, silent members should be probed) and as requiring investment (members should not be absent), but one in which people should be positively regarded (should not be put down after opening up, and should be told when they are likable). These characteristics constitute, in effect, a general encounter group culture. Such expectations are undoubtedly carried directly into the group by members and are presumably reinforced by leader and member behaviors during the early stages of the group.

Norm Differences. Finding such "universals" confirmed the expectation that the intensive personal growth groups, whatever their label, bear many similarities from group to group. To locate meaningful clusters of normative types, however, required an analysis of norm *differences.* Table 8–2 shows that the normative differences among groups were almost bewilderingly wide. On Dimension 1, for example, Group #6's strong approval for high-intensity feeling expression stands in striking contrast to Groups #7, #13, and #5, where such behaviors as touching, expressing caring, crying, and kissing were not disapproved, but were quite clearly not approved, either. The boundaries about appropriate content (Dimension 2) also varied substantially. In Group #3, bringing in problems with others outside the group, discussing one's sex life and dreams, frequent joking, and refusing to be bound by a group decision were all approved. In contrast, in Group #14, bringing in outside material, disclosing to the outside, joking, and bringing a friend to the group were all frowned upon. These normative differences suggest great differences in the two groups in the amount of control asserted internally and in the firmness of the boundaries separating the group from the outside.

Normative Types

Cluster analyses [3] of the data presented in Table 8–2 yielded information on how each group scored on the four major norm dimensions. (See Table 8–3.) The two groups (#6 and #3) which fell into *Type S* (*Intense, disclosing confrontation*), shared high feeling intensity, wide boundaries of what was permissible content, and high appropriateness of confrontation (hostile, judgmental). On the other hand, almost no norms in the area of peer control were evident in these two groups. The normative picture is of a potent, affective, high-intensity climate; the fact that peer control was not approved or disapproved is commensurate with the presence of a charismatic leader around whom the members focused.

Type T (*Distant, guarded*) contained Groups #11 and #15. In both these groups, approval of intense emotional expression was particularly low for positive feelings (kissing, touching, caring), and intense negative feelings (hitting, threatening) were discouraged. In both groups the behav-

TABLE 8-3

Final Norm Types (Groups Classified According to Norm Dimension Scores)

		Norm Dimensions			
		1 Intense Emotional	2 Open	3 Hostile, Judging	4 Peer
Norm Type	Groups	Expression	Boundaries	Confrontation	Control
S Intense, Disclosing	6	High	High	High	Low
Confrontation	3	High	High	High	Low
T Distant, Guarded	11	Low	Low	Medium	Medium
	15	Low	Low	Medium	High
U Here-and-now Confrontation	14	Medium	Low	High	Low
V Nonerotic, Disclosing	5	Low	Medium	Medium	Low
Confrontation	7	Low	High	Medium	Medium
	13	Low	High	High	Low
W "Average Plus"	1	Medium	Medium	Medium	Medium
	8	Medium	High	Medium	High
	12	High	High	Medium	High
X Leader Support	4	High	Low	Low	Low
Y Here-and-now Feelings,	2	High	Low	Medium	High
Peer Support	9	High	Medium	Medium	Medium
	10	Medium/High	Low/Medium	Medium	High
	16	High	Low/Medium	Medium	High
Z Cautionary Peer Support	17	Low	Medium	Low	High

ior of "talking without showing feelings" was unregulated (neither appropriate nor inappropriate). All other groups, except for Group #7, considered such behavior inappropriate. In addition, the boundaries of appropriate content were not especially broad. Although there was moderate to high discouragement of behavior such as withdrawal, indifference, absence, and writing off, such peer control occurred in the absence of warm feeling expression (Dimension 3).

Type U (*Here-and-now confrontation*) includes only Group #14. Its members felt that all confrontational behavior, such as giving advice, saying the other is wrong, probing, interrupting, saying others are unlikable, and shouting with anger, was appropriate. In addition, the members of Group #14 felt that bringing in outside topics or disclosing on the outside, or bringing a friend to the group were inappropriate behaviors. Material such as dreams, or details of one's sex life was judged neither appropriate nor inappropriate. This group appears to have been restricted to here-and-now material. The approval of emotional intensity in this group is moderate, with kissing, warmth, likability, and crying all seen as appropriate behavior.

Type V (*Nonerotic, disclosing confrontation*), which includes Groups #5, #7, and #13 presents a striking normative pattern: no group regulates the behaviors of kissing, touching, showing sexual attraction. In all other groups, except for #11 and #15, such erotically toned behaviors are seen as appropriate. In Type V groups such behaviors could be *talked about,* and private outside material, including sexual activities and dreams, could be discussed, but expressing sexually toned behavior in the group appears to have been ambiguously received. These three groups also approved such confrontational behaviors as giving advice, convincing others, probing, and saying another person is wrong. (The confrontational scores were higher for the Synanon Group #13 where it was also thought appropriate to tell another he is unlikable, to shout with anger, or "put down someone who has just opened up.") Peer control in these groups was not particularly sanctioned. Controlling behaviors, such as trying to take over, manipulating, or dominating were unregulated in the Type V group.

Type W ("*Average plus*") included Groups #1, #8, and #12, which approved intense emotional expression, had broad boundaries on what could be discussed in the group, emphasized peer control and (with the exception of Group #8) were more likely than not to approve of hostile confrontation. Type W groups were "feelingful," believing that touching, caring, saying the other is likable, and pleading for help were all appropriate behaviors, (though hitting and threatening were inappropriate in Groups #1 and #8); they permitted wide ranges of topics; for example, both sexual and dream material as well as outside problems; they did not sanction high levels of confrontation, (probing a silent member was appropriate; shouting with anger was seen as appropriate by Groups #1 and #8 —but Groups #8 and #12 considered "keeping on probing" inappro-

279

priate and peer control was emphasized. Groups #8 and #12 considered manipulation and withdrawal inappropriate; writing off and absence were thought inappropriate in the type as a whole. In Type W groups, the important normative dimensions are in force and extremes are avoided.

Only Group #4 was of *Type X (Leader support)*. The normative pattern seems substantially different from the other types: Although intense feeling expression was highly approved (kissing, touching, liking, caring, and crying), boundaries were moderately narrow—disclosure was cautiously regarded (outside topics were inappropriate, dreams were all right, accounts of one's sex life were unregulated). Confrontation, interruptions, and pushing group members who have had enough were inappropriate; commenting on another's unlikability, shouting with anger, advice-giving, saying the other is wrong, and convincing were unregulated. There seemed also to be relatively few peer control norms in operation; manipulation or dominance were not deplored; only withdrawal or absences were seen as inappropriate. The general picture is one of a relatively high level of emotional expression without peer control, along with moderately narrow boundaries on what content can be brought into the group, and little hostile judging or confrontation. Such a climate could be presumed to be managed and supported mainly by the leader—an inference supported by the finding (Table 8–2) that Group #4 was the lowest-scoring group on the counterdependence dimension, and was among the lowest of the groups in the total number of norms in force (only eighteen of the forty-eight possible). It is as if the members of Group #4 did little to form coherent norms, and did not know what was appropriate or inappropriate.

The four groups in *Type Y (Here-and-now feelings, peer support)* (Groups #2, #9, #10, and #16) all approved positive feelings: touching, saying others are likable, caring, pleading for help, and crying were generally seen as appropriate. Kissing was seen as appropriate in Groups #5 and #16. Along with the emphasis on positive feeling, peer control was strong. Manipulation was disapproved, except in Group #5, where domination was disapproved. Writing other members off and absence were generally disapproved. Hostile, judging confrontation was moderately approved. Behaviors such as saying the other is wrong, probing, convincing, and interrupting were largely unregulated, though shouting with anger was seen as appropriate in Groups #9 and #16, and telling another he is unlikable was considered appropriate in both Groups #9 and #10. Discussion of sexual material was not generally approved and bringing in outside topics was seen as inappropriate, while bringing in problems one had with outsiders was not an issue. Thus the general picture of Type Y is that of valuing moderate confrontation, positive feelings and strong peer control.

Group #17 appeared quite distinct from any other group in its pattern of norms, and comprises *Type Z (Cautionary peer support)*. Peer control was valued more highly than in any other group, but the approved level of emotional expression was relatively low in comparison with most other groups. Telling someone of his likability, or expressing caring, along with touching, were seen as appropriate, but hitting or making threatening remarks were disapproved. Acceptance of confrontation was also relatively low. Alone among all the groups, the members of Group #17 disapproved of saying another is wrong, telling another that he is unlikable, and continuing to probe or push another. Outside problems were considered legitimate, but sexual and fantasy material were not regulated one way or another. Type Z represents peer-control directed toward holding down the level of hostility and of feeling expression.

Norms and Outcomes

How likely were groups with differing norms to yield positive, neutral, or negative outcomes? Table 8–2 suggests some relationships. Looking first at the overall number of norms in force in groups by their late sessions, a modest relationship may be noted: The number of norms in force is slightly related to yield level. The median number of norms for all groups is twenty-three. Of the seven groups with twenty-five or more norms, five are higher-yield groups. Of the six groups with twenty-one or fewer norms, four are lower-yield groups. This makes sense. The recognition of a large number of norms suggests a reasonable degree of stability or consensus, regardless of normative content, which may serve to facilitate learning. Yet, Group #7, with only eighteen norms in force, is a medium-yield group (rank 11); and Group #10 with twenty-seven norms in force, is a low-yield group (rank 16). Thus the issue of normative content must be invoked. Does it make a difference what norms are *about*?

To explore the impact of normative content, scores were developed for each normative dimension by adding the number of norms included (or subtracting if the norm went in the opposite direction from the dimension label), excluding "universal" norms. The first dimension, intense emotional expression, showed no relationship to group yield at Time 2 (rho = .12), largely because the three lowest-yield groups (#4, #10 and #9) highly approved of intense emotional expression. It seems likely that high approval of feeling-expression must be tempered or moderated by other norms if yield is to be high. The second dimension, open boundaries permitting private and outside material,[4] yielded a relationship to group yield which approached significance (rho = .34). The average yield rank for groups above the median in their approval of open boundaries was 4.5; groups which were less approving of open boundaries had an average yield rank of 13.

In general, groups which permit discussion of private and outside material, are tolerant of flight, or can accept the idea of bringing friends to the session, are somewhat more likely to produce higher yield. This finding is at variance with traditional beliefs that encounter groups should deal centrally with here-and-now material and maintain relatively tight boundaries, with minimal flight or change in membership. Such strictures may not be as relevant to the question of group yield as has been expected.

For the third dimension (hostile, judgmental confrontation), no relationship obtained with short-term group yield (rho = .09). Confrontation norms, by themselves, did not affect group yield, and must be tempered by or associated with other normative dimensions to have a positive effect.[5]

The fourth dimension (peer control) correlated .19 (not significant) with outcome. Overall, there is a faint positive trend, depressed by two higher-yield groups (#3 and #6) which had low approval for peer control, and one lower-yield group (#10) with high approval for peer control.

In sum: groups which approve of loose boundaries and do not forbid outside material tended to be higher-yield groups. Groups favoring peer control (considering domination and withdrawal alike as bad) tended slightly to have higher yield, and groups with a larger number of norms, regardless of content, tended slightly to have higher yield.

NORMATIVE TYPES AND INDIVIDUAL OUTCOME

Short-post Outcomes. Table 8–4 presents the effects of differing normative types. Normative Types W ("Average plus"), Z (Cautionary peer support), and S (Intense, disclosing confrontation) achieve the *highest* levels of

TABLE 8-4
Norm Type and Outcome Categories (Short Post)

Norm Type	N	High Learner	Moderate Changer	Un-changed	Negative Changer	Dropout	Casualty	Weighted Impact Average
S Intense, Dis-closing Con-frontation	25	6-24%	5-20%	10-40%	0-00%	2-08%	2-08%	.80
T Distant, Guarded	21	1-04%	6-28%	8-33%	2-08%	2-08%	2-08%	.14
U Here-and-now Confronta-tion	9	0-00%	2-22%	3-33%	1-11%	2-22%	1-11%	.33
V Nonerotic, Dis-closing Con-frontation	43	5-11%	7-16%	14-33%	3-07%	11-26%	3-07%	.07
W "Average Plus"	36	8-22%	13-36%	8-22%	3-08%	3-08%	1-03%	1.06
X Leader Support	13	1-07%	2-15%	3-23%	3-23%	1-08%	3-23%	−.69
Y Here-and-now Feelings, Peer Support	46	4-08%	3-06%	25-54%	5-11%	5-11%	4-09%	−.20
Z Cautionary Peer Support	13	3-23%	2-15%	7-54%	0-00%	1-08%	0-00%	.92
Total	206							

group yield. No generalization can be made across these three types in terms of common underlying dimensions, with the exception that all have medium to high levels of approval of open boundaries. The more confident generalization is that different normative patterns may lead to high yield. For example, the high approval of open boundaries in Type S was accompanied by low approval of peer control, high approval of emotional intensity, and high approval of confrontation. In Type Z, on the other hand, moderate approval of open boundaries was accompanied by low approval of emotional intensity and of confrontation, along with high approval of peer control. Type T (Distant, guarded) also achieved above-average levels of positive change, but these were offset by negative changes.

The *lower-yield* normative types were X (Leader support), U (Here-and-now confrontation), and Y (Here-and-now feelings, peer support). Here there is a bit more commonality: All three types share medium to high approval for emotional intensity, and low to medium levels of approval for open boundaries. Type V (Nonerotic, disclosing confrontation) also had above-average amounts of negative change that were offset by moderate levels of positive change. Type X (Leader support), which induced an especially high rate of casualty and negative change, was characterized by high approval of intense emotional expression and low approval of open boundaries, confrontation, and peer control. The members of this group may have found themselves expressing a good deal of feeling, but without normative supports to regulate procedures and manage confrontation.

More generally, all three types (U, V, X) where the most negative changes occurred did not have norms that supported peer control. In U and V, there was medium to high acceptance of hostile confrontation, and in X of high feeling intensity. Peer-oriented norms which prohibit manipulation and domination, and discourage withdrawal and indifference may well be needed to protect members against negative outcomes. But once again, the picture is not this simple. For example, in Type S (Intense, disclosing confrontation), peer control was low and emotional intensity, open boundaries, and confrontation were deemed highly appropriate. Yet net yield was high. Perhaps the presence of strong clear norms in the three areas compensated for the low acceptance of peer control; perhaps the behavior of the leader (in both Groups #6 and #3, the leaders were active and vigorous) made the difference.

The groups which produced the most *unchanged* members were Y (Here-and-now feelings, peer support) and Z (Cautionary peer support). These types shared high approval for peer control, medium levels of confrontation, and medium levels of open boundaries. The pattern is coherent: It is as if Types Y and Z were "driving with the brakes on"—operating in a way that muted confrontation and held the boundaries somewhat firm. The level of approval for emotional expression may vary considerably, but approval of open boundaries and confrontation is clearly moderate. In

Type Z the caution paid off—no Negative Changers or Casualties were found, and only one person dropped.

Dropping out can also be seen as a function of the normative pattern. As seen in Table 8–4, drops were most frequent in Type V (Nonerotic, disclosing confrontation) and U (Here-and-now confrontation). Other normative types with high approval for confrontation, such as S and T, either highly approved emotionality and open boundaries, or peer control. Type V approved open boundaries, but not emotionality or peer control. U was moderate to low on approval of all three. The implication is that high approval for confrontation is likely to induce dropping out unless supporting norms are present to legitimate peer control, intense emotional expression and open boundaries.

Long-post Outcomes. Table 8–5 shows norm types and long-range effects, as assessed six months after the groups terminated. The figures on Negative Changers are too small to make any generalization. The Unchanged category is figured on the same percentage base (those persons unchanged at Time 2) as the "late bloomer" category; in general, Types S, W, and possibly V were most likely to have "late blooming" rates higher than the average. These three norm types shared high approval of open boundaries and high to medium approval of confrontation. The norms regulating emotional intensity and peer control do not appear to be critical variables in "late blooming." In some way, normative support for open boundaries, and for confrontation, appears to make it more likely that per-

TABLE 8-5

Norm Type and Outcome Categories (Long-Range Effects)

Norm Type	Percent Not Returning[a]	Change Maintenance[b]	Late Bloomer[b]	Became or Stayed Negative[b]	Recovered[b]	Backslider[b]
S Intense, Disclosing Confrontation	30	7/7	3/7	No Negative Changers	No Negative Changers	0/7
T Distant, Guarded	38	1/3	1/6	1/1	0/1	2/3
U Here-and-now Confrontation	14	2/2	0/2	1/1	0/1	0/2
V Nonerotic, Disclosing Confrontation	28	7/9	3/10	1/2	1/2	2/9
W "Average Plus"	27	11/15	2/7	2/3	1/3	4/15
X Leader Support	17	1/2	0/2	3/4	1/4	1/2
Y Here-and-now Feelings, Peer Support	24	5/6	7/16	4/5	1/5	1/6
Z Cautionary Peer Support	08	3/4	1/7	No Negative Changers	No Negative Changers	1/4
Totals	26	37/48	14/57	12/16	4/16	11/48

[a]Figured on base of persons supplying Time 2 data.

[b]Figured on base of those persons for whom movement (up or down) was possible or on starting base of Unchanged, Negative, or Positive change.

sons originally untouched by the group experience will show net gains six months later. One might speculate that groups encouraging "late blooming" were simply more effective groups generally. This is true for Types S and W; Type V, however, was below average in positive effects, and Type Z, a high-yield climate, had unimpressive "late blooming" rates, so that the normative explanation seems more likely.

In sum, it appears that diverse normative types can lead to high yield at termination. Moderate to high approval for loose group boundaries, however, seems systematically important. Groups with tighter boundaries, but with moderate to high approval for emotional intensity, tended to achieve lower yields. Negative outcomes seemed more likely (in three out of four normative types) when approval for peer control was low. Groups which highly approved confrontation without regulating emotional intensity or boundaries or with little peer control tended to have more Dropouts.

Six months later, it appeared that maintenance of positive change was most likely for members from groups which originally approved intense emotional expression. "Late blooming," or movement from an initially unchanged to a positive-change position occurred in only a quarter of those for whom such movement was possible, but more often where the group climate favored loose boundaries and confrontation.

NORMATIVE TYPES AND CHANGE INDICES

Did differing normative patterns affect change indices differently? The answer is yes, for about a quarter of the thirty-three change indicators at both termination and follow-up. Since it is almost impossible, practically speaking, to disconfound the effects of different leader styles and temporal arrangements from the effects of norms, statistical manipulation was used to control for these effects, as well as for differences in initial scores on the change indices.[6] Table 8–6 summarizes short- and long-post relationships. When leader and temporal effects were controlled, only two variables, "experiencing" of values and leniency of self-concept, showed significant differences according to normative type at both short and long post. Except for these two variables, outcome differences which stemmed from unique normative climates did not endure at long post. Figure 8–1 shows graphically which types of normative climates were associated with gains or losses on the thirty-three outcome indicators at termination.[7]

Attitudes and Values. Looking at the three indices which showed the strongest statistical differences (see Figure 8–1), it appears that Type S (Intense, disclosing confrontation) moved its members away most from values emphasizing "experiencing" ("just letting things happen"). Types T (Distant, guarded) and V (Nonerotic, disclosing confrontation)—both low-warmth groups—moved away from change-oriented values. Type X (Leader support) increased change-orientation. Type Z (Cautionary peer support) increased its members' self-orientation, and Type S (Intense, disclosing confrontation) decreased it.

Figure 8–1 also shows that Type W ("Average plus") members experienced most change in seeing encounter groups as safe and beneficial, and moved somewhat away from self-orientation. Members of Type S (Intense, disclosing confrontation) also saw encounter groups as safer and more beneficial and genuine; their values moved away from an "experiencing" orientation, and they were less growth-oriented, and less self-oriented. Members of Type Z (Cautionary peer support) saw encounter groups as safer

TABLE 8-6

Outcome Measures Showing Significant Differences Across Normative Types

| | Significance Level | | | |
| | Short Post | | Long Post | |
Variable	Norms, with Leader Style Held Constant	Norms, with Leader Style Uncontrolled	Norms, with Leader Style Held Constant	Norms, with Leader Style Uncontrolled
Attitudes and Values				
5. Values: Experiencing Orientation	.11	.06	.04	.08
6. Values: Changing Orientation	.002	.31		
13. Life Space: Growth Orientation			.06	.45
15. Life Space: Self-Focus	.06	.31		
18. Life Space: Intimacy Emphasis			.08	.14
Interpersonal Behavior				
2. Self-View of Behavior: Feeling Sensitivity			.09	.42
11. Coping Style: Active			.06	.58
22. FIRO: Control Wanted from Others	.02	.03		
23. FIRO: Control Expressed by Self	.02	.10		
Self				
8. Self-Concept: Leniency	.03	.04	.07	.15
27. Self-Ideal Discrepancy: Interpersonal	.08	.18		
Conceptions of Others				
9. Concept of Others: Adequacy			.09	.39
33. Friendship: Relationship with Closest Friend			.006	.03
External Relations				
3. Interpersonal Environment: Peer Communication	.14	.09		
4. Interpersonal Environment: Freedom for Anger			.09	.16

and more beneficial, became less growth-oriented but more self-oriented, and emphasized interpersonal values.

Members of Type T (Distant, guarded) groups saw increased safety in encounter groups, became less change-oriented, and much less growth-oriented. Those in Type V (Nonerotic, disclosing confrontation) also saw more safety in encounter groups, increased their growth orientation considerably, and placed less value on interpersonal and intimate aspects of their life space.

Though members in the low-yield Type X (Leader support) group saw encounter groups as somewhat more safe, they saw them as phonier and less beneficial. They changed more than those in other types toward valuing change, but placed less emphasis on growth, and moved away from intimacy. Members in Type U (Here-and-now confrontation) groups saw encounter groups as more dangerous, less beneficial, and decidedly phony. They also increased their emphasis on growth, interpersonal and intimacy values. Members of Type Y groups (Here-and-now feelings, peer support) saw encounter groups as more phony, moved toward less growth orientation, and tended to move away from interpersonal orientation.

In the attitude-value domain, the most coherent impact of norms appears to have been on attitudes toward encounter groups, with more successful groups inducing positive changes and less successful ones moving in the opposite direction.

Interpersonal Behavior. Members of Type X (Leader support) increased significantly in acceptance of control from others, while those in Z (Cautionary peer support) decreased; in both cases the change seems congruent with the normative climate. The other difference was on expression of controlling behavior, which increased most in Y (Here-and-now feelings, peer support), and decreased somewhat in S (Intense, disclosing confrontation).

Looking at extreme scores in the higher-yield groups, it may be noted that for Type W ("Average plus") there were no differences from other groups; for Type S (Intense, disclosing confrontation) there is a decrease in the expression of controlling behavior, along with a decrease in the acceptance of affection from others. Type Z (Cautionary peer support) was associated with increased sensitivity to feelings, a reduction in use of defensive, avoidant coping styles, less acceptance of control, and more expression of affection. Unlike other groups, Type Z did not decrease in acceptance of affection. In moderate-yield groups, Type T (Distant, guarded) moved toward less acceptance of affection, which seems congruent with group norms. Type V showed no differences in scores from other groups. In lower-yield groups, Type X (Leader support) induced more interpersonal inadequacy than any other group, reduced sensitivity to feelings, increased defensive coping styles and increased acceptance of control—a glum picture. Type U (Here-and-now confrontation) increased interpersonal adequacy and sensitivity to feelings, along with adequate coping (and defensive coping), reduced the acceptance and expression of control, and

FIGURE 8-1

Norm Types and Specific Outcomes

Attitudes and Values

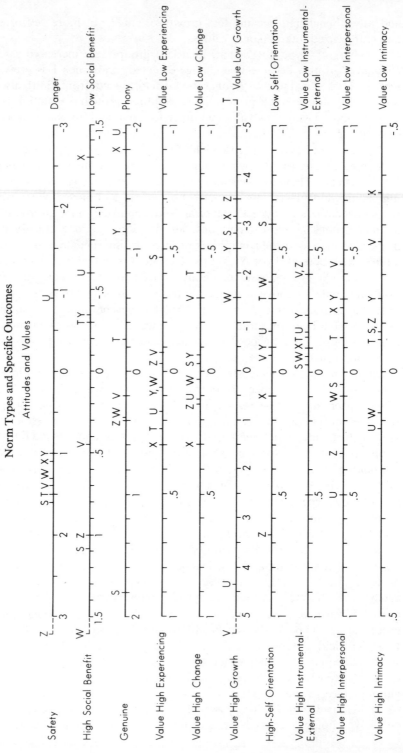

FIGURE 8–1 (*Cont'd*)

Norm Types and Specific Outcomes

Interpersonal Behavior

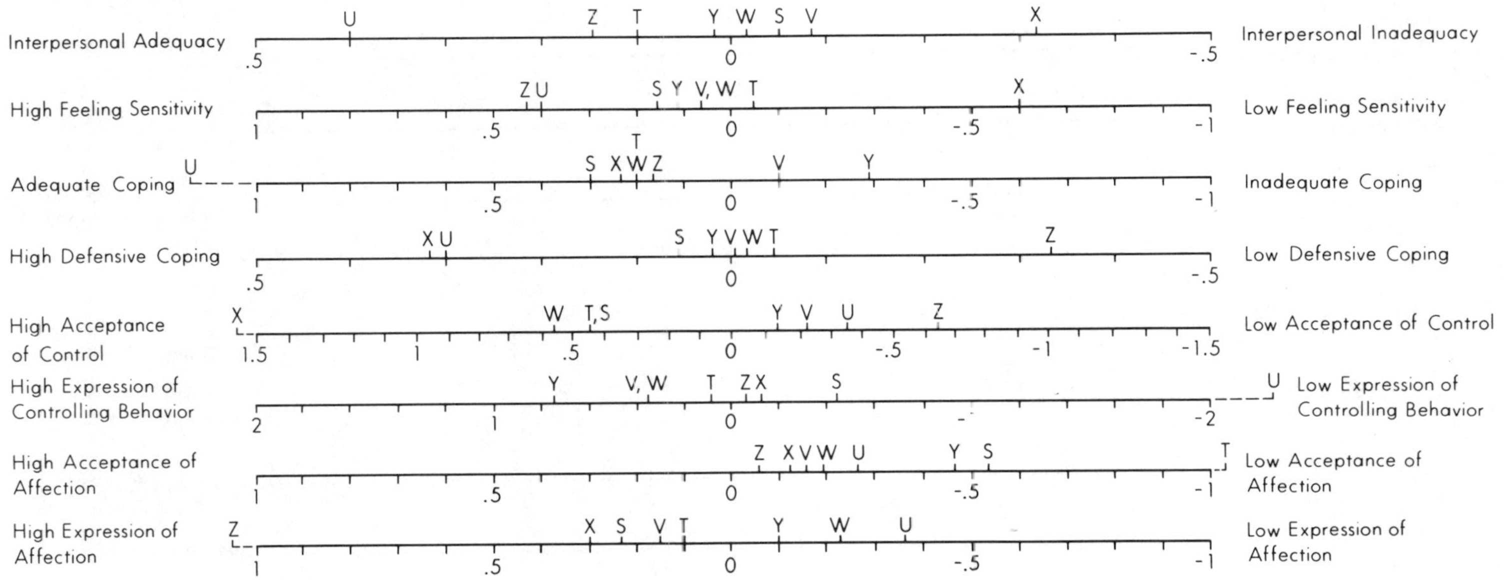

Interpersonal Adequacy
Interpersonal Inadequacy
High Feeling Sensitivity
Low Feeling Sensitivity
Adequate Coping
Inadequate Coping
High Defensive Coping
Low Defensive Coping
High Acceptance of Control
Low Acceptance of Control
High Expression of Controlling Behavior
Low Expression of Controlling Behavior
High Acceptance of Affection
Low Acceptance of Affection
High Expression of Affection
Low Expression of Affection

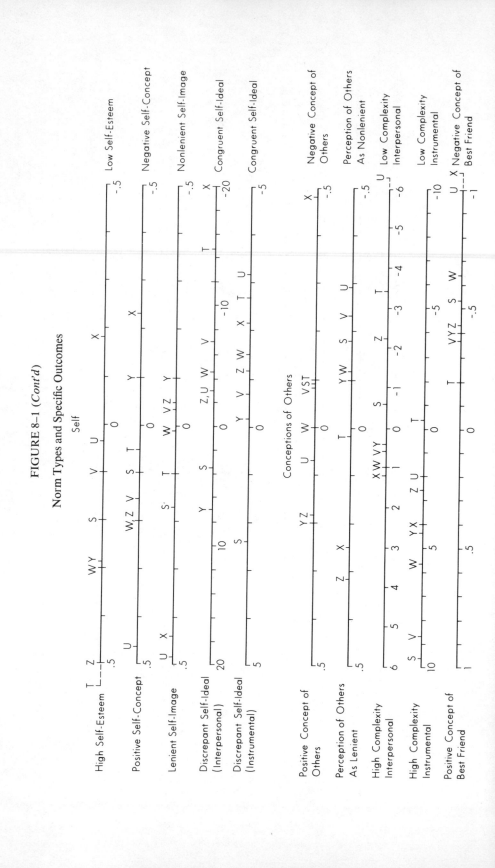

FIGURE 8–1 (*Cont'd*)

Norm Types and Specific Outcomes

FIGURE 8-1 (*Cont'd*)

Norm Types and Specific Outcomes

External Relationships

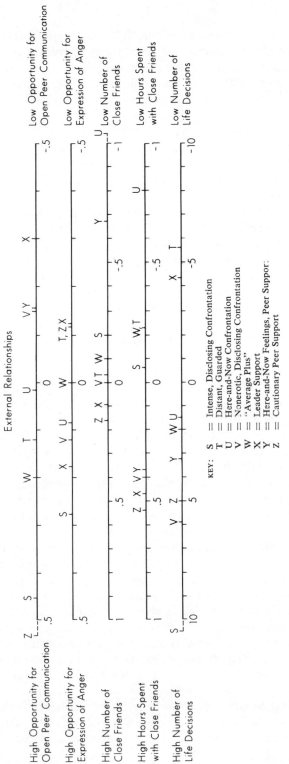

KEY:

S = Intense, Disclosing Confrontation
T = Distant, Guarded
U = Here-and-Now Confrontation
V = Nonerotic, Disclosing Confrontation
W = "Average Plus"
X = Leader Support
Y = Here-and-Now Feelings, Peer Support
Z = Cautionary Peer Support

reduced expression of affection; the picture is mixed. Type Y (Here-and-now feelings, peer support) reduced adequate coping, increased controlling behavior, and (possibly) the acceptance of affection from others. There are occasional examples of congruence between normative climate and changes in interpersonal behavior, but the picture is certainly not that of a one-to-one correspondence.

Self. Leniency of self-concept was one statistically significant change: The low-yield Types X and U increased this, while the other low-yield Type Y decreased it slightly. These differences do not seem especially congruent with normative content. The other change noted was in interpersonal self-ideal discrepancy. Again the pattern is puzzling: Types X (Leader support) and T (Distant, guarded) improved (decreased) self-ideal discrepancy, while Types S (Intense, disclosing confrontation) and Y (Here-and-now feelings, peer support) worsened it.

Among higher yield types, Type W ("Average plus") increased self-esteem and positive self-concept; Type S (Intense, disclosing confrontation) increased self-ideal discrepancy (interpersonal) and (marginally) self-esteem; and Type Z (Cautionary peer support) increased self-esteem and self-concept. The moderate-yield Type T (Distant, guarded) increased self-esteem substantially, along with improving interpersonal and instrumental self-ideal discrepancy; a surprise when one considers the normative content. Type V (Nonerotic, disclosing confrontation) may have improved self-ideal discrepancy (interpersonal) slightly. Among lower-yield types, Type X (Leader support) decreased in self-esteem and self-concept, increased in leniency of self-image, but improved self-ideal discrepancy in the interpersonal area. Type U (Here-and-now confrontation) increased positive self-concept and leniency and moved toward more congruence between self and ideal (instrumental). Type Y (Here-and-now feelings, peer support) increased in self-esteem, decreased positive self-concept and leniency of self-image, and increased discrepancy between interpersonal self and ideal. Once again, it is hard to see clear correspondence between normative content and changes in the self-system area.

Conceptions of Others. Among higher-yield types, members of Type W ("Average plus") increased slightly, unlike those in other groups, in complexity of their interpersonally oriented views of others (see Figure 8–1). Type W members also showed a trend toward increased complexity in the instrumental domain and became more negative toward their best friends. Type S (Intense, disclosing confrontation) members increased their instrumental complexity substantially and became more negative toward their best friends. Type Z (Cautionary peer support) members became more positive toward others and saw others as more lenient. Here the content of norms seems to have made a difference: The peer-oriented Type Z members were less willing to judge others negatively and saw them with somewhat less complexity. In the moderate-yield Type T (Distant, guarded), a decrease may be noted in perceptual complexity (interpersonal). Unlike those in all other types, Type T members did not change in the complexity of their instrumentally oriented views of others. Among lower-yield types, Type X (Leader support) members became considerably more negative about others, although they saw them as more lenient, and retained rather than reduced their level of complexity in viewing the interpersonal aspects of others. Type U (Here-and-now confrontation) members saw others as nonlenient and as less complex and also saw their best friends more negatively. Finally, Type Y (Here-and-now feelings, peer support) members became more positive toward others. All in all, it is difficult to connect normative content to changes in views of others.

External Relations. The significant difference (see Figure 8–1) was in peer communication: Group yield is consistently related to change on this outcome. The high-yield Types Z, S, and (possibly) W improved on it, and the low-yield Types X and Y worsened. Low-yield Type U showed no change. Considering high-yield types, Type W ("Average plus") showed no change except on (possibly) peer communication. Type S (Intense, disclosing confrontation) improved on peer communication, on opportunities for expression of anger, and on the number of life decisions made. Type Z (Cautionary peer support) members improved on peer communication, reduced their perceived opportunities for the expression of anger, and were less likely than those in any other group to reduce the number of close friendships and to spend more time with close friends. They also made a moderately high number of life decisions. The congruence between normative content and the changes in Type Z members is quite straightforward. Among moderate-yield types, members of Type T (Distant, guarded) saw little change in opportunity for expression of anger, and made fewer life decisions. Type V (Nonerotic, disclosing confrontation) members felt they had less opportunity for peer communication, spent more time with close friends, and made more life decisions.

Among lower-yield types, Type X (Leader support) members felt they had fewer peer communication opportunities, but more for expressing anger, did not change their number of close friendships, spent more hours with close friends, and made fewer life decisions. Members of Type U (Here-and-now confrontation) groups decreased in number of close friends and time spent with them. Members of Type Y (Here-and-now feelings, peer support) groups reported reductions in peer communication opportunities and chances to express anger, and fewer close friends but more hours spent with them. The picture of lower-yield types tends to be one of increased restriction in the interpersonal environment. In general, one gets the feeling that yield differences and, in Type Z, normative content, relate reasonably well to change indicators in the external relations area.

On balance, the connections between normative type and change indices do not come across as substantial. Normative climates which encourage higher yield tend to increase favorable attitudes toward encounter groups, enhance self-picture, and improve opportunities for interpersonal relations outside the groups, but these things do not seem to be a direct function of the normative *content,* as such.

The Formation of Norms

The preceding discussion indicates that norms are not a minor part of a group's life and are related to general outcome, though rarely to specific outcomes. In general, the final state of the group's norms predicts about as much variance in outcome as does the particular type of leader behavior noted in the group. Given this linkage between normative climate and the yield of groups, the question of how such norms become developed is of considerable interest. What in fact determines the final normative state of affairs in an encounter group? Is it in some way a function of the leader's behavior or the expectations members bring to the group? [8]

LEADER STYLE AND GROUP NORMS

Perhaps there are some meaningful linkages between a leader's general style and the sort of norms that develop in his groups. The intercorrelations between the four basic leader style dimensions, the six norm dimensions,[9] and ranked group outcomes, are presented in Table 9–1, p. 311.

Groups with open boundaries are most closely associated with the leader behavior dimension which involves strong attribution or meaning and the provision of coherence in understanding individual feelings and behavior in the group. Leaders who provide such cognitive support turn out to have groups in which the boundaries are looser.

Secondly, it appears that groups with norms favoring intense emotional expression have leaders who express a good deal of caring. The normative dimension of intense emotional expression is heavily loaded with positive affective behaviors such as touching, commenting on likability, kissing, expressing caring, and the like; it may be that the caring leader models such behavior inducing the sense that it is appropriate. The leader's emphasis on meaning-attribution at the individual level also seems associated with this norm.

Groups in which the leader provides a great deal of emotional stimulation are not associated with approval of counter-dependence. This relationship meets expectations for the charismatic leader, who by magical or other means tends to discourage the expression of counterdependence, and evokes admiration and respect. The issue is not whether the charismatic leader invites dependence, a normative quality unrelated to leader stimulation, but that counterdependence—challenges directed toward the leader —is perhaps seen as inappropriate when forceful leader inputs are constantly supplied.

Finally, there is a tendency for dependence behaviors to be approved when the leader's style is that of caring, as if warmth and support tend to reinforce a paternalistic view of the leader's role. The norm of intense emotional expression is also positively related to the dependence norm; suggesting that intense expressions of feeling are also seen as more appropriate in groups where the leader stands as a protective, benevolent figure.

These findings, however, do not indicate direction. They do not clarify whether the leader's attribution of meaning tends to induce approval of open boundaries, or whether seeing open boundaries as appropriate somehow encourages the leader to provide cognitive inputs. Similarly, they do not reveal whether high emotional stimulation by the leader dampens counterdependent behavior and causes negative valuing of it by group members, or (to be extreme) whether the absence øf approval for counterdependent behavior somehow induces high emotional input from the leader.

Given such ambiguity, it may be useful to examine the preliminary expectations of the leader, the sort of student who came to the groups, and more direct evidence on the source of the norms which finally emerged in the groups.

LEADER EXPECTATION, SUBCULTURAL EXPECTATION, AND GROUP NORMS

Prior to the group, each leader was asked to indicate how appropriate or inappropriate the forty-eight behaviors on the norms instrument would have been for groups he ran in the past. Similar data were not collected from group members, but were collected from controls, who constituted a reasonably good sample for assessing the general subcultural (Stanford) expectations for encounter group norms which group members might be expected to bring to sessions with them.

The question of interest is: Of the group norms which actually emerged late in the life of each group, how many were prefigured in the leader's expectations, and how many in the members' expectations (assuming that these were largely similar to those of their control group compatriots)?

Tables 8–7 and 8–8 present the findings. When specific norms were examined, the leaders' expectations were in fact realized for a third of the forty-eight norms, across fifteen groups. The parallel figure for general subcultural expectations is less. There is a source of considerable error, however, in leader's expectations as to typical group norms: Leaders tended to say that almost all behaviors were typically approved or disapproved in their usual groups. They used the "uncertain" category very rarely (7 percent of the time). In contrast, the control group members, in the aggregate, invoked the "uncertain" category 57 percent of the time.[10] The leaders' expectational certainty had in general resulted in a higher rate of active disconfirmation (11 percent of the leaders' expectations

295

TABLE 8-7

Leader Expectations and Final Group Norms
(Overall Percentages for Fifteen Groups)

Leader Expectations	Final Norms			
	Inappropriate	Unregulated	Appropriate	Totals
Inappropriate	9.9	22.2	6.8	38.7
Uncertain	0.7	5.9	0.8	7.3
Appropriate	3.9	25.6	24.2	54.0
Totals	14.5	53.7	31.8	

NOTE: Expected-to-final correspondence: 34.1%, plus 5.9% of "uncertain" expectations which emerge as uncertain. 10.7% disconfirmations.

TABLE 8-8

General Subcultural Expectations (Control Group)
and Final Group Norms (Overall Percentages for Seventeen Groups)

General Subcultural Expectations	Final Norms			
	Inappropriate	Unregulated	Appropriate	Totals
Inappropriate	9.5	8.5	0.5	18.5
Uncertain	6.1	37.6	13.0	56.7
Appropriate	0.2	7.2	17.5	24.9
Totals	15.8	53.3	31.0	

NOTE: Expected-to-final correspondence: 27.0%, plus 37.6% of "uncertain" expectations which proved "uncertain" in the final norms. 0.7% disconfirmations.

were reversed from inappropriate to appropriate or from appropriate to inappropriate, while only .7 percent of the control groups' expectations were thus disconfirmed).

So whose expectations were more in accord with the final normative state? It appears to be a trade-off. The leaders had more specifically defined expectations (expected that norms would in fact emerge for nearly all of the norm items). As a result, they achieved more "hits" and made more decisive errors. They underestimated considerably the actual degree of norm uncertainty (lack of normative regulation) that turned out to exist in these groups.

The general subcultural expectations which control group members had were more conservative: only about half of the forty-eight items were expected to emerge as actual norms; thus the number of "hits" and the number of disconfirmations were both lower. But the general subcultural expectations correctly "predicted" that a substantial amount of behavior would remain unregulated in the groups.

EXPECTATION CONFIRMATION AND GROUP YIELD

Was the fulfillment or disconfirmation of leaders' norm expectations related to group yield? Of seven high-confirmation leaders (above the mean of 34.1 percent), five had higher-yield groups (outcome ranks of 3, 1, 5, 4, 7, 8, 14); of eight low-confirmation leaders (outcome ranks of 12, 9, 16, 17, 13, 15, 6, 11), only two had higher-yield groups. Cut the other way, the average high-yield leader had 44 percent of his expectations confirmed; moderate-high, 34 percent; moderate-low, 29 percent; and for low-yield, 29 percent (rho = .67). The average high-confirmation group had a yield rank of 6.0; low-confirmation groups averaged out at 12.4—a substantial difference.

Did high-yield leaders have more realistic expectations, or were high-yield leaders more able to induce the norms they had been successful in inducing in prior groups? Did low-yield group leaders have unrealistically high expectations about the normative clarity of their past groups, which they projected on to the present group? Or did their expectations in fact reflect the normative state of affairs in their previous groups which for some reason they were unable to replicate in the study groups? Let us see.

First, how did normative expectations of the control group relate to norms of groups of different yield levels? Of ten groups above the mean confirmation of subcultural expectations, seven were higher yield groups. Of the seven low-confirmation groups, two were higher yield groups. Only one group (#10) was seriously deviant (high confirmation, low yield). Cut the other way, high-yield groups averaged 31 percent confirmation of subcultural expectations, while the other groups ranged from 24 to 27 percent (rho = .47). The spread is narrower than for leaders, whose expectations tended, on the average, to be more frequently confirmed than were the control group's. But, on the face of it, it is *not* the case that high-yield group leaders were solely effective in imposing their desired set of norms on the group. Rather, they were simultaneously able to create conditions where their own norm expectations *and* general cultural expectations were realized. Low-yield groups proved less effective in doing both.

One striking thing found about cultural expectations is that in only four of the seventeen groups (averaging 1 percent of the items) were *any* general cultural expectations for group norms actively disconfirmed. The general expectations which group members bring, in other words, form a powerful set of constraints which are rather unlikely to be reversed in the actual normative state of affairs.[11] The leaders' expectations, on the other hand, were reversed about 11 percent of the time, suggesting that leader influence on group norms is largely restricted to strengthening existing expectations, or converting uncertain expectations into decisive norms.

When particular types of norms were examined, we found that leaders most frequently were accurate in expecting norms regulating the amount of emotional expression and norms about confrontation—for both types of

297

norms between 40 to 50 percent of leader expectations were confirmed. In contrast, norms about the content boundaries and degree of peer control were confirmed only about 25 percent of the time.

Summary

Groups with more norms and those approving looser group boundaries, and to some extent peer control, had higher yield. Normative patterns differently influenced about one quarter of the thirty-three change indices. With a few exceptions, there did not seem to be clear linkages between the content of group norms and the change indices. The normative climates present in higher yield groups tended to improve attitudes toward encounter groups, self-image and interpersonal relationships with persons outside the groups, but it appeared that (with the exception of the boundaries norm) there could be different normative paths to high yield.

Some meaningful associations were noted between leader style and the emergent group norms: norms favoring open boundaries were more often found for leaders who provided a clear conceptual framework for individual change; caring leaders seemed to have groups with more intense emotional expression; counterdependent norms were less likely for leaders who provided caring.

Groups in which *both* leaders' expectations and general subcultural norm expectations were met had higher yields, though confirmation of leaders' expectations was more closely related to group yield. Almost no subcultural norm expectations were reversed by the actual norms which emerged.

NOTES

1. One possible additional feature of group norms assumes particular salience in the encounter group setting. Though data are lacking, there are good theoretical reasons to believe that norms, employed for a significant period of time, or under conditions of high potency or saliency, tend to become internalized as attitudes of individual members. For example, active experience with a norm indicating that it is a good idea to analyze here-and-now events in the encounter group may tend to encourage allegiance to such behavior in other settings (that is, a social system property sometimes becomes internalized as a person property). Much of the success of families' efforts to socialize their children can perhaps be explained in this way, but it is not known whether experience with norms in temporary systems (such as encounter groups) does in fact induce attitude change (see Miles, 1964).

2. An initial effort at this proved unsatisfactory. An inverse correlation analysis (Q analysis) was performed, using the seventeen groups as variables and correlating

them with each other, considering that each group contained five cases (the first five factors). This strategy did not produce a coherently clustered set of groups. The factor scores, incorporating eight to twelve different items and based on continuous scores which were often sums of "inappropriate" and "appropriate" responses, were far removed from the actual normative situation in the groups.

3. Inverse correlation analysis (Q analysis) was performed on the data in Table 8–2. In order to differentiate groups maximally, universal norms, such as "asked for reactions or feedback," and norms which were regulated by almost no groups, such as "said he thought the leader should have the biggest responsibility for planning and guiding group activities," were eliminated. The net cluster scores shown in Table 8–2 were inversely correlated, and the results subjected to a McQuitty linkage analysis.

A hierarchial cluster analysis was also performed (HICLUS—a Hierarchical Cluster Analysis Program. S. C. Johnson, Version 1S, November, 1968. FORTRAN IV Level H. Stanford Computing Center. See also Johnson, 1967). This method essentially works from a matrix of the distances between all seventeen groups, using the six scores, and clusters them according to their relative degree of connectedness. In the HICLUS program, the six dimensions were weighted as follows: I, 11.5; II, 8.5; III, 5.3; IV, 315; V, 2.0; and VI, 4.0. These were based on the eigenvalues of the original factor analysis, adjusted slightly for added and omitted items. The final clustering thus gave most weight to the first three clusters, with some contribution from cluster VI.

The dependence dimension (5) and the counterdependence dimension (4) each contributed less variance than did the peer control dimension. In addition, the empirical range of norms in force on these dimensions was so narrow that they contributed little or nothing to understanding the normative types; they are thus omitted in Table 8–3. The high-scoring counterdependence groups were #3, #5; low, #4. The high-scoring dependence group #16, low, #15. (See Table 8–2.)

4. Normative *approval* of self-disclosure, and self-rated *amount* of self-disclosure go together (r = .56).

5. Approval of hostile behavior tends to go with actual angry behavior, as rated by observers (r = .28). Of the eight groups having more angry (as vs. harmonious) climates, only two were below the median score on approval of hostile confrontation. As discussed in Chapter 9, an angry climate late in the group life was negatively correlated with group yield.

6. Multivariate analysis of covariance, MESA 98.

7. Only short-post effects of normative climates are shown, since such effects are most likely to be visible immediately; and the working N is larger.

8. An additional possibility is that norms form in encounter groups through the administration of rewards and punishments. Leader style and leader/member expectations, in this view, may say less about norms than does sanctioning behavior.

9. Table 9–1, page 311, also illuminates relationships among norm dimensions. It is useful, in passing, to note that the strongest relationship (negative) is between the confrontation norm and that for peer control, suggesting that the primary purpose of the "anticontrol, antiwithdrawal" norm is to defend members against hostile confrontation and judgmental demands. This pattern had already been noted in Types Y and Z.

10. If between 60 and 75 percent of control subjects expected the behavior to be inappropriate or appropriate, scores of −1 and +1 were given, respectively; if between 75 and 100 percent of control subjects expected the behavior to be inappropriate or appropriate, scores of −2 or +2 were given. All other proportions received 0 ("uncertain"). Given the size of the control group (sixty-nine) it seemed less appropriate to demand the sixty-seven percent concurrence, as with the actual encounter group members. Using the sixty-seven percent cutoff would have enlarged the "uncertain" category for control group expectations substantially; as it was, the amount of uncertainty in control group expectations was very close to the net amount of uncertainty in final normative conditions. Leaders were scored −2 for "definitely inappropriate," −1 for "somewhat inappropriate," 0 for "uncertain," and +1 and +2 for corresponding degrees of appropriateness.

11. Leader #6, a highly charismatic person, was able to reverse the expectations

that hitting other members and making threatening remarks were inappropriate. In Synanon (Group #13), the expectation that writing another member off was inappropriate was reversed. Groups #10 and #16 reversed the expectation that social and political questions should be discussed in encounter groups.

CHAPTER 9

Other Group Characteristics Affecting Outcomes

Powerful effects upon outcome have been attributed in research literature and practitioner lore to several overriding features of small groups beyond their leadership or normative characteristics. In many experimental studies cohesiveness has been shown to strengthen group effects on the person. Similarly, the emotional tone or climate of the group has been associated with productivity. Schutz (1958) has reported that highly compatible task groups were more productive, whereas others (Harrison and Lubin, 1965) studying training groups have suggested that moderate compatibility yielded higher net learning than extremely high or low compatibility.

Practitioners often stress the salience of what is discussed—some attest that what makes the difference is keeping to what is happening currently within the group, while others stress the essentiality of personal, historical material. In recent years, certain schools of group therapy and encounter have placed much emphasis on the temporal arrangements that characterize the group—that is whether the experience is massed into a concentrated block of time or spaced over several sessions. Finally, debate has remained through countless professional meetings over whether focusing on individual, interpersonal, or total group issues renders greater success.

Since the seventeen groups varied in respect to each of these conditions, they offered the opportunity for comparative analysis of their effects on what participants carried away from the experience. Since particular group conditions have been differently associated with outcome depending upon the age of the group (Miles, 1965), in the present study cohesiveness and group climate were measured at early and late meetings of the groups.[1]

301

COHESION

Cohesion has been defined in small group literature as an aggregate score of individual attraction measures: Groups in which many members feel strongly attracted to the group may be expected to stay together, resist disruption, and exert stronger effects on their members. Member attraction to the study groups was measured at an early and late meeting through a seven-point scale ("Feelings about the Group," see Appendix II), which included ratings of liking/disliking for the group, how likely the group was to enable the attainment of personal goals, attraction to other participants, and how included the participant felt in the activities of the group.

The cohesiveness questionnaire was first administered between the ninth and fifteenth meeting hours of the groups. On a possible score range of 7–45, the seventeen groups achieved an average score of 31.5 (s.d. = 3.1).

FIGURE 9–1

Group Cohesiveness (Late) vs. Ranking of Group Yield (Time 2)

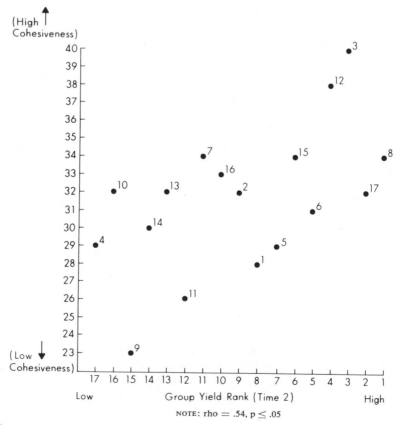

NOTE: rho = .54, p ≤ .05

A rank-order correlation between early cohesiveness and outcome effects as measured by group yield suggested a modest positive relationship (rho = .35, p = .11). The same questionnaire was again administered between the twenty-first and twenty-seventh hours and yielded an average score of 31.6 (s.d. = 4.1). At this administration, as seen in Figure 9–1, a stronger relationship obtained between cohesiveness and group yield (rho = .54, p ≤ .05) chiefly through the effects of high-yield Groups #3 and #12 and low-yield Groups #9 and #11. For groups with middle-range cohesiveness scores, the association was considerably weaker.

CLIMATE

Intensity. At the close of each group session, observers filled out twelve semantic differential scales asking for judgments of the overall group climate on such dimensions as tense/relaxed, fast/slow, and angry/harmonious.[2] A factor analysis of these scores produced two general factors, one dealing with the relative potency or strength of the group's climate (involvement intensity) and the second dealing with the expression of anger (harmony/anger). Involvement intensity was defined as the sum of the three climate items loading highest on the first factor (involved/uninvolved, close/distant, and strong/weak).

The range of possible scores on involvement intensity was 3–21: the mean for early sessions was 40.4 (s.d. = 10.6). No relationship was obtained between intensity and group yield (rho = .28, n.s.). The rank-order correlation, however, during the late sessions was .56, a clear positive relationship (see Figure 9–2). The positive relationship between involvement intensity and outcome is primarily due to the low involvement intensity scores of the four lowest yield groups (#4, #10, #9, and #14). Group #13 was an exception; though its involvement intensity scores were moderately high, its yield level was in the bottom third of the groups. Thus, climate intensity was associated with outcome when measured late in the group life, but not when measured early.

Why should this be? Perhaps the vital issue is one of timing. Too much intensity early in the group may facilitate churning and excitement, but not the necessary trust and stable relationships necessary to produce a corrective emotional experience. Groups which start with all rockets blazing may never establish a foundation of mutuality and safety. Once a solid, coherent group is formed, however, emotional intensity seems necessary for change; otherwise members do not risk, do not make the affectual investment so vital for shifts in behavior and self-conceptualization. Late cohesiveness and late emotional intensity seem an ideal brew for facilitation of personal learning.

Yet early cohesiveness hardly goes with outcome. Early cohesiveness may be based on different factors than late cohesiveness. Members may be attracted to their group for such reasons as coziness, comfort, a lack of conflict, a gratification of dependency needs. Group #10 (Esalen Eclectic)

FIGURE 9–2

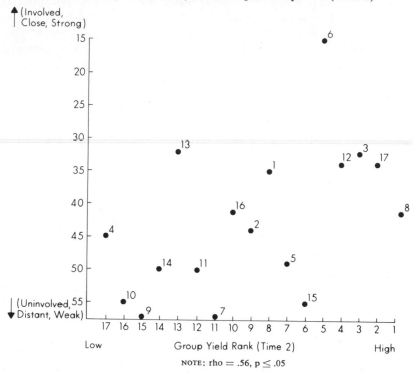

Climate: Involvement Intensity vs. Ranking of Group Yield (Time 2)

NOTE: rho = .56, p ≤ .05

is a case in point. The leader heavily structured the group. Members were spared both the anxiety stemming from the initial situational ambiguity and the frustration of facing a leader who would not (in the traditional sense) lead. Group #10 had a very high early cohesiveness score which later in the life of the group declined considerably. It may be that group members, late in the group, are attracted to their group if they are valued by the other members and if they sense that the group is facilitating their locomotion towards the fulfillment of personal goals.[3]

Climate: Harmony. Are angry or harmonious groups more likely to produce member learning? High levels of anger might be an indication of considerable group authenticity, hence more learning could occur. On the other hand, anger could be an indication of unresolved power struggles and unstable group structure and could serve to impede learning. Similarly, high levels of harmony could be seen either to facilitate or obstruct growth. Observer ratings for the adjective pair "angry/harmonious" were used as the index of harmony. The range of this score was 1–7 and the obtained mean across all groups was 4.0 (s.d. =0.9) for the early sessions and 4.1 (s.d. =0.87) for the late session.

The rank-order correlation between harmony level and group yield early in the group was .02 (n.s.), late .52, significant beyond $p \leq .05$ (see Figure 9–3). Anger experienced in the latter part of the sessions as a strong feature of the climate was negatively associated and harmony positively associated with positive outcome. The relationship obtains, however, only for extreme groups. Group #6 (and Group #15) remain as high-anger deviants from the general relationship, but it is worth note that the level of harmony in Group #6 increased a good deal (from 2.0 early to 3.1 late). On the other side, Groups #16, #7, #11 (and especially #4) were deviants from the obtained relationship: they were rather harmonious, but experienced moderate to low amounts of gain. On balance, the evidence leans toward the interpretation that a reasonable degree of harmony makes for more learning and fewer negative outcomes.

INTERPERSONAL COMPATIBILITY [4]

The "interchange" compatibility index developed by Schutz (1958) was used to assess interpersonal compatibility. On this index, the lower the

FIGURE 9–3

Climate: Harmony (Late) vs. Ranking of Group Yield (Time 2)

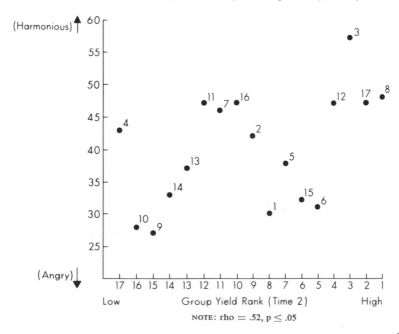

NOTE: rho = .52, p ≤ .05

score, the greater the similarity across all pairs of group members on the amount of interaction they prefer in the "control" and "inclusion" areas of interpersonal relations. The possible score range was 0–24, the mean score for all groups, 9.1 (s.d. = 1.6). No substantial relationship obtained between compatibility and group yield (rho = .28, n.s.). Furthermore, the relationship is not a simple curvilinear one as suggested by the work of Harrison and Lubin. Groups with moderate levels of compatibility, at least within the range found (slightly above the theoretical midpoint of the scale), were *not* more likely to be higher yield groups.

CONTENT EMPHASIS

There is a good deal of emphasis in the encounter group movement on the analysis of here-and-now experiences, those transactions occurring within the sight and hearing of the persons assembled. This stands in contrast to the assumption in many therapy groups, which often encourage the introduction of current and historical material about relationships outside the group, dreams, and the like. The study leaders varied considerably in their preference for inside or outside material, which might be expected considering their differences in training and working assumptions.

To measure content emphasis, observers were asked at the close of each meeting to indicate the percentage of time the group had spent in that meeting in discussing outside topics, defined as "material not common to the current here-and-now or the shared history of the group as a group." Examples of outside content were suggested including campus events, current personal experiences, politics, or interaction among members on the outside.

On the average, the seventeen groups spent 43 percent of the time discussing outside topics (s.d. = 17.7), a surprisingly high figure for a sample of groups containing several leaders supposedly oriented toward a here-and-now emphasis. No relationship obtained between emphasis on outside material and outcome (rho = .18). Nor was the amount of emphasis on here-and-now material related to encounter group labels. For example, Group #11, a Rogerian Marathon, which might be presumed to focus on here-and-now material, spent 70 percent of its time on outside topics. Even the two NTL T-groups, whose leaders represented the training tradition with perhaps the strongest commitment to here-and-now focus, spent 36 percent and 37 percent of their time on outside material. Heavy here-and-now emphases ranging from 70 to 80 percent appeared in Group #10 (Esalen Eclectic), Group #6 (Psychodrama), Group #16 (Tape Group), and Group #3 (Gestalt). Emphasis on outside material occurred ranging from 60 to almost 80 percent in Group #7 (Psychoanalytic), Group #11 (Rogerian Marathon), Group #8 (Transactional Analysis), and Group #12 (Eclectic Marathon).

Since outside material might include either personally oriented and clinical material or flightful, abstract material, outside content was further analyzed to ascertain the proportion devoted to personal material. After each meeting, observers were asked to divide the total time spent on outside topics among several categories, including "personal history (years ago)," "personal (current)," "race," "larger social issues (included those pertaining to the Stanford Campus)," and "abstract" (philosophy, general discussion on trust). To arrive at a general measure, the percentage estimates for current and historical personal material were multiplied by the total percentage of time spent in discussing outside material. This analysis indicated the groups as a whole averaged 21 percent of time spent on personal outside topics (s.d. = 10.8). As portrayed in Figure 9–4, no relationship obtained between content emphasis and group yield. Figure 9–4 offers support for the view that psychiatrists may have focused more on outside personal material: this is the case for four of the five leaders who were psychiatrists. The five leaders who were clinical psychologists are not

FIGURE 9–4

Content Emphasis (Personal, Outside) vs. Ranking of Group Yield (Time 2)

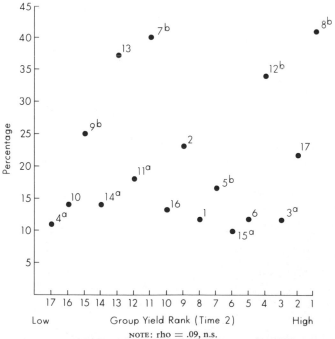

NOTE: rho = .09, n.s.
[a] Leader is a clinical psychologist who professionally is a psychotherapist.
[b] Leader is a psychiatrist.

FIGURE 9–5

Content Emphasis (Inside, Personal) vs. Group Yield Rank (Time 2)

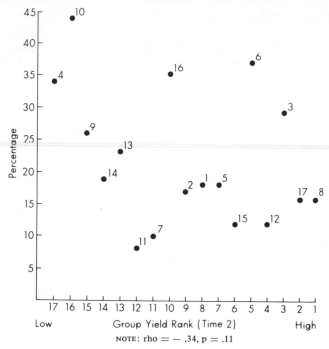

NOTE: rho = − .34, p = .11

distinguished from the other seven groups. Group #13 (Synanon) had a strong outside personal emphasis, like that of the four psychiatrists.

A more precise analysis of inside content in which only personal here-and-now content was considered indicated that the seventeen groups averaged 22 percent of their time on personal inside topics (s.d. = 13.3). As seen in Figure 9–5, personal inside material achieved a modest negative relationship with group yield (rho = − .34; p = .11). The relationship is mainly accounted for by low-yield Groups #4 and #10, which emphasized inside personal material, and high-yield Groups #8, #17, #12, and #15, which did the converse.

PERSONAL FOCUS

Encounter groups differ considerably in the degree to which they focus on one person at a time. Some leaders in effect do individual therapy in the group, working with one member, while the rest form an audience. Others encourage other forms of interaction, such as going around the group, working in smaller groups, or engaging in general discussion.

Observers were asked to allot the group's work time to one of six work patterns: monologue (one person holding forth), dialogue (two persons relating, talking to each other), focusing on one member (someone in group becomes main topic of discussion), going around the group (turn-taking, one after another, shifting of focus systematically), subgroups (groups actually talking in two or more subgroups), and general discussion (no discernible pattern). The average time spent focusing on one member was 31.3 percent (s.d. = 16.1). The relationship between individual focus and group yield rank was insignificant (rho = −.17); one more indication that personal focus, *as such* does not necessarily lead to learning.[5] Actually, only two groups spent substantial amounts of time focusing on one person. Group #13 (Synanon) spent 71 percent of its time "putting the game" on an individual, and Group #6 (Psychodrama) focused on individuals 61 percent of the time. All other groups spent 36 percent or less time, down to the 7 percent spent by Group #17 (Tape).

MASSED VS. SPACED TIME USE

Massed group sessions, taking place over a weekend, or a one or two week continuous period, are said by many encounter leaders to promote the breakdown of defenses, the creation of a more intense affective climate, and the reduction of distractions from outside the group experience. On the other hand, it has been frequently claimed that massed experiences without the opportunity to test and extend learnings outside the group may result in short-run gains but less long-run, durable change.

The seventeen groups varied considerably in their deployment of time over the life of the project. For example, Group #1 met ten times over eight weeks. At the other extreme, Group #12 had a twenty-hour weekend meeting, sandwiched between two shorter meetings shortly before and after the marathon.

To develop a usable measure of temporal arrangement, the distribution of the sessions in each group was used to compute the proportion of total group time occupied by the longest single, uninterrupted session.[6] The average total time spent in the longest single session was thirty-seven percent (s.d. = 24.6). Figure 9–6 indicates a clear positive relationship of time use to group yield. Of the six groups which spent 50 percent or more of their time in a single session, four were higher-yield groups. Only Groups #4 and #11 deviated from the general pattern. And, of the six top-ranking groups in terms of yield rank, all used 40 percent or more massed time. For the limited time range examined in this study, massed sessions were, relatively speaking, more efficacious.

Causes and Effects

In examining several group conditions which have been claimed to be associated with different levels of group yield, the variables of group cohesiveness, involvement intensity, harmony, as well as the degree to which a

FIGURE 9–6

Massed vs. Spaced Time Use vs. Group Yield Rank (Time 2)

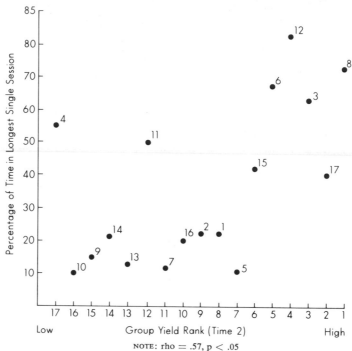

NOTE: rho = .57, p < .05

marathonlike approach was used were all significantly predictive of gains at reasonably good levels (correlations of .5).

Individual focus, interpersonal compatibility, the total amount of time spent in discussion of personal (over interpersonal, group, or other matters) did not turn out to be meaningfully related to outcome. The "here-and-now" shibboleth voiced by many encounter group leaders, which implies that focusing on internal-to-the-group material, current feelings, and cognitions is the sole route to gain in the intensive group experience was found to give way to the opposite condition: material from outside the group was more associated with gains.

Findings have been presented in Chapters 7, 8, and 9 that suggest a positive relationship between outcome and certain characteristics of the group —how the leader behaves, what behaviors are regulated in the group through norms, the level of group cohesiveness, type of emotional climate, and temporal arrangements. Table 9–1 shows the intercorrelations among those group conditions found to be significantly related to outcome; the four basic leadership dimensions, and the four norm dimensions. Substantial associations exist between group cohesiveness, climate, temporal arrangements, certain normative dimensions, and leader behavior. The

310

correlations, however, underestimate the associations. For example, considering norm types and leader types (rather than single dimensions), the most successful leader type (B), and the most successful norm type (W) are identical. On the other hand, as suggested in Chapter 8, norms are certainly not totally the product of leader behavior.

Given that members were randomly assigned to groups, it seems reasonable that the first order of causality would be leader behavior. As we know from the examination of leader behavior and norms, however, no direct evidence was available which would suggest that there was an identity between norm and leader behavior. An analysis of causality is further complicated by the particular distributions of the groups along the dimensions of cohesiveness, climate/intensity, climate/harmony, and massed/spaced time use.

To illustrate with the question of the contribution of massed sessions to outcome: obviously the simple linear correlation (.57) does not isolate the singular effect of this variable uncontaminated by the effects of norms on

TABLE 9-1

Intercorrelations of Group Conditions, Norm Dimensions, and Leader Dimensions

	B	C	D	E	F	G	H	I	J	K	L	M
A Group Yield Rank (Time 2)[a]	.54	.56	.52	.57	.12	.34	−.09	.19	.16	.46	.61	.05
B Group Cohesiveness (Late)		.33	.58	.43	.21	.57	.08	.14	.26	.25	.38	.24
C Climate: Involvement-Intensity (Late)			.20	.51	.48	.47	.20	−.25	.70	.57	.45	.22
D Climate: Harmony (Late)				.47	−.05	.39	−.28	.07	−.02	.42	.12	−.04
E Massed Time Use					.30	.37	−.12	−.02	.40	.53	.45	.02
F Norm: Intense Feeling Expression						.24	.23	−.10	.35	.45	.40	.39
G Norm: Open Boundaries							.29	−.27	.25	.28	.53	−.06
H Norm: Hostile, Judging Confrontation								−.71	.30	−.22	.17	−.11
I Norm: Peer Control									−.33	−.01	−.01	.25
J Leader: Emotional Stimulation										.30	.43	.39
K Leader: Caring											.16	.58
L Leader: Attribution of Meaning												.00
M Leader: Executive Function												

[a]The correlations in this row are rank-order correlations.

NOTE: An obtained r of .45 is significant at the .05 level.

leadership style. Unfortunately, the number of groups involved makes the use of appropriate statistics (partial correlations) suspect, so it is difficult to assess statistically the independent contribution of each of these group conditions as they affect outcome.[7] A simple review of the findings on leader style and group conditions, however, will illustrate the point. Figure 9–6 which shows the groups that utilized massed sessions (50 percent or more of their time in one continuous session) indicates that only leaders drawn from the three relatively more effective leadership styles (Type A, Energizers; Type B, Providers; and Type C, Social Engineers) used massed time. Thus the analysis cannot compare highly unsuccessful and highly successful groups but must be limited to the relatively successful ones. Looking first at the three Type B leaders (Groups #8, #12, and #1) the two most successful Type B leaders used massed meetings, contrasted to the least successful Type B leader who did not. Of the four Type A leaders, the two most successful and the one least successful used massed time, while the moderately successful did not; of the three Type C leaders, the least successful used massed learning, the two most successful did not. Although it is impossible to disentangle the relative contribution of leader style and contrast it to the temporal format a leader uses, clearly, the utilization of massed temporal format cannot, in and of itself, be said to lead to productive outcomes; there is no evidence that leaders, no matter what their style, who use massed learning would be more successful than ones who did not.

A similar analysis was conducted for cohesiveness. Controlling for leader style—that is, comparing groups within a similar leader style which were above or below the mean on cohesiveness—the analysis revealed that for the Type A leaders, the two highest on cohesiveness were first and third most successful of the A leaders; the two groups low on cohesiveness were ranked two and four in success among the A leaders (the ranks are relative to each leader style). For the B leaders, the two most successful were high on cohesiveness, the lowest ranking group was low on cohesiveness. Type C reversed itself; the most successful and least successful were low on cohesiveness, with the mid-ranked on success high on cohesiveness. For Type D, the most successful was high on cohesiveness; the least successful low on cohesiveness; similarly for Type E leaders. Both Tape Groups fell above the mean on cohesiveness, although the more successful Tape Group was somewhat lower on cohesiveness. In general, cohesiveness appeared to make an independent contribution to the success of the group and in this sense can be treated as an independent characteristic of the group beyond leader style. (Note in Table 9–1 that none of the four basic leader dimensions was highly correlated with level of cohesiveness.)

An examination of the intensity of the emotional climate of the group similar to those carried out for cohesiveness and massed/spaced temporal arrangement did not provide independent support that high involvement (although correlated .56 with outcome), could be considered an independent contributor to outcome. Involvement intensity appears so highly related to leader style that the distribution of high and low involvement intensity across leader types was too narrow to allow analysis. Of those cases, the most successful Type A groups and Tape Groups were found high in involvement intensity. This did not hold, however, for the Type B group, in which the most successful was lower in involvement intensity than the next two ranked Type B leaders. For Types C, D, and E, all groups under these leadership styles were low in involvement intensity. And among them, the order of gain was not associated within the range of involvement intensity.

In conducting a similar analysis for harmonious climates the independent contribution, beyond leader style, was indeterminate. For Type A leaders, the most and least successful were high on harmony; those in between were low on harmony. For Type B leaders, the relationship to harmony was that the most successful B leaders had highly harmonious groups; the least successful had low harmonious groups. For Type C leaders, relationshops were reversed; the most successful had low harmony, the next two had high. Both Type D leaders were indistinguishable on this variable. For the Type E leader, the most harmonious had the most success, the low harmony the least success. Both Tape Groups had high levels of harmony, and the more and less successful Tape Groups could not be distinguished on this variable. Descriptively attempting to control for the effects of leader style and parcel out the independent contribution of group conditions is admittedly crude, but serves to highlight the mitigation which seems warranted in interpreting the relationship between group characteristics and outcome presented in this chapter. Only in the case of cohesiveness is there sufficient evidence to suggest that, regardless of leader style, its presence will have a beneficial effect on outcome. Both massed/spaced temporal arrangements and group climate appear more closely associated with particular leader styles.

Although a similar analysis could in theory have been conducted for normative types, the number of norm types (eight) over seventeen groups was too large to make it feasible.

NOTES

1. "Early" sessions were defined, in the case of groups which had only weekly meetings, as the first 50 percent of the sessions. A number of groups had massed (marathonlike) sessions at some point in their lives. If such sessions were held before the half-way point, the beginning of the marathon session was usually used as the dividing point between "early" and "late," on the assumption that the climate within the marathon session was more likely to be homogeneous.

2. The range of possible scores on involvement intensity was 3–21; the mean dur-

ing the early sessions was 40.4 (s.d. = 10.6); late, 42.7 (s.d. = 11.4). No relationship was obtained between intensity and group yield (rho = −.28 n.s.). The twelve semantic scales proved to be rather reliable (item reliabilities averaged .63). After they had made independent ratings, which formed the basis of these reliability estimates, the observers discussed their reasons for rating with each other, and arrived at a final consensus rating for each item.

3. The finding also appeared in an earlier study (Miles, 1965) in which it was shown that variables such as personal involvement and amount of feedback received during a two week training laboratory showed very little relationship to outcome during the first week, but significant relationships during the second week. This study was carried out with individuals rather than groups as the unit of analysis.

4. We are indebted to Herbert Wong for this analysis. The score was computed by summing the "Expressed" and "Wanted" scores for control and affection for each group member, and computing the summed dyadic differences among all group members, then dividing by the total number of dyads in the group. Absolutely speaking, we do not know what "low," "moderate," or "high" levels of compatibility might be using this method, and must restrict our generalizations to this sample.

5. To test whether person orientation in general was associated with positive outcome, the percentages of group time spent on inside and outside personal material were added, yielding a total of 43 percent of time spent across all groups on personal focus. (s.d. = 11.7) The rank-order correlation of −.16 was not significant.

6. "Uninterrupted" was strictly defined, except in the case of Group #8 whose marathon session was spread over three adjacent days: 9 p.m. to midnight on April 23rd, 9 a.m. to 9 p.m. on April 24th, and 9 a.m. to 4 p.m. on April 25th. These sessions appeared to us to be close enough together to fall into our "massed" definition. In all other cases, the marathon experience was uninterrupted by breaks (formal) for sleeping, or occurred during an entire day, as in Group #11's 9 a.m. to 9 p.m. marathon on April 12th and its 9 a.m. to 9 p.m. marathon on May 10th.

7. A Kendall partial rank correlation coefficient was computed between the four group conditions highly associated with positive outcome, and the two major leader dimensions that have been associated with positive outcome—Caring and Meaning-Attribution. The results of this analysis indicate that the correlation between cohesiveness and group yield is reduced from .54 to .48 when amount of Caring behavior is partialled out and .41 for Meaning-Attribution. Climate involvement is reduced from an initial .56 correlation to a .36 when controlling for Caring behavior and .37 when controlling for Meaning-Attribution. Climate, harmony, which shows a .54 correlation to group yield is reduced to .41 when Caring is controlled for and .58 Meaning-Attribution (thus Meaning-Attribution has no effect on the relationship between harmonious climate and outcome). Finally, the association between massed use of time for group sessions which showed a .57 association with positive yield is reduced to a .44 when Caring is controlled for and a .42 when Meaning-Attribution is controlled for. Overall, these partial correlations (in which no statistical tests for significance exist) suggest that one or both of the major dimensions of leader behavior do reduce the association between group condition and outcome. The partial correlation is less dramatic when leader style which is a combination of all four leader dimensions is taken into account.

CHAPTER *10*

Who Shall Learn and Who Shall Falter?

What were the participants like as they arrived at the threshold of the encounter groups? Why did they come? What did they hope would happen? Did these things make a difference? Did they influence the kind of experience participants had in the groups and the kind of learning they took away?

Of those who were studied, many came to the groups free of pressing personal problems. Some came out of curiosity, others for stimulation, exhilaration, a turn-on. Some wanted "feedback," a chance to explore their personal uncertainties with others. They sought self-validation, a chance to find out "Am I acceptable, am I lovable, do I match up to others?" Some were desperate for human contact, and sought the encounter group to escape alienation. Some felt they bore the scars of a life gone wrong and turned to encounter for relief or salvation, as they might have formerly turned to religion or psychotherapy. Some brought values of freedom, openness, the "new world image" which they saw as embodied in the encounter setting; others were less committed but wanted to taste. Some of the participants had already been in an encounter group and wanted to repeat or recapture the emotional quality. Some entered in doubt, others in dauntless anticipation.

Prior to the time a participant entered one of the encounter groups, data were gathered on five aspects of his personal makeup which might influence the impact of the group upon him: His *expectations and attitudes* toward the experience, including his feelings and prior experience relative to such issues as expressivity or intimacy, that might be relevant in the encounter context; his *values* pertaining to personal change, experiencing, achievement, and so on; his *psychological adequacy* or degree of pathology; certain *personality traits* such as suspiciousness and authoritarianisms; and *interpersonal conceptions* regarding significant others in his social environment.

315

In all, thirty-seven indices of the participant's personal status prior to his involvement in the study groups were assessed.[1] Each of these thirty-seven characteristics was matched against the participant's status at the end of the experience, classified in terms of High Learner, Moderate Changer, Unchanged, Negative Changer, Dropout, or Psychological Casualty. Table 10–1 shows the thirty-seven indices of prior personal status and the relative power of each in predicting outcome status.[2]

TABLE 10-1
Test of Significance for Outcome Prediction

	Main Effects	Contrasts with Unchanged				
		High Learners	Moderate Changers	Negative Changers	Drop-outs	Casualties
Attitudes and Expectations						
1. Felt Interpersonal Adequacy				.17		
2. Feeling Sensitivity		.13				
3. Opportunities, Open Peer Communication	.08	.04		.06		.13
4. Opportunities, Expression of Anger			.16			
5. Anticipation of Change	.06	.20		.004		
6. Attitude—Safe-Danger		.08				
7. Attitude—Social Benefit				.17		
8. Attitude—Genuine-Phony						.14
Overall p	.50					
Personal Value Systems						
9. Life Space—Growth	.18				.03	.09
10. Life Space—Self-Orientation	.07				.002	
11. Life Space—Hedonism	.10	.18			.08	.07
12. Life Space—External	.20		.12		.05	
13. Life Space—Academic	.001		.003	.11	.002	
14. Life Space—Social-Political						
15. Life Space—Interpersonal	.004			.05	.001	
16. Life Space—Intimacy	.16			.02	.15	
17. Value—Experiencing	.04	.003				
18. Value—Changing	.20	.17	.12			
Overall p	.004					
Psychological Adequacy/ Pathology						
19. Self-Esteem	.11	.01				.10
20. Positive Self-Concept	.02	.19	.02	.18	.16	.09
21. Self-ideal Congruence— Interpersonal						
22. Self-ideal Congruence— Instrumental						
23. Coping—Adequate	.01	.001				.05
24. Coping—Defensive					.09	
Overall p	.08					

TABLE 10-1 (continued)

	Contrasts with Unchanged					
	Main Effects	High Learners	Changers	Negative Changers	Drop-outs	Casualties
Personality Traits						
25. Acceptance of Control (FIRO)				.16		
26. Expressing Controlling Behavior (FIRO)						
27. Acceptance of Affection (FIRO)						
28. Expression of Affection (FIRO)		.10				
29. Suspiciousness	.01		.11		.001	
30. Authoritarianism (F Scale)						
31. Lenient Self-Image						
32. Life Space—Decisions					.05	
Overall p						
Conceptions of Others						
33. Positive Conception of Others	.15	.18	.10			.07
34. Others As Lenient			.18	.11		
35. Complexity—Interpersonal						.11
36. Complexity—Instrumental	.08	.15	.20	.06		
37. Positive Conception of Best Friend	.001			.001	.02	.005
Overall p	.005					

Expectations and Attitudes

The assessment of a participant's expectations centered on whether or not he anticipated the encounter group as capable of helping him to change, and how much he believed the group would be safe, genuine, relevant. Before starting the group, each participant was asked to rate himself on a list of personal characteristics commonly considered to be learning goals of encounter groups. For such goals as expressivity, self-understanding, intimacy, and sensitivity to others he indicated where he thought he was now and where he thought he would be after the encounter experience. Another inventory asked the participant to rate how much opportunity he felt his current environment offered to engage in expressive, intimate, trusting situations, with open "feedback," and how much he thought the encounter group would provide such opportunity. These data were converted to render four summary scales: interpersonal adequacy, feeling sensitivity, opportunities for open peer communication, and opportunities for feeling-expression.[3] It also gave an Anticipation scale: How much the participant thought the encounter group would offer personal change and new opportunities for positive emotional experience.[4] The extent to which participants positively valued the forthcoming experience was assessed on three attitude scales: safety / danger, social-beneficial / nonbeneficial, and genuine / phony.

What did these eight measures foretell of a person's outcome status? Overall, they are only moderately predictive. The most powerful predictors were the level of anticipation and the participant's rating of his current environmental opportunities for open peer communication. The High Learners and Negative Changers had the most distinctive pattern of expectations and attitudes, and showed the largest difference from the Unchanged. Casualties could be predicted only at a much lower level of probability. Neither the Moderate Changers nor the Dropouts were differentiated from the Unchanged by their pre-existent attitudes and expectations. Figure 10–1 shows the means for each attitude and expectation scale that discriminated at least one outcome group.[5] (Nonsignificant scales are omitted.)

High Learners (*HL*) entered the encounter groups viewing themselves as deficient in feeling sensitivity, as not understanding their own inner feelings and being insensitive to others' feelings. They felt their environment was deficient in having few opportunities for open peer communication. Their anticipations were the highest of all participants. They foresaw the encounter group as able to provide relevant opportunities and to effect changes in those areas where they felt deficient. They expected more and, in many ways, received more. Of interest is the attitude the High Learners had toward encounter groups; they were the only group who perceived encounter groups as somewhat risky or dangerous. It would seem that the High Learners felt a need for the encounter group and expected it to work for them but at a price beyond that of admission.

Those who changed negatively (*NC*) offered the sharpest contrast to the High Learners in their attitudes and expectations. They were people whose net learning scores at the end of the experience were opposite to the High Learners. Their personal status profiles at the onset of the group evidenced the same contrast to those of the High Learners. They rated their own behavior as interpersonally adequate at the start of the encounter group, and saw themselves as having many opportunities for open communication with their peers; they anticipated little change from the encounter group experience.[6] Again, unlike the High Learners, the Negative Changers perceived the encounter group as safe and, also, as phonier than other participants did. As compared both to the High Learners and the Unchanged, Negative Changers appeared to need less, anticipate less, and fear less, possibly because they were doubtful about whether encounter groups were really capable of helping individuals.

The participants who became *Psychological Casualties* (*CS*) rated themselves lowest in interpersonal adequacy (deficient in relating to others) but high on feeling sensitivity (understanding themselves and others); they saw themselves as having significantly fewer opportunities for open peer communication than did the Unchanged. They saw encounter groups as safe and as very genuine, attitudes distinct from the more suspicious or cautious High Learners. Thus the Casualties came to the encounter groups with a generally favorable attitude and saw themselves as needing the group to correct certain relationship problems.

The *Dropouts* (*DR*) and the *Moderate Changers* (*CH*) were not distinguished from the Unchanged on any of the attitudinal-expectational variables. They clustered at the midpoint relative to the other outcome groups.

Personal Value Systems

Encounter groups are high value-induction systems; they represent a clear, articulated value alternative for many participants. Two types of values were analyzed: personal values relevant to the particular culture of encounter groups, and more generalized values bearing on the life space of the participant. To assess personal values relevant to encounter groups, each participant was given a list of values emphasized in encounter group culture, such as high expression of feeling, sensitivity, novelty, flexibility, changing, intimacy, understanding; he then indicated how important each of these was to him.

Two scales were generated from these data. One measured the importance of *experiencing* (being flexible and letting things happen, sharing, having new experiences, expressing one's self) to the participant; the other, the importance of *changing* (changing relationships, learning how others view me). The participant's responses to an open-ended question on what he saw as most important at the time he entered the encounter group yielded several categories regarding the type of values he primarily emphasized: Whether internally oriented, placing primary emphasis on growth, self-realization, personal pleasure, and so on; or externally oriented, emphasizing values related to achievement, political/social issues, and so on; or relationship-oriented, emphasizing communion, love, and so on.[7]

Table 10–1, which lists all the values assessed, makes clear that the values participants brought to the encounter groups were powerful predictors of subsequent outcome status—in fact, the most powerful. The overall predictive power of values is apparent from the evidence in the table; almost all ten value scales discriminated among the outcomes. All of the outcome groups differed significantly from the Unchanged, especially the Dropouts and High Learners. The Casualties and Moderate Changers showed least contrast to the Unchanged with respect to the predictive power of values. Figure 10–1 shows the means for each of the statistically significant values' scales.

FIGURE 10–1

Predictors of Outcome

Attitudes and Expectations

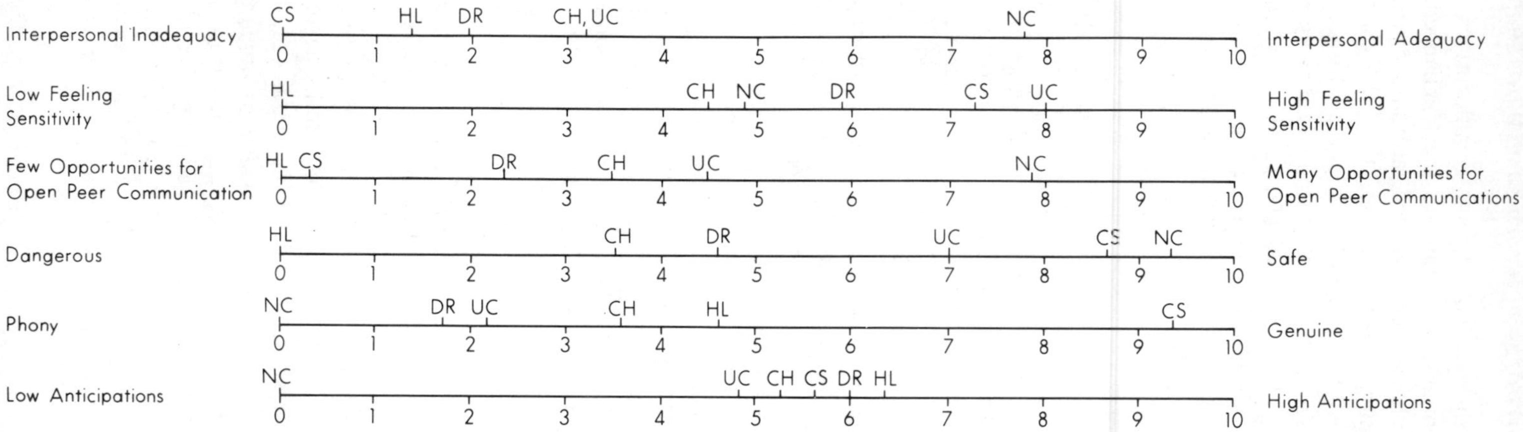

Interpersonal Inadequacy   CS 0 — HL 1 — DR 2 — CH,UC 3 — 4 — 5 — 6 — 7 — NC 8 — 9 — 10   Interpersonal Adequacy

Low Feeling Sensitivity   HL 0 — 1 — DR 2 — 3 — CH 4 — NC 5 — DR 6 — CS 7 — UC 8 — 9 — 10   High Feeling Sensitivity

Few Opportunities for Open Peer Communication   HL CS 0 — 1 — DR 2 — CH 3 — UC 4 — 5 — 6 — 7 — NC 8 — 9 — 10   Many Opportunities for Open Peer Communications

Dangerous   HL 0 — 1 — 2 — 3 — CH 4 — DR 5 — 6 — UC 7 — 8 — CS 9 — NC 10   Safe

Phony   NC 0 — 1 — DR UC 2 — 3 — CH 4 — HL 5 — 6 — 7 — 8 — CS 9 — 10   Genuine

Low Anticipations   NC 0 — 1 — 2 — 3 — 4 — UC CH CS DR HL 5 — 6 — 7 — 8 — 9 — 10   High Anticipations

FIGURE 10–1 (*Cont'd*)

Predictors of Outcome

Personal Value Systems

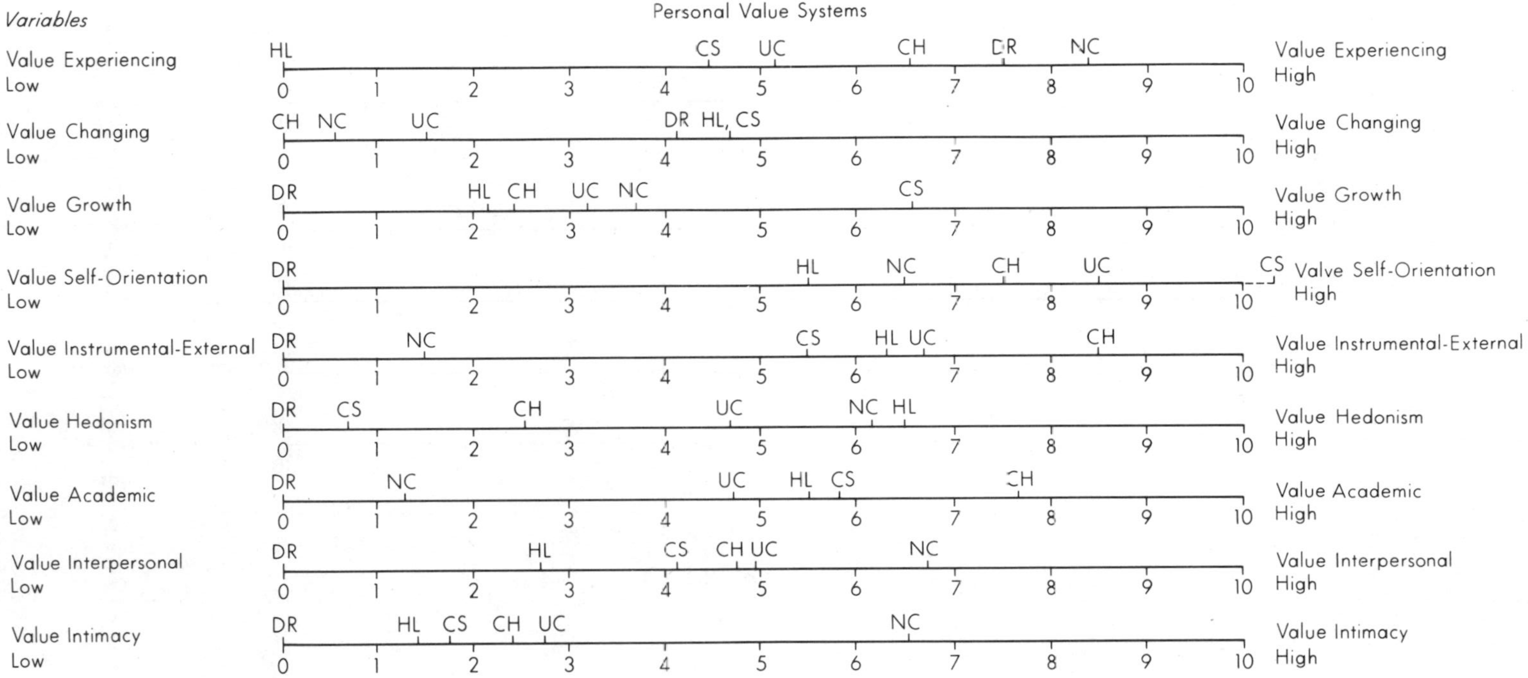

Variables

Value Experiencing
Low — HL, 0 1 2 3 4 CS 5 UC 6 CH 7 8 DR NC 9 10 — Value Experiencing High

Value Changing
Low — CH NC, 0 1 UC 2 3 4 DR HL, CS 5 6 7 8 9 10 — Value Changing High

Value Growth
Low — DR, 0 1 2 HL CH 3 UC NC 4 5 6 7 8 9 10 — Value Growth High

Value Self-Orientation
Low — DR, 0 1 NC 2 3 4 5 HL 6 NC 7 CH 8 UC 9 10 — CS Value Self-Orientation High

Value Instrumental-External
Low — DR, 0 1 NC 2 3 4 5 CS 6 HL UC 7 8 CH 9 10 — Value Instrumental-External High

Value Hedonism
Low — DR, 0 CS 1 2 3 CH 4 UC 5 6 NC HL 7 8 9 10 — Value Hedonism High

Value Academic
Low — DR, 0 1 NC 2 3 4 UC 5 HL CS 6 7 8 CH 9 10 — Value Academic High

Value Interpersonal
Low — DR, 0 1 2 3 HL 4 CS CH UC 5 6 NC 7 8 9 10 — Value Interpersonal High

Value Intimacy
Low — DR, 0 1 2 HL CS CH UC 3 4 5 6 NC 7 8 9 10 — Value Intimacy High

FIGURE 10-1 (Cont'd)

Predictors of Outcome

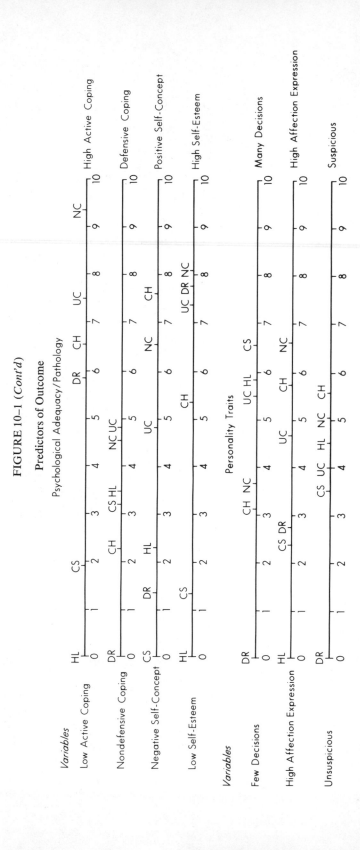

FIGURE 10–1 (Cont'd)

Predictors of Outcome

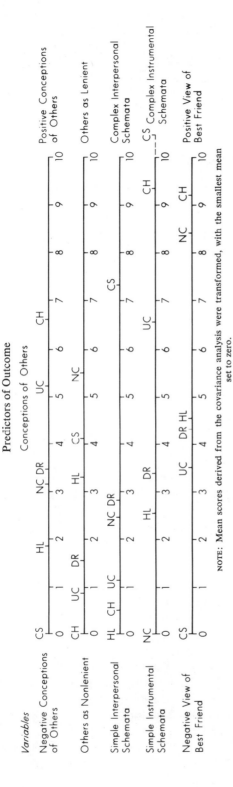

NOTE: Mean scores derived from the covariance analysis were transformed, with the smallest mean set to zero.

KEY:
HL = High Learners
CH = Moderate Changers
UC = Unchanged
NC = Negative Changers
DR = Dropouts
CS = Psychological Casualties

The High Learners stood out from all other outcome groups in under-valuing *experiencing* and in emphasizing *changing*. Such a value orientation in a context of low self-ratings on interpersonal adequacy and feeling sensitivity, as well as their feeling of a deficit in environmental opportunities, suggests that they may have felt more under the press of personal problems to be solved than others did. Perhaps they came to encounter groups with a highly specific "task focus" much like many patients who enter psychotherapy. Their interest was not in the experience, the novelty, the opportunity to feel something different, but rather in the opportunity to change. On most other values, the High Learners showed only moderate interest. They were somewhat above average in hedonistic values and below in relationship values.

The Dropouts were unique in their general life values when compared to those who remained in an encounter group regardless of outcome status. They were significantly low in growth orientation, as well as in self and external orientations. They did not emphasize hedonistic or academic values, nor did they focus their values on interpersonal relationships. Their entire value structure reflected diminished interest in most of the attraction potential in encounter groups, perhaps expressive of the tenuous ties they were to develop to the groups. Their low-order investment in life issues of common interest to other students may have mirrored the tentative, "not-yet-invested" personality qualities that characterized the Dropouts (see Chapter 5).

The Negative Changers (NC) emphasized values of experiencing and de-emphasized those concerning change. They were high in growth values, similar to the High Learners on hedonism, and low in academic interest. They emphasized intimacy and interpersonal values. Primarily, Negative Changers were distinguished by their emphasis on person relationship and their low interest in vocational or intellectual values. So far, the portrait of the value priorities of the Negative Changers suggests they entered the encounter groups not feeling very needy (a major distinction between them and the Casualties) and anticipating little change. They strongly identified with one core aspect of encounter group culture, experiencing, "letting things happen." The Negative Changers call to mind an image of the encounter group buff, interested in such groups for their immediate experiential attributes and not their instrumental potential for change.

Moderate Changers were undistinguished by their values paralleling their "middleness" in the attitude-expectation area. They resembled the Unchanged in their emphasis on externally oriented type values, especially the academic. They did not appear to represent as distinct a cluster of value-orientation as the more extreme outcome classifications, the High Learners or those who, on balance, experienced negative outcomes of any type (Negative Changers, Dropouts, and Casualties).

The value structure of those who became Casualties was characterized by a unique emphasis on growth. The Casualties expressed a very high personal commitment to changing, to growing, to developing. Perhaps the intensity of these orientations was an expression of their neediness, their desire for salvation. This may explain part of the problem these individuals experienced in the encounter group; their hopes for change were perhaps far beyond the realistic limitations of a thirty-hour experience. The other major value area that distinguishes the Casualties from other groups was their low interest in Hedonism, in pleasurable sensory activities. The Casualties were not "swingers" in the value domain. They did not subscribe to contemporary claims about the value of experiencing. Rather, they expected the encounter experience to offer direct personal benefit, therapeutics.

The relationship of an individual's value system to his potential for gains or losses does not allow the formulation of a simple hypothesis such as that those individuals entering into learning situations in which their values (beliefs) are highly discrepant from the dominant values, and where pressure exists to behave in accordance with group beliefs, will be among those most changed; nor does it allow the formulation of an hypothesis which suggests that individuals with highly discrepant values who find themselves in a highly value-laden situation will be in difficult circumstances, leading to extrusion from the group or the suffering of severe psychological distress. Nonetheless, both of these observations are somewhat supported by the findings.

The picture is clearest in the case of those who dropped out (were extruded); their value structure was most discrepant from the values inherent in the general characteristics of encounter group culture, particularly their low investment in growth and relationship values. In contrast, the High Learners were individuals whose values mirrored some aspects of the encounter group culture, the emphasis on changing and on hedonism; their devaluation of Experiencing, however, places them in opposition to a dominant motif of the encounter group. Perhaps some degree of discrepancy between the values of the person and the encounter culture was necessary in order for positive benefits to occur; yet, too great a discrepancy between the individual's values and the group's, such as that shown by the Dropouts, may predict failure rather than success.

Perhaps the closest match of the dominant encounter group values can be found among the Negative Changers. More than any other group, they fit the value stereotype associated with encounter groups, so that it is unlikely that they experienced any major discrepancies between what they valued and what the encounter group culture presented.[8]

The, at best, loose fit of both hypotheses concerning the relationship of values to outcome most likely stems from the probable contradictions, or at least complexity, of values. It is likely that most encounter group leaders emphasize two sometimes opposed values: Encounter groups are a place to experience, to live, to enjoy, to feel; and encounter groups are a place to learn, to change, to develop. Unfortunately no good evidence is at hand on this, although the goals questionnaire (see Chapter 2) suggests considerable communality among leaders.

These data suggest that experiencing and changing are two quite distinct value dimensions; it may be that a simple hypothesis, which relates the participant's value-orientation to his outcome status, cannot be formulated at least partly because of the dual focus characteristics of encounter group culture.

Psychological Adequacy/Pathology

Of all the variables that have been tested against psychotherapeutic outcome, psychological adequacy/pathology has been most often studied, and has most often showed relationships to outcome. Patients who were psychologically healthier when they entered psychotherapy have been reported more likely to benefit the most from psychotherapy. It is, however, hazardous to extrapolate directly from psychotherapy research to encounter groups. Although some participants come to encounter groups with psychotherapeutic goals, many enter to experience, to satisfy curiosity, to test out, to meet people. The outcome classification system employed in this study further complicates such a comparison because the negative outcome groups (Negative Changers, Dropouts, Casualties) are not only those who did not benefit or showed no effects; rather they represent individuals in whom measureable negative effects (not noneffects) were determined. Comparable outcome classifications are not characteristic of psychotherapy research.

Bearing in mind these qualifications, the relationship between psychological adequacy/pathology and outcome in the encounter context was tested via seven indices, including ratings by an experienced clinician using a sentence completion test to assess the degree of pathology (the model used by the clinician to rate pathology was based upon a psychoanalytic model of object cathexis),[9] self-esteem (assessed by the Rosenberg measure), and a scale derived from the Personal Description Questionnaire which assessed Positive Self-Concept (how well-disposed the person was to himself). In addition to these measures in the self area, two self-ideal discrepancy scales were included, based on the notion that one aspect of psychological adequacy would be reflected in the assessed correspondence between ideal image and self-image. Finally, two measures of coping based upon the Personal Dilemma Test were included: A scale assessing adequate coping strategies based upon wide variety of interpersonal resources; and a scale, defensiveness, assessing strategies of avoidance or psychological denial.

Overall level of psychological adequacy/pathology was a significantly powerful predictor of subsequent outcomes (see Tables 10–1 and 10–2).

TABLE 10-2
Clinical Ratings of Pathology
(Percentages)

Level of Pathology	Outcome Classifications					
	High Learners	Moderate Changers	Unchanged	Dropouts	Negative Changers	Casualties
No Signs	55	40	49	29	19	11
Minor Signs	15	40	31	35	44	56
Disturbed	30	20	19	35	38	33

The most powerful aspects of this dimension were the adequacy of coping strategies, positive self-regard, and level of self-esteem. Clinical ratings of pathology were associated moderately. The degree to which an individual's self-concept matched his ideal image was not predictive of subsequent outcome. High Learners and Negative Changers were the most discriminated from the Unchanged on these indices.

The overall finding that the level of psychological adequacy / pathology as a person enters an encounter group is predictive of outcome matches the expectation set by psychotherapy research. As shown in Figure 10–1, the relationship between psychological health and success is complex. The High Learners and Casualties were both low in adequacy of coping, low in positive self-regard, and low in self-esteem. These findings present a complex picture in which the two extreme outcome groups, those who benefited considerably and those who experienced psychological harm, are similar. This challenges the view that the psychologically healthy should be expected to benefit most. On the other hand, the High Learners showed fewer signs of psychopathology than did the Casualties (see Table 10–2).

Similar to Bradburn's findings on happiness, it may be that psychological adequacy is not contiguous (on the same dimension) with psychopathology, but that these describe two relatively independent areas. (The correlation between pathology ratings and adequacy of coping, for example, is under .20.) Thus, it is almost impossible to predict who would benefit greatly from encounter groups and who would become Casualties on the basis of assessments on psychological adequacy / pathology. Both outcomes show low levels of psychological adequacies (again perhaps suggesting their "Patient" goal orientation), but there is only marginal evidence that some of them (more frequently those who became Casualties) were psychologically more ill. The close correspondence between those who were High Learners and those who became Casualties is dramatically portrayed in this area. We have previously noted a similar correspondence in both the attitudes and value areas, and will discuss this in more detail in the last section of this chapter.

It is instructive to note in regard to the issue of prediction that Moder-

327

ate Changers did not resemble High Learners in psychological adequacy / pathology; they showed relatively high levels of psychological adequacy and low levels of psychopathology. On measures of psychological adequacy they resemble the Negative Changers in all but one important way; Negative Changers much more frequently showed signs of psychopathology than Moderate Changers. The Dropouts were undistinguished from the other outcome groups in level of psychological adequacy / pathology.

Personality Traits

Information on several personality traits was available from a number of instruments administered to participants prior to their entering the encounter groups. These instruments were administered, however, for purposes other than assessing personality traits as outcome predictors, so that they constitute a somewhat less than ideal package for such a purpose.

Several of the measures that were available, however, had been shown in previous studies to play some role in predicting success in both group therapy and sensitivity training. The FIRO B Test yielded four scales measuring interpersonal orientations: Acceptance of control from others, expression of control, acceptance of affectional behavior from others, and the expression of affection. Two scales which measured the personality traits of suspiciousness and authoritarianism (the F scale) were examined for their predictive potential. The Life-Space Questionnaire, which indicated the number of important decisions a person had made during the six months prior to entering the encounter group, although not strictly a "personality measure," was used to provide some data on the degree to which important self-induced changes (decisions) were taking place in the individual.

As perhaps was to be expected from the "grab-bag" quality of available information on personality traits, the overall power of personality traits to predict was low (see Table 10–1). Only suspiciousness showed high statistical significance. The only outcome group to show a unique pattern on a personality trait was the Dropouts (see Figure 10–1), who had made the fewest decisions in the six months before they entered the encounter group, and showed the least suspiciousness.

As discussed in connection with attitudes, expectations, and values, those who terminated prematurely from the encounter group experience appeared to start off having less need for the experience and less investment in it. Their extremely low number of major life decisions may represent a lack of involvement in changing their lives or, perhaps, a feeling that they were not in control. It is of interest that the Dropouts were the least suspicious of all encounter group participants. This may reflect a characteristic of naivete; Dropouts, like babes in the woods, may have entered the encounter group experience unthinkingly and, at the first hint of danger, reacted in extreme by leaving.

Little can be gleaned from the findings on personality traits. The range and breadth of the measures available and their theoretical relevance to outcome is suspect, although several of the instruments have been used previously for relating personality traits to outcome. Old stand-bys like the F scale have little value when studying a population of college students like those found at Stanford. Measures of interpersonal orientation, although having shown some relationship in previous studies, may not be appropriate to the conditions involved here. The range in type of encounter group studied was indeed broad; it may very well be that certain personality traits match particular types of experiential learning situations better than others. This issue has not been explored in the context of this study.

Nevertheless, it is reasonable to conclude that the ability to identify those who will benefit from those who will endure high risk can be done much more efficiently by using measures of a person's attitudes, expectations, and values than by measuring selected personality traits or level of psychological functioning.

Conceptions of Others

Conceptions were assessed by the Personal Description Questionnaire and the Friendship Semantic Differential. For the former test, descriptions of four people who were personally important to the participants were indexed on such traits as comfort with others, responsibility, enthusiasm, influence, sincerity, sympathy, reliability, activity, thoroughness, competency, anxiety, and so on. Four general scales were developed from this instrument: the positiveness of the individual's perception of significant others; the degree to which he saw significant others as lenient; the degree to which he differentiated among the four significant others in terms of adjectives describing interpersonal traits and adjectives describing instrumental traits; a series of items describing the individual's relationship to his closest friend, good/bad, pleasurable/painful, warm/cool and so on.[10] These items yielded a scale assessing the positiveness of the person's orientation to his closest friend.

The way people saw their interpersonal world, their images of significant others, before they entered the encounter group were strongly associated with subsequent outcome (see Table 10–1). A positive conception of significant others, especially one's best friend, rendered a particularly powerful prediction. Outcome was also associated with the degree to which an individual perceived others in his world as being differentiated along instrumental lines.

The Casualties were the most distinctive outcome group based on conception of others, followed closely by the Negative Changers and the Moderate Changers. Figure 10–1 shows the mean scores for each outcome group on the five indices of conceptions of others. The Casualties began the encounter group with a very negative conception of their best friend and of their network of "significant others." They thought of their "significant others" as being highly differentiated both in their personal attributes and their skills on achievements. The Moderate Changers were the outcome group most highly differentiated from the Casualties. They began the encounter group with a positive conception of their best friend, and did not differentiate among "significant others" in interpersonal aspects although they did in the instrumental aspects. The Moderate Changers appeared as individuals who had fond feelings towards people they considered important. High Learners were not particularly distinct from other outcome groups in their interpersonal conceptions, except that they tended not to differentiate their "significant others" in relation to skills and achievements. Negative Changers were generally positively inclined toward others. They were distinguished from other groups in their perception of significant others as lenient; they made the least differentiation among the people important to them with respect to achievement and skill. Conceptions of others proved an ineffective predictor of Dropout status.

In general, the findings on interpersonal conceptions suggest that those who became Casualties were more likely to begin their encounter group experience with a relatively jaundiced view of their interpersonal world and to make rather minute distinctions among people they considered important. Their view of significant others is sharply contrasted with that of the Moderate Changers, who had a positive imagery of others and did not tend to differentiate among them to the degree that Casualties did.

Summary and Conclusions

The personal characteristics of participants clearly play a role in whether the encounter experience will render success or failure. Significant relationships among certain characteristics of a person, particularly his values and his conceptions of others, were associated with subsequent outcome. These findings take on added weight in light of the effort to randomize participants and the indisputable differences in the impact of various groups (see Chapter 3 on outcome relative to group differences), both factors which would operate to dilute the influence of personal characteristics. To illustrate: It is probable, given the randomization of participants, that those with the personal characteristics associated with becoming Casualties were present in groups that did not produce Casualties, a consideration which weakens the case on predicting Casualty status from the personal characteristics of the participant.

The two most powerful predictors of subsequent outcome were the values the person brought to the encounter group and his conceptions of others, his interpersonal schema. Knowing these two facts about a participant permits a prediction at a relatively high level of confidence of the consequences to be expected for such a person if he were to participate in an encounter group. Another observation worthy of note, but not surprising, is that by and large it is easier (more predictively powerful) to discover aspects of the person related to extremes in outcome, both positive and negative, than it is to identify personal characteristics to discriminate among more moderate positive or negative reactions to encounter group experience. The High Learners, Dropouts, and Casualties were much more distinct in their pre-encounter characteristics than the Moderate Changers or the Unchanged. This may be another way of saying that the extreme groups tended to be more homogeneous in specific characteristics than did the broad middle range.

A COMPARISON OF EXTREMES—
HIGH LEARNERS AND CASUALTIES

Some remarkable similarities in psychological attributes at the onset of the encounter group have been revealed on several assessments between those who made the largest gains (High Learners) and those who reaped ill consequences from the encounter groups (Casualties). Both groups expressed especially strong need for the experience, and both were radically affected by it. Particular aspects of adequacy or pathology play a role in the psychology of the Casualties, and they appear to play a similar role in the lives of the High Learners. Both groups show a pattern of inadequate coping, low self-esteem, and low self-regard. But they differ in level of pathology; few High Learners were rated as showing signs of clinical psychopathology. If the interest were in the practical application of these findings, how could those who are most likely to become Casualties be screened out, while, at the same time, maximizing the number of individuals who could benefit most from the encounter group experience?

The key to answering this question lies in the detection of discernible differences between the two extreme groups. One may be that those who became Casualties overvalued changing and developing. Their very high growth score suggests that the Casualties may have entered the encounter group with the expectation that it would offer them salvation. Such a speculation is borne out by the major difference between the Casualties and the High Learners in respect to attitudes: Although needing much and expecting much, the High Learner initially had a cautious view of encounter groups. In contrast, the attitude of the Casualty toward the forthcoming encounter experience was totally positive and uncritical. He was perhaps overly eager to be influenced or unrealistically hopeful. His freedom from the initial caution evidenced in the High Learner may also have meant this difference: High Learners expected to find pain in the growth process; Casualties expected pleasant magic to be worked upon them. If so, when pain was experienced, the High Learner was not required to alter his expectations (he experienced no dissonance), whereas the Casualty may not only have been shocked by the demand for his own involvement in the change process; he may have been moved to perceive the encounter as another light that failed him.

Such a possibility is supported by the finding that the major psychological difference between those who became Casualties and those who became High Learners lay in their conception of others. The Casualties expressed a misanthropic view towards others who were important to them, even their closest friend. Perhaps their extremely negative and discriminatory view of others made it difficult for them to utilize an experience that is basically interpersonal; or perhaps they assigned to the demands of their cohorts in encounter a repetition of the disappointments they must have associated with their other acquaintances.

NEGATIVE OUTCOMES

At the end of the encounter groups, approximately 30 percent of those beginning were assessed as having reaped a negative benefit from the experience. The experiences of those with negative outcomes, whether Dropouts, Casualties, or Negative Changers, were relatively similar in the group insofar as certain relationships or experiences occurred (or did not occur) to these people which appeared to be associated with their outcome status (see Chapters 11 and 12). The assessment of their personal attributes, however, makes clear that the communality characteristic of their experience in the group is not reflected in what they were like before they entered the group. At the onset of the encounter groups they were markedly dissimilar people. On the basis of what they were like before they started the experience, the dropouts could not, in reality, become Casualties. They did not have the psychological makeup of those who were eventually to become Casualties. Similarly, the Negative Changers in terms of their personal characteristics were not likely to have dropped out of the group or become Casualties.

In expectations and attitudes, what similarity there was among the three negative outcome groups was found between the Dropouts and the Casualties. Both were low in their self-ratings of interpersonal adequacy and their ratings of their environments as providing opportunities for open communication with peers. Both were moderate in their anticipations of the benefits (how much change they expected). They did not resemble one another in attitudes toward encounter groups. The Negative Changers and Casualties were alike in seeing encounter groups as safe; the Dropouts and Negative Changers were alike in seeing encounter groups as phony. In this sense, no negative outcome group resembled another, generally, in attitudes.

Resemblances in the values of the three negative outcome groups were few. The Dropouts had the most distinct pattern of values, values that in general were at variance with all other groups. The Dropouts resembled the Negative Changers in their low valuation of external events, particularly academic, and in their high valuation of experiencing. They were unique among the three groups in emphasizing both experiencing and changing as a value in the encounter group culture. By and large it is reasonable to conclude that these three outcome groups did not resemble one another in the value area.

Even more remarkable is the lack of resemblance in the areas of psychological adequacy and personality traits, where on almost all dimensions the three groups touched the range of possible scores from high to moderate to low. They clearly began the experience in very different ways.

In the conceptions of others, Dropouts and Negative Changers were similar. Both groups tended toward positive conceptions of others, and held similar conceptual models of their "significant others." They differed in that the Negative Changers tended to see their interpersonal world more moderately than the Dropouts, and they perceived their friends in more positive terms. Dropouts and Negative Changers resembled each other in this area more than either resembled the Casualties.

The only generalization that can be made is that in some ways the Dropouts resembled the Negative Changers and in some ways the Casualties. The points of correspondence between Negative Changers and Casualties are much fewer, however. They appear to represent very different kinds of people.

Viewing these findings on the negative outcome groups in conjunction with those reported in Chapter 12 on the mechanisms of learning and those on psychosocial relationships (Chapter 11), it appears that, while the relationship a participant has to the group and the particular kinds of experiences he undergoes influence whether he will learn or falter, the type of negative outcome is more related to the attitudes, expectations, and personal qualities he brings to the group than to group conditions.

POSITIVE OUTCOMES

As a group, the Moderate Changers were the least distinguished from the Unchanged. They entered the encounter groups with a high positive self-regard and a positive view of others. They were distinct in their concern for academic and social-political values. On most other parameters, perhaps most importantly on their expectations and attitudes toward encounter groups and the degree to which they valued personal change, they were middle of the road. The Moderate Changers entered the encounter groups with a generally positive but not an extreme orientation. They neither rejected nor were ready-made converts to the encounter culture.

They felt their current life-style was relatively comfortable; they accepted themselves, and felt no pressure to make radical changes in themselves or in others. They had made a relatively low number of major life decisions before entering the encounter situation.

It is again instructive to reflect on the experiences the Moderate Changers had in the groups (see Chapters 11 and 12). Moderate Changers and High Learners, although quite distinct in their values, attitudes, and numerous personality qualities prior to their entrance into the groups, by and large had similar relationships to the group and experienced the group in similar ways. What appears to make the difference between them was that High Learners entered the groups under much more tension; they needed more, wanted more, expected more, and felt more dissatisfied with their life than those who changed moderately. The Moderate Changers were able to use the encounter group for growth but appeared not to be in desperate need of it. They differed from the Unchanged primarily in having a somewhat more positive view of themselves and others. They could be said to be the most psychologically well-adjusted group among the participants.

What a person enters with tells us something about what kind of experience he will have in an encounter group. It is perhaps most dramatic in distinguishing individuals within the extreme categories of a positive or negative outcome. Becoming a High Learner is a result of how one entered a group as well as of his experiences within the group. It is impossible to distinguish between the *experiences in the group* of High Learners and Moderate Changers. Similarly, sharp differences exist between Negative Changers, Casualties, and Dropouts, not in their experiences in the groups but in what they were like when they entered, and how they anticipated the experience before they got started in it.

Despite the wide variety of experiences participants had in the encounter groups, and in the range of leader styles to which they were exposed, the findings indicate that it is possible to maximize the number of individuals who will benefit from an encounter experience and to minimize the number who will reap a negative yield. Despite all the variations that occurred among the groups, certain qualities of the person, his expectations, attitudes, and values and how he viewed others and himself, made a difference in how he utilized the experience. Using some of the guides suggested in these findings, it is quite feasible to develop screening devices that would allow individuals entering encounter groups to be appropriately placed to minimize pain and maximize gain. Even in situations where exclusion (screening out) based upon assessment of attitudes, expectations, and personal qualities of the applicant is neither feasible nor philosophically comfortable, the identification of high-risk people would allow specialized intervention without exclusions. The provision of informed consent, letting the person know that, because of the kind of person he is and what he expects from the encounter group, he is in a high-risk position, might reduce risk.

NOTES

1. Those familiar with psychotherapy research will recognize the conceptual sources of several of these indices; they echo the findings of investigators who have studied characteristics of the person entering psychotherapy. Other measures are appropriate only to the encounter context.

2. A multivariate analysis of variance (MESA 98, covariance subroutine) was used to test the relationship between the initial status of participants and outcome status. Because of the association of Time 1 scores and sex, covariance analysis was used to partial out sex effects. Two analyses were computed; the first tested the main effects of each variable—its efficiency in discriminating among outcome groups. The second, a contrast analysis, compared each of the outcome groups to the Unchanged group, which was used as a referent for evaluating all other outcome statuses.

3. Principal component analysis. For items see Chapter 3.

4. The Anticipation scale, a difference score between where the person rated his current status and where he expected to be, is affected by both ratings. The statistic used to evaluate anticipations was the step-down F, the independent contribution of anticipation after the scales describing current behavior and opportunities were partialed out.

5. Note that the Unchanged group is frequently close to the midpoint on these scales. If the contrasts were computed, for example, between the High Learners and the Negative Changers, significance levels would have been appreciably increased. Therefore, in examining the figures, means more distant from the group in question would frequently be statistically significant at a higher level than the contrast with the Unchanged group.

6. It should be recalled that placement into one of the six outcome classifications (High Learners, Moderate Changers, Unchanged, Negative Changers, Dropouts, and Casualties) was based on several indices including peer judgments as well as test responses. Thus, it is unlikely that "regression to the mean" explains, for example, the perception of the Negative Changers at onset as interpersonally adequate, because of the large number of methodologically and statistically independent methods used for classifying outcome status.

Although based on a difference between the individual's rating of his current interpersonal adequacy, feeling sensitivity, and environmental opportunities, the anticipation score does not completely account for the low anticipation of the Negative Changers. A step-down analysis of variance in which anticipations were assessed after partialing out the effects of self-ratings of adequacy and feeling sensitivity, as well as environmental opportunities, revealed that Negative Changers' anticipation scale was still significantly related.

7. Correlations between the first set of values and the second were low, with only one out of sixteen correlations being at the .20 level.

8. The value structure of the Negative Changers is characterized by a high emphasis on experiencing, coupled with a low emphasis on instrumental value of changing. In addition, they emphasize growth, hedonism and interpersonal and intimacy values while de-emphasizing values associated with the external world—social-political and academic.

9. The clinical rating was not included in the overall analysis since the judgments were categorical; (1) no sign of pathology (41 percent of participants); (2) some slight but relatively insignificant indications of disturbance but not of the magnitude which would suggest pathology (35 percent); and (3) some signs of emotional disturbance (25 percent).

10. Principal component analysis. See Chapter 3 for details.

CHAPTER *11*

Person-Group Relations: Their Effects on Learning

Like any small face-to-face group which has a life over a period of time, an encounter group is a highly complex social system. The interface between the person and social system can be described along a number of dimensions. Certainly within an encounter group, role differentiation is a necessity for the social system to operate smoothly. Certainly each individual assumes a specific status in the group. Not all members are perceived in the same way by their coparticipants: Some are liked more than others; some are seen as having more influence than others; some may be "called upon" when a wry sense of humor or some other tension reducing behavior "seems required." Not all members get an equal share in the distribution of the group's resources. Some, for example, acquire more of the group's attention. Membership, that elusive but yet critical feature of groups, is not equally distributed: Some of the participants have the experience during the life of the group of being more central than others; others are peripheral and may experience painful feelings over being outside the "bosom of the group."

There are many features of group life that describe a person's relationship to the group. The focus here, however, is not the spectrum of relationships participants may have had to their groups but rather those that may have played a role in the change process. The interest is in those aspects of the person's psychological relationship to his group that were instrumental in affecting outcome status.

Three issues pertaining to psychosocial relationships were examined: Member role, feelings of belongingness (attractiveness of the group and the leader), and membership/deviant status. The selection of relationships to study was guided by previous research on sensitivity-training groups and group psychotherapy, certain particular characteristics of encounter groups, and some limiting conditions posed by the character of the study itself.[1]

336

Unfortunately, the literature is relatively mute in helping to select robust psychosocial dimensions that show promise in relating to outcome. The most promising is cohesiveness (a group property) and its individual manifestation, a feeling of belongingness or attraction to the group. The tendency of encounter groups to be high value-inducing systems, making explicit demands on participants for feeling, thinking, and believing in certain ways, suggested that an examination of the conditions surrounding membership might prove productive.

Member Role and Outcome

At the end of the third session and seventh session of each group, each participant was asked to rank everyone in the group from the most to least, including himself but excluding the leader, on eighteen items such as who characteristically responded warmly to others, took risks, worked easily with others, had the most influence, and so on. Table 11–1 shows the results of a factor analysis on these data (seventh session).[2]

Four dimensions were extracted from the factor analysis: The "VCIA role" (Value Congruence, Influence, and Activity), "accommodation," "self-understanding," and "ability to learn." Only two are relevant to the present discussion since the factors describing those who had "self-understanding" and "ability to learn" are not roles assumed in relationship to the group.

VCIA (Value Congruence, Influence, Activity) is a label which describes people who, in the eyes of their coparticipants, exhibited behavior in harmony with encounter group values: risk-taking, spontaneity, openness, expressiveness. These characteristics are behaviors in the group that fit into valued behavior in the encounter group context. Other aspects of this role, as described on the sociometric, were helping the group and responding warmly. Judgment of who in the group was influential and who was active are highly correlated (.88 and .84) with the factor of being a VCIA. Participants perceived as VCIA's were also those who were thought to play a critical role in the encounter group culture. They were valued, influential individuals who may have been seen as serving a "leadership function" in the special circumstances of the encounter group.

Accommodation described the role played by people who gave, who lent support, who worked easily with others. It was a role that resembled what has been described in small group literature as the socioemotive or maintenance role: It leavened communication among individuals and diffused conflict.

The role a person plays within the context of the group can, of course, change. Correlations of individual scores on these two dimensions from early in the sessions to near the end of the encounter group suggested con-

TABLE 11-1

Factor Analysis of Sociometric Questionnaire

Items	Factor 1 Value Congruence, Influence, Activity	Factor 2 Accommo- dation	Factor 3 Self- Under- standing	Factor 4 Ability to Learn
1. Responds warmly to others	.62	−.59		
2. Expresses own feelings openly and directly	.88			
3. Is tuned-in, aware of what is happening in the group	.84			
4. Responds angrily to others	.36	.82		
5. Has told intimate things about him/herself	.65			
6. Does a lot to help the group move along in its work	.88			.31
7. Takes risks, is willing to try things, not cautious	.92			
8. Is spontaneous, does things freely, on the spur of the moment	.88			
9. Is out of the group	−.87			−.29
10. Listens to feedback from others, doesn't get defensive		−.85		
11. Is in touch with own feelings and aware of what's happening inside	.57	−.41		
12. Is flexible, lets things happen, doesn't act rigid	.57	−.66		
13. Sees self clearly, doesn't kid self about own strengths and weaknesses		−.26	.87	
14. Shows a contradiction between words and feelings		.23	.87	
15. Works easily with others, coop- erates without any difficulty	.40	−.79		
16. Amount of influence	.90			.22
17. Amount of learning	.26			.88
18. Level of activity	.84			.37

NOTE: Factor loadings less than .20 are omitted.

siderable stability for the VCIA role (r = .73), but much less so for the accommodating or maintenance role (r = .57). However, these correlations still leave room for a reasonable amount of change between these two points in time.

What about the congruence between the role others perceive a person to occupy and his own perception of his role? The correspondence between self-perceived role and perceptions of others was moderately high for the VCIA role (initially, .69 and towards the end of the meetings, .49); for the maintenance role the relationships were .49 and .32 respectively. A person's own perception of his role changed over time more than others' perception of his role.

As suggested in Table 11–2 by the relatively low degree of differentiation among the five outcome classifications, the relationship between the role a person played in the group during the early meetings, whether defined by his peers or by himself, was not strongly associated with outcome status.[3] An examination, however, of the same roles as defined by peers during the later encounter sessions indicates that those who became Casualties and those who were Negative Changers significantly declined in performance of the VCIA role as seen by peers. In contrast, High Learners significantly increased in this role. This finding suggests that those who ended the encounter group with a high positive gain were perceived toward the latter part of the meetings by their coparticipants as occupying a high-status, valued role in the group as compared to those who suffered negative consequences from the encounter group experience.[4] Whatever the behavior or attributes of the person in the early sessions that led peers to perceive an individual as a high or low VCIA person, they were attributes or behavior that were not directly associated with future outcome.

TABLE 11-2
Sociometric Status

	Mean Scores				
	HL	CH	UC	NC	CS
Self-Defined Role					
1. VCIA Early Sessions	10.4	10.8	10.0	12.0	9.4
2. VCIA Late Sessions	11.0	10.9	10.6	11.4	8.5
3. Accommodating Early Sessions	6.4	6.8	7.0	7.5	6.1
4. Accommodating Late Sessions	6.3	6.7	7.0	6.5	5.1
Peer-Defined Role					
5. VCIA Early Sessions	10.1	10.4	9.5	10.7	10.4
6. VCIA Late Sessions	11.0	10.1	9.6	9.9	9.2
7. Accommodating Early Sessions	5.9	6.7	6.0	6.8	6.0
8. Accommodating Late Sessions	6.1	6.0	6.6	6.6	5.8
	Mean Change				
9. VCIA Peer Defined[a]	+0.6	−0.1	+0.2	−0.5	−1.6
10. Accommodating Peer Defined	+0.2	−0.5	+0.3	−0.3	−0.2

[a] $p = .05$, one-way analysis of variance.
KEY: HL = High Learners; CH = Moderate Changers; UC = Unchanged; NC = Negative Changers; CS = Casualties; VCIA = Value Congruence, Influence, Activity.

The finding that it is only later in the sessions that peer perceptions of persons who play the VCIA role articulate with outcome suggests that this role is not solely a property of the person (having these characteristics prior to entering the encounter group), but rather arises from the complex interplay of behavior within the social context of the group.

Table 11–2 also shows findings relevant to the accommodation role. Outcome groups were not differentiated either early or late in the group life, excepting perhaps that the Casualties saw themselves, and were perceived, as less accommodating than any of the other groups.

The analysis of the relationship between the two roles and outcome suggests a relationship between a role which focuses around value congruence and influence and the person's outcome in terms of learning or ill effects. A role focusing around the accommodation or maintenance function in groups did not relate to a person's outcome status.

Did those individuals who became the most influential individuals in an encounter group and who learned the most become learners because they were able to call upon more of the group resources? As active influential people, were they able, for example, to receive more feedback? Or, on the other hand, did their behavior, which expressed many of the core values of the encounter group, receive reinforcement from their coparticipants and leader? Could the lack of association between outcome and the accommodation role be explained because these behaviors were not reinforced? An influential role would afford a person more command over the resources, more influence on how the group operated, and, perhaps, the subjective experience of more satisfaction in the situation and with the group. Positive reinforcement, "being liked" or "seen as attractive," would make the environment more positive to a person than being perceived by the group as a negative, disturbing, distracting individual. Let us turn to an analysis of the attractiveness of the group as a way of shedding some light on the meaning of this role differentiation.

Attractiveness of the Group

During the early sessions and again toward the end of the group, participants were asked to fill out a questionnaire used to assess the attractiveness of the group. It included items such as: I like my group; I feel that working with this particular group enables me to obtain the personal goals for which I have sought an encounter group; if most of the members in my group decided to dissolve the group by leaving, I would try to dissuade them. If you could replace members of your group with other "ideal" group members, how many would you exchange? To what degree do you feel that you were included by the group in its activities? Compared to other groups, how well would you imagine your group works together? [5]

TABLE 11-3

Attractiveness of the Group

	Early Sessions		Late Sessions	
	Mean[a]	Percent of Participants Showing Very Low Attractiveness	Mean	Percent of Participants Showing Very Low Attractiveness
High Learners	32.7	16	34.2	15
Moderate Changers	34.7	06	35.9	06
Unchanged	32.5	16	32.4	26
Dropouts	30.7	23	29.0	38
Negative Changers	27.3	75	22.7	66
Casualties	28.4	27	26.5	54

[a]High score = high attractiveness, possible range of score: 7-45.

NOTE: An analysis of variance among outcome classification showed a $p \leq .005$ in the early sessions and a $p \leq .001$ for the late sessions.

Table 11–3 shows the mean scores and degree of differentiation of each outcome group on belongingness during the early sessions and during the late sessions. It demonstrates significant differences among outcome groups. High Learners, Moderate Changers, and Unchanged tend to be high in attraction to the group; the Negative Changers, Dropouts and Casualties tend to be low. These differences are even greater late in the session. As shown in Table 11–3, the same relationship can be expressed in terms of the proportion of individuals having scores in the lowest quartile. Thus, for example, in the later sessions, individuals who felt no attraction to the group rarely changed (five out of forty-nine people).

These findings clearly demonstrate the potency of this psychosocial relationship to the group, this feeling of belongingness or sense of membership and inclusion in the group. Those who did not experience the group in this way were individuals who suffered negative consequences from their participation in the group. These findings mirror many from other studies (Back, K. W., 1951; and Cartwright and Zander, 1962), and suggest a process which may be critical in explaining why some learned or faltered.

Member evaluations of the leader are another perspective for looking at an aspect of the attractiveness to the group.[6] At the termination of the group, each member was asked to evaluate his leader on a set of six seven-point scales: competency; would like to be in a group with him again; admired him as a person; approved of his leadership techniques; felt that he understood our group; and effective. Analysis (significant at $p \leq .001$, one way analysis of variance) revealed that the High Learners ($\bar{x} = 27.4$) and Moderate Changers ($\bar{x} = 27.9$) evaluated their leaders in a more positive way than did the Unchanged ($\bar{x} = 22.8$), Negative Changers ($\bar{x} = 16.6$), and Casualties ($\bar{x} = 16.1$).

The strong relationship between evaluations of leader and participant outcome suggests that liking a leader has as much to do with one's relationship to the group as do the properties of a particular leader. A rank-

341

order correlation of a score, based on group evaluations of the leader (a score based on the sum of member judgments) and total outcome score for that group, yielded a rho of .46. A scatter plot of this correlation revealed that there was a close correspondence between very high impact groups and member evaluation. However, low impact groups also showed many high leader evaluations; of the seven low change groups, five had leader evaluation above the sample mean. The strong relationship shown between member evaluation of leader and outcome thus suggests that even in groups with unattractive leaders (defined by mean scores of all participants' evaluations), those who changed were more likely to see the leader as more attractive; conversely, in groups with high leader attractiveness, those who were unchanged or negatively changed, were likely to see the leaders as less attractive.

Participants who were more attracted to the group were those who were more likely to be learners (High Learners and Moderate Changers) than those on the opposite end of the outcome continuum. In conjunction with the finding that learners were also more likely to play a valued, influential, active (VCIA) role in the group, these findings add weight to the conclusion that those who benefited from the group did establish a characteristic psychosocial relationship, differing from those who did not learn.

Deviance

Perhaps the two most powerful experiences an individual can have in a group arise, on one hand, from the aforementioned sense of belongingness and, on the other hand, from a deviant status which may render a psychological state of isolation. Belongingness (feelings a person has about the group) and deviance (a special case of how the group feels about a member) are not necessarily polar opposites. Individuals can be low in belongingness and not have deviant status; it is even possible for a participant in a group to have some characteristics of deviant status and still experience some aspects of belongingness.

We conceive of deviancy in a group as behavior in opposition (showing overt signs) to the norms of the group. The consequences of such norm violation are predictable. The group initially attempts to "change" the deviant, to bring him around, to get him to conform to the norms. If this process fails, the deviant's status in the group is usually changed. In extremes, he may be extruded from the group; more frequently, he is psychologically isolated. Previous studies (Gross, N., Mason, W. and McEachern, A., 1960; Pepitone, A. and Wilpizeski, C., 1958; Emerson, R., 1945) on deviance suggest three effects of deviant status: (1) extrusion from the group, (2) focusing of the group's attention on the deviant, and (3) psychological consequence for the deviant member, such as lowered self-esteem, unhappiness. This would lead to the expectation that in the encounter context the Negative Changers, Dropouts, and Casualties would include more cases of deviant status than those who maximally used the encounter group experience (the High Learners and the Moderate Changers), and those participants who remained relatively untouched by the experience.

As an indication of such status in the encounter groups, deviancy was defined as norm misperception. The assumption was that if a participant misperceived the norms of his group, he could not regulate his behavior in a way the group would consider appropriate; thus he was more likely to become a deviant, that is, to violate the norms of his encounter group. A Norm Misperception score, based upon discrepancy from the group perception of the prevailing norms, was computed for each participant. Using these discrepancy scores, the one to three members in each group who most misperceived the norms were defined as deviants. More than three would have been statistically impossible, for norms were defined as agreements shared by most of the members of the group. (See Chapter 8 for a full description of the norm measures.)

Table 11–4 shows both the mean discrepancy scores and the percentage of individuals in each outcome classification who were "norm discrepant,"

TABLE 11-4

Deviance

	Norm Misperception		Peer-Defined Out of Group		Self-Defined Out of Group	
	Early Meeting	Late Meeting	Early Meeting	Late Meeting	Early Meeting	Late Meeting
High Learners	3.77[a]	4.73	1.93	1.89	1.92	1.37
N = 26	16%[b]	24%	27%	11%	19%	04%
Moderate Changers	3.79	4.68	1.96	1.99	1.59	1.51
N = 36	17%	28%	27%	30%	14%	19%
Unchanged	3.51	4.56	2.09	1.97	1.81	1.63
N = 70	14%	27%	33%	27%	13%	11%
Negative Changers	3.50	5.38	1.87	1.91	1.79	1.94
N = 17	24%	29%	14%	18%	21%	24%
Dropouts	5.82	7.91	1.96	1.90	1.75	2.33
N = 17	35%	32%	35%	24%	07%	37%
Casualties	4.75	6.50	1.88	2.19	2.00	2.23
N = 10	30%	20%	11%	55%	22%	25%
Levels of Significance[c]	.21	.19	.45	.32	.55	*.009*

[a]Mean score.

[b]Percent of "deviants," based on absolute score adjusted for each group. For self-defined out of group, absolute rating; for received score, lowest 2 or 3 per group, usually 2.5 score; (overall $\bar{x}$ = 2.0, s.d. ± 0.5) for norm; 8-point discrepancy (overall $\bar{x}$ = 6, s.d. ± 1.5).

[c]Analysis of variance.

who showed extreme scores. Individuals were defined as discrepant if they deviated by more than one standard deviation from the mean discrepancy score. The table indicates that a higher percentage of norm discrepant individuals were found among the Negative Changers, the Dropouts, and the Casualties during the early sessions of the encounter groups. The mean scores for the Dropouts and the Casualties are particularly high compared to all other groups, suggesting that they misperceived far more norms than, for example, the Negative Changers who had a mean score similar to the positive and neutral outcome groups, despite their high percentage of discrepancy.

What were some of the consequences during the encounter group itself of such misperception of the group norms? If those who misperceived the norms were truly deviant, it would be expected for other members to perceive them thus. Early in the sessions and then again in the latter half of the encounter group, participants were asked on a sociometric questionnaire to judge which of their peers were "out of the group." The data displayed in Table 11–4 indicate that in the early sessions there were no systematic associations between peer-defined deviance (being out of the group) and outcome status. In fact, the mean scores for the Negative Changers, Dropouts, and Casualties were lower (less out of the group) on the average than the High Learners, Moderate Changers, and Unchanged. The data thus suggest that during the early sessions (usually the third meeting) the Negative Changers and Casualties, in particular, were very central to the group. During the later sessions, however, more than half of the Casualties were perceived by their peers to be "out of the group," only one out of ten of the High Learners.[7]

Although highly tentative (the analysis of variance proved not to be statistically significant overall), these findings are consistent with the expectations regarding deviance. Early norm misperception, which may have led to a deviant status in the group, probably channeled attention of the peers on the deviants in an attempt to change them, to pull them into the group, not to define them "out of the group." Perhaps only after such effort seemed unavailed did the peers come to acknowledge a member as deviant or "out of the group."

The relationship between norm misperception and the self-perceptions and peer perceptions of being out of the group is instructive. During the early meetings 13 percent of the persons who misperceived the norms saw themselves as out of the group, and only 20 percent of them were perceived by their peers as being out of the group. In contrast, during the later meetings, over one-third (36 percent) of those who misperceived the group norms saw themselves as out of the group, and over half of all of those who misperceived the norms (58 percent) were seen by their peers as being out of the group. The differences between the early and late meetings lend credence to the interpretation that a process occurs by which the peers do not perceive the deviant as being "out of the group" until they see that he resists their efforts to have him conform to the group norms.

Participants' own perceptions of being "in the group" or "out of the group" are also presented in Table 11–4. These data indicate perceptions similar to the peer judgments. During the early sessions individuals were relatively undifferentiated with regard to feeling out of the group, excepting perhaps the Casualties who had a higher mean score than any other group. By the later meetings, however, as with the peer perceptions, only one High Learner perceived himself as "out of the group"; this is contrasted with a quarter of the Negative Changers, a third of the Dropouts, and a quarter of the Casualties. Overall, the evidence on the relation of deviant status to outcome must be viewed circumspectly; it is indirect and statistically not powerful. The data are suggestive, however, that norm misperception, and consequent deviant status, may explain some part of how certain participants fared ill in the encounter group.

Summarizing the cumulative meanings of the three vantage points on participants' psychosocial relationships to the encounter group which have been explored (member role, feelings of belongingness, and deviant status), it would seem that psychosocial relationships may more powerfully explain those who failed in encounter groups than those who succeeded. The data are forceful in suggesting that only rarely are individuals who have a low sense of cohesion able to achieve learning in an encounter group. Of the combined High Learners and Moderate Changers groups, only five individuals were low in cohesiveness. Achieving a sense of belonging, however, does not itself guarantee success; it is the lack of it that guarantees failure. Although the data on deviance are not statistically as robust, nor theoretically simple, a similar conclusion can be reached. Those who experience deviant status in an encounter group are more likely to be failures, but success is not assured by a nondeviant status. Achieving prominence in an encounter group, having a role that is influential, is associated with success. Most likely the reinforcement and the probable command of more of the positive resources of such groups explain this relation.

Unlike the findings reported in Chapter 10, "Who Shall Learn and Who Shall Falter?," in which characteristics related to outcome show large differences among High Learners and Moderate Changers as well as those who became Casualties and those who were Negative Changers, the results on psychosocial relationships suggest a similarity in the relationship between Casualties and Negative Changers to the group. It may be that the psychosocial relation of the person to the group differentiates only crudely between those who benefited and those who did not benefit. High Learners and Moderate Changers may have had the same sets of experiences, but they were differentiated because of the kind of people they were and not because of the experience or relationships they had.

It thus appears that the psychosocial relationship an individual has to the encounter group provides the floor upon which productive work can take place. Without this base, the learning opportunities of the group are less available.

NOTES

1. Since the major "experimental condition" was leader behavior, the central explanatory variable became the leader and differences among the leaders. Under such "experimental conditions," the degree to which influential psychosocial relationships can be found is limited; not because they may not be as powerful, but because of the specific experimental condition guiding this study. It would, however, be possible to construct groups in which the major differences were focused around psychosocial relations. For example, it would be quite feasible to develop a research project similar to the one carried out as described in this book in which leader styles were constant but groups were composed (instead of random selection) to enhance or limit cohesiveness. Under such an arrangement, the influence of member attraction to the group might have been greater than will be reported in this chapter.

2. In order to assess characteristic behavior in the group setting, we designed a sociometric instrument which included eighteen peer nomination items and three ranking items (each group member was asked to rank all members, including himself but excluding the leader, on the dimensions of "weight" or influence, amount of learning, and amount of talking).

For each peer nomination item, such as "responds warmly to others," the respondent was asked to name the two or three group members who had acted *most* like the description in the group meetings so far, and the two or three members who had acted *least* like the description. He was also asked to explicitly identify his self-perceived behavior as being "most," "least," or "in the middle."

The rankings received by group members were adjusted for size of group by the following formula:

$$PR_x = \frac{N_L + L - X}{N}(100)$$

where X = average rank received by a particular group member
PR = percentile rank
L = lower limit of the rank interval in which x is located
N_L = number of ranks below L
N = number of people in the group

This results in a percentile ranking score indicating the subject's position in his group; it is comparable across groups of differing size.

The peer nomination portion of the instrument thus provided us with three measures: self-perceived behavior, behavior as seen by others (the "received" score), and the congruence between these two, defined as the proportion of other group members who agreed with the individual's self-perception.

3. The lack of strong associations between role and outcome may in part be the result of measurement artifacts. The sociometric questionnaire was of a forced-choice variety, thus limiting the number of individuals who could be rated high or low within any one group. For groups in which large numbers of learners occurred or for groups that contained no learners, the under-representation or over-representation of outcome categories and sociometric status would create an underestimate of the true relationship between role and outcome.

4. The VCIA role is not simply another name for being perceived by the partici-

pants as having learned a lot. The factor analyses of the sociometric questionnaire on which these roles are based indicated that peer judgments of learning are independent, forming a separate factor unrelated to the other roles developed from the factor analysis. This independence is particularly strong in the latter part of the meetings; perceptions by peers of who changed showed some relationship to the VCIA role in the early sessions, but not in the late. Nor is the role of the VCIA identical with sheer amount of activity. An analysis of activity rates as judged by peers indicated no significant differences either early in the meetings or late among the outcome groups. In fact, the most active participants were drawn from among the negative outcomes both early and late in the sessions.

5. Belongingness scores were based on a sum of these items. The items were drawn from a larger pool and on the basis of homogeneity and internal consistency used as a single score to assess attractiveness of the group.

6. Correlations between attractiveness and evaluation of the leader were .21 in the early sessions and .41 in the late sessions. Stated another way, of the seventy participants high on group attractiveness, fifty showed high evaluations of the leader. Of the seventy-nine participants who expressed low attractiveness, forty-nine also expressed low evaluation of the leader. Comparable figures in the late sessions were fifty-two of seventy-five participants, and fifty-one of seventy-five participants.

Correlations between the two sociometric roles, group attractiveness, norm misperception, and leader evaluation revealed that during the early group sessions two sociometric roles, VCIA and accommodation, were associated with attractiveness, non-norm misperception, and liking of the leader. However, at the later meetings the accommodating role was moderately associated with group attractiveness and non-norm misperception in a positive direction (.20 correlations). Group attractiveness, as already mentioned, was associated with leader evaluation; it was also associated at the later sessions with low norm misperception.

7. An examination of the relationship between outcome and norm discrepancy, self-defined status as out of the group, and peer defined status of being out of the group reveals the following: the mean outcome scores for participants not classified as norm discrepant was +.56, for those who were norm discrepant, −.11; for self-defined out of the group (during the later meetings) −.29, compared to those who did not so define themselves, +.61; peer defined out of the group, +.17 compared to −.56 for those not so defined for their peers.

CHAPTER *12*

How People Learn in Encounter Groups: Mechanisms of Change

If there is any theory underlying encounter groups, it begins from assumptions about particular kinds of events or experiences that a person should undergo in order to grow. Prescriptions are often simply put: "to express freely," "to experience totally," "to reveal one's secret thoughts and feelings," "to give and receive feedback," "to be open and honest." Events and experiences of this genre are usually thought of as essential components of encounter, although they are often acknowledged to be more difficult to accomplish then to prescribe.

It has been shown in Chapter 3 that some encounter groups are more effective than others in their capacity to produce individual growth. Some sources of these differences in effectiveness—leadership style and group norms—were explored in other chapters. In the present chapter, the processes that make up the experiences and activities of the participants in the group are weighed in terms of their effects on personal learning. A host of such processes or learning mechanisms have earned attention in the literature and vernacular of encounter. Some have recurrently been regarded as the primary conditions of the personal change process. For that reason, they have been subjected to intensive analysis here. Such mechanisms are: *expression of intense personal feelings, self-disclosure, feedback* (receiving information about one's behavior that can be accepted), *experiencing strong emotions,* and *cognitive learning* (the discovery or reinterpretation of something about oneself, self-insight, or receiving cognitive information that can be adapted for oneself).

Several other mechanisms are treated more summarily, partly because they have been perceived more peripherally in the field, and partly because the study has yielded fewer data through which to examine them. These included a number of processes which may occur only in a group context such as: *communion,* the capacity to experience unity with the group; *altruism,* the experience of being helpful to others; *spectatorism,* learning from being in a situation where others are having critical emotional experiences; the *discovery of similarity* between one's own and others' problems; and *active versus passive involvement* in the group process.

Finally, attention is given to three other mechanisms which may operate either in the dyadic or group context: *advice* from other participants or the leader on how to deal with important life problems or relationships; *modeling* behavior or styles of problem-solving observed in the group; and experiencing the *group as a symbolic representation of the primary family,* reliving, in an aware manner, early family experiences.

The evaluation of the role of such mechanisms in encounter group learning required data on two central questions: (1) Did activities or events of these types occur regularly among participants? (2) If they occurred with relative frequency, were they associated with learning? The problems attendant on the selection of an appropriate strategy for studying the processes of interest are readily apparent when one considers how likely it is for a participant to feel that he has experienced intense emotion, or insight, or communion with the group, but without evidencing any behavioral manifestations that would be discernible to an observer. In the case of self-disclosure, one man's intimate "confession" might be a casual cocktail party comment for another. It is well-nigh impossible to judge a particular behavior as self-disclosure without knowing how private the content is considered by the person who offers it.

Although coparticipants, being embedded in the same matrix as the participant, might have been more in touch with the emotional valence of events for their cohorts than outside observers, even the more acquiescent could be expected to have a low level of tolerance for "head-oriented" research questions during the life of an experience which asked them to "engage their affects" and "avoid head trips." Thus prudence suggested that the range of requests on coparticipants be kept as economical as possible, and that the participant, himself, be looked to as the primary source of data.

To minimize the resistance that a structured research schedule might engender in participants, an idiographic procedure was emphasized which simply asked that participants at the end of each session write a brief paragraph answering the questions: "What was the most important event (for you personally) in the group today? Why was it important?" Approximately 1,500 descriptions of critical incidents were generated through this procedure. Critical incidents described averaged 7.5 per participant. Those who dropped out of the groups, of course, contributed far fewer incidents, so that the participants who completed the sessions actually averaged closer to nine contributions of critical incidents. The method of analysis employed required two raters to code each incident into twenty-two different categories based on: *The event,* what the respondent was referring to that had happened in the group that session; *Who,* how the event related to the respondent, whether he initiated or received it, whether it involved other participants, whether it referred to the group as a whole; and *Respone,* how he felt about the event in relationship to himself.[1]

As shall be seen in the subsequent treatment of the various learning mechanisms, these classifications of the critical incidents comprised the primary data brought to bear on the analysis (Table 12–1). Another major source of data was provided by a questionnaire, "How Encounter Groups Work." (See Appendix II.) This was administered at termination and requested participants to indicate the relative importance of fourteen aspects of encounter group experience to their own learning (did not apply, applied somewhat, definitely an important part of my experience leading to learning) and, of those items scored definitely important, to indicate which were thought to be the two most important.

TABLE 12-1
Basic Twenty-two Categories of Critical Incidents

	Learners		Unchanged		Negative Outcomes	
Event						
1. Expression of Feeling	15% ⎫		19% ⎫		12%ᵃ ⎫	
2. Expression of Positive Feeling	06% ⎬ 34%		05% ⎬ 35%		09% ⎬ 45%	
3. Expression of Negative Feeling	13% ⎭		11% ⎭		24%ᵃ ⎭	
4. Experience Positive Feeling	05% ⎫ 09%		09% ⎫ 12%		07% ⎫ 12%	
5. Experience Negative Feeling	04% ⎭		03% ⎭		05% ⎭	
6. Feedback	12%		15%		14%	
7. Insight	05%		04%		05%	
8. Self-Disclosure	21%		19%		18%	
9. Abstract Discussion	18%		15%		07%	
Who						
10. Active Self	29%		30%		28%	
11. Passive Self	09%		11%		21%ᵃ	
12. Not Self	40%ᵃ		26%		36%ᵃ	
13. Group	22%		32%		15%ᵃ	
Response						
14. Love	15%ᵃ		20%		16%	
15. I'm Like Others	03%		06%		02%ᵃ	
16. Altruism	03%		01%		03%	
17. Personal Mastery	08%		08%		09%	
18. Group Mastery	07%ᵃ		14%		05%ᵃ	
19. Empathy	04%		04%		05%	
20. Negative Feeling	22%ᵃ		15%		29%ᵃ	
21. Insight	18%ᵃ ⎫ 36%		13% ⎫ 32%		15% ⎫ 27%	
22. Information	18% ⎭		19% ⎭		12%ᵃ ⎭	

ᵃPercent indicates statistically significant $p \leq .05$, analysis of variance contrasting Learners to Unchanged; and Negative Changers to Unchanged.
NOTE: Figures in italics indicate significant contrast with Unchanged group.

Table 12–9, page 372, presents the fourteen items. The items reflect many of the same events coded from the critical incidents. The instruments differ, however, in that the solicitation of critical incidents offered no structure suggesting what was important.[2] Moreover, the learning mechanism instrument placed the participant in an evaluative-retrospective framework where he was asked to consider, to reason, to think about a large body of experience. This is quite different from the immediacy of response requested on the critical incidents.

Expressivity

A central theme running through much of encounter methodology is that expressivity is a crucial step in the growth process as well as a desired outcome. Some leaders emphasize the expression of positive feelings toward other human beings; others place more emphasis on the expression of negative feelings, especially hostility and anger. Some leaders encourage expression about important life events, others encourage the letting go, particularly of negative feelings, toward others in the group. The usual assumption in the latter case is that, unless the person is "freed-up" to express negative feelings toward others directly and openly, the road to personal growth will be blocked. This emphasis in encounter groups harkens back to the early libido-hydraulics thinking of Freud in which stifled emotions were viewed as the major impediment to mental health and the major etiology of symptomatology.

The emphasis on expressivity in encounter group ideology is echoed in the importance the participants placed upon expressing positive and negative feelings, even prior to their entry into the group. Participants rated the expression of feeling as one of the top three out of eleven aspects of encounter groups that were personally important to them; the other two were interpersonal sensitivity and understanding their inner selves. Moreover, of the fourteen types of experience seen as helpful in his learning, the average participant rated expressing feeling as third, preceded only by feedback and the discovery of similar thoughts, feelings, and behaviors in himself and others (see Table 12–9, p. 372). Thirty percent of all participants perceived expression of feeling as very important or the most important in helping them learn in the group. Over a third of the events chosen by participants as the most important to them in each meeting focused on expressivity, although over two-thirds of the events selected involved the expression of feeling by other people rather than self-expression. The emphasis placed on expressivity by encounter leaders (see Chapter 2 for illustration and relevant data) reflected or matched the participants' perception that expression of feeling was truly an important contribution to their growth.

TABLE 12-2

Expressivity and Learning

	Learners	Unchanged	Negative Outcomes
(a) Expression of Positive Feeling, Positive Consequence	21%	20%	13%
(b) Expression of Positive Feeling,[a] Cognitive Effect	09%	13%	*00%*
(c) Expression of Positive Feeling, Negative Consequence	09%	07%	10%
(d) Expression of Hostile Aggressive Feelings, Positive Consequence	05%	09%	03%
(e) Expression of Hostile Aggressive Feelings, Cognitive Effect	02%	03%	00%
(f) Expression of Hostile Aggressive Feelings, Negative Consequence[aA]	05%	04%	*10%*
(g) Expression of Feelings of Despair, Disappointment, etc.	05%	07%	10%
(h) Self-Rating of Expressivity, Early Sessions	4.01	3.82	3.92
(i) Self-Rating of Expressivity, Late Sessions	4.44	4.04	4.14
(j) Importance in Learning of Expressing Feelings[c]	36%	26%	*15%*

[a] $p \leq .10$; [b] $p \leq .05$; [c] $p \leq .01$.

Percents in italics show significant contrast; e.g. item (b) indicates that the Negative Outcome group was significantly different when compared with the Unchanged.

NOTE: The entries into the table for items (a)-(g) represent the number of individuals who experienced this event at least once, (significance levels were computed by 2 series of X^2, Learners vs Unchanged and Negative Outcomes vs Unchanged) as well as analysis of variance. In the latter case, scores were computed for each individual case. When statistical significance was found for only the variance analysis, the designation *A* is used. (h)-(i) are mean scores (one way analysis of variance) and (j) is the number of individuals who rated expression feelings as "definitely an important part of my experience leading to learning" (a 3 on the scale) or "one of the two most important aspects of the group leading to my learning" (a 4 on the scale).

Is the perceived importance of expressivity reflected in differences among those who learned, those who were unchanged by the encounter group experience, and those who experienced negative effects?[3] In other words, can expressivity be instrumentally associated with outcome? Did those who benefited from the encounter group express more positive and negative feelings or did they express them in contexts which were supportive rather than unsupportive?

Table 12–2 presents all of the available information on expressivity relevant to those questions. Items (a)–(g) represent the participants' responses to the question asked at the end of each meeting, "What was the most important thing that happened to you in today's meeting and why was it important?" These seven items contain all of the coded responses in which the event the participant selected related to the expression of affect.

The first three items refer to positive affect; the second three to hostile, aggressive expressions; the seventh (g) to other negative affects, such as despair or disappointment. The responses were classified according to the affect context described; thus item (a) represents those instances where a person expressed some positive feeling and, through the interaction with the group or his own evaluation, experienced it as positive:

Joe (leader) had asked for final reactions and Cindy had just finished with some of hers. I felt much further from Lynn than at any other meeting, which disturbed me. I told her, and we exchanged some comments which left me still upset. Emily then said I didn't show my emotion and all of a sudden I really wanted to but was helpless. John took Lynn's arm and said, "I like you, etc." and told me to do the same, which I did and felt really good about it. I was able to do something that I've been wanting to do; I felt relieved at re-establishing some contact with Lynn and I hope I can overcome this "aloofness" others sense and I feel.

Item (b) represents a positive expression of feeling in which the consequence for the person was some cognitive learning, usually of an "insightful nature":

When the group was trying to pick an object which corresponded to his impression of each member. . . . During my turn I had trouble placing some people and ease in placing others. My reaction was to wonder how I make judgments about people. It illustrated to me how and in some cases why I place people in categories—how easily and how hard—the more I've talked to a person, generally the harder it was to find a symbol for them.

Item (c) represents the expression of positive feelings in which the circumstances produced a negative consequence (as seen through the eyes of the participant):

When I helped Vivian go through Jeff to get out of the door. I'm a chicken—I waited till Vivian attacked him before I helped. Physical confrontation scares me.

Item (d) represents the expression of hostile aggressive feelings in a positive context:

I expressed my resentment toward X and Y, who seem to form one of the three factions within the group. It's the first time I've said anything negative about anyone, and I'm glad others in the group had similar feelings (although they didn't express it before).

Item (e) is the expression of hostile aggressive feelings in which some cognitive growth eventuated:

. . . got exceptionally pissed at one guy and told him so. He thought that I, in talking to someone else in the group and telling that guy what I really thought he felt, was playing an ego trip game, that I was a pompous idiot. Well I thought that he was playing a game whereas I wasn't. Ironic. I got pissed at him, Dick suggested that we arm wrestle. We did. He is bigger than I am and should have won right away. He didn't—he just let me struggle. Then he said that he enjoyed watching me struggle—I knew that he was sincere in saying so. Before, when I was pissed at him I kept telling him that he was pissed with me. He kept denying that he was pissed. When he said the above sincerely, I learned to listen to him. Perhaps he wasn't pissed. I am learning to listen.

Item (f) represents an expression of hostile feelings in a negative context:

X had failed in communicating with Y and Z, was being comforted (more or less) by several people. I pulled him out and wrestled with him. I was disgusted at his not feeling, in a way I wanted to (I did) hit him, because I've felt as he did and know that this method would do nothing, and because he'd hurt them. I was disappointed that it did nothing.

Item (g) connotes the expressions of other negative affects regardless of context: "I was being emotional for the fifth time—what a bore."

The remaining items in Table 12–2 refer to other measures of expressivity. Item (h) represents a self-rating of degree of expressivity in the early sessions of the encounter group. These were seven-point scales, with seven being *a great deal* and one *not at all*. Item (i) represents the same scale given to the participants during the later sessions of the meetings. Item (j) is from the instrument, "How Encounter Groups Work," in which the individual is given a series of fourteen "learning mechanisms" after the series of sessions. He is asked to indicate which of these were important in his learning, from *did not apply* to *the most important part of my experience leading to learning,* on a four-point scale.

Self-ratings of the amount of feelings expressed [Table 12–2, items (h)–(i)] did not discriminate among those who learned, those who remained unchanged, and those with negative outcome. In the tendency to be expressive, the overall trend was upward for each of the three outcome groups; participants felt they expressed more affects later in the life of the group than in the beginning, an unsurprising finding. Encounter groups are based upon encouraging expressivity and these self-ratings reflect the overall, although small, increase in such expression. Another way of arriving at a similar finding was to ask the frequency of expressivity as reflected in the critical incidents. These data are shown in Table 12–1. They indicate that, of all the events participants indicated as critical, learners cited expressivity 34 percent, the unchanged 35 percent, and those with negative outcomes 45 percent. These differences are not significant. However, when a breakdown is done in terms of positive-negative feelings, they do suggest that significantly more hostile, aggressive events were cited by those negatively affected (negative changers, dropouts, and casualties). Although events involving expressivity were seen as important by both leaders and participants, the amounts of both positive and hostile aggressive feelings were quite similar for all three outcome statuses; if anything, those with negative outcomes demonstrated somewhat more expressivity, albeit of a hostile aggressive kind, than the learners.

When the context in which the expressive behavior was demonstrated was taken into account [items (a)–(g)], it is clear from Table 12–2 that there were no statistically significant differences among the learners and the unchanged. Although those who experienced negative outcomes expressed a similar amount of positive feelings, these positive feelings did not lead to insight and were slightly less likely to be expressed in a positive context. Similarly, as already indicated, those with negative outcomes expressed somewhat more hostile aggressive feelings and were more likely to experience the event negatively. The findings make clear that, despite the perception of both leaders and participants of expressivity as a salient aspect of the encounter group experience, such events are not uniquely associated with learning in encounter groups. Those who changed could not be distinguished from those whose status was unchanged at the end of the encounter group experience either in amount or kind of expressivity.

Expressivity appears to play some role in the experience of those who had negative outcomes. Although expressing at least the same amount or more positive feelings, the negative changers appeared unable to utilize these expressions for cognitive learning, particularly insight. In other words, their expression did not lead to a certain kind of growth experience. Expressions of hostile aggressive feelings, somewhat higher among those showing negative outcomes, were more often experienced as negative. In contrast, the learners and the unchanged, when they expressed hostile feelings, perceived such expressions as leading to positive consequences, often insights.

The data are mute as to why those who had counterproductive outcomes could not utilize expression of feelings as did those who experienced productive outcome. Possibly they were treated or perceived differently by their peers, who reacted to them in indifferent ways; or they may have expressed feelings at inappropriate times or in styles that differed subtly from other participants. Possibly, too, they "misread" other people's reactions to their expressions of feeling.

An examination of amounts and type of expressivity among the seventeen encounter groups (analysis not shown) showed no statistically significant differences. This is still another indication that expressivity is not an instrumental act directly associated with outcome in encounter groups. The significant differences in outcome, which have been demonstrated earlier among the groups and leader types, were not reflected in similar differences in the number of expressive events their respective participants cited as critical to them.

It is impossible, of course, to assess the converse of the expressivity hypothesis, what the groups would be like with respect to outcome if little or no expression of both positive or negative feelings occurred. It may well be that, for encounter groups such as these, a relative absence of expressivity would have produced dismal results; and it may be that for the groups studied, expressivity was maintained beyond some critical point

355

where it became a nonissue, not directly related to individual outcomes. The evidence points, however, toward the conclusion that expressivity (perhaps like catharsis) is a dramatic event which may have received, because of its high visibility, much more credit for change than it deserves. Though people may feel good about getting out feelings and may believe that it is instrumental in their learning, no evidence yet supports the belief that expressivity *per se* is specifically associated with differences in individual growth.

Self-Disclosure

Perhaps no other event characteristic of the encounter group gets more popular attention than revelation or self-disclosure, the explicit communication of some personal information that the participant believes the group would be unlikely to acquire unless he himself disclosed it. Moreover, the person must consider this information to be highly private, of such a nature that he would not disclose to everyone who might inquire about it (Culbert, 1967). The importance attributed to self-disclosure among the public accords with the place revelation has been awarded by such theorists as Jourard (1964) and Mowrer (1964) who have hailed self-disclosure as the primary mechanism and *sine qua non* of growth.

In 20 percent of the events they deemed critical, participants singled out examples of self-disclosure (See Table 12–1). Of considerable interest, however, is that only a quarter of these examples referred to the respondent's own self-disclosure; the rest referred to events in which other participants had self-disclosed. The poignancy to others of self-disclosure as an event in the group is emphasized by the frequency with which participants selected others' revelations as the event of the session personally most important to them. Overall, at least a third of the participants in the encounter group experience had one or more experiences of a significant (their perception) self-disclosure.

The importance for learning, however, as perceived by the participant was considerably below what would be expected from the frequency with which it was cited as a critical event. Compared to other events, it ranked twelfth out of the fourteen learning mechanisms participants evaluated at the end of the encounter group experience.[4] Only 18 percent of the participants (compared to 30 percent for expressivity or 50 percent for feedback) rated self-disclosure very important or most important for their learning.

Table 12–3 (constructed similarly to Table 12–2 on expressivity) presents the data derived from the critical incidents related to self-disclosure. A person's self-disclosure was analyzed according to the consequence he attached to it.

Self-disclosure with a positive consequence:

TABLE 12-3

Self-Disclosure and Learning

	Learners	Unchanged	Negative Outcomes
(a) Self-Disclosure, Positive Consequence	17%	21%	13%
(b) Self-Disclosure,[b] Insight	*23%*	10%	10%
(c) Self-Disclosure, Negative Consequence	11%	05%	07%
(d) Self-Rating—Amount of Self-Disclosure, Early Sessions	3.4	2.9	3.1
(e) Self-Rating—Amount of Self-Disclosure,[a] Late Sessions	4.3	3.4	3.5
(f) Importance in Learning of Self-Disclosure	25%	13%	18%

[a] $p \leq .10$.
[b] $p \leq .05$.
NOTE: Figure in italics indicates significant contrast with Unchanged group.

The group had split up into pairs, after long periods of silence, after a period of touching the other, as a way of introduction. I felt that I wanted to talk and I did a lot. I didn't feel that I was held back from saying anything, and I did say some things that I felt were important to me. It was the first time I had ever spoken to anyone that I had never even seen before about things that meant a lot to me. We talked about experiences that had affected us personally. This was to a girl that I had never even been introduced to. I didn't even know her name until later.

Self-disclosure which leads to insight:

When I brought up the topic of suicide, I was quite upset, and somewhat afraid to talk about this with the group, because the experience of X's suicide is still bothering me quite a bit. After talking about suicide in rather general terms, hearing Y give a psychiatrist's thoughts, I felt somewhat relieved, maybe just in bringing the subject up. It showed that I'm not yet over the shock of the suicide, as I thought I was—thought the guilt had been relieved, which it has not. It also helped to talk and bring out some of the feelings that have been bottled.

Self-disclosure experienced as negative:

We had to tell you we felt depressed or whether I came feeling close and happy and excited—often blah—I felt in my stereotype of quite—I tried to explain how I felt—felt misunderstood—nobody seems to care so why should I?

An analysis (Table 12–1) of the total amount of self-disclosure reported in the critical incidents revealed no significant differences among the learners, unchanged, and those with negative outcomes. An inspection of Table 12–3, however, does show that those who were classified as learners used self-disclosure in quite a different way than either the unchanged or the negative outcomes groups. Self-disclosure for the learners led to more discovery about the self, more insight, than did similar amounts of self-dis-

357

closure for the unchanged and the negative outcomes. This difference is reflected in the self-ratings of amount of self-disclosure [In this group I have talked about intimate details of my life a great deal (7) not at all (1)].[5] During the early sessions no differences obtained among the learners, unchanged, and negative outcomes; by the later group sessions, however, those who learned felt that they had disclosed more.

The increase among the learners in the amount of self-disclosure during the later meetings of the encounter groups suggests that perhaps those who utilized self-disclosure for productive learning carried on such disclosures in a supportive context, whereas others rendered such disclosure before the group could respond to them in a helpful way. It is likely that it is quite different in effect to reveal important things about oneself in a situation of trust and mutual support than to do the same kind of revealing in a context which has not yet acquired these properties. There is every reason to suppose that such conditions are more likely to be present late than early in the history of an encounter group. This may explain the observation that the learners, who showed a similar amount of revelation to that of the unchanged and negative outcome groups in the early sessions, markedly increased at the later sessions in the amount of revelation.

Self-disclosure plays an important role in learning if, and only if, certain other conditions are present. Self-disclosure *alone* does not appear to be a mechanism that is associated with differences in the amount of learning. If the participant who self-discloses is able to utilize such self-disclosure for cognitive learning, then the productivity of the disclosure process is enhanced. The finding that the most productive self-disclosure most likely takes place in the later sessions of the encounter groups perhaps indicates that, to be useful, self-disclosure must take place in a context in which the responses to it show understanding and support. The different kinds or different intensities of self-disclosure appear not to make a difference. The examples of self-disclosure from the critical incidents suggest that the material that is disclosed shows only subtle and perhaps unimportant differences. More important is the context of the self-disclosure as the person experiences it and the meaning that he attaches to the act.

The increased amount of revelation among the learners towards the later part of the encounter group experience is reflected in their recapitulation, six months after the end of the encounter group, of the amount and type of self-disclosure they experienced in the group (see Table 12–4). Participants were asked to indicate how much they had revealed in the encounter group, compared to other situations prior to their entrance into the group. The self-disclosure questionnaire inquired about revelations of past life material; feelings at the moment; feelings of happiness and pride; sexual feelings; fears, weaknesses, and feelings of inadequacy; and personal goals, wishes, and plans. A six-point scale ranging from "Things that I have never told anyone before" to "I did not talk at all about this in the group" was used for each of these areas.

TABLE 12-4

Type of Self-Disclosure[a] (Long Post) Outcome Group—Mean Score

Type	Learners	Unchanged	Negative Outcomes	Total
Past Life Details[b]	*3.8*	3.3	3.0	3.4
How I Felt at the Moment[c]	4.2	3.9	*3.2*	3.8
Feelings of Happiness or Pride[c]	*3.3*	2.6	*1.8*	2.7
Sex Life	2.8	2.5	2.5	2.6
Feelings of Fear or Weakness[c]	3.8	3.7	*2.9*	3.5
Personal Goals	2.8	2.6	2.1	2.5

[a]t-test comparisons between Learners and Unchanged, and Negative Outcomes and Unchanged. Scores range from 6 to 1; 6 = never told anyone before; 5 = that I had told one or two people before; 4 = told to my closer friends; 3 = that I had told in bull sessions; 2 = that I had told to casual acquaintances; 1 = I did not talk about that at all in the group.

[b]$p \leq .10$.

[c]$p \leq .05$.

NOTE: Figures in italics indicate significant contrast with Unchanged group.

Learners felt they had disclosed more about their past life and about their feelings of happiness or pride than did those who were unchanged. An examination of the level of self-disclosure of learners compared to that of the unchanged on details of their past life revealed that those who were unchanged were much more likely than learners not to have revealed such material at all (21 percent versus 10 percent). The groups did not differ in the number of first-time disclosures; only three of forty-eight learners had made first-time disclosures of details of their past, and only four of fifty-seven unchanged had done so. A similar pattern obtained in revealing things they felt happy or proud about; only one learner and only one of the unchanged group indicated he had revealed something of this type for the first time. The differences occurred because few learners felt they had not revealed at all in this area (10 percent), while nearly a third of the unchanged said they had never revealed feelings of happiness or pride.

Thus, if the participants' recollections about the kind and level of disclosure mirrors their actual disclosure in the group, it appears that the primary type of self-disclosure does not involve material that heretofore has never been communicated to others; rather it appears to be revelations of deeply personal material that may have been shared with one or two others in the past, but now have been shared with a group of "relative strangers." The utility of self-disclosure in the encounter group appears to be a matter of the interpersonal context in which the act occurs. It is probably useful only when the intention of sharing of deeply personal material is understood, appreciated, and correctly interpreted by the collectivity. Finally, it is the perspective gained from this material, whether it is accompanied by cognitive learning, that appears to make the difference in terms of learning from self-disclosures.

Those who experienced negative outcomes showed the lowest scores in all types of self-disclosure, and were significantly distinguished from those who were unchanged in disclosing fewer feelings that occurred to them within the group, particularly happy or proud feelings and feelings related to fear or weakness. Again, they did not differ radically in making fewer first-time disclosures (such were rare for all outcome types), but rather in that many more of those with negative outcomes felt they did not disclose at all. They felt they did not share either their happy or proud feelings or their fears and worries with the group.

A detailed breakdown of the type and amount of self-disclosure for all participants revealed that the highest levels of self-disclosure occurred in the areas of current feelings, the lowest in the areas of personal goals. For each of six areas, we found that: 20 percent of the participants did not talk about their past life, while 8 percent revealed something they had never told anyone before; 6 percent did not talk at all about feelings they had at the moment, while 12 percent revealed feelings of the moment of a kind they had never told anyone before; 31 percent did not reveal at all feelings of happiness or pride, while only 2 percent revealed they had never told anyone such feelings before; 47 percent did not disclose any information about their sex life, while 4 percent revealed material about their sex life which they had never told anyone before; 20 percent did not reveal feelings of fear or weakness, while 8 percent revealed such feelings that they had never told anyone before; 33 percent did not reveal feelings in the area of personal goals, and only one percent revealed personal goals they had never told anyone before.

Clearly, disclosing "here-and-now feelings" was a primary revelation experience in the encounter groups. Material about one's past life and fears and weaknesses followed as the most frequent occurrences. The overall number of "first-time revelations" was small. Disregarding the content of the revelation, 16 percent (thirty-two) of all participants had made a first-time revelation in the encounter group. Of these, 31 percent (ten) were learners, 41 percent (thirteen) were unchanged, and 28 percent (nine) were negative outcomes.

The poignancy rendered by self-disclosure is frequently reflected in the participants, not by what they themselves disclosed, but by the importance they attributed to what others disclosed. Perhaps it is because self-disclosure increases this high degree of responsiveness in others that the importance of such events has been exaggerated. Self-disclosure is implicated in successful outcome, but the data make it difficult to maintain that it is an essential condition of change. Many of the study participants experienced significant learning without ever self-disclosing in the encounter group.

Feedback

Of all learning mechanisms associated with personal change and development through groups, feedback (receiving information about oneself from others, information that the receiver believes is important and useful) is unique to the group situation. It probably does represent one of the most classical assumptions about group change processes, inasmuch as it received systematic attention in the original thinking of Lewin and his students, and was crucial in guiding their development of sensitivity-training, or T-group methodology.

The hallowed status accorded to feedback by many theoreticians and practitioners who direct their energies toward groups for personal growth and change is reflected in the importance with which the study participants viewed events of this character. Feedback was ranked at the very top of all of the aspects of the encounter group which participants, at termination of the groups, felt had helped them to learn. Half of the participants considered feedback as central to their learning or among the one or two group experiences that were truly useful for them. Out of each hundred events cited in the critical incidents, thirteen involved feedback, and 70 percent of these were concerned with the person receiving feedback; the others involved a small number of cases where the participant gave feedback or cited the importance to himself of feedback directed to someone else.

The events cited that involved feedback were analyzed according to: (1) Association with a positive feeling or response: "People's reaction to me. It made me strong." (2) Association with some cognitive learning.

I was trying to say something that the members of the group could really feel enough about to respond and X made me aware that I was talking about a very personal experience on a high level of abstraction. When I am aware that I've really only circumscribed what's so personal to me, I'm much more able to say what I'm getting at. This has carried over outside the group.

(3) Association with an event that the participant experienced negatively:

We gave feedback on each other and from two people who I am very attracted to I got good feedback from. My feelings were mixed. I was very happy they liked me as much as I liked them. I don't trust either of our feelings, however, because I'm not sure they would hold up on the outside.

The analysis of those events classified as feedback is presented in Table 12–5. Feedback was seen as important by all participants, regardless of outcome type. Two of the three analyses of feedback showed significant differences, feedback associated with cognitive responses and feedback associated with negative feeling responses. The direction of the differences, however, is quite surprising. Significantly fewer learners had experiences involving feedback which led to cognitive learning; in contrast, a large number of both the unchanged and negative changers cited situations involving feedback with cognitive learning as salient. This unexpected finding is contrary to what would be expected from much of the previous theorizing about feedback and its definitive role in personal learning.[6]

Item (c) of Table 12–5 presents data on feedback associated with negative feeling response and indicates that those who had negative outcome significantly differed from the other outcome groups in more frequently citing events in which the feedback they received engendered negative feelings within themselves. The greater occurrence of this type of event for those who negatively changed or became casualties is not surprising. As discussed in Chapter 11, they in general seem to experience events in groups as negative, so that the greater occurrences of feedback associated with negative events, information they receive which they perceive as hurtful rather than helpful, fits in as a particular example of the pattern already described.

The contrast between the use of self-disclosure for cognitive insight and such use under a feedback condition is dramatic. Self-disclosure, when used for some type of cognitive learning, is directly implicated as a mechanism associated with those who reaped positive outcomes from the encounter groups; feedback used for cognitive learning is associated with those who were unchanged or had negative outcomes. Perhaps the differences in effectiveness stem from the likelihood that achieving some cognitive mastery through one's own actions (self-disclosure) to arrive at self-understanding is a different experience than achieving such understanding through the action of others (feedback, being a recipient). Unfortunately, the data available cannot provide an answer for such a speculation.

The Experience of Emotions

The inability of modern man to experience intense emotions may be seen as a primary diagnosis underlying much of encounter group methodology. The mutilation of this skill has been described by many as at the very core of what is responsible for human problems and what needs to be corrected—hence, the emphasis on increasing sensory awareness and on the stimulation of physical feelings and emotion-provoking experiences. Many of the structured exercises which are practiced repeatedly in many encounter settings and which are used to induce meditation, inner fantasy, heightened interpersonal responsiveness, and so on, are partly aimed at revitalizing what are considered atrophied pathways to intense feelings about one's inner life, one's body, and one's relationship to others.

We were particularly interested in the experience of love. Perhaps much too much has been written through the ages on the curative aspects of experiencing love for it even to be singled out for questioning. It is not sur-

TABLE 12-5

Receiving Feedback and Learning

	Learners	Unchanged	Negative Outcomes
(a) Feedback, Positive Feeling Response	11%	12%	16%
(b) Feedback, Cognitive Response[a]	*17%*	25%	26%
(c) Feedback, Negative Feeling Response[a]	08%	09%	*16%*
(d) Importance of Feedback in Learning	53%	53%	34%

[a] $p \leq .10$.

NOTE: Figures in italics indicate significant contrast with Unchanged group.

prising, given the long historical emphasis on the experience of loving and being loved, that encounter leaders have used this as a prime example of what it is they hope to bring to their participants.

Table 12–6 shows the analysis of experiencing. Item (a), positive emotions, refers to those events, based on the critical incidents, in which the participant focused primarily on positive experiences:

Probably the most significant was feeling another person's face. It's something I rarely do and it gave me a *completely* new perspective of that person. Her (!) face gave itself a totally new understanding to me once I had felt it—I felt I knew her very well after having had contact with her. It gave me an opportunity to relate to someone on a very personal relationship very quickly. It was valuable because I found it quite rare.

X—she's just great—right there—head screwed on right. I dig people whose heads are screwed on right.

Item (b) refers to those events that the individual reported, again focusing on the experience, but in these instances the experiences were on balance negative feelings:

TABLE 12-6

Experience of Emotions

	Learners	Unchanged	Negative Outcomes
(a) Positive Emotions[c]	*19%*	33%	31%
(b) Negative Emotions	21%	22%	26%
(c) Experience of Love in Which the Self Was Involved[a;c]	*06*	10	10
(d) Experience of Love When Only Others Were Involved	58%	70%	*45%*

[a] Mean Scores rather than percent of people are shown here.

[b] $p \leq .10$; [c] $p \leq .05$.

NOTE: Figures in italics indicate significant contrast with Unchanged group.

I felt I used too much brute force in breaking out of the circle and I didn't use intelligence. I think I took advantage of others and regret it.

I loved X and had to touch her, put my arm around her. I copped out. I gave myself the reason that it would appear awkward to others, I was ripping at a straitjacket I had put on myself. I committed suicide. I copped out.

Items (c) and (d) are drawn from "the response" part of the Critical Incident Questionnaire. They are ones in which the participant has cited an event and in which the meaning the event had for him was an experience of love. Item (c) refers to the experience of love in which the self participated in the event to which the response is given; in other words, the person was an actor in the event he selected to which he had the experience of love. Item (d) refers to those incidents in which the events selected by the participant were not ones in which he himself was a direct participant. However, the experience of the person was one of love stimulated by the events he observed.

Table 12–6 indicates that for three of four items, significant differences exist among the outcome groups. Of considerable interest is the fact that learners report significantly fewer positive emotional experiences *qua* experience than do both unchanged and negative outcomes. They also report fewer love-type responses to events that they were actively involved in. Differences are not apparent for the negative experiences. Lastly, the experience of love in response to situations taking place outside the self, among others in the group, shows that the learners and unchanged were signficantly higher than the negative outcomes.

Intense emotional experiences occurred with relative frequency in the encounter groups. One out of ten times in responding to the question, "What was the most important thing that happened to you today?" participants focused solely on the experience without acknowledging the event in which such an experience took place. Nevertheless, the data suggest that these experiences were not specifically associated with learning. Those who were unchanged or had negative outcomes cited such experiences significantly more often than the leaders. Feelings of love appear not only to be not enough but, even more, to be "too much."

The events and experiences reported in the critical incidents were often rather powerful and at times gripping emotionally. Why should they be under-represented among those who learned, more frequent among the unchanged and negative outcomes? Might this reflect differences in orientation to the encounter group experience? We have previously noted (in Chapter 10) that the learners, and particularly the high learners, were more likely to focus on the change potentials of the group and minimize the experiential potential. In sharp contrast, the negative changers in particular emphasized the experiential and minimized the change aspects. The data presented in Table 12–6 reflect a similar distinction. The learners selected out fewer emotional experiences; conversely, the negative changers selected out and participated in events that were fitting with this interest in experiencing.

Experiencing love in response to what was happening to others in the group [item (d)] was least frequent among those who had a negative outcome. Perhaps this represents some unwillingness or inability or lack of interest in the others. If what was central to those who changed negatively in the group was their own experiencing, then they would not focus on having such experiences through identification with others but would rather emphasize strong, intense positive emotions in which they were centrally involved. Perhaps, too, those who experienced negative outcomes were generally more frustrated in the group, and had somewhat more of a survival kind of orientation. Their ability to identify with others would, under such a psychological set, be limited.

Cognitive Learning

Although the dominant motifs of encounter groups would not lead one to expect cognitive processes to be important learning mechanisms in the encounter context, as previously noted in Chapter 7 many encounter leaders invested substantial amounts of time or interventions aimed at achieving cognitive learning. The participants also considered cognitive learning important in their experience. Approximately 30 percent of the responses to the critical incidents contained some reference to cognitive learning; about half of these referred to insight and half to deriving information. Of the fourteen mechanisms participants ranked in terms of importance to their own learning (see Table 12–9, p. 372), *Understanding,* "understanding why I think and feel the way I do; discovering previously unknown or unacceptable parts of myself," was ranked fifth; *Genetic Insight,* "insight into the causes and sources of my hang-ups; learning that some of the things I am are related to earlier periods of my life," was rated low, tying for the eleventh rank.

What about the role of cognitive experiences in outcome? Table 12–7 presents the data bearing on this question. Item (a) shows the proportion of total insight responses for the learners, the unchanged and negative outcomes; item (b), a similar total for the obtaining information. Although these two types of responses certainly overlapped, an attempt was made to rate separately insight which yielded information and insight which was seen as involving deepened understanding of the self. Insight responses contained an answer to the question "why" as well as an answer to a "what" question. Obtained information was used for cases where the participants described events but didn't seem to respond emotionally. Items (c), (d), and (e) represent a breakdown of the insight category in which insight responses were divided according to: (c) if insight was primarily self-

TABLE 12-7

Cognitive Learning

	Learners	Unchanged	Negative Outcomes
(a) Insight, Total Proportion of Response[b]	*18%*	13%	15%
(b) Information, Total Proportion of Response[b]	18%	19%	*12%*
(c) Insight, Active Participation in Event— Percent of People[b]	34%	28%	*19%*
(d) Insight, Recipient of Event—Percent of People[b]	18%	22%	*35%*
(e) Insight, Other Events—Percent of People[b]	*53%*	28%	32%
(f) Insight, Importance in Learning[c]	*37%*	08%	12%
(g) Understanding, Importance in Learning[b]	*43%*	22%	12%

[a]$p \leq .10$; [b]$p \leq .05$; [c]$p \leq .01$.

NOTE: Figures in italics indicate significant contrast with Unchanged group.

generated; (d) if the participant's insight stemmed primarily from others providing information or reactions for the recipient. In (c) the person was a central actor in the event; in (d) he was the recipient of an event; and in (e) the event occurred among others.

Prior to considering the relationship between cognition and outcome, it is worth commenting on what conditions or events in the group generated insight responses in the critical incidents. This analysis will also highlight some of the differences between insight and obtaining information. Using the nine basic events as reported in the critical incidents (expressivity, experience, feedback, etc.), we found that insight responses occurred frequently in response to almost all types of events (that is, with one exception—insight responses were rare to experiential events). On the other hand, obtaining information primarily occurred when the event had to do with a discussion situation, forty percent of the total information responses were in this area. Very few of the obtained information responses occurred when the event contained strong emotions, suggesting that the two basic types of cognition are probably psychologically distinct.

Insight plays a significant role in learning as can be seen from Table 12–7. Those who were classified as learners reported more insight experiences and seemed particularly able to use the experience of others for developing insight, item (e). They evaluated Understanding and Genetic Insight as central mechanisms explaining the benefit they received from the encounter groups, items (f) and (g). In contrast, those who experienced negative outcomes, although reporting relatively numerous cases of important insights, did point to other cognitive learning mechanisms, such as obtaining information, to the extent that both the learners and unchanged did. Of more dramatic interest were the situations under which those in the negative outcome group obtained insight. Rarely were they situations where they were active participants, rather they were situations where they received insights others gave to them. At the end of the encounter group experience, those in the negative outcome groups rated understanding relatively low as a learning mechanism.

The discovery that cognitive learning played such an important role in the lives of the participants was an unexpected one. The mythology that surrounds much of the encounter group field had suggested that such processes were eschewed by both leaders and consumers and that the prescription not to take "head trips," so frequently an admonition of encounter leaders, would have diminished the importance of such a learning mechanism. As we have seen, both in the chapter describing leader behavior and now in mechanisms of learning, cognitive factors play an important if not crucial role in such learning. (Recall that in our prior discussion of self-disclosure in this chapter, self-disclosure associated with cognitive processes was the crucial aspect of this mechanism that generated learning.)

Recall also, the previous discussion of feedback. There it was noted that the negative outcome group reported the highest incidence of cognitive learning. Perhaps a distinction must be made between insight developed where the self is active, like self-disclosure, and insight where the individual is a passive recipient, like feedback. It is the former instance that is strikingly associated with those who learned.

Other Mechanisms of Change

The events that commonly occur in encounter groups and are associated with the production of personal learning include several types beyond the five just discussed. They have, however, gained less prominence in the relevant literature and the present study has rendered somewhat less information about them. Some of these events have received greatest attention in the literature of group psychotherapy because they can occur only in the group context: the phenomena of communion, altruism, spectatorism (spectator therapy), the discovery of similarity, and the experience of the group as a recapitulation of the primary family. Three other mechanisms —modeling, obtaining advice, and experimenting with new behavior—fit either group or dyadic contexts (although with some important modifications). They are also analyzed here relative to their association with learning.

EXPERIENCE OF COMMUNION

Surely a most powerful attribute unique to the group is its ability to provide its members with a feeling of oneness with others, a sense of belonging to a collectivity. Many leaders of the encounter movement have

TABLE 12-8

Other Mechanisms of Change

	Learners	Unchanged	Negative Outcomes
(a) Experience of Communion[c]	52%	66%	*29%*
(b) Altruism, Percent of Total Responses[b]	03%	*01%*	03%
(c) Importance of Altruism[a]	*36%*	17%	*00%*
(d) Spectator Therapy, Positive Feeling Response	59%	55%	55%
(e) Spectator Therapy, Cognitive Response[c]	*50%*	25%	41%
(f) Spectator Therapy, Negative Feeling Response[c]	29%	17%	*55%*
(g) Discovery of "I'm Like Others", Percent of Total Responses[b]	03%	*06%*	02%
(h) Importance of Similarity	43%	29%	32%
(i) Doer, Percent of Total Events	29%	30%	29%
(j) Receiver, Percent of Total Events[c]	09%	11%	*21%*

[a] $p \leq .10$; [b] $p \leq .05$; [c] $p \leq .01$.

NOTE: Figures in italics indicate significant contrast with Unchanged group.

postulated encounter as a corrective to what they view to be a major need of contemporary society, to recapture a sense of community. In an era where issues of alienation gain growing attention, it seems reasonable to speculate that communion is one of the driving, if unverbalized, needs participants seek to meet through engagement in encounter groups.

The indices employed here to assess communion are viewed as primitive indicators of only one aspect of this experience. Out of all the incidents participants cited as critical, approximately a fourth were selected out because they focused on the group as a whole. These incidents were further sorted to include only those where a personal sense of participants' responses reflected positive affective feelings: love, feelings of similarity, altruism, mastery, empathy. As, for example, "the feeling of community created between the nine of us was very warm and human. People were beginning to communicate honestly." The percentage of participants who cited one or more of these experiences during the group is shown in Table 12–8, item (a). A significant portion of learners and unchanged experienced one or more of such events; both groups contrasted signficantly to those with negative outcomes, who reported only half as many of such experiences.

The analysis indicates that the experience of communion was (1) an important one for a large number of those who participated and (2) not uniquely associated with learning. It is, however, sensitive to individuals who left the encounter group with negative outcomes; a subanalysis of the differences between those who were classified as negative changers and casualties revealed that the casualties, in particular, seldom experienced communion. The analysis of communion mirrors that described in Chapter 11 regarding attraction to the group; it perhaps represents only a dramatic instance of the general feeling of belongingness associated with cohesiveness. Those who experienced the encounter group as negative and were altered in harmful ways were individuals who could not or would not sufficiently identify with the group as a collective unity and experience a feeling of identity.

ALTRUISM

The experience of being helpful to others has been underlined by many writers in the field of group psychotherapy as a significant curative event for the neurotic. They have pointed out that the low self-esteem and poor conception of self so characteristic of neurotic patients often prevents them from experiencing the feeling of being genuinely helpful to another human being. The group context has been heralded as a medium of psychotherapy insofar as it provides an opportunity for such experiences, in contrast to individual therapy.

An analysis of altruism [Table 12–8, items (b) and (c)] was performed to investigate whether an analogous experience in the encounter group could prove beneficial to the participants. Item (b), which is derived from the critical incidents, indicates that responses coded for altruism were rare. An example of such a response would be: "I hope we—the group and I —personally have helped him to overcome his apprehensions." Despite the significant differences between both the learners and those with negative outcomes and the unchanged, the low proportion of such responses suggests that altruism may not be central as a mechanism of learning in encounter groups. It is not without importance, however. At termination, 36 percent of the learners saw altruism as an important mechanism, while none of the negative outcome group perceived it as an important part of their experience despite their frequently reporting such incidents during the group sessions.

Similar to the analysis of communion, this finding suggests that those who reaped negative benefits from the encounter group not only experienced it as a negative for their own gain, but also as a situation in which they did not perceive their own roles as being useful to others. It is perhaps not surprising that, at the end of the encounter group experience, perceiving little benefit to themselves, they could not believe that they had in any way helped other human beings.

SPECTATORISM

This is again a concept borrowed from group psychotherapy where it has been applied to patients who appear to learn something useful by being in a situation where others are having critical and significant emotional experiences. The assumption underlying the postulation of such a mechanism is that such situations clarify issues which are critical to the spectator. It has been used to explain the enduring puzzle in which learning seems to occur for some patients who, though they appear to "sit on their hands" during the entire experience, saying little and relating little to others, yet end up with positive feelings and productive changes. It is a "mechanism of learning" that has not been formally explored, although the work of Bandura (1969) on imitative learning may have relevance to the clinical observations which have been offered on spectator therapy.

This issue was explored in the present study because the participants often reported as critical events that happened to others in which they were not actively involved. These events usually involved other persons in a situation characterized by strong affects (both positive and negative) or situations where other participants had received feedback or had self-disclosed; in other words, situations in which the person who reported the incidents was a passive observer.

The data relevant to spectatorism are presented in items (d), (e), and (f) of Table 12–8. Item (d) refers to events in which the participant as a passive observer had a positive feeling response; item (e) refers to an event in which the person reported some cognitive gain through observing others' affective experiences; item (f) refers to events in which the respondent reported a negative feeling such as anger or disgust. As indicated in Table 12–6 events such as these, where the participant as a spectator underwent a personal response, occurred frequently among all participants. Learners, however, contrasted with those who were unchanged in that they more frequently cited events which led to a cognitive response; those who reaped negative outcomes differed from the learners and unchanged in that they much more frequently cited events involving others to which they responded with negative feelings.

These findings mirror those reported regarding self-disclosure. Much more frequently than other participants, those who learned in the encounter groups used spectator situations for cognitive learning. For example, they utilized personal self-disclosure as a source of insight. Here, for spectator type events, they utilize others' experiences as a source for personal insight. We also see again that those with negative outcomes experienced others' positive emotional states negatively; they appeared unable to step outside the bounds of their own person and identify with the actual feelings of others.

DISCOVERY OF SIMILARITY

Patients in group therapy often report as one of the most salient aspects of the experience the discovery that they are not alone or unique, that others have similar negative feelings and problems. As a mechanism of learning in encounter groups, such events were cited in the critical incidents relatively infrequently. As shown in item (g) of Table 12–8, those who were unchanged cited the discovery of similarity much more frequently in their critical incidents than either the learners or the negative outcome groups.

At the end of the encounter group, participants ranked the discovery of similarities second only to feedback; differences among outcome groups did not occur. However, when each of the outcome groups was ranked according to the fourteen mechanisms on the questionnaire (table not shown), it is the unchanged and negative outcomes who accorded a group a rank of one or two, while the changers ranked it fourth. This distinction between those who learned and those who did not suggests that although important for all, the learners "went beyond" this type of experience to other types they considered more crucial, while those who were unchanged or had negative outcomes were more likely to emphasize the discovery of similarities as important. It is as if the latter groups were "fixated" on a learning mechanism common to the early sessions of the group which, because they did not move beyond, caused them to be cut off from other significant experiences.

ACTIVE VS. PASSIVE INVOLVEMENT

To assess the effect of active as opposed to passive involvement in learning, critical events in which the respondent, himself, had been involved were classified according to whether the person had initiated or received the event. Over twice as many of the events described as critical involve the person as an active participant rather than as a recipient: expressing feelings, self-disclosing, and so on [see Table 12–8 items (i) and (j)].

The amount of active participation did not significantly differ among outcome groups; outcome types did differ, however, in the number of critical events they cited in which they were passive recipients. Those who experienced negative outcomes were more frequently involved in events they considered critical in which they were recipients.[7] Primarily, these were events in which others expressed feelings toward them, or gave them feedback, or where they were the object of discussion, or where insight was offered to them. As discussed in Chapter 11, those with negative outcomes were more frequently deviants, increasing the likelihood that the group would focus on them, that they would be targets of the group. The data presented here underscore this distinction in the relationship of the negative outcome group, and suggest that being targeted for the group's attention may have been a crucial difference in the experience of negative outcomes compared to that of all other participants.

OTHER MECHANISMS

A number of other processes have been considered by others to play a role in change: advice-getting, modeling, experimenting with new forms of behavior, inculcating hope, and perceiving the group as a family. We can, unfortunately, say relatively little about these mechanisms, for our base of data is slim. We have to rely totally on what participants said in response

TABLE 12-9

Perceived Learning Mechanisms[a,b]

	Learners	Un-changed	Negative Out-comes	Overall Mean	Overall Rank
1. The group members and/or leader gave me some direct *advice or suggestions* about how to deal with some life problems or with some important relationships	<u>43%</u>	26%	21%	2.18	4
2. *Helping others*, being important to others, giving part of myself to others has been an important experience for me and has resulted in a change in my attitude toward myself	<u>36%</u>	17%	<u>00%</u>	2.03	8
3. The important issue was that I was an *involved member of a group*; I felt close to the other members	<u>40%</u>	22%	10%	2.09	7
4. I was able to *express feelings* very fully; I was able to say what I felt rather than holding it in; I was able to express negative and/or positive feelings toward others	36%	26%	<u>15%</u>	2.21	3
5. I was able to use others as *models*, to pattern myself after another member and/or leader. Seeing how others approach problems gave me ideas of how I could; seeing others take risks in the group enabled me to do the same	30%	20%	15%	1.96	9
6. The group was, in a sense, like my *family*. Rather than pass through blindly, however, I was able to understand old hang-ups with parents, brothers, and sisters. It was like reliving, only in a more aware manner, my early family experience	<u>36%</u>	11%	05%	1.27	14
7. The group helped me understand the type of *impact I have on others*; they told me honestly what they thought of me and how I came across	53%	53%	31%	2.61	1
8. I learned that *"we're all in the same boat."* My problems, feelings, fears are not unique, and I share much with others in the group	43%	28%	31%	2.32	2
9. Getting insight into the *causes and sources of my hang-ups*; learning that some of the things I am are related to earlier periods of my life	<u>36%</u>	07%	10%	1.75	11.5
10. The group gave me *hope*; I saw that others with similar problems and experiences were able to grow and to overcome their hang-ups	<u>21%</u>	17%	10%	1.74	13

TABLE 12-9 (continued)

	Learners	Un-changed	Negative Out-comes	Overall Mean	Overall Rank
11. The experience that despite the availability of others, I must still face life alone and *take ultimate responsibility for the way I live*; learned to face the basic issues of life and death, thus living a life less cluttered with trivialities	23%	14%	26%	1.77	10
12. The group helped me by encouraging me to *experiment* with new forms of behavior, by working out difficulties with some other member(s), by doing and saying things that I have not previously done with others	35%	26%	<u>15%</u>	2.11	5.5
13. *Revealing* embarrassing things about myself and still being accepted by others	24%	12%	11%	1.75	11.5
14. *Understanding why I think and feel* the way I do; discovering previously unknown or unacceptable parts of myself	<u>43%</u>	22%	05%	2.11	5.5

[a]Percent of people who rated the item as the most important or very important mechanism of their learning.

[b]( ) underlined percents indicate $x^2 = .05$ level of significance when compared to the unchanged group. ( ) indicates $x^2 = .10$ level of significance.

NOTE: Significance levels on the questionnaire must be regarded with caution, for the number of items checked varied considerably by outcome status. Learners saw many more events as meaningful than did the Unchanged and Negative Changers. Their significance levels are obviously overinflated, on eight of the fourteen items, outcome groups were significantly differentiated, both by an analysis of variance procedure (using scores of 1, 2, 3, 4, for each item) and by Chi Square analysis.

to fourteen descriptions of ways people have learned in encounter groups for information (see Table 12–9).

Advice-getting, while an important component in such lay-led programs as Alcoholics Anonymous or Recovery, Inc., would be viewed by most professionals involved in psychotherapy or other forms of induced personal change as an unimportant process in learning. Not so for the study participants; receiving advice was ranked fourth among fourteen learning mechanisms. More surprising, as shown in Table 12–9, learners much more frequently cited this as crucial. To those who learned, prescriptive advice appeared important in a proportion far beyond the normal expectations of most professionals. Although this finding may be "interpreted" to mean that to acknowledge receiving advice was a shorthand way of saying "someone cared for me" or "I got feedback," the data unfortunately are insufficient to confirm such an interpretation. The finding must stand: Receiving advice significantly distinguished those who made gains and appeared to be an important road to learning for many of the participants.

Modeling, as a learning mechanism, implies that the participants have taken other participants in the group or the leader as models to follow in behavior and style of life. Modeling was ranked ninth out of the fourteen learning mechanisms; twenty-five percent of all the participants perceived modeling as a highly important aspect of their learning. It appeared to play a role among all participants regardless of their outcome status and, as will be discussed in Chapter 14, modeling appeared as a prime process among those who were able to maintain their learning. Aside from this relationship to maintenance, the data do not provide any information on the unique or special contribution of modeling in the change process.

Experimenting with new forms of behavior has been venerated as a change process in the earliest writings on classical forms of sensitivity training. The study participants perceived experimenting with new behavior as an important aspect of their learning, ranking it tied for fifth place; thirty percent of the participants saw it as central in their own learning or among the two most important of the fourteen. Experimentation did not discriminate among outcome groups, however, and in this sense cannot be said to be uniquely related to learning. Similar to modeling, experimenting appeared to play a unique role in the maintenance of change (see Chapter 14), but was insensitive to an analysis of primary outcome.

Inculcating hope, the feeling that one can change and that the group can be responsible for such change has been described, particularly by Jerome Frank (1961), as crucial in psychotherapy. Overall, the study participants ranked hope as relatively unimportant (thirteenth); only 18 percent saw it as very important or among the two most important mechanisms of learning. Differences within the major outcome categories were observed. Of interest is that those who became casualties emphasized hope more than any other outcome groups. (The contrast between the casualties and those who were negative changers is instructive; a third of the casualties perceived hope as very important or among the two most important mechanisms, whereas none of the negative changers similarly perceived hope.) Second to the casualties in stressing hope were the high learners. Just under a third of that group perceived hope as among the most important mechanisms. The findings concerning hope are reminiscent of other similarities among high learners and casualties (see Chapter 10), and may again reflect the more intense need for the encounter experience in these two groups and their anticipation of change. Hope, it may be seen, did not discriminate among those who were most successful and those who were the biggest failures.

Perceiving the group as a family, a frequent analogy used by group therapists to explain the symbolic meaning of group treatment for some patients, received scant support as important in the view of participants, who ranked it last of the fourteen mechanisms. Of some importance, however, is the finding that those who changed were three times more likely to see this analogy as at least somewhat important in their learning. Those who were unchanged or incurred negative outcomes rarely referred to the

374

group as a family in evaluating the learning potential of their encounter group.

Overall Implications

A large number of processes have been considered that could be implicated in change or learning in groups. These mechanisms have been studied through the eyes of the participants, using primarily data called for at the end of each meeting. Participants gave their views of the activity of the day they felt to be most critical for their own learning, as well as some of the reasons why they saw these events as critical. From these raw data, coding schemes were developed to analyze learning processes. Thus, the findings must not be taken as reflecting observed antecedent-consequent relationships from an external framework; the data do not report how much the participant actually engaged in any kind of behavior. Information on whether he engaged in a particular behavior at all is confined to his own day-to-day perceptions. The analyses of learning mechanisms have also employed data gathered at the end of the encounter group experience on participants' ratings of the relative importance to their own learning of fourteen "mechanisms" of learning.

The findings based on these data are somewhat surprising, insofar as a number of the "favorite processes" implicated as crucial to change in encounter group theory and in the literature of related fields failed to show associations with learning. The number of events that differed between the learners and those who were unchanged was small and primarily involved cognitive learning. The expression of anger, of rage, the experience of profound emotions, the receipt of feedback, self-disclosures in and of themselves, appeared not to differentiate markedly those who learned and those who remained unchanged. It was only when cognitive events modified these experiences that statistically significant differences obtained among the learners and those who remained unchanged.

As is perhaps all too common, the data speak more loudly on the experience of those who reaped negative benefits. It is possible to be much more definitive about the experiences and events or the lack of experiences and events that were related to negative change. Despite the fact that those who experienced negative outcomes were as active (took as large a share of group time, see Chapter 11) as the learners, overall it seems as if these participants were less able to take advantage of the experiences available in the encounter groups. This is particularly dramatized by their under-utilization of mechanisms surrounding events that did not directly involve them. Those with negative outcomes, for example, were less able to reap cognitive learnings under the condition of spectatorism. It could be concluded that they were less able to identify with the group.

375

Perhaps a major distinction between those who learned and those who did not is that the learners appeared to be people who could take the role of others, who could step into another person's shoes and feel with him, as well as get some perspective for themselves through this process and make some useful analogies to their own cases. It might be speculated that in the encounter group context, where time per person is scarce, learners are people who, more than those who reap ill effects, can maximize their time by rendering more from processes in which they are only indirectly, vicariously, or empathetically involved.

Do these findings on learning mechanisms mean mechanisms heretofore thought to be instrumental in encounter groups are irrelevant? Not so. More frequently than not, the data imply that events such as the experiencing or expression of strong affect were perceived as crucial by the participants. Although these experiences or events are not unique to those who learn in the group (for those who did not learn cite as many), the data do not bear on the question of what the absence of these events might have meant for the group. Can one have an encounter group without the expression of hostile feelings? Can one build an environment for personal learning without a modicum of disclosure? Although there are no empirical bases to answer such questions, it seems reasonable to think not. It is unreasonable to assume that events so nearly universal in occurrence within the encounter context could arise independently in each case.

It may be that many of the mechanisms which are associated with encounter groups and thought to be critical to learning are not simply related to learning, itself, but rather to the building of an environment upon which people can draw for learning.

NOTES

1. The original coding system contained twenty-two *Event* categories representing several examples of feeling expression, experience of feelings, processes of feedback, insight, self-disclosure, and discussion. These twenty-two categories were subsequently condensed to nine basic events. The reduction was based on the relative frequency of events. The original coding system, for example, contained seven categories referring to negative experience: hostility, frustration, suppression, fear, nervousness, rejection, and uninvolvement. As the frequency of each of these specific events was small, they were reclassified as experience of negative feelings. The second classification, *Who,* contained four categories. The third classification, *Response,* originally contained thirteen categories which were reduced to nine on a similar principle as described for the *Event* category reduction.

Table 12–1 (page 350) shows the basic twenty-two categories used to classify critical incidents, nine *Event,* four *Who,* and nine *Response,* as well as the proportions for each of the three outcome groups. Each critical incident is represented in the three classifications of *Event, Who,* and *Response* and each classification adds up to 100 percent. This three-way classification system provided a means of classifying any single critical incident into one of 324 subclassifications: nine *Event,* four *Who,* and nine *Response.* The analysis of learning mechanisms presented in the chapter involves various combinations from the 324 theoretically possible. For most of the analyses, the number (proportion) of the total represented for each outcome group is used; for others, since participants usually responded only once within any classification (that is, over the series of nine critical incidents each participant provided, only one of the nine times was his reference to a particular *Event-Who-Response* combination), the scores represented are based on a dichotomy of the percentage of people who provided at least one such combination.

2. The critical incident measure is based upon the saliency of the event to the individual, and is not a direct reflection of amount of behavior. It has the advantage of assessing the meaning of group events to an individual more directly from that individual's framework and, in this sense, assesses importance; on the other hand, by forcing the individual to choose a single event as most important, it has the inherent disadvantage of losing the participant's perspective on other events that occurred in the same group session and that he may have considered especially salient. It might also force a response that "nothing" was particularly important to the participant.

3. An initial analysis using the six-category outcome classification (High Learners, Moderate Changers, Unchanged, Negative Changers, Dropouts, and Casualties) indicated that differences on most of the variables explored to study mechanisms of change among the High Learners and Changers were negligible; and although some minor differences existed between the Negative Changers and Casualties, overall they were similar. Hence for ease of presentation, outcome categories were combined: Learners (High Learners and Moderate Changers), Unchanged, and Negative Outcomes (Negative Changers and Casualties). Dropouts were excluded since the number of cases with data was too small to warrant analysis.

4. The definition of self-disclosure given to the participants in the questionnaire was confining, "Revealing embarrassing things about myself and still being accepted by others," and may have influenced the low ranking.

5. A previous analysis of self-ratings of revelation and peer ratings of revelation revealed considerable agreement between these two measures. The findings reported by Roberts in an unpublished dissertation (Roberts, 1971) using data from the Group Experience Project, indicate some degree of validity to the self-ratings of self-disclosure reported in this chapter.

6. The failure to find that the amount and condition under which a person receives feedback relate to positive change may reflect both the shortcomings of the methodology employed here to assess feedback, as well as speak to the process through which feedback becomes useful to the person. We know little about the content of the feedback the person receives. Also, it should be borne in mind that the measures do not reflect the actual frequency of feedback the participant received, but rather represent the participants' own experience of events involving feedback which he considers important in his learning. Although feedback has been referred to for over twenty-five years as a central mechanism of learning in sensitivity groups, the empirical base for supporting its importance is slim and replete with methodological problems that make the findings difficult to interpret. For example, a study by Miles (1965) found feedback to be positively associated with short-term, self-perceived, and leader-perceived changes, but not with change as measured for the participants on their back-home job. In other words, it appears as if feedback has been demonstrated to be effective in the person's evaluation or the leader's evaluation of their change, but appears not to be instrumental in measuring outcomes in terms of external data. Another interesting finding from Miles' study is that feedback received during the first week as evaluated by participants did not relate to change, while feedback as evaluated by the participants after the experience, at the end of the experience, was related to their own evaluation of change and leader evaluation which were made at the same point in time. Perhaps the positive associations are based on these simultaneous judgments in a context where the participants equate useful feedback with having learned. Myers et al. (1969) showed that the systematic induction of feedback led to increased interpersonal sensitivity. However, as the authors point out, the discrepancy measures used are open to several equally valid interpretations aside from the functional utility of feedback.

In an attempt to clarify the role of feedback, the relationship between feedback and leader style was analyzed; overall, as expressed in the critical incidents, participants with Type B leaders (who produced the highest number of positive outcomes) evidenced the smallest number of events involving feedback. The highest number were cited by members of the Tape Groups and groups led by Type C leaders (the two leadership styles next most successful to the Type B leaders in producing outcome.) Nor did an analysis of feedback with cognitive responses help. Such incidents were most numerous in the Type F leader groups (the least successful) and Type C leaders, and were lowest in number in both Type B (high success) and Type E (low success) leaders.

7. As discussed in Chapter 11, activity rates of learners, unchanged, and negative outcomes did not differ.

CHAPTER *13*

Interracial Encounter

Do encounter group participants evidence significant change in intergroup, as well as interpersonal, attitudes? Does interracial content in the encounter context modify the stance of whites toward blacks? Are particular patterns of personal change in encounter groups associated with intergroup attitude change, or may such changes be better explained by conditions outside the person, such as the race of the leader or the racial composition of the group?

Whatever the answers, sufficient experiental programs have been designed over the past two decades on the assumption that better self-understanding leads to improved relations between the races to warrant raising such questions. The encounter study, taking place at a time when race was a paramount issue for black and white Stanford students, seemed apt for the examination of such relationships.

It may be remembered that during the academic year of 1968–1969, when the study got underway, issues of student militance and black separatism were rampant on campuses throughout America. Stanford was no exception. In an effort to respond to student demands for black studies, Stanford inaugurated a course in Race and Prejudice in the Fall Quarter. According to those who developed the course, great effort was expended to assure the highest quality of instruction and to provide content of depth and breadth. Nonetheless, by Winter Quarter discontent with the course was broadside. In some sections, discussion of lecture content gave way to explosive confrontations between white and black students which rivaled any embroilments typifying encounter. Black students, following the pattern then becoming prevalent on many campuses, began to demand separate discussion groups, arguing that, when free of comparison with or subtle intimidation by whites, they could speak more freely and learn more. This set of affairs in fact became the happenstance causing the encounter study to be executed under Stanford auspices. Surprised by the negative response to the Race and Prejudice course, its staff approached the encounter group investigators with questions about alternative, experienced-based designs that might be more responsive to the needs voiced by the students.

379

Launched in this context, the initial conception of the encounter group study was that it would test the impact of varied encounter formats on interracial attitudes, as well as on those dimensions of change discussed in other chapters. The claim of black students that racial composition functioned as a crucial variable in learning was expected to constitute a major research hypothesis. The situation also seemed opportune for testing older assumptions about interracial contact as an antidote to negative interracial relationships. Carrying official course credit, the encounter research groups were viewed as a third-quarter variation of the Race and Prejudice course, expressly providing for the generation of issues which only accidentally had come to the fore in the prior two quarters. While it was made clear to all prospective leaders and participants that they were under no obligation to deal with racial issues (or any other preordained content), announcements of the groups as a course offering noted their potentiality as a context for penetrating exploration of interpersonal issues centering in race. Indeed, several leaders attested to the racial dimension of the investigation as among the attractions the assignment held out for them.

It was expected that most of the black and white students who had previously elected the Race and Prejudice course would register for the encounter groups, allowing the groups to be systematically varied to include several all-white, all-black, and racially mixed groups. Of several varied approaches to interest black students, however, including frequent announcements in black student publications and through black student organizations, as well as face-to-face meetings of black students with the research team, none met with success. This was partly because recruitment got underway at a time when most black Stanford students were deeply involved in time-consuming political activities and partly because of the black students' expressed mistrust of the researchers, even though a black psychologist aided in the original research planning.

Thus, of the 210 encounter group registrants, only 29 percent had undertaken at least one quarter of the earlier course in Race and Prejudice. Although twenty-five black students participated in pretesting, only fourteen of these also took the post-tests. Several others attended some encounter group meetings, but only seven black students went through the entire experimental sequence. Of the eighteen groups, a sufficient number of black students participated to allow only four to be racially mixed—two under black, and two under white leadership.[1]

The failure to involve black students in the encounter groups is far less surprising now as we glance back at the events of 1968–1969 than it was to the investigators at the time. Black students' and their elders' dissatisfaction with integration as a remedy for race-determined inequities was manifested from coast to coast in increasing adherence to organizations favoring militance and separatism. Less than a year before, massive unrest among black Americans had been sufficient to cause a Presidential study commission to cite racism as American's number one social problem.

380

Panaceas urgently advanced in the mid-sixties, such as the Job Corps, Head Start, and judicial mandate had been seen to fall far short of anticipation. Black unemployment continued to be disproportionately high, school desegregation went slowly, urban housing available to blacks remained inadequate, and accusations of police brutality created occasions for angry outbursts here and there throughout the nation.

At the same time militant political ideologies culminated on American campuses in student demands for autonomous black studies programs and separate black social organizations and in free schools which taught black history and encouraged the development of black culture. The natural hairstyle and the dashiki became the visible symbols of adherence to the cultural revolt and to the total liberation movement. A new generation of militant black leaders had arisen to command the respect and inspire the actions of black youth, and formerly integrated civil-rights organizations were undergoing structural changes in the direction of greater separatism.

The new black movements, which were growing rapidly in cities throughout the nation, had their counterparts at Stanford. Its first sizable group of black students had been admitted only three years earlier under a policy of relaxed admission standards. Although the twenty-one black students who entered Stanford in 1966 averaged scores on college boards appreciably lower than the Freshman class as a whole, no special tutorial program was available to them, and there were very few black upperclassmen to aid in their adjustment (*Trans-Action,* 1971). By the winter of 1968, efforts to make the university more responsive were underway. A Black Student Union enlisted the energies of many of the black students, who joined in varying degrees with the leaders' demands that Stanford change the ways it selected faculty, admitted students, defined its curriculum, and awarded credits and degrees. Specific demands were for open enrollment, the abolition of "white" standards for appointments, admissions, and performance, and the full commitment of the school to a racial revolution. Some stressed the need for autonomous departments of black studies, separate housing, and social facilities for blacks. Many participated in strikes or vandalism intended to force the compliance of the university, while others were more moderate in their positions with regard to the use of force.[2]

Like other major campuses across the country, Stanford had an extremely active antiwar contingent in 1968–1969, whose activities and ideology cut across racial lines. The peace movement shared with the black liberation movement the call for total personal commitment to massive social and cultural change. While the peace movement made use of a variety of techniques, its armamentarium included the achievement of more widespread personal control over social decision-making processes and the establishment of social structure permitting the widest possible range of individual freedom. Politicization of students was viewed as an essential first step. Thus, the two movements, despite many differences, shared an em-

381

phasis on the responsibility of the common man for his own fate. White student leadership, partly in response to the separatist platform of the black students, turned major attention to the promotion of antiwar activities, and also called for militant, direct action against those Stanford programs perceived as aiding the military complex.

It is within this context of black disillusion with conventional democratic forms and increasing adherence to an ideology of militance and separatism, coupled with radical challenges to old values among whites, that the data presented in the present chapter must be evaluated. The unavailability of a sufficient sample of black students meant that attitude change could be assessed only for the white participants; the unprecedented interracial climate at the time of the study meant that many assumptions underlying earlier research on race attitudes, such as those associating separatist values with prejudice, had to be laid aside for conceptions more appropriate to a changing ideology.

White Racial Attitudes: A New Configuration?

While a plethora of studies have documented relationships between race attitudes [3] and behavioral or psychological variables, they were all performed when minorities were using peaceful means to secure full civil rights and integration into American society (Campbell and McCandless, 1951; Deutsch and Collins, 1951; Jahoda and West, 1951; Titus and Hollander, 1957; Christie and Cook, 1958; Yarrow, Campbell, and Yarrow, 1958; Selltiz and Cook, 1962; Cook, 1962; Williams, 1964; Peabody, 1966). During the years between 1930 and 1965, when many studies of racial attitudes were undertaken, attitudes that deviated from the ideal norms of rationality in making judgments, justice toward all, and tolerance, or "sympathetic identification with the underdog" were typically defined as prejudiced (Schuman and Harding, 1963). Writing in the early 1940s, Gunnar Myrdal (1964) produced a massive indictment of the discriminatory, castelike racial practices characterizing every American social institution. Arnold Rose (1947) published a book-length review of *Studies in the Reduction of Prejudice,* many of which made use of the rubric employed by Myrdal to evaluate the attitudes and other behaviors of white Americans. Not only was color-blindness generally considered to be the appropriate measure of lack of prejudice, but the appeal to conscience and rationality was frequently believed to be the key to attitudinal and behavioral change.

The striking contrast between these types of dimensions and the militant, separatist banners of 1968 makes clear why it was deemed necessary, for the present study, to develop an attitude measure tailored to the current situation. A series of items based both on the investigators' hunches and items drawn from Protest and Prejudice (Marx, 1967) were cast into a multiple-choice Race Questionnaire which was administered to all participants and controls several weeks before and a month after the encounter groups were conducted (see Table 13–1). Roughly, the major purposes of the Race Questionnaire were to measure "attitudes of acceptance toward blacks in general and toward current black activities and demands," as well as to gather associated information about the respondent's view of his own role in the contemporary scene, his social values and outlook on the future, and his emotional response to racial interactions. Items were included to permit definition of the respondent's ideological or political orientation as well as to provide insights into less transparent, deep-rooted personality variables related to the former.[4]

Since some items that formerly might have been used as indicators of prejudice against blacks (for example, a statement emphasizing cultural or biological differences) might in 1968 be indicators of identification with black liberation, no *a priori* judgments were made about whether particular items indicated a favorable or unfavorable stance toward blacks. Instead, items were factors analyzed to determine their organization and direction and to derive empirical summaries of race attitudes.[5]

The four factors emerging from this analysis accounted for 40 percent of the variance in responses to the Race Questionnaire. *Separatism / Black Power* grouped items directly related to the goals and strategies employed by black leaders on campus. *Personal Responsibility* expressed the white student's conception of his own role in racial matters on campus. *Mistrust* included expressions of fear or perceptions of hostility, alienation, distrust, or difference. *Liberalism* expressed faith in ideas and procedures which characterize a conventional liberal approach to racial issues.

In addition to these four factors, three other *a priori* attitude measures were used: an *Authoritarianism* scale (the F scale), a *Suspiciousness* scale ("I worry quite a bit about what people think of me; I am suspicious of people who try to be different from everybody else; I am suspicious of whites who try to help blacks"), and a *Militancy* scale (six items prefaced by the caption "The following are alternative means for accomplishing one's desired ends," and listing actions ranging from peaceful demonstrations to guerilla warfare). Information was also gathered on the respondent's activities related to black problems and black issues: the amount of time he spent in volunteer activities such as tutoring, and his friendships across interracial lines.

As indicated by the means presented in Table 13–1, the average white participant rejected separatism/black power concepts, but accepted personal responsibility for improving race relations and felt optimistic that gains could be made. He recognized the presence of interracial hostility and the possibility of interracial distrust; but he rejected the idea that he

383

TABLE 13-1

Race Questionnaire Items,[a] by Appearance in Factors

Separatism/Black Power Factor (Mean = 2.66)	Factor Loading Weights[b]
A "Black Studies Program" must be autonomous; that is, the program must be answerable only to itself and not to the college	+.69
The most meaningful path to "equal status" is separatism for blacks with things under their own control and direction	+.66
Black students ought to be able to have all-black dormitories if they want them	+.62
All administrators of a "Black Studies Program" must be black	+.61
Black students' demands to the college should be presented as "non-negotiable"	+.61
Standards should be lowered to admit any member of a minority group who wants a college education	+.61
I am against the use of destructiveness, abusive language, and the threat of violence	−.60
It is the responsibility of every white student to do everything he can to help the blacks on campus get what they say they want	+.56
I would be willing to have my tuition raised in order to support special programs for black students	+.48
I wouldn't marry someone of another race, not because I feel any prejudice but because in this society there would be so many problems to deal with	−.34

Personal Responsibility Factor (Mean = 3.27)	Factor Loading Weights[b]
Personally, I do not believe that there is anything I can meaningfully do to help make things better between blacks and whites	−.70
I came to college to get an education, not to solve the black-white problem	−.62
I would be willing to donate at least four hours per week tutoring minority group students admitted to this university who want assistance	+.55
I am getting fed up with this whole black-white issue	−.51
I am optimistic about some meaningful solution to racial problems on campus	+.37

Mistrust Factor (Mean = 2.62)	Factor Loading Weights[b]
With members of another race I still have the feeling that they don't really *trust* me	+.77
No matter what I do or say black students treat me as if I were a racist	+.72
I feel scared and intimidated by blacks	+.51
If I had to choose between a doctor of my own race and one of another race, when it comes to illness and trusting someone with my life, I'd choose a doctor of my own race	+.41
Only a black person can really understand another black	+.31

TABLE 13-1 (continued)

Liberalism Factor (Mean = 3.47)	Factor Loading Weights[b]
There should be no limit set on the number of black students admitted to any college or university	+.63
"Separatism" and "Black Nationalism" are short-run means to get power and respect, not long-term solutions to the black-white problem	+.49
Absolute equality in everything is the only solution to the black-white problem	+.42
The natural hairstyle is more attractive for black people than straightened hair	+.37
When groups like the Black Panthers carry firearms it is simply a threat and not truly serious	+.31

[a]Responses to all items were based on a five-point scale, ranging from strong agreement (5) to strong disagreement (1).

[b]A (−) designates that disagreement with the item was associated with the factor scale.

was considered a racist by blacks without regard to his behavior or that he was afraid of blacks. He expressed commitment to democratic procedures and equalitarian goals. On the three additional dimensions tested, the average respondent revealed himself to be nonauthoritarian, unsuspicious, and in favor of militancy.

An intercorrelation of the seven attitude measures indicated two main clusters: one included separatism/black power, militancy, and personal responsibility, and the other included suspiciousness, mistrust, and authoritarianism. Further, separatism/black power and suspiciousness were negatively correlated, as were militancy and suspiciousness, and personal responsibility and mistrust. The clusters represent a rough ordering of attitudes according to an ideology-personality trait classification. There was no significant link established, however, between authoritarian attitudes and overt opposition to conventional liberal positions. Instead, current black demands for militancy and separatism were negatively related to authoritarian personality characteristics, suggesting that the respondents expressed freedom from racial prejudice by sympathy for black power demands. The relatively high endorsement of militant tactics, evidenced in the present sample, is not congruent with the implications of earlier work on authoritarianism and racial prejudice. This reversal may reflect the changed ideological climate which accepted violence for the achievement of racial equity. Such ideas had virtually no expression among students in the 1950s. At that time, militancy was generally associated with totalitarianism and white supremacy. During the 1960s militancy had acquired positive value as a tactic for achieving racial equity.

The Intergroup Impact of Encounter

Change in social attitudes has been a goal and promise of sensitivity-training workshops since they were inaugurated on the American scene. The implication, too, had already been present that the increased interpersonal sensitivity included those of another race or culture, as well as other people like oneself. As Kahn (1963) put it, "the theory of T-groups implies that reduction in prejudice would be one of the results of a general increase in sensitivity to the needs of others and insight into one's own behavior as it affects others." While there has been little research bearing directly on the assumed linkage, such expectations have gained a great deal of implicit empirical support from the considerable body of literature which has established associations between interracial contact and positive interracial attitudes (Amir, 1969). A host of studies has suggested that intergroup contact leads to a reduction of stereotype and prejudice under certain conditions: when it occurs frequently; involves intimate, rather than casual, relations; involves persons of equal status or minority persons of high status; when it has institutional support; when it is pleasant or rewarding in outcome; and when the members of both groups are interacting in functionally important activities toward the achievement of common aims requiring their cooperation.

The racially mixed encounter groups at Stanford satisfied enough of these conditions to suggest the utility of comparing their effect on the attitudes of their white members with those induced in all-white groups. In addition, other aspects of the study had identified both individuals and groups which had been most successful in achieving personal growth, so that it was possible to ask whether such personal gains led to increased acceptance across racial lines, as some have suggested.[6] The presence of both a black and white leader of the racially mixed groups allowed another lens to be held up to questions which have been raised about the impact of the race of the person in authority on racial attitude change.[7] Finally, the data were amenable to the analysis of the effects of such differences as amount of emphasis on direct discussion of racial material, sex of the participant, and amount of formal or informal contact with blacks outside the encounter group.

Participation in the encounter group *per se* cannot be credited with the induction of viable attitude change (see Table 13–2). Neither participants nor controls underwent radical shifts from the favorable to the unfavorable stance, or vice versa, on any of the seven attitudinal dimensions. Before and after the encounter experience, both participants and controls favored militant tactics, felt personally responsible for improving race relations on campus, and endorsed the general principles of a liberal democratic philos-

386

TABLE 13-2

Effects of the Encounter Experience on Attitudes

	Encounter Groups (N = 154)	Controls (N = 63)	All White Groups (N = 128)	Black-White Groups (N = 26)	Black Leader (N = 6)	White Leaders (N = 20)	Much Race Content (N = 24)	Little Race Content (N = 30)	High Learning Groups (N = 39)	Low Learning Groups (N = 30)
General Attitudes										
Authoritarianism										
Time 1	19.7	19.7	19.8	19.4	20.7	19.4	19.6	19.8	19.7	19.9
Time 2	20.1	20.4	20.1	20.0	18.5	20.0	19.0	20.7	19.6	20.5
Militancy										
Time 1	19.3	18.3	19.6	18.2	20.8	17.2	20.5	19.7	20.6	19.6
Time 2	20.7	19.5	20.7	20.7	21.8	20.3	21.9	21.5	21.9	20.4
Suspiciousness										
Time 1	8.3	8.2	8.4	7.9	8.2	8.0	8.3	8.6	8.5	8.4
Time 2	8.5	8.4	8.5	8.6	9.0	8.8	8.7	8.4	8.8	8.6
Racial Attitudes										
Separatism/Black Power										
Time 1	27.4	25.8	27.5	26.7	27.8	25.1	28.7	27.9	29.8	26.3
Time 2	28.8	27.1	28.7	29.7[a]	27.5	28.8	30.0	29.6	30.3	27.1
Personal Responsibility										
Time 1	19.2	19.3	19.1	19.3	17.8	18.7	18.7	19.2	19.1	19.1
Time 2	18.5	18.9	18.4	19.0	17.5	18.4	18.0	19.1	18.8	17.3
Mistrust										
Time 1	13.1	13.6	13.3	12.4	9.5	12.9	13.8	13.0	13.0	13.9
Time 2	13.8	14.2	13.7	14.4[a]	10.5	14.1	13.3	14.0	13.8	14.3
Liberalism										
Time 1	17.1	17.4	17.2	16.5	18.7	16.5	17.4	16.7	17.2	17.5
Time 2	17.0	16.8	17.0	16.5	19.5	16.3	16.4	17.2	16.6	17.2

[a] $p < .05$.

ophy. Before and after involvement in the encounter groups, participants, like controls, were below midpoint on authoritarianism, suspiciousness, and mistrust and did not give substantial endorsement to black power demands. All this is to say that the experience in encounter groups demonstrated no effects that could not have occurred otherwise.

Racially mixed groups, however, did exhibit changes in racial attitudes, as compared with groups composed only of white students (see Table 13–2).[8] White students in racially mixed groups significantly increased in their support of separatism/black power and also in their mistrust, but students in all-white groups did not. White students in the racially mixed groups also evidenced substantially varied attitudes before they had been in the encounter groups, whereas after the encounter experience their attitudes followed a more organized pattern. They now saw negative relationships between separatism/black power and suspiciousness, between mistrust and personal responsibility, and between liberalism and authoritarianism, as well as maintaining the positive association they revealed in pretesting between separatism/black power and militancy. When the encounter groups which were successful[9] in effecting personal learning were compared with those which produced little personal change, no differences were revealed sufficient to support the expectation that such change could imply improved racial attitudes. Similarly, the amount of emphasis on racial content or the race of the leader was not signal in their impact on racial attitudes. Sex difference in racial attitudes change was also tested, but none was demonstrated.[10]

Now, what of the relationship between individual change via the encounter experience and racial attitude change? When changes in attitudes toward separatism/black power and mistrust, the two factors affected by participation in racially mixed groups, were correlated with thirty-three measures of individual change, only one variable was associated ($r = .19$) with separatism/black power, and only one ($r = .19$) with mistrust (see Table 13–3). Clearly, changes in racial attitudes were not associated with changes in the person's value-attitude system, his self-concept, or his concepts of other people, nor were they associated with particular personality traits, levels of pathology, or other dimensions. These findings leave no room to assume that there is any relationship between the achievement of personal change or learning in an encounter group and change in racial attitudes.

In summary, relative to the influence of encounter groups on attitudes of whites toward blacks, only one condition, mixed racial composition, proved effective. The simple fact of being in an encounter group is not enough, even for those people who evidence significant personal change. Nor does it matter if attention is particularly drawn to racial issues through such devices as discussion, role-playing, and so on, if no blacks are in the group. On the other hand, black leadership produced no more change than white leadership in groups of mixed racial composition. These findings are

TABLE 13-3

Outside Contact and Attitudes of White Students[b]

Attitudes	Race Course		Volunteer Work		Black Friend	
	Yes (N = 51)	No (N = 172)	Yes (N = 29)	No (N = 206)	Yes (N = 48)	No (N = 127)
General						
F Scale	18.7	19.8	19.5	19.6	19.7	19.7
Militancy	21.2	18.5	20.3	18.9	18.5	18.9
Suspiciousness	8.2	8.2	7.8	8.3	8.8	8.2
Race						
Black Power	30.6	25.6	31.0	26.0[a]	26.6	26.3
Personal Responsibility	19.7	19.0	20.9	18.8[a]	20.3	18.5
Mistrust	14.0	13.0[a]	13.5	13.2	12.3	12.7[a]
Liberalism	17.2	17.1	17.5	17.1	17.5	16.8

[a]$p < .05$.

[b]One-way analysis of variance scores were computed for each participant by unit-weighting and summing items, with sign as determined by the factor analysis. In addition to these, scores on the F Scale, Militancy, and Suspiciousness were obtained by summing values of items. A tabulation of other characteristics of the fifty-one students who took the Race and Prejudice course shows that only six of these claimed a friend of another race, only fifteen had contacts with blacks through volunteer activities, and only one claimed both.

supportive of the contact hypothesis which has been presented in earlier studies of racial attitudes.

Outside Encounter

The vigor of the contact variable, as opposed to all other experimental conditions that tested the influence of the encounter experience on interracial attitudes, calls forth the question of whether the effects which were demonstrated must be attributed to contact within the encounter context. This conclusion is hard to espouse *a priori*. The data available on the study participants allowed the effects of interracial contact within the encounter context to be compared with contact in three situations outside the group: through prior participation in the Race and Prejudice course, through volunteer activities (generally tutoring) to aid black students, and through a friendship with at least one black student.

The three contact variables were associated with several significant differences in response patterns as measured on the attitude scales at Time 1 (see Table 13–3). Those who claimed at least one close friendship across racial lines and who, therefore, may be assumed to have had an equal-status, informal, and intimate type of racial contact, looked essentially like liberal students did a college generation or so ago. They differed significantly in acceptance of personal responsibility and were lower in mistrust than their counterparts who claimed no friendships across racial lines.

Empathy for blacks was expressed as support for separatism/black power for the students who had taken the Race and Prejudice course and for the students who had tutored or done other volunteer work with blacks. Students who had had these experiences showed differences from those who had not in their support of separatism/black power. Students who participated in the Race course were also significantly lower in authoritarianism than those who had a volunteer work experience. In contrast, those who had done volunteer work felt significantly more personal responsibility than did the participants in the Race course.

Up to this point, the students who engaged in volunteer activities or who had the Race course looked like the hypothetical antiauthoritarian, who is open and unbiased in underlying personality characteristics and, similarly, sympathetic to blacks in surface ideological commitments. Their sympathy now encompassed an appreciation for the black liberation movement. Insofar as such a classical picture also attaches an expectation of trust and freedom from prejudice, an important difference obtained particularly in the students who were involved in the Race and Prejudice course. Like their counterparts in the mixed encounter group (and less like those who engaged in less combative forms of interracial contact) these students increased in mistrust at the same time that they expressed increasing identification with the prevailing black ideology in their support of separatism/black power and militance. Thus it appears that while contact explains and increases ability to understand black needs as determined by that group's own, rather than the white man's criteria, a distinction must be made between those situations where the conditions of contact are relatively benign and those where they involve confrontation and conflict. The data speak clearly that in the latter case alienating forces are set at work that are not witnessed in the former. It may be that the particular conditions of contact in the encounter groups and in the Race and Prejudice course simply brought to the fore fears that were always there but not formerly recognized.

Observer ratings of emotional climate fixed the mixed encounter group as more angry than the all-white encounter groups, despite the frequency of confrontative interaction noted for many of the white groups.[11] Although direct evidence was not available on the climate of the Race course, indications from the faculty responsible for the course were that angry outbursts were commonplace.

Implications

Psychological changes, even if profound, involving changes in a person's value structure, conceptions of self and of others, do not in and of themselves in today's world insure that the individual will alter his attitudes toward blacks. Perhaps the findings would have been different if the participants were not already committed to a liberal ideology; perhaps under such circumstances changes of the person would have affected racial attitudes. The message is clear, nevertheless, for a population similar to the one studied at Stanford, that experiential groups, encounter groups, cannot be expected to alter racial attitudes in and of themselves.

What about the effectiveness of encounter groups that bring together both blacks and whites? The findings are clear here also that only in mixed groups can encounter groups change racial attitudes. The question still remains whether such attitude changes as were observed are desirable. It seems reasonable to assume that the increase in positive attitudes toward separatism/black power indicates a greater identification with and perhaps a greater understanding of the black position in today's world. More difficult to understand and to evaluate is the increased mistrust or fear of blacks associated with participation in racially mixed encounter groups. Students who increased on this dimension were saying that "the members of another race are still of the feeling that they don't really trust me; no matter what I do or say, black students treat me as if I were a racist; I feel scared and intimidated by blacks. . . ."

The increased arousal of fear in white students as a consequence of such experience may represent an undesired outcome for many college administrators. An alternative understanding of this increase may be more appropriate, however. There is abundant evidence for the justification of black rage in our society; yet a group of liberally oriented middle- and upper-middle-class college students, such as those who participated in the encounter groups, may have had little prior experience with such feelings. Their awareness of the implications of the current black ideology and their "misunderstanding" of black feelings is perhaps more dangerous than the admission to themselves that they as whites are fearful of the feelings of blacks. Fear is perhaps a better or more useful affect than guilt.

It may very well be that what has occurred as a result of participating in the interracial encounter is that the white students were able to admit and verbalize fears that were there all the time. The data alone do not support one or the other of these interpretations of white students' increased mistrust of blacks. Correlations between scores on mistrust of black and all other variables used in the study, however, yield two of the four highest correlations with coping strategy. Those who had higher mistrust or fear of blacks tended to use adequate coping procedures and did not use defense mechanisms such as avoidance or denial; those who had more fear or mistrust of blacks perceived themselves as more adequate individuals. The correlations are small; however they do support a position that the increase in mistrust of blacks evidenced in the interracial encounter groups may represent a positive step for it is associated with perceptions of adequacy and of adequate coping and particularly with low use of avoidance or denial mechanisms.

What are the implications of these findings for policy on college campuses with regard to black-white relations? Identifiable attitude changes have been associated with interracial encounter groups. Is this a policy of choice? Should such groups be encouraged?

In the abstract, if one can accept a positive interpretation of the meaning of the changes, the answer would appear to be yes. It should be recalled, however, that the course in Race and Prejudice may have similar effects on racial attitudes, analogous to those of the encounter groups themselves.[12] Although the conclusion that it was the personal confrontational quality of the course, rather than the course content, is speculative, it is not lightly to be dismissed that the Race and Prejudice course had similar effects on the attitude system to those generated by highly experienced encounter leaders. It is as if the skills associated with such leaders made little difference. Positive results from racial encounters or confrontation, telling it like it is, exposing white students to black attitudes on a personal level, can occur without the skills and leavening of encounter leaders. On the basis of the evidence at hand, there is no unique or special role one can attribute to encounter groups in the area of racial attitudes. If it is the face-to-face confrontation that enabled these attitudes to change or induced these changes, many alternative contexts might be considered.

NOTES

NOTE: Credit and appreciation to Betty A. Goldiamond ("Social Determinants of Racial Attitudes, With Special Reference to the Effects of Encounter Group Experience." Ph.D. Dissertation, University of Chicago, December, 1971) for the data analysis and much of the writing presented here.

1. Only three groups contained black students from Stanford. The fourth, Synanon, was composed of Stanford white students and whites and blacks from Synanon.

2. During Spring Quarter, 1969, a group of black Stanford students ransacked the University bookstore.

3. Although systematic differences abound within social psychology in the definition of attitude, most investigators appear to be in accord with Kramer's (1949) omnibus definition of attitudes as dispositions to think, feel, and act in certain predictable ways toward particular stimulus objects.

4. These items will be recognized as from the F scale. While earlier research seeking to establish the link between authoritarian, antidemocratic traits and the overt expression of racial prejudice were not uniformly successful, Flowerman, *et al.* (1950) concluded that the F scale was a valid measure of prejudice; Goldstein (1952) confirmed that a general tolerance-prejudice factor exists and that an authoritarian syndrome closely associated with prejudice is "quite real." Campbell and McCandless (1951) reported that the F scale correlates substantially with a variety of prejudice measures, including ethnocentrism and xenophobia; and Steckler (1951), studying black college students, found a moderate covariance between anti-Negro, antiwhite, and ideological militancy-pacifism sentiments on the one hand and F on the other.

5. The factor analysis was based on the MESA 85 program, which provides a

varimax rotation with several options. Model 1, a principal components analysis which develops a correlation matrix with ones in the diagonal, was employed. The number of factors rotated is controlled by three input parameters: (1) the maximum number of factors to be considered for rotation was limited to five, (2) the minimum eigenvalue to be included in rotation of associated factors was set at 1.00, and (3) factors with less than three loadings greater than .30 were not rotated. With these restrictions, ten rotations resulted in varimax convergence. The factors obtained were uncorrelated with each other.

6. One study (Rubin, 1967) of black and white participants in a two-week long summer program in sensitivity training, which attempted to relate changes in self-acceptance to changes in "human-heartedness," found that those who increased most in self-acceptance increased significantly more in human-heartedness than those who decreased in self-acceptance or increased only a moderate amount.

7. Several studies have indicated that contact with high status minority group members has resulted in a reduction in stereotyping or prejudice toward other minority group members. In addition, in a recent review article summarizing racial "experimenter effects" in experimentation, testing, interviewing, and psychotherapy, Stattler (1970) concluded that "positive attitudes (of whites) toward blacks can be induced by a black experimenter or by a black-white experimenter team." The experimenters' race has been demonstrated to yield different effects in subjects' attitudes or preferences in several studies (Trent, 1954; Kraus, 1962; Freedman, 1967; Summers and Hammonds, 1966). Dreger and Miller (1968), in their review of comparative psychological studies of blacks and whites in the United States, 1959–1965, warn that it is "widely recognized that in ethnic attitude research the race of the experimenter or interviewer is a significant variable." On the other hand, Greenwald and Oppenheim (1968) concluded that the experimenters' race was not a significant variable affecting doll preferences of northern Negro children, and Morland (1966) failed to find experimenters' race a significant variable in a study investigating racial preferences of northern and southern Negro preschoolers.

8. A dissertation by Markley (1969), on the effects of interracial dormitory rooming at Northwestern University and Oberlin College, is directly relevant. The author reports that, while control subjects (white students rooming with other whites) moved toward attitudes favoring integration and cooperation in civil-rights work, the respondents who had black roommates changed in their attitudes in the direction of those of the black students. That is, they were more likely to (1) endorse black self-determination, (2) affirm the need for black power, and (3) feel that whites should leave Negro civil-rights work to Negroes and solve their own problems. They tended, with the blacks, to endorse lower class background as a better qualification than upper for governing the country and to view urban race riots as legitimate expressions of rage and violence.

9. Successful Groups: 2, 6, 8, 12; Unsuccessful Groups: 4, 5, 9, 10; High emphasis on racial content: 5, 6, 12. Low: 2, 3, 8.

10. Since sex effects have frequently been found in studies of racial prejudice, their failure to appear in the study is unexpected.

11. To test the hypothesis that the mixed encounter groups were characterized by combativeness, observer ratings of group climate were examined. Two scales were appropriate, the degree of tension and amount of anger. The racially mixed encounter groups were contrasted (t test) with all white encounter group; on a seven-point scale Tense—Relaxed, mixed had a mean of 3.8 (low score = more tension), all white, 4.1. These differences were not significant. On the scale Angry—Harmonious, mixed, 3.5; all white 4.3, significance at a $p \leq .05$. Data suggest that the mixed groups were characterized as being more angry but not necessarily more tense.

12. Comparisons between the encounter group effects on attitudes and the Race course's are, at best, speculative. In the former, change could be assessed, while the latter involved only a Time 1 comparison between students who took the course and those who did not. Thus, the "effects" of the course are only speculative and indirect.

CHAPTER *14*

Processes of
Maintaining Change

WITH JAN ALLEN

Educators and clinicians both puzzle over why changes endure in some and not in others, yet little systematic attention has been given to explaining what influences the maintenance of change. Of the forty-eight study participants who showed clear gains when the encounter groups were ended (for whom Time 3 data were available) thirty-seven (77 percent) had maintained the changes, while for the rest the changes achieved were evanescent. A year after the encounter groups were ended, a group of participants were studied who at termination had appeared to profit from the encounter groups. The interest was to explore how Maintainers differed from Nonmaintainers—in personal characteristics and in their experiences during or subsequent to their participation in the groups. Did Maintainers do anything different from Nonmaintainers? Did they develop strategies for maintaining change, for example? Or were Maintainers and Nonmaintainers different kinds of people before they entered the groups?

A provisional definition of visible learners was established because the study of maintenance was executed before the outcome classifications presented in Chapter 3 were developed. A year after the groups terminated, thirty-four participants were identified who had given high positive testimony at the end of the groups and who at that time had also been rated by their leader or coparticipants as high positive changers.[1] Of these, thirty were interviewed; four more who were unavailable for interview filled out a questionnaire based on the interview format. Each interview was tape recorded and a rater evaluated how much each respondent had used or undergone any of twelve processes which had been tentatively identified as possibly relevant to maintenance of change.

The maintenance interview [2] consisted of three parts: (1) Several changes the student had reported at Time 2 were introduced; he was asked to talk about the kinds of things he felt had encouraged him to maintain the changes or to return to old patterns; (2) the student was asked to rank statements which represented the maintenance variables according to their importance and then explain his choices; (3) the student was presented with a hypothetical situation in which he was asked to give advice about maintaining change to a person who was just finishing an encounter group.

The Variables

Lacking previously developed theoretical guidelines to aid in the identification of salient dimensions of maintenance, twelve processes or maintenance variables were tentatively posited, drawn from earlier interviews and observations of the study groups and participants, clinical hunches of colleagues derived from their experience with maintenance processes, two pilot studies, and selected psychotherapy literature, e.g., Kelman, 1963; Hobbs, 1962.

The twelve variables represent different conceptual levels and are not mutually exclusive. Furthermore they are not defined as necessarily enhancing maintenance. As some of the illustrations suggest, certain phenomena may suppress or discourage maintenance. The twelve variables were categorized into four areas: active behavior, reinforcement, cognition, and psychological characteristics of the person.

ACTIVE BEHAVIOR

Experimenting. This included any active behavior (practice, effort, trial and error) of the participant to utilize what he learned or experienced in the encounter group. Participants often reported that trying out new responses, such as interpersonal openness, involved considerable risk and thought.

You also do have to work on changing your behavior, you have to make a conscious effort.

Take whatever you've learned and use it.

In addition to hard work and risk, experimenting also had its rewards. Referring to his relationship with a girlfriend, one participant said:

We made more of a conscious effort to experiment with things, about being honest, and saying how we really felt at the moment, and this has brought us so much closer.

Refinement. Closely related to experimenting, this variable refers to the adjustment or modification of new responses. It takes time to consolidate new responses; one must often tone them down and take into consideration the appropriateness of the time and place and responses of other people before they can be integrated constructively into one's way of life. In interviews participants mentioned adjustment, getting perspective, achieving a balance, and patience. Participants related humorous accounts of overly enthusiastic behavior, of coming on too strong after the encounter groups. Some used the movie *Bob and Carol and Ted and Alice* as an illustration.

Well, I would say one thing . . . not to rush into, let's say the postgroup period, overenthusiastically, like I almost did, just run around freaking out. Because, man, that's what you really look like you're doing after coming out of one of those things. I kind of even put off a few people, just because I was saying "Oh, no, you're wrong. That's no way to think, that's uptight. That's negative and we should be positive," and all that sort of shit. There are deeper things you learn in the group than just the immediate. I would say just play it cool and keep that stuff in mind. . . . When you're starting to feel screwed up in about a month, which you will, just try and keep those in your head.

I'd like to emphasize that I don't believe in being completely honest . . . because as I found out, in this type of a living situation I really believe in tact. . . . I think you should try to think what you're going to say and decide, "Well, gee, I'm in a bad mood right now," you know, and not say it. Or say it and say, "I'm in a really bad mood, this could be the reason why I'm saying this," you know, rather than saying something harmful and really not meaning it at all. . . . You have to understand the other person, too, how he's going to react, and if he understands what you're talking about.

Both these examples evidence cognitive activity, overt behavior, and an ability to perceive the consequences of behavior and modify it accordingly.

Spontaneous Orientation. Some participants reacted negatively to the concept of planning for or working on change. They stressed the importance of acting on new learnings, but in contrast to experimenting and planning, they emphasized action as a naturally occurring, spontaneous, unthought-out process. They explicitly devalued cognitive, reflective, or practice-oriented behavior, and gave the impression that they were starting to function in new ways very naturally by just flowing with it, just "doing it."

I find it much better to just kind of live it without thinking, just kind of let yourself come out in whatever happens.

Just do it whenever you have the opportunity. If some situation comes along and you think "Well, I ought to do that and assert myself," or something like that, then you ought to go and do it instead of thinking about it.

I have doubts about working on changes. I don't think that the kind of change involved here can be worked upon.

I really object to the whole notion of working on it, because it's not like school work . . . that you learn it and then go work on it or something. It's sort of a, more of a, change in what you are and how you react, and you either remain that way and keep acting that way, or you don't . . .

Talking with Others. This variable included talking in depth with others about experiences in the group and their impact on the person, feelings about the group, changes made, and experiences since in maintaining changes. In most cases, participants felt discussion with others was useful for getting perspective on the experience, sorting out what had happened since the group, reflecting on new behavior, or exploring it further. Sometimes experiences were shared with others who had also been in encounter groups.

I'd also get together with someone I'm very close to who was also in Synanon, and we'd discuss and compare the effects we'd been having on people . . . he found very similar reactions. He would confront people even more strongly than I would. It was very helpful because we both found the same thing . . . rejection.

Right after the group I talked to three or four more people who were not in my group but in other groups. We sort of compared notes and talked really deeply about how we'd changed and things. It was really sort of a uniting feeling, because we were definitely at a deeper level of communication than I have ever achieved with those particular people.

REINFORCEMENT

Reactions of Other People. Participants described specific reactions which other people had to them as they tried out new behavior after the encounter group. They also emphasized the importance of obtaining support or encouragement from others.

I've had a positive experience with a lot of my friends . . . I'm making it sound like it was really easy to start being honest with people, and it isn't; I mean it was a little bit scary too. But my experiences have just been positive.

The only factor I guess that would make a difference are the people you're with. If you put yourself with people that have no sensitivity to what you've learned or what you've become, then you'll probably lose it. But if you're with people that at least respect that and are willing to try to be that way too, you'll probably be happier.

Sometimes I blurted out something that I felt about some person right at that moment, I mean he was almost stunned that I even said it . . . it'd be some kind of situation where all of a sudden I would be really uncomfortable with what that person was saying, and I would say, "I don't particularly like what you're saying and I don't feel very good about you right now," and he would sort of shake his head and say, "What? What's that got to do with anything?" And a couple of experiences like that and I became a bit more hesitant about saying what I was thinking or feeling.

Self / Intrinsic. Some participants answered the question, "What helped you keep up that change?" with statements like, "I just feel better," "I'm just happier being that way," or "Relationships conducted this way are so much better that they naturally continue." Apparently these participants saw changes, especially those in interpersonal relationships, as intrinsically rewarding or as creating psychological states which were rewarding. The variable is based on the psychological principle that if a behavior or set of circumstances result in feelings such as happiness, satisfaction, "feeling better," such states would in turn reinforce the behavior which produced them. Some students called newly adopted responses "self-reinforcing."

Some of these things you just kind of do, like they're so good you just pick them up and keep on doing them.

I like to understand, and it makes me much happier when I can understand the other person's side, I feel so much better than being narrow-minded.

Impact of Discrete Events. Often a significant external event occurred which the participant believed had an important influence on whether or not he maintained learning and change. Examples included getting married, going to Europe, changing majors, developing a philosophy of life, political events. Sometimes the events were fortuitous; sometimes they were the result of decisions growing out of the participant's experiences in the encounter group.

Impact of the Environment. Many participants mentioned the *lack* of positive reinforcement from the normal environment. They described how easy it was for the group experience to become remote and for them to fall into a rut. Some participants conveyed the sentiment that there was a cold, indifferent, and immovable world out there which is hard to counteract.

That type of bubbly enthusiasm . . . gets cooled quickly in a dorm or fraternity atmosphere where you're back in the normal routine of things.

In daily life, you can't be blatantly honest all the time . . . I don't know exactly what it is, if in the outside world you have to rely more on dishonesty and playing games or what. I almost hate to admit that that's the way it is but it seems more comfortable if you do that . . . I kept running into these disappointments and frustrations and realized that the outside world just isn't the same as the encounter group."

COGNITION

Group As Referent. Some participants associated their current life situations and some aspect of the encounter group experience, such as an event which took place in the group, a particular group member or the leader, or some psychological issue.

You can draw a sort of analogy between the situation in the group and the situation outside of the group, and the group situation gives you a kind of start for this.

The function of these associations was usually stated quite explicitly. Some involved the memory of an incident which the student still used as the basis for insight or generalization. One student recalled the way in which a man and a woman in his group had worked through some knotty problems in their relationship. As he thought about this later, the student realized that one source of conflict was their inability to listen to each other, and he has become more aware of his own tendency not to listen to others.

The memory of certain group situations sometimes functioned as a model for current behavior:

I would flash back to the group situation, like I would be talking to someone who is either asking me for advice, was confused about an issue, or talking about maybe something personal, or something he had to do in his life, like making decisions. I would think back to the group where we turned something like that out to the group and got all sorts of suggestions . . . I would think back to the group and remember the importance of getting a lot of things said.

It made me much more aware of an emotional level of existence which I have flashed back on and compared myself with. You know at times when I'll be in a certain situation I'll compare myself to how it was in the encounter group situation and that kind of emotional existence.

Although students usually reported that incidents from the group would flash into mind spontaneously, for some referring back to the group sometimes involved more sustained thought and reflection.

Analysis and Thought. This variable refers to thinking about or analyzing current feelings, situations, or behavior which are connected in some way with the maintenance of change. The emphasis is on reflection, introspection, and trying to understand, and can include the assumption of a general diagnostic stance toward certain problems or the application of a particular psychological model to a situation.

The way I maintained that was just by thinking about it consciously when I'm in that situation . . . conscious awareness of what you want to change is important, just keep that in mind.

It's OK to react, but at the same time you have to put aside reaction a little bit and look at it, and say, "What's really happening here is . . .

Like the technique of my leader was partly Transactional Analysis, the Parent-Child type thing. And sometimes when I'm really confused about things I stop and ask myself, "What the hell is making me do that? My God, is it a response to all the shitty things my mother did to me as a kid . . . or was it a response that I'm making of my own accord?" That's a fairly complicated theory and I didn't learn it totally by him explaining it for an hour or two during the group, but it kind of gave me some guidelines to go on. It does help a bit and makes you think back.

As this last example illustrates, some of this analytic activity had been taught and encouraged in the encounter group; in this sense, it can be seen as a group outcome in its own right.

Planning for Change. This variable refers both to specific plans the participant formulated to effect learning or change, and to a general intention to act on change or learning after the group. For some, the idea of making plans evoked negative reactions; they felt that deliberate planning violated the spirit of the encounter group; they stressed the natural, spontaneous occurrence of new behavior after the group. Others felt, in retrospect, that some planning would have been helpful in maintaining change.

I probably said at one time or another when I was still very emotionally involved with this and just coming down off that into the routine, I probably said, you know, like, "I've made some major changes and I'm going to keep up with them," and I think if I'd been pressed at that time to say what my plans were, if there were any that were very well thought out, that were objective, then I probably could have carried them out.

PSYCHOLOGICAL ASPECTS

Personal Characteristics. This variable refers to aspects of the person's makeup which he feels have affected the process of change maintenance. Some participants, during the interview, suggested that certain traits they possessed helped or hindered their ability to maintain change. Most of the examples were stated as having a positive effect on maintenance, e.g., flexibility, or a commitment to growth.

Findings

The tape recorded interviews were rated for the presence of each of the twelve variables of change maintenance.[3] Findings are presented in Table 14–1 for the total sample (N = 34) as well as the reduced sample (N = 23, seventeen Maintainers and six Nonmaintainers). The smaller sample can be treated with greater confidence, inasmuch as the Nonmaintainer sample is more precisely defined.

Maintainers did more about maintaining change in several ways: first, more Maintainers experimented with new behavior than Nonmaintainers. More Maintainers also made attempts to refine new responses in light of the kinds of reactions those responses evoked. They gave the impression that this was a complex, ongoing process which demanded the ability to perceive and reflect on the consequences of a trial run, and then to decide about how the behavior should be adjusted. Refinement seemed to be a transitional process which occurred for a time while new responses were being more comfortably worked in with the person's life style. (The actual

TABLE 14-1

Number of Subjects Mentioning Importance of Twelve Maintenance Processes

Variable	Maintainers (N = 17)	Nonmaintainers (N = 17)	Significance Level Maintainers (N = 17)	Significance Level Nonmaintainers (N = 6)
Behavioral				
Experimenting	10	5	.17	.10
Refinement	6	2	.11	.12
Spontaneous Orientation	5	6		
Talking with Others	5	1	.09	.18
Reinforcing				
Reactions from People	10	8		
Self/Intrinsic Rewards	12	7	.17	.13
Impact of Events	13	7	.08	.02
Impact of Environment	5	8		
Cognitive				
Group As Referent	4	3		
Analysis and Thought	8	5		
Plans	4	2		
Personal Characteristics	4	0	.05	

process was of course not as conscious and deliberate as this discussion makes it sound; however, all these elements seemed to be involved.)

More Maintainers talked in depth to others about the changes that they had experienced. These conversations about the encounter group and its outcome seemed like active attempts to assimilate the group experience or to work toward an understanding of what had happened since the group. Clearly, these were more than simple conversations; students described discussions which touched upon profound personal issues, involving self-disclosure, rejection, and risk.

The words "changes" and "new behavior" have been used in a general way thus far. Although students talked about a variety of changes they had made, the one which stood out most clearly in their descriptions was "openness," and it was in reference to openness that participants most often experimented and refined new behavior after the group.

More Maintainers reported that important things had happened since the group ("Impact of Events") which had affected whether or not changes were maintained. The events were not described as incidents which just happened to the person. The participants seemed to take an active stance toward important events, rather than being the passive recipients of reinforcement. Even in cases where the event was disruptive or painful, students were able to do something about what was happening to them. For example, one student's brother was killed in a traffic accident. The student was able to express his feelings about the loss to his friends; something new for him, and something which he said he had learned in the group.

This eased the stress he was experiencing, and enabled him to be more understanding of his parents' need for his support.

In other cases, the event had been initiated by the student himself, often as the result of a major decision which was influenced by the group experience:

I came to grips with myself about last spring and summer, that swimming was taking me away from people, and that's where I wanted to be. Like I was out swimming in the morning, swimming in the afternoon, exhausted in the evening, and what kind of relationships can you have with people when you're exhausted all the time and gone all the time? I just couldn't stand that any more . . . I was getting into myself and realizing why I was trying to win races and be competitive and all that sort of thing. I'm kind of out of swimming now and I am confident about that decision.

This student lost a stipend for withdrawing from athletics; the decision to quit was a major event for him, the concrete expression of a change in values. Perhaps the main point to be made here is that major events did not stand alone as happenings which simply reinforced the maintenance of change either positively or negatively. Students were proactive; they worked with the events, often drawing upon what they had learned in the encounter group to enable them to deal with an event or to initiate it.

Somewhat more Maintainers than Nonmaintainers talked about positive feeling states (e.g. "feeling better," "being more satisfied") resulting from new behavior, or the intrinsic worth of new ways of interacting. Simply put, certain types of behavior seemed to be self-rewarding. Maintainers expressed pride and exhilaration at being able to behave in ways which they have long regarded as desirable and praiseworthy. This may be associated with the stance Maintainers took in regard to trying out new behavior, and the intrinsic reward they felt from these trials.

Thus, based upon the findings presented in Table 14–1, experimenting, refinement, talking with others, self/intrinsic rewards, and impact of events were characteristic strategies of Maintainers. It is clear from Table 14–1 that a number of the strategies and events thought to be implicated in maintenance were reported more frequently by the Maintainers than the Nonmaintainers. Table 14–2, which shows that approximately twice as many Nonmaintainers reported no experiences in the active and cognitive areas, provides more dramatic evidence of the different use of maintenance strategies in the two groups.

In addition to learning about participants' actual experiences with maintenance, the interviews were analyzed for factors which they thought influenced maintenance in general. Participants were asked to give advice about how to maintain change to a hypothetical friend who had just finished a group experience. Occasionally participants also volunteered some generalizations gleaned from personal experiences since the group. These statements were tested for differences between Maintainers and Nonmaintainers. Except for two areas, Maintainers and Nonmaintainers seem to

TABLE 14-2

Frequency of Maintenance Processes

	None	1	2	3	4
Active Behavior					
Maintainers (N = 17)	3	7	3	3	1
Nonmaintainers (N = 17)	8	7	1	1	0
Reinforcing Variables					
Maintainers (N = 17)	0	4	4	7	2
Nonmaintainers (N = 17)	3	4	6	3	1
Cognitive Variables					
Maintainers (N = 17)	5	6	5	0	
Nonmaintainers (N = 17)	10	4	3	0	

have held similar views of what influences the maintenance process. Both groups stressed the importance of others' reactions, talked about the importance of experimenting, and so forth. More Maintainers, however, stressed the importance of thinking about or reflecting on what one is doing about change, of pausing to analyze problem situations, and so forth ("Analysis and Thought", p = .02). One Maintainer gave this advice to a hypothetical friend:

I'd probably advise him to be moderately reflective about himself, you know, and sometimes take time out to just think about things, and problems he had, and try to get back to the root of the problem . . . you know, be fairly analytical.

In contrast, more Nonmaintainers stressed the impact of the environment on change (p = .04). They emphasized the view that a person could be squelched or supported by a broad, undifferentiated force ("Impact of Environment") which he does not direct or could not counteract. The Maintainers, in other words, stressed an active internal process rather than one in which the person is simply the passive recipient of influence.

These data seem to indicate that Maintainers and Nonmaintainers dealt with the task of maintaining change in different ways. Maintainers were both more proactive and more cognitive in their posture toward maintenance. Experimenting, refinement, and talking with others all involve an interaction between overt behavior and cognitive activities such as recognizing and assessing the consequences of trying out a new response. It should be stressed that the interaction between outward behavior and cognition is important. Neither cognitive activity alone (as represented by the three cognitive variables) nor action without reflection ("Spontaneous Orientation") were related to successful maintenance.

The study of maintenance variables demonstrated that the Maintainers and Nonmaintainers behaved differently after the group, but does not explain how such differences came about. Three hypotheses were explored which might account for Maintainer-Nonmaintainer differences: (1) that maintenance was linked to certain group characteristics; (2) that Maintainers and Nonmaintainers had different kinds of experiences in the encounter group; (3) that Maintainers and Nonmaintainers were different kinds of people before they entered the group.

Since these analyses did not depend on interviews, all Maintainers (N = 36) and Nonmaintainers (N = 18) were used, as defined by the outcome classification system presented in Chapter 3.

(1) It seems unlikely that successful maintenance is linked to certain group characteristics since data reported in Chapters 3 and 7 indicate that Maintainers were fairly evenly distributed across the groups.

(2) Maintainers and Nonmaintainers were compared on the mechanisms of learning described in Chapter 12, using the same statistical technique. Two variables significantly differentiated the two groups.[4] More Maintainers than Nonmaintainers reported experimenting with new behavior during the group (p = .02). More Maintainers reported incidents involving active insight (p = .02), that is, insight which was generated by something the person himself did. Although it is not possible to establish a causal relationship, it is striking that a subset of Maintainers reported similar processes in postgroup life (that is, experimenting and refining new behavior, and the importance of cognitive activity in the maintenance process). In the same way that cognitive activity involved thinking about the consequences of one's experimental efforts after the group, active insight during the group may have been a consequence of experimenting. Not only was active insight associated with positive change, but it discriminated even further in the sense that it separated out the long-term learners (Maintainers).

(3) Thirty-seven indices assessing attitudes, expectations, values, psychopathology, personality traits, and conception of others were analyzed to explore whether Maintainers and Nonmaintainers were different kinds of people before they entered the encounter group. Table 14–3 lists the five statistically significant differences found between the Maintainers and Nonmaintainers. (See Chapter 10 for a complete list of the variables and a description of the statistical technique employed.) Two differences were found in the area of *Expectations and Attitudes*. When they entered the encounter groups, Maintainers saw themselves as lacking sensitivity to others' feelings and lacking understanding of their own feelings. In contrast, Nonmaintainers rated themselves as very sensitive in these two areas, in fact as more sensitive than any of the other outcome groups. Nonmaintainers also perceived encounter groups as potentially very dangerous, whereas Maintainers acknowledge some danger, but not an extreme amount. In the area of personal values, the Nonmaintainers place a significantly greater emphasis on growth and development than Maintainers. This orientation toward personal growth also articulates with certain encounter group values. Thus, the Nonmaintainers entered the group already "in tune" with

TABLE 14-3
Personal Characteristics Prior to Group

Variable	Mean		Level of Significance
	Maintainers	Nonmaintainers	
Expectations and Attitudes			
Feeling Sensitivity	−.285	.083	.09
Safety/Danger	26.2	24.9	.09
Values			
Growth	18.5	34.1	.06
Interpersonal			
Wanted Affection	6.3	4.8	.05
Positive View of Best Friend	31.7	29.7	.02

group values; they had two pieces of "basic equipment" which Maintainers seemed to lack. Maintainers and Nonmaintainers were most different in their approach to interpersonal relationships. Maintainers held a more positive view of their best friends, and they were more willing to accept affection from other people.

Implications

What have these investigations established about maintenance? In the post-group period Maintainers clearly behaved differently toward their learning. This difference was not related to the particular group they were in since the incidence of maintenance and nonmaintenance was distributed across groups. There were, however, some interesting Maintainer/Nonmaintainer differences in pregroup attitudes and values and in the mechanisms of change used during the group experience.

Before entering the group, the Maintainers perceived themselves as being deficient in both understanding of their own feelings, and sensitivity to others' feelings. Furthermore they were less "growth oriented" than Nonmaintainers and perceived encounter groups as moderately risky, in contrast to Nonmaintainers who viewed them as exceedingly dangerous. One might consider whether in some basic areas the Maintainers experienced dissonance in the encounter group, because encounter group values emphasize personal and interpersonal sensitivity and personal growth. The Nonmaintainers, who felt satisfied with themselves in these areas, may have felt more comfortable in the group.

Although perceiving themselves as deficient in certain important interpersonal skills, the Maintainers appeared to be more open to influence in an interpersonal situation. Their readiness to accept affection from others and their perception of others as positive and benign suggest that they may have been better prepared to work in the interpersonal context of the group. In what way these personal characteristics of Maintainers may have enabled them to utilize the groups differently from the Nonmaintainers is open to several possible interpretations. It is clear, however, that the Maintainers were more likely to use experimentation and active insight as learning processes. Perhaps they made heavier use of these processes in the group because they were more comfortable about interpersonal situations, as well as more motivated by feelings of interpersonal sensitivity.

There is a tentative implication in these findings more *useful than any specific findings:* that participants can do something about maintaining change after the group. Although the findings hint that successful maintenance may be enhanced by certain aspects of personal makeup, they imply no necessary link. It is theoretically possible for a member to engage in some of the activities discussed (for example, experimenting, refinement) whether or not he has some of the personal characteristics that were associated with maintenance.

Perhaps the main implication of this study is that the chances are that one will not naturally maintain what was gained from an encounter group experience. A participant needs to take action, to try out new ways of being, to think about the consequences of his new behavior, and so forth. The kinds of activities which seem to promote successful maintenance do go against the grain of some strongly held encounter group values. Action which also calls for conscious effort and thought may seem at face value to clash with the values which cluster around spontaneity. Such a clash is not inevitable. The students who described these reflective processes as instrumental to their success did not report them as severely inhibiting spontaneity or expressivity.

NOTES

1. This selection procedure actually yielded fifty-eight students; only thirty-five, however, could be reached for interviewing. (One of these thirty-five was a previously undetected Casualty, and was deleted from the maintenance sample.) Later analysis of the remaining thirty-four participants who comprised the maintenance sample revealed that twenty-three met the final criteria for positive change presented in Chapter 3. Of these twenty-three, seventeen maintained their change at Time 3 according to the same criteria. The eleven remaining visible learners (who perceived themselves and who leaders and peers perceived as having made substantial positive changes in the groups) neither met the index criteria of positive change nor maintained change at Time 3 according to interviews or their own testimony. Separate analyses of the group of seventeen and the group of eleven yielded findings comparable to those for the group of thirty-four, as is seen later in the chapter.

2. See Jan Allen, "Maintenance of Change after Encounter Groups," unpublished Ph.D. Dissertation, Department of Psychology, The University of Chicago, 1972, for

a detailed description of the interview and a review of literature pertinent to the maintenance variables.

3. To ascertain reliability of the maintenance variables a second rater coded ten interviews which had been randomly preselected using a statistic developed especially for nominal category systems, a reliability coefficient of .76 was obtained. (See Cohen, 1960.)

4. For the comparison, all those who learned were divided into Maintainers and Nonmaintainers. Recall that the group of learners could be distinguished from others who were unchanged or experienced negative outcome. Given the previous finding that those who learned were different, the possibilities of further distinguishing among the learners is obviously limited.

CHAPTER 15

Structured Exercises

WITH SUSANNE DRURY

The popular usage of structured exercises represents a curious source of dissonance within a movement defined by the theme of humanism and geared toward transcending the depersonalizing processes of a production-line culture. And, indeed, as a solution to an existential problem, these prescribed experiences have aroused heady controversy. Argyris (1967), the most outspoken critic of this form of packaged learning, insists that prescriptive leader interventions lead to an unproductive learning climate and to unstable gains. Others claim that structured exercises are effective in producing changes and are better than letting the group members spend many sessions groping aimlessly and uncertainly for some understanding of the ways they habitually behave (Fagan, 1970).

For many encounter leaders and consumers, structured learning experiences symbolize the encounter movement. Since such prescriptions for leader intervention have become readily obtainable through manuals such as *Joy* (Schultz, 1967),[1] untold numbers have been encircled by their co-participants, closed their eyes, and let themselves fall backwards, as an exercise in trust.

As is all too common in this field, no empirical evidence exists that might help settle the issue. In this chapter, the use of structured exercises is examined in relation to how much people learn, what they learn, and how lasting the learning is. It should be evident from the preceding chapters that it is often difficult to find simple relationships between what a leader does and what participants take away from the group. Accordingly, in the present discussion, structured exercises are examined not only in terms of their effects on outcome; such dimensions as climate and cohesiveness are also examined in relationship to the use of structured exercises in order to elucidate how the use of structured exercises influences conditions thought to be important to encounter group learning.

Analytic Procedures

A structured exercise was defined as a leader intervention that includes a set of specific orders or prescriptions for behavior. These orders limit the participant's behavioral alternatives. If a leader said, for example, "Go around the room and tell each member of the group what you think of his behavior in the last twenty minutes," he would have outlined a structured exercise. The behavioral sequence by which interpersonal interaction will occur has been specified. A group member can choose to carry out the exercise or not, but if he does the exercise, the behavioral alternatives available to him are limited by the instructions. If a leader said, "What do you think of what the other group members have been doing in the last twenty minutes?", he was not considered to be introducing an exercise. The content of the interpersonal transaction has been specified, but the participant may choose the process of the interaction. He might talk about how he sees one member of the group; he might describe his feelings about the group in general to the leader; or he might address comments to several group members.

Some leader interventions are very clearly structured exercises. For example, when a leader sets up a psychodrama, assigning roles as "alter egos" to group members and asking the protagonist to set the scene, he has specified the actions through which the group members will work on their problems. If the leader asks the group members to pick partners and share with the partner what they fear the most, what they like the most, and what they like the least, he controls the process of the interaction. Group members will interact in pairs; the pairs will be chosen in some specified way; the pairs will interact for a specified length of time; each pair will discuss the same content.

In some interventions that involve a single person in interaction with the group or one other group member, it may be more difficult to judge whether the leader is specifying the action. In the present study, an intervention that could be rephrased as a question was not called a structured exercise even if it was phrased in the imperative. For example, a leader saying, "Name three things you are afraid of," would not be counted as a structured exercise because it could be translated as "What three things are you afraid of?" If the leader said "Tell John three things you are afraid of," the instruction was considered an exercise because the leader specified the actions to accompany the answer to the question.

Structured exercises may be primarily verbal or primarily nonverbal; they may prescribe activities for all of the group members or for only one or two group members; they may intend change for all of the group members or primarily one person. These dimensions were used to distinguish four types of exercises. Psychodrama exercises were added as a fifth type because they are treated as a special type of exercise in the literature.

In "group nonverbal exercises," the whole group does something without talking. Group members may be asked to pay attention to bodily or sensory information, to arrange themselves into a statue that represents feelings about the group, to follow another group member while blindfolded, to mill around the room without talking, and greet other group members nonverbally, or to pick the person who feels the most distant and stare at him.

Exercises in which members of the group all give each other feedback or all have a fantasy around a theme were classified as "verbal group" exercises. They often involve the group forming into subgroups with part of the group observing while another part interacts.

"Psychodramas" are activities in which the leader sets up a role-playing scene involving two or more people, such as one group member as himself in interaction with the leader or another member as his parent. Psychodramas may also be directed toward the learning of the whole group. In one psychodrama, the group members took the roles of blacks and whites and staged a confrontation as a way to learn more about their "racist feelings." [2]

"Group-on-individual" exercises are activities in which the whole group interacts with one member on his individual problem. This category includes either verbal and nonverbal exercises, such as the group members massaging one member, the group giving feedback to one member, or the group lifting and rocking one group member.

"Individual" exercises are activities directed toward one or two group members. For example, arm-wrestling between two group members, one person going around and expressing his feelings about each group member, or role-playing activities in which the protagonist plays all the roles.

Structured exercises are only one of a number of ways that a group leader controls the interaction in his group. Questions explicitly structure the content of the group interaction and implicitly demand certain kinds of behavior. Regardless of the style in which they are introduced, however, structured exercises are the most explicit way in which a group leader dictates how the time in the group will be spent. In groups where many exercises are used, the leader has more control over what the group will do in a given block of time.

There were two sources of data on differentiating the study groups in terms of the use of structured exercises. Observer records of leader statements provided information about the number of exercises each leader introduced. The number of exercises introduced in each of the nine groups in this sample [3] was counted by collecting all of the leader statements recorded by observers that fit the definition of a structured exercise. Since exercises varied a great deal in complexity, it was thought that the number of exercises introduced might not accurately reflect the predominance of

TABLE 15-1

Number of Exercises Introduced,

Their Predominance, and Psychological Saliency

Leader Type	Group Number and Group	Average Exercises Introduced per Session	Complex Individual	Simple Group	Psychodrama	Complex Group	Weighted Average Types of Exercises per Session	Proportion of Critical Events Cited As Exercises
F	10 Esalen Eclectic	5.2	11	10	1	16	7.1	40
A	3 Gestalt	4.9	6	2	1	11	4.8	39
	12 Eclectic Marathon	2.1	0	2	0	10	4.0	51
C	11 Rogerian Marathon	2.0	1	1	8	8	4.7	24
B	1 T-group	1.6	3	2	0	3	1.4	12
C	2 T-group	2.5	6	5	0	3	2.5	6.5
C	5 Psycho-drama	1.2	0	2	7	1	1.9	7
E	7 Psycho-analytic	0	0	0	0	0	0	0
B	8 Transactional Analysis	.9	2	0	0	2	.8	16.5

structured exercises in a group's interaction. Weights were therefore assigned to each exercise on the basis of the judged amount of time they would ordinarily take. Simple individual exercises were weighted zero; simple group and complex individual exercises, one; psychodrama exercises, two; and complex group exercises, three.

The second source of data about the centrality of structured exercises in a group was the number of times that members saw structured exercises as critical group events, that is the psychological salience of structured exercises in a given group.

Table 15–1 shows the average number of exercises introduced per session; the number of complex individual, simple group, psychodrama, and complex group exercises; a weighted average number of exercises per session; and the proportion of all events cited as important that were structured exercises.

Based on the predominance of exercises in the group interaction and the psychological salience of exercises in each group, four groups were designated as high exercise groups (#3, #10, #11, #12) and five as low exercise groups (#1, #2, #5, #7, #8).[4]

TABLE 15-2

Frequency of Overall Change Designations in High and Low Exercise Groups

Group	Average Yield Score	High Learners	Moderate Changers	Total Changers	Un-changed	Negative Changers	Casual-ties	Drop-outs	Total Nega-tive
High				29%	53%				18%
Exercise	.27	4	10	14	26	2	3	4	9
Low				42%	30%				28%
Exercise	.56	14	8	22	16	7	2	6	15

The Impact of Exercises on Participant Outcome

Table 15–2 shows the outcome status of participants in the high and low exercise groups at Time 2. Although exercise use did not significantly differentiate all outcome classifications, the high exercise groups did produce significantly fewer High Learners (p = .02). In general, the data presented in Table 15–2 suggest that high exercise groups were less effective in producing Changers (42 percent for the low exercise groups versus 29 percent for the high exercise groups). A group-by-group examination of the number of Learners suggested, however, considerable variability among the groups classified as high and low exercise. Thus, for example, the number of Changers in the high exercise groups were 4, 0, 2, and 8, while the number of Changers in the low exercise groups were 3, 3, 4, 2, and 10. Such variability within groups classified according to exercises does suggest that other conditions existent in the group may have been more influential than the simple use or nonuse of structured exercises. Another view of this variability may be gained by looking at the overall gain or yield scores: all low exercise groups produced some gain (.22, .20, .28, .09, and 2.0), while the high exercise groups showed considerably more variability (.91, − .63, 0.0, and .80). The variation in outcomes associated with high exercise use suggests that some leaders may be less able than others to utilize exercises effectively to benefit the group. A more conservative interpretation is that exercises are irrelevant to producing positive change (there are other leader strategies that seem more productive) and that exercises used in concert with some leader styles may be counterproductive.

EXERCISES AND THE MAINTENANCE OF LEARNING

A frequent criticism of leader strategies that utilize exercises has been based on the argument that when a person does not discover his own solutions to learning dilemmas his learning will fade away as soon as the group is over. An examination of Time 3 data indicated that twelve of the sixteen Changers in low exercise groups (75%), compared to five of the eight

Changers in the high exercise groups (63%), maintained their changes. A comparison of these two frequencies indicated a level of significance (p = .07) which suggests a trend for Learners in low exercise groups to maintain their learning at a higher rate than Learners in high exercise groups. These findings are offset to some extent, however, by the observation that seven of twenty-six (26 percent) of the Nonchangers at Time 2 in the high exercise group were "Late Bloomers" at Time 3 compared to only three out of seventeen (17 percent) of the Nonchangers in the low exercise groups. This difference proved to be significant at a p = .05 level. Thus, the finding that there is a trend against maintenance of learning in high exercise groups is somewhat vitiated by the observation that a higher proportion of Time 2 Nonchangers moved in positive directions. These two conflicting trends as well as the fact that close to 30 percent of the sample did not return at Time 3 make an inconclusive case for or against the utility of exercises to yield lasting changes.

TYPES OF LEARNING UNDER CONDITIONS OF HIGH AND
LOW EXERCISE

The basic thirty-three change variables described in Chapter 3 were analyzed to determine whether certain ones were associated with high or low exercise use. Significant differences (multivariate analysis of covariance) between the high and low exercise groups obtained on only three of the thirty-three variables. Members of high exercise groups increased in their use of adequate coping mechanisms, experienced increased opportunities for open peer communication, and decreased in the number of decisions they made about their lives outside the group.

At Time 3 the difference between high and low exercise groups in specific changes became more marginal: The differences in coping strategies disappeared; however, members of high exercise groups did maintain their perception of their environments as containing more opportunities for open peer communications, while the members of low exercise groups increased even further in the number of decisions they were making about their personal lives.

The potency of structured exercises as a form of leader interventions is thus not impressive. At best they appear irrelevant; at worst, more likely to be ineffective than effective. Unfortunately the data do not permit a clear-cut answer to the questions of how structured exercises affect outcome. Too many other aspects of leader strategy and style as well as group conditions appear more important.

The Psychological Experience with Structured Exercises

The immediate psychological experience created by exercises was studied by examining participants' descriptions of critical incidents, the personally significant group incident each described at the close of each meeting. Critical incidents involving exercises were compared with an equal number of contributions of the same participant of critical incidents not involving exercises. The critical incidents were coded into nine categories: [5]

1. Group closeness—feelings of warmth, closeness, and trust in the group: "It brought the group closer together, permitted them to make closer contact." "Really got a feeling of group closeness, all just people." "People seemed to touch one another . . . a friendly atmosphere."
2. Changes in group interaction: "The activity made the six of us use more teamwork and therefore feel like a group and closer—I feel more trusting now." "This was great because everyone could relate something of themselves through their fantasies and that everyone had them obligated to open themselves up to others." "Some of the more quiet members opened up."
3. Self-understanding—as displayed in understanding causes of behavior, information about how one is seen in the group, the realization that one has been ignoring realms of sensory or bodily experience, and new information about one's attitudes or feelings, for example: "I found it very hard to argue from a white point of view." "I decided that I must not be trying too hard to get close to people and resolved to try more." "It allowed me to properly gauge my own feelings." "It showed me that violence is dangerous only when hostility exists beforehand." "I realized how much more aware I became of other senses when my eyes were closed. The effect was overpowering."
4. Expression of feeling—valuing the opportunity the event provided to tell others how one felt, for example: "I was able to open up more easily." "It was the first time I had ever spoken to anyone I had never met before about things that meant a lot to me." "I was put in the center and forced to talk."
5. Experience of feeling—experiencing anger, dependency, aloneness, fear, and so on, when the importance or newness of the feeling was emphasized, for example: "I felt totally dependent on the other person. I felt helpless and weak . . ." "It was good to be allowed to do this since we are often alone anyway in the group. The feeling (of being alone) became very intense and almost pleasant." (Feelings that were simply reactions to the activity like "It was pleasant," or "I was angry at Dr. X for asking me to do something I didn't want to do" were classed as miscellaneous responses.)
6. Identification—feelings aroused through identification with another group member, for example: "I only recently realized how prevalent it's been for me to deny my loneliness." "I was able to relate very strongly to the feeling of alienation and resentment."
7. New feelings about another group member—a change in feelings about someone in the group, for example: "I felt closer and more understanding

about her now, but her emotional reaction was not as genuine as I had expected." "I was glad to see X get involved."

8. Miscellaneous positive—all responses with positive affect about the exercise that wouldn't fit any other category, for example: "It turned me on." "It was interesting."

9. Miscellaneous negative—all responses that described negative affect.

Table 15–3 shows participant responses to all exercises and participant responses to a sample of nonexercise events.

Structured exercises did not differ very much from other group events in the kinds of responses they generated. There was a tendency for structured exercises to provoke less identification and fewer negative reactions than other types of group events, but the group closeness responses were the only kind of responses that exercises generated significantly more often than nonexercises. About one quarter of all events, exercises and nonexercises, led participants to describe self-understanding as a response to the event.

Different types of exercises, however, were found to produce different kinds of psychological experiences in the group. Feelings of group closeness were frequently associated with nonverbal and verbal group exercises, as well as group-on-individual exercises. Changes in the interaction of the group were more often generated by group verbal exercises. Feelingful expressions were associated with verbal group exercises and individual exercises, particularly exercises which stressed members pairing with one another. Self-understanding was most likely to be encouraged by psychodrama, both for the audience and the protagonist in the psycho-

TABLE 15-3
Responses to Exercises, Nonexercises

Response	Nonexercises		All Exercises	
	Frequency	Percentage	Frequency	Percentage
Group Closeness	8	4.0	30	15.0
Changes in Group Interaction	23	11.6	21	11.5
Self-Understanding	40	20.2	50	25.5
Feeling Expression	30	15.2	23	11.5
Feeling Experience	12	6.1	11	5.5
Identification	18	9.1	9	4.5
Charged Feelings About Group Member	19	9.6	15	7.5
Miscellaneous Positive	31	15.7	30	15.0
Miscellaneous Negative	17	8.5	8	4.0
Total	198	100	197	100

drama. Self-understanding, in the sense of paying attention to previously ignored senses, was associated with nonverbal group exercises.

Effects of Structured Exercises on Group Processes

Cohesiveness. High exercise groups were significantly more cohesive both in early sessions and later in the group.[6] Thus, it is clear that the use of exercises, although not radically affecting participants' outcome nor even the nature of their psychological experiences in the group, does appear to have a significant effect on one important group variable, cohesiveness.

Self-Disclosure. An analysis of the amount of revelation judged by the observers in the high and low exercise groups revealed insignificant overall differences. There was a striking difference in the amount of observer-rated, here-and-now revelation that occurred in the first two sessions (six hours) of high and low exercise groups, but by the third session, low exercise groups had "caught up" in intensity of revelation. Nor did the amount of self-disclosure as judged by the participants themselves discriminate among the high and low exercise groups. Exercises did not hold up overall as uniquely precipitating self-disclosure.

Climate. The effect of exercises on the emotional tone or climate of the group was determined from observer ratings of the emotional tone of the groups at the end of each meeting (see Chapter 9). The comparison between low and high exercise groups revealed no significant differences in the emotional tone or intensity of the groups. Contrary to the supposition by leaders who use such devices, they do not in and of themselves create intense experiences.[7]

Underlying Issues. The impact of exercises on thematic characteristics of the group was also examined. (See Drury, "The Effects of Structured Exercises in Encounter Groups," 1972.) In all, observers were asked to rate the presence or absence of thirty-three themes, divided into six general areas: goal setting, power and influence, relatedness, expressivity, feelings, and type of coping. Simply put, a theme represents a judgment of "the underlying issue" concerning the group as a whole. The presence of a theme usually indicates an area of concern, an issue the members are "working on" (Whitaker and Lieberman, 1964). This investigation revealed a number of significant differences between the low and high exercise groups in the particular themes they emphasized. The low exercise groups focused significantly more on setting directions and making up their minds how to proceed. They were more concerned, in addition, with issues of closeness and distance between people. They emphasized such themes as affection, trust/mistrust, and genuineness/not genuineness. In contrast, high exercise groups focused on themes expressing both positive and negative feelings. If the theme is understood as an indicator of what concerns the groups, it is perhaps not surprising that in high exercise groups, where leaders provide considerable direction for how to work, setting goals and working out procedures and so on are not salient issues. These findings support Argyris' speculation that exercises take a function he and many other leaders believe the group should handle. Issues of closeness, relatedness, and trust are also not as germane in highly structured groups; to some extent exercises resolve these issues for the members. Expressivity, a common goal of structured exercises, was reflected in the extent that members of high exercise groups focused on these issues. Perhaps the rapidity by which feelings are expressed and private thoughts are disclosed in high exercise groups makes this issue a primary concern for the members.

Participants' Theories About How the Groups Worked

At the termination of the encounter groups, participants were asked to indicate what sorts of experiences were instrumental in their learning (How Encounter Groups Work). Although participants in both the high and low exercise groups emphasized feedback and receiving advice as most important experiences in their learning, more participants in high exercise groups cited the acceptance of personal "responsibility for the way I live," as an important aspect of their learning. They also stressed the opportunity to experiment with new behavior. In contrast, participants in the low exercise groups cited the opportunity to "understand the causes and sources of my hang-ups" and "to understand why I think and feel the way I do" more frequently than participants in low exercise groups. Chi-squares for these four responses were $p = .04$, $p = .04$, $p = .10$, and $p = .11$, respectively. The use of exercises thus appears to have oriented participants toward placing greatest value on activity and existential encounters; in contrast, groups that did not emphasize exercises oriented participants more toward valuing introspection and understanding.

The findings discussed thus far have not clarified why structured exercises have become so popular and widespread. Clearly, the outcome data do not explain the popularity of such a leader strategy. Structured exercises are probably less likely to lead to productive outcome.

More clues to the popularity of exercises are suggested in the findings on group conditions and learning mechanisms. Structured exercises do produce groups that are more attractive to the participants (cohesiveness) and probably minimize certain basic issues of goals and relationships among members which often make members uncomfortable. These considerations suggested that an analysis of participants' overall reactions to the encounter experience and to their leaders might offer further understanding of the contagious popularity of structured exercises as a leader style.

Table 15–4 presents mean scores of participants' testimony, leader eval-

TABLE 15-4

Evaluation of Group and Leader

	High Exercise		Low Exercise	
	Short Post	Long Post	Short Post	Long Post
Desires to Be in Another				
Group with Leader	4.3[a]	4.2	4.2[b]	2.8
Liked Techniques	4.4[b]	4.7	4.6[b]	3.1
Understood Group	4.9[b]	4.6	4.3	3.9
Effective	4.5[b]	4.3	4.2[a]	3.2
Liked As a Person	4.9	4.2	4.7	4.5
Competent	5.2[b]	5.1	5.1[b]	4.2
Group Pleasant	4.5	4.0	4.1	3.8
Turned On to Group	3.8	3.6	3.5	3.2
Group Constructive	4.8[a]	4.2	4.3	4.2
Learned a Lot	4.0[c]	3.5	3.2	3.2
Frequency of Active				
Proselytizing	—	8/33[c]	—	3/33

[a] $p \leq .05$.
[b] $p \leq .01$.
[c] $p \leq .10$.

uations, and proselytizing behavior in high and low exercise groups. At termination the leaders of high exercise groups were seen by participants as more competent, more understanding of the group, and more effective than leaders of low exercise groups. Participants liked the techniques that high exercise leaders used, and were more likely to want to be in another group with the same leader.

Participants clearly liked leaders who used more exercises. Perhaps as Goldstein, Heller, and Sechrest (1966) suggest on the basis of research on patient expectations, leader-centered groups are more attractive to participants at least initially. The leader of such a group will be better liked in early sessions of the group. Leaders who introduce many exercises are allowing group members to look to them for guidance on what to do about the initial aimlessness of the group; this may induce more positive evaluations of the leader because of the reduced anxiety and frustration. Participants may also interpret a leader's ability to offer concrete, well-defined activities as an index of his competence. The use of exercises was also found to generate feelings of warmth and closeness which may also have induced positive evaluations.

An examination of leader evaluations six to eight months after the groups terminated showed that the high exercise group members continued to see the leaders as more competent, more effective, more active, and using better techniques than did members in low exercise groups. Members of high exercise groups had even more positive feelings about the leader at the follow-up than they did immediately after the group.

418

MEMBERS' EVALUATION OF THE EXPERIENCE

As shown in Table 15–4, on two of the four testimonial scales adminis-tered at termination, those who participated in high exercise groups saw the groups as more constructive and felt they had learned more than their counterparts in the low exercise groups. Six to eight months later, how-ever, as seen in Table 15–4, although high exercise group members main-tained their perception of the leaders as competent, they devaluated the constructiveness of the experience, so that their judgments were no differ-ent from the members of the low exercise groups. This finding supports Argyris' opinion that the effects of leader-directed activities are more tran-sitory because group members do not experience what happens in the group as a product of their own activity. Their decreased enthusiasm echoes the previous lower rate of change maintenance for the participants in the high exercise groups when compared to the low exercise groups.

The information displayed in Table 15–4 on proselytizing behavior indi-cates that in keeping with their more positive leader evaluations, members of high exercise groups were more active proselytizers—they frequently urged their friends to join such groups. It is thus abundantly clear that leaders who make considerable use of structured exercises in their reper-toire will be liked, judged competent, and generate enthusiastic, active pros-elytizing participants.

Appraisal

Analysis of the impact of structured exercises shows that they are neither the royal road to existential bliss nor a robust means of inducing change in in-dividuals. On balance, exercises appear at best irrelevant in that they do not yield markedly different results whether they are used or not; more likely, it can be inferred they are less effective in general than more unstructured strategies. Unfortunately, too many other factors of climate and leader strategy enter into such an equation to speak conclusively about the singu-lar contribution of exercises in relationship to an individual's learning.

Still, as the encounter movement has grown, so has not only the general use of exercises but also the wholesale diffusion of encounter group "pack-ages" which include a set of identical experiences proposed for worldwide use.[8] The evidence presented here suggests an explanation. Exercises en-hance the esteem of the leader; participants believe he is more competent if he uses exercises and they are more enthusiastic about him and about how much they have learned. Their enthusiasm about the personal benefit of the experience is short-lived, but that is usually unknown to the leader where leader-participant relationships are severed when the group is ended. Exercises "take the heat off" the leader at no cost to his prestige with the group and probably enchance his business, since it is more likely than not that leaders who use structured exercises will produce members who proselytize.

In many ways, the effects of exercises ape the effects induced by the Energizer (Type A) leaders who generate initial enthusiasm, perceptions of competence, and high rates of proselytizing, although they are not among the most successful in producing learning. Perhaps exercises are a means by which leaders may emulate the effects of the founders of their respective movements, movements which have been developed by highly charismatic individuals. Not everyone can possess charisma; yet, as demonstrated in Chapter 7, in general, leaders perceived themselves as charismatic although their members did not. Exercises offer a solution to the problem of transferring charisma, democratizing its magical properties. Anyone can learn to use them and thereby gain, if not a semblance of charisma, at least the appearance of technical proficiency. Exercises truly make the encounter movement egalitarian—all can be leaders and some can be gurus, for the skills are simple and the manuals are many. What better way to provide a sense of charismatic power or to escape the questions that beleaguer leaders whose methodology requires careful, knowledgeable assessments of the needs and the readiness of the person and of the characteristics of the group.

The demonstrated power of exercises to increase cohesion may also explain their popularity. If, as many have speculated, encounter groups have taken hold because there are fewer and fewer sources of communion in contemporary life, the experience of momentary togetherness, without the concomitant responsibility required by communion in the real worlds of religion, family, community, or corporation, may for many be enough to be worth their participation in an encounter group.

NOTES

1. See also J. W. Pfeiffer and J. B. Jones (1969); Goodwin Watson, *Manual of Structured Exercises* (1969); and C. Hills and R. B. Stone (1970).

2. The "psychodrama" category does not include role-playing in which one group member plays all the roles in some fantasied scene. A scene in which a group member carries on a dialogue with his father by playing both himself and his father was classified as an "individual" exercise rather than psychodrama.

3. The criteria used to sample groups were balance of leader types and return rates for the long post. In addition, the Tape Groups were excluded. One leader, #6, Psychodrama, was excluded because the leader style is unique in utilizing such props as lights and music, structures which could not readily be measured by the methods used in this study. The nine groups chosen were an Esalen Eclectic, a Gestalt group, Rogerian Marathon, an Eclectic Marathon, two T-groups, a Psychodrama group, one Psychoanalytic group, and one Transactional Analysis group.

4. There are three other variables that have been shown to have significant relationships with outcome. These three variables are leader type, norm type, and session distribution. Although there were no high exercise groups with a laissez-faire leader and no high exercise groups with nonerotic, disclosing, confronting norm patterns; and no low exercise groups had energizing or high structure leaders or charismatic or distant-guarded norm patterns, neither was exercise use synonymous with one or two leader or norm types. Three of the four high exercise groups had a "massed" distribution of group sessions, while only one of five low exercise groups had "massed sessions," so the effects of exercises cannot be clearly separated from the effects of session distribution.

5. The coding procedure for the critical incidents used in analyzing structured exercises differs from the methods previously described in Chapter 12. The coding scheme described here was specifically developed to be sensitive to the potential effects of structured exercises.

6. The mean cohesiveness for high exercise groups in the early sessions was 34.8, for low exercise groups 31.4; the mean cohesiveness in the late sessions for high exercise groups was 34.5, for the low exercise groups, 30.9. Both these differences were significant beyond the .01 level.

7. A separate analysis of the amount of nonverbal exercises leaders used (observer ratings) was available for all groups studied. A rank order correlation between number of nonverbal procedures and involvement intensity was a $-.24$.

8. It is of interest to compare the elevated position that exercises have come to enjoy in the contemporary encounter scene with what happened in the early years of sensitivity-training as developed by NTL where the trend over the first decade was increasingly to eliminate structured experiences (skill-groups).

CHAPTER *16*

Implications for Practice

The encounter group movement has generated a series of well-worn statements purporting to comment on group processes and outcomes. Most of those have the quality of "lore," and have not been previously empirically tested. In the light of the present study, a number of such statements can be seen as "myths"; false, unfounded generalizations.

"Feeling, Not Thought." Much encounter group practice attacks cognitive functioning as sheer rationalization and defensiveness and stresses the importance of "gut" feelings as the basic coin of exchange. Yet the study repeatedly demonstrates that thought is an essential part of the learning process. High Learners reported more critical incidents which involved the presence of insight and the reception of cognitive information, and they also rated understanding and insight as important factors in their learning. The sheer experiencing of positive feelings was *less* for learners than for those unchanged by the experience. Self-disclosure and the expression of positive feeling led to personal gain primarily when accompanied by cognitive insight. Leaders who supplied clear conceptual organizers, especially for the meaning of individual behavior, achieved better outcomes. After the group, those who maintained their learnings buttressed their experimenting, proactive behavior with careful self-monitoring and clarifying discussion with others. They also stressed the importance of analysis and reflection in their advice to others for effective maintenance. All in all, it appears that the myth should be revised to read: *Feelings, only with thought.* Humans have minds, and it appears they need to use them in encounter groups and afterward, if benefits are to ensue.

"Let It All Hang Out." The popular stereotype, and the belief of many encounter group participants and leaders, is that unalloyed expressiveness and full-scale self-disclosure are essentials for learning. Only if the learner stops inhibiting his impulses, and removes the barrier between his private experience of self and his publicly communicated views, can he make genuine progress: So goes the shibboleth.

The study implies that considerable qualification of this view is in order.

Implications for Practice

Expressing positive feelings, with either positive or negative consequences, was not done more by learners than by those who remained unchanged or received negative outcomes. Expressing negative feelings, if the consequences were negative, was more frequently done by those who received negative outcomes. Groups with norms stressing the importance of intense emotional expression did not achieve higher yield. Leaders who demand more feelings through evocative, challenging, stimulating behavior were, on the average, likely to induce more casualties. Self-disclosure, by and large, was not as intimate, frequent, or as dramatic in the study groups as has been supposed and did not, in and of itself, lead to learning. Increased "openness" toward others after the group was the most frequently reported learning, but such openness seemed most effectively maintained when it was subject to self-monitoring and modulative refinement.

Less pithily, and more cautiously, the revised maxim might read: *Let more of it hang out than usual, if it feels right in the group, and you can give some thought to what it means.* The expression of feelings or private information, as such, doesn't lead to learning, and shouldn't be demanded.

"Feedback Is the Core Experience." From the beginning of the self-analytic group movement, the reception of information about the impact of the self on others has been considered a central feature of learning. Feedback of previously defended-against or unknown information is seen to arouse energy for learning via "unfreezing" of existing patterns, and to provide information on the results of alternate behavioral strategies.

Though participants judged feedback the most important learning mechanism, feedback followed by a positive response (the usual condition thought to be most useful for learning) was *not* reported more frequently by learners than by unchanged or negatively changed persons. Nor did these categories of persons differ in their judgment of the importance of feedback. Furthermore, contrary to what might have been expected from the findings on cognition, feedback followed by a cognitive response was reported *less* frequently by learners than by others. Finally, feedback followed by a negative feeling response was more frequent for those who changed negatively as a result of the experience. It also appeared that leaders who achieved the highest level of group yield had groups in which the smallest number of critical incidents involving feedback were reported. The next most effective leader types, however, had groups citing the largest number of feedback incidents. So although feedback is almost universally seen as important, valued by group members, and almost always supported by the group norms, reported incidents involving feedback yield a mixed picture.

Perhaps all that can be said here in the way of an alternate maxim is: *There's more to learning than feedback.* Our findings conflict with some earlier studies in training groups (Miles, 1965), and with a whole host of studies on "knowledge of results" in the study of skilled performances. The group conditions supporting effective feedback need much more speci-

423

fication, and the properties of feedback which are useful to the learner need clarification. Clearly more inquiry is needed—especially inquiry which does not take the centrality of feedback processes for granted.

"Getting Out the Anger Is Essential." For some encounter group practitioners, the experience and expression of basic rage is the essential for a "breakthrough." For others, the use of anger as a basis for confrontation and challenge, and for disconfirmation of existing self-images, appears an extremely important tool. Yet this study suggests that expression of anger may be more dysfunctional than helpful in encounter groups. Those groups in which the climate during the second half of the groups was angry rather than harmonious proved to have lower yields, by and large. Those who dropped from the groups very frequently proved to be conflicted about expressing anger or receiving it. Attack and rejection by leader or group, both of which involve anger, were prominently associated with the production of casualties. Those who were casualties, or received negative outcomes, were more likely than others to report the expression of hostile, aggressive feelings. Finally, groups in which the norms favored hostile, confrontational behavior were not higher in yield.

The evidence favors the view that sustained levels of anger are unproductive in encounter groups; in addition to challenge, it appears that persons need love and support in order to learn. (Note, in passing, that High Learners were more likely to view salient others positively, while those receiving negative outcomes were more negative and judgmental; high maintainers were closer to their best friends than were nonmaintainers and more willing to accept affection. High anger levels may imply a less stable group system;[1] even where anger is relatively institutionalized, as in Synanon groups, negative consequences from attack and rejection were likely. So: *Getting out the anger may be OK, but keeping it out there steadily isn't.*

"Stay with the Here-and-Now." This admonition has been made by leaders, and by willing members, since encounter groups and their ancestors began. Focusing on current feelings and behaviors of the self and others is thought to be a central criterion for encounter group success; those who deviate are frequently accused of "flight," of being unwilling to become involved in the group. It is quite correct that encounter groups do gain much of their intensity from a here-and-now focus: Discussion of what is normally forbidden in polite or task-oriented conversation involves breaking taboos and releases a good deal of excitement. Yet the study demonstrated that the proportion of time a group spent on matters internal to the group was unrelated to outcome. Rather, groups in which the normative boundaries were relatively loose (e.g., permitted joking, the discussion of outside relationships, and sexual and dream material) were groups which (a) in fact did discuss more outside personal material; (b) had a higher average level of self-disclosure; and (c) had higher group yield. Learners tended to disclose more during late sessions of their groups, particularly details of

424

their lives, along with feelings of happiness and pride. Negative changers disclosed fewer such feelings, along with fewer feelings of the moment, and feelings of fear and weakness. (It is correct that here-and-now feelings were disclosed more frequently, across all groups, than other sorts of private material: the point is that such disclosure, while it may be necessary, is not sufficient for gain.) Our revised maxim might be: *Here-and-now is not enough; add the personal there-and-then.*

"There Is No Group, Only Persons." Many encounter group leaders tend to focus their primary attention on the individual. Some use procedures akin to "individual therapy" in the group.

Yet, though the leader or the members may not be attentive to them, group conditions do influence learning. Those marginal to or deviant from their groups tended to receive negative outcomes; those attracted to their groups and whose behavior embodied encounter group ideals (risk-taking, spontaneity, openness), and who were active and vigorous in the hierarchy of interaction, learned more. Groups in which peer control was only weakly favored by group norms tended to have more casualties. Groups in which appropriate behavior was more clearly defined (groups with more norms) had higher yield; groups with norms favoring moderate levels of emotional intensity, moderate confrontation, looser boundaries, and peer control had the highest yield.

The normative climate of groups appeared to predict outcome about as well as did the style of the leader. It was also found that groups that were more cohesive in the latter part of their lives had higher yields. So did groups in which climate was relatively harmonious and relatively involved and intense.

The conclusion is inescapable: *Group processes make a difference in personal learning,* whether or not salient attention is paid to them by leaders or members.

"Encounter Groups Are Safe." Prominent encounter group practitioners, and organizations sponsoring such groups, have reported minimal negative effects on members. Rogers (1970), for example, quotes a conclusion from Gibb's (1970) review of research, "There is little basis for the widespread concern among lay groups about the traumatic effects of group training," and says, "It is good to see this ghost laid to rest." He discounts reports of damage as stemming from rumor, and suggests that those believing such rumors are threatened by the disruptive possibilities of personal change. To support this conclusion he cites Gibb's review: only one of 1200 persons studied had a negative experience. What were the findings (Batchelder and Hardy, 1968)? Over a number of years, a large portion of the YMCA professional staff had been involved in sensitivity training and organizational development laboratories totaling approximately 1200 in all. A questionnaire was sent to 1,725 YMCA facilities asking for information regarding the chief staff officers' impressions of the value of such training; responses were received from 790 of these 1,725

installations. As part of the study, the investigators sampled from some of the installations for determining the base of criticism, ". . . it should be noted that the sample of critics was not deemed to be representative of YMCA professional staff, since it was not the purpose to generalize for the total population, but rather to obtain a sample which would assist in the identification and classification of issues, problems, and concerns." In other words, sixteen individuals were chosen for interview purposes so that the investigators could describe the issues that critics within the YMCA had about such training. Interviews were conducted with the sixteen (note out of 1,725 installations). "Six respondents expressed the opinion that individuals have experienced severe personality disorientation during sensitivity-training. . . . A systematic effort was made to track down each of these alleged severe negative experiences and four cases were finally identified for follow-up. Data gathered from careful interviews with the participants themselves, their work supervisors, their trainers, etc., suggested that only one of the four had any enduring negative reaction." Nowhere in the data presented by these investigators, as the widely circulated comments of Gibb and by Rogers imply, were the other 1,196 participants investigated, nor did the original investigators make any claim to have done a systematic inquiry into negative reactions. Thus, to quote the figure one out of 1200 appears to serve the function of myth-making, rather than providing adequate data to "lay the ghost to rest."

Our study did find group experiences damaging to 8 percent of those who began the groups, a figure which most people would not consider "safe." The ghost, in short, is not at all laid to rest. It appears that previous studies of encounter groups, and the claims of practitioners, tend to minimize negative effects. This minimization seems explained by limited follow-up contact with members after the group, insufficiently careful attention to the existence of negative outcomes during the group, and ideological rejection of "negative effects" as a meaningful concept.

So encounter groups are not as safe as claimed. Furthermore, this study found that persons who came to the groups with strong wishes and hopes for change, and considered the groups to be "safe" were rather more likely to be at risk, to be vulnerable to perhaps unexpected attack and rejection. Persons who came to the groups with equivalently strong hopes, but with an attitude of moderate skepticism about the safety of group experience, were likely to learn a good deal. Interviews with a number of persons who attended higher-risk groups, but did not become casualties, showed that they were able to protect themselves through withdrawal, lower involvement, and distance. (Such devices also served to block positive learning to some extent.)

An associated submyth is that "high-risk equals high-yield," the belief that some groups achieve strong gains for some members, perhaps at the price of damage to others. Only one of the groups studied even came close to this model; it included four high learners and two casualties. In all

426

other groups, the presence of many learners and the presence of many casualties were mutually exclusive.

So: *Encounter groups can be dangerous,* and their danger is not counterbalanced by high gain.

"Enthusiasm Equals Change." Advocates perceive self-reports as the most trustworthy data (Rogers, 1970); critics tend to dismiss the reports of participants as the result of a temporary turn-on, as a form of quasi-religious fervor, or as conversion to the view that encounter groups are good for everyone—a conversion occurring in parallel with a marked lack of noted behavior change. This study does show that participants became more positive in their attitudes toward encounter groups, seeing them as more safe places to be, and that they also engaged in proselytizing behavior. Can participant testimony be trusted, or is it an ephemeral glow? Positive testimony was inflated over our assessments of change, lending weight to the "enthusiasm" view. At termination only 57 percent of those who gave positive testimony actually did receive positive benefit; however, at six-month follow-up, 76 percent of those giving positive testimony actually benefited. So, just after the group there is a good deal of unfounded enthusiasm, but if several months have elapsed, we can be more confident that participants' views are trustworthy.

While the data show that participant enthusiasm wanes with the passage of time, participants' judgments of the worth of the experience are not to be discounted when looking back at the experience some six to eight months later. Perhaps the maxim might be changed to: *Enthusiasm must stand the test of time.*

"You May Not Know What You've Learned Now, But When You Put It All Together . . ." The idea that "late blooming" may take place weeks or months after the end of an encounter group is an attractive one, which justifies disappointing experiences to members and leaders alike. The encounter group experience is sometimes seen as a stirring, unfreezing, or shaking-up experience; if a process of refreezing or consolidation has not taken place during the group, the natural hope is that it will do so afterward. This study indicates that such formulations are nearer wishful thinking than reality. Late blooming occurs in a minority of those unchanged at termination and almost never in those who leave with negative outcomes. Our revised apothegm should be: *Bloom now, don't count on later.*

"It All Washes Out When You Leave the Group." One of the most ancient pieces of folklore in the encounter group field is that while members may leave the group with a "glow," it will fade and their behavior will generally return to pregroup levels, as they are faced with pre-existing role expectations and pressures.[2] There is some justification for this belief in that initial enthusiasm levels of participants dropped somewhat, yet 78 percent of those members who received positive benefit from the groups maintained these gains six months later, a figure which decisively washes out the supposed "washout effect."

Some meaningful reasons for maintenance of change were found. Self-reported changes were more likely to be maintained if the changer was confident of future maintenance. Changes were maintained more when the learner engaged in active experimentation with new behavior and talked actively with others about learning (here again cognitive supports seem important). The appropriately revised motto might be: *If you learned, most likely you'll keep it.*

Implications for the Leader

A most striking implication of the study findings is the humbling one which requires that encounter leaders abandon a Ptolemaic conception of the process of change. Change does not revolve around the solitary sun of the leader; the evidence is strong that psychosocial relations in the group play an exceedingly important role in the process of change. When leaders were interviewed at the onset of the study the great majority stressed that it was important for members to express greater honesty toward others, to receive feedback about their interpersonal behavior, to experiment with a wide range of new behaviors, to get close to others, to learn to care for other people, to "get in touch with their feelings"; few leaders, however, expressed an awareness of the powerful effects upon learning of the relationships between the member and the rest of the group.

What implications may we draw from this? Our intent is not to demonstrate the conceptual shallowness of the leaders in our project. We have repeatedly stressed that the group leaders were experienced and deemed highly competent by their colleagues. The implication in our view is that our research demonstrates that there are factors influencing change which occur in the substratum of the group outside of the leader's level of awareness. Given their invisibility, it is not surprising that these factors have not been appreciated in most leadership approaches. Indeed most leaders have fashioned their style and their theory of change from their personal observations of their groups; clinical style has rarely been influenced by research findings. Exceedingly competent leaders may be unaware of significant factors responsible for their success. And the process does not end there. Many highly successful leaders assume a responsibility to transmit their techniques to others. The result is that they establish training institutes in which they teach their techniques as they conceptualize them, and fail to pass on their intuitive, unconscious utilization of the psychosocial factors which bear on their success. Too often these teachers transmit only epiphenomenal behavioral characteristics which are idiosyncratic and irrelevant or insufficient to explain that leader's effective outcome.

Consider some specific illustrations of the teaching of epiphenomenal behavior. Several of our leaders were convinced of the efficacy of the "hot seat" approach—the technique of focusing the entire energy of the group on one person for long periods of time. Some of the leaders encouraged the group members to center on one member whereas other leaders devoted extended periods to one-to-one work between themselves and each of the group members. Yet the "hot seat" approach bore no relationship to outcome. Some of the most successful group leaders (Leaders #3 and #8), as well as some of the least successful leaders (Leaders #4 and #13) were highly committed to this technique. Structured exercises provide another example. Many of the leaders considered structured exercises highly related to outcome. Yet, some of the lowest yield leaders (Leaders #4, #10, #11) as well as some of the higher yield leaders (Leaders #3 and #12) also used a large number of structured exercises. At the same time, the most successful (Leader #8) and some of the least successful (for example, Leaders #5 and #9) used extremely few structured exercises.

The identical point can be made considering a number of other highly prized leadership techniques, for example, total here-and-now focus, emphasis on extremely intensive emotional expression, high self-disclosure, being "shaken," or specific theoretical constructs, such as Gestalt therapy or Transactional Analysis. We have already commented on the fact that one Transactional Analytic leader led a highly successful group whereas the other Transactional Analytic leader led a highly unsuccessful group; one Gestalt therapy leader led a high-yield group whereas the other Gestalt therapy leader led the lowest yield group. It is unnecessary to belabor this point further. Without further information about the change process, high-yield leaders may be convinced that it is the "hot seat" technique, or structured exercises, or intense emotional expression, or the "here-and-now," or a transactional interpretation of personality that is responsible for their effectiveness. Perhaps another point is that some low-yield leaders were unaware that they had been ineffective. Accordingly, such leaders may attempt to transmit *their* techniques to students.

Our findings do not deny the importance of the leader in determining the course and outcome of the group. They suggest, however, that the nature of his role be more precisely described. The leader has both a direct and indirect role: he attempts to change members by his *personal interaction with each individual* in the group, and he has a *social engineering* function in which he indirectly contributes to outcome by helping to construct a group which is an effective agent of change. Too often encounter group leaders have an imbalanced view of these functions: They attribute far too much importance to the direct contributions of the leader; and overlook the more subtle but more important indirect functions. We do not intend to imply that the direct functions are unimportant. The leader's person and behavior loom very large in the course of the group, and he is generally endowed by the group members with surplus meaning and power which stems from irrational and archaic sources. Accordingly, we shall return to these direct functions in greater depth shortly, but first we shall discuss the implications of our findings for the too-often-overlooked indirect functions of the leader.

The division of the leader's functions into direct and indirect ones is arbitrary. His functions may be placed along a continuum: At one end are those behaviors in which he engages to increase the eventual potency of the social system which he is attempting to construct. On the other end of the continuum are behaviors oriented toward immediate therapeutic effects upon individuals. Obviously there is a blurred boundary between the two, but we can without difficulty cite several findings which explicate indirect functions.

INDIRECT FUNCTIONS

Chapter 11 demonstrates that there is a role members can assume which is correlated with positive yield. This role is one in which the individual engages in behavior that is valued by the group (activity, risk-taking, spontaneity, openness, expressiveness, helping the group, responding warmly to others) and which enables him to influence other members of the group. Members with high VCIA (Value Congruence, Influence, Activity) behavior tend to have positive outcomes, while members with low VCIA behavior tend to have unchanged or negative outcomes. This is hardly a surprising finding; social-psychological research has demonstrated time and time again that social forces in the environment are powerful influences on the shaping of behavior. Not only do high VCIA members tend to be rewarded for their behavior in the group by being highly valued, by being liked and respected by other members and thus having their own positive self-images reinforced, but also the very types of behavior which are reinforced seem to have intrinsic value which will serve them well in their life outside the group. In striking contrast to the success associated with the VCIA role, the deviant in the group is quite likely to have a negative learning experience. Rarely did anyone have a positive outcome who had deviant status. How attractive each member considered the group is another important determinant of outcome. Only rarely in our study (five out of fifty-nine members) did a member with low attraction to the group end the group with positive outcome.

Such findings may be of considerable importance for the group leader who wears blinders in the group which allow him to focus only on the work done between him and other members. It means both a shift in emphasis and a shift in technique. The leader should simply become more aware of the importance of the role that each member assumes in the group. If there is a member of the group who the leader notes occupies a position of extraordinarily little influence among the other members, whose comments are rarely heard, and who is in general undervalued by them, then he does well to reflect seriously upon this situation. The same may be said for attraction to the group and deviancy. If a member has exceedingly low attraction to the group and this position is permitted to go unaltered, then the chances of his benefiting from the group are exceptionally slim. The leader must regard with concern any member who occupies an extreme deviant position; he stands an excellent chance of suffering either a negative outcome or even casualty status.

Effort to identify and correct problems in psychosocial relationships in the group is crucial, not only for the personal growth or avoidance of negative outcome of the particular member concerned but also for the entire group. There are probably certain developmental tasks which small groups must accomplish in the early course of their evolution and there are few things more inhibitory for a group than an obviously troubled member who diverts the group time and energy.

Before the leader can make ameliorative moves, he must have methods of appraising the psychosocial situation he must alter. Perhaps the first and most important maneuver the leader can undertake is a phenomenological shift: He must attempt to view the experience from the experiential position of each of the members. It is striking how often group leaders failed to recognize the strong impact on some individuals of what they had thought to be a somewhat trivial event. Inquiry into what each member considered the critical event of the meeting reminded us again that each individual constitutes his own world and his own affective relationship to that world. Thus what appeared to be from the leader's stance a mild rebuttal was sometimes experienced as cataclysmic for some isolated individuals who have had little group experience. The leader must appreciate the tremendous force and power of group pressure to fully appreciate the experience of each member. There is considerable social psychological research to demonstrate the power of group pressure which may be constructive or destructive to group members depending on how it is harnessed and utilized. If, as Asch and Sherif have shown, group pressure may distort perception of primary sense data, it is likely that group pressure can influence the perception of one's basic worth.

Secondly, we encourage the leader to develop methods by which he may explicitly inquire into the psychosocial structure of the group. We suggest a broadening of the definition of feedback. Feedback is a concept used in encounter groups to connote the process of members and the leader giving other members information about their interpersonal presentation of selves. We suggest that the leader, too, obtain process and role feedback at frequent intervals throughout the group. The practice is one quite consonant with the general flow of the encounter group since these groups differ from ordinary task groups in that they are self-reflective: They both act and observe their activity. Depending upon his personal style the leader can use a number of various techniques to obtain information about the role that each of the members is assuming in the group and the general attraction of the group for each of the members. Some leaders may prefer to do ongoing assessments of these parameters through written questionnaires: our Attraction to the Group questionnaire is an exceedingly simple one requiring only a couple of minutes for administration. The influence hierarchy, or deviance, can be easily assessed by the periodic administration of simple sociometric instruments.

Other leaders will find the administration of written questionnaries awkward or dissonant with their general style, and may prefer to obtain the same information through verbal inquiry. Naturally, in a verbal consensus, the leader will have to take note of and attempt to neutralize the effect that group pressure will have toward producing conformity among the members. For example, members may be disinclined to disclose publicly their lack of attraction to the group. There is ample social-psychological research to suggest the wide differences between public and private disclosures in which group members are willing to engage. Members might be asked to arrange themselves in the room at a distance from the center which depends on how much in or out of the group they perceive themselves to be. The leader can obtain considerable information, however, from explicit inquiry. He can ask members at appropriate intervals whether or not they feel they are considered valuable by other members of the group, whether or not they feel they are listened to, whether their opinions are sought after. They can be asked at which point they felt most a member of the group and at which point they felt less a member of the group. Our purpose is not to suggest specific procedures; technique must vary according to the leader's personal style and the characteristics of the specific group. What we wish to emphasize is the nature of information which the leader must acquire.

We suggest that the leader take serious note of a member with minimal attraction to the group. He may pose this as an issue for the entire group to discuss, he may facilitate that member's exploration of some of the sources for his minimal attraction to the group. Some members may find the group unrewarding because they perceive that the group will not fulfill some of their expectations. Either of these issues can be a fruitful area of exploration when made explicit. Unrealistic expectations can be examined and altered in such a way that the member and the group arrive at a realistic appraisal of what can still be accomplished in the remaining time. If the leader feels that a member's low attraction to the group is immutable, then he must come to terms with our findings that suggest that that particular member has virtually no likelihood of profiting from the group experience. We would defend the position that the leader explore with the group member the wisdom of his continuing in the group. Although most group members assume a strong obligation to "stick it out" until the end of the group, the leader might help the group re-examine these rules so that the member may have total freedom in deciding whether it is sensible for him to continue exposing himself to what has proved to be a nonviable learning environment.

Implications for Practice

Once the leader discovers that certain members are suffering because of low approval and acceptance by the group, it is often sufficient merely to call attention to this state of affairs. If an accepting and caring substratum has been built in the group, then the group members with the leader's assistance will find ways to help the deviant re-enter the mainstream of the group. Some balance must be struck between the group interacting freely, moving along spontaneously, and on the other hand striking an attitude of self-reflection regarding the fulfillment of its primary task. If a member is eager to enter and to benefit from the group and is not able to accomplish that, the group can generally find ways of coming to his aid. One other tack for the leader to take is to attempt to increase the group's tolerance for individual differences. Groups vary in their ability to allow members to participate at their own pace without attempting to batter down defenses too quickly and to reject those members who do not quickly adopt group values and accepted modes of behavior. If there is a deviant in the group who is deeply troubled and so disturbed that he does not consciously express or recognize his deviant role, then the chances of negative outcome may be quite high. We suggest that the leader consider as one of his options the withdrawal of such obviously troubled members from his group.

This is an easy decision in retrospect. For a large number of the Casualties one can say, "If only the leader had removed him from the group in the first or second meeting . . ." In time-present, however, in the heat of the life of the group, asking a member to leave is an extraordinarily difficult and painful decision. The leader will wonder whether he is correct. Perhaps things will simmer down. Perhaps the subject is merely a provocateur who characteristically reacts to new situations in this manner. One can never be sure. And yet there are times when the leader must listen to his best judgment and make such a decision. It is an extreme move and obviously maximum tact must be employed. Such advice to members is often best presented around the issue of "fit" in the group and the poor climate for his personal learning. The leader is well-advised to make arrangements for further discussion privately with the member during which time he explains in some detail the reasons for his decision and, if he deems advisable, raise the question of psychotherapy.

How will the other members of the group respond to such a decision and action on the part of the leader? Our experience subsequent to this research has been that, if the group member involved is obviously disturbed, the other members will be more relieved than threatened. Their trust in the leader is further reinforced by his concern for the member and by his responsible behavior in seeing the individual privately for further discussion and for suggestions for other ways to obtain help.

The study of the normative structure of the group reveals the important impact of group norms on yield. We can appreciate the importance of indirect functions of the leader when we note that the normative structure of the group may vary considerably for two leaders who have similar styles and may be associated with widely different outcomes.

It appears that leaders are by no means the sole, or perhaps even the most important source of group norms. Group norms are associated with the expectations that members and leaders have for their group. It is difficult for leaders to reverse strong expectations entering members have about the norms of their group. Leaders influence norms most heavily by strengthening existing expectations of the members or by converting some ambiguous or uncertain expectations of group members into decisive norms. We also found that those leaders who were successful in converting a large percentage of their pregroup expectations into norms were those leaders who had the highest yield groups and conversely, those leaders who had many of their anticipations disconfirmed tended to lead low-yield groups.

What implications do these findings have for leadership technique? First, they further press the leader to abandon some omnipotent notions about his influence on the group. It is clear that normative structure as well as psychosocial relations have a potent influence on group outcome. Furthermore, the leader's role in the formation of group norms is limited, and is an indirect rather than a direct function. The most specific guideline that can be drawn from these findings is that it is of the utmost importance that the leader assess the group members' expectations about the form and the rules that their group will assume. He may obtain this information by employing specific instruments such as the ones used in our study or he may make a more informal inquiry into the members' expectations about the group. If he fails to appreciate the members' expectations for the group and attempts to introduce opposing norms, then he may find himself struggling against some rather potent forces in the group. The leader can most powerfully influence members' expectations which are uncertain or ambiguous. This implies that he should pay more attention to pregroup orientation of his group members; if he is more explicit to prospective members about what they can reasonably expect in the group, he can assist members to make an informed decision about entering the group and decrease the likelihood of having severe deviants in the group.

DIRECT FUNCTIONS

What have the findings to say about the immediate, personal impact of the leader on the members of the group? There are implications for several aspects of leader behavior: cognitive input, stimulation, transference, leader responsibility, and clinical skills. Time and again it has been revealed through this study that cognitive factors are far more important in producing positive outcome in encounter groups than is generally realized. What implications does this have for the leader? It is important to point out that there is no evidence that any particular conceptual framework was more or less effective in producing positive outcome. Nor is there evidence that any leaders were successful in actually teaching a particular framework to their group members: Members in Transactional Analytic groups did not retain any complex transactional conceptual scheme, nor did members of the psychoanalytic group internalize its explanatory system. What the members did learn in the group was a general strategy which they could employ in understanding and resolving problematic areas. They were able to assume a diagnostic observing stance toward important life dilemmas. The specific types of coping strategies internalized were at times disarmingly simple. What seemed to be the most important thing was that people whom they had grown to respect (the leaders and other members of the group) advocated a reflective, self-conscious attitude toward coping.

If members assimilate only crude approximations to a specific conceptual framework, does this not argue against a leader grounding himself fully in the theoretical underpinnings of some theory of change? We think not. When confronted with a bewildering amount of inchoate information, it is to be expected that leaders would search for methods to organize or classify it. In much the same way that nature abhors a physical vacuum, so does a man abhor ideational randomness. Thus most group leaders and psychotherapists can operate more comfortably and effectively if they have some central organizing conceptual framework; this holds even though the particular content of the framework may make little difference. We do not mean to take a nihilistic stance toward the formulation of theory; nor do we mean to say that there are not particular kinds of knowledge that effective leaders must have. We have already argued for a framework which relies heavily on the recognition of psychosocial forces in the environment of the group, and now we suggest that it is important for the leader to organize experience according to some intellectual framework and to plan moves accordingly. This allows him not only to function with comfort but, by his very posture toward conceptual organization, also provides invaluable model setting for group participants and helps participants organize their personal experiences.

Stimulation input by the leader bears a curvilinear relationship to outcome: A moderate amount seems optimal, too much stimulation input leads to high-risk groups, and too little to laissez-faire, apathetic, high dropout groups. High challenge or high confrontation by the leader is not only unnecessary for change but is negatively correlated with outcome. On neither the group nor the individual level was high risk a bedfellow of high gain.

From the point of view of the individual, our data could give no support to the adage that a person must first be shaken up if he is to change. Quite the contrary. We found that the individuals who were adversely affected by the group at the end of the group experience did not "put it all together" and assimilate their learning in the postgroup period. Of our entire experimental sample, only one individual who had a negative outcome at the end of the group moved over to the positive outcome side of the ledger six months later.

The leader looms very large in the emotional life of the group. Try as he will he cannot shuck all the irrationally based trappings of his role. Transference is an inevitable accoutrement of the leadership role in the group and will occur even when the leader very forcibly attempts to abdicate the leadership role. The surplus meaning that the leader has for the participants results in his words and actions having considerable power to help or to harm. Interviews with learners indicated that the leader's support and acceptance was of considerable value for some individuals in helping them to increase their evaluation of self-worth. Other members, through their constructive interaction with the leader, were able to re-evaluate and to alter their relationships with parents or parental surrogates. Others identified strongly with the leader's world view and *modus operandi;* for example, even months later they might deal with a personal dilemma by trying to remember how the leader would have considered or handled a similar situation.

Conversely, strong criticism, negative judgment or rejection by the leader was received by some members as an exceedingly important indictment. Recall that the majority of the Casualties reported having been deeply affected by an attack or rejection by the leader. Some of the Casualties recalled months later some of the negative statements of the leaders with extraordinary vividness. Why did the leaders attack or reject certain members? High-attack leaders shared several characteristics: An unwavering faith in themselves, their product, and their technique, a sense of impatience—changes must be made *now*—a tendency to impose their values on their subjects, a failure to recognize signals that vital defenses are prematurely crumbling, and a failure to differentiate between individuals; they operated as though all individuals needed to make the same changes.

The acquisition of certain clinical attitudes and perspectives is an important part of the training of the leader. An encounter group leader must have a deep appreciation for the tenacity and the self-preservatory function of defense mechanisms. They cannot be battered down; patience, working-through, and time are essential companions of change. Change is a complex process of recycling as the member and the leader spiral repeatedly around recalcitrant areas of resistance. To attack an individual in an effort to dislodge him from familiar defensive niches is crude and often counterproductive; to attack him punitively because he refuses to comply with the leader's timetable and route for change is ignorant and censurable. Furthermore, the sophisticated leader must appreciate and learn to harness transference in the service of change. Timing, patience, resistance, and transference have been overlooked in the avalanche of new enthusiastic change efforts.

436

Implications for Practice

It is important that leaders have enough experience with the difficult business of inducing change in people that they do not oversell their product, either to members of their group, or to themselves. Leaders who invest themselves in achieving the "breakthrough" tread an especially treacherous path. Change is hard work, and although "breakthroughs" occur in the group they are preceded and followed by considerable and deliberate effort. Our findings on the maintenance of learning demonstrate that changes are more likely to remain with an active, risk-taking posture toward the learning accrued. These are more than academic points, since several participants suffered ill effects from the group precisely in this manner. They entered the group with highly unrealistic expectations of what they might accomplish in a short period of time. In the group, some schizoid individuals confronted and were defeated by their lifelong maladaptive interpersonal patterns; they terminated the group far more discouraged than ever about the possibilities of obtaining help in the future.

ARE LEADERS RESPONSIBLE?

Some of the group leaders argued that they bore no responsibility for what happened to the members of their group. One leader put it that the members of the group had formed a contract with him in which each of them assumed responsibility for himself; whatever happened in the group, then, was not his but each member's responsibility. As his group progressed he concluded that he would just "have a good time." We suggest that such a view of the leadership role is particularly misguided and dangerous. It fails to consider that the leader has vast importance in the group, not only because of the surplus meaning which is placed upon him by the group members, but also because of his unique position in the group to harness, for better or for worse, powerful group forces.

This leadership position is even more dangerous when it is coupled with a "no exit" approach. Participants in the group then are placed in an extraordinarily bewildering paradox: They have signed a "contract" (written in a language which they cannot understand because the group is a new experience for them) which states that they have to assume responsibility for themselves in the group. At that point they are placed in a social system from which it is difficult to escape or to proceed counter to a group current which may or may not be in their best interest. The leader of the most successful group took exactly the opposite posture, and very much assumed personal responsibility for what occurred in the group. He explicitly worked to elaborate supportive, trusting norms, and in addition helped group members make their own decisions about how much work they wanted to do. A hallmark of his approach was to ask an individual upon whom the group was focusing, "Do you want to continue on this, do you want to do any further work on this area?" If the group member implied that that was all he wanted to do, the leader, without censure, shifted the focus onto another member.

437

THE PROCESS OF CHANGE

A study of the actual process through which the individual undergoes change bears general implications for the leader relevant to both his direct and indirect functions. Only when a leader understands the process of change can he make an informed decision about the kinds of experience he should attempt to provide for members. Previous considerations of the process of change in encounter groups have generally been contaminated by another characteristic of these groups—"potency." There is general consensus that encounter groups are potent; from their earliest days experiential groups have had a powerful, compelling quality. Unfortunately, in the adulation of things potent, the *raison d'etre* of the group—personal growth or change—has often been forgotten. Indeed at times encounter group *aficionados* have so obfuscated the concepts of potency and change that the two terms have come to be used synonymously. We would argue for a disentanglement of the two terms. "Potency," as it is generally used in regard to encounter groups, refers to the ability to provide an emotionally charged, moving experience; potency in this sense does not refer to the ability to effect change. What do we know about the relationship between "potency" and change? The study suggests that emotional "potency" was associated with change, perhaps even a necessary but by no means a sufficient condition for change.

What are the qualities of the encounter group which contribute to a heightened emotional potency? It appears potency is evoked by certain basic experiences ("the intensive group experience") that the small group provides for its members. The majority of participants reported that the group helped them to experience and express their feelings, to obtain feedback about themselves, to make them aware of their interpersonal impact upon others, to understand that they are like other people, to reveal themselves, and to experience a deep sense of involvement with a group.

On the face of it, these experiences seem to provide a sound platform for the process of change. Yet the intensive group experience is not equivalent to the change process: The critical differences, we believe, are accent and temporal perspective. If the accent is on the intensive experience for the purpose of having an emotional experience, then change is not likely to ensue. Alexander pointed out decades ago that we have emotional experiences all of our lives without ensuing change; it is essential that the experience be a *corrective* emotional experience. Study participants who were oriented toward having an intense or novel experience for its own sake showed less benefits from the groups. Not only must individuals experience deep emotion, but they also must be helped to objectify the experience in such a way as to provide meaning for the future.

The very core of the intensive group experience is the focus on the here-and-now, a focus which we suggest goes beyond pure, mindless experiencing. The here-and-now approach is basically a self-reflective one: Participants alternatively experience and examine their experience. The examination of the experience provides them with some type of cognitive framework which, if sound, will have generalizability. The participant must be able to carry something out of the group experience that is more than a simple affective state. He must carry with him some framework, though by no means necessarily well-formulated, which will enable him to transfer learning from the group to his outside life and to continue experimenting with new types of adaptive behavior. A well-balanced intensive group experience, then, with accent on *reflection* as well as experience and with a focus both on the present and on the future application of the present experience may be a potent vehicle for change. Most small groups will spontaneously evolve into a social unit which provides the affective aspects of the intensive group experience; the leader's function is to prevent any potential obstruction of the evolution of the intensive experience, and in addition to be a spokesman for tomorrow as he encourages group members to reflect on their experiences and to package them cognitively so that they can be transported into the future.

Advice to the Participant

By and large, it is safe to predict that encounter group leaders will be only modestly influenced in their style of practice after perusing this book. Words on paper have a poor track record in altering overt behavior—especially that involved in such a complex performance as group leadership. Almost anything said here to leaders (collect data from group members on who has been hurt in your groups; build a clear contract with group members; use informed consent; pay attention to group forces, and so on) has an essentially exhortational character. Such prescriptions might have influence if designed as part of a systematic leader training program carried out when the leader is reasonably "plastic." But as advice to the presently operating leader, they will probably have little efficacy.

Advice to the encounter group participant, however, is another matter. It is quite feasible to make a number of suggestions to persons who are considering entering an encounter group which will minimize the possibility of negative outcomes and make positive outcomes more likely. The model here is consumer education. *Caveat emptor.* The buyer is in a clear position of power over his or her own decisions. He can decide to go to a group, or not; and can choose a particular type of group. To some extent, the participant can monitor and control his or her own participation during the life of the group, and he can choose to leave it. The participant has most at stake, and is in a good position to utilize information from a study like this one.

Before Deciding to Enter. For those considering attending an encounter group, the findings of this study encourage, first, some self-assessment. What are one's hopes for the experience, and one's own views of self? Persons who feel essentially cut off from other people, dislike their own behavior, and see it as less than adequate, and, in addition, believe that the encounter group experience will somehow beautifully, magically, and safely liberate them from themselves, should take care. Such inflated expectations—and they are perhaps too easy to caricature—can lead not only to frustration, but to negative outcomes. It is simply suggested here that potential group entrants examine realistically where they are, and what they might hope, practically speaking, to obtain from the experience. It should be kept in mind that one's chances for clear positive benefit are only about one in three. A person who feels, essentially, that he or she is in psychological distress should ordinarily be considering counseling or psychotherapy rather than an encounter group experience.

Another sort of useful pregroup decision activity is data collection from past group participants. Persons who have been in groups led by the particular encounter group leader being considered should be talked to, preferably several months after their group experience. The most productive question is: "Would you like to be in a group again, led by this leader?" Negative answers should be taken rather seriously. Positive answers should be taken skeptically; one should talk to another group member, or preferably several. Past group members can also profitably be asked about the general group climate, especially the degree to which, in the latter part of the group, anger and attack took place. Such groups should be entered with caution, if one's hopes for learning and for avoiding negative effects are high.

Questioning past group members as to whether anyone got hurt in the group, and getting details of this, is also especially productive in locating groups which might be damaging.

If, after reconnaisance, one has decided to attend a particular group, assessment of the realism of hopes and expectations for the experience and one's own degree of skepticism or trust about the experience is in order. Mild skepticism, the attitude that the group can be used for one's purposes, but may not automatically be the best or safest of environments, appears to be the most productive stance.

During the Group. Particularly during the first half or so of the group's life, it will pay to be recurrently aware of one's own position in the group, and to operate, if possible, in ways that induce the realistic feeling that one is a comfortably active member of the group. Persons who, by the middle of the group, find that they have been largely passive, "out of it," do not like the group particularly, do not sense that they are respected and liked by other members, never have a feeling of "communion" with them, and do not feel able to disclose their inner thoughts and feelings, will probably get little out of the group experience.

Implications for Practice

It may be argued that one's position in the group is not wholly under one's control—that others define it. That is correct to some extent. By and large, however, if one becomes aware of his position in the group, and treats improving it as a secondary learning objective, the position can be altered. The person who, for example, reports that "I feel out of the group and wish I could be more in," tends to alter others' views of his position, so that their behavior usually shifts toward welcoming and support. Similarly, active behavior directed toward important and valued group goals, such as open expression of feelings, acting freely and spontaneously, taking risks, and being aware of what's happening in the group, tends not only to be personally rewarding, but improves one's own position in the group. Passive, withdrawing, demanding, or hostile behavior does not do so. The option of leaving the group if it is proving steadily unproductive, stressful, or damaging should always be kept open. Not all persons and all learning environments can be perfectly matched.

Generally speaking, it is easier to give data-based advice on how to avoid negative outcomes than it is to suggest ways of guaranteeing positive gain. It appears, however, that there are many different pathways to gain, assuming that the learner is able to avoid the traps of overoptimism, blind trust in the goodness of the group or the leader, and being out on the edge of the group. Avoiding these traps permits—but does not guarantee—achievement of positive learning goals.

There is one suggestion which will encourage positive gains, however: For those who maintain an active, *thoughtful* stance toward what is occurring in the group and in their own awareness, durable gains are more likely. Efforts to think about the encounter group experience and its meaning, contrary to what is often asserted, are likely to make for more learning. Keeping a diary or journal is an easy way to accomplish this, especially if its contents are occasionally discussed with others.

After the Group. Some realistic assessment should be made of what has been learned (or not learned). That, more likely than not, is what will be retained and carried away from the experience. The hope that "it can all be put together" at some time in the future is a relatively slim one. Secondly, after the group has receded in time, some reduction in positive feelings can be expected. But to the degree positive learnings were in fact achieved, maintenance of gains is quite likely. More maintenance will occur if one experiments actively with new behavior, taking a self-monitoring stance. This requires some modulation and refinement, rather than all-or-none operations. Using others for active feedback and discussion aids in the process of stabilizing learnings. It appears rather important to be reflective, to *think* about one's behavior and its meaning in the post-group setting. All in all, a relatively proactive, thoughtful stance seems most productive. It should be said, though, that giant efforts of will do not seem required: Many of the gains reported by our participants were intrinsically satisfying and self-rewarding, so that the reward and reinforcement supplied by others may be less crucial than many people have supposed.

NOTES

1. The formulation "getting the anger out," in passing, implies a fixed and latent amount of aggression existing in persons, a dubious assumption at best. Anger, among other things, is a function of frustration, especially frustration seen to be nonlegitimate (Horwitz, 1963); these are properties of social systems as much as they are of persons.

2. This belief has been partially supported by uncritical and widespread quoting of an early study on foreman training carried out by Fleishman, Harris, and Burtt (1955)—a study invariably interpreted to mean that foremen trained in human relations principles lost their new learnings because of job counterpressures. Yet Fleishman *et al.* found nothing of the sort. They did *not* follow a particular group of foremen back to the job, but instead compared successive groups of foremen who had been in training during previous periods. There was no way to tell whether the successive cohorts of foremen were or were not already different in their human relations attitudes, regardless of the training.

CHAPTER *17*

The Role of Encounter Groups in Society

Are encounter groups good or bad? Should people go to them? Should their development be encouraged? Do they really help? Clearly some of those who participated in the encounter groups emerged differently at the end from those who did not. Some of these differences would be seen by most (although not all) as positive changes, and some would be seen by most (but not all) as negative changes. To say that one-third of the participants benefited in ways that, for most, could be identified both at termination and half a year later might appear to some as an impressive figure, to others as an insubstantial amount. Some would see the goblet as two-thirds empty, some, as one-third full. How does one balance the observed rates of benefit with the rates of destructive outcomes found among the participants? Some perspective may be gained on this question by examining information from two activities sharing some of the same goals as encounter groups—psychotherapy and education.

ENCOUNTER VS. PSYCHOTHERAPY OUTCOMES

Comparisons are risky. Our participants by and large did not enter the encounter groups with a mindset of "patienthood." The measures of outcome generated in this project are not totally comparable to outcome measures used in psychotherapy. The best data available on outcomes are from individual psychotherapy, not group psychotherapy. Despite these qualifications, it is instructive to note the rates of success in well-conducted psychotherapy research, and compare them to success and failure rates noted in the encounter groups. Before examining the studies of psychotherapy, it is useful to point out that the thrust of much psychotherapy outcome research (Bergin and Garfield, 1971) suggests that (1) the duration of therapy (the number of hours) is not related to rates of success; (2) type

443

of criteria used, such as test behavior, therapist ratings, patient sympton checklist, and the like do produce different rates of success (an observation that we have found all-too-true in the encounter group research); (3) there is a slightly greater likelihood that experienced therapists will produce more success than inexperienced ones (recall that in the encounter groups studied, highly experienced practitioners were used); and (4) there is a tendency for more rigorous designs for measuring outcome to produce slightly more favorable outcome rates. (The structure of the present research would match the criteria Bergin and Garfield used to assess adequacy of designs, such as adequate control group and multiple outcome indices.)

Using Bergin and Garfield's survey of selected outcome studies published between 1952 and 1969, nine studies [1,2] were selected to compare success rates in psychotherapy with the rates of success in the encounter groups. Criteria for inclusion from Bergin and Garfield's sample for this comparison were studies that (1) used outcome criteria beyond the therapist rating and patient self-perception (test responses, external judges, and the like) to assess outcome; (2) studies that met Bergin and Garfield's criteria of good or fair design; (3) studies that reported percent improvement; and (4) studies where the patient population was not psychotic.

The percent of improvement reported in these nine studies ranges from a low of 33 percent to a high of 87 percent, yielding a mean of 67 percent and a median of 71 percent. In the encounter groups, the success rate ranged from zero per group to 80 percent, with a mean of 33 percent and a median of 33 percent.[3] The comparison is obviously crude, since it is difficult to find exact matches between the encounter group outcome measures and those used in psychotherapy research. The criteria of change employed in the present case may be more exacting; moreover, it should be stressed that the comparisons are between the general effects of psychotherapy across many different therapists and of encounter across many different encounter leaders. Nevertheless, taken this way, these rates of effectiveness suggest that across all the encounter groups studied, the ability to effect change is modest when compared to that of psychotherapy.

The readiness of patients to change may account for some of these differences, although what data are available on psychotherapy suggest that those more well-integrated (better ego strengths, less psychopathology, and so forth) are likely to be more successful, a finding which suggests that the students studied in the encounter groups would be the more positively biased sample. The greater apparent success of psychotherapy might also be explained in that patients may have more needs or desire to change. Although directly comparable data are unavailable, the finding that many of the students entered with relatively high expectations does not lend itself to such an argument.

How do the rates of damage noted in the encounter groups compare to similar findings in the psychotherapy studies? The data from psychotherapy studies are less clear; the criteria used, the adequacy of the studies, and the differences in terms of patient diagnosis make comparisons difficult.[4] In some studies (for example, Weber, Elinson, and Moss, 1965), it has been found that psychotics had a deterioration rate much higher than neurotics. Bergin and Garfield (1971) report a figure of approximately 10 percent overall negative impact for the studies they have reviewed. How does this rate compare to the rate of negative impact found in the present study? Eliminating those participants who dropped out for psychological reasons to achieve most comparability to psychotherapy research, the rates of 8 percent Casualties and 11 percent Negative Changers, or an overall rate of 19 percent (omitting Dropouts), is close to double that of the overall rate of negative impact reported in psychotherapy literature. It appears, thus, that, overall, encounter groups are less successful in positively changing individuals when compared to psychotherapy and are more likely to induce deteriorative effects than psychotherapy.

ENCOUNTER VS. THE EFFECTS OF COLLEGE EDUCATION

Studies which have examined changes in individuals over their careers in college offer another perspective for comparison to the effects of encounter groups. Of particular interest is an excellent study by Katz (1968) of changes in college students from their freshman through senior year, which was conducted, in part, on the same college campus (in 1961–1965) as the encounter group study. Katz and Associates noted that a third of the men and about half of the women said that they had changed greatly in personal characteristics. Fewer indicated changes in morality, politics, and religion.

In response to an open-ended questionnaire asking, "How have you changed since the Fall of 1961?" a third of those who responded indicated they had become more self-confident, more poised, and felt more independent—for example, in the willingness to express and stand up for one's beliefs. Less frequently, but still relatively often, students also described themselves as having become more stable, as having achieved self-understanding, self-satisfaction, self-criticism, a better-defined philosophy and interests, better emotional control, and the ability to face limitations. Next in frequency they reported changes in their awareness of others— better relationships with people or greater tolerance of their behavior or convictions—and often they reported changes in the direction of increased intellectual activity and curiosity. Katz and Associates point out that general changes noted were improved heterosexual relationships, the ability to express impulses more freely, and increased ability to pursue their own desires. "They lessened previous restrictive and constrictive controls and they adopted more tolerant and permissive attitudes toward the behavior of others." The authors suggest that major personality reorganizations such as suggested by Erikson's identity theory were not the rule. Rather, seg-

445

ments of character, such as more adequate self-conceptions and lessening of previous masochistic tendencies in relationship to others were more frequently noted.

Over half of the students studied by Katz and Associates reported much greater self-understanding. About half said that during their college years, it had become less difficult for them to feel close to people. Their sense of personal mastery was relatively high. Less change was reported in values. About a fifth reported much change in their moral views, their religious views, and their political views. A third reported much greater freedom to express their feelings and desires.

In indicating their most meaningful experience during their college career and how it affected their lives, the largest proportion pointed to self-understanding, self-awareness, or self-evaluation. This percentage was increased by those who listed improved self-confidence and increased meaning to life. Second in order of frequency were responses that fall under the heading of relationships to others; insight into others, greater awareness of the world, and greater tolerance.

Katz and Associates also examined personality changes as measured through the personality inventory. "The major results suggest that changes from freshman to seniors reflect a movement toward greater openmindedness and tolerance, a rejection of a restricted view of life, and a humanization of conscience. . . . Along with the changes in the direction of greater psychological freedom, there is some evidence of the greater capacity for feeling close to others."

The Katz and Associates studies used questionnaire and interview data which methodologically cannot be compared to the encounter group research strategy. What is impressive, however, is the similarity of characteristics or qualities students used to discuss the general college experience. What was important and how they felt they changed markedly resembles the changes noted in students in the encounter groups. Whether the demonstrable changes induced by some of the encounter groups in some participants were otherwise unobtainable benefits, or whether the group experience simply accelerated the rate of "normal development" is impossible to disentangle.[5] The inescapable conclusion in either case, however, is that although *some* people make important changes as a result of their experience in *some types* of encounter groups, viewed as a *total activity,* across all types of encounter groups, the effects of encounter groups are not massive in number or substantially different in kind from those reported for collegiate experience as a *total* activity.

CHANGING VALUES AND VALUING CHANGE

Consistently, the encounter groups were found to have maximum effect on the values of the participants, whether participants were compared with controls or differences among the seventeen groups were assessed. The special sensitivity of values is further emphasized in the finding that the values with which participants entered the encounter groups were one of the two strongest predictors of overall outcome status. Although these value shifts were often unique to the individual, the most characteristic among participants was an increased valuation of personal growth and change. This finding supports the recent suggestion of Kurt Back (1972) that encounter groups have taken on the character of a social movement because of their emphasis on the "mythology of change":

> We can see here the value put on change, on the regeneration of experience, pure and simple. . . . The impression that sensitivity training is worthwhile, that a usually rigid group of modular men can form a unit, and that "real" scientists conduct a meeting, makes the change experience acceptable. The vocabulary of change, change agents, gut learning, spontaneity, authenticity, is all directed toward some change in everyday life, no matter what. In the same vein, Kenneth Burke has put forth a concept of the "God-term," the term which represents the principal value in a society. Change might be such a term now. . . .

Viewed from the perspective in which Back places the encounter group movement, it is not surprising that the most common effect on participants is in the area of value shifts and, particularly, in increasing the valuation of personal growth and change.

A NEW TECHNOLOGY?

If the chief effect of encounter groups is to heighten the valuation of personal change, it must be remembered that they have also been thought to have provided a new technology for human change and growth. Has the array of activities that are generally associated with the encounter group movement made a substantial contribution to the development or appreciation of techniques to enhance change or growth in people? Is there anything really new in what they do? It should be eminently clear by now that a consideration of these questions cannot begin with an examination of the technological contributions of the various theoretical orientations currently existent in the encounter field. Theoretical orientation did not correspond to what our leaders did, nor did it correspond to the degree of benefit or risk for the participants. Simply knowing the theoretical label an encounter leader attaches to himself tells little about what he will do as a leader or about how much he will help people grow.

Four basic dimensions were found to describe the activities of encounter leaders: Stimulation, Caring, Meaning Attribution, and Executive Function. Except for Stimulation, these dimensions in a general way will remind those familiar with the small group literature of other "functional theories" of leader behavior in small groups. Certainly what we have termed Executive Function, the management aspects of leader behavior, and the Caring function correspond to the two parameters postulated by Bales, the oft-cited socioemotional and task functions of leadership. Meaning Attribution, a tongue-twisting abstraction to describe an array of leader functions that have to do with interpreting or labeling or other behavior aimed at creating a cognitive perspective in the participants is again a dimension of leader behavior that has been observed in studies of task, therapeutic, and educational settings. While the dimensions which emerged in studying encounter leader behavior are not identical to those described in earlier studies, they do share similarity with other analyses of leader behavior. Only the dimension of encounter leader behavior which we have called Stimulation seems to represent an unusual technological contribution of the encounter group movement. Certainly stimulation represents a core aspect of "inspirational" teaching or leadership. Yet, in the past decade educators and psychotherapists have increasingly eschewed excessive stimulation. Recall that Stimulation encompasses a large variety of encounter leader behaviors such as confrontation, personal revelation, demonstration, stagings, which in the eyes of some have become synonymous with change-oriented groups which depart from earlier forms. Our findings speak clearly that Stimulation is not *in and of itself* a productive behavior and leaders very high on this characteristic were not only modest in gain but high producers of negative outcomes. Thus a functional analysis of what encounter leaders actually do has isolated as characteristic of the encounter technology only one dimension, of which the efficiency for inducing positive personal growth is doubtful.

The contribution of the encounter technology can also be analyzed by considering the application of structured exercises. Although certainly in use long before the current explosion of encounter techniques (by NTL trainers in the earliest Bethel laboratories, or, of course, prior to that by Moreno in the employment of role-playing for psychotherapy) the complexity, variety, and frequency with which structured exercises are employed is distinctively characteristic of the encounter ethos. Again, the evidence does not demonstrate this characteristic of the encounter technology to be a highly effective instrument for personal change.

Perhaps the most dramatic examples of the failures of the encounter technology are supplied by the findings presented on several processes frequently purported to be the key experiences through which individuals grow and develop in encounter groups. Many of these experiences have been systematically built into the core of encounter methodology because they have been seen as the critical ingredients which are absent in contemporary everyday experience. None has been more widely acclaimed in encounter ideology than expressivity—the expression of warm, positive feelings or angry, hostile feelings. Yet, expressivity did not appear to be instrumentally related to gain or benefit from an encounter group. Even so hallowed an activity as self-disclosure needs to be accompanied by cognitive processes to maximize its benefit.

The analyses of norms and other group characteristics, as well as of the relationship of the person to the group, point to the important, if not critical, contribution of properties and characteristics of the group as a social system. The relationship of the person to the group (membership/deviancy), how attracted he is to the group, or how attracted the group is to him, the norms that govern what is talked about and how it is talked about, and the sources of control (leader/peer) in a group, all play a role in determining whether a person will benefit or not in a group. The yield of particular learning mechanisms, such as self-disclosure, is clearly governed by the type of normative structure the group develops. Cognitive factors which are neither unique to the encounter technology nor *universally characteristic of it* are seen to be central to learning in encounter groups; group experiences and leader behavior that facilitate a cognitive perspective are most productive. These are not new thoughts about how people can utilize groups to learn and grow. What is more to the point is that they have been unappreciated by many who lead encounter groups and that ignoring these conditions which affect how people learn in a small group may vitiate the best intentions of the most dedicated leader.

Most encounter group theories, and certainly the technology, seem to assume that all participants in encounter groups need the same set of experiences so that a similar set of techniques will do for all. The evidence presented on how different people are when they enter encounter groups and how different their roles are in the groups, as well as how differently they make use of what experiences they have, suggests that individual variation is still as much a factor as has been indicated since the work of Galton. Individual variation of this degree warrants questioning the assumption implicit in the rigid application of specific techniques that all people need to change in the same way or that all can learn in the same way.

Examining the contribution of specific characteristics of the encounter movement to the development of a new technology for inducing change does not suggest that the "new techniques" or, as they have been referred to by some, the "new therapies" are in and of themselves highly potent methods for changing behavior.

IS TRAINING THE ANSWER?

Could our conclusion about the relative impotence of encounter as a mechanism for personal change be erroneously explained as a function of the inadequacy of the technology rather than the competence of the leaders? We think not. Most of the leaders were prestigious, "senior" encounter leaders, highly experienced and well-regarded representatives of their orientations. In our own observations of these leaders as they worked with participants we tried to ask how well each leader applied his own framework or "theory of change." Our most poignant observation on this point concerned Leader #6—a leader who had a highly articulate theory of how people change and what he needed to do in order to change them. This leader used numerous techniques to generate basic rage in a participant, a state that he believed necessary for fundamental change. Given this orientation, Leader #6, in our estimation, was exceedingly skillful in moving toward his goal. He possessed sensitive diagnostic skills so that he "knew" what material would generate this state in an individual. He could orchestrate the situation using structured exercises and dramatic backgrounds of music and changing light with consummate skill to generate a situation that would rapidly stimulate an experience of profound rage. The impression gained from observing him was that his sense of timing was superb. To an outside observer the level of stimulation, confrontation, onslaught, involved in his approach may have looked like sheer madness but within his own framework, Leader #6 was a skilled tactician who knew what to do, when to do it, and when to stop. Yet, he was not an unusually successful leader, and two participants reaped severe harm from his group.

One or two leaders were seen by us as not possessing high levels of skill in the sense here defined. By and large, however, our impression was that most of the leaders were competent, a few consummate masters at their trade, yet our judgments of competence did not correspond exactly with the success or failure rates these leaders produced. The intended point is that the level of skill was less the problem than the assumptions many of the leaders made about how people change and about the requisite techniques to achieve individual change. The questionable effect of much of what goes on in encounter groups to induce change is thus, in our view, less a failure in skill than of theory and technology.

Many professionals have over the years become increasingly concerned about the "proletarianization" of encounter group leadership, the "everyman can become a leader" theme. We, of course, did not study nonprofessionals, so that our findings cannot be used either to support or question the use of nonprofessionals. They do imply, however, that control over the excesses to which the critics of encounter point is not automatically guaranteed by censure of the use of nonprofessionals. Our leaders, all professionals, displayed as broad a spectrum of practices as it is reasonable to expect of a nonprofessional sample. Moreover, they varied greatly in what results they produced. On this evidence, success or the deterrence of harm is not guaranteed merely by the appropriate degrees or the ordinary clinical skills thought by some to be so critical in leading encounter groups. The argument here is that more fundamental than the degree of professionalization are the ill-founded assumptions about what operations make for positive change in human beings. Those who are interested in the professionalization of the encounter movement may better serve their cause by articulating the conditions necessary for successful low-risk change which might characterize the work of professionals and nonprofessionals alike, than by assuming that certification establishes subscription to such conditions.

THE CONFUSION OF LIKING WITH LEARNING

If we are correct in suggesting that the fundamental problem in encounter groups is incorrect technology, it seems well to ask how this error came into existence and why it is maintained. Encounter groups are brief, intense experiences; they are truly encounters that rely on the immediate present. A group of strangers assemble, interact intensely, and then become strangers again. Our data indicate few relationships among participants that endured beyond the groups,[6] although the participants were all undergraduates on one college campus. This does not mean that the groups themselves or the people in them were quickly forgotten; members recalled events and people in their group with vividness but not their names. Nor should such information be taken to imply that true intimacy, true relationships did not occur in the group. It is perhaps an all too general morality which would suggest that intimacy as an emotional experience requires permanence. It is our impression as well as the impression of many of the participants that deep but temporary relationships occurred in the groups. What is suggested, however, by the transitory quality of the group relationships is a shared agreement among participants that the groups were truly encounters; intense events but with little requirement to persist beyond the existence of the group itself.

Under such conditions how do encounter leaders judge the instrumentality of their activity; how do they know when they are being helpful, useful, providing situations for people to grow and develop? Clearly, they must get their feedback from the events that transpire in the group and immediately at its end. Much of what encounter leaders do appears to have one clear-cut and predictable result—to increase the enthusiasm and involvement of the participants. (This is not meant to imply that this is a motivation for encounter leaders' behavior.) We have previously suggested that high stimulation, the behavior most characteristic of encounter leaders, is associated with members' perception of high gain based on their testimony after the groups. The use of structured exercises, which we have suggested is a substitute leader behavior for true (personal) charisma, has an equivalent effect; members perceive themselves as having been in productive learning environments and clearly perceive leaders who use many such exercises as being competent. Thus if leaders judge their utility by members' perceptions, they will receive positive signs. Stimulation and structured exercises also rapidly induce cohesiveness, shared perceptions of being in an attractive situation. The ambiance that characterizes highly cohesive groups produces a generalized feeling of well-being, a feeling that cannot help but have an impact on the leader. Stimulation and high use of structured exercises also has been seen to induce postgroup proselytizing which in turn induces others to undertake the experience.

How do leaders judge how well they're doing during the group? Again some of the same feedback processes occur. Leaders value spontaneity, expressiveness, openness, and self-disclosure and work from theoretical propositions from which they derive that these are the mechanisms *par excellence* which can induce learning or growth in the participants. The findings presented in Chapter 12 clearly suggest that the expressions of strong positive or negative feeling, a great amount of self-disclosure in and of itself, and the experience of intense emotional events are not mechanisms that uniquely maximize member learning. They are, however, vivid, intense experiences in participants' minds, and thus the leaders whose techniques are oriented toward producing them come to believe that they are "right on." Perhaps both members and leaders have contributed to the construction of an elaborate mythology which specifies that where there is stimulation (or expressivity, or self-disclosure) there also will be learning; a mythology for which there is evidence, not of learning, but of involvement, of liking what is happening.

Perhaps we have erred in examining encounter groups as if they were activities organized primarily for people-changing. Perhaps we have demanded evidence that is inappropriate to the major meaning of encounter groups as enterprises *not for people-changing, but for people-providing.* Perhaps the import of encounter groups lies not in how many people leave them with new ways of thinking about and responding to themselves and the world they live in and new strategies for coping with life. Perhaps there is a much simpler need that encounter groups are engineered to provide efficiently and effectively—that of momentary relief from alienation, which some have called the most prevalent illness of our times.

COMMITMENTLESS COMMUNION

"Sensitivity training is thus an excellent synthetic community experience for a population that has lost the meaning of community but not its sentimental appeal." (Back, 1972) Those aspects of leader strategy that are characteristic of encounter groups are superbly engineered to provide intense, meaningful, transitory relationships to others. They satisfy a deep hunger for the individual who experiences a sense of normlessness, a chronic boredom, or any other symptoms usually associated with the term alienation. This quality of encounter groups should not be associated with irresponsibility for, at their best, encounter groups provide intense, personal experiences with others in a responsible manner. People are bound together and do feel responsible for one another. There is no evidence in our findings which would suggest that a prime attraction of encounter groups is "headless" release or legitimization of impulsive acting out, as often seen by their most vociferous critics. Every report collected in the study suggests that (except for occasional untoward incidents) the technology used by encounter leaders does create caring for one another among the participants. Witness, for example, the frequent identification of participants with one another as reported in their critical incidents and their sense of empathy and responsiveness to others' joys and sorrows.

The Role of Encounter Groups in Society

What is unique to the situation is that the responsibility and feelings for others are severely limited in space and time. Encounter groups are happenings that are salient and significant and meaningful for most of the participants at the time they take place and perhaps understood by all as being sufficient as such. Unlike the case with many other institutions to which people have looked for communion—most notably the family and the church—no pledge to the future is exacted as the price of belonging, no permanent commitment to particular individuals or particular ideas is required to experience the joys of membership. Blessed as "the tie that binds" may be, it is a satisfaction won at a higher price in more enduring social systems than encounter groups.

The techniques encounter leaders use to create excitement, to create closeness, to create openness become more understandable viewed in this perspective. The psychological meaning to participants of the well-known "trust-walk," the exercise which perhaps most epitomizes the encounter movement, may be clearer when viewed as functioning not to change people but to provide them with a replica of an experience felt to be too rare or too costly to acquire from the interactions of everyday life.

The idea that the prime function of encounter groups in our society rests upon their ability to provide engagement, involvement, and relationship has been noted by others (Slater, 1971; Rogers, 1970; Back, 1972). The analysis we offer differs primarily from these authors' in that they have identified relief from alienation as the role of encounter groups in society on the basis of a functional analysis. We have arrived at a similar conclusion based not on an external reference point, but rather by asking the question "What sort of functions do the modal activities of leaders in encounter groups provide?" Note, too, in sharp contrast, for example, to Rogers' perception of encounter groups, that although we believe that the groups are superbly engineered for this transitory and temporary but meaningful experience with regard to people-providing, our data offer sparse evidence that such experiences in and of themselves lead to altered states in the person beyond the confines of the group. Within the limits of our measurement techniques, the kind of closeness, the type of human experience offered in the encounter group does not appear to be an "irreversible experience" serving, as Rogers suggests, as an internal reference point which has consequences for the person beyond the confines of the experience.

Rosenthal (1971) has offered an explanation of the function of encounter groups in our society which stresses the ritualistic or ritual-providing characteristics of encounter groups. While such a conception is not identical to the theme of people-providing, the identification of ritualistic characteristics is harmonious with a view that it is communion or social integration which people seek from encounter groups.

Do the conclusions regarding the people-providing rather than people-changing emphasis imply that encounter groups cannot play a productive

453

role in facilitating human progress? By no means. The modern day encounter group and its forerunner, sensitivity-training, are learning contexts that have grown out of twenty-five years of recent human experience and resemble countless activities developed during centuries of the prescientific era of human change. They are activities that address themselves to basic human needs, and some have estimated that over five million people have sought them out. The type of groups examined in this study represent the end product of an overdeveloped spiral in which innovations of one year become the stagnant establishment of another year. In the pell-mell rush to become the new miracle cure, the fundamental discoveries about the potency of the small group for change that gave birth to a movement dedicated to expanding human potential have been harnessed to service excesses beyond the limits of productivity.

Yet the underlying principles are simple and still meaningful. Encounter groups excel in their ability to involve and to provide a setting in which certain basic human activities associated with productive change can occur. When one strips away the excesses and the frills, the ability of such groups to provide a meaningful emotional setting in which individuals can overtly consider previously prohibited issues cannot be ruled out as an important means for facilitating human progress. The notion, as simple as it is profound, that by creating a social microcosm based upon principles which are involving on the one hand and different from ordinary life on the other, remains sound. The opportunity for individuals to learn something about themselves by explicitly using others' reactions to their behavior is meaningful. The affirmation of self through the overt (rather than as in normal life, covert) comparisons with peers does provide a new dimension to ordinary human experience. The sanctioning of a group of peers that become important for expressing and experiencing emotions *and being able to talk about* such feelings is a basic process for enhancing human potential. It is an experience that is not easily duplicated in the ordinary course of living. In other words, encounter groups, at their best, provide a setting for engaging in processes that are not usually available in the degree to which many apparently desire and perhaps need them.

What went wrong? As the use of encounter groups expanded at an explosive rate, and the prophets became many, the basic assumptions about what it is people need and under what conditions they can grow and develop were stretched into grotesque shapes with a loss in perspective and balance. Some encounter leaders distinguished themselves on the principle that if freeing up human beings to express emotions was good, then progress could be enhanced, intensified and speeded up by greater and greater dosages. For others, if developing closeness and the basic human respect and trust for others was a good, then more and more love made faster and expressed at increasingly intense levels would be even better. For others, if the ability to talk about previously unrecognized or unspoken aspects about oneself was a good, then the total stripping of self and the total disclosure of all hidden recesses was even better, and techniques were developed to facilitate and speed up this process. If providing a setting for human growth and enhancement required that this setting not be constrained by the ordinary mores and mutual expectations of society, then a total and instantaneous sweeping away of the fabric of mutually acceptable restraints in social relationships was seen as the answer. The encounter group scene became like a science fiction portrayal of basically sound procedures; procedures so misshapen by excess that they no longer served their original function.

Synergistic with this emphasis on better and faster technologies were the spiraling demands and expectations placed upon the encounter group: Increasingly, participants came seeking salvation or radical change in themselves, in their life-style, in their relationships to others, burdening the providers with providing even further satisfactions. Rather than a learning setting, the group was seen as a place for radical surgery. The leader, the resource person, the conductor, the individual who could enhance the basic learning setting became the guru, the person who could provide change for all no matter what the demand. Rather than the learner using and shaping the setting, he became increasingly a passive tool under the increased direction of omniscient gurus. Rather than providing a setting in which the ordinary societal constraints on communication were removed as a means of providing a learning context, the encounter group became a setting for basic personality changes, for radical transformations—the repository for the ubiquitous and unmet needs of an avaricious clientele.

What initiated this chain of events? Whether it was the seeker or provider is perhaps unimportant to disentangle. What is important is to recognize both the promise as well as the limits of a technique. Encounter groups present a clear and evident danger if they are used for radical surgery in which the product will be a new man. The danger becomes even graver when both the provider and the seeker share such a perception. Encounter groups are a disappointment if we place on them the burdens of the plight of modern man and ask why have they not done more. If we unburden them from such magical expectations and unlock them from the burden of use no matter what the problem, no matter who the person, and begin to perceive them simply as an otherwise unprovided social context for humans to explore and express, then perhaps we can begin to seek more systematic and less dogmatically derived information on how that context may best be shaped to make a meaningful contribution to the resolution of human problems.

NOTES

1. The nine studies are: Person, 1967; Bieber, 1962; Koegler and Brill, 1967; Gottschalk, Myerson and Gottlieb, 1967; Shore and Masimo, 1966; Schjelderup, 1955; Orgel, 1958; Shlien, Mosak and Dreikurs, 1962; Rosenthal, 1955; and Imber, Nash, Stone and Frank, 1968.

2. The comparison between outcome in encounter groups for a population whose dominant orientation to the experience was personal growth, change, or enhancement with patient populations, in whom the dominant motivation was relief from distress and symptoms, further stretches the credibility of such a comparison. Although the nine studies selected for comparison purposes rely on outcome indices beyond symptom relief, the issue cannot totally be ignored. Specifically, the Person study involves test scores, behavior ratings and social behavior; the Bieber study involves behavior change; Koegler measured behavior as well as patient and therapist ratings; Gottschalk utilized research interviews and self-ratings; Shore and Masimo utilized tests as well as behavioral change ratings; the Schjelderup inquiry employed questionnaires, therapist ratings, and observer ratings; Rosenthal used test material questionnaires and research interviews; and Imber *et al.* used patient, interviewer, and observer ratings. Each relied to some extent on target distress. None of these studies covered the range of areas examined in the encounter group project in which values, interpersonal behavior, coping strategies, self-characteristics, conceptions of others, ratings by significant others, as well as the leader ratings and peer ratings were utilized.

In addition, the average length of time in treatment was greater for the psychotherapy studies reviewed, an average of fifty-two hours with a median of forty hours, compared to the thirty hours in the encounter group. Also, all except for Person's study involved individual therapy, rather than a group context. Thus, we may be dealing with more intensive experiences in therapy, we may be making comparisons between groups of individuals who have greater needs to change and reduce distress, and thus may more easily show improvement compared to the relatively well-functioning group of students who participated in the present study.

3. Another perspective for comparing rates of positive benefit in the encounter group with those reported in the psychotherapy literature may be gained from an examination of Table 3–6 in Chapter 3. The measures most analogous to those of symptom improvement in psychotherapy outcome research are self-ratings of deficiencies students felt characterized their interpersonal behavior when they entered the encounter groups. Looked at this way, 24 percent of the students felt they improved in their interpersonal behavior beyond chance variation in the scale, a rate low in comparison to the percent rate of symptom improvement reported in the psychotherapy studies. Note, however, that 24 percent represents a significantly larger proportion than controls. The area of self, which includes self-esteem and self-ideal discrepancy, is another area comparable in some respects to indicators employed in psychotherapy research. In this area, 43 percent of the participants improved beyond chance variation, compared to 25 percent of the controls. Self-reported gains, a third area of comparability, yielded increases in 57 percent of the participants. Finally, leaders rated approximately 30 percent of the participants as "much improved." In general, these percentages are lower than those reported in the psychotherapy literature for similar—not identical—change indices. Again, although several factors mentioned previously mitigate these comparisons, overall effect of the encounter groups for changing individuals were modest when compared to much of what is reported in the psychotherapy literature.

4. The data presented in the psychotherapy literature on deteriorative effects are drawn on the average from less adequate studies and do not have the same research methodology used in the encounter group project to follow the total populations beyond the limits of the treatment. Our own findings, discussed in Chapter 5,

clearly indicate that had such a research strategy not been employed, the rates of negative change noted would have been considerably lower. The discrepancy in methodologies for "discovering" negative effects of treatment thus may be based not on the true rates of each activity, but rather on the differences on methods for locating cases. Again, caution on the adequacy of the comparisons between psychotherapeutic endeavors and encounter groups must obviously be exercised.

5. The "normal development data" from the Katz and Associates study used for comparison with the effects of participation in encounter groups involves disparate time periods. Katz studied his students over a three and a half year period; participants in encounter group studies were examined over nine months.

6. An average of between one and two people per group stated they had formed new friendships in the group; only five participants from three groups said that the groups had met after termination; and six months after the group, participants could, on the average, recall the names of no more than five of those who had participated in their group.

APPENDIX *I*

Questionnaires Used to Measure Outcome

Attitudes toward Encounter Groups

During the past few years, groups variously labeled as sensitivity-training or encounter groups have grown greatly in a variety of settings. Such groups have been used as: a place to provide people opportunities for self-exploration, as a means of personal change, as a way of aiding in intergroup conflict, as a mechanism for dealing with current urban problems, as a hoped-for new educational direction, and as a means of changing organizational life.

The rapid expansion of encounter groups has not been without its critics. The following are a series of statements about the value of and problems with such groups. How closely do these opinions fit your own? Please indicate your agreement or disagreement by circling the phrase that most closely fits your own opinion.

(1)	(2)	(3)	(4)	(5)
Strongly Agree	Agree	Have an Open Mind	Disagree	Strongly Disagree

1. The open and direct expression of feelings toward one another in a group usually degenerates into criticism without leading to productive change.   D/S

2. Encounter groups are at the forefront of what needs to be done. They offer a unique way of breaking down the barriers between people.   SB

3. The situations that arise in encounter groups have no relevance to the real world.   SB

4. People play the sensitivity game—they give out a lot of caring and bluntness, but it's just a thing they do to earn group acceptance.   G/P

5. Encounter group experience is good preparation for living in a really democratic society.   SB

6. Encounter groups encourage people to be open and frank too fast.   D/S

7.   I think this would have been a better world if every child had started in encounter groups in the first year of school.   SB

8.   In these times of black-white impasse we ought to be spending a lot more money on encounter groups as a way of opening up channels of communication.   SB

9.   A person's individuality is frequently pushed aside in encounter groups.   D/S

10.   The first exciting thing that's been on the education horizon in the last decade.   SB

11.   Group members develop the ability to be more direct about their feelings, but it's artificial because they really don't have to take responsibility for the consequences of what they say.   G/P

12.   It is a hit-and-run kind of relating that gives the illusion of being in contact.   G/P

13.   Although some may learn, too many people get hurt in encounter groups.   D/S

14.   Encounter groups are one of the few places where genuine feelings can be expressed and received.   G/P

15.   Just an adult plaything.   G/P

16.   Emphasis on encounter groups detracts from individual responsibility to society.   D/S

17.   Encounter groups are the modern equivalent of a lonely hearts club.   G/P

18.   People may be forced to reveal things against their better judgment.   D/S

19.   People are attracted to encounter groups because of their own personal needs; the groups operate on too emotional and personal a level to be much use in solving social problems.   SB

20.   We are raised with all sorts of inhibitions that prevent us from relating to others; encounter groups help us to become more truly ourselves.   G/P

21.   If businessmen, military men, and politicians went through the experience of an encounter group, they would be less likely to treat other people the way they do now.   SB

22.   This kind of intense experience is more than some people can take.   D/S

23.   People express their genuine selves in encounter groups.   G/P

24.   Since the relationships in a group are only temporary, people may behave cruelly and irresponsibly toward each others.   D/S

D/S = Danger/Safety   SB = Social Benefit

G/P = Genuine/Phony

Personal Anticipations [1]

Participation in an encounter or T-group is a very personal thing. In many ways it is a human laboratory in which each person can meet a variety of needs, carry away a range of learnings, and find many different kinds of experiences. We are interested in knowing, from your perspective at this time, some of the ways you anticipate how, if you were to participate, an encounter group might be meaningful to you.

The following seven items refer to some of the ways previous participants have used such group experiences.

First, read through the entire seven items and show by putting an X on the line—how you would describe yourself *as you are now*.

After you've completed the seven items, read through them again and show—by putting a circle on the line—where you think you would be at the end of an encounter group experience.

1. Seldom express my true feelings to others.   Usually express to others what I feel inside.
2. Difficult to know how others feel and think about me.   Usually know how others feel about me.
3. Would like to change some of the ways I relate to people.   Pretty satisfied about the way I relate to people.
4. Hard for me to get close to others.   Easy for me to get close to others.
5. Frequently don't understand my inner feelings.   Usually understand my inner feelings.
6. Often am not sensitive to how others feel.   Usually am sensitive to how others feel.
7. Difficult for me to be spontaneous.   Easy for me to be spontaneous.

REMINDER: Now read through the seven items again and indicate with a circle where you think you'll be at the end of the encounter group experience.

The following eight items represent how some people have viewed their experiences in encounter groups.

First, read through the entire eight items and show—by putting an X on the line—to what extent in your own life *as it is now* you have an opportunity for such experiences.

1. Items 1–15, ten-point scales; items 16–26, seven-point scales. The questionnaires were given to the participants at the end of the encounter group and then again at the long-post follow-up. The original questionnaires covering items 1–15 with the participants rating were readministered. Thus each participant had before them how they had filled it out prior to entering the groups. The questionnaire covering items 16–26 (values) were administered without benefit of the original scores.

After you've completed the eight items, read through them again and show—by putting a circle on the line—the extent to which you think an encounter group would give you such an opportunity.

8. Rarely have a chance to get information from others about my behavior.

   Have as many opportunities as I need to get feedback about my behavior.

9. I do not have enough opportunities to know others deeply.

   I have enough situations where I can know others deeply.

10. Rarely have an opportunity to have an open and honest encounter with my peers.

   I have as many open and honest encounters with my peers as I want.

11. Not enough opportunity to share with peers.

   Many opportunities to share with peers.

12. Rarely get the chance to have novel experiences.

   Have a number of opportunities to have novel experiences.

13. Rarely have a chance to put others straight.

   Have many opportunities for putting others straight.

14. Seldom in situations where I can trust other people.

   Often in situations where I can trust other people.

15. Seldom in a situation where I can get out all the anger I feel.

   Often in a situation where I can get out all the anger I feel.

REMINDER: Now read through the eight items again and indicate by a circle the extent to which you expect the encounter group will provide such an opportunity.

You have just completed a list of items in which you described where you are now and some of your anticipations about group experiences. We would like to know which of these possibilities offered in the encounter group experience are personally important to you. Please read the following statements and indicate their importance to you by marking the line at the place that best reflects your feelings.

EXTREMELY
IMPORTANT   UNIMPORTANT

16. Being able to express my feelings. _____

17. Being able to tell it like it is. _____

18. Learning about how others view me. _____

19. Being sensitive to others' feelings. _____

20. Having new experiences. _____

21. Being flexible and letting things happen. _____

22. Expressing anger directly to people. _____

23. Changing some of the ways I re-
    late to people.   _____
24. Becoming closer to others.   _____
25. Understanding my inner self.   _____
26. Sharing with peers.   _____
Other ways this experience may be important to you._____

Racial Attitudes

Please indicate your agreement or disagreement with the following statements by circling the phrase that most closely fits your own opinion.

(5)	(4)	(3)	(2)	(1)
Strongly	Somewhat	No	Somewhat	Strongly
Agree	Agree	Opinion	Disagree	Disagree

1. Only a black person can really understand another black.
2. All administrators of a "Black Studies Program" must be black.
3. A "Black Studies Program" must be autonomous; that is, the program
   must be answerable only to itself and not to the college.
4. Absolute equality in everything is the only solution to the black-white
   problem.
5. As open-minded as I think I am, I must admit I feel a reaction when I
   see black and white students on campus holding hands.
6. The natural hairstyle is more attractive for black people than straightened hair.
7. Someone who says that Negro noses and lips are not as aesthetically
   pleasing as those of other races is showing his prejudice.
8. I wouldn't marry someone of another race, not because I feel any prejudice, but because in this society there would be so many problems to
   deal with.
9. If I had to choose between a doctor of my own race and one of another race, when it comes to illness and trusting someone with my life,
   I'd choose a doctor of my own race.
10. I am against the use of destructiveness, abusive language, and the
    threat of violence.
11. I am getting fed up with this whole black-white issue.
12. Standards should be lowered to admit any member of a minority
    group who wants a college education.
13. Black students ought to be able to have all-black dormitories if they
    want them.
14. The most meaningful path to "equal status" is separatism for blacks
    with things under their own control and direction.

15. Personally, I do not believe that there is anything I can meaningfully do to help make things better between blacks and whites.
16. I am optimistic about some meaningful solution to racial problems on campus.
17. "Separatism" and "Black Nationalism" are short-run means to get power and respect, not a long-term solution to the black-white problem.
18. There should be no limit set on the number of black students admitted to any college or university.
19. No weakness or difficulty can hold us back if we have enough will power.
20. People can be divided into two distinct classes—the weak and the strong.
21. Getting to the top is more a matter of luck than ability.
22. Most people will go out of their way to help someone else.
23. You sometimes can't help wondering whether anything is worthwhile anymore.
24. Nowadays a person has to live pretty much for today and let tomorrow take care of itself.
25. If you try hard enough, you can usually get what you want.

(5)	(4)	(3)	(2)	(1)
I Would Participate	It's OK for Others But Not for Me	I Have No Clear Opinion	I'm Somewhat against Them for Others	I'm Strongly against Them for Everyone

26. Peaceful demonstrations.
27. Strikes.
28. Occupying offices.
29. Destructive acts.
30. Confrontations with demands and threats.
31. Guerilla warfare.

(5)	(4)	(3)	(2)	(1)
Strongly Agree	Somewhat Agree	No Opinion	Somewhat Disagree	Strongly Disagree

32. I worry quite a bit about what people think of me.
33. I like to hear all sides of an argument before I make up my mind.
34. I am suspicious of people who try to be different from everybody else.
35. To tell the truth, I would be afraid to take part in demonstrations.
36. I am suspicious of whites who try to help blacks.
37. How long do you think it will be before there is complete equality between blacks and whites in this country?

(5)	(4)	(3)	(2)	(1)
Under 10 years;	10–20 years;	21–50 years;	51–100 years;	Over 100 years.

(5)	(4)	(3)	(2)	(1)
Strongly	Somewhat	No	Somewhat	Strongly
Agree	Agree	Opinion	Disagree	Disagree

38. It is the responsibility of every white student to do everything he can to help the blacks on campus get what they say they want.
39. With members of another race I still have the feeling that they don't really trust me.
40. No matter what I do or say black students treat me as if I were a racist.
41. Black students' demands to the college should be presented as "Nonnegotiable."
42. When groups like the Black Panthers carry firearms it is simply a threat and not truly serious.
43. On the whole, black people are more in touch with their emotions, more spontaneous, less controlled, than whites.
44. I feel scared and intimidated by blacks.
45. I came to college to get an education, not to solve the black-white problem.
46. I would be willing to have my tuition raised in order to support special programs for black students.
47. I would be willing to donate at least four hours per week tutoring minority group students admitted to this university who want assistance.
48. If a black student acts as if I were to blame for how blacks are treated in this country, my first reaction is likely to be to:
    Get angry—Feel he's right—No feelings—Feel a little bored by it—Wish he'd be more reasonable.
49. I devote time and participate in activities related to black problems.

    Please check all those that apply:

    ——BSU;   ————Hrs/week;   ——————Helping plan the black studies program————————Hrs/week;   ————Tutoring ————Hrs/week;   ————Recruitment of students ———— Hrs/week;   ————Recruitment or selection of faculty ———— Hrs/week;   ————Other ————Hrs/week.

Personal Dilemmas [1]

Listed below are a number of incidents that most people encounter in their day-to-day lives. Some or all of these situations may have occurred to you during the past six months. We are interested in having you think about these events. For many of these "events" a number of examples may come

---

[1] Seven-point scales. The set-up of 19 scales is given for each of the three "personal dilemmas" described by the respondent.

to mind. Choose the one that seems to you most puzzling—where you weren't sure you knew what to do—the one that was a dilemma for you personally. We'd like you to briefly describe an actual example of each of these events.

1. Wanted to change something in your personal life.
2. Had a problem with a close friend, but you weren't sure of what to do.
3. Had a problem with school or work, but weren't sure of what to do.

Now look over the personal situations you've just described and think about what you would do *if you had to face each of these dilemmas tomorrow*. Now, rather than write out what you would do, we would like you to check on the following scales how likely it is you would respond in these ways to each of the personal situations you described above. You may of course check as many as seem appropriate to represent what you would do if you had to face the problem tomorrow.

Very Likely   Very Unlikely

1. Try to see the humorous aspects of the situation.
2. Take some positive, concerted action on the basis of your present understanding of the situation.
3. Not worry about it, everything will probably work out fine.
4. Talk it over with the person(s) in the situation to see if you can work it out.
5. Try to put yourself in the other's shoes.
6. Become involved in other activities in order to help keep your mind off the problem.
7. Draw upon your past experiences from a similar situation.
8. Seek some professional help or advice.
9. Get out of the situation.
10. Get your feelings out by talking to someone.
11. Make several alternate plans for handling the situation: after all, you never know which one might work.
12. Try to get some perspective by talking it over with a friend.
13. Re-examine your own thoughts and feelings—do a lot of inner looking.
14. Express your feelings "as they are" to the other person(s).
15. Try something experimental to see if it works.
16. Try to reduce your tension by, e. g., smoking, drinking, exercise.
17. Act spontaneously—do the first thing that comes to mind.
18. Be prepared to expect the worst.
19. Seek additional information by reading up on the situation.

Personal Description Questionnaire

We would like to record some of the ways you see yourself and others. You will be asked to describe four people you know, plus yourself, on a number of characteristics in this questionnaire.

Think of four people whom you know fairly well, and whom you will see fairly often in the next couple of months. This latter condition is necessary because you will be asked to describe the same people again some time after the encounter group experience.

In selecting from among the people you know, please try to pick persons who are as *different* from one another as possible, so that the four you choose will represent a diverse and varied group among the people you know. One way of doing this is to pick two people who *stand out* for one reason or another. It doesn't matter why they stand out—it may be because of something they have done, a relationship they have with you, some particular characteristic they have, a position they hold, or perhaps just because they seem unusual or different or special to you.

Then, for the remaining two people, pick each one to be as different as possible from one of the first two. When you are through, you should have a fairly diverse set of people to describe.

Your task is to describe the four persons and yourself (as you really are now—"S"—and as you would like to be—"L") on these scales. Show how these people and yourself are similar and different on each characteristic by placing the number identifying the people you are describing in the letters identifying yourself in the boxes of the scale.

REMEMBER: If you place two people's numbers in the same box, it means that you consider them essentially the same on the characteristics represented by the scale. If you place them in different boxes, it means you consider them different in some significant way on that characteristic.

7	6	5	4	3	2	1
☐	☐	☐	☐	☐	☐	☐

1. Comfortable with others—Uncomfortable with others
2. Genuine—Artificial
3. Lenient—Strict
4. Shows Feelings—Hides Feelings
5. Accepts Suggestions—Rejects Suggestions
6. Responsible—Irresponsible
7. High Ability—Low Ability
8. Enthusiastic—Unenthusiastic
9. Influential—Uninfluential
10. Relaxed—Tense

11. Sincere—Insincere
12. Undemanding—Demanding
13. Outspoken—Reserved
14. Sympathetic—Unsympathetic
15. Accepts Help—Rejects Help
16. Reliable—Unreliable
17. Active—Passive
18. Low Status—High Status
19. Well Adjusted—Maladjusted
20. Prefers Not to Direct Others—Prefers to Direct Others
21. Demonstrative—Undemonstrative
22. Constructive—Destructive
23. Thorough—Careless
24. Competent—Incompetent
25. Involved—Uninvolved
26. Low Prestige—High Prestige
27. Unworried—Anxious
28. Frank and Open—Evasive
29. Considerate—Inconsiderate
30. Accomodating—Stubborn
31. Dependable—Undependable
32. Informed—Uninformed
33. Interested—Unconcerned
34. Optimistic—Pessimistic
35. Happy—Sad

Table of Correlations "Basic" Thirty-three Variables
Time 1 Scores for Total Sample (N = 274)

Variables:	1	2	3	4	5	6	7	8	9	10	11	12	13	14	15	16	17	18	19	20	21	22	23	24	25	26	27	28	29	30	31	32	33
1. Safety/Danger																																	
2. Social Benefit	34																																
3. Genuine/Phony	41	48																															
4. Value Experience	-15	-26	-27																														
5. Value Change	-11	-12	-15	00																													
6. Value Growth	02	04	04	-20	00																												
7. Self-Orientation	07	02	10	-07	01	30																											
8. Instrumental-External	-09	-05	-08	08	14	15	12																										
9. Interpersonal	-02	02	12	00	08	-01	26	26																									
10. Intimacy	-02	02	00	-05	-03	10	28	18	53																								
11. Interpersonal Adequacy	06	02	06	-04	27	-09	00	-01	06	06																							
12. Feeling Sensitivity	-04	-07	-06	-01	11	-05	00	-08	-06	00	-01																						
13. Adequate Coping	12	27	04	-22	17	00	00	-01	07	-01	17	10																					
14. Defensive Coping	-11	00	-20	14	-02	11	-03	-01	-10	01	-06	03	-01																				
15. Wanted Control	00	-10	-01	-01	02	11	10	-02	-02	-02	-15	-01	-04	04																			
16. Expressed Control	-03	-04	-02	14	-09	-05	-06	-02	-09	-15	-07	03	02	08	-12																		
17. Wanted Affection	06	07	10	07	02	-08	06	-01	15	06	04	-09	-02	-06	08	03																	
18. Expressed Affection	-01	03	04	03	11	-18	01	-07	10	02	19	04	07	-05	02	09	43																
19. Self-Esteem	-04	-02	-02	10	28	-04	02	07	23	10	42	15	10	-01	-17	01	02	13															
20. Positive Self	-04	10	04	-13	26	-04	03	04	15	07	50	07	12	-12	-14	08	01	14	46														
21. Lenient Self	-01	03	04	-12	03	-03	05	-09	06	01	09	08	-04	-04	07	-18	04	00	-03	00													
22. Self-Ideal—Interpersonal	04	01	03	01	-07	-07	02	03	06	-03	-05	-16	07	-03	01	01	10	-01	-08	-10	-15												
23. Self-Ideal—Instrumental	05	13	11	-15	01	-01	11	09	07	01	04	-13	07	-07	01	-02	10	-02	-16	-03	17	25											
24. Positive Others	-01	08	01	-13	13	12	03	03	04	06	09	07	08	-07	08	01	08	-03	09	55	03	-03	03										
25. Lenient Others	01	-02	-06	-07	-13	09	-05	-14	-14	-02	00	00	-18	08	05	-06	-05	-12	-17	-19	32	-02	-01	00									
26. Complexity—Interpersonal	04	07	11	04	-16	11	-01	09	14	03	-17	-02	07	02	11	06	03	04	-11	-31	-15	17	00	-52	-10								
27. Complexity—Instrumental	-07	08	-04	10	-04	00	03	11	13	01	-20	17	-03	07	03	-01	15	05	01	-05	-15	-01	09	04	-14	26							
28. Best Friend	05	05	10	-13	11	-07	03	-04	13	08	08	00	07	-17	00	-06	05	10	09	06	03	08	08	17	-05	-06	06						
29. Opportunity for Peer Communication	01	-03	-06	-14	17	-04	-02	02	10	04	61	00	20	-10	-05	-10	03	13	30	47	03	-13	02	22	-03	-24	-10	15					
30. Opportunity for Anger Expression	07	-07	00	00	05	-02	-02	-01	08	06	09	13	-05	06	-02	00	-05	-02	13	11	02	03	07	-01	10	-06	-07	-09	02				
31. Number of Close Friends	-01	13	19	-02	11	03	05	-02	07	-06	23	-02	18	-14	-04	-07	23	22	15	25	02	-04	09	08	-14	-06	08	30	27	-05			
32. Hours Spent with Friends	01	05	08	-07	12	-08	-03	-08	16	01	17	-16	07	-06	01	-13	03	10	01	19	09	12	13	16	-06	-09	01	26	25	05	42		
33. Decisions	04	-02	01	10	17	12	20	21	15	12	-09	-04	05	-04	01	-06	-02	-02	-03	-07	05	-05	-05	-06	08	08	05	07	-09	00	03	02	

NOTE: Reliability estimates are based upon test retestability over a one-year period for the control group (N = 69). When published information on reliability was available, these are the figures used; they are marked by an asterisk. Attitudes toward encounter groups—Danger .56, Social Benefit .62, Genuineness .56, Value Experience .56, Value Change .32, Value Growth .45, Self-Orientation .43, Instrumental/External .02, Interpersonal .33, Intimacy .16, Interpersonal Adequacy .73, Feeling Sensitivity .67, Adequate Coping .43, Defensive Coping .50, Wanted Control* .71, Expressed Control* .74, Wanted Affection* .80, Expressed Affection* .73, Self-Esteem .75, Positive Self .79, Lenient Self .72, Positive Self .45, Best Friend .45, Opportunity for Peer Communication .62, Opportunity for Anger-Expression .46, Number of Close Friends .62, Hours Spent with Friends .33, and Decisions .11.

APPENDIX *II*

Questionnaires and Rating Schedules Used to Measure Group Conditions, Psychosocial Relationships, and Mechanisms of Change

Observer Checklist of Leader Behavior [1]

A. *Evocative Behavior*—Leader interventions designed to get the *person* or *group* to respond. The seven categories under this heading differ in intensity of demand for response.
  1. Inviting, Eliciting (.35) [2]
  2. Questioning (.47)
  3. Reflecting (.55)
  4. Calling On (.66)
  5. Challenging (.75)
  6. Confrontation (.80)
  7. Exhortation (.85)

B. *Coherence Making, Perspective Building, Cognitive Learning*—Leader interventions designed to get the *person* or *group* to look at something; to change, alter or freshen their perspectives on themselves or on the group.
  8. Explaining, Clarifying, Interpreting (.69)
  9. Comparing, Contrasting, Finding Similarities (Comparing one's behavior with another's) (.70)
  10. Summarization—providing an historical perspective for the in-

---

[1] *The task:* We are interested in the type and frequency of certain kinds of behavior associated with group leaders. Your task is to rate occurrence. Look at the form of behavior, *not* the success or failure, of the leader's intervention. Try to ignore the *leader's motivation* for the behavior; doing this will probably increase your accuracy. Note that some of the leaders you observe may use only a *limited* number of forms repeatedly, while others may cover a *wide* range of forms. Try not to err either on the side of "wanting to check off a lot of items," or of locking into your "general" image of the leader.

[2] Interjudge reliability based on eighty-nine observer pairs, gammas computed on 4×4 contingency tables.

dividual or group. (Comparing over time, reflecting on behavior or feelings of individuals or the group) (.69)

11. Inviting Members to Seek Feedback (.62)
12. Providing Framework for How to Change (.54)
13. Providing Concepts for How to Understand (Instructing group about meaning of body posture, tone of voice, interpersonal games) (.71)

C. *Support*—Affective, relationship dimension of leader behavior; helping, rewarding *individual* or *group*.
14. Protecting (.85)
15. Support, Praise, Encouragement (.71)
16. Offering Friendship, Love, Affection (.72)

D. *Management*—Leadership behavior directed toward how people are working, relating to one another, and how the group is functioning, progressing.
17. Stopping, Blocking, Interceding (.80)
18. Suggesting Procedure for the Group or a Person (.76)
19. Managing Time, Sequence, Pacing, Starting and Stopping (.71)
20. Focusing (Drawing attention to something that happens to the group or what someone said or did) (.57)
21. Suggesting or Setting the Rules, Limits, Norms (.78)
22. Suggesting or Setting Goals or Directions of Movement (.74)
23. Decision Task (Suggesting that the group needs to make a decision, act planfully, or gauge itself, etc.) (.89)
24. Decision Making (Group faces an overtly expressed dilemma or decision point; leader makes a decision for the group) (.94)

E. *Use of Self*—Leader behavior in which the primary thing is the focus on self to accomplish some learning purpose in the group.
25. Reveals His Own Here-and-Now Feelings (.69)
26. Reveals His Own Personal Values, Attitudes, Beliefs (.87)
27. Draws Attention to (focuses on) Himself As an Issue to Be Dealt with by the Group (Either in leadership role or personal qualities) (.80)
28. Participates As a Member in the Group, Involves Himself Personally (.81)

Leader Style Categories [1]

1. *Interpreter of Reality*—Attaching meaning to a person or a group's behavior. The issue here, no matter what the particular phrasing, is that

[1] Interjudge reliability based on eighty-three observer pairs, gammas computed on 3×3 contingency tables.

some kind of explanation is being suggested for consideration that a particular individual or individuals may not be overtly recognizing some aspect of their feelings or behavior. The leader may name it, he may suggest that we look into it, he may tell a person directly what he's feeling. In general, understanding how it is and what people are feeling is an important goal for this kind of leader. $(g = .54)$

2. *The Releaser of Emotions*—A free-swinging "gutsy" expression of how one really feels is important.
    A. The leader may accomplish this by some form of suggestion. $(g = .60)$
    B. The leader may accomplish the same end by *demonstrating* himself his own expressive parts. He may become the risk-taker, expressing the anger, or the warmth, or the love, etc., in a sense showing how it is to be done. $(g = .82)$

3. *The Personal Leader*—This is a leader who expresses considerable warmth, acceptance, and genuineness, and a real caring for specific other human beings in the group. His style is characterized by the establishment of specific, definable, personal relationships with particular individuals in the group, and by working with them in a caring manner. $(g = .78)$

4. *The Social Engineer*—Here the emphasis of the leader's behavior is on the conditions people establish in the group, in other words, on group-building, group characteristics, how the group is working, etc. Such an approach is highly inferential for specific behaviors. Leaders who utilize it may make frequent references to the group, raise issues about how the group is working. However, "social engineers" may also make individual comments, and the critical features to identify such a leader is the intent of the intervention. Does he seem to be concerned with the way the group is working? Do his interventions, even if seemingly geared toward one individual, have the effect of moving the group ahead? $(g = .68)$

5. *The Charismatic Leader*—This is a very personal style of leadership, where the leader is at the center of the group's universe. It is through his own personal powers and force of personality that the group moves ahead and people in it have specific experiences. Such leaders may make group-centered or individual-centered comments, and it would be difficult to define such a leader by any specific comment, but rather the general feeling that he gives you, that it is by sheer weight of "personal attractiveness" (shamanlike) and his personal powers, that people are made to move. $(g = .84)$

6. *The Teacher*—The basic intervention here is like a movie director, who stops the action and focuses on particular behavior (group or individual) in which the intent of the "stopping the action" is to have the partic-

472

ipants learn about particular behavior cues, emotions, personal learnings, etc. He is essentially asking the group to reflect upon some action, and unlike the "interpreter of reality" leader, he may not be providing the answers, but rather asking that the group provide these answers. He is more tentative than the interpreter of reality. (g = .27)

7. *The Resource Leader*—This is a particular kind of stance toward the group, in which the leader attempts to communicate that he's there to be used in the way the group would like. He himself has nothing overt that he wants the group to do, but rather, he has a different vantage point, from which he can contribute. This tends to be a relatively low-keyed, noninterventionist position, and again is perhaps not tied to specific interventions, but rather to the lack of frequent interventions and a particular communication to the group that it's up to them to find out how they want to use him. Such leaders may overtly try to diminish the status differences implied by the role of the leader. (g = .87)

8. *The Challenger*—Personal confrontations are central. Such leaders may be characterized by frequent dialogues with individual members. A value is placed on personal confrontation, and shaking up or unsettling may be a primary learning condition. Challenging assumptions people hold about themselves and some refusal to accept easily people's views of self may be characteristic behavior. (g = .85)

9. *The Model*—This quality of leaders cuts across the previous eight. To what extent does the leader signal, in some form or manner, that he encourages the participants *to be like him* in style, values, behavior, or beliefs? This will be a highly inferential judgment based on signals from the leader. Note: Actual instances of participants being like the leader are not the source of data. (g = .69)

Observer Reliability

Observer reliability was computed for each session of each of the group meetings in which two observers were present (N = 90). Unless otherwise stated, the figures given are correlations. If the figure is preceded by a "g," reliability is computed using Gamma. Here-and-now revelation .73, number of people who revealed here-and-now feelings g = .68, then-and-there revelation .36, number of people revealing then-and-there feelings .47. Observer rating of content and work pattern. Percentage outside .79, percentage abstract discussion .47, percentage social issues .71, race (outside) .74, personal history .62, personal outside .49, personal inside .50, interpersonal .58, group .66, leader .38, race .75. Work pattern, monologue .56, dialogue .40, focus on one .62, going around .73, subgrouping .37, nonverbal exercises g = .74. Observer rated climate. The reliability is for each of the items (note that climate is reported as two basic factor scores). Tense .36, open .61, warm .67, formal .50, involved .70, close .66, angry .60, happy .48, alive .77, intense .74, fast .75, strong .72. Items below .50 were eliminated from consideration in the factor analysis.

Reliability of categories used for leader behavior is reported on specific instruments in this appendix.

Do's and Don'ts

Whether or not you have ever been in an encounter group before, we'd like to know your feelings about certain aspects of "group life." Over a period of time, any group tends to build up do's and don'ts—ideas about what is appropriate or inappropriate, to do or not to do, *in that particular group*.

Please think about being in an actual group. Suppose, after having been in the group for some time, that a new member whom you know were about to join it, and asked you to give him an idea of what went on in general in the group.

He might ask, "If a member of the group were repeatedly late, how would the others feel?" You might answer, "They would feel that it was somewhat inappropriate," or "They would have a mixed reaction." If your friend kept asking different questions of this sort, he would gradually form an idea of what the appropriate and inappropriate behavior in the group was.

For each of the items below, please indicate how appropriate or inappropriate you think the item would be in your group. Write in the number that shows your best estimate of how the group would feel.

+2 Definitely Appropriate; +1 Somewhat Appropriate; 0 Mixed Reaction; −1 Somewhat Inappropriate; −2 Definitely Inappropriate.

How do you think the group would *feel if a member:*

- ——— 1. Said little or nothing in most sessions.
- ——— 2. Talked about the details of his sex life.
- ——— 3. Brought up problems he had with others who weren't in the group.
- ——— 4. Kissed another member.
- ——— 5. Tried to take over the leadership of the group.
- ——— 6. Asked for reactions or feedback (How do you see me in this group?)
- ——— 7. Focused his comments on what was going on in the group.
- ——— 8. Frequently joked.

——— 9. Pleaded for help.
———10. Offered the leader a ride home after the group session was over.
———11. Challenged the leader's remarks.
———12. Said he was not getting anything from being in the group.
———13. Described his dreams and private fantasies.
———14. Disclosed information about the group on the outside.
———15. Warmly touched another member.
———16. Gave advice to other members about what to do.
———17. Appealed to the leader to back him up.
———18. Interrupted a dialogue going on between two people.
———19. Brought a friend to the group session.
———20. Said another member's behavior was wrong and should be changed.
———21. Told another member he was unlikable.
———22. Talked about killing himself.
———23. Kept bringing in topics from outside the group.
———24. Frankly showed sexual attraction to another person in the group.
———25. Refused to be bound by a group decision.
———26. Was often absent.
———27. Shouted with anger at another member.
———28. With strong feeling told another member how likable he is.
———29. Wrote another member off, saying he didn't matter.
———30. Tried to manipulate the group to get his own way.
———31. Hit another member.
———32. Told another member how much he cared for her.
———33. Talked about important political or social questions in the group.
———34. Told the group off, saying that the whole experience was silly and worthless.
———35. Told another member exactly what he thought of him.
———36. Acted indifferently to other members.
———37. Kept on probing or pushing another member who had said, "I've had enough."
———38. Talked a lot without showing his real feelings.
———39. Dominated the group's discussion for more than one session.
———40. Put down another member who had just "opened up" with some personal feelings.
———41. Said he thought the group should take more responsibility for deciding what activities should go on.
———42. Cried.
———43. Tried to convince people of the rightness of a certain point of view.

475

——44. Said he thought the leader should have the biggest responsibility for planning and guiding group activities.

——45. Probed another member who was silent.

——46. Resisted the leader's suggestions on procedures.

——47. Made threatening remarks to other group members.

——48. Showed he had no intention of changing his behavior.

Leadership Questionnaire

Each of the boxes below contains four words describing qualities of leadership. From each group of four words, circle the one word or phrase that best describes your group leader; *choose only one from each group*. Please read and answer each question in turn, without reference to the previous or following questions. Thank you.

A. Inspiring (C); Loving (L); Comradely (P); Has expertise (T).

B. Giving (L); Related (P); Solid (T); Really believes in what he's doing (C).

C. Relaxed (P); Competent (T); Imposing (C); Caring (L).

D. Knows his stuff (T); Has a vision (C); Warm (L); One of us (P).

E. People want to be like him (C); People want to be with him (L); Easy to get close to (P); Convincing (T).

F. Understanding (L); Stimulation (C); Intelligent (T); Easy to follow his lead (P).

G. A nice guy (P); Decisive (T); Genuine (L); A very special person (C).

H. Knowledgeable (T); Has a sense of mission (C); Sympathetic (L); Easy-going (P).

I. Dramatic (C); Open (L); A friend (P); Rarely makes mistakes (T).

J. Kind (L); Makes people feel special (C); Thoroughly democratic (P); Skilled (T).

C = Charisma; L = Love;
P = Peer; T = Technical

Sociometric Questionnaire
The Members of This Group

Please think over the things that have happened during the life of this group, up to the present. What we would like is your own best estimate of what different people, including yourself, have been doing in the group.

Below is a list of descriptions of behavior. Take the example, "Comes to meetings on time." First, look at *yourself* carefully. Would you say you are one of the three people who has acted MOST like this, one of the three in the group who has acted LEAST like this, or are you somewhere in the MIDDLE? Write "Me" in the place where you think you belong.

Then consider the other group members; who are MOST like this? Write in their names. Who is LEAST like this? Write in their names. Do not include the group leader or the observers—only group members. Do not bother with those you consider "in the MIDDLE."

MOST like this   In the MIDDLE   LEAST like this

_____   _____   _____

1. Responds warmly to others.
2. Expresses own feelings openly and directly.
3. Is tuned in, aware of what is happening in the group.
4. Responds angrily to others.
5. Has told intimate things about himself or herself.
6. Does a lot to help the group move along in its work.
7. Takes risks, is willing to try things, not cautious.
8. Is spontaneous, does things freely, on the spur of the moment.
9. Is out of the group.
10. Listens to feedback from others, doesn't get defensive.
11. Is in touch with own feelings and aware of what's happening inside.
12. Is flexible, lets things happen, doesn't act rigid.
13. Tends to magnify or overreact on racial issues.
14. Sees self clearly, doesn't kid self about own strengths and weaknesses.
15. Shows a contradiction between words and feelings.
16. Works easily with others, cooperates without any difficulty.
17. Tends to minimize, deny or smooth over racial issues.
18. Is comfortable with self as a member of his or her own race.

Now we would like you to think over the members of your group, including yourself. Put them in a ranking on the questions below. This may not be too easy to do, but give your best estimate. Don't include your leader or the observers.

19. How much weight do different people's ideas swing in the group? Who is able to get the group to do what he or she wants?
       HAS THE MOST WEIGHT   HAS THE LEAST WEIGHT
20. How much do different people seem to be learning in the group. Who has evidence of change and growth?
       HAS LEARNED THE MOST   HAS LEARNED THE LEAST
21. Taking all the sessions or time in the group sessions so far, how much have people talked? Who has spoken a lot?
       HAS TALKED THE MOST   HAS TALKED THE LEAST

Feelings about the Group

Answer the following questions in terms of your feelings at the present time. Circle the best answer.

1. In the group I have talked about intimate details of my life.
   A great deal—Very much—Much—Some—A little—Very little—Not at all.

2. I have expressed my feelings of irritation, annoyance, sorrow or warmth in the group.
   A great deal—Very much—Much—Some—A little—Very little—Not at all.

3. When expressing feelings of irritation, annoyance, sorrow, or warmth, I feel:
   Extremely comfortable—Very comfortable—Comfortable—Slightly uneasy—Uneasy—Very uneasy—Extremely uneasy.

4. Since the last session I have thought about the group:
   All of the time—Most of the time—Much of the time—Some of the time—A couple of times—Once—Not at all.

5. I like my group:
   Very much—Pretty much—It's all right—Don't much care—Dislike it a little—Dislike it—Dislike it very much.

6. I feel that working with this particular group will enable me to attain my personal goals for which I sought an encounter group.
   Definitely—Very likely—Likely—Uncertain—Unlikely—Very unlikely—Definitely not.

7. How often do you think your group should meet?
   (a) Much more often than at present (b) More often than at present (c) No more often than at present (d) Less often than at present (e) Much less often than at present.

8. How well do you like the group you are in?
   (a) I like it very much (b) I like it pretty well (c) It's all right (d) Don't like it too much (e) Dislike it very much.

9. If most of the members in your group decided to dissolve the group by leaving, would you try to dissuade them?
   (a) I would try very hard to persuade them to stay (b) I would try to persuade them to stay (c) I would make a slight attempt to persuade them to stay (d) It would make no difference if they left or stayed (e) I would definitely not try to persuade them to stay.

10. If you could replace members of your group with other "ideal" group members, how many would you exchange? (Excluding the leader.)
    (a) None (b) One (c) Two (d) Three (e) Four (f) Five (g) More than five.

11. To what degree do you feel that you are included by the group in its activities?

(a) I am included in all the group's activities (b) I am included in almost all the group's activities (c) I am included in most of the group's activities (d) I am included in some of the activities, but not in others (e) I don't feel that the group includes me in many of its activities (f) I don't feel that the group includes me in most of its activities (g) I don't feel that the group includes me in any of its activities.

12. How do you feel about the group leader?

(a) He couldn't be better (b) I am extremely satisfied (c) I am satisfied (d) I guess he's OK (e) I have many doubts (f) I am dissatisfied (g) I am extremely dissatisfied.

13. Compared to other groups in the course, how well would you imagine your group works together?

(a) Probably the best (b) Much better than most (c) Above average (d) Average (e) Not quite as well (f) Not nearly as well (g) Probably the worst.

How Encounter Groups Work [1]

The following are some aspects of the encounter group experience which others in the past have found useful in helping them grow and learn. Please review in your mind the course of your encounter group; read all these items; then make a decision and indicate for each item whether it was an aspect of your group that was important for your learning.

1. The group members and/or leader gave me some direct *advice or suggestions* about how to deal with some life problems or with some important relationships.

2. *Helping others,* being important to others, giving part of myself to others has been an important experience for me and has resulted in a change in my attitude toward myself.

3. The important issue was that I was an *involved member of a group;* I felt close to the other members.

4. I was able to *express feelings* very fully; I was able to say what I felt rather than holding it in; I was able to express negative and/or positive feelings toward others.

5. I was able to use others as *models,* to pattern myself after another member and/or leader. Seeing how others approach problems gave

---

[1] Four-point scales: "Did not apply to my learning in the group"; "Applied somewhat"; "Definitely an important part of my experience leading to learning"; "The two most important experiences."

me ideas of how I could; seeing others take risks in the group enabled me to do the same.

6. The group was, in a sense, like my *family*. Rather than pass through blindly however, I was able to understand old hang-ups with parents, brothers, sisters. It was like reliving, only in a more aware manner, my early family experience.

7. The group helped me understand the type of *impact I have on others;* they told me honestly what they thought of me and how I came across.

8. I learned that *"we're all in the same boat."* My problems, feelings, fears, are not unique and I share much with others in the group.

9. Getting insight into the *causes and sources of my hang-ups;* learning that some of the things I am are related to earlier periods of my life.

10. The group gave me *hope;* I saw that others with similar problems and experiences were able to grow and overcome their hang-ups.

11. The experience that despite the availability of others, I must still face life alone and *take ultimate responsibility for the way I live;* learned to face the basic issues of life and death, thus living a life less cluttered with trivialities.

12. The group helped me by encouraging me to *experiment* with new forms of behavior, by working out difficulties with some other member(s), by doing and saying things that I have not previously done with others.

13. *Revealing* embarrassing things about myself and still being accepted by others.

14. *Understanding why I think and feel* the way I do; discovering previously unknown or unacceptable parts of myself.

REFERENCES

American Psychiatric Association Task Force. 1970. *Encounter Groups and Psychiatry.*

Amir, Y. 1969. Contact hypothesis in ethnic relations. *Psychological Bulletin* 71: 319–342.

Argyris, C. 1967. On the future of laboratory education. *Journal of Applied Behavioral Science* 3 (2): 153–183.

Asch, S. E. 1951. Effects of group pressure upon the modification and distortion of judgments. In H. Guetzkow (Ed.), *Groups, leadership and men.* Pittsburgh: Carnegie Press. Pp. 171–190.

Back, K. W. 1951. Influence through social communication. *Journal of Abnormal Psychology* 46: 9–23.

———. 1972. *Sensitivity training and the search for salvation.* Russell Sage Foundation.

Bandura, A. 1969. *Principles of behavior modification.* New York: Holt, Rinehart and Winston.

Batchelder, R. L. and Hardy, J. M. 1968. *Using sensitivity training and the laboratory method.* New York: Association Press.

Bates, A. P. and Cloyd, J. S. 1956. Toward the development of operations for defining group norms and member roles. *Sociometry* 19: 26–39.

Bebout, J. 1971. Talent in interpersonal exploration project. (Personal communication.)

Bergin, A. E. and Garfield, S. (Eds.). 1971. *Handbook of psychotherapy and behavior change.* New York: Wiley.

Berne, E. 1961. *Transactional analysis in psychotherapy.* New York: Grove Press.

Bieber, I. 1962. *Homosexuality: A psychoanalytic study.* New York: Basic Books.

Buchanan, P. 1967. Evaluating the effectiveness of laboratory training in industry. In E. A. Fleishman (Ed.), *Studies in personnel and industrial psychology.* Homewood, Illinois: Dorsey.

Bunker, D. 1965. Individual applications of laboratory training. *Journal of Applied Behavioral Science* 1: 131–48.

Burke, K. 1952. *A grammar of motives.* Englewood Cliffs, N.J.: Prentice-Hall, Chapter 2.

Campbell, D. T. and McCandless, B. R. 1951. Ethnocentrism, zenophobia, and personality. *Human Relations* 4: 185–192.

Campbell, J. P. and Dunnette, M. D. 1968. Effectiveness of T-group experiences in managerial training and development. *Psychological Bulletin* 70: 73–104.

Cartwright, D. and Zander, A. 1962. *Group dynamics*. Evanston, Illinois: Row Peterson and Co., Chapters 7 and 8.

Christie, R. and Cook, P. 1958. A guide to published literature relating to the authoritarian personality through 1956. *Journal of Psychology* 45: 171–199.

Cohen, J. A coefficient of agreement for nominal scales. 1960. *Educational and Psychological Measurements* 20 (1): 37–46.

Congressional Record. June 10, 1969. H4666–4679.

Cook, S. W. 1962. The systematic analysis of socially significant events: A strategy for social research. *Journal of Social Issues* 18: 66–84.

COPED (Cooperative Project for Educational Development). 1970. Final Report, Contract OEG 3–8–08069–43 (010). Project No. 8–0069. U.S. Office of Education. Volume I: Research Outcomes.

Culbert, S. A. 1967. *The interpersonal process of self disclosure: It takes two to see one*. Explorations in Applied Behavioral Science Vol. 3. New York: Renaissance Editors.

Deutsch, M. and Collins, M. E. 1951. *Interracial housing: A psychological evaluation of a social experiment*. Minneapolis: University of Minnesota Press.

Dreger, R. M. and Miller, K. S. 1968. Comparative psychological studies of negroes and whites in the United States: 1959–1965. *Psychological Bulletin Monograph Supplement* 70 (3): Part 2, 1–58.

Emerson, R. Deviance and rejection: An experimental replication. 1945. *American Sociological Review* 19: 688–693.

Etzioni, A. 1968. *The active society*. New York: Free Press.

Fagan, J. The tasks of the therapist. 1970. In J. Fagan and I. L. Shepert (Eds.), *Gestalt therapy now: Theory, techniques, applications*. Palo Alto: Science and Behavior Books.

Feuer, L. 1969. *The conflict of generations*. New York: Basic Books.

Fleishman, E. A., Harris, E. F., and Burtt, H. E. 1955. *Leadership and supervision in industry*. Bureau of Educational Research Monograph No. 33. Columbus, Ohio: The Ohio State University.

Flowerman, S. H., Stewart, N., and Strauss, M. 1950. Further investigation of the validity of "authoritarianism" as predictive of ethnic prejudices. *American Psychologist* 5: 307–308 (abstract).

Frank, J. 1961. *Persuasion and healing*. Baltimore: Johns Hopkins Press.

Freedman, P. I. 1967. Race as a factor in persuasion. *Journal of Experimental Education* 35: 48–52.

Gibb, J. R. 1964. Climate for trust formation. In L. P. Bradford, J. R. Gibb, and K. D. Benne (Eds.), *T-group theory and laboratory method*. New York: Wiley. Pp. 279–309.

———. 1971. The effects of human relations training. In A. E. Bergin and S. Garfield (Eds.), *Handbook of psychotherapy and behavior change*. New York: Wiley. Pp. 829–862.

Goldstein, A., Heller, K., and Sechrest, L. B. 1963. Patient's and therapist's assessments of the same therapist. *Journal of Consulting Psychology* 27: 310–318.

Goldstein, M. 1952. General tolerance-prejudice and the authoritarian syndrome. Unpublished doctoral dissertation, Princeton University.

References

Gottschalk, L. A., Myerson, P., and Gottlieb, A. A. 1967. Prediction and evaluation of outcome in an emergency brief psychotherapy clinic. *Journal of Nervous and Mental Disease* 144: 77–96.

Gottschalk, L. A. and Pattison, E. M. 1969. Psychiatric perspectives on T-groups and the laboratory movement: An overview. *American Journal of Psychiatry* 126: 823–39.

Greenwald, H. J. and Oppenheim, D. B. 1968. Reported magnitude of self-misidentification among Negro children: Artifact? *Journal of Personality and Social Psychology* 8: 49–52.

Gross, N., Mason, W., and McEachern, A. 1958. *Explorations in role analysis.* New York: Wiley.

Harrison, R. 1962. The impact of the laboratory on perception of others by the experimental group. In C. Argyris, *Interpersonal competence and organizational effectiveness.* Homewood, Illinois: Irwin Press.

Harrison, R. and Hopkins, R. 1967. The design of cross-cultural training: An alternative to the university model. *Journal of Applied Behavioral Science* 3 (4): 431–460.

Harrison, R. and Lubin, B. 1965. Personal style, group composition and learning. *Journal of Applied Behavioral Science* 1 (3): 286 301.

Hills, C. and Stone, R. B. 1970. *Conduct your own awareness sessions.* New York: Signet Books, New American Library.

Hobbs, N. 1962. Sources of gain in psychotherapy. *American Psychologist* 17 (11): 741–747.

Horwitz, M. 1963. Hostility and its management in classroom groups. In N. L. Gage and W. W. Charters, Jr. *Readings in the social psychology of education.* Boston: Allyn and Bacon. Pp. 196–211.

House, R. J. 1967. T-group education and leadership effectiveness: A review of the empirical literature and a critical evaluation. *Personnel Psychology* 20: 1–32.

Imber, S. D., Nash, E. H., Stone, A. R., and Frank, J. D. 1968. A ten-year follow-up study of treated psychiatric outpatients. In S. Lesse (Ed.), *An evaluation of the results of the psychotherapies.* New York: Charles C Thomas.

Jaffe, S. J. and Sherl, D. J. 1969. Acute psychosis precipitated by T-group experience. *Archives of General Psychiatry* 21: 443–449.

Jahoda, M. and West, P. S. 1951. Race relations in public housing. *Journal of Social Issues* 7: 132–139.

Jeffries, B. 1969. Personal communication.

Johnson, S. C. 1967. Hierarchial clustering schemes. *Psychometrika* 32 (3).

———. 1968. HICLUS—A hierarchial cluster analysis program. Version 1S, Fortran IV Level H. Stanford Computing Center.

Jourard, S. M. 1964. *The transparent self: Self disclosure and well-being.* Princeton: Van Nostrand.

Kahn, R. 1963. Aspiration and fulfillment: Themes for studies of group relations. Unpublished manuscript, University of Michigan.

Katz, J. and Associates. 1968. *No time for youth.* San Francisco: Jossey-Bass, Inc.

Kelman, H. C. 1963. The role of the group in the induction of therapeutic change. *International Journal of Group Psychotherapy* 13: 399–432.

Kelman, H. C. and Parloff, M. B. 1957. Interrelations among three criteria of improvement in group therapy: Comfort, effectiveness, and self-awareness. *Journal of Abnormal and Social Psychology* 54: 281–288.

Keniston, K. 1968. *Young radicals*. New York: Free Press.

Koegler, R. and Brill, Q. 1967. *Treatment of psychiatric outpatients*. New York: Appleton-Century-Crofts.

Kramer, B. M. 1949. Dimensions of prejudice. *Journal of Psychology* 27: 389–451.

Kraus, S. 1962. Modifying prejudice: Attitude change as a function of the communicator. *Audiovisual Communication Review* 10: 14–22.

Laing, R. 1967. *The politics of experience*. New York: Pantheon Press.

Luke, R. A., Jr. 1972. The internal normative structure of sensitivity training groups. *Journal of Applied Behavioral Science* 8(4):421–437.

McNemar, Q. 1949. *Psychological statistics*. New York: Wiley.

Markley, O. W. 1969. Having a Negro roommate as an experience in intercultural education. Unpublished doctoral dissertation, Northwestern University.

Marx, G. 1967. *Protest and prejudice*. New York: Anti-Defamation League of B'nai Brith.

Miles, M. B. 1964. On temporary systems. In M. B. Miles (Ed.), *Innovation in education*. New York: Teachers' College Press. Pp. 437–490.

———. 1965. Changes during and following laboratory training: A clinical-experimental study. *Journal of Applied Behavioral Science* 1: 215–242.

———. 1969. The development of innovative climates in educational organizations. Educational Policy Research Center, Stanford Research Institute, Menlo Park, California, Research Note EPRC–6747–10.

Morland, J. K. 1966. A comparison of race awareness in northern and southern children. *American Journal of Orthopsychiatry* 36: 22–31.

Moscow, D. 1971. T-group training in the Netherlands: An evaluation and cross-cultural comparison. *Journal of Applied Behavioral Science* 7 (4): 427–448.

Mowrer, O. H. 1964. *The new group therapy*. Princeton: Van Nostrand.

Myers, G., Myers, M., Goldberg, A., and Welch, D. 1969. Effects of feedback on interpersonal sensitivity in laboratory training groups. *Journal of Applied Behavioral Science* 5 (2).

Myrdal, G. 1944. *An American dilemma: The Negro problem and modern democracy*. New York: Harper and Brothers.

News and Reports. 1969. NTL Institute, 3.

Orgel, S. Z. 1958. Effect of psychoanalysis on the course of peptic ulcer. *Psychosomatic Medicine* 20: 117–125.

Peabody, D. 1966. Authoritarianism scales and response bias. *Psychological Bulletin* 65: 11–23.

Pepitone, A. and Wilpizeski, C. 1960. Some consequences of experimental rejection. *Journal of Abnormal and Social Psychology* 60: 359–364.

Person, R. W. 1967. Relationship between psychotherapy with institutionalized boys and subsequent community adjustment. *Journal of Consulting Psychology* 31: 137–141.

Pfeiffer, J. W. and Jones, J. B. 1969. *A handbook of structured exercises for*

References

human relations training. Vols. I–III. Iowa City: University Associates Press.

Philosophers and kings: Studies in leadership. 1968. *Daedalus,* Summer.

Psathas, G. and Hardert, R. 1966. Trainer interventions and normative patterns in the T-group. *Journal of Applied Behavioral Science* 2 (2): 149–169.

Reich, C. A. 1970. *The greening of America.* New York: Random House.

Roberts, J. 1971. Self disclosure and personal change in encounter groups. Unpublished dissertation, University of Chicago.

Rogers, C. 1970. *Carl Rogers on encounter groups.* New York: Harper and Row.

Rose, A. 1947. *Studies in reduction of prejudice: A memorandum summarizing research on modification of attitudes.* Chicago: American Council on Race Relations.

Rosenberg, M. 1965. *Society and the adolescent self image.* Princeton, N. J.: University of Princeton Press.

Rosenthal, B. 1971. The nature and development of the encounter group movement. In L. Blank, G. Gottsegen, and M. Gottsegen (Eds.), *Encounter: Confrontation in self and interpersonal awareness.* New York: Macmillan Press. Pp. 435–468.

Rosenthal, D. 1955. Changes in some moral values following psychotherapy. *Journal of Consulting Psychology* 19: 431–436.

Rubin, I. 1967. The reduction of prejudice through laboratory training. *Journal of Applied Behavioral Science* 3: 29–49.

Sata, L. 1967. Unpublished study.

Sattler, J. 1970. Racial "experimenter effects" in experimentation, testing, interviewing, and psychotherapy. *Psychological Bulletin* 73: 137–160.

Schjelderup, H. 1955. Lasting effects of psychoanalytic treatment. *Psychiatry* 18: 190–133.

Schuman, H. and Harding, J. 1963. Sympathetic identification with the underdogs. *Public Opinion Quarterly* 27: 230–241.

Schutz, W. C. 1958. *FIRO.* New York: Holt, Rinehart and Winston.

——. 1966. *The interpersonal underworld.* Palo Alto, California: Science and Behavior Books.

——. 1967. *Joy.* New York: Grove Press, Inc.

Selltiz, C. and Cook, S. W. 1962. Factors influencing attitudes of foreign students toward their host country. *Journal of Social Issues* 18: 7–23.

Shaevitz, M. H. and Barr, D. J. 1970. *Encounter groups in a small college: A case study.* La Jolla, California: University of California at San Diego, Mimeographed.

Shlien, J. M., Mosak, J. J., and Dreikurs, R. 1962. Effect of time limits: A comparison of two psychotherapies. *Journal of Counseling Psychology* 9: 31–34 (a).

Shore, M. F. and Masimo, J. L. 1966. Comprehensive vocationally oriented psychotherapy for adolescent delinquent boys: A follow-up study. *American Journal of Orthopsychiatry* 36: 609–615.

Siegel, S. 1956. *Nonparametric statistics for the behavioral sciences.* New York: McGraw-Hill.

Stock-Whitaker, D. 1964. A survey of research on T-groups. In L. P. Bradford, K. D. Benne, and J. R. Gibb (Eds.), *T-group and laboratory method*. New York: Wiley. Pp. 395–441.

Summers, G. F. and Hammonds, A. D. 1966. Effect of racial characteristics of investigator on self-enumerated responses to a Negro prejudice scale. *Social Forces* 44: 515–518.

Titus, H. E. and Hollander, E. P. 1957. The California F scale in psychological research: 1950–1955. *Psychological Bulletin* 54: 47–64.

Trans-Action. 1971. Roundup of current research. Vol. 8 (4): 4.

Trent, R. D. 1954. The color of the investigator as a variable in experimental research with Negro subjects. *Journal of Social Psychology* 40: 715–725.

Watson, G. 1969. *Manual of structured exercises*. Newark, N. J.: Newark State College Laboratory of Applied Behavioral Science.

Weber, J. J., Elinson, J., and Moss, L. M. 1965. The application of ego strength scales to psychoanalytic clinic records. In G. S. Goldman, and Shapiro, D. (Eds.), *Developments in psychoanalysis at Columbia University: Proceedings of the 20th Anniversary Conference*. Columbia Psychoanalytic Clinic for Training and Research, New York.

Whitaker, D. S. and Lieberman, M. A. 1965. *Psychotherapy through the group process*. New York: Atherton Press.

Williams, R. M., Jr. 1964. *Strangers next door*. Englewood Cliffs, N. J.: Prentice-Hall.

Wilner, A. R. 1968. The theory and strategy of charismatic leadership. *Daedalus*, Summer.

Work, H. 1971. Written communication.

Yalom, I. 1970. *The theory and practice of group psychotherapy*. New York: Basic Books.

Yalom, I., Houts, P., Newell, G., and Rand, K. 1967. Preparation of patients for group therapy. *Archives of General Psychiatry* 12: 416–427.

Yarrow, M. R., Campbell, J. P., and Yarrow, L. J. 1958. Acquisition of new norms: A study of racial desegregation. *Journal of Social Issues* 14: 8–28.

INDEX